# An Introduction to Islam

## Fourth Edition

Frederick Mathewson Denny
University of Colorado at Boulder

Routledge
Taylor & Francis Group
LONDON AND NEW YORK

First published 2011, 2006, 1994 by Pearson Education, Inc.

Published 2016 by Routledge
2 Park Square, Milton Park, Abingdon, Oxon OX14 4RN
711 Third Avenue, New York, NY 10017, USA

*Routledge is an imprint of the Taylor & Francis Group, an informa business*



Credits and acknowledgments borrowed from other sources and reproduced, with permission, in this textbook appear on page 410-411.

ISBN: 9780138144777 (pbk)

Cover Designer: Suzanne Duda

**Library of Congress Cataloging-in-Publication Data**
Denny, Frederick Mathewson.
An introduction to Islam / Frederick Mathewson Denny. — 4th ed.
p. cm.
Includes index.
ISBN-13: 978-0-13-814477-7 (alk. paper)
ISBN-10: 0-13-814477-X (alk. paper)
1. Islam. I. Title.
BP161.2.D46 2011
297—dc22

To Alix, Josh, Sydney, Mike, Jake and Ian

# Contents

# Preface

The reception of the first three editions of this book has been very gratifying. I am particularly honored to have had it adopted by many colleagues who teach college-level courses on introductory Islam with high Muslim student enrollments.

Although I have not always heeded the advice of thoughtful colleagues and students, I have attempted to make this fourth edition better where possible, without losing the book's broad topical plan. In addition to numerous minor revisions, additions, and corrections, there are significant new elements in this edition.

## WHAT'S NEW TO THIS EDITIION?

- I have added a "General Introduction to Islam's Basic Teachings and Practices" at the very beginning of the book to provide readers with a preview of what is to come after reviewing (in Chapter 1) pre-Islamic Near Eastern civilizations and religions that set the stage for Islam and contributed enduring customs, traditions, values, beliefs and cultural legacies.
- I have provided pronunciation tips for Arabic-Islamic words printed in Roman transliteration (at the end of the General Introduction).
- The Suggestions for Further Reading section at the end of the book has been considerably updated and expanded.
- Key terms have been listed at the beginning of each chapter and printed in bold type the first time they appear and are defined in the text.
- A new section on Islam in West Africa has been added to Chapter 14, featuring the great charismatic Sunni leader Usman dan Fodio (1754–1817 C.E.).
- Additional Qur'an passages in English translation have been quoted to flesh out important discourses more fully.
- An entirely new global map of Muslim population percentages by country has been created, showing not only the main historic Muslim population centers of the Middle East, Africa, and Asia, but also global regions (e.g., Europe and the Americas) to which Muslims have been migrating in increasing numbers in recent decades.
- A new subsection ("Islamic Law and the State in the Present Age") has been added at the end of Chapter 9 ("Law and the State in Classical Islamic Formulations"), bridging that traditional treatment to the modern age, which is treated much later in the text.

- Some additional explanatory material on Islamic feminism has been added to the text in Chapter 15.

Many colleagues and students have provided valuable suggestions for improving the book over the years. Most have been named in the earlier editions. I want to acknowledge most gratefully the following persons for their continuing helpful comments, useful information, and suggestions as I prepared the fourth edition: Amir Hussain, Nelly van Doorn-Harder, David Valeta, Ruth Mas, Amila Buturovic, Mahdi Tourage, and Mustansir Mir.

I also want to express profound gratitude to Sarah Holle, my most patient, gracious, and helpful Project Manager at Prentice Hall, who greatly helped me to envision the new edition and did much at a detailed level to see that everything hung together properly, and to the following reviewers: Erin Stiles, California State University–Sacramento; Kent Jackson, Brigham Young University; and Mark Soileau, Albion College.

I lovingly dedicate this fourth edition of *An Introduction to Islam* to my wife Alix, our son Josh, our daughter Sydney, her husband Mike, and their baby sons Jake and Ian.

Frederick Mathewson Denny

INTRODUCTION

# A General Introduction to Islam's Basic Teachings and Practices

The classical Islamic religious tradition and civilization emerged in the Arabian Peninsula and its surrounding regions, eventually extending from the Atlantic Ocean in the west, across both north and sub-Saharan Africa, the Nile River to Central Asian regions, and onward to South and Southeast Asia. Muslims, the people who follow Islam's teachings, today comprise the second largest religious community in the world, with approximately[1] 1.57 billion members, following Christianity's worldwide population of approximately 2.3 billion. The word "Islam" is an Arabic word meaning "surrender, submission," specifically to the one universal god known as Allah in Arabic. One who submits to Allah and commits to the teachings and practices of Islam is called a "Muslim," a "submitter."

Allah is the same god worshipped by Jews and Christians, who are fellow monotheists (believers in only one god) who came before Islam in the ancient Near East. Arabic-speaking Christians call God Allah, and the opening passage in the Arabic translation of the Old Testament-Hebrew Bible book of Genesis states: "In the beginning **Allah** created the heavens and the earth." All three religions recognize themselves as being part of a shared heritage reaching all the way back to the Biblical patriarch Abraham (ca. 1750 B.C.E.), who is considered to be the principal figure in the founding of the ancient Israelite religious tradition, which later developed into the Jewish religion, known as Judaism, which in turn served as a major foundation for both Christianity and Islam. The basic teachings and practices of Judaism and Christianity will be reviewed in Chapter 1, because they figure importantly in some of the fundamental dimensions of Islam, which followed them historically.

But before we provide a brief introductory survey here of the basic teachings and practices of Islam, we must also acknowledge the importance of much older political, social, cultural, and religious traditions in the ancient Near East, extending from the ancient Egypt of the Pharaohs in the Nile Valley east to the Mesopotamian civilizations of Tigris and Euphrates civilizations in the region of contemporary Iraq. Those traditions will be briefly surveyed in Chapter 1, before we turn to Abraham and what is today often called the extended family of "Abrahamic" traditions of Judaism, Christianity, and Islam.

Muslims consider their religion, Islam, to be the fulfillment of the Jewish and Christian traditions. Muslims believe the Qur'an, "the Recitation," Islam's holy scripture, to have been revealed in Arabic language segments from Allah to the Prophet Muhammad by the archangel Gabriel over a period of twenty-two years (610–632 C.E.). There are in the Qur'an numerous references to Jewish and Christian history and beliefs as well as many of their important persons, such as Adam, Noah, Jonah, Abraham, Isaac, Ishmael, Moses, David, Solomon, Ezra, John the Baptist, Jesus, and Mary. The Qur'an declares Jews and Christians to be the "People of the Book," meaning the Holy Bible. The Qur'an teaches that it is the final and complete message of Allah, repeating important aspects of the previous scriptures, but correcting errors and deviant beliefs and practices that accumulated over the centuries. An oft-cited Qur'anic passage (Sura 3, verse 110) strongly states, as a contemporary commentator has phrased it, that "the logical conclusion of religious history is a non-sectarian, non-racial, non-doctrinal, universal religion, which Islam claims to be." Allah addresses the Muslims in the passage as follows: "Ye are the best of Peoples, evolved for humankind, enjoining what is right, forbidding what is wrong, and believing in Allah. If only the People of the Book had faith, it would have been best for them. Some of them are believers, but most of them are sinful."

Following are the five basic beliefs required of Muslims, which are presented in detail in Chapter 5: (1) faith in the absolute unity of God; (2) belief in angels and their important work as messengers and helpers of God; (3) prophetic messengers and divinely revealed scriptures; (4) the final judgment, including a "doctrine of the last things," with some similarities to Zoroastrian, Jewish, and Christian teachings; and (5) the divine decree and predestination. This last one has been one of the most frequently and passionately discussed of the beliefs, because of its tension with human free will, which Muslims also believe the Qur'an teaches.

In addition to the five beliefs just listed are five required ritual practices, known as the "Five Pillars" of Islam: (1) the *Shahāda,* or "bearing witness," that "There is no god but God" and "Muhammad is the messenger of God"; (2) the worship service, known as *Salāt,* performed five times daily (early morning, noon, mid-afternoon, sunset, and evening); (3) *Zakāt*; "legal almsgiving," of a certain proportion of one's wealth annually for the good of others and the community of believers generally; (4) *Sawm,* "fasting," during the month of Ramadan from before dawn until sunset; and (5) the annual pilgrimage to Mecca, known as the *Hajj,* at least once in each Muslim's lifetime, if resources and circumstances allow. A sixth pillar is sometimes included in discussions of required acts of worship, namely, *jihād,* "striving, exertion" in the service of God by every Muslim as a central dimension of one's personal struggle to be a strong, sincere Muslim. The term may also refer to armed combat against enemies of Islam, but only in self-defense.

What has been presented here briefly is a bare minimum of what is expected of Muslims with respect to beliefs and practices. We shall see ahead details and variations, as well as spiritual attitudes, practices, and organizations that help inspire and sustain the religious life of Muslims and bring them to *falāh,* "success, prosperity" in this life and the next. This concept is parallel in some ways to the Christian notion of "salvation."

## SOME PRONUNCIATION TIPS FOR KEY ARABIC-ISLAMIC TERMS

***dhimmī*** A member of "People of the Book," that is, Jews or Christians protected under Islamic rule. The Arabic transliteration ***dh*** is a single consonant that sounds like the English hard "th," as in "this." The double "m" is pronounced intensively, as are double consonants in German words. The first vowel "i" is pronounced like the "i" in "this"; the second, long Arabic "i," with the macron line over it, is pronounced "ee" as in bee. The word is thus pronounced: **thim-mee.**

***ṣalāt*** The formal prayer–worship service observed five times daily. The opening "s," with a dot beneath, has an intensive pronunciation but is not hard as is the "s" in English "easy." The first "a" is pronounced like the "a" in "raw." The "a" with the macron line is long and pronounced like the "a" in latitude. The word *ṣalāt* is pronounced much like the final two syllables of the common English expression "thank-***salot,***" except that the final syllable sounds like "lat" in "latitude."

***sharī'a*** Islamic law. Pronounced "sharee-uh," with the "uh" (as in English "uh-huh") begun with a throat sound a bit like when the doctor tells you to say "ahhh."

This intensive sound is the Arabic consonant *'ayn* and is the same as the intensive opening sound of the "a" in "Arab" when pronounced by a native speaker.

***madhhab*** "muth-hub" School of Islamic law, not in the sense of a "law school," but of a tradition of legal thought and practice. Recall that ***dh*** (above, in *dhimmī)* is pronounced like "th" in "this." The letter transliterated as ***h*** is one of two "h" sounds in Arabic, namely, the soft one, which sounds like an English "h." (There is another "h" sound that is intensive, like when one breathes hard on glass to put some moisture on it. This latter "h" is in such Arabic words *ḥadīth,* usually transliterated into English with a dot beneath as follows: ḥpronounced "hhuh-deeth" (the final "th" is with a soft "th" sound, as in "think," unlike the hard "th" sound in *madhhad above.*)

***qur'ān*** "qoor-on" (ending as in the English word "on") Islam's Holy Scripture. Arabic has two "k"-like sounding letters, transliterated into English respectively as ***q*** and ***k***. *"q"* is pronounced deep in the throat, whereas "k" is like English "k" or hard "c" (as in "cat") and used in Arabic words such as *kitāb* (meaning "book"). The English apostrophe (') marks a glottal stop in Arabic orthography, called a *hamza,* which may either begin or end a vowel sound. So, in properly pronouncing *qur'an,* the speaker ends the "r" sound and then says "on."

***dīn wa dawla*** "deen wa dow-la" "Religion and state." This phrase has traditionally been a practical definition of Islam.

## NOTE

1. As estimated in a comprehensive study of more than 200 countries by The Pew Forum on Religion and Public Life study "Mapping the Global Muslim Population: A Report on the Size and Distribution of the World's Muslim Population," Copyright Pew Research Center 2009. www.pewforum.org p. 1.

PART ONE

# Religion and Common Life in the Pre-Islamic Near East

CHAPTER

1

# Early Civilizations and the Origins of Judaism and Christianity

### KEY TERMS

**Old Kingdom**
**Osiris**
**Isis**
**Ma'at**
**topocosm**
**Mesopotamia**
**Gilgamesh**
**Hammurabi**
**Israelites**
**Allāh**
**ethical monotheism**
**prophet**

## EGYPT THE LAND

Islam arose in the same part of the world that witnessed the rise of civilization, including writing, large-scale agriculture, long-distance trade both by sea and by land, and a number of great religious traditions. From their beginnings, the civilizations of both Egypt and Mesopotamia placed religious symbols, beliefs, and practices in prominent positions. The Egyptians believed their wonderful land and its ordered people to be a gift of the gods, who deserved in return continuous praise, thanksgiving, and service. The Mesopotamians considered themselves to be the stewards of their land, which was believed to be a vast estate ruled by the gods in heaven. At the center of both systems was a ruler who had sacral and priestly as well as political, economic, judicial, and military functions and qualities. In Egypt the pharaoh was believed to be a god as well as a human, and so he provided a link between the earthly and heavenly realms. Actually, there seems to have been no sharp distinction made between the two, for, as the great American Egyptologist John Wilson has put it, the Egyptians lived in a "consubstantial" universe in which humans, animals, gods, and inanimate nature were intimately and harmoniously interrelated.[1] This helps explain the confidence that marked Egyptian religious, political, artistic, and social expression in its formative and classical periods, extending roughly from 3000 to 2200 B.C.E. and known as the

View of the medieval Cairo skyline, facing the pyramids. (*Source:* Frederick Mathewson Denny)

**Old Kingdom.** This was the "pyramid" age, during which most of the characteristic institutions and concepts pertaining to Egyptian civilization were begun and perfected. For centuries, indeed millennia, afterward, Egyptians looked back to this period and drew from it inspiration for continuing tasks as well as comfort in periods of failure and disintegration. The great innovator Ikhnaton (d. ca. 1353 B.C.E.), who instituted a monotheistic cult nearly a thousand years after the fall of the Old Kingdom, clearly meant to return to the original pattern that exalted the pharaoh above all else on earth and worshiped him as the good god.

The Egyptians' general optimism and confidence, reflected in their graceful and imaginative funeral art, for example—which both protected and provided for the dead—was at least partly a product of topography and climate. The Nile valley is a place greatly blessed by nature. The weather is generally mild most of the year, and the soil is rich and loamy, coming as it did until recent times in the annual inundation from central Africa. With irrigation, there is almost always sufficient and sometimes abundant water. Goods and people are easily and cheaply transported from one part of the narrow valley to another on the Nile, whose current flows north toward the sea, whereas the prevailing wind blows south, thus enabling propulsion either by wind or current in both directions. The land is both contained and guarded by steep walls in the valley and hostile deserts on both sides, and to the north the swampy delta and the Mediterranean Sea effectively check incursions from the outside, provided the minimal necessary defensive outposts are maintained, especially along the Gaza Strip between Palestine and Egypt. As Herodotus said, "Egypt is the gift of the Nile."[2] Throughout its ancient existence as a major Near Eastern power, Egypt capitalized on its unique endowments and its sense of miraculous emergence and continued maintenance from the interaction of sun, soil, and moisture.

### *Egypt's Ancient Religion*

The annual inundation of the Nile, bringing forth once again the life-giving green crops, symbolized as well as embodied the cycle of life, death, and resurrection that the Egyptians came to embrace through the cult of **Osiris.** Originally, Osiris was thought to have been the king of Egypt.[3] His jealous and treacherous brother Seth, who is traditionally associated with the desert and its scorching winds, contrived to kill Osiris so as to ascend to the throne himself. The body of Osiris, trapped inside a beautiful box, floated out to sea and eventually washed up at Byblos, on the Phoenician coast. The devoted wife of Osiris, **Isis,** searched all over for her husband's body, finally discovering it in a pillar of the palace of the king of Byblos. Returning with the body to Egypt, she hid it and herself in the delta marshes, where she succeeded in reviving Osiris enough to become impregnated. Seth, out hunting one night by the light of the moon, came upon the body of his brother, which he cut up into pieces and strewed all over Egypt. The penis was dropped into the Nile, where it was eaten by a fish. Isis, who from this time forward was often depicted as a grieving woman, flew in her form as a kite all over the land in order to find the parts of Osiris's body. Wherever she found one, she dedicated a temple at the spot, burying the part there. (One version has her reassemble the body and then become impregnated by it, a mythological explanation of the widespread occurrence of Osiris worship.) After a while Isis gave birth to a son, Horus, who was always identified with the falcon. Later, when Horus grew up, he avenged his father's murder through a tribunal of the gods, who found Seth guilty. Horus thus became the rightful ruler. Thereafter the living pharaoh was thought to be Horus, and the dead pharaoh, Osiris.[4] Horus kept watch over Egypt as a just and mighty ruler, eventually adding to his falcon symbolism the powerful symbolism of the sun. Since the earliest of times birds of prey and the sun have been royal symbols, for who else can oversee vast regions at one glance, dive down swiftly to deal with disturbances, and make the soil fertile? In the person of the pharaoh, the forces of nature are harnessed to those of politics and justice by means of religious symbolism and ritual. In addition, Osiris continues to live and bring new life through the power of the Nile and the green vegetation associated with its annual floods after the dry season.

***Religion and Afterlife.*** During the period of the Old Kingdom, as each pharaoh died, he became Osiris, and his successor became Horus. As Osiris, the pharaoh continued in an external life of happiness and pleasure. As the centuries went by, the nobles and then the common people came to share in this identification with Osiris, through elaborate rituals of burial and continued tomb maintenance. James Henry

Breasted, the pioneering Egyptologist, named this phenomenon the "democratization of the Osirean afterlife."[5] It seems to be one of the first explicit doctrines of life beyond the grave to have appeared in world religious history. Significantly, such an afterlife was dependent on having lived a good life on earth. The supreme Egyptian virtue was **Ma'at,** "justice," depicted in the form of a woman with weighing scales and a feather. At a postdeath trial, really a last judgment, the newly deceased was questioned and examined and his or her deeds were weighed on Ma'at's scales of justice. If the verdict was damnation, a fearsome-looking crocodilelike monster was on hand to devour the victim. But if the verdict was innocence, then the happy soul was ushered into the Elysian Fields. There seems to have been much litigation in the afterlife on the part of deceased persons seeking a good outcome. And both the living and the dead continued to have relations with each other and could affect each other for good or ill.[6]

Ideas of justice, final judgment, and punishment or reward that have descended from ancient Egypt became central to the Abrahamic religions, of which Islam is the youngest. Although there are structural similarities in the ancient Egyptian and the Christian, Jewish, and Islamic doctrines of individual judgment and either punishment or blissful afterlife in a kind of heaven, the details are quite different. Christianity, Judaism, and Islam feature a resurrection of the body, whereas the ancient Egyptians embalmed the body for a postmortem existence based in the tomb. The Christian, Jewish, and Islamic forms of afterlife do not have any necessary connection with a specific geographic location, whereas Egyptians had always

A deceased Pharoah appears before the goddess of justice, Ma'at (Valley of the Kings). (*Source:* Frederick Mathewson Denny)

dreaded dying and being buried away from their sacred land. Ancient Egypt had multiple geographies of death, one of which was an idealized version of the land and the Nile in heaven.[7] Whenever possible, the remains of Egyptians who died abroad were transported back to the Valley of the Nile for a proper funeral, which included the journey across the Nile to the land of the Westerners, where the sun sets each day over the cemeteries. Of course, other differences are connected with the diversity of gods in ancient Egypt and the roles they played in the funerary cult, as in many other dimensions of the cultural and religious system.

***Religion and "Topocosm."*** Ancient Egypt, like other traditional agriculture-based civilizations in Mesopotamia, the Indus valley, and China, unified into a symbolic and ritual system the land, the people, and the founding myths. This complex but harmonious interrelationship of the individual, society, time, and location centered in the agricultural–seasonal cycle has been given by an American specialist in comparative religion, Theodor Gaster, the name of **topocosm.**[8] It is a union between place (*topos*) and world structure (*cosmos*). Thus, the crops, their planting, and their harvesting are not subject merely to the vicissitudes of a particular territory. They also are connected to the universe through a cosmology and a pattern of seasonal ritual repetition that ensures regularity and harmony. All of the settled agricultural peoples with whom the ancient Hebrews and, later, the Arabs came into contact shared more or less in a topocosmic world view, whether in Babylon, Canaan, or Egypt.

Nomadic pastoralist peoples have tended to be ambivalent toward religious systems that are rooted in the intimate relationship between agriculture and a settled population. At the most superficial level, pastoralists have despised the peasants for their slavery to the soil. At a more profound level, the Hebrew of the Mosaic covenant, for example, has been at pains to resist the comforts and securities of fertility cults based on the relationship between the female earth and the male lords of the clouds and storms: Ashtoreth and the Baals. After Israel settled into an agricultural mode of existence, there was a considerable accretion of topocosmic elements in the religion that became Judaism. This can be seen most clearly in some of the seasonal festivals, such as Tabernacles (harvesttime) and Passover (springtime), as well as the holy geography of Eretz Yisrael, the "Land of Israel." Although Islam, as we shall see, is relatively free from topocosmic dimensions, it places great emphasis on the sacred enclaves of Mecca and Medina. The specific symbolism and ritual practices connected with them will be considered later.

## MESOPOTAMIA THE LAND

In **Mesopotamia** the situation is strikingly different. There is no seasonal regularity, as in Egypt. Rather, one season of sufficient rain, mild winter, and bearable heat may be immediately followed by a period of scorching desert winds, with no moisture, to be capped off by a severe winter. The climate, in short, is capricious and damaging as often as it is nurturing.[9] What is more, the topography is relatively open and vulnerable to outside and possibly aggressive populations. Mesopotamia has been ruled by many different groups over the millennia. The peasants, however, have remained the same, although new peoples have migrated and settled there from time to time. Abraham's migration from Babylon would have been neither possible nor appealing to most people in Mesopotamia (see Gen. 11:31), but Abraham came from a seminomadic, pastoralist background, it seems.

### *Mesopotamia's Ancient Religion*

Our records indicate that the Mesopotamians generally had a more pessimistic view of life than their Egyptian neighbors did. This life is full of toil and stress, and there is nothing to be expected after it. The ancient Babylonian story of **Gilgamesh** is a reminder that all humans have is their present life. When the hero Gilgamesh was journeying in quest of the one man who could give him the secret of eternal life, everyone told him that his hope was futile.

> Gilgamesh, whither are you wandering?
> Life, which you look for, you will never find.
> For when the gods created man they let
> death be his share, and life
> withheld in their own hands.
> Gilgamesh, fill your belly—
> day and night make merry,
> let days be full of joy,
> dance and make music day and night.
> And wear fresh clothes,
> and wash your head and bathe.
> Look at the child that is holding your hand,
> and let your wife delight in your embrace.
> These things alone are the concern of men.[10]

The ending of this story is unhappy and frustrating. Gilgamesh is unable to accept his fate and the fate of all mortals. The best that one can do is to surrender fatalistically to death as the final fact. This view was shared by the pre-Islamic Arabians, as we shall see when we examine some of their poetry.

***Religion and Culture.*** The peoples of Mesopotamia—the dimly perceived Sumerians, who first civilized that region, the better-known Babylonians and Assyrians, both Semitic peoples, and others—have been assertive, aggressive, innovative, and creative throughout most of their histories. This was also the case with the peoples who later came to dominate Mesopotamia, such as the Persians and the Greeks, both Indo-European peoples. Writing was first invented by the Sumerians in Mesopotamia,[11] and from there it spread to Egypt and other lands. The first codified law, the Code of Hammurabi, was drawn up in Babylon nearly eighteen centuries before Christ. Mesopotamia was also the site of significant advances in mathematics, astronomy, and architecture. In Egypt, the people and the gods were in basic conformity, with the pharaoh at the apex of the human system, exercising justice and authority as a god who also participated in human life. Although it was surely important to maintain this intricate relationship as well as local ritual patterns, there was a general conviction that all would go well. Indeed, Egypt was remarkably stable through the centuries. The Egyptian worldview and way of preserving the system of human, animal, divine, and plant life was an impressive exercise in consistency. The prayer of the ancient Egyptian was not "May tomorrow be different"; it was "May tomorrow be like today and like yesterday."

But Mesopotamia was quite different. In Egypt, the cosmic order was a gift of the gods, whereas in Mesopotamia it had to be achieved by combining a great variety of cosmic and transcendent wills. As Thorkild Jacobsen stated, the Mesopotamian's "understanding of the cosmos tended therefore to express itself in terms of integration of wills, that is, in social orders such as the family, the community, and, most particularly, the state. To put it succinctly, he saw the cosmic order as an order of wills—as a state."[12] At the top of the human order was the king. He was not at all like the pharaoh, for he was mortal and highly vulnerable. The gods above him were regarded as the real rulers of earth, and their wills were inscrutable and capricious, reflecting the unstable and threatening climate. Indeed, the divinities of Mesopotamia were identified closely with the elements. At the top was Anu, the sky god; then there was Enlil, the storm god. These two were central in the realm of political and military power. Enki was the god of the earth but took the form of water, which moves on and under the earth in sometimes unpredictable ways. The earth itself was regarded as feminine, but passive and fertile. There also were lesser gods and goddesses. In actual political life, the human leaders and custodians of power regarded themselves as working on a vast estate owned by the gods in heaven. When there were changes, such as revolts or conquests, they were regarded as tied to the will of the gods. A successful leader therefore had to be attuned to the nature and roles of his superiors. He kept in touch by means of an elaborate ritual and divining cult, focused in a temple that dominated the center of each city-state. Mesopotamian kingship was invested with what the people understood to be the "Enlil functions." The king's task was to maintain internal order, security, and productivity by means of justice and the wise management of the lands and irrigation systems. Added to this was the responsibility of protecting the people from invaders from outside and extending the state's power and prestige.

Although the human *as human,* even at the level of royalty, was weak in the presence of the gods, nevertheless there came from time to time a ruler who was thought to embody the will and power of the cosmic authorities. When this happened, the highest gods usually lent their power to the god of a particular city-state. One such locality was Babylon, whose patron and protector was the mythical god Marduk, who in primordial times had vanquished Tiamat, the demon-goddess of chaos. The great sacral king **Hammurabi** characterized his position in memorable lines:

> When lofty Anu, king of the Anunnaki, and Enlil, lord of heaven and earth, who determine the destinies of the country, appointed Marduk, the firstborn, Son of Enki, to execute the Enlil functions over the totality of the people, made him great among the Igigi, called Babylon by its exalted name, made it surpassing(ly great) in the world, and firmly established for him in its midst an enduring kingship whose foundations are (as) firmly grounded as (those of) heaven and earth—then did Anu and Enlil call me to afford well-being to the people,
>
> me, Hammurabi, the obedient, god-fearing prince, to cause righteousness to appear in the land,
>
> to destroy the evil and the wicked, that the strong harm not the weak and that I rise like the sun over the black-headed people, lighting up the land.[13]

***Religion and Authority.*** Although this passage appeared at the beginning of Hammurabi's great law code, the yearning for justice had been a hallmark of human aspirations throughout the ancient history of Mesopotamian and Egyptian civilizations. These peoples had always believed that justice came from the gods and that when there was a high level of harmony, amity, stability, and material prosperity on earth, it was because of their conformity with the cosmic structure. In Hammurabi's prologue to the laws, he is seen as the agent of Marduk, who in turn derived his authority from Enlil and Anu. The king became the executive on earth. When something went wrong with this arrangement, it was thought that the gods had taken the Enlil functions away from the king and given them to someone else. This view is comparable to the classical Chinese notion of the Mandate of Heaven, which was bestowed on its emperors. In Mesopotamia, then, the sovereign could be replaced or at least sternly taken to task for failures. Power moved from city-state to city-state through the centuries. When a rival leader began to dominate in a region, the people came to recognize the shift in focus of the Enlil functions, and they would accordingly shift their allegiance. This actually had the effect of unifying larger and larger regions under a common mythic structure in regard to the possession and exercise of power. This development is especially evident when the complex, interdependent structures of irrigation are considered.

Without stability and a hierarchical state structure, it would have been impossible to maintain a state-grade society with all the material and social benefits that it provided. In Mesopotamia, especially from the time of Hammurabi's Babylon, and in Egypt, but in somewhat differing ways, justice was regarded as the highest good. In the ancient hydraulic civilizations of Mesopotamia and the Nile valley, justice was considered crucial to the maintenance of the social, political, economic, and cultural pattern. It was grounded in reality and thus secured and applied within what can be called a *religious* context. The laws of humankind were regarded as coming from the gods. In Mesopotamia we can see the origins of the idea of divine revelation in the form of law as scripture handed down by the gods.[14] In Egypt, although revelation in the sense of prophecy and texts descending from heaven was rare, the very presence of the pharaoh in the midst of his people meant that Ma'at (justice) was available.

## THE ORIGINS OF JUDAISM

A remarkable liturgical passage is found in the Hebrew Bible book of Deuteronomy, a rehearsal of the historical experiences of a special people in covenant with their God:

> A wandering Aramean was my father; and he went down into Egypt and sojourned there, few in number; and there he became a nation, great, mighty, and populous. And the Egyptians treated us harshly, and afflicted us, and laid upon us hard bondage. Then we cried to the Lord the God of our fathers, and the Lord heard our voice, and saw our affliction, our toil, and our oppression; and the Lord brought us out of Egypt with a mighty hand and an outstretched arm. . . . (Deut. 26:5–8)[15]

This is a very different kind of sacred story than is found in the experiences of peoples in Egypt and Mesopotamia, who were so closely identified with their land from the beginning of time. To be sure, the account in Deuteronomy is about God's bestowing land on his chosen people, but this came to be only after a historic struggle. And the struggle continued long after the land was settled.

The "wandering Aramean" is Jacob, the third patriarch of Israel, who led his people down into Egypt from Canaan during a period of famine. The story is the climax of the Joseph saga in Genesis 37–50. The **Israelites**[16] first appear in the Bible in the story of Abraham, their traditional ancestor (Gen. 14:13). These people were a seminomadic class that moved about in search of good grazing in the hill country of Canaan, having moved there from Mesopotamia.

## ABRAHAM

Abraham is venerated by Jews, Christians, and Muslims as the father of faith. They all trace their traditions back to him, the Jews in a quite literal genealogical sense, for Abraham was, according to the biblical record, the grandfather of Jacob, whose name became Israel. The Arabs also trace their genealogy back to Abraham, but through a different line. The Christians and Muslims—the non-Arab Muslims, in any case—are more like adopted grandchildren of the patriarch Abraham, but this in no way lessens their conviction of being peoples of God who had inherited the way of faith that Abraham is believed to have pioneered.

Terah, Abraham's father, took his family—including his son Abram (later Abraham) and Abram's wife Sarah—from their home in Ur of the Chaldeans (that is, Babylon) to Haran, a hilly region near the headwaters of the Euphrates. They were headed, eventually, for Canaan and a new life. After Terah's death, the Lord said to Abram:

> Go from your country and your kindred and your father's house to the land which I will show you. And I will make of you a great nation, and I will bless you, and make your name great. . . . (Gen. 12:1–2)

Abraham and his family went to Canaan and were told that their descendants would one day inherit the land.

### *Abraham's Religion*

We are not sure of the precise details of Abraham's religion,[17] but the whole bears some resemblance to the contemporary nature religions. We read of several names for divinity in Genesis, such as El Shaddai ("the God of the Mountains"), El Olam ("the Everlasting God"), and El Bethel ("the God of Bethel"). El is a common name for God throughout the Fertile Crescent, from Canaan to the Persian Gulf. It has the same root as the Arabic *ilāh,* "god," which when combined with the definite article, *al-,* becomes ***Allāh,*** literally "the god," or God. The Bible admits that when Abraham's ancestors still lived in Mesopotamia, they were polytheists. (See Josh. 24:14)

The struggle from Abraham's time (ca. 1750 B.C.E.) onward was to serve faithfully the one Lord who had called them to Canaan. This did not mean that other gods did not exist; it simply meant that they were not to be served by this particular people. But this is not properly monotheism, because it does not deny the existence of other gods. Later, after Moses and the Sinai covenant, the Jews came to embrace a proper monotheistic doctrine. But they did this only after a considerable length of time had elapsed. It was not until the Israelite prophet Amos (ca. 750 B.C.E.), at least, that there appeared a clear notion that the God of Israel was also God of *other* peoples. (See Amos 9:5-8)

### *Isaac*

Added to the notion that God is one is the conviction that he is just and good and requires righteous behavior from his creatures. This is **ethical monotheism,** and it became the foundation of all three Abrahamic religions: Judaism, Christianity, and Islam.

The patriarchs of Israel—Abraham, Isaac, and Jacob—appear to the reader who is conversant with the history and culture of the Arabs as very much like the kind of Bedouin chieftains, known as *shaykhs,* who have from time immemorial provided political, moral, and military leadership as a sort of "first among equals" in their tribes. These patriarchs and their remarkable wives and womenfolk, who were indeed matriarchs (e.g., Sarah, Hagar, Rebecca, and Rachel), breathe the air of the desert encampment and the hillside flocks more than that of the village and city of the civilized world. There is much in their stories, as contained in the Book of Genesis (12–end), that an Arab of both pre-Islamic and Islamic times would find familiar and congenial. A good example is the story of Abraham and the strange visitors (Gen. 18:1–15) who were received with all the splendid hospitality for which the Arabs and other Near Eastern peoples are famous. The visit was a divine one, as Abraham himself gradually learned, and the angelic visitors told of the coming of a son to Abraham through his until-then barren wife Sarah. When Sarah overheard the men's conversation about this, she laughed, saying to herself derisively, "After I have grown old, and my husband is old, shall I have pleasure?" Some months later Isaac, which means "he laughs," was born to the old couple.

But Abraham already had a son by Hagar, Sarah's Egyptian maid, whom Sarah had given to her husband as a proxy so that Abraham would have a son to carry on his line (a very important thing to an Israelite or Arab). The son born to Abraham and Hagar was named Ishmael (Ismāʿīl in Arabic). One day, Ishmael was playing with little Isaac. Sarah, watching them, was prompted to say to Abraham: "Cast out this slave woman with her son; for the son of this slave woman shall not be heir with my son Isaac" (Gen. 21:10). Abraham was upset at this turn of events, but God commanded him to do as Sarah wished. Abraham's name would live through Isaac's line, but Ishmael's line would also be a nation, "because he is your offspring." Hagar and Ishmael were sent away with water and bread into the wilderness. When the water was gone, Hagar placed the child under a bush, for she could not bear to see her child die. But God heard little Ishmael's weeping and, through an angel, said to Hagar:

> "What troubles you, Hagar? Fear not; for God has heard the voice of the lad where he is. Arise, lift up the lad, and hold him fast with your hand; for I will make him a great nation." (Gen 21:17–18)

Then God showed Hagar a well of water, which saved the two. Ishmael grew up in the wilderness, becoming an expert archer. Much later, as we shall see, the Arabs and, through them, the Muslims traced their spiritual lineage back to Abraham through Hagar and Ishmael, regarding themselves as that "great nation" that God had promised to create.

When Isaac became a boy, his father was commanded by God to take him into the mountains and sacrifice him as a burnt offering. (Muslim sources have Ishmael as the intended offering.) In a dramatic scene, Isaac asked his father where the sacrificial animal was. "God will provide himself the lamb for a burnt offering, my son," Abraham replied. Then Abraham prepared an altar and bound Isaac so as to slaughter him with a knife. As he raised the knife over his son, an angel called out:

> "Abraham, Abraham!" And he said, "Here am I." He said, "Do not lay your hand on the lad or do anything to him; for now I know that you fear God, seeing you have not withheld your son, your only son, from me." And Abraham lifted up his eyes and looked, and behold, behind him was a ram, caught in a thicket by his horns; and Abraham went and took the ram, and offered it up as a burnt offering instead of his son. (Gen. 22:11–13)

This episode shows most vividly the faith for which Abraham is remembered. Abraham was leaping into the unknown, risking his most precious possession: his son. He was commanded to destroy the very thing that God had promised to protect and enhance: his posterity.

### *Abraham's Covenant with God*

At the core of this religious consciousness was the covenant relationship between God and Abraham and, through Abraham, with the Israelites. This was a special relationship that entailed "chosenness." The great covenant passage is Genesis 17:1–21, whose opening lines deserve quoting here:

> When Abram was ninety-nine years old the Lord appeared to Abram, and said to him, "I am God Almighty; walk before me, and be blameless. And I will make my covenant between me and you, and will multiply you exceedingly." . . . And I will give to you, and to your descendants after you, the land of your sojournings, all the land of Canaan, for an everlasting possession; and I will be their God. (Gen. 17:1-2, 8)

The mark of the covenant was circumcision, performed on all males who partook of the covenant relationship, in Abraham's time and forever afterward. Anyone not circumcised would be cut off from Abraham's people and regarded as a breaker of the covenant (Gen. 17:14). Interestingly, God declared (Gen. 17:19–21) that he would establish his covenant with Isaac and not with Ishmael; yet he had Ishmael circumcised on the same day as his father was (Gen. 17:26). But the Bible's interest is obviously in Abraham's posterity through Isaac's line, as Ishmael drops from sight in the narrative a little later. Jacob, Isaac and Rebekah's clever son (see Genesis 25:19–50 for the remarkable saga of a hustler who grew into a holy man), would be renamed Israel after a mysterious spiritual passage. His twelve sons would then be the founders of the legendary "Twelve Tribes of Israel" who settled Canaan.

## MOSES

There is not sufficient space here to recount in greater detail the story of the patriarchs. But you should have enough background information to understand the significance of Abraham and his covenant with God. Later, the Israelites lived in Egypt for four centuries and then were rallied to the old covenant by Moses, one of the most remarkable individuals in human history. His story is related in the Book of Exodus. The Sinai covenant, with the gradual revelation of the Torah (divine "instruction"), which includes at its heart the Ten Commandments (Exod. 20:1–17), was the foundation, together with the great and terrible events surrounding it—the Passover, the Exodus through the Red Sea (ca. 1250 B.C.E.), the wandering in the Sinai wilderness, and the entrance to the land of Canaan under Joshua—that form Israel's national consciousness.

In a real sense, Israel's history begins with Moses,[18] as the patriarchs and other ancestors would become fully understood in relation to Israel only after the Sinai events. We shall see later that Muhammad, the prophet of Islam, bears a striking resemblance to Moses in that he also called a whole people to righteousness and obedience to God and led them through a kind of exodus, called the *hijra,* to a new land and life in Medina. What is more, God revealed a holy law to Muhammad, too, in the Qur'an. The divine legislation revealed to the Muslims is believed to be essentially the same that was earlier sent down to Moses and the Israelites at Sinai. The Ten Commandments in the Book of Exodus have parallels in the Qur'an. The relationships of the two leaders to their respective lands were very different, but both Moses and Muhammad saw their great work to be, in part, a renewal of Abraham's faith and a fulfillment of God's promise to Abraham.

### *The Israelites' Religion*

The children of Israel, after Moses, entered the land of Canaan and gradually subdued it, but not without great bloodshed and the displacement of the resident population. The record of this era is preserved in the biblical books of Joshua and Judges. As the Israelites settled, they became enmeshed in the characteristic assumptions and practices of an agriculturally based existence. There ensued a tradition of extreme tension between the exclusive covenant with Yahweh,[19] the "Lord," and the arrangements of a more topocosmically oriented temperament and life structure. In a sense this was a struggle between the nomadic and the sedentary types of life. The relative freedom of the patriarchs'old nomadic ways, which seems to have enhanced the sense of divine guidance and presence across a variety of topocosmic frontiers, gave way to the greater security of life lived in a close relationship to the soil.[20]

This later culture included a polytheistic type of religion featuring the creative interrelationship of the feminine and masculine modes of being. Canaanite religion had much more in common with the old systems of Mesopotamia and Egypt than it did with the religion of Moses, which had been developed and ingrained first of all in a nomadic environment. Moses himself became aware of this while living in exile in Midian after fleeing Egypt because of his killing an Egyptian (see Exod. 2:11–15). He married into the Midianite tribe and apparently came to know its religion as the son-in-law of Jethro, the priest of Midian. Mount Sinai seems to have been a sacred Midianite shrine, and in any case, these people were distant blood relatives of the Israelites (see Gen. 25:2).[21]

## LATER RELIGIOUS DEVELOPMENT

Fundamental to the covenant idea, first established with Abraham and later renewed and considerably extended at Sinai into specific laws and obligations, is a conviction that the historical process itself is religiously significant. This is in some ways the most revolutionary aspect of Israelite religion.[22] In contrast with the comforting, stable patterns of life lived in harmony with the sacred social order of a hierarchical system based on an agrarian economy, the new, historically alert vision was marked by a sense of entering the future with expectation and a sense of adventure. This required also the ability to review the past in relation to the covenant faith. A peculiar philosophy of history was created, which viewed Israel's fortunes as directly related to its covenant keeping. When Israel obeyed God and upheld the laws, it was rewarded with success and God's protective presence. But when the people strayed from their covenant responsibilities, God punished them. This cyclical view is known as the

"Deuteronomic" view of history,[23] because it is first discerned in the books of Deuteronomy and Judges, whose editorial viewpoints were influenced by that school of thought. It became a fundamental feature of later Near Eastern religion.

Although the Israelites read their past history as the sequence of covenant renewal and covenant breaking and their corresponding divine responses, throughout much of their history, the most significant thing always was God's repeated forgiveness of his wayward children. God's compassion and fatherly love were always, in the final analysis, greater than his wrath and justice. The experience of renewal over and over again convinced the Hebrews that there was something mysterious and wonderful in their history. This gave rise to what more recent thinkers have come to call *salvation history,*[24] the record of God's gracious purposes worked out in the crucible of human historical conflict and decision. This is why Abraham's faith is basic: It provided the means for true historical existence in which humankind could develop in a dynamic and creative manner, free from the tutelage of the archaic structures of authority. The important thing was decision, not blind conformity. The subsequent experience of many of the world's peoples has been a witness to the revolutionary developments that Israel first introduced into human history, by treating that very history as an arena of meaning rather than as simply a cycle of primordial repetitions.

## THE PROPHETS

Well before even the northern exile, there arose a class of Israelite leaders who discerned in Israel's troubled and tragic events God's just punishment for the people's continual breaking of the covenant. These leaders are known to us as **prophets** (sing., *nevi*; pl., *nevi'im*; cognate of the Arabic *nabī*). In the simplest sense, a prophet is a person who transmits a message from God, about the divine world, to humans. Antecedents of the Old Testament written prophets can be traced back into the distant past to the religiously enthusiastic and charismatic personalities who spoke forth in the name of their Lord. Indeed, these earlier prophets were given to ecstatic, frenzied utterances. When they lost control and gyrated wildly, people regarded them as being possessed by God's spirit. These prophets joined the Israelite armies and went, escorting the holy ark of the covenant (containing the tablets on which were written the Ten Commandments), into battle with the troops, shouting encouragement and frightening the enemy by their fierce gestures.

Later on, the vocation of prophet became more sharply defined as a type of independent voice calling the people back to their covenant responsibilities. As the schools of prophets developed, some were loyal to the kings of Israel, while others denounced in the name of God the status quo of a smug populace and its priesthood and royalty. The faithful became convinced that God's living words were being conveyed through his messengers, thus strengthening the Israelites' sense of God's continuing guidance, power, and, especially, judgment.

### *Amos*

The prophet Amos denounced the Israelites as luxury-loving, vain, and insensitive people who substituted ritual for compassion and punctilious observance of Israel's liturgical calendar for conscientious attention to the needs of the downtrodden.

> I hate, I despise your feasts, and I take no delight in your solemn assemblies. . . . Take away from me the noise of your songs; to the melody of your harps I will not listen. But let justice roll down like waters, and righteousness like an everflowing stream. (Amos 5:21, 23–24)

What is a prophet? The conventional understanding is that he or she is someone who can foretell the future. This was part of what the Israelite prophets did, but it would be a mistake to center our understanding on that alone. The sort of divining of the future of which the great prophets were capable was based on a clear moral vision rather than on occult powers. If the people disobeyed the Lord, then ruin would surely come. This did not require extraordinary perceptions, but a basic grasp of what it meant to be faithful to the covenant, which contained reciprocal obligations and conditions. The great prophets—and here is meant those who have left the most lasting impression on the Jews and Christians, who know them through the Bible—were not so much *foretellers* as *forth tellers.*[25] That is, they spoke fearlessly and independently against the abuses and sins of their own times, predicting dire consequences if the people did not mend their ways and fulfill their covenant obligations to God, who always fulfilled his. This is the heart of ethical monotheism: It matters cosmically whether one is faithful to the covenant with God, and the prophets spoke in the name of God, convinced that his spirit was with them for the task.

### *Hosea*

The prophets did not, like Amos, speak only of God's terrible punishment of those who strayed from his commandments. Nowhere is this seen more clearly than in the Book of Hosea. Hosea took a wife who was a prostitute and who had committed adultery more than once. Although the children born of adultery lived in his house, Hosea somehow continued to feel compassion and even love for his undeserving wife, Gomer. This mysterious process of faithfulness to the faithless one created for him a vision of the divine steadfastness in the covenant that the people kept breaking. Hosea was to Gomer as God was to wayward Israel. The climax of this wonderfully tender yet righteous prophecy is as follows:

> When Israel was a child, I loved him, and out of Egypt I called my son. The more I called him, the more they went from me; they kept sacrificing to the Ba'als, and burning incense to idols. Yet it was I who taught Ephraim [i.e. the Northern Kingdom of Israel] to walk, I took them up in my arms; but they did not know that I healed them. (Hos. 11:1–3)

Then comes an interlude pronouncing harsh judgment upon the ungrateful, idolatrous Israel: The people will be subjected to Egypt and Assyria, and because of their rebelliousness, they will be made slaves. But then there wells up in the prophetic message the following, unexpected words of God:

> How can I give you up, O Ephraim! How can I hand you over, O Israel! . . . for I am God and not man, the Holy One in your midst, and I will not come to destroy. (Hos. 11:8, 9)

## FROM ANCIENT ISRAELITE RELIGION TO JUDAISM

With God there was always another chance, and the Jews, who were the heirs of ancient Israelite religion of the Torah and Temple priestly rites, deepened their understanding of his stubborn love and faithfulness. Later, Islam would come on the world scene with a profound conviction of the divine compassion and forgiveness, thus extending the beliefs that came into being in ancient Israel. Isaiah, who foretold the return from exile in Babylon, saw even in the lowest moments of Israel's suffering and dejection a redeeming dimension. Could it be that in the greatest sorrow and hurt there could come forth saving strength? Isaiah told of a certain servant of the Lord who shouldered the sins of the world and, like a sacrificial lamb without blemish, brought about reconciliation and healing. (See Isaiah 53:2-6)

By this time, the Israelites realized, or their prophets had, that God was Lord over all the earth. Even though Israel had been chosen, all would eventually be called upon to serve God. Over the centuries after the exile of captive Judeans in Babylon, Israel still suffered tragic reverses, finally coming under the heel of the Roman Empire. From the distant past, Israel remembered the hope for a divine deliverer, someone who would restore the glory of the kingdom of David. This was the messianic hope, the expectation that God would send an "anointed one" to deliver Israel from its travails and enemies. As the centuries went by, this turned into an eschatological hope: God would redeem Israel (e.g., the Jewish people) and usher in a new age at the end of the historical process. So the interim command was to listen, look, and wait faithfully.

The second temple in Jerusalem was destroyed by the Romans in 70 C.E. and never was rebuilt. By then most of the Jews had dispersed to other regions of the Near East and Mediterranean world. Biblical and temple Judaism were things of the past. The new era was based on what is called *Rabbinic Judaism,* a religion that focuses on the study of the Torah and its commentary and related literature, known as the *Talmud.* Huge scholarly projects were undertaken in both Palestine and Babylonia, which produced two different (but related) Talmuds, each taking its name from the place of its origin. Rabbinic Judaism is really "classical" Judaism. It never featured a close cultic relationship with any particular geographic region but always had held Jerusalem and the old land of Israel to be very special and holy.

When the Islamic religion spread throughout the Mediterranean and Near East in the seventh and eighth centuries, it came into direct contact with flourishing Jewish communities in Mesopotamia, Egypt, and North Africa. But before those encounters, Muslims and Jews had been fatefully involved with each other in Arabia, especially in Medina, where there was a large Jewish population when in 622 C.E. Muhammad and his followers founded the *umma,* the "community" of Islam. Over the centuries, Muslims and Jews continued their often fruitful relations.[26] Indeed, both religions have much in common, especially their strong emphasis on law and faithful observance of moral and ritual obligations within solid community structures.[27]

## AWAITING GOD'S MESSIAH

The Jews were awaiting God's Messiah so that they could be delivered from the oppressive rule by outsiders. The days when Israel had been a self-governing entity, preserving its covenant faith and temple rituals without having to please external interests, had become a very distant memory by the time the Romans occupied Palestine. The Roman Empire was an international, intercultural, cosmopolitan commonwealth on a scale unprecedented for its longevity and stability. One element of the Romans' administrative genius was their willingness to permit regional belief systems and cults to operate unhindered, as long as they were not subversive and as long as the peoples engaged in them also paid allegiance to the Roman authority. By the time of Jesus, this was centered in the person and office of Caesar, the emperor.[28]

But some in the Roman province of Palestine plotted to overthrow the foreign occupiers by means of terrorism and armed rebellion. These so-called Zealots were convinced, or at least hoped, that God would show his favor by sending his Messiah in the form of a military liberator, like David. Then the covenant people of Israel would be vindicated and rewarded for their steadfast faith.

Other Jews had already adopted the contemplative, disciplined life of a purified community apart from society. Such was the Dead Sea community of Essenes, who lived austere lives of patient devotion and strict observances as they awaited God's deliverance. Still others concluded that life had to go on being lived and planned for in the normal ways while acknowledging the Roman authority as an evil to be endured and, if possible, kept sufficiently satisfied so as not to arouse it to punitive reprisals, which were frequent enough, anyway. These last were the majority in Palestine, from the priestly and cosmopolitan Sadducees and scholarly and Torah-observant Pharisees down to the simple Jews who lived humble lives as peasants, laborers, artisans, traders, and fishermen.

## JESUS OF NAZARETH

It was into this last group that Jesus of Nazareth was born during the reign of Caesar Augustus, as the Gospel of Luke tells us. Jesus, of humble birth and circumstances, grew up to be one of human history's few world-shaking figures, comparable in his impact to Moses, Confucius, Buddha, and Muhammad. Perhaps nearly a fourth of the population of the earth today would rank him as first among this company, for that is the estimated proportion of Christians in the world.

Little is known of Jesus' childhood and young adulthood before he embarked on the public ministry of preaching the kingdom of God and calling the lost to salvation and eternal life.[29] But Jesus' actual message, as contained in his parables and preaching, was not entirely original.[30] Nearly everything had been expressed before in some form, especially by rabbis, even though no one had ever put so many of the highest spiritual ideas of the ancient world into such a memorable and convincing synthesis. But virgin births, the performance of miracles, incarnations, resurrections, sacrifices, and ascensions to heaven all had been known before, if not in the Jewish world, then in the cults and traditions of other peoples of Southwest Asia and the Mediterranean basin.[31]

### *Jesus' Message*

What was so special about Jesus, then? The answer to this cannot be found in his teaching; it can be discerned only in his life. Jesus did not so much preach a message as he *was* a message. The Hebrew scriptures knew of God's love and selfgiving through his forgiveness and renewal. Jesus knew the Hebrew Bible and quoted from it often: It was by his time a common legacy of the Jews. The passage from Isaiah quoted above proves to what depth the Jewish spirit could reach when trying to understand God's ways regarding humans. But it was not until Jesus that the notion of selfless, redemptive love was fully realized in a human life. This is Jesus' uniqueness in the history of religions. God does not tell us what Jesus is; rather, Jesus shows us what God is like. The people who left all else behind to follow Jesus came to believe—sometimes demonstrating their conviction through death—that in Jesus, God had come into this risky, doomed world of deceit, hatred, prideful rebelliousness, and murderous rivalries. God came not as a Zealot avenger or as an exalted, wise king of Israel but as a simple human being who ate bread, felt temptation, enjoyed the company of others, worked and worshiped alongside his people, had to have faith in the absence of cheap tricks, and spilt his blood as a sacrifical victim nailed to a Roman cross as a common criminal. Not the sort of messiah that most people expected—or wanted: a humiliating sort of savior. But his followers were overwhelmed by the belief that Jesus was indeed the promised Messiah.

### *The Gospels*

In order to account for Jesus' unprecedented power in the hearts and minds of his community after his resurrection, some of those who wrote memoirs of the life of Jesus and related events (which contained the "good news" of Jesus, known as the Gospel) reached way back into history and even before history to explain their Messiah's position in the cosmic scheme of things. The earliest Gospel, that of Mark, began with Jesus' baptism by his cousin John. But the somewhat later Gospel of Matthew traced Jesus' ancestry all the way back to Abraham, showing that he was destined to be the renewer and savior of Israel. Luke's Gospel went back even farther by tracing Jesus' genealogy all the way back to Adam, the first human being, in order to show that he had been sent to redeem all humankind, and not just the Jews. Jesus became the "New Adam," who offered the human race another chance at righteousness and completeness, the "fullness of life" that was at the core of salvation. But John's Gospel went back to before human or even world history to the timeless beginnings. For John, Jesus was the Logos, or "Word" of God, who descended from heaven in fleshly form as a human being. This is the incarnation, the "Word made flesh."(See the Gospel of John 1:1-5; 9-14, 18) This boldest of theological assertions provided the broadest possible scope for relating the mission and message and person of Jesus, called the Christ (Messiah), to the world.

***The Popularity of Jesus' Message.*** Jesus came at a period in Near Eastern and Mediterranean history when many different peoples were awaiting deliverance from the confining and deadening ways of the past. The varied mystery cults of the period often were centered in the belief in a personal savior (Greek *soter*). The expectation of a definitive event was expressed by the Greek term *kairos,* which is usually translated as the "fullness of time," the time of special happenings and peculiar quality, not like mere chronological progression. The presence of Jesus on earth came to be viewed as a time when eternity invaded the normal flow of events and transformed it into an epochal point on which all subsequent events would hinge. The presence of Jesus was a foretaste of God's final kingdom. The Last Supper, before Jesus' betrayal and crucifixion, was a rehearsal and portent of both Jesus' passion and, beyond that, the heavenly feast in God's presence.

## PAUL

The early church was first composed of Jews who believed Jesus to be the Messiah, the expected one. But before long the message began to spread beyond Israel. The apostle Paul, who had for some time persecuted the Christians, even consenting to the death by stoning of the first Christian martyr, Stephen (Acts 7:57; 8:1), later became the most zealous of missionaries to the Gentiles. He was particularly well qualified, by background and training, to translate the Gospel of Jesus into Hellenistic modes of discourse for the salvation of those who had not been part of the covenant people of Israel. This was a revolution in Jewish practice—and the Christian movement would be thought of as a Jewish movement for a number of years[32]—because it related the saving acts of God to all peoples, at least potentially.

### *Paul's Message*

Paul's great themes were the freedom in the spirit and the lordship of Jesus Christ. Contrasting the new dispensation in Christ with the old legalistic teaching of the

Torah, Paul insisted that God was calling people to a responsible and effective life as free beings, justified by their faith through the grace of God in Christ. This meant that works of law were outmoded and even deadening. Christ came as a fulfillment, not as a continuation of the Torah. From the time of Jesus onward people would be called to newness of life in communion with the spirit of Christ. Paul contended that sinful humankind could not justify itself by obedience to the Jewish Law. At most, according to his analysis in the Epistle to the Romans, people could use the Law to measure how far they had fallen from righteousness. Abraham's righteousness, as Paul saw it, came not from works of obedience to law but from faith (Rom. 4:13), as did that of all others after the renewal brought about in Jesus Christ.

Paul's Hellenistic background (he was born and raised in Tarsus, in Asia Minor, and was a Roman citizen), combined with his training as a Jewish Pharisee and his knowledge of the Torah, enabled him to develop a theology for both Gentiles and Jews. This was crucial in the transmission and development of the Christian message in the wider world of the ancient Mediterranean cultures. Paul made three major missionary journeys, starting new churches and visiting established ones and advising, correcting, inspiring, and renewing them. His letters to some of his early congregations have endured as essential statements of doctrine and practice in the canon of the New Testament. That is, they became "scripture," regarded as inspired by God. The work of Paul extended the Gospel to a wider world of need and aspiration, making the movement a world religion. Although Jesus is the *sine qua non* of Christianity—"that without which nothing"—Paul was in a real sense the "second founder" of the tradition.[33]

## CHRISTIANITY

Christianity appeared at a time when there were many diverse religious movements—especially mystery cults, both Oriental and Hellenistic—competing for allegiance in the Mediterranean and Near Eastern worlds.[34] Although some of them were attractive and satisfying, Christianity alone survived as the one that gave the most to the greatest number of spiritually thirsty souls. This was in great degree because it was the most open and accepting of all the creeds, especially in the social sense. Women, the poor, and the outcast all were welcome. The universalism of Christianity had its ideological roots in the teaching of Isaiah, but the actual testing of it required the life and especially the crucifixion and resurrection of Jesus, plus the theological pioneering of Paul and other intellects and personalities of the early generations, including John, who gave the world the Logos ("Word") doctrine of the preexistent and eternal Christ.

### *Christianity and Rome*

Christianity as a social and religious movement grew to maturity in a position of political powerlessness. But its convictions regarding a "kingdom of God" gave it hope for the future. At times it was severely persecuted by the Roman authorities, who regarded both the "stiff-necked" Jews and the "cannibalistic" Christians (they ate the "body" and drank the "blood" of their god) as subversive in their refusals to sacrifice to Caesar as a god. This, of course, would have been idolatry to the children of Abraham, whether Jew or Christian. Both groups of believers, with some tragic exceptions, refused to submit to Caesar and thus were guilty of undermining the civil religion that Rome regarded as a major means of maintaining stability and security. But Christianity continued to spread throughout both the East and the West. Finally, in the fourth Christian century there came along a Roman emperor, Constantine, who recognized and appreciated the virtues of the illegal religious movement and contrived to bring it into the empire's orbit. He himself became a Christian and worked hard throughout the remainder of his life to use the Christian religion to unite and strengthen his empire.[35] Indeed, before many more years Christianity, because of its enormous appeal to diverse people in the vast Roman Empire, became its official religion, largely for political reasons. But this was not universally regarded as a good thing, for it meant that citizenship as much as personal commitment would make people at least nominal members of the church.

## CHRISTIANITY AND JUDAISM

The Christians soon became a much larger movement than the Jews, because of their missionary emphasis and the peculiar appeal of their message and style of life to a wide variety of peoples. Until the coming of Islam, it was the most successful and powerful religious venture in Europe, the Mediterranean, and the Near East.

The Jews had already spread throughout the Mediterranean, as well as in Mesopotamia, long before the coming of Christianity. The Jews have always been concerned about the proper observance of ritual duties and obeying God's Law, though relatively less concerned about creedal or doctrinal issues, apart from how they related to ethical and devotional matters. Thus, Judaism is characterized by what we may call *orthopraxy,* that is, a dedication to "correct" *(ortho) "practice" (praxis).* Christianity, in contrast, is characterized more by *orthodoxy,* from the Greek term meaning "correct opinion" or doctrine. We make this comparison here for emphasis and not to suggest either that Judaism has no strong regard for correct doctrine or that Christianity does not strive to perform correctly its liturgical and communal duties. Judaism, however, is a religion of law, whereas Christianity emphasizes freedom from law, so as to follow spontaneously the Holy Spirit's guidance.

### *Islam, Christianity, and Judaism*

Islam, as we shall see, resembles Judaism much more than it does Christianity, in that law and duty became more urgent than did theological reflection or creedal definition. Neither Judaism nor Islam has an official, comprehensive creed, although each has summaries of doctrine and minimal statements of belief that are generally agreed upon. But Judaism and Islam never became close religious partners, despite their mutual affinities. Islam developed a strong missionary emphasis quite early in its history. Christianity, from the beginning, was a missionary religion, too, and like its later rival was extremely territorial and aggressive in extending its sway, politically as much as doctrinally. And the new scripture that Christians collected into the canon of the New Testament contributed immeasurably to the spread of the faith. Although the movement very early ceased to be regarded, either by itself or by others, as a Jewish sect, it continued to consider itself as the heir to the covenant history of Israel. The Jewish Bible became part of the Christian Bible, but (for Christians) it was to be no more than a preparation for the Gospel, an "old covenant" that was fulfilled in the "new covenant" of Jesus.

The historical dimension of Israelite and Jewish faith continues in Christianity.[36] We shall see that the third of the Abrahamic religions, Islam, is also devoted to that mysterious, transcendent God of history who is believed to have called Abraham from Mesopotamia, spoken to Moses from the burning bush, delivered the children of Israel from bondage in Egypt, tested and deepened Jewish faith and devotion during the exile in Babylonia, instilled in his worshipers a love for Torah study in their life of dispersion, and spread through his apostles and martyrs the paradoxical message of redemptive love that triumphs through suffering.

## NOTES

1. In Henri Frankfort et al., "Egypt: The Function of the State," in *The Intellectual Adventure of Ancient Man* (Chicago: University of Chicago Press, 1977), pp. 62–69.
2. The "Father of History" lived around 484–425 B.C.E. He traveled to Egypt and other foreign lands from his native Greece and wrote about them in his great *History.*
3. The version of the Osiris–Isis–Horus myth sketched here is very abbreviated and does not take into account any variations of detail or arrangement. There is no narrative, such as is suggested by my summary, in any ancient Egyptian literature. It was not until Plutarch (ca. 46–120 C.E.), the Greek biographer and essayist, that a coherent narrative of the Osiris legend was composed. This work is entitled *De Iside et Osiride* ("Concerning Isis and Osiris") and is available in translation, a very good one being that by J. Gwynn Griffiths (Cardiff, Wales: University of Cardiff Press, 1970). The elements of Plutarch's narrative and many regarding Osiris and Isis are found in ancient Egyptian texts and iconography. For a technically expert analysis, see Henri Frankfort, *Kingship and the Gods* (Chicago: University of Chicago Press, 1948).
4. The pharaoh as Horus when living and Osiris when dead is a structure that was brilliantly analyzed by Frankfort, in *Kingship and the Gods,* pp. 36–47.
5. James Henry Breasted, *The Development of Religion and Thought in Ancient Egypt* (New York: Harper Torchbooks, 1959). Now rather dated, this book nevertheless remains a classic and is still well worth reading.

6. John Baines, "Society, Morality, and Religious Practice," in *Religion in Ancient Egypt: Gods, Myths, and Personal Practice.* Ed. by Byron E. Shafer (Ithaca: Cornell University Press, 1991), p. 151, n. 79, and pp. 151–153.
7. Th. P. von Baaren, "Afterlife: Geographies of Death," in *The Encyclopedia of Religion,* vol. I, ed. Mircea Eliade (New York: Macmillan, 1987), pp. 116–120.
8. Theodor H. Gaster, *Thespis: Ritual, Myth and Drama in the Ancient Near East,* rev. ed. (New York: Harper Torchbooks, 1966), p. 24.
9. See Thorkild Jacobsen, "Mesopotamia: The Cosmos As a State," in Frankfort et al., *Intellectual Adventure of Ancient Man,* especially pp. 125–128.
10. *Ibid.,* pp. 210–211.
11. See the presentations of "firsts" that Samuel Noah Kramer has compiled under the title *History Begins at Sumer* (New York: Anchor Books, 1959).
12. Jacobsen, in *Intellectual Adventure,* p. 127. The remainder of this paragraph is based on Jacobsen's discussion.
13. *Ibid.*, p. 193.
14. Humans did the actual writing down, of course, but it was believed that legal and ritual matters were the will of the gods, written down in heaven as well as on earth. See Arthur Jeffery, *The Qur'an As Scripture* (New York: Russell F. Moore, 1952), p. 9. For an absorbing study of humankind's earliest religious texts, see Samuel Noah Kramer, *Sumerian Mythology,* rev. ed. (New York: Harper Torchbooks, 1961).
15. All biblical quotations are from *The Oxford Annotated Bible with the Apocrypha* (New York: Oxford University Press, 1965).
16. We use "Israelites" to denote the related peoples, beginning with Abraham, who later came to be known as "Jews," from the Judeans who experienced exile in Mesopotamia in the sixth century B.C.E.
17. For a clear and authoritative review, see James Muilenburg, "The History of the Religion of Israel," in *The Interpreter's Bible,* vol. 1 (New York and Nashville: Abingdon Press, 1952), pp. 292–348.
18. A penetrating interpretation of Moses and his role is by Martin Buber, *Moses: The Revelation and the Covenant* (New York: Harper Torchbooks, 1958).
19. Yahweh is the most important name for God in the Jewish Bible. It is also very mysterious and means something like "I will be what I will be." Jews came to observe a strict taboo against uttering this holiest of names. By contrast, no such name taboo developed in Islam concerning Allah.
20. I am indebted for this and related insights to H. Frankfort and H. A. Frankfort, "The Emancipation of Thought from Myth," chap. 12 of *The Intellectual Adventure of Ancient Man* (Chicago: University of Chicago Press, 1977), especially pp. 363–373.
21. For an interesting but inconclusive discussion in favor of "Kenite [that is, Midianite] Yahwism" as a source of Moses' religious ideas and practices, see Norman K. Gottwald, *A Light to the Nations: An Introduction to the Old Testament* (New York: Harper & Row, 1959), pp. 131–134.
22. See Robert S. Dentan, ed., *The Idea of History in the Ancient Near East* (New Haven, Conn.: Yale University Press, 1955), especially Millar Burrows' article, "Ancient Israel," pp. 99–131.

23. A sophisticated (and rather technical) recent discussion of the Deuteronomic view of history is by Norman K. Gottwald, *The Tribes of Yahweh: A Sociology of the Religion of Liberated Israel, 1250–1050 B.C.E.* (Maryknoll, N.Y.: Orbis Books, 1979), pp. 140–149 and passim.
24. For a review of theories of *Heilsgeschichte,* the original German expression translated as "salvation history," see C. R. North, "Pentateuchal Criticism," in *The Old Testament and Modern Study,* ed. H. H. Rowley (London: Oxford University Press, 1951), pp. 73–76.
25. This distinction has been made by many scholars and is contained in the meaning of the term *prophet.* There was in ancient Israel a strong sense that the prophet was a "seer," too. A full analysis is by Johannes Lindblom, *Prophecy in Ancient Israel* (Philadelphia: Muhlenburg Press, 1962).
26. An authoritative and unsentimental survey of Muslim–Jewish relations, especially in the Middle Ages, is by Solomon Dob Fritz Goitein, *Jews and Arabs: Their Contacts Through the Ages,* 3rd ed. (New York: Schocken Books, 1974).
27. An important recent survey of events and sources is Gordon Darnell Newby's *A History of the Jews of Arabia from Ancient Times to their Eclipse Under Islam* (Columbia: University of South Carolina Press, 1988).
28. Morton Scott Enslin's *Christian Beginnings, Parts I and II* (New York: Harper Torchbooks, 1956) remains a reliable as well as highly readable survey of the Roman period in Palestine. See especially chap. 3, "The Rise and Rule of Herod," and chap. 4, "Tetrarchs, Procurators, and Agrippa."
29. For a historically exacting survey of the evidence for Jesus' biography, see Günther Bornkamm, *Jesus of Nazareth* (New York: Harper & Row, 1959); more recent scholarly opinion is represented by John Dominic Crossan, *The Historical Jesus: The Life of a Mediterranean Jewish Peasant* (New York: HarperCollins, 1991).
30. See *Jesus' Jewishness: Exploring the Place of Jesus within Early Judaism,* ed. James H. Charlesworth (New York: Crossroad Press and the American Interfaith Institute, 1991).
31. A discriminating collection of texts in translation has been edited by Frederick C. Grant, *Hellenistic Religions: The Age of Syncretism* (Indianapolis and New York: Bobbs-Merrill and Liberal Arts Press, 1953). Also strongly recommended is C. K. Barrett, ed., *The New Testament Background: Selected Documents* (New York: Harper Torchbooks, 1961).
32. See Frederick C. Grant, *Ancient Judaism and the New Testament* (New York: Macmillan, 1959).
33. An accessible study of Paul is Leander E. Keck's *Paul and his Letters* (Philadelphia: Fortress Press, 1979); for understanding Paul's larger context, see Wayne A. Meeks' *The First Urban Christians: The Social World of the Apostle Paul* (New Haven: Yale University Press, 1983).
34. A detailed study of various religions and cults in early Christian times is by Harold R. Willoughby, *Pagan Regeneration: A Study of Mystery Initiations in the Graeco-Roman World* (Chicago: University of Chicago Press, 1929). See also Arthur Darby Nock's *Conversion: The Old and the New in Religion from Alexander the Great to Augustine of Hippo* (Oxford, England: Clarendon Press, 1933; Oxford paperback, 1961). See also

Kurt Rudolph, "Mystery Religions," in *The Encyclopedia of Religion,* ed. Mircea Eliade et al. (New York: Macmillan and Free Press, 1987).

35. An accessible synthesis of scholarship concerning this subject is by Ramsay MacMullen, *Constantine* (New York: Harper Torchbooks, 1971).
36. A comprehensive history of Christianity is Williston Walker et al., *A History of the Christian Church,* 4th ed. (New York: Scribner's, 1985).

CHAPTER

# 2 Pre-Islamic Arabia: Beliefs, Values, Way of Life

### KEY TERMS

**Arabian Peninsula**
**Hejaz**
**Semites**
***al-Jāhilīya***
***shaykh***
***ḥilm***
**Ka'ba**
***daughters of Allah***
***ḥajj***
***tribal humanism***
**monotheistic religions**
***hijra***
***ḥanīfs***

## PRE-ISLAMIC ARABIA

The "island of the Arabs," as the **Arabian Peninsula** is known by its inhabitants, is somewhat over one million square miles in area. Because most of the terrain is inhospitable desert or marginally habitable steppe, the population is proportionally sparse. In general, the land slopes from a high, mountainous western border along the Red Sea to lower elevations toward the east, with the exception of such rare up thrusts as the Green Mountain (*al-Jabal al-Akhḍar*) in Oman. The southern region, embracing Yemen and the Hadramaut coast, is affected by the Indian Ocean monsoons. Unlike the rest of the peninsula, it has known a complex civilization in antiquity, related in certain respects to Mesopotamia. Much of the southern sector of the peninsula, north of Hadramaut and northeast of Yemen, is a vast desert known as the Empty Quarter (*al-Rub' al-Khālī*). This is connected by a narrow strip of desert, known as al-Dahnā', to the Nufūd desert in the north, reaching as far as the frontiers of southern Jordan. The western sector of Arabia, from below the latitude of the Sinai Peninsula in the north to about the latitude of al-Ta'if in the south, is known as **Hejaz.** This is the region in which Islam was born and developed, and thus it is often called the "cradle of Islam."

For a region and a complex of peoples who have had such a great impact on world history, the prehistory, archaeology, and antiquity of Arabia are much less well known than those of the other parts of the Near East are. This is due in part to a cautious attitude by the region's modern rulers toward archaeological investigations in their domains. We do know that since early times Arabia has been a major factor in trade between the east and west. One of the most important routes has been along the Red Sea coast between southern Palestine and Yemen. Other routes proceed from Yemen across the desert to central Arabia and then on to Syria, Mesopotamia, or the Persian Gulf.

The Arabs are **Semites,** which means that they speak a language belonging to a large family of related tongues, including Hebrew, Aramaic, and Syriac, as well as ancient Akkadian and Assyrian. It is part of an even larger language group, called *Afro-Asiatic,* which includes the Berber languages, Amharic, and other Ethiopic tongues, ancient Egyptian, and Coptic. The term *Semite* comes from Shem, one of Noah's sons who came forth from the ark after the Flood (Gen. 9:18–19).

There is a popular modern theory that the Semitic-speaking peoples originated in the Arabian Peninsula in prehistory when it was relatively fertile and capable of supporting large populations.[1] With the gradual drying up of the old river courses and the absence of sufficient rainfall, the peoples migrated in waves into the Fertile Crescent, becoming the Babylonians, the Syrians, the Hebrews, the Phoenicians, and others. Thus the area that is now largely desert was the breeding ground of significant populations. This theory has not been proved, but it has had some supporters. Alternative theories place the origins of the Semites in Africa or southern Mesopotamia. It is true that within recorded history, the Arabs seem definitely to have overpopulated their regions. Long before Islam, they migrated in large numbers to the richer, contiguous lands of Egypt, North Africa, the Fertile Crescent, and beyond. It is not so much that the Arabs, or whoever the peninsula's aboriginal inhabitants were, reproduced more abundantly than did other peoples—although they often did—as that the available land and food resources were inadequate to provide for even relatively small increases in population. Thus the critical threshold of maximum population was reached sooner in the more arid, less productive ecosystems of Arabia.[2]

### *The Northern and Southern Branches*

The Arabs traditionally trace their roots back to two major sources: the northerners and the southerners. They consider the southern branch, centered in Yemen, to be the peninsula's aboriginal peoples, whereas the northerners, who settled in Hejaz, Najd, Palmyra, and Nabataea, are thought to have become assimilated to Arabism through a kind of naturalization process. These latter are thought to have descended from ‘Adnān, a descendant of Ishmael. The two branches of Arabs have remained distinct to this day, although Islam did much to narrow the gap between them. The southern branch also regards itself as having descended from biblical forebears: Joktan, the grandson of Shem (Gen. 10:25–26). According to the Bible, other Arabian groups, particularly in the north, sprang from the union of Abraham and his other wife, Ketura (Gen. 25:1–4).

The pre-Islamic Arabian past to which Islam looks back is not the civilized past of the Yemen but the pastoral-nomad dominated past of Hejaz, which is generally considered to have been barbarian and wild. No outside power had ever succeeded in subduing the region, owing to its remoteness, the difficulty of the terrain, and the extreme fierceness of its inhabitants, who possessed certain technical as well as systemic advantages when defending their own territories. The term ***al-Jāhilīya*** is applied to the life and times of the Arabs in Hejaz and surrounding areas during the centuries before Islam. This term means, literally, "the ignorance," but it also includes the notion of barbarism. It is a term coined in Islamic times and is thus intended to discredit the idolatrous and licentious days of old, before the Islamic virtues and habits came to transform, to some extent, the life of the Arabs.

## SOCIAL STRUCTURE AND ECONOMY

Before we describe the pre-Islamic Arabs' worldview, it is necessary to understand something of their social structure and economy, for these are intimately linked with it. The dominant pattern of life was pastoralist, with the people divided into more or less independent tribes. Although these tribes concluded alliances with one another in an *ad hoc* manner as the need arose, such arrangements were fragile and subject to rapid dissolution. A number of towns spotted the landscape, but their inhabitants often were only recently removed from the nomadic way of life themselves and in fact shared the old values to the extent of continuing to trace their lineages by genealogy rather than by location. Genealogy was an important concern of the Arabs, for the preservation of family, clan, and tribal purity and honor was more important than anything else.

But it would be a mistake to think of these people as aimless wanderers. Pastoralists, as nomads everywhere, move their flocks, people, and minimal domestic goods seasonally according to availability of pastureland. They usually do this in a highly regulated, traditional manner. Abraham was an exception, and he must have been strong indeed to have passed through regions where there were sure to have been local pastoralists guarding their water holes and customary grazing grounds, as well as town folk who hated the tribal nomads and, for excellent reasons, feared them as well. The old Arabian way of life was highly conservative, with change coming rarely and finding a welcome even less often. The Arab pastoralists' main means of livelihood was raising camels and sheep, hunting, occasionally serving as bodyguards or escorts to caravans, or being hired out as mercenaries in such fringe areas as the Syrian and Iraqi frontiers, where it was best to buy off the wild aborigines. Another means of gaining goods, if not great wealth, was by raiding. This was done among Bedouin groups as well as between them and sedentary peoples. In the former case, the total level of wealth did not normally increase; it just changed hands from time to time. Only by attacking settled peoples, who produce the goods of this life, could the Bedouin significantly add to their meager possessions. The raiders particularly hoped to capture camels, horses, slaves (especially women), gold, fine fabrics, and other luxury items but often had to settle for much less. The raid, known as the *ghazwa* (*razzia*), was more than a means of adding to the clan's or tribe's store of goods; it was, according to the great authority on the Arabs, Philip K. Hitti, a "sort of national sport," with well-understood rules that included refraining from bloodshed if at all possible.[3] The *ghazwa* was a way of expressing vitality, and it seems to have been highly ritualized as well as fun, at least for the victors. Usually a raid was carried out by a superior force against a weaker one, perhaps a few men in an encampment who were looking after camels. The raiders would often journey to the scene of their planned attack by means of a secret, usually circuitous route, taking up their final position under cover of darkness. A long journey would be made on camelback, with horses trailed along for the dashing attack at dawn.

### *Language and Culture*

The Qur'an (Islam's scripture)[4] contains a vivid early Meccan passage (Sura 100, vss. 1–5) that preserves in poetic form the spirit of a Bedouin raid. Recite the right-hand transliteration to gain a sense of the rhythm.

| | |
|---|---|
| By the snorting chargers, | wa-l-'ā́diyā́ti ḍábḥa |
| by the strikers of fire, | fa-l-muriyā́ti qádhạ |
| by the dawn-raiders, | fa-l-múghīrā́ti ṣúbḥa |
| blazing a trail of dust, | fa athárna bíhi náq 'a |
| cleaving there with a host! | fa wasáṭna bíhi jám 'a |

The meter suggests the rocking motion of a horse. The *wasaṭna bihi jam'a* has an onomatopoeic quality: a sharp sword cutting through something soft, like cloth and flesh. *Wasaṭna* brings to mind the Arabic word for sword, similarly onomatopoeic: *ṣayf,* pronounced with great intensity on the *s* (start saying the word with clenched teeth and somewhat puckered, not smiling, lips.) The raised mark ', as in *jam'a,* is called *'ayn* and is pronounced in the throat, sounding something like the "aaah" that the doctor expects you to utter when examining your throat. It takes much practice to pronounce this properly. The *h* with the dot under it—*ḥ*—is heavily aspirated; it should, when pronounced correctly by the beginner, make steam on a mirror held close to the mouth. (That is exaggerated, but once the clouding of the glass is achieved, then the speaker can tone it down to what it should be.)

### *Tribe and Clan Loyalty*

The Arab habit of raiding developed over the centuries a tradition of skillful weapon handling, and the loyalties associated with certain tribal affiliations provided a cohesion that was passed down through generations. The power that bound people together on the clan and tribal levels is known as *'aṣabīya,* a kind of powerful "group feeling." As one poet expressed it, "Be loyal to thy tribe, its claim upon its members is strong enough to make a husband give up his wife."[5] The basic organization of the social system starts with the family, represented by a tent. A number of tents pitched together make up a *ḥayy,* which constitutes a clan (*qaum*). Several related clans together comprise a tribe (*qabīla*). It is on the clan level, especially, where solidarity reigns. The clan has one ***shaykh,*** or chieftain, and calls itself by one name: Banū Hāshim, for example, which means "the sons of Hāshim" (the Prophet's own clan, which has continued down to this day in the Hashemite Kingdom of Jordan). The blood relationship was not always real, but if it was thought to be authentic, that is what mattered. Sometimes new people were grafted onto the lineage by being adopted or by becoming clients, and before long these people would be regarded as solidly attached.[6]

***Retaliation.*** Bloodshed within a clan left the perpetrator defenseless. The murder of someone outside the clan established a vendetta in which one clan was pitted against another, with anyone considered fair game for retaliation. The *lex talionis* ("law of retaliation") reigned supreme in pre-Islamic Arabia, and sometimes interclan and intertribal feuds continued for many years. They are memorialized in the *ayyām al-'Arab,* the "Days of the Arabs," early chronicles that described such feuds and served, with poetry, as a literary source from which much of our knowledge of the Jāhilīya has been acquired.

***Personal Honor.*** Added to the pride of lineage and blood relationship, with its corollary that the outsider—the nonrelative—was an enemy and to be treated as one wished, is the sense of personal honor. This is known as *'irḍ* and was an individual's most valuable possession. Any attack on one's honor was grounds for deadly retaliation. The dishonor of a man—and it was the males who had *'irḍ*—could come especially through his women. Women were regarded by the Arabs as naturally weak and apt to yield to temptations, sexual and other kinds. A man's honor was protected, according to the poetry, by means of *murūwa,* "manliness."[7] This great virtue included courage, loyalty, and generosity. Courage was displayed in raiding, whereas generosity was expressed in hospitality, which could be lavish. Perhaps the highest virtue possible for a human being was ***ḥilm,*** "forbearance," possessed only by a person of great spiritual as well as physical strength and courage. A man who gave away his last possession would also be remembered as a superior man, especially if it meant slaughtering his last camel. The camel was the measure of wealth and prosperity among the ancient Arabs. A poet boasts:

> O yes, many a fine day I've dallied with the white ladies,
> and especially I call to mind a day at Dara Juljul,
> and the day I slaughtered for the virgins my riding-beast
> (and oh, how marvellous was the dividing of its loaded saddle),
> and the virgins went on tossing its hacked flesh about
> and the frilly fat like fringes of twisted silk. (Mu'allaqa of Imr al-Qais)[8]

It was a great dishonor to be cuckolded or to have a female of one's clan compromised in any way, even by suggestion. But to cover another with dishonor was an occasion for the malicious publication of the details. The same poet, the legendary "Wandering King" Imr al-Qais, again boasts:

> Many's the fair veiled lady, whose tent few would think of seeking,
> I've enjoyed sporting with, and not in a hurry either,
> slipping past packs of watchmen to reach her, with a whole tribe
> hankering after my blood, eager every man-jack to slay me,
> . . . "God's oath, man, you won't get away with this!
> The folly's not left you yet; I see you're as feckless as ever."
> Out I brought her, and as she stepped she trailed behind us
> to cover our footprints the skirt of an embroidered gown.[9]

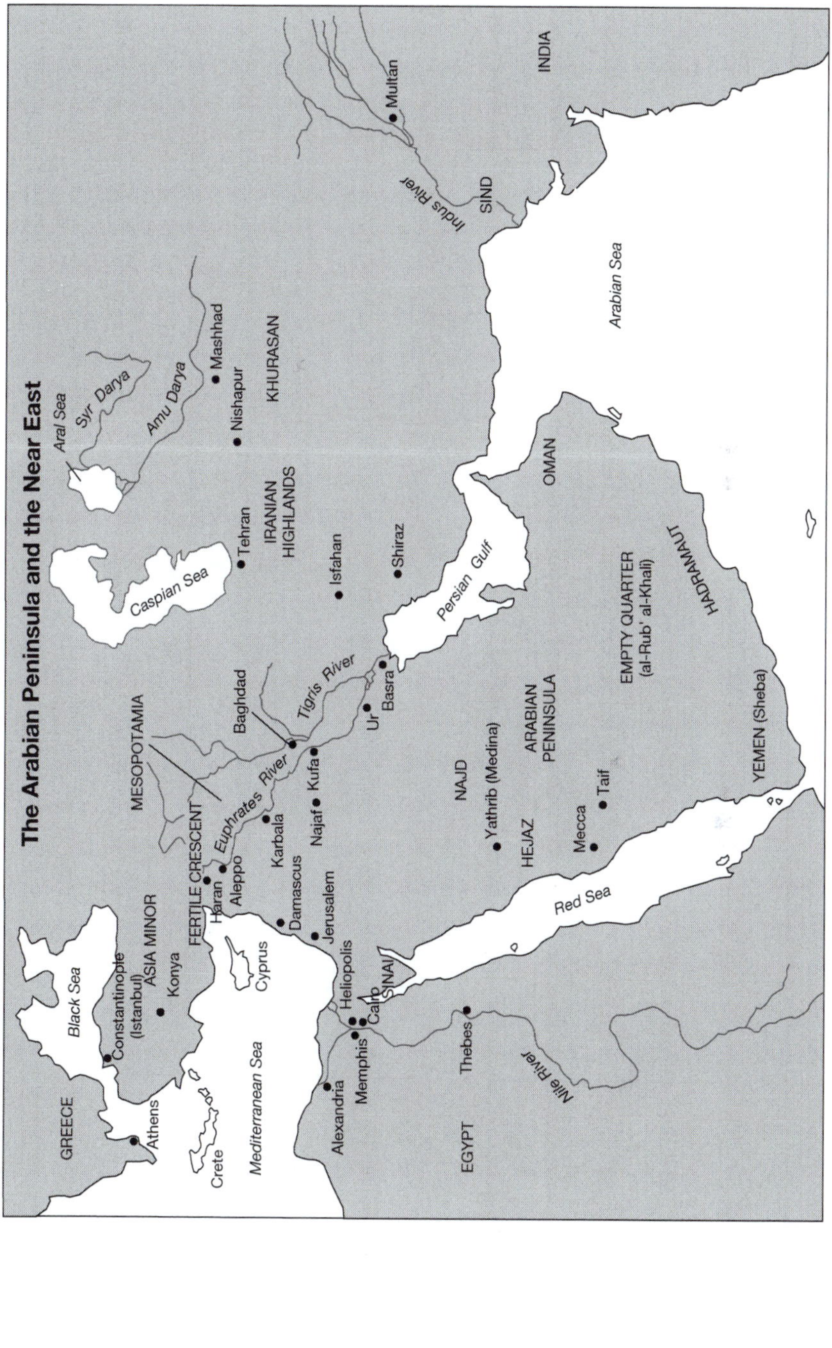


The Arabian Peninsula and the Near East

The rest of the episode is described in standard terms, but with clever twists of the poet's own. The lady in these kinds of poems always has a slender waist, plump thighs, the sidelong glance of a wild gazelle, thick cascading black hair, hips like sand dunes, and on and on through the desert inventory of sensual delights.

***In Praise of Camels.*** If the Arab male was given to meditation on the pleasures of the flesh, this flesh was not by any means limited to the human female sex. Probably more lines of poetry were written in praise of the bard's camel than of his lady. The camel made possible the free life of the desert. It was the technical edge that the Bedouin had over sedentary peoples, allowing them to traverse with a payload long distances through inhospitable territory. So thoroughly intermeshed with other aspects of Arabian existence was the life of camel breeding and so dependent were the Arabs on that stubborn yet omnicompetent beast that the Arab has been called the "*parasite of the camel.*" Indeed, there are said to be over 1,000 words in Arabic that mean camel.[10]

Camel driver, Wādī Rūm. (*Source:* Frederick Mathewson Denny)

## POETRY

The standard genre of poetry was the *qaṣīda,* or "ode." Highly stereotyped and regular, it gave the poet a means of saying old things in new ways. The ode always began with a lament over some lost love, with tears prompted by the view of an old campsite, possibly just uncovered by the shifting sands. After recalling the joys of love and describing the beauty and virtues of his beloved, the poet would often talk about his faithful riding beast, which could carry him quickly away from grief and trouble. One poet, grown old, delighted at the spirit of his also aged camel, which

> yet rejoices in her bridle, and runs still as if she were
> a roseate cloud, rain-emptied, that flies with the south wind,
> or a great-uddered she-ass, pregnant of a white-bellied sire worn lean
> by the stampeding and kicking and biting of fellow-stallions. (Labīd)[11]

The Arabs' predilection for taut bellies and smooth thighs in women is matched or even surpassed by their specifications of camel or horse flesh:

> Perfectly firm is the flesh of her two thighs—
> they are the gates of a lofty, smooth-walled castle—
> and tightly knit are her spine-bones, the ribs like bows,
> her underneck stuck with the well-strung vertebrae,
> fenced about by the twin dens of a wild lote-tree. . . .
> Her cheek is smooth as Syrian parchment, her split lip a tanned hide of
> Yemen, its slit not bent crooked;
> her eyes are a pair of mirrors, sheltering
> in the caves of her brow-bones, the rock of a pool's hollow. (Tarafa)[12]

The poetry goes on for many more lines, ending with "Such is the beast I ride."

Poetry was the major form of artistic expression that the ancient Arabs had. It was more than art, really, because its inspiration was believed to be supernatural and its utterance surrounded by mysterious power. Poetry had its roots in religion, especially in the rhymed prose of the *kāhin,* a sort of shamanistic practitioner whose attunement to surroundings and people, plus a gift for trance and ecstasy, enabled him or her to divine the future, find lost camels, and heal. Among Semitic peoples, ecstatic utterance has always been regarded as a participation in the universe's occult powers. As far back as we can trace magic-religious practices, there have been oracles and poet-seers whose blessings or curses have been potent. In fact, any person's blessing or curse makes a material difference in an event's outcome. In Genesis we find numerous moments of blessing, such as the old, blind Isaac's mistaken blessing of Jacob instead of the firstborn, Esau (Chapter 27). Even though Jacob stole his brother's blessing by means of a trick, a blessing was a blessing, and it stayed with the "supplanter," which is what Jacob means.

A poet is known in Arabic as a *shā'ir,* meaning "one who knows." The poet's knowledge is esoteric knowledge that ordinary people do not possess. It was believed that the poet received his special insights and knowledge from a demonic being called a *shayān* or "satan," or from a *jinnī,* one of those creatures of fire, invisible but usually anthropomorphic, whom the Arabs so often feared. This relationship with demonic beings made the poet a potentially dangerous figure, one whom no one would want as an enemy. Whenever a poet was born into a family or clan—and the "birth" would become known the day the individual exhibited a special gift for verse—it was announced far and wide and celebrated with rejoicing. The special power of the poet was in curses and insults against enemies, or against one's patron's enemies, on the one hand, and panegyric for one's protector and boasting of one's prowess, on the other. A cunningly contrived nickname for an opponent, for example, would stay with the victim forever. The old childhood riposte to name calling, "Sticks and stones may break my bones, but words can never hurt me" would have to be amended in the Arabian setting to read: "Sticks and stones only break my bones, but words can *kill* me!"

Scholars of Semitic languages continue to wonder how, in a largely illiterate culture, the Arabs (at least of Hejaz and central Arabia) were able to develop a common poetic language, which we call classical Arabic.[13] This was different from the tribal dialects, in that it was uniform and transcending. Each year during the truce months a fair was held at 'Ukāz, not far from Mecca, at which poets from near and far would compete with one another by means of *qaṣīdas* composed for the event. This fair gave the Arabs a means of getting to know one another, and it enabled them to celebrate at a very high level their devotion to poetic imagination. Only Mecca, the important trading town with an ancient sanctuary, could claim greater prestige than 'Ukāz. (Mecca's significance is treated later.)

The knowledge of and devotion to poetry was not limited to literary circles, intellectuals, or elites. Practically everyone engaged in it at some level, even if only to learn about interesting things. Without the surviving pre-Islamic poetry, we would know far less than we do about the life of the Jāhilīya Arabs, including their religious beliefs. As an old saying goes: "Poetry is the public register of the Arabs."[14] The Arabs' sensitive appreciation of and prudent regard for the poet's vocation made them especially receptive to the message of the Qur'an, which for Muslims stands as the peerless example of inspired utterance. Although it is not regarded technically as poetry (it is prophecy), the Qur'an is composed in a "clear Arabic tongue" and possesses a kind of "divine magic," which we will investigate later.

## PRE-ISLAMIC RELIGION

The religious beliefs of the pre-Islamic Arabs of the Hejaz included the veneration of stones, wells, trees, and sacred precincts connected with the tribe's origins. Many deities were recognized, and on the eve of Islam, the **Ka'ba,** Mecca's very archaic sanctuary, contained representations of 360 of them. But they do not seem to have been terribly compelling, except when they could be related to the tribe. People made sacrifices at various shrines, and each community or town had its own patron deity.[15]

The divinities were both male and female. Among the latter were three called the ***daughters of Allah:*** al-'Uzza, who was Venus, the morning star, the chief deity of Quraysh to whom human sacrifices were offered; al-Lāt, the goddess whose sacred precincts near al-Ṭā'if were places where no tree felling, hunting, or human killing could take place; and Manāt, the goddess of fate or destiny. The main divinity of the Meccan sanctuary, known as the Ka'ba, seems to have been an anthropomorphic deity named Hubal, who was possibly imported from Moab or Mesopotamia, as the Aramaic name, meaning "vapor, spirit," suggests.[16] Beside him were placed the famous divining arrows that the *kāhins* used to draw lots. The Arabs made pilgrimages to the shrines of their deities and engaged in a characteristic ritual circumambulation of them, known as *ṭawāf.* This circling has been recorded from antiquity and continues to the present in the sevenfold circling of the Ka'ba during the Muslim ***ḥajj,*** or pilgrimage to Mecca. As we shall see, several pre-Islamic ritual practices, especially those connected with the Ka'ba cult in Mecca, were continued by Muhammad, with appropriate mythic and symbolic reinterpretations and corrections.

### *The High God*

Allah was well known in Arabia and was the high god of the great trading city of Mecca and especially of the Quraysh tribe, into which Muhammad was born. Allah, as noted earlier, means "the god" and may thus be translated as "God." He appeared very early in the Arabian tradition and was considered to be the creator and sustainer who, when the people found themselves in extremity, could be called upon for help. The "high god" is nearly universal in the comparative religions of nonliterate, archaic peoples found in the Americas, aboriginal Australia, Asia, Africa, and elsewhere. Typically, the high god created the world, but then left when history began. Lower divinities were then worshipped and supplicated in the normal course of events. But when a calamity struck or when young men were to be initiated into the secrets of the tribe, then the high god's name and relationship to the human order were revealed.

We do not know much about the role and function of Allah in the distant Arabian past, but we should not conclude that he was unimportant or so distant as to be ineffectual. This is the manner in which the high gods of religion always behave. Their marginal and seemingly useless existence is an indicator of their mysterious, transcending power. But the worship of a high god is not the same thing as monotheism, because the high god is the supreme, but not the only, divine being.[17]

### *Tribal Humanism*

The Hejazi Arabs' deepest feelings were possibly rooted in what W. Montgomery Watt, a leading biographer of Muhammad, has called ***tribal humanism.***[18] We have already described the Arabs' social system and how group feeling binds people together, particularly on the clan level. Watt asserts that the constellation of basic attitudes and activities connected with the social group—honor, manliness, hospitality, the equitable distribution of goods, the shaykh as first among equals, raiding as a display of courage, the vendetta, and devotion to one's genealogy—together comprised the real religion of the majority. This is a useful hypothesis, and it accounts somewhat for the recessive character of the indigenous cults that surely existed and had some importance but that did not figure prominently in such records as the poetry. But the poetry had a rather restricted range of suitable subjects—desert encampments, amatory exploits, descriptions of nature, camel eulogizing, panegyric of patrons—and did not lend itself much to religious expression. There are exceptions, but they are rare.

Although unusually shaped stones, as well as trees and springs, were often the markers of sacred sanctuaries—both taboo and faithfully maintained—the Bedouins did not worship stones, trees, and water. Rather, the spirits that were thought to be associated with these objects were what they venerated, supplicated, and propitiated. A sophisticated symbolic process is always at the center of such cult activities, and so terms like *litholatry,* the "worship of stones," for example, quite miss the point. After the coming of Islam, the Bedouin proved themselves quite resistant to the new religion, except in a nominal sense when it suited their purposes. The Qur'an itself despairs of the desert Arabs, who are "stubborn in unbelief and hypocrisy" (9:97), most of them at any rate. Islam did not appeal to the Bedouin largely because it was an urban movement, as we shall see.

On balance, Watt's tribal humanism is an appealing notion, if it remains a provisional hypothesis and open to suitable alteration or expansion as more evidence is gathered in this still-developing field of pre-Islamic beliefs and ritual practices. The word *humanism* in the phrase is the problem, because there is no question of the importance of the *tribal.* However, it is likely that behind the tribe is a sacred origin and that beneath the tribe is a sacred power that keeps it going. Thus the ultimate reference would be beyond the human plane, even though the revered ancestors themselves are human symbols. But humanism also means "locating the source of value in the human," and there is evidence that the Arabs did that, as can be seen in their fatalism, which saw no meaning beyond this life. Tribal humanism is a good way, regardless of where religious-historic research leads, to characterize the more functional aspects of life among the Bedouin of Hejaz and beyond during the period before Muhammad. Watt further argues that with the development of trade in Hejaz and the consequent growth of the towns and a money economy, more and more pastoralist nomads settled down and oriented their lives in a new way, especially in Mecca and Yathrib (later Medina). Thus the old tribal values and customs came to be neglected, especially those that pertained to the fair distribution of goods and the protection of weaker members. According to Watt, this breakdown of tribal humanism provided a condition for the success of Islam.

### *Monotheistic Religions*

There were representative communities of the **monotheistic religions** in Arabia before Islam. The Jews were quite numerous in South Arabia, as well as in Yathrib, the agricultural oasis that became Medina after Muhammad and his fellow emigrants moved there in 622 on their fateful ***hijra.*** There were Christians, too, for example, at Najran in South Arabia. The Meccan caravan community witnessed the traffic of Christians, Jews, and Zoroastrians,[19] and the Meccans were apparently conversant with the main themes and characters of the biblical tradition. It is difficult to imagine that the many passages reflective of that tradition in the Qur'an could have been first recited to people who did not know anything about Moses, Abraham, and Jesus. After all, the Qur'an was intended as a message that the Arabs could understand immediately. This is not to suggest, however, that the knowledge of the old monotheistic faiths was either literate or systematic. Our sources indicate that much of the knowledge of the pagan Arabs in the Hejaz was based on oral traditions at least as much as the Bible, and probably more so. But the extremely laconic character of the sūra of Joseph, for example—the only sustained narrative in the otherwise largely oracular Qur'an—implies that the hearers knew the old story well enough to follow the Qur'an's interpretation of it. We are told that in pre-Islamic times the Ka'ba itself was decorated with pictures, some of which were of biblical subjects: Abraham, angels, Jesus, Mary, and some prophets (unnamed).[20]

There also seem to have been native Arabian monotheists who were neither Jewish nor Christian. The Qur'an calls these people ***ḥanīfs,*** which, according to the way that it is used in that text, can be translated as a kind of "generic monotheist."[21] The term is used to characterize the religion of Abraham, who

> in truth was not a Jew, neither a Christian; but he was a Muslim and one pure of faith [that is, a *ḥanīf*]; Certainly he was never of the idolaters. (3:67)

Interestingly, the Arabic word *ḥanīf* may have been borrowed from an Aramaic word meaning "pagan."[22] However that may be, there seems to be no doubt that among Muhammad's hearers it included a sense of purity and uprightness. The pagan dimension would fit if it meant a distinction between the Christians and the Jews on one side and a supposed Abrahamic core of monotheism in the distant past, which had degenerated into polytheism over the centuries, on the other side. Muhammad and the Qur'an, as we shall see, called for a return to the original Islam, as they regarded it, of Abraham and the patriarchs.[23]

The Roman Catholic Church had long considered Arabia to be a "breeding ground of heresies" (*haeresium ferax*) because of its polytheism and its resistance to regulating the renegade varieties of Christianity that did exist in that area, such as the anathematized Monophysites. Christians never succeeded in evangelizing the peninsula, or any part of it, in the name of the one, holy, catholic, and apostolic Church. Surely what happened in the seventh century was as unexpected as it was startling. The "breeding ground of heresies" had become the "cradle of Islam," and the "evangelization" of Arabia, as well as vast regions beyond, was to be achieved according to a quite different program and under a new imperium.

Rather than draw upon the resources and experience of outside power centers, the Arabs of Hejaz would, under the banner of Islam, mobilize their own considerable means that had been developing in the great mercantile center of Mecca and the large agricultural oasis of Medina. These two cities, especially Mecca, gained vast wealth and regional prestige during the sixth and seventh centuries C.E. Mecca, which was ruled by an oligarchy of leading commercial families when Muhammad was born, was also the most prominent traditional religious center, a goal for pilgrims from throughout the region. Well before the rise of Islam, a close relationship between religious beliefs and practices and economic life had been cemented in the Meccan sanctuary. No Meccan businessperson wanted to see this alliance undermined in any way. But before Muhammad's career as prophet, no one had ever dreamed that Mecca would become a highly lucrative pilgrimage center for much of the world, and not just Hejaz. The breakdown of "tribal humanism" was to be fortuitously resolved by the rise of a new value system for the much more complex and sophisticated social, economic, and political order that was emerging around the time of Muhammad's birth in 570 C.E.[24]

## NOTES

1. Known as the Winckler-Caetani theory, after its principal supporters. Bernard Lewis, *The Arabs in History,* rev. ed. (New York: Harper Torchbooks, 1966), p. 22. For a review of the various theories, see George Barton, "Semites," in *Encyclopedia of Religion and Ethics,* vol. 11, ed. James Hastings, "The Semitic Cradle-Land" (New York: Scribner's, 1921), pp. 379–380.
2. See Xavier de Planhol, "The Geographical Setting," in *The Cambridge History of Islam,* vol. 2, ed. P. M. Holt, Ann K. S. Lambton, and Bernard Lewis (Cambridge, England: Cambridge University Press, 1970), pp. 444–445. De Planhol acknowledges a variety of causes for the Arab-Islamic conquests that witnessed a tremendous outpouring of people from the peninsula. Fred McGraw Donner, in his exhaustive study, *The Early Islamic Conquests* (Princeton, N.J.: Princeton University Press, 1981), emphasizes religious and political as well as economic factors in the Arab conquests and migrations. See especially pp. 267–271 for the author's conclusions, which dismiss the theory that overpopulation was a factor.
3. Philip K. Hitti, *History of the Arabs,* 9th ed. (New York: St. Martin's Press, 1967), p. 25. An absorbing analysis of the *ghazwa,* based on both ethnographic and historical data, is by Louise E. Sweet, "Camel Raiding of North Arabian Bedouin: A Mechanism of Ecological Adaptation," reprinted in her *Peoples and Cultures of the Middle East: An Anthropological Reader,* vol. 1 (Garden City, N.Y.: Natural History Press, 1970), pp. 265–289. See also, in the same volume, Barbara C. Aswad, "Social and Ecological Aspects in the Formation of Islam," pp. 53–73.
4. Unless otherwise noted, the translation of the Qur'an used throughout this book is by A. J. Arberry, *The Koran Interpreted* (New York: Macmillan, 1955), but with the standard "Egyptian" verse numbers.
5. Hitti, *History of the Arabs,* p. 27.
6. The classic Western study of this subject is by W. Robertson Smith, *Kinship and Marriage in Early Arabia* (London: A. and C. Black, 1903).

7. A discussion with many examples is by Ignaz Goldziher, "Muruwwa and Dīn," in his *Muslim Studies (Muhammedanische Studien),* vol. 1, ed. S. M. Stern and trans. C. R. Barber and S. M. Stern (Chicago: Aldine, 1966), pp. 11–44.
8. A. J. Arberry, *The Seven Odes: The First Chapter in Arabic Literature* (London: Allen & Unwin, 1957), p. 61.
9. *Ibid.*, p. 62.
10. Hitti, *History of the Arabs,* pp. 21–22, provides a fair amount of camel lore.
11. Arberry, *Seven Odes,* p. 143. An excellent recent translation of several of the famous odes is Michael Sells, *Desert Tracings: Six Classic Arabian Odes by 'Algama, Shánfara, Labīd, 'Antara, al-A'sha, and Dhu al-Rúmma* (Middletown, Conn.: Wesleyan University Press, 1989).
12. Arberry, *Seven Odes,* pp. 84–85.
13. See the article, "'Arabiyya," in *Encyclopedia of Islam,* new ed., vol. 1, ed. H. A. R. Gibb et al. (Leiden: E. J. Brill, 1960–), p. 565, for a discussion of the emergence of the Arabic "poetical *koiné.*"
14. Cited in Hitti, *History of the Arabs,* p. 95.
15. Relatively little is known for certain about pre-Islamic Arabian religion. One needs to take into account the differences between the Hejaz and South Arabia. A good recent review is Adel Allouche's article "Arabian Religions" in *The Encyclopedia of Religion,* vol. I, ed. by Mircea Eliade et al. (New York: Macmillan and Free Press, 1987), pp. 363–367. A rare early source is Ibn al-Kalbī, *The Book of Idols.* trans. Nabīh Amīn Fāris (Princeton, N.J.: Princeton University Press, 1952). A significant recent study of pre-Islam Arabian myth-making and its incorporation into the Qur'an and Islamic history is Jaroslav Stetkevych, *Muhammad and the Golden Bough: Reconstructing Arabian Myth* (Bloomington and Indianapolis: Indiana University Press, 1996).
16. Ibn al-Kalbī, *op. cit.,* p. 100.
17. For an illuminating comparison of the notions of *supreme* god and *only* god, see Raffaele Pettazzoni, "The Formation of Monotheism," in his *Essays on the History of Religions* (Leiden, Holland: E. J. Brill, 1954), chap. 1; see also Hamilton A. R. Gibb, "Pre-Islamic Monotheism in Arabia," *Harvard Theological Review* 55, no. 4 (1962): 269–280.
18. W. Montgomery Watt, *Muhammad at Mecca* (Oxford, England: Clarendon Press, 1953), p. 24.
19. Or Mazdeans, a strain of Zoroastrianism. This religion is referred to in Arabic as *majūs* and is mentioned once in the Qur'an (22:17). M. Morony, "Madjūs," in *The Encyclopaedia of Islam,* new ed., vol. V, Fasc. 96 (Leiden: E. J. Brill, 1987), pp. 1110–1118.
20. Alfred Guillaume, "The Pictorial Background of the Qur'an," *The Annual of the Leeds University Oriental Society* 3 (1961–1962): 39–59.
21. I am indebted to the late Professor Marilyn Robinson Waldman, Ohio State University, for this felicitous rendering. In her lectures to undergraduates, Dr. Waldman contrasted "generic monotheism" with "brand-name monotheism" (for example, Judaism, Islam).
22. For a review of the evidence and major theories, see Frederick Mathewson Denny, "Some Religio-Communal Terms and Concepts in the Qur'ān," *Numen* 24 (February 1977): 26–34.

23. An excellent review of the evidence connecting Abraham with pre-Islamic Arabian religion is Reuven Firestone's "Abraham's Association with the Meccan Sanctuary and the Pilgrimage in the Pre-Islamic and Early Islamic Periods," *Le Muséon: Revue d'Etudes Orientales,* Tome 104, Fasc. 3–4 (1991), pp. 359–387.
24. See Eric R. Wolf, "The Social Organization of Mecca and the Origins of Islam," *Southwestern Journal of Anthropology* 7, no. 4 (Winter, 1951): 329–356.

PART TWO

# The Coming of Islam: The Prophet, His People, and God's Religion

CHAPTER

# 3 Muhammad and the Early Muslim Community

## KEY TERMS

| | | |
|---|---|---|
| ***ḥadīth qudsī*** | ***islām*** | ***rasūl*** |
| **Qur'an** | ***'ibāda*** | **Medina** |
| **Quraysh** | ***ṣalāt*** | ***umma*** |
| **People of the Book** | ***nabī*** | ***qibla*** |

## BEFORE MUHAMMAD

Even with all their gods, spirits, shrines, poets, *kāhins,* and elegant tribal genealogies, the old desert-dwelling Arabs, especially, appear to have been basically fatalistic. They had no real belief in a transcendent source of personal meaning and thus no hope. The Qur'an captured the essence of these people's dominant conviction:

> They say, "There is nothing but our present life; we die, and we live, and nothing but Time destroys us." Of that they have no knowledge; they merely conjecture. And when Our signs are recited to them, clear signs, their only argument is that they say, "Bring us our fathers, if you speak truly." (45:24–25)

The resurrection of the body was as foolish a notion to most Arabians as it had been to the ancient Greeks.[1] This life is all there is, and so make the most of it. One of the ways in which the Arabs enjoyed life was by drinking wine, and there are many drinking songs that have come down to us, from both the Jāhilīya, when imbibing was not considered to be a sin, and Islamic times, when it has been punished. Tarafa, a pre-Islamic poet who did not wish to waste time, stated:

> So permit me to drench my head while there's still life in it,
> for I tremble at the thought of the scant draught I'll get when I'm dead.
> I'm a generous fellow, one that soaks himself in his lifetime;
> you'll know tomorrow, when we're dead, which of us is the thirsty one.
>
> • • •
>
> I see Life is a treasure diminishing every night.
> and all that the days and Time diminish ceases at last.
> By your sweet life, though Death may miss a lad for the nonce
> he's like a loosened lasso, whose loops are firmly in hand.[2]

The Arabic word that is translated as "Time" both in the Qur'anic passage and the preceding poem is *dahr*: "impersonal, blind fate." A "divine saying" (Arabic, ***ḥadīth qudsī***), those extra-Qur'anic traditions that God is believed to have revealed to Muhammad, deals with *dahr* in a striking manner:

> The son of Adam [that is, humans] vexes me by saying, "Curse Time!" So none of you should ever say, "Curse Time!," for *I am Time,* who causes its night to follow its day, and so, if I willed, could bring them both to nothing. (emphasis mine)[3]

This change constitutes a breakthrough in religious consciousness. All along, behind a seemingly impersonal and capricious fate, was a willing, purposeful, personal God. In this saying God is not claiming to be *dahr;* rather, he is the real power of the universe that the Arabs had mistakenly associated with mere time.

## MUHAMMAD THE PERSON

### *The Early Years*

Around 610 C.E. a prophet was born in Arabia when a voice descended upon a thoughtful, middle-aged man of sensitive feelings.[4] This man, Muhammad ibn 'Abdallah, had taken up the habit of retiring for personal meditation and spiritual cultivation to a cave in a mountainside outside Mecca. He would pack enough provisions for a few days' retreat, after which he would return home for more, in order to pass additional days and nights at Mount Hira. He would often dream, and it was then that the first revelations came to him, "like the morning dawn." A mysterious, personal presence came to Muhammad and announced: "O Muhammad, you are the Messenger of God." Muhammad fell to his knees, trembling all over. He dragged himself to Khadīja, his beloved and trusted wife, saying: "Wrap me up!

Wrap me up!" Then he remained covered up until his terror passed. Another time the presence announced the same thing to Muhammad, causing him to become so distraught and frightened that he was about to throw himself off a high cliff. Then it appeared again, announcing that Muhammad was God's apostle and that the speaker was the angel Gabriel. According to a Qur'anic passage that describes the apparition, the angel was

> one terrible in power, very strong; he stood poised, being on the higher horizon, then drew near and suspended hung, two bows'-length away, or nearer, then revealed to his servant that he revealed. (53:5–10)

Later Gabriel came to Muhammad while he was sleeping. Covering him with a brocaded coverlet on which there was some writing, he commanded Muhammad: "Recite!" "I am unable to recite!" responded Muhammad. Gabriel pressed down the cover so hard on Muhammad that he thought he was about to die. Again Gabriel ordered him: "Recite!" When Muhammad once again confessed his inability, Gabriel pressed down even harder, bringing Muhammad near death. A third time he commanded him to recite, whereupon Muhammad cried out, "*What* shall I recite?" in order to save himself from the pressure. Gabriel replied:

> Recite: In the Name of thy Lord who created,
> created Man of a blood-clot.
> Recite: And thy Lord is the Most Generous,
> who taught by the Pen,
> taught man that he knew not. (Qur'an 96:1–5)

These are the first verses of the **Qur'an** to be revealed. The word *qur'ān* means "recitation," and it refers to individual passages as well as to the entire collected body of recitations that Muhammad was to receive, starting with that terrible day in Ramadān until his death more than twenty years later.

Muhammad the prophet came into being when he was about forty years of age. Muhammad the person was born around 570 C.E., according to traditional dating; he was certainly born sometime between then and 580 C.E. We have little reliable information about his family background, except that he was a member of **Quraysh**—a powerful tribe in Mecca—and of the clan of Banū Hāshim, one of the less prominent groups, although well regarded. Muhammad's father died before he was born, and his mother died when he was only six. As with many boys in those days, Muhammad was sent out to a wet nurse in a Bedouin tribe in the desert, in order to strengthen him and expose him to the purest Arabic language. After his birth, his grandfather 'Abd al-Muttalib acted as Muhammad's guardian and did so lovingly, taking over his rearing when his mother died. But Muhammad's grandfather died only two years later, leaving the boy in the care of his uncle, Abū Tālib, who protected Muhammad in later years when as prophet he began to threaten the polytheistic Meccan oligarchy's sense of well-being.

### *Legends*

Such are the outlines of Muhammad's early years. There also are hagiographical stories. One legend has it that the Prophet's mother, Amina, heard a voice when she was pregnant with him, which stated:

> You are pregnant with the Lord of this people and when he is born say, "I put him in the care of the One from the evil of every envier; then call him Muhammad" [meaning "laudable"].[5]

During her pregnancy Amina saw a light emanate from her body by which she could see certain castles in far-off Syria. Another legend tells of a remarkable happening when Muhammad was traveling on a caravan to Syria that his uncle was leading.[6] The company stayed at Bostra in Syria, a major center of Monophysite Christianity. A monk there named Bahīra had studied a certain book that foretold the coming of a prophet, whose advent would be accompanied by certain signs. Bahīra had never before paid any attention to the Meccan merchants, but he noticed, as this caravan approached, that one of the people was overshadowed by a cloud. When that person, the young Muhammad, pulled up under a shady tree, the shadow followed him, though otherwise the sun shone. Bahīra then did an extraordinary thing: he invited the Qurayshite group to eat with him. He looked for the special person, who would have a mark on him. Not finding him among the diners, he inquired if all the troop had come to partake of the meal. They told him that all were present except for a youth who was guarding the baggage. Bahīra thus had Muhammad brought in, whereupon he proceeded to question him about a number of things.

Muhammad's answers (dealing with such matters as his sleeping habits, details of his person, and so forth) accorded with the old book that the monk had studied. Looking at his back, Bahīra discovered the sign of prophethood, which was said to be like the mark of a cupping glass. Bahīra then asked Abū Tālib who the boy was. When Muhammad's uncle replied that he was his son, the old monk saw through him, and so Abū Tālib confessed that he was his nephew and that the boy's father had died before he was born. Bahīra agreed and then warned Abū Tālib to take Muhammad back home quickly, adding that he should be protected from the Jews, who would do something evil to him if they discovered the truth about his special nature. Muhammad then grew up into manhood under the protection of God.

Some stories even tell of Muhammad's being prevented in interesting ways from leaving his flocks to go into Mecca for a "night on the town." Once he is said to have been distracted from such a goal by a rustic wedding being held on the outskirts. Joining in the festivities, he soon fell asleep. Muslims view Muhammad as sinless and remember such stories as evidences of God's providential arrangement for Muhammad's innocent youth and manhood until he was ready to begin his prophetic career. Whatever the facts may have been, Muhammad achieved early a reputation as an honest and reliable person, as his nickname, al-Amīn ("The Trustworthy"), indicates.

Muhammad grew up in very modest circumstances and had to work hard, most likely in trade, as he grew into adulthood, although he was a shepherd in his youth. When he was in his twenties, Muhammad entered the service of a wealthy widow named Khadīja, as a manager of her caravan. He succeeded admirably in turning a good profit for his employer. Because of his success and his generally excellent character and bearing, Khadīja proposed marriage to him. This was a significant turn for the better in Muhammad's fortunes, and the marriage did much to foster his further development. When they were married, Khadīja is said to have been forty years old, or fifteen years older than her new husband. This would have been around 595 C.E.; but it is possible that Khadīja was somewhat younger because she bore at least six children to Muhammad: four daughters and two sons. Neither of their sons survived childhood.

Muhammad and Khadīja effectively became business partners through their marriage, but we do not know much about that side of their lives. It is possible that Muhammad again traveled to Syria. He did take more and more to a contemplative posture, which apparently included brooding over the low level of moral and social life in Mecca. Muhammad felt sympathy with other people, especially orphans, widows, outcasts, and the poor. He was horrified by such practices as the burying alive of infant daughters, which was still practiced in certain locales in Hejaz. This was done partly for economic reasons, but also, it seems likely, to forestall the possible dishonor that might come to a man through his daughter's foolishness. Later, the Qur'an prophesied that at the Last Judgment the girl buried alive would be asked "for what sin she was slain?" (81:9)

## MUHAMMAD THE PROPHET

Muhammad's call to be a prophet occurred after he had apparently become a highly disciplined spiritual seeker. That is, the vision and the call to "Recite!" did not confront a simple camel driver and small businessman. A telling detail in the main Qur'anic account of the encounter with the apparition on the horizon is that "his [Muhammad's] eye swerved not, nor swept astray. Indeed, he saw one of the greatest signs of his Lord" (53:17–18). Muhammad was able to look straight at the apparition, and the commentators agree that this was without either fright or impudence. This singular experience ushered in the prophetic era of Arabian history when Muhammad began to receive revelations through a special process known in Arabic as *waḥy,* a sort of auditory inspiration.

Actual visions were extremely rare in Muhammad's career as prophet, being limited to the initial call by Gabriel, the miraculous ascension to heaven and the presence of God later on, and one or two others from legendary sources. The verses of the Qur'an were revealed to Muhammad little by little, and he was distinctly aware that they were not of his own conceiving. This point is crucial for Muslims, who regard the Qur'an as being entirely the product of God and not at all of a human being, except for its arrangement, verse numbering, and the names of the sūras (chapters), which were assigned within a generation after his death. Muhammad clearly distinguished what was from God and what was his own opinion throughout his life as prophet.

It should be pointed out that his followers tended very early to regard Muhammad's own pronouncements as also being very weighty. A natural question may be raised: Did people come to believe and obey his message because of its self-evident authority or because of Muhammad's charismatic nature? Probably because of both working simultaneously and synergistically as what one scholar called the "prophetic-revelatory event."[7] This is even more likely when the "divine saying" (*ḥadith qudsī*) is considered. This is a type of utterance believed to have come from God to Muhammad, but not as a *qur'ān* or "recitation." Rather, it is between a *qur'ān* and what Muhammad might have said on his own authority. An example of a divine saying is the preceding one about the Arabs' cursing of time.

After Muhammad's call to prophecy, there was a period when the contacts with his divine source did not recur. This *fatra,* as it is known, continued for a long enough time for Muhammad to feel abandoned and depressed. It is useful to compare this "dark night of the soul" with the experiences of other visionaries and mystics who have been plunged into grave doubt and distress after having reached an exalted state of spiritual awareness. It is a common pattern.

> But after a while the revelations resumed with the following words:
>
> By the white forenoon and the brooding night!
>
> Thy Lord has neither forsaken thee nor hates thee and the Last shall be better for thee than the First.
>
> Thy Lord shall give thee, and thou shalt be satisfied.
>
> Did He not find thee an orphan, and shelter thee?
>
> Did He not find thee erring, and guide thee?
>
> Did He not find thee needy, and suffice thee? (Qur'an 93:1–8)

The biographical elements of this passage are obvious. In fact, the best original source for Muhammad's knowledge is the Qur'an, which is doubtlessly authentic and from the Prophet's mouth. The problem is that the Qur'an is not a consciously historical or autobiographical record, nor does it provide any kind of narrative structure. That must be derived from other sources. But we do get from the Qur'an a vivid and reliable sense of Muhammad's religious experience and worldview. The soul of Muhammad is revealed throughout, regardless of whether one accepts the Muslim view of revelation or the view that the Prophet somehow composed the text himself.

Khadīja was the first to become a Muslim, and her support and comfort of Muhammad during these trying times were of critical importance. Her cousin, Waraqa ibn Nawfal, either a Christian or *a ḥanīf,* was consulted when Muhammad had doubts right after his first experience with the angel. Waraqa knew something of the older scriptures and declared that what had come upon his cousin's husband was none other than what had previously descended upon Moses, the *nāmūs.* This term seems to have been understood by the Arabs as meaning an angelic messenger, especially Gabriel, but it is a corruption of the Greek *nomos,* meaning "law," or Torah. Waraqa also predicted difficult times for Muhammad, because peoples had in the past always tended to reject their prophets. He died not long afterward and so was not on hand to support Muhammad.

## THE QUR'AN

The early message of the highly oracular Qur'an centers on the themes of God's coming judgment of humankind at the end of the world. On the last day the dead will be raised from their graves to stand trial and will be granted eternal felicity in heaven or eternal punishment in hell. Each will receive what he or she has earned, for God is depicted as just. He is also all-powerful, majestic, and holy and is thus deserving of worship and praise. God demands moral behavior from his creatures and especially emphasizes generosity toward others, particularly the poor, the orphaned, the weak, and the outcast. Not only awe and obedience are required; gratitude is just as important.

As time passed, God's compassion and mercy came also to be emphasized. They balance and temper but do not replace God's justice. Yet the divine justice is not impersonal or mathematical in proportion to humankind's deeds. It is expressed in a personal, intentional, and yet inscrutable way. Unlike the Hindu and Buddhist *karma,* in Islam, God's divine justice is subject to forgiveness and erasure, in a relationship with humans that is both mutual and spontaneous. The Qur'an, in fact, continued Judaism's and Christianity's message of ethical monotheism. The Muslims, too, have a strong sense of covenant with God.

The one unforgivable sin, according to the Qur'an, is *shirk,* the "associating" of anything with God (4:48). One who does this is a *mushrik,* an "idolater." The ancient pagan Arabs, of course, fell into this category, but they, as well as all others, were given the chance to turn toward God as Muslims. The Qur'an regards the Jews and the Christians as **People of the Book** (ahl al-kitāb) who, although they possess authentic scriptures from God, have over the generations twisted and corrupted their messages and split up into sects. But some of them accepted the revelation to Muhammad and so would be rewarded (3:199). Generally, the Jews and Christians are invited to become Muslims so as to renew and perfect the religion that was first revealed to Abraham. Otherwise they are to be treated justly (as long as they do not oppose Islam) and in no case forced to convert.

Throughout the Qur'an runs the theme of God's unity, and it is the compromising of this oneness that constitutes the greatest sin. The unity of God is to be reflected in the unity and uniformity of his religion and in unanimity in his community of worshipers. All that the Muslim does is to reflect God's greatness and unity. The most pointed and forceful statement of this central theme is in the Sūra of Sincerity:

> In the Name of God, the Merciful, the Compassionate
> Say: "He is God, One, God, the Everlasting Refuge, who has not begotten, and has not been begotten, and equal to Him is not any one." (112)

The reference to begetting is obviously a major difference from the Christian view of God, but it also refers—probably more immediately—to the ancient Arabian notion of gods' giving birth to gods, as in the case of the "daughters of Allah." For a very brief period, according to one source, Muhammad acknowledged the worship of these three goddesses alongside Allah, but later he realized, by means of revelation, that the permission to do so had come from Satan.[8]

> Have you considered El-Lat, El-'Uzza and Manat the third, the other? [The following words in italics are the so-called "Satanic verses," which, according to one historian-exegete, were later nullified and removed from the Qur'an at God's command:] *These are the intermediaries exalted, whose intercession is to be hoped for. Such as they do not forget.* [The proper divinely revealed ending is as follows:] What, have you males and He females? That were indeed an unjust division. They are naught but names yourselves have named, and your fathers; God has sent down no authority touching them. (53:19–23)

According to this account, Muhammad apparently was very intent on attracting the Meccan merchants to his new religion, and the compromise indicated in the satanic verses seemed a good way to do it. He learned a lesson, it appears. According to the old belief, God's having only daughters suggested a deficiency in virility, and by implication, Muhammad was similarly afflicted: the Meccans could taunt in inventively malicious ways.

## THE FIRST MUSLIMS

'Alī, Muhammad's cousin and son-in-law, was the first male convert to Islam. He later became important as the fourth caliph, or "deputy," to succeed the Prophet as leader of the Muslim community and as first imām of Shi'ism. 'Alī was a spiritual person who himself gained a reputation for religious knowledge and guidance. He was married to Fātima, a daughter of Muhammad and Khadīja. Then Abū Bakr, who became Muhammad's father-in-law and the first caliph, converted to Islam. In the early years there were only a few Muslims, and they were from the humbler classes, with the exception of 'Uthmān, the sole convert from Mecca's oligarchy in the Meccan years. He became the third caliph.

Muhammad's early preaching was warning, and the Qur'an gives one of his titles as "warner." His warnings of the coming judgment and of the woes of those who refused to believe and do good works were apparently received at first with good-natured indifference. But when Muhammad began attacking the Meccan divinities and, through them, the old religious establishment, which was as profitable as it was deeply rooted, the situation became increasingly tense. This seems to have happened after Muhammad was inspired to change the Qur'anic verses pertaining to the three goddesses, which we quoted earlier. From this time onward, the emphasis on God's unity is pronounced. Life became difficult enough for the Muslims that a number of them who were being persecuted were sent to Abyssinia. As a standard source expresses it: "This was the first hijra ['emigration'] in Islam."[9]

Muhammad and his family were spared intense persecution because of his uncle Abū Tālib's protection as head of the Hāshim clan. But others, especially of the lower classes, were given harsh treatment. They were beaten, imprisoned, deprived of food and water, exposed to the midday heat, and otherwise tortured. Bilāl, a black slave who had become a Muslim, was put in the hottest part of the day on his back with a heavy rock on his chest. Then his evil master announced: "You will stay here till you die or deny Muhammad and worship Al-Lāt and al-'Uzzā." Then Bilāl repeated over and over while undergoing such agony: "One, one!"[10] referring to God's unity. Abū Bakr finally reprimanded Bilāl's owner for such inhumane treatment, and he traded a "heathen" black slave of his own for Bilāl. Eventually Abū Bakr freed Bilāl, who became the prophet's chief *mu'adhdhin,* the one who calls the Muslims to prayers. The Quraysh even attempted to have the emigrants forcibly returned from Abyssinia, but the Negus, or ruler of that country, refused to turn them over to Meccan agents.

The move to Abyssinia occurred in about 615 C.E. Those Muslims remaining in Mecca were still being persecuted, and in 619 C.E. there was a crisis when Abū Tālib, Muhammad's uncle and clan protector, died. Leading up to this unsettling turn of events was a prolonged boycott of the Hāshim clan by the majority of the Quraysh tribe. The Muslims did not give in, nor did their pagan protector, Abū Tālib. But after his death, his brother and successor as clan chief, Abū Lahab, a prosperous merchant, withdrew the clan's full protection of Muhammad, and he forced him to admit that his deceased uncle, not having embraced Islam before he died, was now in hell. This was regarded as disrespectful by Abū Lahab (and by the established custom of Quraysh) and deserving of punishment. It seems that Abū Lahab also wanted Muhammad to stop preaching Islam. At any rate, Muhammad began seeking a new site for his community. He visited the town of Tā'if, but the people there rejected and mistreated him. On his return to Mecca, he had to wait on the outskirts until he could find someone to protect him. Muhammad's troubles increased in the same year with the death of his beloved Khadīja, who had always been his mainstay and comforter to whom he confided his innermost thoughts.

## THE DEVELOPMENT OF ISLAM

By this time the basic features of Islam were fairly well developed but it still lacked the kind of community integrity and authority in governmental, judicial, and military matters that it would have in Medina after the great Hijra in 622 C.E. The Arabic word ***islām*** means "submission" or "surrender" to almighty God, and one who submits is called a *muslim* (or *muslima* if female). Islam is an act and not a thing, and it continues in time as a relationship between the servant and his or her master. Each Muslim is an *'abd,* "slave" or "servant" of God. The proper way to commune with God is in worship and praise. The various acts of worship are known collectively as *'ibādāt* (pl.), which is from the same root as *'abd* is and can be translated as "services," in the sense of the work that slaves do for their masters. But in the Islamic context, ***'ibāda*** means worship. It is significant that all three Abrahamic religions attach the meaning of work to worship: the ancient Hebrew *'avodah,* "service" (and an obvious cognate of *'ibāda*), and the Latin *opus Dei,* "work of God," which means prayer and praise, especially in the strictly regulated monastic context.

At the heart of Muslim devotion is the ***ṣalāt,*** or "prayer service," consisting of several cycles of postures culminating in full bodily prostration with the forehead touching the ground. This seems to have been practiced from the beginning as a distinctive aspect of the new movement. The little Muslim group prayed together at night, in houses, but also out in public sometimes during the day, which occasionally brought ridicule and persecution. Praise and thanksgiving seem to have accompanied the prostrations. The gradually increasing amount of revealed recitation (Qur'an) comprised the Muslims' "prayer book." In the Near East, public worship has often been a sign of one's commitment to a party or a program, and it has also been a symbol of submission to authority. Thus, the Muslims, when they prayed publicly, were participating in that old form of allegiance. So were the Meccan leaders when they lined up to pray with Muhammad and the Muslims during the period when the "daughters of Allah" were still worshiped. When the formula was changed in accordance with God's demand that he alone be worshiped, the pagan Meccans' public participation was cut off. From then on the Muslim salat was a badge of difference and independence. As soon as a new convert was made, that person immediately performed the salat with his or her new brothers and sisters.

### *Muhammad's Night Journey and Ascent into Heaven*

Muhammad and his followers continued to observe certain aspects of the old Ka'ba cult in the Meccan sanctuary. One night when Muhammad was sleeping near the holy Ka'ba itself, as he sometimes did when observing a prayer vigil, a remarkable event took place. It is not certain whether it was originally considered to be a spiritual, dreamlike experience or an actual happening.[11] An angel, presumably Gabriel, came to the sleeping Prophet and split open his chest and belly from the throat to the groin, from which he drew out Muhammad's heart and bowels. These were then washed in a golden basin filled with faith (another version has Zamzam water, from the famous spring beneath the Ka'ba shrine) and replaced in Muhammad's body, which was then closed up. Then a small steed was brought, whose name was Burāq. This marvelous animal, often depicted with the head of a woman and the body of a horse, could travel with each gallop as far as the eye can see.

Gabriel then led Muhammad, who was seated on Burāq, through the sky to Jerusalem, where he prayed a two-prostration prayer at the "farthest mosque," as the Qur'an calls the temple there. Then Gabriel led Muhammad up through the seven heavens into the very presence of God. This was the greatest of all of Muhammad's spiritual experiences and gave him the sort of standing among the Muslims that certain other prophets had achieved before him, like Enoch, Abraham, Moses, and Jesus, all of whom had had a personal and direct meeting with God. In later Islamic history, as we shall see, the Sufis, or mystics, placed great importance on Muhammad's night journey (*isrā'*) to Jerusalem and his ascent (*mi'rāj*) above the seventh heaven to God. Later spiritual guides traced their doctrines and authority back through a chain of *shaykhs,* or masters, to Muhammad, who had met with God. It was of course one thing, and marvelous, to have had revelation *descend* from God to Muhammad; it was quite another, and more wonderful and auspicious, for God to have caused Muhammad to *ascend* to his presence.

The Prophet Muhammad's night journey (*isrā'*) and ascension (*mirāj*) to heaven, as depicted in a central Asian manuscript illumination by 'Abd al-Razzāk, ca. 1500. (*Source:* The British Library)

### *The Establishment of Muhammad's Role in Islam*

For some time Muhammad was not regarded as what he was—a prophet and warner—but as a poet (*shā'ir*), a *kāhin,* or just a plain madman (*majnūn*). This is because the role of prophet was not as well established among the ancient Arabs as were those other roles. When people called Muhammad a poet or seer, they were not denying his supernatural knowledge and power; rather they were identifying in traditional ways his gift of inspiration. As indicated in the preceding chapter, the vocations of poet and *kāhin* were prestigious in pre-Islamic Arabia.

There are two terms that apply to Muhammad as prophet: ***nabī*** and ***rasūl.*** The first means "prophet," that is, one to whom God has spoken. The second means "apostle" or "messenger," who is charged with communicating what God has told him to others, usually a specific community. All *rasūls* are *nabīs,* but the reverse is not the case. Muhammad and a relatively few others before him were both *nabī* and *rasūl.* The Qur'an names some twenty-five prophets, of whom five are notable: Noah, Abraham, Moses, Jesus, and Muhammad. Muhammad is regarded as the "seal" (*khātam*) of the prophets, in the sense that he is the last and also that he validates the history of prophecy, like an official seal on a document. The Qur'an regards all previous prophecy as complete and perfect, but the peoples to whom the messages were communicated have distorted and corrupted them. Therefore, Muhammad came to transmit the old true message anew and established through it a universal community, which in Medina was known as the *umma.*

It is important to understand that the main task of both Muhammad and the Qur'an was to restore the primordial monotheistic religion of Abraham, which had degenerated in Arabia over the centuries. Thus Islam is the original and true religion for humankind. This is not to be confused with specific historical details of the Islamic movement introduced in Arabia through the Prophet and the Qur'an. That religion is "name brand" Islam (with a capital *I*). But all true religion is "surrender" to God and, thus, *islām,* in the "generic sense" (with a small *i*). Several Qur'anic passages establish Abraham's primacy:

> People of the Book [that is, Jews and Christians]! Why do you dispute concerning Abraham? The Torah was not sent down, neither the Gospel, but after him. What, have you no reason?. . . . Abraham in truth was not a Jew, neither a Christian; but he was a Muslim and one of pure faith *[h.anīf]*; certainly he was never of the idolaters. Surely the people standing closest to Abraham are those who followed him, and this Prophet [Muhammad], and those who believe; and God is the Protector of the believers. (3:65, 67–68)

The essential unity of the divine message through the generations of prophets is clearly stated in a following passage. (The command "Say" in this, as in many other Qur'anic verses, is addressed by God to Muhammad and his people.)

> Say: "We believe in God, and that which has been sent down on us, and sent down on Abraham and Ishmael, Isaac and Jacob, and the Tribes, and in that

> which was given to Moses and Jesus, and the Prophets, of their Lord; we make no division between any of them, and to Him we surrender [that is, are 'Muslims']." Whose desires another religion than Islam, it shall not be accepted of him; in the next world he shall be among the losers. (3:84–85)

The Qur'an restored the purity of the original message from God. Earlier prophets and their books were authentic, but the message had become corrupted and obscured by the followers of the Jewish and Christian religions.

## THE QUR'AN'S DIVINE MESSAGE

Throughout the Meccan years of Muhammad's ministry, the Qur'an moved from simple and dramatic warnings of the Judgment to stories of earlier prophets, mostly from the biblical tradition, who struggled with their peoples and were persecuted. The record of previous peoples whom God warned—and punished—was laid forth for the unruly and perverse Meccans as a sort of salvation history in which a few persons and groups persevered in the way of God. The manner in which biblical figures and events are woven into the highly oracular Qur'anic text suggests to critics that Muhammad did not know the Bible firsthand. Differences between the Hebrew Bible or the New Testament and the Qur'an do not necessarily imply imperfect knowledge of the Bible. Rather, Muslims are convinced that the Qur'an came directly from God and that it corrects the Bible when necessary. There were also Jewish teaching stories that differed in certain respects from the Bible versions. The only sustained narrative in the Qur'an is the Sūra of Joseph (12), as we noted earlier.

The Qur'an considers itself to be the last divine message to descend. The Arabians had never had a "book," as did the Jews and Christians and others. Through Muhammad, the idolatrous Arabs were introduced to true religion by means of a prophetic message composed in a "clear Arabic tongue." This meant that there would be no excuse for missing the point of God's warning and judging. Looked at in another way, the Arabian Qur'an was a gracious and miraculous gift bestowed on God's highly esteemed people, the Muslims, who are called in one place "the best umma (community) ever brought forth for humankind, bidding to honor, and forbidding dishonor, and believing in God" (3:110). The contents of the Qur'an are complete with God on a "preserved tablet," also known as the "mother of the book" (*umm al-kitāb*) (43:4). It is in heaven.

### *The Conversion of 'Umar*

A final major conversion occurred while Muhammad and the Muslims were still in Mecca. 'Umar ibn al-Khattāb, "a strong, stubborn man whose protégés none dare attack,"[12] according to the standard description, was one day striding forth with his sword in order to kill Muhammad. This dangerous prophet had split his tribe, mocked their traditions, and preached that their gods were worthless, and so 'Umar was determined to rid Mecca of this pest. There was a meeting in progress attended by Muhammad, Abū Bakr, 'Alī, and the Prophet's uncle, Hamza, who himself had only recently become a Muslim—to the great benefit of the community because of his character and powerful physical bearing. A fellow tribesman named Nu'aym—a secret Muslim for fear of reprisal—intercepted 'Umar and told him that he would never get away with killing Muhammad. Instead he should put his own house in order by disciplining and punishing his sister Fātima, who together with his brother-in-law and nephew were at that moment in another house listening to a man recite the Qur'an.

'Umar heard the chanting as he approached the house and was furious as he stormed in. As he was laying hold of his brother-in-law, Fātima rose to defend her husband, whereupon 'Umar struck her in the ear, seriously hurting her. The group then confessed that they were indeed Muslims. 'Umar, suddenly remorseful for his violent attack, demanded to look at the sheet from which the man had been reading, which Fātima had hidden under her thigh. Fātima said that 'Umar could not handle the sheet of Qur'anic passages because he was unclean, being a polytheist. 'Umar then washed himself and was handed the sheet, which contained a portion of the sūra known as TāHā. Unlike most others in Hejaz, including the Prophet, 'Umar could read. After looking at the sheet for a moment he said:

> "How fine and noble is this speech." When he heard that, Khabbāb emerged [from his hiding place in another room, too frightened to confront 'Umar] and said, "O 'Umar, by God, I hope that God has singled you out by His prophet's call, for but last night I heard him saying, 'O God, strengthen Islam by Abu'l-Ḥakam b. Hishām or 'Umar b. al-Khaṭṭāb. "Come to God, come to God, O 'Umar." At that 'Umar said, "Lead me to Muhammad so that I may accept Islam."[13]

'Umar strapped on his sword once again and headed for the house where Muhammad and his companions were meeting. One of them saw 'Umar approaching and warned the rest. Hamza counseled Muhammad to let 'Umar in to see what he wanted. If 'Umar started something violent, they would kill him with his own sword. (Hamza was the only one of the Muslims who could say a thing like that and be believed.) 'Umar entered and was surprised to be met by an angry Muhammad, who seized him and dragged him along the floor berating him for his continuing persecution of the Muslims. Then 'Umar replied that he had come at that very moment to "believe in God and His apostle and what he had brought from God." Muhammad then gave thanks to God in such a loud voice that he could be heard by everyone in the house.

The conversion of 'Umar, and Hamza before him, made it safe for the first time for the Muslims to worship at the Ka'ba. Before that, they had been brutally mistreated there by the Qurayshī polytheists. But no one wanted to tangle with Hamza or 'Umar or with anyone connected with them, for they had loyal and able comrades, too. 'Umar soon learned how difficult the new road was upon which he had embarked. He was insulted and abused by his kinsmen, but he stood firm. Later he became the second caliph and the architect of Islam's great empire: a figure in world history who does not suffer by comparison with Alexander, Caesar, Kublai Khan, or, on a far smaller territorial scale but nonetheless of great importance, Joshua, son of Nun.

As the years went by and 'Umar's simplicity of life and relative poverty became known, people came to follow Muhammad because the intrepid 'Umar recommended him. When 'Umar entered an assembly, people fell silent from respect and fear. He once harshly punished his son who had been caught drinking wine. When the son cried out to his father, "You have killed me!" 'Umar answered, "Then go and tell Allah how your father enforces his punishments."[14] ('Umar had been a heavy drinker before his conversion.) There are many legends about 'Umar that Muslims delight in telling: "His riding whip was feared more than the sword of the tyrants: his conversion was the victory of Islam and an act of God's mercy toward his people." As Islam attracted more and more strong people, it demonstrated its superiority over the old value system, which lacked both the vision and the binding force of a new communal order based on faith rather than kinship and which offered the reward of heaven. Later, the Medinan phase proved this beyond all doubt.

## THE HIJRA

During the pilgrimage season of 620 C.E., Muhammad met a party of men at one of the fairs near Mecca.[15] They were from Yathrib, a large agricultural oasis settlement nearly three hundred miles north of Mecca. Yathrib, also known as **Medina**—which became its usual name because of the phrase *madīnat al-nabī,* "city of the Prophet," although it had also been known as Medina before Islam—had experienced many years of tension and bloody fighting between two major Arab tribes, the Aws and the Khazraj. The earlier Jewish settlers had become outnumbered and occupied an uneasy position between the larger communities. Around 618 C.E. a fierce battle had taken place at Bu'āth between the two tribes. Yathrib had evolved over the generations into an urban type of region, and the old tribal patterns of leadership and order, based partly on the vendetta and law of retaliation, were disastrous in such a heavily populated, socially complex setting. Some sort of stable and evenhanded government was urgently needed. The men with whom Muhammad met were greatly impressed with him, whom they had heard about and wanted to meet. They returned the following year with others, representing most of the groups in Yathrib, and they agreed to become Muslims and to obey the Prophet. A pledge was concluded to this effect. This development must have seemed providential to the beleaguered Muslims.

The following year a large group of seventy-five traveled down from Medina and pledged themselves to fight in Muhammad's cause, if necessary. This was in the early summer of 622 C.E. Muhammad then invited his followers in Mecca to begin emigrating north to Medina, which they did in small, inconspicuous groups, totaling around seventy by September. A few stayed behind in Mecca, and so did Muhammad, Abū Bakr, and 'Alī, planning to move north when all was ready there.

Finally, Mecca became so dangerous for the Prophet that he decided to make his move. A band of Quraysh was plotting to kill him while he slept, all to share in the bloodguilt so that it would be impossible to retaliate. But 'Alī was sleeping in his father-in-law's bed when they came, and they realized they had been tricked. They did not harm 'Alī, and meanwhile Muhammad and his chief assistant, Abū Bakr, had hidden in a cave, where they stayed for three days. Passing by this cave in search of their quarry (according to one legend), the Qurayshī assassins were again fooled by a web that had just been spun across the cave entrance by a providentially positioned spider. "No one is in there, surely," they agreed.

Later, Muhammed and Abū Bakr traveled together to Medina by back roads, reaching the outskirts on September 24, 622 C.E. 'Alī also arrived safely. This year later was officially recognized as the beginning of the Islamic lunar calendar—not the day of Muhammad's arrival but the start of that year, which had been July 16, 622 C.E. This is the Hijra, best translated as "emigration." (The older Western spelling is "Hegira," and the still-common translation "flight" is incorrect.) The Muslims were embarking on a fateful venture, going to something positive more than leaving something negative.

Careful preparations had been made, and many Medinans had already professed their belief in Islam. They were henceforth known as the "helpers" (*anṣār*), and those who made the Hijra were called "emigrants" (*muhājirūn*). Muhammad, demonstrating political insight, arrived last and was greeted by an already-established, loyal constituency. So as not to play favorites in his adopted city, which he was now about to serve as a just outside arbitrator and religious leader, he let his camel roam loose and named its eventual resting place as the site of his home. The land was duly purchased and a large open mosque built, with a couple of small huts for Muhammad's now two wives, with whom he took turns lodging.

### *Medina*

In Medina Muhammad was by no means a ruler, at least in the early years. But by the time he died, in 632 C.E., he was the unchallenged leader in both that city and virtually all of Arabia. In Mecca, Muhammad was the inspired head of a religious sect; in Medina he transformed the little Muslim movement into an incipient world religion, whose universal appeal was demonstrated over the next several centuries by the massive conversions of non-Arab peoples, as well. Since the *hijra* to Medina, the Muslim community has been known as the *umma muslima. Umma* is an Arabic term that refers to human communities united by a common faith.

A valuable document has been preserved since Medinan times, which is often called the "Constitution of Medina."[16] In it is spelled out the organization and structure of the newly reformed political and social life of the troubled oasis community of Yathrib. Although the document is clearly a composite text, written over a number of years, certain generalizations can be made about it. All parties were to cooperate together for their mutual defense, with Muhammad acknowledged as the chief arbitrator under God's guidance. All were to obey God and his Prophet. The Jews were to be considered a religious community (***umma***) alongside the Muslims, sharing in the privileges as well as duties of life in a secure society. The remarkable thing about the Constitution of Medina is that it transformed Yathrib's warring and fractious tribes and clans into a kind of supertribe, bound together not by kinship but by a common religious faith. This was a revolution in the social and political history of Arabia and made possible the eventual unification of the whole peninsula under the banner of Islam. Even though kinship solidarity was not wiped out or even diminished, at least people were beginning to recognize the advantages and opportunities that large-scale cooperation could provide. Islam afforded a transcending allegiance structure with a higher ethical level combined with more adequate safeguards against the destructive traditions of the vendetta and the law of retaliation.

The emigrants needed to find suitable work in Medina, but they were at a disadvantage because of their lack of experience in agriculture, the city's main occupation. They did find manual labor jobs, but those did not appeal greatly. Therefore Muhammad directed their talents and energies toward the old occupation of raiding. He did this in a controversial way, breaking the traditional truce months during which the ancient Arabs refrained from warfare with one another. A number of his followers, dispatched with sealed orders, attacked a caravan bound from Yemen to Mecca, which required a long and circuitous journey. The guards were overwhelmed, and the caravan was diverted all the way to Medina. There was some criticism, mostly because of the threat from an angry Mecca under which the Medinans would now be living, but also because of the break with tradition. Muhammad received a revelation to the effect that although breaking the truce was indeed sinful, the Meccan persecution of Islam was even more so.

> They will question thee concerning the holy month, and fighting in it. Say: "Fighting in it is a heinous thing, but to bar from God's way, and disbelief in Him, and the Holy Mosque, and to expel its people from it—that is more heinous in God's sight; and persecution is more heinous than slaying." (Qur'an 2:217)

This passage is a good example of how a higher allegiance came to substitute for the older way of behaving. The old truce idea was still maintained, but as subordinate to the new prophecy. This kind of compromise and cooptation or preemption was characteristic of Muhammad's immense skill in dealing with the Arabian peoples and their customs. He did not seem to be taking away, so much as rearranging, refocusing, and even restoring. The last was seen especially in the Medinan years, with the gradual arabization of Islam, which was viewed as the restoration of the archetypal religion of Abraham, who was neither a Jew nor a Christian. Other raids were later mounted, both by the Meccan emigrants and their Medinan helpers.

***The Jews in Medina.*** Not many weeks before things came to a head with the aroused Meccans, a significant event occurred in Medina. The Jews, who were viewed increasingly as less than fully cooperative with Muhammad and the Islamic venture and in fact as potentially refractory and even dangerous, were suddenly and dramatically cut off. Up until this time, the Muslims and Jews had prayed together, facing Jerusalem. But during a Friday worship service in February of 624 C.E., Muhammad received an inspiration to turn 180 degrees and face Mecca. He and the Muslims did so and the new ***qibla*** (direction of prayer) led to the aforementioned thorough arabization of Islam. Muhammad apparently considered his former ingratiating incorporation of Jewish worship practices to have been misguided and futile. Thereafter, relations with the Jews of Medina became more difficult until a few years later the Jews were either driven out of the oasis altogether or, in one tragic case, the men were executed for treachery in a battle.

### *The Battle of Badr*

A huge and rich caravan was reported to be en route home to Mecca from Palestine. A large group of helpers and emigrants set out to intercept it at Badr, a group of wells near Medina. Anticipating trouble of this sort, the Meccans had sent north a large force of about 900 men to protect the caravan on the final leg of its journey. Muhammad's 300–man force was outnumbered, but in an amazing display of courage and initiative, it totally outfought the large opposing army. Many prominent Meccans were killed, including the leader of the expedition. The helpers and the emigrants involved were, as a result, more closely unified, and both took home a great amount of booty.

The Battle of Badr was the turning point in the history of Islam as a political and military as well as an expanding religious movement. It has been compared with the Jewish Passover and Exodus as a definitive experience for the Muslims, when their self-confidence and sense of destiny as a people of God were firmly established. Setbacks were yet to occur, some serious, but the Muslims' faith and determination were never seriously shaken after Badr.

As the Qur'an itself reflected on the event, the true magnitude of the Meccan forces was hidden from Muhammad by means of a dream, lest the Muslims become frightened and discouraged (8:43). The Qur'an saw the conflict as having been entirely God's contriving and concluding and as providing the Muslims with confidence and the feeling that God's people could not fail:

> O Prophet, God suffices thee, and the believers who follow thee. O Prophet, urge on the believers to fight. If there be twenty of you, patient men, they will overcome two hundred; if there be a hundred, they will overcome a thousand unbelievers, for they are a people who understand not. (8:65)

In another place (8:9), God told Muhammad that a thousand angels stood behind the Muslims as they fought at Badr. This was in March of 624 C.E., during the second year of the Hijra.

Within the next three years two massive Meccan punitive expeditions were launched against Medina. In 625 C.E. came the Battle of Uhud, named for the mountain where the fighting took place. Oddly, the Meccans, after gaining a decisive victory, gathered together their forces and went home. Uhud, then, was a mixed success for both sides. Muhammad continued to launch raids against various Arab targets, and during the Medinan years he was regarded as a major force by the Bedouin tribes, which concluded many treaties and covenants with him. Muhammad became the center of a congeries of direct relationships with tribes and their leaders, whose lines of submission and agreement radiated outward from him in all directions. Some of the parties to the agreements remained pagan, but it was clearly Muhammad's aim to incorporate them eventually into the umma of Islam. Muhammad had a knack for compromise and delay, pressing his advantage only when all the conditions were ripe.

### *The Battle of the Trench*

In 627 C.E. (A.H., i.e., *anno hegirae,* "year of the Hijra" 5) an enormous force of up to 10,000 men marched forth from Mecca in what was intended to be an Arabian Armageddon. The Medinans could muster only about 3,000 defenders, but a Persian convert suggested to Muhammad that they dig a large trench so as to withstand a long siege. The "Battle of the Trench" turned out to be a stalemate, because the Meccans—and the Arabs in general—did not have a tradition of siege warfare and did not like the long wait involved, preferring attack tactics and speedy, decisive outcomes, in part because of the lack of sufficient forage for their beasts. The Meccans finally retreated and went home after two weeks. The Jewish clan of Qurayza were found out to have been planning a rear attack with the Meccans, and so after the invaders had gone back home, the Jews were attacked in their Medinan stronghold. When the Jews surrendered, the men were executed and the women and children sold as slaves. But this sorrowful conclusion should not be interpreted as anti-Jewish, for it was essentially a response to behavior regarded as treason. The Constitution of Medina had clearly spelled out the Yathrib people's defense responsibilities and the extent of mutual loyalty.

Islam thus became firmly established, and Muhammad was recognized as the greatest single power broker in Arabia. Mecca's prestige visibly waned after the Battle of the Trench. The details of Islamic religious and community life became established, as can be seen in the accumulation of Qur'anic passages that dealt more and more with ritual, legal, practical, and communal matters. This is the great difference between the Meccan period of Qur'anic revelation and the Medinan years. The former were concerned with the central issues of God's nature and the relations between him and his creatures, with the coming judgment prominently featured. The stories of the ancient prophets were repeated in such a manner as to comment on Muhammad's relations with a hostile Meccan environment. In Medina, however, the contents were more prosaic and practical. But it would be wrong to regard the Medinan revelations as less concerned with "religious" matters; the scope of what was *Islamically* religious simply had expanded as the project developed from a minority sect into a substantial new community, sometimes labeled a *theocracy.* From Medinan times, Islam was considered both *dīn wa dawla,* "religion and political order."

### *Mecca*

In the spring of 628 C.E. Muhammad led a host of pilgrims to Mecca. The pre-Islamic Medinans were accustomed to participating in the Mecca pilgrimage, but this was the first time that the young Muslim community of Medina had attempted it. As usual the Medinans were prepared for battle but wished to enter Mecca peacefully. They were met by the Meccans at the gateway to the sacred precincts known as al-Hudaybiya. Muhammad then decided not to lead his people on the lesser pilgrimage (*'umra*) that year, although his idea had been basically peaceful—a sort of testing of the waters. Much to the displeasure of some of his supporters, Muhammad concluded a treaty with the Meccans. Although he returned home that year without making the pilgrimage, the following year he and the Medinans came back for the sacred rites, and the city of Mecca was evacuated for three days so as to avoid a conflict. Muhammad thus demonstrated his goodwill and his adherence to a sacred ritual structure that both the pagan and the Muslim Arabians were dedicated to maintaining. Muhammad had come a long way by the time of the Treaty of alHudaybiya, but so had the Meccans, who now acknowledged his great prestige and power in Arabia.

Muhammad's forces probably could have carried out a successful attack on Mecca during that first visit that ended at Hudaybiya, but Muhammad was patient and statesmanlike. The Medinans did complete their pilgrimage the following year, and it remained peaceful. The following year a killing occurred between the major parties, breaching the treaty, and so the Medinans decided to attack Mecca. Muhammad assembled 10,000 men, an enormous force, and marched south. But the leader of the Meccans, Abū Sufyān, who was, ironically, Muhammad's father-in-law, ventured forth from the city to submit to the Medinans. Muhammad accepted the surrender. Only a few Meccans resisted, and the rest were allowed to go free under an amnesty, provided they adopted Islam. A few dissidents were put to death, but on the whole the conquest of Mecca was bloodless. Likewise it was a spiritual more than a military conquest, with no significant loss of face by the vanquished. No booty was allowed, and those few Meccans who were relieved of their possessions by aggressive Medinans were indemnified. Mecca was converted to a Muslim city with an Islamic government: Muhammad's first important act after entering the city was to go to the Ka'ba and purify it by smashing the polytheistic idols. Thus the sacred sanctuary was rededicated to the original monotheism of Abraham, for according to the Qur'an as well as older Arabian legend, the Ka'ba had originally been built by Abraham and Ishmael as a temple dedicated to the worship of the one true God. But in the intervening centuries the people had degenerated into polytheism and wickedness. Allah had been relegated to a marginal position as merely the "high god" of the Arabians. But with the career of Muhammad, the mysterious Allah had returned to call back his creatures to the pure religion of the *ḥanīfs*.

### *Beyond Arabia*

After the conquest of Mecca, Muhammad began to look beyond Arabia, but he first was generally successful in solidifying his hold on the Bedouin tribes, who were mixed in their feelings because of the loss of regional independence that Islamic community life required. The Bedouin as a whole never took to Islam with the loyalty and drive of the more settled and even urban peoples, who were the most important recruits for the new religion. Contrary to romantic Western notions, Islam was not a religion of the desert, if by that it is meant the daring and dashing Bedouin. Islam was a religion of settled life, and any *hijra* to the places where people lived together in interdependence and mutual trust was regarded as a religious act. It is true, however, that the merchant classes that adopted Islam in great numbers did have a stake in maintaining good relations with the fierce and mobile Bedouin, because the latter made indispensable partners in transporting goods over long distances. The agriculturalists fared less well under Islamic rule, although there was never a strong feeling that working the soil was beneath the dignity of the Muslims as a whole. But to the extent that the nomadic Arabs, or Arabian Muslims relatively recently removed from the old camel-breeding and raiding life, dominated in Islamic affairs, the more agricultural peoples found themselves regarded as somehow inferior in their lifestyle, if not in their essential humanity.

## MUHAMMAD'S LATER LIFE

Little has been said about Muhammad himself in the Medinan years. His personal life was strongly influenced by events, but these in turn were to a considerable measure formed by the strengths and insights of his continually deepening religious life. Muhammad seems to have acquired an inward serenity, which provided stability and patience in difficult times. The discipline that the complex and energetic Medinan career demanded from him was developed during his years of persecution and testing in Mecca. Throughout the Medinan years Muhammad had a full but sometimes trouble-prone family life. After losing Khadīja, Muhammad finally married ten more wives and took two concubines. Some of these marriages were political, but others were merciful caring for otherwise bereft and unwanted women. (The battles of Islam took many victims from the time of Muhammad onward through the generations of conquest far and wide.)

### *'Ā'isha*

After Khadīja, 'Ā'isha was the favored wife of Muhammad. A lively and attractive person, she left us more reports (*ḥadīth*) about the Prophet than anyone else did. She lived long after her husband's death and figured prominently in some of the main events of the umma's post-Muhammadan years. She told some charming stories about Muhammad, revealing him as a loving and warm person of good humor and delicacy in human relationships. She even told about how her husband could beat her in footraces—only after she had become fat.[17] The Prophet once told 'Ā'isha how he could tell when she was angry with him. She would answer a question with "no, by Abraham's Lord" when she was angry, whereas when she was pleased, she would say, "no, by Muhammad's Lord."[18] When 'Ā'isha wanted to watch the Abyssinian soldiers playing their martial games with spears in the mosque courtyard, Muhammad would stand before the window of her house with his cloak spread so as to conceal her. Being the Prophet's wife, she should not be looked upon unveiled. And men's games were not for women's eyes, either: "He would then stand for my sake till I was the one who departed; so estimate the time a young girl eager for amusement would wait."[19]

## *Zaynab*

But Muhammad's household was not always tranquil. His wives sometimes found it difficult to get along peaceably with one another, and Muhammad himself had to be careful to treat each kindly and justly. One especially trying period came when Muhammad became emotionally involved with his own daughter-in-law, Zaynab.[20] She immediately felt his interest one day when he showed up looking for Zayd, his adopted son and Zaynab's husband. Muhammad left abruptly when she told him he was not there, even though as father and father-in-law he had every right to enter the house even when Zaynab was there alone. Zaynab was beautiful, and she and her husband had apparently not been very happy together. After hearing of his father's strange behavior, Zayd sensed its cause and quickly offered to divorce Zaynab so that Muhammad might have her as his own.

This affair over Zaynab caused a great commotion among Muhammad's followers, who regarded such a union as incest, because of the custom of considering adopted children as blood relatives. But God revealed to his prophet that he would permit Muhammad to marry Zaynab, in what became a controversial verse (33:37). 'Ā'isha was not pleased, and some of those in Muhammad's community already suspected him of withholding certain verses of the revelation for personal reasons. In an oblique reference to this, 'Ā'isha reportedly declared: "If the Prophet had concealed anything of the revelation, it would have been those [the verses granting permission to marry Zaynab] he ought to have kept hidden."[21] When the Prophet had happily informed 'Ā'isha of God's decree, she is said to have replied: "Truly thy Lord makes haste to do thy pleasure."[22]

These anecdotes are included here not to cast aspersions on the Prophet or the Muslims. Rather, they are included for their intrinsic interest and as an illustration of some of the source material available to the historian, material that has not been censored or changed. Western non-Muslim readers have sometimes used such material to discredit Islam, but they have taken it out of context and thus lost sight of the original situation. Indeed, Muhammad's contemporaries were not at all scandalized by their leader's human passions. In fact, one legend has Muhammad endowed with the capacity to satisfy all of his wives in a single evening. For Muslims, sexual vigor exercised within legal relationships is a great gift from God, to be enjoyed and used often. Instead, it was the social situation that disturbed people, that is, the violation of custom. But Muhammad's repetition of what God had revealed regarding the matter of Zaynab is what the historian must accept if the larger situation is to be appreciated fully. When the traditional Arabs were convinced that in this case it was acceptable for Muhammad to violate the tradition concerning marriage to adopted daughters, it was a mighty display of charismatic authority by Muhammad. Through him God was intervening and the people were responding.

## MUHAMMAD'S PERSONAL LIFE

We have a few descriptions of what Muhammad looked like, his characteristic dress, the foods he ate, and other personal matters. He was, as 'Alī reported:

> neither very tall nor excessively short, but was a man of medium size, he had neither very curly nor flowing hair but a mixture of two, he was not obese, he did not have a very round face, but it was so to some extent, he was reddish-white, he had black eyes and long eyelashes, he had protruding joints and shoulder blades, he was not hairy but had some hair on his chest, the palms of his hands and feet were calloused, when he walked he raised his feet as though he were walking on a slope, when he turned [for example, to someone] he turned completely, between his shoulders was the seal of prophecy and he was the seal of the prophets, he had a finer chest than anyone else, was truer in utterance than anyone else, had the gentlest nature and noblest tribe. Those who saw him suddenly stood in awe of him and those who shared his acquaintanceship loved him. Those who described him said they had never seen anyone like him before or since.[23]

Muhammad ate little, and in fact together with his family, even in later years in Medina, often went without food because of the people's neglect to bring the household provisions, and it was beneath a prophet's dignity to engage in trade or begging. ('Ā'isha once reportedly said that her husband loved three things in this world: women, perfume, and food but that he succeeded in getting only two of them: women and perfume.) Muhammad mended his own sandals and otherwise looked after his own personal maintenance chores. He always granted people requests and gifts, to the extent of his ability. Once when he was asked to curse the polytheists, he answered: "I was not sent as one given to cursing; I was sent only as a mercy."[24] He took no personal vengeance, but when someone defied God, his activism was stirred up in God's behalf. His tendency to pardon and forgive is best seen in the way he treated the Meccans. The superior Arab of old times was the one who possessed and exercised *ḥilm,* which is the forbearance of the stronger and morally superior toward the guilty and weaker. Few people possessed this virtue, and it could not be faked in a violent, proud society such as Jāhilīya Arabia with its *machismo* code. Thus Muhammad could have crushed Mecca and killed all of its inhabitants without suffering the censure of his fellow Arabs. "They got what was coming to them" would have been the likely verdict. But instead he forgave them in the name of God. And in the subsequent course of events that was seen to have been as just as it was merciful, a great people became Muslim, and the ancient sanctuary was rededicated for all Arabia to serve obediently and gratefully. One of the most beautiful names of God is al-Halīm, "the Forbearing" (that is, exercising *ḥilm*). So one of the highest moral ideals of the Jāhilīya became one of the central attributes of God and his Prophet in the new age that generously (and wisely) continued so much of the old.[25]

### *Muhammad's Death*

The integration of pre-Islamic Arabian religious elements was completed during the pilgrimage in March of 632 C.E. (A.H. 13), which Muhammad led. In his farewell sermon, delivered from a hill overlooking the plain of 'Arafāt, he recited God's words:

> Today I have perfected your religion for you, and I have completed My blessing upon you, and I have approved Islam for your religion. (Qur'an 5:3)

In June Muhammad then died in 'Ā'isha's arms and was buried beneath her house. He had completed his work: all Arabia was united by the religion of Islam, and the Muslims regarded this as the answer to Abraham's prayer, as recorded in the Qur'an:

> My Lord, make this land secure, and turn me and my sons away from serving idols; my Lord, they have led astray many men. Then whoso follows me belongs to me; and whoso rebels against me, surely Thou art All-forgiving, All-compassionate. Our Lord, I have made some of my seed to dwell in a valley where is no sown land by Thy Holy House [the Ka'ba]; Our Lord, let them perform the prayer, and make hearts of men yearn towards them, and provide them with fruits; haply they will be thankful. Our Lord, Thou knowest what we keep secret and what we publish; from God nothing whatever is hidden in earth and heaven. Praise be to God, who has given me, though I am old, Ishmael and Isaac; surely my Lord hears the petition. My Lord, make me a performer of the prayer, and of my seed. Our Lord, and receive my petition. Our Lord, forgive Thou me and my parents, and the believers, upon the day when the reckoning shall come to pass. (Qur'an 14:35–41)

## NOTES

1. Some form of afterlife belief was widespread among Arabians, according to evidence from modern archaeological excavations. See Adel Allouche, "Arabian Religions," in *Encyclopedia of Religion,* vol. 1, ed. Mircea Eliade et al. (New York: Macmillan and Free Press, 1987), p. 366, with citations of relevant literature.
2. A. J. Arberry, *The Seven Odes: The First Chapter in Arabic Literature* (London: Allen & Unwin, 1957), pp. 86–87.
3. For variants and notes, see William A. Graham, *Divine Word and Prophetic Word in Early Islam* (The Hague and Paris: Mouton, 1977), pp. 212–213. The version of the *ḥadīth* translated here is found in *Saḥīḥ. Muslim,* at the beginning of the *"Kitāb al-Alfāẓmin al-Adab."*
4. The following sketch of Muhammad's life relies heavily on the traditional source, *Life of Muhammad: A translation of [Ibn] Isḥāq's Sīrat Rasūl Allāh,* trans. Alfred Guillaume (London: Oxford University Press, 1967), pp. 104ff.
5. *Ibid.,* p. 69.
6. *Ibid.,* pp. 79–81.

7. William A. Graham, *Divine Word and Prophetic Word in Early Islam,* chap. 1.
8. The source for the story of the "Satanic verses" is found only in the Muslim historian and Qur'an exegete Abū Ja'far Muhammad ibn Jarīr al-Tabarī's (d. 923/310) universal history, available in English translation in *The History of al-Tabari,* vol. 9, *Muhammad at Mecca,* trans. and annotated by W. Montgomery Watt and M. V. McDonald (Albany: State University of New York Press, 1988), pp. 108–109. A full and intricate modern analysis of this interesting and controversial tradition is found in W. Montgomery Watt, *Muhammad at Mecca* (Oxford: Oxford University Press, 1953), pp. 100–109.
9. *Life of Muhammad,* p. 146.
10. *Ibid.,* pp. 143–144.
11. The source I have used for this summary is al-Baghawī's authoritative collection of traditions *(ḥadīths), Mishkāt al-Masābīh,* 4 vols., vol. 4, trans. James Robson (Lahore, Pakistan: Sh. Muhammad Ashraf, 1965–1966), pp. 1264ff. (The opening of Muhammad's breast is sometimes identified as an auspicious event of his youth, and separate from the ascension.)
12. *Life of Muhammad,* pp. 155–157.
13. *Ibid.,* pp. 156–157.
14. This and the following quotation are from Tor Andrae, *Mohammad: The Man and His Faith,* trans. Theophil Menzel (New York: Harper Torchbooks, 1960), pp. 130–131.
15. This account of the Hijra is based on *Life of Muhammad,* pp. 198–231; and on W. Montgomery Watt, *Muhammad: Prophet and Statesman* (Oxford, England: Oxford University Press, 1961), chap. 4.
16. It appears only in Ibn Ishāq's *Sīra.* See *Life of Muhammad,* pp. 231–233. A better translation is by W. Montgomery Watt, *Muhammad at Medina* (Oxford, England: Oxford University Press, 1956), pp. 221–225. This document has been discussed thoroughly by R. B. Serjeant, "The Constitution of Medina," *Islamic Quarterly* 8 (1964): 3–16. (Serjeant's dating of the document is convincing.)
17. *Mishkāt al-Masābīh,* vol. 2, p. 691.
18. *Ibid.,* p. 689.
19. *Ibid.*
20. For this summary, I have relied on Maxime Rodinson, *Mohammad* (New York: Vintage Books, 1974), pp. 205–208.
21. From the *Ḥadīth* collection of al-Tirmidhī, as quoted in Rodinson, *Mohammed,* p. 207.
22. As quoted in Andrae, *Mohammed,* p. 154.
23. *Mishkāt,* vol. 4, pp. 1242–1243.
24. *Ibid.,* p. 1247.
25. The relationship between *ḥilm* and *jahl* (destructive folly) is much more complex than can be summarized in a few words. I have based my interpretation principally on the discussion of Toshihiko Izutsu in his *God and Man in the Koran: Semantics of the Koranic Weltanschauung* (Tokyo: The Keio Institute of Cultural and Linguistic Studies, 1963), pp. 203–219. The classic western study of *jahl* is Ignaz Goldziher's "What is meant by 'al-Jahiliyya'," in his *Muslim Studies,* vol. I, trans. C. R. Barber and S. M. Stern (Chicago: Aldine Publishing Company, 1967), pp. 219–208.

CHAPTER

# 4 The Arab Conquests and Islamic Rule: The Struggle for a Unified Umma

## KEY TERMS

***khalīfa*** **and** ***khilāfa***
**Shīʿis and Shīʿa**
***dhimmī***
***mawālī***
**Commander of the Faithful (*amīr al-mu'minīn*)**
***shū ra***
***fitna***
**People of the House (*ahl al-bayt*)**
**Sunnīs (*ahl al-sunna wa'l-jamāʿa*)**
***dīn wa dawla***
***ʿilm al-kalām***

## MUHAMMAD'S HEIRS

Before he died in 632 C.E., Muhammad had not left instructions as to the governance of the umma, nor, according to majority Muslim opinion, had he designated a successor to lead the Muslims. Some of the old guard quickly gathered to decide how to hold the people together and provide stable leadership and some form of continuity. Abū Bakr, ʿUmar, and Abū ʿUbayda took it upon themselves to select Abū Bakr as the first ***khalīfa,*** "deputy," of the Prophet (generally spelled as **caliph** or "calif" in English). They presented this decision in a peremptory manner to the Medinan community, and it was accepted, but not without some degree of resentment. This rather authoritarian and preemptive move on the part of the inner circle of companions went against the old Arabian ideas of tribal leadership, in which the shaykh was selected by a wider consensus as a first among equals who could fairly easily be overruled if he became overbearing.

Muhammad had no male heir, and even if he had had one old enough to assume leadership, it is unlikely that even the Prophet's prestige could have smoothed the way for a son's rule unless that son had had enormous native ability. Being of the Prophet's immediate line probably would not have been sufficient, as seems to have been proved by certain features of the subsequent history of persons who had the closest ties to Muhammad's family. The **Shī'īs**, strong supporters of 'Alī, who emerged during the early post-Muhammad years when the Muslim government was centered at Medina, came to claim that Muhammad had designated 'Alī as his successor well before the Prophet's death. This claim has never been accepted by the majority of Muslims, who eventually evolved into the Sunnīs and consider themselves the mainstream of Islamic faith and practice. The Shī' at 'Alī, "party of 'Alī," developed a peculiar view of Islamic governance centering in the infallible imāms, who descended from Muhammad by way of 'Alī and Fātima.

### *The Ridda*

The **caliphate** (***khilāfa***), as the new form of government soon came to be known, had much to do. After Muhammad had passed from the scene, Arab tribes near and far began to reassess the close associations that they had maintained with Medina under Muhammad's leadership. This development came to be called the *ridda,*[1] "apostasy," and where it took the form of withdrawal from the Medina-centered Muslim rule, it was met by stern military measures on Abū Bakr's initiative and, even more, 'Umar's, who emerged as the real power broker. Muhammad had never succeeded in uniting all of Arabia, either politically or religiously. The regions surrounding Mecca and Medina seem to have been quite well Islamized and subjugated, but more distant territories, such as eastern Arabia, Yemen, and the Hadramaut, had to be forcefully incorporated into the umma during the caliphate of Abū Bakr. But the wars of the *ridda* should not be thought of exclusively as a struggle to reclaim what had been lost after Muhammad's death. In a real sense, they were the first wave of the great Arab-Muslim conquests that were to extend within a generation the new order into all the Near East. The great foreign conquests were important economically for the reunited Arab tribes, which not only realized enormous wealth from them in the form of booty but also soon began to migrate into the new lands as administrators, military garrisons, and settlers.

## THE MUSLIMS' FOREIGN CONQUESTS

The lands lying closest to Arabia were taken relatively easily.[2] Egypt was conquered by the great general 'Amr ibn al-Ās in 640 C.E. What began as a raid on Egypt's eastern frontier in 639 ended with the surrender of the Byzantine army, which had long occupied Egypt. The Arab conquest of Egypt was a costly loss to the Byzantine Empire, because of its great value as a major producer of

Constantinople's agricultural products. The Egyptians were not opposed to the Arab conquest and viewed it as potentially a brighter prospect than continued life under the oppressive Byzantine rule. Similar attitudes existed in other regions that came under Arab rule. The Greek forces retook Alexandria in 645, but they held it for only a short time before Egypt settled permanently into the Islamic and Arabian orbit. The process of Arabization and Islamization in Egypt was very gradual; until the present there has been a substantial Christian (Coptic) minority in the country.

The Islamic movement brought a new religion and new patterns to Near Eastern life, but it also wisely and profitably encouraged the subject peoples to continue many of their old ways. The old citied life of the region continued with new cities taking root and participating in a new internationalism that was made possible by the Arab-Islamic empire, which was centered in Damascus, and the even more cosmopolitan order of the Abbasids, with its capital in Iraq, at Baghdad. The centers of power and culture of the ancient Near East—Egypt, Mesopotamia, and Syria—once again became prestigious and powerful under Islamic rule. It was soon seen to be impossible to manage a vast governmental bureaucracy and administer far-flung regions from so remote a place as Medina. Thus the old centers of Near Eastern influence and trade were revived before long, and business continued as usual, albeit with a new international language (which was fortuitously close to the Aramaic that was still spoken in many parts of the Fertile Crescent) and a universal religion that was quite tolerant of the older faiths, which it resembled in significant ways.

### *Egypt*

In Egypt, the center of power shifted from the Mediterranean coast and Alexandria to the interior and the Nile city of Babilon, next to which Cairo was eventually founded by the Shī'īFātimid dynasty in 969. With the abandonment of the great old Hellenistic cultural and intellectual center of Alexandria at the borders of the Dār al-Islām, the "Abode of Surrender," a long and distinguished era ended. Egypt henceforth looked to the East for political associations and cultural contacts. Large numbers of Arabs eventually migrated to the land of the Nile and intermarried and intermingled with the native Egyptians, to the point that Egyptians to this day regard themselves as both Egyptian and Arab. For centuries, the indigenous Christian Egyptians, the Copts, continued to be numerically dominant, but under Muslim governments.

### *The Dhimmīs*

Throughout the regions that the Islamic governments came to rule, many of the indigenous peoples gradually converted to the new religion. But this process was slow, and there were always significant groups that retained their traditional faiths. But Islam eventually became the majority religion, and the Muslim governments were fairly tolerant, though condescending toward Christians and Jews, especially. Peoples of the Book, whether Jewish, Christian, or Zoroastrian (in the Iranian regions), were granted ***dhimmī,*** "protected" status, in their own enclaves and with their own community rules governing internal matters.[3] These *dhimmīs* came in time to be restricted by a law known as the "Covenant of 'Umar" attributed to the second caliph, although actually enacted long after his time. The Covenant of 'Umar applied only to People of the Book. Polytheists were offered either conversion to Islam or death (although later the Hindus were included among those religious communities possessing sacred books, because of the existence of Vedas and other scriptures as well as the practical political necessity of dealing with a vast and varied people).

The *dhimmīs* were forbidden to build new houses of worship on new sites, but they could repair existing ones. They were not allowed to publicize their religion in order to attract new adherents, but they had the freedom to maintain their own forms of worship and belief, passing them down from generation to generation. They were required to wear distinctive clothing, to treat Muslims with respect and deference, and to pay a poll tax, known as *jizya*. The jizya was paid in lieu of the zakāt, which the Muslims were required to pay. In addition, there was a land tax known as *kharāj*.

The *dhimmīs* could not bear arms, ride horses, or serve in the military, but they were granted protection from enemies of the state. For many generations in the early centuries of the Islamic movement, the *dhimmīs* often occupied high and honored positions in government. Their talents and long experience in the civilized centers of the Muslim empire were sorely needed, indeed often indispensable. It was some time before the rougher tribal peoples, who constituted the leadership of government, would be able to deal with the complex and subtle details of advanced bureaucracies and cultural institutions. Gradually, however, the vigorous new people from Arabia intermingled with the sophisticated and sedentary older ones, and a true Islamic civilization came into being. When this had been achieved, the *dhimmīs* and other minorities dwindled into regional ethnic groups, though sometimes of significant size—as in Egypt—but without political or military power. Although the letter of Islamic law regarding the *dhimmīs* was somewhat harsh, the application of it varied greatly from place to place and period to period. For the greater part, the People of the Book have been treated tolerantly and respectfully by the Muslims, far more so than could be said of non-Christians in predominantly Christian lands over the same centuries (the Western Middle Ages down to modern times) or even of minority Christian bodies that lived independently of Rome. The Jews, especially, flourished under Muslim rule in such places as Iraq, Egypt, and the Maghrib (especially Spain). Though there were periods of persecution and tragedy, they were rare. But this is not to say that Christians, Jews, or Zoroastrians necessarily welcomed life under Islamic governments.

### *The Iranian Plateau*

The Iranian plateau, extending to Khurasan in what is now northeast Iran and Afghanistan was much more slowly brought under Islamic-Arabic control. But when it had finally been subjugated, it provided some of the most powerful recruits for the new movement in the form of tribal-nomadic peoples of great military ability as well as sophisticated peoples of ancient culture. Because the Zoroastrian faith of many of the Indo-European Iranians was often a royal creed, without the grassroots strength and tradition of Christianity, Judaism, or other old creeds, it declined rather rapidly after it lost the Persian royal favor. The fire temples, the sacred ritual centers of Zoroastrianism, continued for some time, but the religion was treated somewhat more harshly than were the other "book" traditions.

## EARLY MUSLIM GOVERNMENTS AND THE SPREAD OF THE UMMA

In the early phases of the Arab conquests, the invading armies tended to settle in garrison cities. Kūfa in Iraq, Fustāt in Egypt, Kairouan in Tunisia, and others like them provided a safe environment for Muslim armies to preserve their cultural, social, and especially religious integrity while remaining safe from the native peoples and their ways. A strong sense of both Arab superiority and Islamic purity seems to have contributed to this practice of standing somewhat aloof. For a considerable period, the victorious Muslim armies did not consider their task to be conversion but, rather, subjugation of the conquered peoples.

Some of these peoples wanted to become Muslim before such an idea gained strong momentum among the original Muslims who had spilled out of the Arabian Peninsula seeking booty and land. Thus there came into being a special class of non-Arab Muslim converts known collectively as ***mawālī,*** from the Arabic term *mawlā,* meaning "master." That is, many Iranians, Egyptians, Palestinians, and others attached themselves as clients to an acknowledged Arabian tribal lineage and thus appropriated enough of the old tribal identification to be admitted gradually into full membership in the new order. This new synthesis evolved in an international and intercultural environment of assimilation to Islamic ideals, Arabic language, and tribal kinship patterns, whereas the politically dominant Muslim class, made up principally of Arabs, adopted some of the ways of the older civilized peoples and preIslamic times.

It is interesting to follow the progress of Islamization and Arabization through the spread of tribal, clan, and family names throughout the regions that Islam came to dominate.[4] It is true that many Arabs migrated into these regions, but it is equally true that many of the Arab names added to the populations were of peoples who changed their names through the *mawālī* system. These people moved to the vicinities of the garrison towns and served the leadership class of Arab Muslims through skilled and unskilled labor, markets, and so forth, thus transforming the garrison into a city of complex structure.

The rulers became greatly concerned that the *mawālī* would become so numerous that the state's financial integrity would be seriously undermined. After all, if everyone became Muslim, who would pay the poll tax? The Arab minority was challenged by this non-Arab movement that had become Muslim and wanted some of the success of the recent generations. To no small extent the old Persian ruling class was involved in the *mawālī* movement, and in general it was composed of non-Arabs.

After a while it allied itself with the developing Shīʻa movement and its evolving religious notions, which included Arab as well as non-Arab sources and participants. But we must first understand the genesis and early development of that tradition before we describe the ways that it engaged the support of the *mawālī,* in some fateful political ventures a little more than a century after the death of Muhammad.

### *Abū Bakr and ʻUmar*

As we observed earlier, a group of Muslims arose who were especially devoted to ʻAlī and the family of the Prophet as the rightful heirs of the Muslim leadership.[5] This movement began early in the history of the caliphate and gained strength during the years in which ʻAlī, Muhammad's son-in-law, himself sought to be recognized as leader. The much older Abū Bakr was selected first, but he served as caliph only from 632 to 634 C.E. before dying.

In an age-respecting society such as Arabia, the leadership usually fell to the older and presumably wiser members of the clan or tribe. The word *shaykh,* after all, means "old man," one with gray hair. Thus it is not difficult to understand why ʻUmar became the next caliph; he had in fact been making crucial decisions during Abū Bakr's reign and later became one of the greatest military leaders and forgers of world empire in the history of humankind. It was ʻUmar who was first accorded the title, to remain with his successors until the caliphate died out six centuries later, of **Commander of the Faithful** (***amīr al-mu 'minīn***).

### *ʻUthmān*

When ʻUmar was attacked in 644 by a resentful servant, before he died he realized the trouble that a search for his successor could bring, and so he appointed a committee, called a ***shūrā,*** to represent the Muslims in selecting a new caliph. Much to the surprise of most, the person chosen was ʻUthmān, a member of the Qurayshī aristocracy of Banū Umayya. He was the weakest candidate and thus a compromise of powerful rivals. ʻUthmān, personally respectable and pious, had been the only Meccan of high status to embrace Islam in the early years before the Hijra. But he was not widely admired as a leader and was a far cry from ʻUmar or Abū Bakr in courage and military initiative. Then, when he became caliph, he also came to be viewed by some as a notorious nepotist, appointing his kinsmen to choice positions and neglecting the less exalted but supposedly equal Muslim brothers of humbler social and economic background. ʻUmar had earlier appointed another Umayyad, Mu'āwiya, as governor of the new province of Syria. He was ʻUthmān's nephew. This able and resolute warrior and administrator figured importantly in the later showdown between ʻAlī and his followers and those new Muslims who represented the old Meccan oligarchy.

ʻUthmān achieved one thing that somewhat mitigated his otherwise unfavorable record as caliph: he had the Qur'an collected and put into an authorized recension, thus preserving intact the precious message and averting serious dissensions among Muslim groups that were already beginning to quarrel over variant readings of the text. This major accomplishment was realized by a commission headed by

Zayd ibn Thābit, who had been Muhammad's last amanuensis and seems to have aided his master in beginning a collection before the Prophet died. According to the most authoritative traditional sources, the 'Uthmānic recension was promulgated throughout the empire, and all the other early codices—collected by private individuals—were ordered destroyed.[6] This official text is substantially the one that the Muslims use to this day, although it was some centuries before technical matters of voweling, standardizing the writing system, and accounting for dialectal variants were smoothed out.

'Uthmān reached a sad end by being assassinated in his own house in Medina by a band of dissident Egyptians who because of a grievance had stormed the undefended compound. 'Uthmān's power was prestige alone, so without a personal bodyguard, he was easily cut down by the mutinous Arab troops back from their post in Egypt. Abū Bakr and 'Umar had been strong leaders, commanding the respect of the Muslims, but 'Uthmān ended up as a sorry figure who could not stir even his fellow Medinans to protect him. This event has festered in the soul of Islam since that dark day, for it showed an ominous weakness in the political system. The changes in the habits and traditions of the Arabs since the death of Muhammad, particularly in the political and social spheres, and the establishment of a vast empire with the beginnings of a centralized administrative system were what really lay at the base of the ***fitnas,*** "trials, temptations"—civil wars, actually—that began with the death of 'Uthmān. It is fruitless to speculate whether things would have turned out much differently had the third caliph been a forceful leader. His successor, who had a powerful personality, certainly had tremendous problems from which he himself could not finally escape.

## 'Alī

'Alī became caliph after the death of 'Uthmān in 656, but when the chance came he hesitated because of the unpromising circumstances. The Medinans, the Ansār, were solidly supportive, but other groups, especially those from Mecca, like the old Arab aristocracy of the Umayyads, were bitter and refractory. 'Alī had become caliph because one of their chief members had fallen. What made things worse was 'Alī's failure to protect 'Uthmān when he was being attacked, although he appears not to have either encouraged the event or condoned it. Then, after he became caliph, 'Alī did not punish the perpetrators of the deed. What is more, he withdrew or canceled many of the appointments that 'Uthmān had made. 'Uthmān thus became a rallying point for the development of a powerful Umayyad movement, later to become established in Damascus as a dynasty that ruled for almost ninety years.

'Alī moved the capital from Medina to Kūfa, one of the garrison cities on the desert edges of Iraq. He had strong support there, and it made strategic sense to concentrate the government's power near the center of the ancient Mesopotamian civilization. The Islamic movement was rapidly spreading to the north and east, and Kūfa was in a good location for centralizing the administration, being also within convenient and unobstructed reach of Hejaz, across the desert routes. 'Alī knit together a basically unified coalition of peoples in Iraq, but his relations with his enemies worsened.

'Ā'isha, along with Talha and Zubayr, Meccans who resisted 'Alī's ascendancy, stirred up trouble against the new caliph by playing on both sides of the fence. They had been implicated in the action against 'Uthmān but were conveniently "out of town" when the tragedy occurred. Then they raised a hue and cry against 'Alī for failing to punish the killers. These three organized an armed force and traveled from Mecca all the way to Basra, in Iraq, to challenge 'Alī. But they were soundly defeated in the "Battle of the Camel," the name given to the encounter because it raged around the camel on which 'Ā'isha was riding in her howdah and which was finally cut down after all of 'Ā'isha's bodyguards had been killed. Talha and Zubayr were killed, but the Prophet's impetuous and imperious widow returned to Medina, where she lived out her long life in relative serenity and gained wide renown for her copious memory concerning the Prophet's life and sayings.

But this conflict between 'Alī and 'Ā'isha was an exceedingly painful affair, because of its family dimension. The first generation of Muhammad's family, connected with Khadīja and the Prophet, was different from that of Muhammad's later marriages with an assortment of women. 'Ā'isha admitted that the one person she had ever been jealous of was Khadīja, whom, she knew, the Prophet had loved even more than her. But 'Ā'isha commanded the respect, even the reverance, of the Muslims as the Mother of the Faithful.

It would be unthinkable to treat the principal characters and events connected with the **People of the House**(***ahl al-bayt***), as the Prophet's family are known, as less than exalted personages, and all Muslims are united in this common regard for them. But it is instructive that the sources we have concerning some of them and their exploits are as absorbing as is the best fiction one can find about heroic families and their destinies. The Muslims have lovingly preserved these sources as parts of the great saga that is so intimately intertwined with the coming of Islam to humankind. Both the assets and the liabilities of these people are portrayed, for it is only God's mighty acts and his command of submission and obedience that are pure and perfect. Our earliest records of Islamic history do not portray the principal actors as anything other than what they were: human and imperfect. Later, however, a different attitude came to dominate as the hagiographical temperament took hold, especially at the level of popular religion.

### *Mu'āwiya*

Most of the Islamic provinces recognized 'Alī's caliphate at Kūfa, but Syria refused. Its governor, Mu'āwiya, a nephew of 'Uthmān, boldly and stubbornly refused to step down for the newly appointed governor sent by 'Alī. Events were leading toward war between Mu'āwiya and the caliph, but the Syrians themselves had to be convinced that it was worthwhile. This is a complex issue, far transcending the question of bringing justice in the wake of 'Uthmān's assassination, although that matter provided useful emotional and even religious fuel for the fire that was being kindled. Iraq had permitted large-scale Arab immigration, to the point that it was becoming difficult to manage the land and the economy. Syria under Mu'āwiya regarded itself as a special case, in that it served as the military buffer between the enemy Byzantines and the Islamic heartland. Major new infusions of Arab settlers would upset the balance in Syria and annoy the natives, it was felt. 'Alī wanted free migration to all parts of the empire, whereas Mu'āwiya favored a highly conservative approach on the matter. 'Umar and 'Uthmān both had pursued policies much closer to Mu'āwiya's, and they both had strongly supported the young and capable Mu'āwiya, thereby giving him a continuing prestige among the Muslims even after they had left the scene. Mu'āwiya and 'Alī thus were rivals, and Mu'āwiya succeeded in mounting a military expedition to challenge 'Alī. Mu'āwiya was so intent on this that he even concluded an unfavorable treaty with the despised Byzantine-Christian forces, so as to protect his rear. The symbolism of this act is a reminder of what the Muslims should have been accomplishing as the "best umma" ever brought into being. This first great *fitna* fatefully separated the Muslims and is still felt.

***The Decisive Battle.*** The two armies met in May 657 at Siffīn near the upper Euphrates River. There was some desultory combat in the form of skirmishes, but no one really wanted to fight, and so they turned to negotiations. Mu'āwiya demanded the punishment of 'Uthmān's assassins, at the least. He seemed also to favor a new *shūrā*, or council, to choose a caliph who would be acceptable to all parties. The sides finally engaged in battle, but it was halted by a clever trick just as 'Alī was winning. The Syrian cavalry put copies of the Qur'an on their spear points and faced 'Alī's men with the cry "Let God decide!" Relieved, the two armies stopped fighting, but 'Alī was well aware of what arbitration at this point would likely cost him. He gave in to his supporters and agreed that he would accept whatever decision emerged from negotiations between the parties, the Iraqis on one side and the Syrians on the other.

'Amr ibn al-Ās, who had suggested the stratagem of hoisting the Qur'an on spears, was the arbitrator for the Syrians. (He was the same person who had earlier conquered and then governed Egypt.) The arbitrator for Iraq was selected over 'Alī's strenuous objections. He was Abū Mūsā al-Ash'aarī. Both arbitrators were highly qualified to meet together, for each knew his province well, having been long involved in their settlement and governance. Abū Mūsā was neutral regarding 'Alī, whereas 'Amr was hotly and loyally pro-Umayyad. 'Alī's great mistake was to agree to any arbitration at all, because it put his caliphate into question and reduced him in the eyes of some of his staunchest supporters to the same level as Mu'āwiya, as at most a pretender to the highest office of the umma.

Some of these supporters, disgusted with his agreement to arbitrate, left 'Alī and became the *khawārij* (Khārijites), an often-extremist sect that in different forms continued for some years after. Their name in Arabic means "those who go out" or "split off." They were a rigorously Qur'anically based movement, fiercely egalitarian and dedicated to divine justice. They had wanted 'Alī to rectify the errors and misdeeds of 'Uthmān's administration, considering the matter of punishing his killers already resolved. 'Alī was finally able to neutralize most of these *khawārij* in a battle, but the remainder went their own ways and even set up a rival caliph, who never had any power beyond their circles. Their position was that "even an Abyssinian slave," if he were a good Muslim, could be caliph.

***'Alī's Downfall.*** Meanwhile 'Alī's regime was falling into shambles. The arbitration efforts went against him, and Mu'āwiya even seized Egypt for his side, a stunning economic loss to 'Alī, as it had been to the Byzantines when the wily 'Amr ibn al-Ās first took the rich Nile province. Then the Umayyad forces mounted disruptive raids into Iraq. 'Alī was nearing the end of his resources and options when he was murdered by one of the Khārijites in 661, thus ending a relatively brief and disappointing reign as caliph. 'Alī continues to be recognized as a great Muslim, especially as a religious adviser and guide. For the Shī'a, he later became regarded as an infallible, divinely guided imām, or "leader," second only to Muhammad and in fact continuing the perfect type of spiritual and political leadership that his father-in-law had offered.

The Shī'a were always to have a tragic dimension to their existence, starting with the untimely death of Fātima, a daughter of Muhammad and Khadīja and a wife of 'Alī. Dying after a period of ill health during the caliphate of Abū Bakr, she was the mother of two succeeding imāms, Hasan and Husayn, who were, respectively, the second and third Shī'ī imāms after 'Alī. Her position among the Muslims is exalted and later included being regarded as "virgin," the perfect embodiment of womanhood, and "queen of the women of paradise."

After 'Alī was killed, his son Hasan ruled as caliph (as well as second Shi'ī imam) for six months, but then abdicated his power to Mu'āwiya, who then soon succeeded in being recognized as the caliph throughout the Islamic world. Mu'āwiya ruled from Damascus and ushered in the era that later Islamic historians characterized contemptuously as the "Arab kingdom." Muslim purists reacted to the establishment of the Umayyad dynasty much as Samuel, the last judge of Israel, reacted to the people's call for a king to rule over them. A king is merely a human tyrant, but a caliph is one who rules as deputy of God's apostle and, in a sense, of God himself. In calling the Umayyads "kings," then, a forceful and ironic statement was made about the nature of their leadership and the perceptions of those whom they governed. The age of the "rightly guided" caliphs came to a tragic end with 'Alī ibn Abī Tālib, the fourth caliph and the third to die a violent death.

## TWO APPROACHES TO POLITICS AND RULE

Although it is not incorrect to call the supporters of 'Alī by the name Shi'īs by the time of his death, it should apply only in a social and political sense. The religious doctrines and imamology of Shi'ī Islam developed much later. But it is also premature to name as Sunnīs the Umayyads and their majority at this early date. The *ahl al-Sunna wa'l-Jamā'a,* the full Arabic name for the **Sunnīs**—meaning "The People of the [Prophet's] Sunna and the Community"—were fully recognized as the majority of Muslims only after the establishment of the major law schools and the rejection of certain forms of rational, speculative theology in the third century after the Hijra. Even so, there arose in early Islam two distinct approaches to politics and rule.

A leading American anthropologist, Clifford Geertz, adapting a suggestion of W. Montgomery Watt, a recognized authority on early Islamic history, has characterized the two approaches as *intrinsicalist* and *contractualist.*[7] The first refers to a special charisma or power in certain individuals, in the present context the descendants of Muhammad through 'Alī and Fātima. This approach brings to mind the old sacral kingship patterns of the ancient Near East. Watt has argued that the South Arabian tribes, strong supporters of 'Alī, had inherited an ancient tradition of divine kingship, probably influenced in antiquity by Mesopotamia. It is difficult to know for certain whether Watt's thesis is sound, although it is an intriguing one. What is certain is that 'Alī's admirers, not all of whom were of South Arabian extraction, did come to look for spiritual as well as political guidance from the fourth caliph and his progeny. For them, Muhammad's charisma continued in that line, and thus each succeeding imām had an intrinsic authority.

But the majority of Muslims preferred a more representative approach to selecting leaders, and Geertz has characterized them as *contractualist* in political procedure (sharpening Watt's term *constitutionalist*). This approach refers to a leader on whom a representative sampling of the people had bestowed their approval by means of an oath of allegiance, called *bay'a.* This old and essentially Arabian form of selection and political loyalty appealed more to the masses. It suited the Arabs, as well as the somewhat populist peoples of Egypt and Syria who had come under Muslim rule. For those who were later called Sunnīs, the Prophet's charisma had become "routinized," to borrow Weber's model, in the umma itself.[8] This process had only begun by the end of the era of the rightly guided caliphs, but it indicated how the memory and living tradition of Muhammad were becoming institutionalized in the attitudes and habits of his people. The more consensual and representative nature of Sunnism will be examined in Chapter 9 and contrasted with Shī'ī political theory. A fateful *ḥadīth* ("saying") of Muhammad states: "Truly, my Umma shall never agree together upon an error." Sunnī Muslims have used this statement to support their contractualist ideal of government and to imbue it with supernatural force, whereas the Shī'īs have concentrated their attention and devotion on the remarkable individuals who descended in the special line of imāms that makes possible the intrinsicalist theory about who should rule the Muslims.

## THE SPREAD OF THE ISLAMIC EMPIRE

The Umayyads were effective rulers and greatly extended their hold over the world into which Islam had been first introduced by the great conquests. An especially important goal was the subjugation of the Byzantine Empire, and the Damascus caliphs kept up the pressure on Constantinople, in the process becoming highly skilled sea as well as land fighters. It was during the Umayyad period that Islam was firmly established in Europe: Spain was largely subjected to Muslim rule by 718 C.E.

Summer raiding parties crossed the Pyrenees into France but were repulsed by Charles Martel at the famous Battle of Poitiers in 732. Muslim navies dominated vast stretches of the Mediterranean by that time, and the southern shoreline, as well as the coast of Spain and the easternmost coasts, were under Muslim domination.

By the mid-eighth century, the Islamic empire constituted the dominant power system across the arid zone from the Atlantic to the frontiers of India. In certain parts of this expanse the conversion to Islamic values and Arab styles was relatively easy and free from dislocation or shock, as, for example, among the Aramaic-speaking populations of Syria, Palestine, and Iraq. The Arabs brought a new version of a basically familiar religious and ethical system to peoples whose native language was also in the Semitic family and closely related to the language of the Qur'an. The Persian rulers of Iraq during the Sasanian period immediately before the Arab conquests had far less of a cultural and linguistic advantage than did the uncouth warriors who swept in from the desert. The long-established natives tended to be more often Semitic than Indo-European. This was not, of course, the case in Spain, or Iran, or India. And Constantinople, although it eventually fell to the Islamized Ottoman Turks in 1453, never would have easily yielded its Greek and Christian soul to the followers of Muhammad but was instead overwhelmed by superior human resources in the form of Turkish tribes that gradually altered the landscape as well as the population of Asia Minor. The leadership of the Eastern church then moved to Moscow, which, after Constantinople, became the "Third Rome."

### *Mu'āwiya the Leader*

Mu'āwiya was one of the greatest leaders of Islamic history, with a personality and leadership style that were deeply informed and molded by *ḥilm* (forbearance), as a recent study shows. Although he was characteristically successful in both arbitration and on the battlefield, he treated his defeated foes with magnanimity and respect, thereby winning them over to his ideas. Throughout his reign he was able to reconcile conflicts and resolve grievances between parties. He greatly strengthened the central government in Damascus, yet all the while cultivated the persona and style of an Arab shaykh, a first among equals. He took the middle road and sought the loyalty and respect of disparate constituencies. He even succeeded in gaining the support of prominent admirers of 'Alī and his side. Because he all along steadily built up a powerful military in Syria, Mu'āwiya, like Teddy Roosevelt, walked softly and carried a big stick.

The first requirement for exercising *ḥilm* is possessing the potential to annihilate one's opposition, if necessary. There was something fascinating and appealing to his fellow Arabs about Mu'āwiya, who had infinite patience, perfect timing, and the ability to make his guests feel honored and indulged while protecting them from their enemies and themselves. It must not be forgotten that he also represented the most influential clan of Quraysh. Arab nobility increases over generations, and it did not make any difference that the Umayyads were now Muslims, because customs die slowly in that part of the world when honoring the superior types.

### *The Tragedy at Karbala*

Mu'āwiya initiated a dynastic line that much later was severely criticized for its worldliness and ruthlessness. In fact, with some exceptions, the Damascus caliphs worked hard to lead in a manner that reflected and ingrained Islamic values and held the subject peoples in a secure bond with a centralized administration. The ancient Arabs did not like hereditary succession, but Mu'āwiya shrewdly gained the support of his *shūrā* in order to see his son Yazīd readied for the throne after he died. Indeed, his son was almost as capable a leader as his father was, and he succeeded to the caliphate without serious trouble.

But Iraq's relations with the Syrian administrators were worsening, and the Arab Muslims there began to favor Husayn, the grandson of the Prophet and a son of 'Alī and Fātima, as leader. Recall that his elder brother, Hasan, had reigned briefly after the death of their father. Husayn was enthusiastic about going to Kūfa to receive the support of the members of the Shī'a there and then to set about establishing himself as the rightful leader of the Muslims, probably first in Iraq and later elsewhere. Together with his family and a few loyal supporters, Husayn advanced on Kūfa only to be ambushed at nearby Karbala. The entire company was massacred, except for the women and children, who were taken in bonds to Damascus together with the severed heads of Husayn and his followers. (In those days, before news photos, displaying the enemies' heads was a common way of publicizing something like the death of a movement.)

This shocking event occurred in 680 and marked the beginning of Shī'ism as a religious-political movement with a strong element of tragedy. Husayn gradually was

View of the great shrine of Husayn at Karbala, where the tragic martyrdom occurred in 680 C.E. (*Source:* Abdulaziz A. Sachedina)

hailed as a great martyr and Imam and even as the prototype for God's redemption of the Shīʻa at the end of the historical age. Shīʻism created a doctrine and style imbued with some of the pessimism and suffering of ancient Mesopotamia, combined with the hope for a savior, who in the folk myths, is a composite of Jesus and Tammuz. To this day, especially in Iraq and Iran, a "passion play" called *ta'ziya* is performed each year in commemoration of Karbala.

### *The Shīʻite Movement*

Although the Shīʻite movement was seriously interrupted in that it was unable to place a caliph-imām at the head of the umma, it drew strength from the tragedy of Karbala and attracted new followers who desired to see the Prophet's descendants reach their deserved place in the system. The next twenty or so years proved to be difficult ones for the Umayyads, but finally, with the reign of Walīd (705–715), the dynasty was restored and the empire's territory was extended, occupying Sind to the east and Spain to the far west.

During this period the *mawālī* were becoming numerous and also restive, because of their second-class status in the order of society and economy that the Arab-dominated leadership had designed. Both Shīʻite and Khārijite opposition were seriously harming the Umayyads. The former were especially successful in gaining the support of large groups of *mawālī,* who essentially had non-Arab backgrounds. The Shīʻa stirred up the desire for a descendant of Muhammad to be ruler so that the people, Arab and non-Arab alike, could return to the kind of egalitarian system that the early umma had enjoyed in Medina.

There is a degree of romanticism in this view, but it was powerful as propaganda, and it also expressed the non-Arab Muslims' yearning for justice. The Umayyads were increasingly depicted as Arab tyrants, preserving the best of life for themselves and consigning the rest of the people—the majority—to an inferior existence. The Shīʻīs made much of the universalism and egalitarianism of the true Islamic order and became strict readers and interpreters of the Qur'an in this regard. The movement that gained momentum against the Umayyads was in important respects highly religious and idealistic, but also intertwined with more practical political, social, and economic concerns. This has always been a characteristic of Islam: that it is both ***dīn wa dawla,*** "religion and political order" or "state."

## THE ABBASIDS

The core of the revolutionary movement that swept away the Umayyads was in distant Khurāsān, in the northeast. Calling themselves the ʻAbbāsids, after al-ʻAbbās, a paternal uncle of the Prophet, the leaders insisted that only by means of a caliph who was in the Prophet's house (*ahl al-Bayt*) could the umma resume its godly course. For obvious reasons, these Abbasids easily gained the support of the ʻAlid loyalists, as well as many *mawālī* and Arab tribesmen. But almost immediately, the Abbasids undermined their Shī'ite confederates by advancing their own choice as future leader of the umma. His name was Abū Muslim, and he was a remarkably effective leader. A *mawla,* he was given an Arabic and a Muslim name. But he was always acting in the name of one from the house of the Prophet, to be named later. At Merv he raised the black flags of revolution, a well-known regional symbol of a coming messianic deliverer. Black became the traditional color of the house of 'Abbas. The cause was considered just, and so the revolt proceeded, with Abū Muslim's forces battling their way to Iraq, where in 750 the Umayyad caliph and his army were beaten at the Great Zāb, near the Tigris. Caliph Marwān II fled to Egypt, where he was later murdered. Almost all of the remainder of the Umayyads were killed, and this effectively prevented a return of the dynasty. Only one escaped, who later founded an Umayyad dynasty in far-off Spain, but the young 'Abd al-Rahmān's adventures cannot detain us here.

Abū Muslim was a strong man, but the revolution had other elements, and it was agreed that the new caliph absolutely had to be a kinsman of the Prophet and be acceptable to all parties. Finally, therefore, Abū al-'Abbās was selected as Amīr al-Mu'minīn, "Commander of the Faithful," and he reigned for four years (749–754). He was succeeded by his more powerful older brother, Abū Ja'far, who showed the others that he would be a strong caliph and no figurehead. He fought a counterrevolution to achieve this goal and went so far as to execute Abū Muslim in order to make his control total. He reigned as *al-Manṣūr,* "The Victorious," continuing his predecessor's practice of using divine names to show his devotion to the revolution's religious aspects. The Shī'ites were pushed aside once their usefulness was over, and the Abbasids continued ruling much as the Umayyads had done, but saying that they were returning the umma to its primitive state, with equality and brotherhood. In actuality, the Abbasids came more to resemble the old Persian shahs as "oriental despots" than they did the more rustic and humble "rightly guided" caliphs of Medina before the *fitnas.*

### *The Abbasids' Cultural Contributions*

The Abbasid age was the glorious period of medieval Islamic civilization, during which its classical institutions and ways of thinking were developed and perfected. Jurisprudence, which was the Islamic science above all others; systematic theology (***'ilm al-kalām***), which was subordinate to law and not the "queen of the sciences" as in medieval Christendom; Arabic philology, grammar, and rhetoric, which were far more than antiquarian disciplines because of the importance of the Qur'an; and Greek-style philosophy—all were explored and perfected before the Gothic cathedrals of Europe were even conceived.

In addition, Arabic *belles lettres,* known as *adab,* delighted many in the Muslim lands, as did especially poetry, that heritage from the Arabian past that continued as perhaps the finest of the secular artistic and literary forms, even among the majority who did not descend from desert ancestors. A new Persian literature also arose in this era. The Abbasid period was the age of the *Arabian Nights,* of Aladdin and his lamp, of Sinbad the Sailor, and of the weird and unpredictable genies who inhabited the imaginations as well as the stories of the Muslim peoples. Great progress was made in science, mathematics, and medicine. The classical treatise on medicine of Ibn Sīna (Avicenna), the tenth-century Persian scholar, was still used as a medical school textbook in eighteenth-century Europe. The theologians and philosophers of Abbasid times, like Ibn Sīna, al-Fārābī, and al-Ghazālī, as well as the later Ibn Rushd, known in Latin as Averroës, provided most of the impetus as well as the models for medieval Christian scholastic theology at Paris, Oxford, and Cambridge universities.

The peak of Abbasid power and creativity under Hārūn al-Rashīd roughly coincided with the period of Charlemagne in the West (ca. 800 C.E.). In fact, the two rulers were well aware of each other and exchanged envoys as well as lavish gifts. Although the Abbasid period experienced cycles of relative power, cohesion, and unity of purpose as well as administration, there were at least as many cycles of weakness, ineffective rule, and corruption, which caused the Muslims great hardship and regression. The Abbasid capital was established in the new city of Baghdad shortly after the revolution (758). The palace compound was constructed on a round plan, which from above resembled a *mandala,* complete with cardinal points and symbolism of universal domination as exemplary center.[9] The site of the new city, known in Arabic as *Madīnat al-Salām* ("City of Peace"), was conveniently located to take advantage of both Tigris and Euphrates trade and communications (although it was actually situated on the Tigris). It was also strategically positioned to withstand aggression from outside the region. In a way, this Islamic capital resembled more than anything else the city-states of ancient Babylon. It is ironic that when the new religious community had to establish its institutional structure in an imperial context, it should have been forced by geography and ancient precedent to adapt itself in a manner that was as far removed as possible from the old Arabian style. Maybe there is a law of empires that requires any ruler who is successful in such a world crossroads as Mesopotamia to assume the style and symbols of rule that had been pioneered and perfected at the dawn of civilization in that matrix of large-scale hydraulic agriculture.[10]

### *The Abbasid Leadership*

In Abbasid times the caliph was referred to as the Presence and enjoyed such imposing titles as "The Shadow of God on Earth" and "The Caliph of God," the latter significantly omitting the word *rasūl,* which was the original wording of the phrase, translated as "The Caliph of the *Apostle* of God." "Caliph of God" (*Khalifat Allāh*) had been applied first to the Umayyad caliphs, but it came to be better suited to the much more lordly style of their successors. Whereas in Umayyad times the Muslims were divided roughly into Arabs and *mawālī*—and this, remember, was one of the main issues in the call for revolution—by Abbasid times all the Muslims were more or less equal in that they were both far removed from their exalted leader in Baghdad. When a minister or other official went in to the Presence with a report or on some matter of business, he routinely carried his shroud over his arm. Off to the side, near the caliph, always stood the executioner, ready to carry out his master's command instantly. Many chambers and doors separated the caliph from the palace's outer rooms, so that visitors—especially foreign emissaries—would be suitably awed when they approached the caliph's inner sanctum.

The stories of the *Arabian Nights* often tell of the exploits of the popular Caliph Harūn al-Rashīd ("Aaron the Rightly Guided"), Charlemagne's contemporary, who delighted in prowling the back streets of Baghdad by night, together with a few close companions. Legend has it that he would dress as a commoner and seek out corruption. On discovering a crooked merchant or a thieving artisan, he would thrust aside his shabby cape and reveal his royal identity before bringing the surprised and condemned criminals to quick justice. Some stories show a worldly, winebibbing, cynical side of court life in high caliphal times. Baghdad had become a world capital, with all that such a position implies. Incredible wealth existed alongside extreme poverty, and every type of human being sought a way to preferment in that glamorous but risky environment. Persons of low estate could be elevated instantly through cleverness or royal whim, to positions of prestige, authority, and, above all, wealth. The reverse was also the case.

## OTHER MUSLIM PEOPLES

### *Turks*

The mid-tenth century witnessed the end of the caliph's absolutist rule. For some generations, Turkish tribes had been migrating into the Iranian highlands, Iraq, and contiguous areas. From their ancestral homelands in the Altai Mountains of Central Asia these vigorous and fearless horse nomads of the steppes became regional strong men, who increasingly acted as military princes in their own localities, while giving some sort of recognition to the caliph as supreme head of the Muslims. In Baghdad the real power went to a new figure, the "Prince of Princes" (*Amīr al-umarā'*), who was head of the army. The caliph from then on stood for the spiritual and communal values of the umma only. In addition to various Turkish waves, other eastern nomadic groups also exerted great influence on the waning caliphate. For some time, beginning in the mid-tenth century, Persian soldiers of Shī'ite persuasion held the caliph virtually a prisoner in his own palace, using him as legitimator of their own policies. These were the Buwayhids, a tribal group.

After the ninth century, the Persians came to the fore in literature, philosophy, medicine, music, and especially the religious sciences. Of course they wrote in Arabic, but they represented a tradition of learning and scholarship that was native to the Iranian regions and extended well into Central Asia. If the tenth and eleventh centuries, especially, were times of great weakness in the caliphate, they were also times of brilliant achievement in the areas just mentioned. In fact, this period has been called the "Renaissance of Islam" and reached its apex in the life and work of

Courtyard of the Mosque of Ibn Tulun, Cairo, showing the ablution area (left) and the "Ziggurat" style minaret. Ninth century C.E. (*Source:* Frederick Mathewson Denny)

the Persian theologian, philosopher, and mystic al-Ghazālī (d. 1111), of whom more will be said in Chapter 10, which deals with Islamic mysticism.

The Turkish peoples took readily to Islam, having had before a religion, shamanism, that was especially appropriate to Central Asian steppe peoples living under the open sky. As the Turks became Muslim, they became so in a staunchly Sunnī way, especially their leadership, and have remained so to this day. Yet they also had a mystical and ecstatic bent, probably stemming from their aboriginal shamanic beliefs and practices. They were excellent horsemen and fighters and impossible to resist when they set their minds to something. Eventually a prominent group of them established the great Ottoman Empire, with its capital Constantinople, whose name had been changed to Istanbul. They carried Islam well into eastern Europe and threatened Western countries even into modern times.

### *Mongols*

In the thirteenth century a new Asiatic nomadic power arose, farther to the east than the Turkish homelands. The Mongols, also horse people of the steppes, became organized into an unprecedently powerful confederation under Genghis Khan. He conquered great expanses of Central Asia, and his sons went even farther to dominate China, Russia, and the Near East as far as Syria. In 1258, Hulagu, a grandson of Genghis Khan, attacked Baghdad, which he sacked and burned to the ground, and executed the last Abbasid caliph. The Mongols devastated most of the lands that they crossed. Iran and Iraq were changed almost beyond recognition, although they eventually recovered, assimilating a degree of Mongol style and mentality as they did, especially in their art. Large numbers of Turkish people from Central Asia were also involved in the Mongol conquests. In later times, especially in Russia, the tribal peoples of Mongol and Turkish heritage became collectively known as Tatars. Just as the Mongols and Turks came to the old Islamic centers in the Middle East from their remote Central Asian domains, the Islamic faith likewise penetrated those very domains later and became established as far as western China, where it still commands a prominent religious community of many millions. Obviously, the Islamic rulers exploited to their benefit the ancient overland trade routes linking the Middle and Far East.

***The End of the Abbasid Caliphate.*** So ended the Abbasid Caliphate. The institution was transferred to Cairo, but there it eventually failed. The Ottoman Turks took the title of caliph after 1517 and breathed some of the old spirit and prestige back into the institution. Indeed, the period leading up to 1258 has often been regarded as the Golden Age of Islam. It is beyond our purposes to prove or disprove that point, but it is true that the Muslims experienced a great loss in the wake of the Mongol devastation of the ancient capital on the Tigris. Yet Muslim power and culture did not reach their heights until well after the Mongol debacle. In the fifteenth century, three great Islamic empires arose and were absolutely dominant from the subcontinent of India to the Mediterranean and Europe: these were the Mughal (named after Mongol) dynasty of India, the Sāfavid dynasty of Iran, and the Ottoman dynasty of the Eastern Mediterranean, Asia Minor, and southeastern Europe. The Sāfavids established Shī'ism as the official religion of their domains, and Iran has remained Shī'ī to the present day. Never before the period of these three great "empires of gunpowder times," as the historian Marshall G. S. Hodgson called them, had there been such a concentration or extent of Islamic power.

### *Islamic Spain and Egypt*

Spain endured an equally powerful and creative western extension of the umma. From the time of its conquest, and later, migrations of peoples from the Near East and the Maghrib (the "West") settled in Spain. A separate Umayyad dynasty, with its own rival caliph, prospered in Spain during Abbasid times. The cultural, literary, and scholarly accomplishments of the Spanish Muslims do not suffer by comparison with those of the central Islamic regions. Egypt, Syria, Iraq, and Iran had their Ibn al-Fārid, al-Shāfi'ī, al-Junayd, and al-Ghazālī, but al-Andalus (Andalusia) had its Ibn Hazm, Ibn Rushd, Ibn Khaldūn, and Ibn al-Arabī, not to mention the immortal scholar-sage, Maimonides, a Jew who was culturally Spanish-Arab and wrote in Arabic as well as Hebrew. It was mainly through Spain (but also through Rhodes and Sicily) that Europe learned about the new sciences of Islam and the manuscript tradition of ancient Greek philosophy, which was lovingly and skillfully translated into Arabic and edited by Muslim scholars.

Finally, a Shī'ī dynasty was established in Egypt in the mid-tenth century. Known as the Fātimids, after the Prophet's daughter, and originating in North Africa, they founded the city of Cairo in 969 and a short time later established the Azhar University, which became and remains the greatest single religious training center in the Islamic world. Fātimid Cairo is the Cairo of the *Arabian Nights,* equal in its own way to Baghdad, its rival to the East. The dynasty lasted for over a century, but Egypt never embraced Shī'ī Islam, the faith of its rulers. From Fātimid times, however, Egypt increasingly became the main intellectual and political power in the central Islamic regions until the rise of the Ottoman Empire in the fourteenth century.

## *Islamic India, Asia, and Africa*

Islam has always been closely associated with the Arabic-speaking parts of the world, that is, most of the Middle East, including North Africa. But Islam is a world religion, with most of its adherents living outside the Arab world and even the Persian and Turkish-speaking regions. Alone among the Abrahamic religions, Islam also became a major religion in Central, South, and Southeast Asia. India was converted by both conquest and peaceful preaching. The first incursion of Arab Muslims into India was made shortly after the death of Muhammad. There were numerous subsequent invasions and migrations, but it was not until around 1000 C.E. that Muslim armies under Mahmūd of Ghazna, in Afghanistan, began subjugating northwest India in earnest. The sultanate of Delhi was founded in 1206, marking the beginning of a long period of Muslim dominance, first in north India, and later, under the Mughals, in nearly all of the subcontinent until British colonial times. The Muslims are still a sizable minority in India and an overwhelming majority in Pakistan and Bangladesh. From about the thirteenth century, Muslim traders from India led in the Islamization of Malaysia and Indonesia. Usually, the urban and coastal areas became Islamic first. By the sixteenth century Islam had achieved a dominant position in the Malaysian archipelago, especially on Java and Sumatra. It is interesting to note that Sufis, or those practicing the mystical forms of Islam, were very important in introducing a largely peaceful, persuasive element into this new faith. This ensured tolerance for the older traditions, often incorporating them into a new blending of spiritual wisdom and meditative practice. The extent to which the older indigenous as well as Buddhist and Hindu ideas, symbols, and attitudes continued in the Islamic period attest to this view. From the archipelago, Islam reached up into the southern Philippines, where it still continues to be strong.

Africa south of the Sahara was first exposed to Islam along the eastern littoral, sometimes called the "Swahili coast." Traders were prominent in spreading the word as they sailed their ships around the horn of Somalia and on down to the regions near Zanzibar (now part of Tanzania). Islam's progress in the interior of Africa was slow for a long time, but within the last two centuries it has made major gains in many regions of the continent, outpacing Christianity in the present century. As in Indonesia, Islam has tried to accommodate the indigenous beliefs and practices, producing a faith that is not so formally strict as that in some of the long-established Muslim countries of the Middle East.

## ISLAM'S ACHIEVEMENTS

From its inception, Islam has been a religion of settled peoples, of the town and city. This observation may sound odd in light of the importance of the Arabian environment in which it was founded. But as we saw in an earlier chapter, the Bedouin were never particularly religious, although they served admirably in spreading Islam beyond the borders of Arabia. Although Islam is largely an urban phenomenon, especially in its devotional practices, the religion has appealed to many pastoralist and nomadic peoples across the expanses of the Afro-Eurasian landmass, more so than any other world religion. Urban dwellers and pastoral nomads have profited from close cooperation involving trade over long distances. The merchants had to have reliable and secure transportation, which the well-positioned camel breeders were able to provide. This occupation gave them an income and the opportunity to use their native initiative and daring in turning a profit for both themselves and their employers. And the common bond of Islamic faith transcended regional and kinship-based affinities to allow an interregional, indeed international, order to flourish.

In his great interpretation, *The Venture of Islam: Conscience and History in a World Civilization,*[11] Marshall Hodgson argued that Islam fulfilled the dream of peoples in the great urban and trade regions between the Nile and Oxus rivers and beyond by bringing a religious, social, and political order that recognized the validity of agreements across a variety of linguistic, ethnic, cultural, and geographic

The mosque-tomb complex of the Muslim saint, Sunan Giri (late 1400s), in Gresik, North Java, Indonesia. He was one of the Wali Sanga, "Nine Saints" who brought Islam to Java. The stacked "Mt. Meru" roof of the mosque reflects earlier Buddhist styles. (*Source:* Frederick Mathewson Denny)

barriers. The one true God witnesses covenants and agreements made among his people, and thereby a type of business integrity emerged based on Islamic justice and fair dealing. This achievement was made possible by an urban-based international Islamic order, the first such order ever to have been established in the long history of the region. (Not the first large-scale empire, of course, which is a different phenomenon.) Indeed, the original unification of Arabia, which only could be accomplished—as it was—under something like Islamic rule, was based in the urban centers of Mecca and Medina. Forever after, moving to a city, a place where people dwell together in amity and under a common law and worship together in the Friday mosque, has always been a meritorious act.

## NOTES

1. For a balanced discussion of the *ridda* wars, see Elias Shoufani, *Al-Riddah and the Muslim Conquest of Arabia* (Toronto and Buffalo: University of Toronto Press and the Arab Institute for Research and Publishing, 1973).
2. Fred McGraw Donner's *The Early Islamic Conquests* (Princeton, N.J.: Princeton University Press, 1981) is highly recommended as an introduction to the complexities of the subject. See also M. A. Shaban, *Islamic History A.D. 600–750 (A.H. 132): A New Interpretation* (Cambridge, England: Cambridge University Press, 1971).
3. For a detailed discussion of *dhimmī* status, see A. S. Tritton, *The Caliphs and Their Non-Muslim Subjects: A Critical Study of the Covenant of Umar* (London: Frank Cass, 1970).
4. See Nehemia Levtzion, ed., *Conversion to Islam* (New York and London: Holmes & Meier, 1979). See also Richard W. Bulliet, *Conversion to Islam in the Medieval Period: An Essay in Quantitative History* (Cambridge, Mass.: Harvard University Press, 1979). Bulliet traces conversion through name changes. A richly diverse collection of essays on Christians in Muslim lands is *Conversion and Continuity: Indigenous Christian Communities in Islamic Lands, Eighth to Eighteenth Centuries,* ed. Michael Gervers and Ramzi Jibran Bikhazi (Toronto: Pontifical Institute of Medieval Studies, 1990).
5. See S. H. M. Jafri, *The Origins and Early Development of Shi'a Islam* (London: Longman, 1979).
6. A new thesis, which argues that Muhammad succeeded in achieving a final redaction of the Qur'an before his death, has been published by John Burton, in *The Collection of the Qur'ān* (Cambridge, England: Cambridge University Press, 1977).
7. Clifford Geertz, *Islam Observed: Religious Development in Morocco and Indonesia* (New Haven, Conn.: Yale University Press, 1968, and Chicago: University of Chicago Press, 1971), p. 76. Watt's terms are *autocratic* and *constitutionalist* and are found in his *Islamic Philosophy and Theology* (Edinburgh: Edinburgh University Press, 1962), p. 53. The ideas are more fully discussed in Watt's *Islam and the Integration of Society* (Evanston, IL.: Northwestern University Press, 1961), especially pp. 104–108.
8. A convenient introduction to charisma theory is the collection *From Max Weber: Essays in Sociology,* ed. H. H. Gerth and C. Wright Mills (New York: Oxford University Press, 1946), pp. 245–252, 297.

9. Jacob Lassner, in *The Shaping of 'Abbāsid Rule* (Princeton, N.J.: Princeton University Press, 1980), argues against a *mandala* symbolism in his learned and clear description of the topography of Baghdad. We do not adopt the *mandala* idea in more than a heuristic sense. For a stimulating argument in favor of the cosmographical point of view, centering on a borrowed *mandala* motif, see Charles Wendell, "Baghdad: *Imago Mundi* and Other Foundation Lore," *International Journal of Middle Eastern Studies* 2 (1971): 99–128.
10. For a suggestive analysis of Mesopotamian agricultural irrigation and its relationship to patterns of rule, see Robert M. Adams, *Land Behind Baghdad* (Chicago: University of Chicago Press, 1965). Adams brings the discussion to Islamic times in Iraq.
11. Three volumes (Chicago: University of Chicago Press, 1974). See especially vol. 1, Chap. 1, "The World Before Islam."

PART THREE

# The Islamic Religious System

CHAPTER

# 5 The Basic Beliefs and Worship Practices of Islam

## KEY TERMS

***shahāda***
***tawḥīd***
***īmān***
***'ibāda* and *'ibādāt***
***ḥadath***
***wuḍū***
**ghusl**
**niyya**
***miḥrāb***
***adhān* and *mu'adhdhin* ("muezzin")**
***masjid***
***imām***
***takbīr***
***khuṭba***
***zakāt***
***ṣawm***
***jihād***

## THE FIVE DOCTRINES OF ISLAMIC FAITH

> *Lā ilāha illā Allāh. Muhammad rasūl Allāh.* ("There is no god but God. Muhammad is the messenger of God.")

This "testimony," known in Arabic as ***shahāda,*** is the closest thing to a creed in Islam. It is sufficient simply to utter it once in one's life, freely and as a believer, to become a Muslim. Then all of the other elements of belief and the prescribed duties become immediately incumbent on the one who has testified by means of the shahāda. The basic doctrines of Islam can be classified under five headings, which are collectively called *īmān,* meaning "faith."

### *Faith*

The first doctrine is faith in the absolute unity of God, which is more than an intellectual assent to a proposition. The technical word for monotheism is ***tawḥīd,*** which means "making [God] one" by means of devotion and refusal to compromise on this point. Recall poor Bilāl under the heavy stone in the hot sun, who nevertheless persevered in *tawḥīd* by exclaiming "One! One!" Another name for Muslims is *muwaḥḥidūn,* "unitarians," or more dynamically, "upholders of the divine unity." God is transcendent, far above all that we can think or say about him. He does not beget, nor is he begotten (Sūra 112). Consequently, a doctrine such as the Christian Trinity is unacceptable and even offensive to Muslim sensibilities, because it suggests *shirk,* the "associating" of something with God, which is the one unforgivable sin in Islam. Later, in Chapter 8, we shall examine the more formally theological issues connected with God: his being and nature, attributes, and activities, all of which are founded, first, on his oneness.

### *Belief in Angels*

The second doctrine is the belief in angels and their important work as messengers and helpers of God. Although most of the great angels are good creatures of God, one is evil. That is Iblīs, or Satan, who was cast out of heaven after he refused God's command to bow down to Adam (Qur'an 7:11–18). Iblīs has a great host of evil followers of angelic origin. The angels, which have no sex, are made of light, whereas humans are created from clay. There are several angels mentioned by name in the Qur'an (for example, Jibrīl/Gabriel; Mīkāl/Michael; as well as Hārūt and Mārūt, both fallen angels). In addition to the angels are the supernatural beings, created of fire, known as *jinn* (sing., *jinnī*). These were introduced in Chapter 2 as the invisible beings that possess poets, filling them with special awareness and power in speech. One who is possessed by a *jinnī* is rendered *majnūn,* "bejinned," meaning "insane." The *jinn* are much lower than the angels, being in most respects like humans. They have limited life spans, are either male or female, and can be either good or evil. The Qur'an speaks of some of them as having been converted to Islam (72:1–19). Generally they are feared by humans, for they are associated with the spooky and uncanny dimensions of life. So, although the stated doctrine is "belief in angels," this heading also includes other supernatural beings.

### *Prophets and Scriptures*

The third belief concerns revealed scriptures and prophetic messengers. Muhammad was the last in a long and noble line of prophets who had been entrusted with bringing scriptures to their peoples. All prophets receive their revelations from God by means of *waḥy,* "suggestion," or "idea-word inspiration."[1] All scriptures are entirely God's work, but peoples before Islam—the Jews and the Christians—had corrupted their original messages to suit their own inclinations. The Qur'an, then, is the purest extant scripture on earth, because it has been preserved from tampering. God sent it as a mercy to humankind, so that they might be brought back to the original, true faith of Abraham. Moses was given the Tawrāt (Torah), David the Zabūr ("Psalms"), and Jesus the Injīl ("Evangel," "Gospel"). The Qur'an lists some twenty-five prophets in a line from Adam to Muhammad: Adam, Nūh (Noah), Idrīs (Enoch), Ibrāhīm (Abraham), Ismā'īl (Ishmael), Ishāq (Isaac), Ya'qūb (Jacob), Dāwūd (David), Sulaimān (Solomon), Ayyūb (Job), Yūsuf (Joseph), Mūsā (Moses), Hārūn (Aaron), Ilyās (Elias or Elijah), al-Yasa' (Elisha), Yūnus (Jonah), Lūt (Lot), Hūd, Shu'ayb, Sālih, Dhu'l-kifl (Ezekiel), Zakariyya (Zecharia), Yahya (John), 'Īsā (Jesus), and Muhammad. Most of these names are also biblical, although David, Solomon, Adam, Abraham, and several others are not considered by Jews and Christians to be prophets. Hūd, Shu'ayb, and Sālih are old Arabian prophets with no clear biblical counterparts. With the exceptions of Ezekiel, Elijah, Elisha, Zecharia, Jonah, and John the Baptist, none of the usually recognized biblical prophets appear in this list.

Muhammad's belief in the close association between the prophetic messengers and the books sent down from heaven derives from ancient ideas in the Near East of the relationship between written language and divine revelation.[2] Although most of the prophets that the Qur'an itself names are not generally regarded by Jews and Christians as being book bearers, those written prophets who are claimed by both of the earlier Near Eastern monotheisms fit the general pattern that Muhammad and the Qur'an perpetuated. It is not clear to what extent such major Hebrew prophets as Isaiah, Jeremiah, Amos, and Hosea were known to Muhammad and his Arabian contemporaries. They are not mentioned in the Qur'an, though in certain stylistic respects their books are similar to portions of the Qur'an. But their contents are very different, with the exception of Amos, which emphasizes the divine judgment on a sinful, unfaithful people. In fact, all four books contain judgment and warning passages similar to those in the Qur'an. But in regard to the peculiar qualities of Yahweh's love and holiness, climaxing the "suffering servant" passages of Isaiah 53, the views of the Qur'an and the Bible part significantly.

Poster with the shahāda inscribed on it. The large letters read: *Lā ilāha illā Allāh,* "There is no god but God." The small cluster of black letters in the upper left read: *Muhammad rasūl Allāh,* Muhammad is the Messenger of God." (*Source:* Frederick Mathewson Denny)

### *The Final Judgment*

The fourth fundamental Islamic belief is in a final judgment, around which cluster the details of Islamic eschatology, or "doctrine of the last things." Many of the specifics of the Qur'an's teaching concerning the Last Judgment have parallels and antecedents in other Near Eastern traditions, especially in Zoroastrianism, Judaism, and Christianity. But the Qur'anic system, later greatly elaborated by the theologians, is unique and came to exert its own special influence on medieval eschatological thought and symbolism in not only non-Muslim regions, particularly Western Christendom (for example, Dante's *Divine Comedy*), but also Asia. The doctrine of a final judgment of humankind is a corollary to the doctrine of *tawḥīd,* for it reveals the moral nature of God in relation to his creation. These two beliefs should be viewed as closely associated with each other. The judgment is the test of *tawḥīd,* but the divine unity both precedes and subsists beyond the "last things." Those faithful devotees of God and his true religion not only survive but also emphatically triumph on the Judgment Day, because they are included within the divine scheme of salvation and reward. The Sufis, or Islamic mystics, emphasize the ultimate union of the slave with his master, as will be seen and analyzed in some detail in Chapters 10 and 11.

***The Last Judgment and the Qur'an.*** The Last Judgment is set forth in many Qur'anic passages as the denouement of the historical process. It is known by such names as "the Day of Doom" (*yaum al-dīn*), "the Last Day" (*al-yaum al-ākhir*), "the Day of Resurrection" (*yaum al-qiyāma*), "the Hour," "the Day of Distinguishing" (the saved from the damned), and others. The final judgment period descends swiftly, heralded by a peal of thunder, a shout, or a trumpet blast. The natural world is then turned upside down, as depicted in the powerful sūra known as "The Darkening," with its prophetic symbols of the reversal and inversion of the normal world order:

> When the sun shall be darkened, when the stars shall be thrown down, when the mountains shall be set moving, when the pregnant camels shall be neglected, when the savage beasts shall be mustered, when the seas shall be set boiling, when the souls shall be coupled, when the buried infant shall be asked for what sin she was slain, when the scrolls shall be unrolled, when heaven shall be stripped off, when Hell shall be set blazing, when Paradise shall be brought nigh, then shall a soul know what it has produced. (Qur'an 81:1–14)

No self-respecting Arab normally would ever leave his pregnant camel alone, particularly in her tenth month (as the Arabic original indicates) when the birthing takes place. The camel was the Bedouin's most valuable single possession. Yet juxtaposed in the same passage is the practice of female infanticide by live burial (lest blood be spilt and pollution entail). Moving mountains would be an especially frightening phenomenon, because in ancient Arabian cosmology they were thought to be the tent pegs of the firmament. In short, all of the usual natural and economic and social customs and processes will be interrupted and ended on the Last Day.

Then all humans, whether long dead or still alive, will be assembled before God the judge. This was a peculiarly unsettling doctrine to the Arabians, who did not normally believe in a bodily resurrection before the coming of Islam. One of the Qur'an's mightiest achievements was to change completely this attitude toward one of religious dread of judgment *after* life and the grave. Time, *al-Dahr,* "like an ever-rolling stream," had simply obliterated human lives in the view of pagan Arabia. But God had other plans. Each human being has a record book that will be examined at the Judgment, with each individual being handed his or her book in either the right or the left hand. This is symbolic of the association of the right with goodness and purity and the left with evil and pollution. As in Muslim social relations, so also at the Judgment, the giving of something into the left hand symbolizes contempt. It is important to note that in a society in which the protection and support of powerful clan members and patrons were normal and expected aspects of surviving difficult trials and judgments, the Qur'an insists that each person stands before God absolutely alone. No one can intercede between God and a person, without God's permission on the Last Day. The general theological interpretation of this Qur'anic point came to be that Muhammad will be able to intercede in certain cases, especially where the sin has been great. But the Qur'an itself is not explicit on this point.[3] Greater support is found in the *Ḥadīth*, the record of Muhammad's own sayings and acts.

The final outcome is either eternal paradise or eternal hell, the former a blissful retreat and the latter a horrible punishment by fire. There are numerous descriptions of both heaven and hell in the Qur'an, with considerable specific detail. Hell is known as *jahannam,* and is cognate with the Hebrew *gehenna.* The most common name is simply "the fire" (*al-nār*). There are punishing angels there who do not allow the damned any respite from their sufferings, which in addition to burning include drinking boiling water and eating a very bitter fruit. Heaven is often referred to as "the garden" (*al-janna*), and this is a fitting symbol for luxuriant sheltered ease in a hot desert climate. All is comfortable and well appointed in the garden, where the saved recline on soft cushions and enjoy good food and a heavenly drink that thrills and satisfies without intoxicating. The descriptions are vivid and detailed, but most important are heaven's spiritual joys, whose appeals far outdistance the more physical delights that obviously were attractive to the rough soldiers of Arabian Islam. The earlier Meccan period of the Qur'an includes mention of beautiful young women "with swelling breasts, like of age" (78:33) to the saved. Although these *ḥūrīs,* as they are called, are a permanent part of the heavenly society, it is also believed that husbands and wives and their children will be together in heaven (13:23). The descriptions of heaven in the Qur'an do not comprise a unified or specific and systematically delineated landscape; they are more symbolic of bliss and joy than anything else. But they have had an enormous influence on the Muslims, whether interpreted symbolically or literally.

### *The Divine Decree and Predestination*

The fifth and final fundamental Islamic belief is the "divine decree and predestination," known in Arabic as *al-qaḍā wa 'l-qadar.* This doctrine has been one of the most frequently and passionately discussed of all Islamic tenets. It has its basis in the

Qur'an, which nevertheless does not unequivocally support the proposition that God decrees and determines all that happens from all eternity and "records" our acts and destinies down to the tiniest detail. A typical Qur'anic passage concerning predestination is "whomsoever God guides, he is rightly guided; and whom He leads astray, they are the losers" (7:178).

The Qur'anic view of the matter is impossible to pin down as either predestinarian or in favor of free will, for both views are embraced or at least implied: "He leads none astray save the ungodly such as break the covenant of God after its solemn binding, and such as cut what God has commanded should be joined, and such as do corruption in the land—they shall be the losers" (2:26). There is a tension in this Qur'anic message between God's foreordaining and humankind's choosing. Certainly that message proclaims God's inscrutable, just, and sovereign decree, but it also describes a religious law and engenders a spiritual attitude that is unintelligible without moral responsibility. If this issue is joined only on the level of human logic, then it will probably end up in favor of predestination. But God is far above what his creatures can imagine or comprehend, and his acts cannot be gauged by human measures.

The sayings of the Prophet Muhammad tend to be more predestinarian than the Qur'an is. Muslim, one of the two collectors of *ḥadīths* that the Muslims regard as soundest, transmitted the following:

> 'Abdallāhb. 'Amr reported God's messenger as saying, "God recorded the fates of all creatures 50,000 years before creating the heavens and the earth, and His throne was upon the water."[4]

A famous Shī'ī pronouncement on this matter comes from the Imām Ja'far al-Sādiq (d. 756), who, when asked about *qaḍā* and *qadar,* replied that it was a forbidden topic of discussion:

> It is a deep sea, venture not into it. . . . It is an obscure path, walk not along it. . . . It is one of Allah's secrets, do not talk about it. . . . He who attempts to seek knowledge of it goes contrary to Allah's command, disputes His sovereignty, and is probing into His secret and His veil, [whereby] he has assuredly incurred the wrath of Allah, so his abode will be Gehenna. What an evil destination.[5]

### The Doctrines and Orthodoxy

The foregoing doctrines comprise what we may call Islamic orthodoxy, "right belief," expressed by the Arabic word ***īmān,*** "faith or belief." One who has faith is called a *mu'min.* In the Qur'an, faith is clearly regarded as superior to surrender, *islām.* But there is no faith without surrender, although there can be surrender without faith, as the Qur'an makes clear:

> The Bedouins say, "We believe [that is, have īmān]." Say: "You do not believe; rather say, "We surrender" [that is, are Muslims]; for belief has not yet entered your hearts." (49:14)

Although belief is required as well as surrender, it should be emphasized that it is as much God's gift as humankind's doing. Belief, interestingly, is perfected and proved in service to God, service that includes worship acts performed according to strict rules and procedures.

*Orthodoxy* is not the best term to use when characterizing Islam's sense of right religion. A better term is *orthopraxy,* which means "right practice" and comes much closer to the reality of Muslim devotion and obedience to God. Here Islam is closer in spirit and practice to Judaism than to Christianity. Christianity stresses doctrinal clarity and understanding by means of creeds, dogmas, and theologies. Islam and Judaism, on the other hand, view religion as a way of life and a ritual patterning of that life under God's lordship. There is a great sense of security in both traditions in maintaining proper worship and following divine guidance by "commanding the good and forbidding the evil," as the Qur'an puts it. It is because of this affinity along the lines of orthopraxy that Muhammad regarded the Jews of Medina as natural allies in the development of the godly community, or umma. The fact that a Jewish–Islamic religious blending did not succeed does not mean that fundamental similarities and structural as well as functional affinities were lacking; it was because of the Jews' and the Muslims' differing views on the provenance of Muhammad's prophecies.

## THE FIVE ACTS OF WORSHIP

Our contention that Islam is more an orthopraxy than an orthodoxy does not mean that matters of doctrine and belief are unimportant, far from it. Rather, they are incorporated into performance in a configuration of worship and daily life. Islam calls upon human beings to be doers of the truth, and not just hearers and speakers of it. There are five basic, minimal acts of devotion to God, sometimes called the "pillars of Islam," but in the Muslim context they are better known as ***'ibādāt,*** "acts of worship" (sing., ***'ibāda***). All Islamic law books begin with ritual duties, the pillars. But even before one reaches the detailed instructions and regulations connected with the pillars of worship (*ṣalāt*), almsgiving (*zakāt*), fasting in the month of Ramadān (*aum*), and the pilgrimage to Mecca (*ḥajj*), one must first understand the crucial place of purification, known as *ṭahāra.* "Purification," according to Muhammad, "is half the faith." In another place, the Prophet said, "The key to paradise is prayer [*ṣalāt*] and the key to prayer is purification."[6]

## PURIFICATION

Purification is both spiritual and physical.[7] The spiritual kind is achieved through an aware, dedicated life in which kindness, concern for others, gratitude and openness to God, and sensitivity to moral issues dominate. Physical purification is achieved by means of specific ritualized acts and is maintained by means of avoidance. Unless one is in a state of purity, one may not handle the Qur'an, perform the *ṣalāt,* circumambulate the Ka'ba, or perform the running rite (*sa'y*) in Mecca (both of which are part of the hajj, or "pilgrimage"). There are varying degrees of impurity, as we shall describe, but even minor impurity bars one from the aforementioned ritual privileges. An understanding of Muslim teachings, attitudes, and practices concerning ritual purity and pollution can take the student far toward appreciating the Islamic way of life, because purification and related issues constantly intersect the Muslim's life. Before describing the purity required of those who worship and the types of pollution that the believer seeks to avoid, it will be of interest to provide some examples of the ways in which purification concerns surface in everyday life.

### *The Uses of the Right and Left Hands*

The right hand is considered to be clean, whereas the left is unclean and generally inauspicious. Remember that the wicked on the Day of Judgment will have their books of deeds handed to them in their left hands (or, alternatively, from behind their backs). One should never, in an Islamic context, touch someone with the left hand or extend it in greeting or bestow a gift or other object with the left hand (barring obvious and unavoidable exceptions, such as when a person's right hand has been amputated). The left hand is symbolically unclean, but even more it may retain actual, physical pollution because of its use in toilet operations and other tasks that bring believers into unpleasant but necessary contact with filth. In any event, the left is associated with actual impurity. (Someone who works as a butcher, tanner, farmer, undertaker, or physician regularly comes into contact with pollution, beyond what an ordinary person does. Yet everyone is vulnerable to pollution because of humankind's biological nature: urination, excretion, passing wind, sleeping, fainting, and male and female orgasm all pollute the person.)

Further, one should enter a privy left foot first and leave right foot first. On the other hand, one enters a mosque right foot first and exits left foot first. Further still, one does not wear shoes in a place of worship but goes about barefooted or wearing socks or slippers.

One eats with the right hand, or at least one puts only the right hand into the common dish. In many Muslim cultures, one does not use the utensils common in the West. The use of the fingers is not due to a lack of knowledge of knives, forks, and spoons; it is from preference for a traditional way of eating in which the food is enjoyed tactilely from the moment it is grasped, and people share this most basic and necessary of activities by dipping into a common bowl or platter, thus symbolizing their mutual dependence. It is not considered a breach of etiquette to hold a morsel of food or an orange, apple, or drinking cup in the left hand. Muslims are not rigid, being always on guard against ritually prohibited or suspect behavior in the area of simple matters such as eating.

A non-Muslim guest is unlikely to be made to feel ashamed or embarrassed for committing small errors caused by ignorance of custom. The cultivation of Islamic patterns of propriety and purification is gentle and gradual, depending mostly on correct example. Far worse than an innocent extending his or her left hand into the rice and lamb dish would be a Muslim host's annoyed gesture of disapproval; for hospitality is a sacred trust, reflecting God's gracious gift of life to all creatures. This is not to say that a good host would feel constrained from mentioning this to his or her guest in a tactful manner, thus opening what is always an interesting topic of conversation. (But, as we shall see in Chapter 12, conversation while eating is not universally desired.)

## RITUAL IMPURITY

Impurity is of two types. The type external to the person is called *najāsa.* It is some impurity that becomes attached to the skin of a person or soils the clothes or prayer place. It is not caused by the believer, but it must be removed before ritual purity can be achieved. The other type is called *ḥadath* and is caused by the person's engaging in or experiencing certain activities. Examples of *najāsa* are wet discharges from humans or animals, like urine, blood, pus, and feces. Sweat, milk, saliva, and tears from living animals are considered to be clean. Two of the four Sunnī law schools (to be described in Chapter 9) even regard human semen as clean (the Shāfi'ī and Hanbalī schools). Wine and all other alcoholic beverages are *najāsa* and contaminate whatever they come into contact with, such as, food. Discharges from pigs and dogs, but especially the former, are considered to be very impure. Although it is usually sufficient to wash once the impure matter from cloth or a prayer place or the skin, or until the stain and smell are removed, the *najāsa* of a pig or dog needs to be washed seven times, mixing a little dust with the water. The dog, however, unlike the pig, is not regarded as being especially impure by all law schools, although in Muslim countries one does not often find people keeping dogs as pets and pampering them, as many Western non-Muslims do. (There is nothing wrong with keeping dogs for herding and other farm purposes or for security or hunting. The saluki is highly prized as a hunter's companion in desert Arabia, but it is carefully distinguished from other canines as a special case.)

### *Minor and Major ḥadath*

***Ḥadath*** is of two types: minor (*al-ḥadath al-asghar*) and major (*al-ḥadath al-akbar*). Minor *ḥadath* is caused by sleeping, evacuating urine or feces, breaking wind, intoxication, fainting, touching the human genitals with the palm of the hand, and skin contact between mutually marriageable persons, especially if it is sexually arousing. (Accidental contact is not thought by most legists to entail *ḥadath.*) Sleeping and fainting may sound like strange circumstances to the outsider, but they both render the person vulnerable to *ḥadath* because of lack of control. Impurities can enter the open mouth, and the natural bodily processes may occur, like breaking of wind, nocturnal ejaculation, and so forth. (Semen is considered by some not to be *najāsa,* but it is always an occasion that brings major *ḥadath,* because of the orgasm.)

Major *ḥadath* is contracted by seminal emission, whether or not intentional. Female orgasm brings major *ḥadath* only if a wet secretion accompanies it. Sexual intercourse, whether licit or illicit, in which there is even partial penetration, also brings major *ḥadath.* (Kissing, fondling, and embracing, even while undressed, does not pollute in a major way.) Other causes of major *ḥadath* are menstruation and post-partum bleeding. The major impurity brought about by human sexuality is collectively known as *janāba.* It should be noted that Islam does not consider sexuality as evil in any way. In fact, marital sex is considered a form of *'ibāda,* "worship." Considerations of ritual or ceremonial purity do not imply feelings of guilt or filthiness associated with sexuality. They are just part of Islam's complex and precisely regulated orthopraxy.

One of the reasons for relating these kinds of details is to become aware of and appreciate the Islamic attention to life. (Judaism's concern for *halakhah,* "the way things are done," is a close parallel.) Far from being considered as an intrusion into everyday life, regulations like those connected with *ṭahāra* enable the believers to live their lives fully aware of their relationship to God. Being a slave of God requires that even the humblest activities have a ritual meaning, even if that meaning is an expression of avoidance of impurity.

### *Removing Impurity*

***Ablutions.*** Minor *ḥadath* is removed by means of ablutions, called ***wuḍū.*** They are prescribed in the Qur'an:

> O believers, when you stand up to pray wash your faces, and your hands up to the elbows, and wipe your heads, and your feet up to the ankles. If you are defiled, purify yourselves; but if you are sick or on a journey, or if any of you comes from the privy, or you have touched women, and you can find no water, then have recourse to wholesome dust and wipe your faces and your hands with it. (5:6)

As the believer performs the ablution, certain short recommended prayer utterances, known as *du'ā,* are included in the ritual washing. For example, when the nose has been washed, the believer may say: "O God! Let me enjoy the sweet smell of Paradise," or when the feet are being bathed, one may say, "God, Make my feet firm on the Path, on the Day when the feet easily slip away from the Path!" When the hands are washed, the believer may pray, while washing the right hand, that on Judgment Day he or she will receive his or her book of deeds in that hand. The washing proceeds in a regulated manner, with the right side of the body being cleaned first, after the manner of the Prophet. There are minor variations in the manner of performing the *wuḍū,* depending on which law school prevails in one's area or background; but on the whole it is a fairly uniform procedure, as indeed are all acts of worship across the world of Islam. Islam enjoys greater ritual unity than does any other major religious tradition—and even more, in the modern periods, than Judaism does. As discussed in Chapter 4, the sectarian divisions of Islam have as much to do with political issues as with religious practices. The basic beliefs, the *īmān,* are the

Cairo boys performing *wuḍū*, "minor ablution," before noon salat. Cairo, mosque of Muhammad 'Al. (*Source:* Frederick Mathewson Denny)

same for all Muslims, but so are the ritual practices, which, as has been observed, contain most of what is essential to Muslim orthopraxy.

***Baths.*** Major *ḥadath* is removed by means of a full and careful bath, known as **ghusl,** which proceeds, like *wuḍū,* in a precisely regulated manner. It requires more time, of course, and is performed far less often. It is recommended that Muslims take a bath before attending Friday mosque prayers. In addition to the ritualized bath, the Muslims pay close attention to their mouth and teeth by proper use of the *siwāk,* or toothbrush. The traditional brush is made from a twig of a tree that grows in Arabia. The Prophet cleaned his mouth and teeth often, regarding a clean mouth and pleasant breath as essential to prayer. He is reported as having said, "The prayer before which the toothstick is used is seventy times more excellent than that before which it is not used."[8]

There is a special procedure to follow when water is not available. It is called *tayammum* and means using clean sand, soil, or dust. One simply pats the dry, clean material and proceeds with the motions of the ***wuḍū,*** or minor ablution, with the exception that the feet are not treated. In a building, one may pat a carpet or cushion or stuffed furniture so that some dust is raised. *Tayammum* is good only for the *fard* ("required") prayer that is to be immediately performed. Unlike the ablution with water, it cannot preserve the worshiper in a ritually pure state, even in the absence of *ḥadaths* being contracted after the salat. It is obvious that Islamic worship, although demanding and frequent, is not designed to impose undue hardship on the believers. *Tayammum* is a good example of the flexible preparation for worship.

***Circumcision.*** Another purification practice is circumcision, about which we shall say more in Chapter 12. It is often called simply *ṭahāra* and extends also to females, whose "circumcision" involves excision of part of the clitoris. Female circumcision, also known widely as *sunnat,* is not universally regarded by Muslims as being required or even desirable, and it is not practiced everywhere. But male circumcision is so strongly endorsed—although not mentioned in the Qur'an—as to constitute, in the popular understanding of the religion, the sine qua non of being Muslim. Food prohibitions and other forms of ritual avoidance will be discussed later.

### *Reasons for Purification*

This consideration of purification is preliminary to a consideration of Islam's major devotional duties. Purification, then, both logically and temporally precedes worship. It is, in fact, a sort of entry into sacred time and space. As one washes, one is symbolically as well as physically separated from the mundane marks of normal living and working and made new for the conscious entry into the presence of God. One is always with God in some sense, of course, and no Muslim is considered to be impure at anytime *per se*—he or she merely experiences a temporary state of impurity; but in worship there is a special intentionality at work that raises the relationship to one of mutuality, in which the slave forthrightly yet reverently addresses the Master. Just as prayer is invalid without purification, so also is it worthless without proper intention, known as **niyya.** *Niyya* is required, in fact, before any ritual performance as well as other important activities, such as finding a marriage partner. *Niyya* ensures a proper mental and spiritual attitude, free from both rote repetition and casualness. It is an exact analogue to the Jewish *kavanna,* even to the point of including the sense of spontaneity and freshness in the presence of God. *Niyya* is specific in that it is dedicated to whatever the worshiper is setting out to do. For example, if someone is planning to perform a prayer in which three cycles of prostrations are to be included, he or she says that in the *niyya* uttered before the observance begins. And one's *niyya* is required to be kept in mind throughout the prayer performance, both so as to carry it out correctly and to be prevented from external distractions.

## THE PILLARS OF ISLAM

This chapter opened with the first pillar, the testifying—*shahāda*—that "there is no god but God" and that "Muhammad is the Messenger of God." The law books, which always begin with ritual practices, usually do not discuss the shahāda at any length, because it is considered to be properly a part of *īmān,* "faith," and so is considered in great detail in the books on *tawḥīd,* the "science of the divine unity." The shahāda, then, is a matter of orthodoxy, "doctrinal correctness," whereas the remaining four pillars are chiefly concerned with orthopraxy. Yet they should be considered as minimal obligations, a kind of outline of the faith, and not the whole religion.

### *Ṣalāt: The "Worship Service"*

The foundation of Muslim devotion is the ritual prayer service known as *ṣalāt* (hereafter salat). God addresses the "believers," that is the Muslims, in Sura 5:55: "Your friend is only God, and His Messenger, and the believers who perform the prayer (salat) and pay the alms (*zakāt*), and bow them down. Whoso makes God his friend, and His Messenger, and the believers—the party of God (*ḥizb Allah*)—they are the victors" (5:55). Although in English the term *salat* is often translated simply as "prayer," that is a little misleading if it means the personal type of prayers of petition, intercession, or invocation associated with private Christian devotion. That sort of prayer is known as *du'ā*. Though a prominent aspect of Muslim personal piety, it is not the same as salat. The salat is an intense, highly regulated, formal observance that features cycles of bodily postures climaxing in complete prostration in an orientation toward the Ka'ba in Mecca.

***Time and Location.*** Muslims are required to perform the salat five times daily: early morning (*ṣalāt al-fajr*), noon (*ṣalāt al-ḍuhr*), mid-afternoon (*ṣalāt al-'aṣr*), sunset (*ṣalāt al-maghrib*), and evening (*ṣalāt al-'ishā'*). In addition, the Friday congregational service (*ṣalāt al-jum'a*), which features a sermon (*khuṭba*), and the salats of funeral and the two eclipses (sun or moon) are also required. (Required practices in Islam are known by the term *farḍ* or *wājib,* the performance of which is rewarded and its neglect punished.) There are also salats that are "recommended" (*sunna*—performance rewarded, neglect not punished): supererogatory prayers offered along with the five *farḍ* ones, the salat of the two major annual festivals (performed in congregation), and a number of others.

Friday noon *ṣalāt* at open-air mosque in Kuala Lumpur, Malaysia. (*Source:* Frederick Mathewson Denny)

It is strongly recommended that the salats be observed as near to the beginning of their proper daily periods as possible. There are mitigating factors, however, if this proves to be impossible, because of work shifts in a non-Islamic society, travel, sickness, and so forth. In some cases the salats may be shortened or combined. There are certain prerequisites for salats. Purification is the first one, as has already been noted and described. Next is the proper covering of the body: from the navel to the knees for males, and the whole body with the exception of the hands, face, and feet for females. This covering is known as *sitr.* Proper intention, *niyya,* is required, as has also been noted. Finally, the worshiper is required to face in the direction of Mecca; this is known as *qibla* and is marked in mosques by a niche, called ***miḥrāb.*** Muslims are required always to face the *qibla* to the best of their ability. It is not uncommon for Muslims nowadays to carry small "Mecca finders" with them on their travels, which are compasses with the coordinates for Mecca indicated for many different locales. The idea of *qibla* is a dramatic symbol of the unity of the Islamic umma worldwide, for during the salat the worshipers all face a common central point and direct their spiritual energies toward it. This is a powerful implosion of religious energy and makes the Muslims feel an intense common purpose and unity. When the Muslim performs the salat, he or she is in a sense participating in the heavenly journey of the Prophet Muhammad; a little personal *mi'rāj* is made.

***The Call to Prayer.*** As the time for the salat begins, the ***adhān,*** "call to prayer," is recited in a loud, clear voice by the ***mu'adhdhin*** **("muezzin")** from atop a minaret or mosque roof or any appropriate place that will allow the call to carry. The call to prayer is as follows, first in Arabic and then in translation:

1. *allāhu akbar* ("God is most great"), four times.
2. *ashhadu an lā ilāha illā allāh* ("I testify that there is no god but God"), twice.
3. *ashhadu anna muḥammadan rasūl allāh* ("I testify that Muhammad is the Messenger of God"), twice.
4. *ḥayya 'al al-ṣalāt* ("Hurry to prayer"), twice.
5. *ḥayya 'alā al-falḥ* ("Hurry to success [sometimes translated as "salvation"]), twice.
6. Only before the early morning salat: *al-ṣalāt khayrun min al-naum* ("Prayer is better than sleep"), twice. The Shī'ī̄s do not include this phrase. Instead, they say *ḥayya 'alā khayr al-'amal* ("Hurry to the best activity") twice in each *adhān* of the daily five.
7. *allāhu akbar* ("God is most great"), twice.
8. *lāilāha illā allāh* ("There is no god but God"), Sunnīs once, Shī'īs twice.

The Muslim preference for the human voice as the means of summoning the believers to worship is in stark contrast with the Christian use of the bell or, in the Arabia of Muhammad's time, a wooden clapper, and the Jewish use of the *shofar,* a kind of trumpet made from a ram's horn. The *adhān* is usually cantillated and thus resembles the sound of Qur'an chanting. After the call to prayer comes the *iqāma,* the command to rise up and actually begin the service. Its wording is almost identical with the call, but it is uttered in a lower tone and quite rapidly, with no pauses.

***Actual Observance.*** It is recommended that Muslims observe the salat in a mosque, but it is permissible to pray at home, at work, or even outdoors, provided the prayer place is clean and free from distractions. The word *mosque* comes from the Arabic ***masjid,*** which simply means "place of prostration" and in no way implies that there must be a building for the purpose. The Prophet's mosque in Medina was simply a large open courtyard in front of his house. Although the salat can be performed alone—in which case the worshiper utters the *adhān* by himself or herself facing the *qibla*—it is meritorious to perform it with another or with a group. In that case, one person must serve as *imām* or leader for the other(s), by standing out in front before the *miḥrāb.* Even if only two are performing the salat together, one must serve as ***imām*** for the other. The *imām* acts as a pattern for the rest to follow, so as to preserve the required precision and order of the service. Any Muslim of moral life and sincere faith may serve as *imām* so long as that person is familiar with the procedure. This position is not a clerical one; there is no ordained clergy in Islam. All Muslims are required to know the salat and other devotional duties, which are learned from childhood. This broad-based knowledge and training is yet another reason for the remarkable ritual uniformity across the umma.

The Suleimaniye Mosque built between 1550 and 1556 by the great architect Sinan. Istanbul, Turkey. Note the thin "pencil" minarets. (*Source:* Frederick Mathewson Denny)

In congregational prayer in which there are only males or a mixture of males and females, only males may serve as *imām*. Females must worship behind males, and there is always a space between the rows of males and females when the two sexes are together. (In some places it is rare to find females in mosques during salat. In others, the sexes are separated by a sheet or tentlike partition.) A female may not serve as *imām* for males. This is because her menstrual period might come and also because of the subordinate position of women, as dictated by the Qur'an. Finally, it is regarded as unseemly for a woman to be seen from behind by men, because the posterior portion of the body is raised during the prostration when the forehead touches the floor.

The salat begins with the *niyya's* being declared softly by the worshiper to himself or herself. The worshiper stands erect, facing the *qibla,* with his or her hands raised to the side of the head with the thumbs nearly touching the earlobes. The ***takbīr*** (*Allāhu akbar*—"God is most great") is recited, marking the entry into the special, sacred time of the salat. From this time until the end, all attention and energy are focused on the correct performance of the rite. The worshiper then recites the opening sūra of the Qur'an, with the hands either hanging loosely at the sides or folded gently in front beneath the chest. Another brief sūra or a group of verses is then recited. After another *takbīr,* the worshiper bows, saying "Glory be to God." Then the worshiper returns to a standing position and praises God. Next, he or she

Interior of the Sultan Hasan mosque, Cairo. The niche to the left of center is the *miḥrāb,* showing the *qibla,* or "direction" to Mecca. The canopied staircase to the right is the *minbār,* or pulpit, where the Friday sermon is preached. (*Source:* Frederick Mathewson Denny)

swiftly and fluidly descends to a prostrate position, with knees and toes on the floor and the forehead touching the floor with palms flat on the surface on either side of the head. This is the climax (though not the end) of each cycle within the salat. Uttering another *takbīr,* the worshiper assumes a sitting position, with a specific arrangement of the legs and feet and palms resting on the thighs. Then a second prostration is performed, ending with *takbīr.* Finally, the standing position is resumed, and this marks the end of a *rak'a,* the discrete, basic cycle of postures and utterances of which all salats are composed.

Near the close of the salat the worshiper, in a sitting position, pronounces the *tashahhud,* a testimony to the unity of God and the apostlehood of Muhammad, followed by a calling down of blessings on the Prophet and his family. Then a short *du'ā* may be said. Finally, the worshiper utters the "peace" two times, turning the head in either direction each time, saying: "Peace be upon you all and the mercy and blessings of God." With this the salat is concluded. The "peace," or *taslīm,* is considered to be directed to one's fellow Muslims and, beyond them, to all humankind who are in need of God's guidance and blessing. It is also thought to be a benediction on the two recording angels who are poised by either shoulder, thus reminding the believer of his or her great responsibility.

The number of *rak'as* required varies with each of the daily salats: two in the morning, four at noon, afternoon, and evening, and three at sunset—seventeen in all that are *farḍ.* The supererogatory *rak'as,* known as *nawāfil,* can number up to thirty-four in a single day.

***The Friday Salat.*** The Friday salat is observed at the time for noon prayer and requires a congregation. Whereas the minimum number of persons required to comprise a congregation is two for the regular daily salats, the Friday one, depending on what Islamic law school prevails, requires five, seven, or forty persons. In congregational salat, the worshipers line up in straight rows with military precision and spacing. The *īmām* stands out alone in front facing the *miḥrāb,* if there is one. Before attending Friday salat, one should take a bath, brush his or her teeth, and apply perfume, if available. Only males are required to attend the service. One should start out early and not be in a hurry. Although Friday is not a day of rest like the Jewish and Christian sabbaths (there is none in Islam), it is not uncommon for businesses in Muslim regions to close, at least during the salat. (Often Muslims do take the day off, and so Thursday night becomes a favorite time for dinner parties, shopping, and socializing because one can "sleep in" the following morning.)

The most prominent and unusual feature of the Friday salat is the sermon, called ***khuṭba,*** which is preached in two parts, with the *īmām khaṭīb,* "preacher," taking a little rest between them, seated on the top step of the *minbār,* or pulpit, a raised canopy with a staircase. The *khuṭba* is devoted to the recitation of a portion of the Qur'an, which provides the subject of the sermon. Generally, the message includes an exhortation to the Muslims to obey God and actively follow and apply the precepts of Islam. Although often the delivery is passionate and dramatic, after Muhammad's example, sometimes the *khuṭba* resembles a scholarly lecture. But it

Men performing noon salat in open-air setting. Notice that one is serving as *imām* for the other two. (*Source:* Frederick Mathewson Denny)

should not be long, for as the Prophet is reported to have said, "The length of a man's prayer and the shortness of his sermon are a sign of his understanding, so make the prayer long and the sermon short, for there is magic in eloquence."[9]

The salats of the two festivals, which will be described in the following sections on fasting and pilgrimage, and the salats of the funeral, the two eclipses, and others are variations on the daily salat. The funeral salat, however, is performed standing throughout and is rather brief. It will be considered in greater detail in Chapter 12, as the final "rite of passage."

### *Zakāt: Legal Almsgiving*

The earliest documents we have concerning Muslim practices—the Qur'an and other contemporary and somewhat later sources—speak often of calling the people to worship by means of the salat and of almsgiving by means of the ***zakāt.*** "Pay the prayer, and pay the alms, and obey the Messenger—haply so you will find mercy" (Sura 24:56). These two basic religious activities are clear indicators of the importance of the vertical relationship between humankind and God through prayer and obedience, on the one hand, and the horizontal relationship of Muslims with one another through the giving of one's wealth, on the other. Next in importance to worship is concern for others, both individually and as a community of Muslims. The zakāt is a legal, obligatory act and considered part of one's service to God, as a technical part of worship in the sense of *'ibāda.* Zakāt is not to be confused with charity, which is known as *Ṣadaqa.* Muslims are commanded to give charity often and freely, with emphasis on discretion and concern for the feelings of the recipients. Zakāt, however, is more like a tax, payable once a year and computed as a percentage of one's various forms of wealth. A manual of Islamic practices written for English-speaking converts describes zakāt as being owed on "three C's: cash, cattle, and crops."[10] The Arabic word *zakāt* has as one of its meanings "purity," and although that sense is secondary, it does apply as a characterization of the wealth remaining to the owner after the alms tax has been paid. That is, the wealth is purified for the use of its owner. If no zakāt has been paid on it during the year in which, according to Islamic law, it was due, then the property is considered to be illicitly held and "unclean." This, again, is a powerful symbol of Islam's sense of community.

***To What It Applies.*** The computation of zakāt on the various types of property to which it applies can be complicated, and we shall not describe it in detail here.[11] The categories of property are (1) cash, gold, and silver; (2) merchandise used in trade (but not personal possessions used in ordinary living, like automobiles, clothing, houses, and jewelry); (3) minerals extracted from the ground; (4) ancient treasure from before Islam (if from the Islamic period, it must be returned to its owner, if possible); (5) cattle, by which is meant oxen, cows, buffaloes, camels, sheep, and goats; and (6) crops from tilled land.

Before zakāt is owed, a minimum amount of each type of wealth must be owned, called *niṣāb.* For the first four categories, it is a value equal to ninety grams of gold, but the tax is due only if the property has been owned for a full lunar year. The zakāt is computed at the rate of 2.5 percent of the amount over the *niṣāb,* except for ancient treasure, whose rate is 20 percent. The *niṣāb* for cattle varies: five camels, thirty cows (or oxen and buffaloes), or forty sheep (or goats). For crops it is 1,400 pounds (but the *Ḥanafi* school of law requires zakāt on any size of harvest.) The zakāt due on livestock is variable and proportional and can only be hinted at here. For example, on five camels it is a baby camel of either sex. On thirty-six heads it is a two-year-old female camel; on ninety-one heads it is two female camels aged three years; and on more than 130 heads it is a two-year-old female camel for every thirty additional heads or a three-year-old female for every forty heads.

Zakāt is owed only by Muslims who have reached their majority (which most schools consider to be sixteen, provided the individual has declared himself or herself to be an adult), and the person must be sane. Zakāt on crops is to be paid at harvest time, on minerals when extracted, and on treasure when found. All else is owed at the end of the year, provided it has been owned for that full year. The categories of zakāt recipients are mentioned in the Qur'an as

> the poor and needy, those who work to collect them [that is, alms], those whose hearts are brought together [meaning converts to Islam who have lost their possessions because of their faith], the ransoming of slaves, debtors, in God's way [for good works, like scholarships, missionary projects, charitable, cultural, and educational institutions], and the traveller. (9:60)

Traditionally in Muslim countries, the zakāt was collected by the government and distributed according to set patterns, covering the various categories of recipients. Nowadays zakāt is a matter of individual conscience, although some Muslim governments are responsible for collecting it. One who intends to give zakāt may select a worthy recipient or cause and go ahead and give it. If the alms is for someone who might be made uncomfortable or embarrassed by receiving it, then it is permissible to make the gift anonymous or withhold information as to its source as zakāt. It is recommended that when given by an individual, zakāt be for local cases of need. When those needs have been met, then it is permissible to give the alms for more distant causes and needs.

***The Reasons for it.*** Zakāt is a highly beneficial practice, both for the society of Muslims and for individuals. As an act of worship, and a required one at that, it is not to be regarded as a favor that the giver does for his or her fellow Muslims. God is the ultimate giver, and the one who makes the right *niyya* before giving the mandatory alms is aware of that and therefore is engaged in a pure act. The same applies to receiving zakāt, although understandably it is wise as well as considerate to manage the giving and receiving in a dignified and sometimes discreet manner. The Qur'an (73:20) teaches that those who "perform the prayer, and pay the alms, and lend to God a good loan [that is, without interest]" will be repaid a greater reward. The paying of zakāt is, then, partly a matter of enlightened self-interest.

There is, in addition to the zakāt, another kind of alms, called *zakāt al fiṭr,* the cost of one day's food for one needy person for the feast of the breaking of the Ramadān fast. Everyone who can must pay this. A husband pays it for his spouse(s) and himself, as well as for any children in the household. Normally this special alms is given at the end of the fasting month, but it can also be given earlier in the month.

## *Ṣawm: Fasting During the Holy Month of Ramadān*

One of the Muslims' best-known religious acts is the monthlong daytime fast, known in Arabic as ***ṣawm,*** during the ninth lunar month of Ramadān. From before dawn until sunset, those who are observing the fast are forbidden from eating, drinking, smoking, and having marital relations. In addition, one may not chew or swallow any external matter or take medicine through any orifice. (It is permissible to receive necessary injections either in the muscle or vein.) Breaking the fast intentionally is a very serious breach and carries substantial penalties. Eating or drinking unintentionally, however, is forgiven and does not break the fast. An example would be coercion; another would be momentarily forgetting what one had intended. One may brush one's teeth; rinse one's mouth; wash the body; swallow saliva; use external medications, ointments, and perfume; and even kiss one's spouse and children without breaking the fast. But intentional breaking of the fast is punishable—if it is the very serious breach brought on by sexual relations—by being required to fast sixty days, to feed sixty people the equivalent of one meal each, or to give charity equal to a meal to sixty persons. This penalty is known as *kaffāra,* meaning "reparation, penance." If the fast has been deliberately broken by eating, drinking, or smoking, then one may renew one's vow and abstain for the rest of the day. But one should observe an additional day's fast after Ramadān to make up for the lapse. Fasting is prohibited for pregnant or menstruating women or to women who have just given birth. They must make it up later.

Travelers may keep the fast only if no undue hardship is experienced; otherwise they must make it up later. Old and feeble persons as well as minor children are exempt, as are the sick and insane. If the old and feeble can afford it, they should give a full meal to a needy person for each day of fasting missed. Children are encouraged to fast but should not be coerced in any way or punished harshly when they fail. As for the insane person, no religious duties are required at all. It is recommended that one eat immediately after the sun has set. One may then eat another, lighter meal before the next day's fasting begins, preferably just before dawn.

***A Joyful Time.*** Fasting in Ramadān is a demanding spiritual discipline and enhances one's awareness of one's dependence on God and essential similarity with other human beings, especially the poor and hungry. Thus, one's religious awe is renewed, and one's regard for others is made keener. Notice the twofold relationship of verticality and horizontalism that we observed when describing the salat. The same is true of the zakāt and *ṣawm.* But Ramadān is by no means a lent, as in Christianity. It is a time of serious reflection, to be sure, but it is not a sad or even a somber period. Ramadān nights are joyful times, when friends and extended families gather for food and singing and simple entertainments. The mosque is visited, and some men even spend several days and nights there in spiritual retreat and vigil. This is known as *i'tikāf* and is especially meaningful when observed during the last ten days of Ramadān, during one of which nights the Qur'an was first revealed. This "night of power," as it is known, is "better than a thousand months; in it the angels and the Spirit descend, by the leave of their Lord, upon every command. Peace it is, till the rising of the dawn" (Sūra 97:3–5). No one knows for certain just which night it is, but it is odd numbered. Some say it is the twenty-seventh, but that is not universally accepted. In Cairo, for example, Ramadān nights are occasions for book buying at reduced rates near the old theological training center of the Azhar University. Sufi brotherhoods hold an open house at their specially erected tents near the medieval mosques, where one can be refreshed and inspired by recitations from old devotional texts and come into contact with spiritual advisers. The reciting of the Qur'an can be heard throughout Muslim neighborhoods long into the night.

***A Sacred Time.*** Ramadān is one of the Muslims' most sacred times. The Qur'an states:

> the month of Ramadan, wherein the Qur'an was sent down to be a guidance to the people, and as clear signs of the Guidance and the Salvation so let those of you, who are present [i.e. in one's home] at the month, fast it; and if any of you be sick, or if he be on a journey, then a number of other days; God desires ease for you, and desires not hardship for you; and that you fulfill the number [of required fasting days], and magnify [i.e. praise] God that He has guided you, and haply you will be thankful. (2:185)

In addition to being the month during which the Qur'an first descended, it was also the month in which the fateful Battle of Badr took place in A.H. 2. Ramadān is the only month mentioned in the Qur'an (2:185). Muslim scholars have noted several other auspicious events that took place during the month:[12] Husayn, son of 'Ali and grandson of Muhammad, was born on the sixth; Khadīja died on the tenth; Mecca was occupied by the Muslims on the nineteenth; 'Alī died on the twenty-first, having been born on the twenty-second; and the eighth Shī'ī Imām 'Alī al-Ridā died on the twenty-first. The name of the month comes from a root meaning "summer's heat," and therefore dates back to the time when the Arabs observed a calendar that coincided with the regular seasonal cycle.

***The Muslim Lunar Year.*** The Qur'an explicitly designates the moon as the measurer of time (10:6) and forbids the old intercalation practices that made the lunar year come out even with the solar year by periodically adding extra days or months. Thus the Muslim year is shorter than the solar year by approximately eleven days, causing it to fall back by that much each solar year, with the base solar year being 622 C.E. Because of this, Ramadān and its fast will fall in all of the natural seasons every thirty-three solar years. This variability is regarded by the Muslims as a mercy from God, in that it distributes the hardships as well as the consolations due to season and location that the believers experience in connection with ritual observances. Fasting in winter is easier than in summer, because of the temperature and length of daylight. Likewise, performing the hajj is less debilitating in the cooler months.

The Muslim lunar year has twelve months, as the Qur'an itself stipulates (9:37), and begins with *Muḥarram,* followed by *Ṣafar, Rabī 'u al-Awwal, Rabī 'al-Akhir, Jumāda al-Ūlā, Jumāda al-Ukhrā, Rajab, Sha'bān, Ramaḍān, Shawwāl, Dhū al-Qa'da,* and *Dhū al-Ḥijja.* Of these there are four months regarded as sacred: *Muḥarram, Rajab, Dhū al-Qa'da,* and *Dhū al-Ḥijja.* In them no fighting is allowed, except in cases of self-defense against idolaters. The names of the months come from pre-Islamic Arabia and are yet another example of the spirit of intelligent compromise that accompanied the transition from the Jāhilīya value system to Islam. Each month is reckoned as beginning with the sunset immediately following the first appearance of the new moon. (The day begins at sunset, too.)

This *hilāl* moon, as it is called, must be ocularly witnessed by trustworthy men, usually religious scholars. Scientific astronomical reckoning has been mastered since early Islamic times and even suggested as a sensible substitute for the quaint practice of gazing at the heavens, but the old practice has persisted until now, causing some confusion and irregularity across the Islamic world, because of weather, location, and so forth. The new moon at the beginning of Shawwāl is especially anxiously awaited, because it signals the end of the Ramadān fast and the entry into a festival known as the Feast of Fast Breaking (*'īd al-fiṭr*), one of two canonical festivals in the Islamic year (the other being the "Feast of Sacrifice" during the hajj). On the first day of Shawwāl a special congregational salat is observed, featuring two

The new, or *hilāl,* moon is the principal marker of the passing months in the Islamic religion. Here it is included as a design element above the dome of a mosque in Cairo. (*Source:* Juan E. Campo)

*rak'as,* additional *takbīrs,* and a *khuṭba.* The day is spent in giving thanks for having been able to complete the fast.

***Other Occasions for Fasting.*** In addition to the Ramadān fast, there are others of a supererogatory kind that are based on Muhammad's practice. Certain days of the year are recommended for fasting, such as any six days in Shawwāl and the ninth, tenth, and eleventh days of Muharram. One may also choose other times for fasting, but it is preferable to fast in moderation. Muhammad generally fasted several days each month—three according to 'Ā'isha's testimony—and, of course, the whole month of Ramadān. Fasting is prohibited on the two major feast days, as well as on the following three days of the greater feast (*'īd al-aḍḥā*), which features animal sacrifices and rejoicing over the gift of life. It is recommended, further, that Friday not be selected as a day for fasting, although it is permissible if it falls within a long fasting period.

The Holy Ka'ba in the Grand Mosque, Mecca. The dark cloth covering, embroidered with Qur'anic verses in gold thread, known as the *kiswa*, is manufactured anew for each year's Hajj, whereas the old one is divided up and given to pilgrims. (*Source:* Mehmet Biber/Photo Researchers, Inc.)

### *Ḥajj: Pilgrimage to Mecca*

The final pillar of Islam (hereafter hajj) is also the most dramatic and developed of all Muslim ritual practices.[13] The pilgrimage to Mecca during the holy pilgrimage month of *Dhū al-Ḥijja* [literally, "(the one) with the hajj"] is held annually. It is required once in each Muslim's lifetime, but only if he or she is legally an adult, as well as both physically and financially capable. The last stipulation means enough money to cover the expenses of the journey as well as providing for dependents while away from home. Usually, people who intend to perform the hajj have already saved for many years, for the trip is costly. It is frowned upon to borrow money for the purpose, because all debts must be paid before the hajj is valid. The money that has been set aside for the pilgrimage must have been "purified" by means of zakāt. Finally, one's will should be drawn up before departure, so that in case of death on the journey, one's heirs and executors may be able without trouble to settle the estate—that is, the portion not regulated in a specific way by Islamic inheritance law. The preparations for hajj are a solemn leave taking of one phase of a person's life so as to move on to a new, higher, and more fulfilled stage. The saying of goodbyes and the drawing up of the will symbolize the acceptance of death in total submission to God's will, whatever it might be.

This leave taking is made even more vivid when, before entering the sacred precincts of Mecca, the pilgrim dons the ritual garb called *iḥrām,* which symbolizes the state of purity when certain things are no longer permitted. This is, to borrow from the ritual expert Arnold Van Gennep's useful analytical language of rites of passage, a true "separation" as the believer enters a "liminal" phase, "betwixt and between" the old status and the new.[14] The white pilgrimage garb intensifies the other-worldly atmosphere of the hajj and symbolizes, at least in part, the grave clothes as well as ritual purity.

Every Muslim going on hajj knows perfectly well some of the dangers that he or she may encounter: dangerous seas, possible air crashes, suspect food and drink in out-of-the-way places, epidemics, and bad people. Recent years have seen tragic losses of life in airplane crashes in which the passengers were pilgrims traveling to or from Hejaz. There is a memorable treatment of this theme in the opening chapters of Joseph Conrad's novel *Lord Jim,* in which some 800 Mecca-bound pilgrims are left to their fate by the officers of the steamship *Patna* after it hit an object and began to sink in the middle of the night. However, the listing ship was discovered the next day and taken in tow to the nearest port, with all the passengers safe. (Conrad's source was an actual pilgrim ship called the *Jeddah,* which was abandoned by its officers in 1880 but was towed safely to Aden.)[15] One who dies while performing the hajj is considered a martyr and earns entrance into paradise.

***The Believers.*** The hajj is a powerful symbol of the worldwide unity of the Muslim community. The believers, who for many years have directed their prayers toward Mecca, converge on the actual location, thus fulfilling a life's wish of being at the center. The Ka'ba, a black-draped cubical structure in the middle of the Mecca sanctuary, is a true *axis mundi,* where heaven and earth and the aspirations and loyalties of all Muslims meet. It is the "navel" of the earth, as some old sources characterize it. The unity of the Muslims is also seen in the white *iḥrām* garb that the male pilgrims are required to wear. This two-piece seamless garment reduces its wearers to an essential oneness of status, erasing their distinctions based on wealth, education, class, language, and ethnicity. All pilgrims recite at least some of their prayers in Arabic, again demonstrating the religion's unifying power. On the other hand, the female pilgrims wear clothes that are native to their home regions: brightly colored saris from India and Indonesia, flowered prints from central and south Africa, simple gowns from North Africa, sensible suits and dresses from Turkey and Egypt, and so forth. Women may wear a simple, white, *iḥrām* type of garment, but it may not be like the men's, because it would reveal too much of their upper body and arms. Thus, the male pilgrims through the *iḥrām* symbolize Islam's unity and egalitarianism, and the women through their great variety of dress symbolize the diverse and creative character of Islam as a global community of faith.

***The History.*** The hajj proper is observed on the eighth through the twelfth days of Dhū al-Hijja, the last month of the lunar year. The last three months are designated as the hajj season, because the pilgrims start to arrive at the beginning of Shawwāl. Many others also spend the month of Ramadān in Mecca and then stay on for the hajj. This is very meritorious. Besides the hajj proper, which we shall describe later, there is the "lesser hajj," known as *'umra,* which is similar to the hajj in its rites observed in Mecca. But the hajj proper also features essential rites outside Mecca. The *'umra* can be performed at any time, but the month of Rajab is especially auspicious.

The antecedents of the Islamic hajj date back to the distant Arabian past, and we can observe a number of continuities from it. Perhaps here we may see most plainly the ingenious blending of the native Arabian with the Abrahamic and monotheistic patterns of the ancient Near East. Muhammad rededicated the Ka'ba and its ritual structure to God in a manner that he insisted restored the pure religion of Abraham and his people. During the hajj, one is made aware of how potent the Abrahamic element is in Islam's sacred history.

***The Ritual.*** Pilgrims enter the holy precincts of Mecca through a number of gates or checkpoints, called *mīqāts.* Non-Muslims are forbidden to advance beyond these points. Medina, to the north, is also forbidden to non-Muslims. At the *mīqāts,* the *iḥrām* is donned by the male pilgrims, and all pilgrims renew their *niyyas,* or "intentions" of making the hajj. Many pilgrims arrive in Hejaz at the port city of Jidda, either by sea or air. They proceed toward Mecca through the *mīqāt* of al-Hudaibiya (where the fateful treaty was concluded between Muhammad and the Meccans). The state of *iḥrām* that the pilgrims enter is in keeping with the nature of the region, which is known as a *ḥaram* ("sanctuary"), using the same Arabic root *(ḥ-r-m)* that denotes sacredness, taboo, purity, or forbiddenness, depending on specific context. One who is in the sacred state of *iḥrām* is called *muḥrim.* This ritual state is open to both males and females (although only males are required to wear the special garb). Certain things are forbidden: sexual intercourse, clipping the nails, hunting, wearing perfume or jewelry, cutting the hair, uprooting living things, arguing, talking about the opposite sex, and the like. Women must keep their heads covered, and men are required to keep them uncovered.

Approaching Mecca and throughout the hajj, the pilgrims constantly recite the *talbīya:*

> I am here, O my God, I am here! (*labbayk allahumma labbayk*)
> I am here, Thou art without any associate, I am here!
> Praise and blessing belong to Thee, and Power.

Arriving in Mecca, the pilgrims enter the sacred mosque through the gate of peace (*bāb al-salām*), reciting Qur'an verses, especially the following:

> And say: "My Lord, lead me in with a just ingoing, and lead me out with a just outgoing; grant me authority from Thee, to help me."
>
> And say: "The truth has come, and falsehood has vanished away: surely falsehood is ever certain to vanish." (17:80–81)

This begins the *manāsik al-ḥajj,* the "rites of pilgrimage." They are at times complicated enough to require special knowledge, which is provided by guides who accompany the pilgrims through the several days of observances. It is also common to see little illustrated booklets on *manāsik al-ḥajj* for sale at newsstands and kiosks in Islamic cities and towns or included in the Friday editions of newspapers, like Cairo's *Al-Ahrām,* early in the hajj season.

One of the central ceremonies of the hajj is a circumambulation of the Ka'ba, known as *ṭawāf,* seven times in a counterclockwise direction. This is performed three times during the hajj: at the beginning, after the ritual haircutting when the blood sacrifice has been completed, and before leaving Mecca at the end of the hajj. Tradition holds that Abraham and Ishmael used to circle the Ka'ba in this manner, and Muhammad certainly did, often. The circumambulation of sacred stones is recorded in other parts of Arabia and seems to be a pattern of religion there from early times. Embedded in a corner of the Ka'ba is the famous "black stone," which is a sign of God's covenant with Abraham and Ishmael. The Prophet used to touch it when he passed, and pilgrims follow his example, also kissing it and meditating near it. In the crush of *ṭawāf* during the hajj, however, it is impossible for most pilgrims to get near the stone, and so they simply extend their arms toward it, reciting the *talbīya.*

After the *ṭawāf,* the pilgrims perform a two-*rak'a* salat at the Place of Abraham, so-called because it is believed the patriarch worshiped there when building the Ka'ba, and there is a stone marking the spot. After the salat, the pilgrims perform the rite of *sa'y,* a walking and jogging sort of circuit back and forth between the two nearby hills of Safa and Marwa. This commemorates the experience of Hagar, who, having been cast out of Abraham's house at Sarah's insistence, wandered in the wilderness with little Ishmael, searching for sustenance. Hagar, in a panic, ran back and forth seven times between the two hills, chasing mirages that appeared before her. Meanwhile, Ishmael kicked the ground where he had been left, and a spring miraculously welled up from underneath the spot where his heel struck the ground. This became the Well of Zamzam, whose water continues to be to Muslims what the Jordan River water is to Christians, and it is bottled and carried home by pilgrims to provide as a memento and, even more, a holy relic of the sacred center of Mecca. The pilgrims proceed with the rite of *sa'y* by walking along a long corridor. At certain points they break into a trot, but it is not unduly difficult to complete the rite. In all, seven courses are made between the two hills, each involving a distance of 443 yards. When this is finished, the *'umra,* or "lesser hajj," is complete. A haircut is required at this point, which may be accomplished simply by removing a symbolic amount of hair from the head or beard.

Proceeding into the hajj proper, the pilgrims leave Mecca and travel to the little town of Minā, a few miles away. On a vast plain called 'Arafāt an enormous tent city has been constructed for the multitudes, which nowadays may exceed three million people. At 'Arafāt the pilgrims reflect on Abraham's great decision to sacrifice his only son, Ishmael, at God's command.[16] On the ninth of the month the pilgrims must stand from noon until sundown in meditation and praise of God. Many climb the hill that stands at the center of the plain. This *wuqūf,* or "standing ceremony," is the heart of the hajj, and if the pilgrim fails to observe it, the whole pilgrimage will be null and void. Pilgrims experience a special closeness to God as well as to their Muslim brothers and sisters during this long afternoon of repentance and prayer.

When the sun has set, the pilgrims pack up for the trip to Muzdalifa, an open plain on the way back to Mecca. As quickly as possible, all the tents are moved there amidst incredible confusion. At Muzdalifa the *maghrib* (sunset) and *'ishā'* (evening) salats are combined, after which the pilgrims collect forty-nine pebbles that will be thrown during the following days at a symbol of the devil. This stoning ceremony also is reminiscent of Abraham and Ishmael. When father and son were going to the place where Ishmael was to be sacrificed, the devil whispered to Ishmael not to go through with the madness. Ishmael then picked up some small stones and threw them at the evil apparition. The pilgrims continue to honor the faith and courage of the father and son through this rite, which also has spiritual value for each person's struggle with temptations and evil.

On the tenth day of Dhū al-Hijja, the pilgrims sacrifice animals in commemoration of Abraham's sacrifice of the ram, which was provided in place of Ishmael after the old man's faith had been tested. This is a joyful event, which Muslims all over the world share in as the Feast of Sacrifice (*'īd al-aḍḥā*), or the Great Bairām. It is the greater of the two canonical Muslim feasts each year, the other being the Feast of Fast Breaking, described earlier. It goes on for three days and gives Muslims a chance to rejoice together through prayer, visits, and eating good things. Whoever sacrifices must share a third with a needy person, a third with a neighbor, and keep the final third for his own household. On the hajj, the flesh may be eaten by the sacrificer as well as distributed to others, but the skins must be distributed to the

The Prophet's tomb in Medina. Pilgrims visit this city to pay their respects, although such a visit (*ziyāra*) is not part of the hajj, nor is it required. (*Source:* Ministry of Information, Saudi Arabia)

poor. The animals—sheep, goats, cows, camels—are taken in hand, their head is pointed toward the *qibla,* and a quick cut is made through the jugular vein and windpipe with the words of the *basmala* being pronounced: "In the Name of God" (*bismillāh*). All of the blood must be drained before the flesh is ritually acceptable for eating. In fact, Muslim food regulations have certain similarities to Jewish practices of koshering food (*kashruth*).

After the sacrifice, the pilgrims perform the ritual of getting a haircut, known as *taqsīr.* It may be a real haircut or shave but can be accomplished, as with the similar ritual after the *'umra,* by cutting the nails or simply removing a bit of hair. This rite marks the end of most of the restrictions of the state of *iḥrām.* The white garment may be set aside, but sexual relations are still prohibited. At this point, the second *ṭawāf* is usually made, and the pilgrims find it to be sometimes a long, drawn-out affair because of the crowds. The next three days are known as the "days of drying flesh," in reference to the sacrificial victims' flesh, which used to be cured in the sun. Nowadays the Saudi government, which hosts the hajj, is trying to find ways of preserving the great quantities of meat for humane distribution where it is needed.

After a final stoning of the devil, the pilgrims perform a farewell *ṭawāf,* and the hajj is ended. Some, however, also perform a farewell *'umra* and thus must again don their *iḥrām* garments. Many, if not most, Muslims then journey north to Medina for the "visit," known as *ziyāra,* to the Prophet's tomb and other important historical sites. This is not part of the hajj and is in no sense required, but Muslims love to pay

Pilgrimage art from upper Egypt, which shows to passersby some of the details of the holy places and the long journey. (*Source:* Yvonne Haddad)

their respects to Muhammad. According to a *hadīth* of the Prophet, "Whoever visits my tomb, my intercession will be granted to him."

### *A Sixth Pillar: Jihād*

Sometimes a sixth pillar is included in discussions of *'ibādāt,* "acts of worship." It is ***jihād,*** meaning "striving, exertion" in the way of God. Most often it is translated in the West as "holy war," but that is only one aspect of the phenomenon. Muslims recognize a greater and a lesser *jihād.* The greater is the individual's personal struggle with his or her base instincts and lack of faith and devotion. This is a spiritual type of *jihād.* The lesser *jihād* involves, if necessary, armed struggle against the enemies of Islam, although it should be only in self-defense. The Qur'an commands that "there shall be no compulsion in religion" (2:256). *Jihād* as exertion is definitely aimed at the spread of Islam, but by peaceful means like preaching, travel, establishing educational institutions, and setting a good example. However, extremist Muslims in all times have considered *jihād* in the form of military aggression against infidels as an Islamic duty. *Jihād* as warfare is generally aimed at righting a wrong and has even been proclaimed by one Muslim group with reference to another. Today, sometimes such a call to *jihād* is heard in troubled parts of the Islamic world.[17]

This chapter has described the basic ritual duties of Islam. It should be understood that they comprise a sort of *minimum* of what is required for the religious life. The devotional life of Muslims is not essentially an external pattern of ritual observances, but an integrated and continuous frame of mind and habits that expresses itself in worship, fasting, almsgiving, and the other acts. The pillars, as described in this chapter, were not in their fully developed form at the time of Muhammad's death. The emerging systems of Islamic jurisprudence did much to regulate them in the kind of detail that the official handbooks contain, a process that took several generations.

## NOTES

1. Fazlur Rahman's interpretation–translation of the term. See his *Islam* (New York: Anchor Books, 1968), p. 26.
2. A well-documented discussion of the idea of scripture in the Near East is by Arthur Jeffery, *The Qur'ān As Scripture* (New York: Russell F. Moore, 1952), especially chap. 1.
3. See 2:255; 10:3; 20:109, passages that say that there is no intercession with God on the Last Day, except by his permission. The mainstream of Islamic interpretation has regarded this as meaning that Muhammad is permitted to intercede. Fazlur Rahman rejects this interpretation in his *Major Themes of the Qur'an* (Minneapolis and Chicago: Bibliotheca Islamica, 1980), pp. 31–32.
4. Al-Baghawī, *Mishkāt al-Masābīh,* vol. 1, trans. James Robson (Lahore, Pakistan: Sh. Muhammad Ashraf, 1965–1966), p. 23.
5. Quoted in Arthur Jeffery, *Islam: Muhammad and His Religion* (New York: Liberal Arts Press, 1958), p. 154.

6. M. Muhammad Ali, *A Manual of Ḥadīth* (Lahore, Pakistan: Ahmadiyya Anjuman, 1951), pp. 41–42.
7. For this distinction and much of what follows on the "pillars," I am indebted to the clear, detailed handbook by Muhammad Abdul Rauf, *Islam: Creed and Worship* (Washington, D.C.: The Islamic Center, 1974), pp. 21–46.
8. *Mishkāt,* vol. 1, p. 80.
9. *Ibid.,* p. 293.
10. *Islamic Correspondence Course* (Fort Collins, Colo.: The Muslim Students' Association of the United States and Canada, n.d.), Unit 5B, "Poor Due," p.4.
11. The details included here are from Abdul Rauf, *Islam: Creed and Worship,* pp. 103–107.
12. Al-Bīrūnī, *The Chronology of Ancient Nations,* trans. and ed. C. Edward Sachau (Frankfurt, West Germany: Minerva GMBH, 1969), pp. 303–331.
13. I am very grateful to Dr. Abdulaziz A. Sachedina, of the University of Virginia, for much of the information and structure of this section. He has been on hajj a number of times and is also an academic expert in Islamic studies.
14. Arnold Van Gennep, *The Rites of Passage,* trans. M. B. Vizedom and B. L. Caffee (Chicago: University of Chicago Press, 1960).
15. Joseph Conrad, *Lord Jim,* introduction by Morton Dauwen Zabel (Cambridge, Mass.: Riverside Press, 1958), p. xiii.
16. The Jewish biblical story has Isaac as the intended victim, as was observed in Chapter 1 (see Gen. 22:1–14).
17. There is a vast literature on *jihād.* A reliable overview is Rudolph Peters, "Jihad," in *The Encyclopedia of Religion,* vol. 8, ed. Mircea Eliade et al. (New York: Macmillan and Free Press, 1987), pp. 88–91. An excellent full study is Majid Khadduri, *War and Peace in the Law of Islam* (Baltimore: Johns Hopkins University Press, 1959).

# CHAPTER 6 The Nature and Function of the Qur'an

**KEY TERMS**

| | | |
|---|---|---|
| ***'ilm al-tajwīd*** | ***tilāwa*** | ***ta'wīl*** |
| ***qirā'a*** | ***tafsīr*** | ***i'jāz al-Qur'ān*** |

## LANGUAGE, FORMAT, AND CHRONOLOGY

The word *qur'ān,* as mentioned earlier, means "recitation," which refers to individual passages as well as to their collection in the book that Muslims possess. A codex, that is, a bound volume, is called in Arabic a *muṣḥaf,* which is a common synonym for the Qur'an when preceded by the definite article, as in *al-Muṣḥaf,* "the Book." Another synonym for the Qur'an is *al-Kitāb,* "the Writing," or "the Book." (But "the Holy Book" in Arabic is "*al-Kitāb al-Muqaddas,*" which convention limits to the Holy Bible.) Other names for the Qur'ān, mentioned in the text itself, are *al-Furqān,* "the Criterion" (between truth and falsehood), *al-Hudā* "the Guidance," and *al-Tanzīl,* "the Downsent" (that is, "revealed from above"). Only in recent times have Muslims taken to calling their scripture "the Holy Qur'an," influenced by English translations, especially in India. There is nothing wrong with the name, but it is not a traditional or idiomatic one. The most common name for the Islamic scripture among Muslims is *al-Qur'ān al-Karīm,* "the Noble (or Gracious) Qur'an."

### *Oral and Written Transmission*

The Muslims have handed down the Qur'an through the ages by both oral and written means. The former has always been considered to be the primary mode of transmission, reflecting its original revelation to Muhammad through the archangel Gabriel. During the early generations of the Islamic movement, for more than its first two centuries, in fact, written Arabic was not developed enough to preserve precisely every sound and thus needed the help of oral knowledge. That is, in some respects, the bare consonantal text (without the vowels marked in to indicate active or passive voice, mood, tense, and so forth) is like shorthand. The native speaker knows exactly how to pronounce a written phrase, but the non-Arab who has learned the language as a second tongue or native Arabs speaking different dialects will not know in every case exactly how to pronounce the text from only the "defective script," as it is called. An example of what is meant by a script that lacks vowels is the following rough approximation, which you should try to decipher:

> w hld ths trths t b slf vdnt tht ll mn r crtd qul tht thy r ndwd b thr crtr wth crtn nlnbl rghts tht mng ths r lf lbrt nd th prst f hppnss. (We hold these truths to be self-evident, that all men are created equal, that they are endowed by their Creator with certain unalienable Rights, that among these are Life, Liberty and the Pursuit of Happiness.)

This illustration does not quite duplicate the situation of the Arabic-speaking context, but it does suggest something of the problem. Actually, the Arabic consonantal script does have some vowels that are written out at all times, but two of these can also be consonants (the Arabic *wāw* is both like the English *u* and *w,* whereas the *yā* is like the English *y* as in "yes" and in "baby"). Another problem of the old Arabic script was that certain forms for consonants could not be readily distinguished from others, as if we were to use a *b* to stand also for *t* and soft *th* sounds. All of this detail has been included to emphasize the importance of a correctly learned oral prototype from Muhammad, which later was written down.

The written Qur'an, then, was originally corrected by the remembered oral Qur'an, although from early times the relationship between the two was close. Although Muhammad is reported not to have been able to read or write, there were many in his environment who could. But they were limited by the incomplete written script of their day. It was not until nearly 300 years after the death of the Prophet that what is called a "standard exemplar" of the Qur'anic text was perfected. That technical term refers to a completely voweled and otherwise precisely marked text that could be used for copying purposes.

### *Conventional Format*

The format of the Qur'an is not a product of revelation, but of convention. There are 114 chapters, called sūras, arranged roughly according to length. They progress from the longer ones in the earlier portions to the shortest ones at the end. The first sūra is an exception: a short prayer called "The Opening" (*Al-Fātiḥa*), which occupies a position in Islam parallel to the Lord's Prayer in Christianity. We may call the traditional arrangement of the sūras the "canonical" ordering, in that it is official. There is also a chronological arrangement of sūras, according to when each was revealed. There is not unanimous agreement about every sūra's historical time of origination, although there is a general consensus about most of them and also about certain individual passages of sūras. Most Muslims do not believe that the Qur'an was revealed in any manner that would suggest it was a response to historical circumstances in a causal sense. The divine will is inscrutable and far above all that humans can say or understand about it. Qur'an scholars call the specific circumstances connected with revealed passages "occasions of revelations" (*asbāb nuzūl al-Qur'ān*). The occasions are not *causes,* but simply incidents or events that have been remembered—most often from reports from Muhammad (*ḥadīths*).

Unfortunately, the reports themselves are not always dated, and so the best we have is a crude connection with an actual historical event to, at most, a relative date (as between *x* and *y,* but precisely where is unknown). Certain events are referred to directly in the Qur'an. An example is the Battle of Badr:

> And God most surely helped you at Badr, when you were utterly abject. (3:123)

However, all we can discern in this passage is that it was revealed after Badr, but not precisely when. It must be Medinan and after A.H. 2, but we cannot tell whether it was immediately after Badr or several years after. Another passage refers to the awkward incident when 'Ā'isha was mistakenly left behind when her caravan packed up and continued on its journey. Her attendants thought she was in the curtained litter on the back of her camel, but she was actually off looking for a lost necklace. A young man who had lagged behind the rest discovered 'Ā'isha and brought her back to Medina on his camel, all the while maintaining a dignified distance from the Prophet's wife. But tongues started wagging, because in that gossipy and scandal-mongering society, unrelated males and females alone together constituted prima facie evidence of adultery or fornication. After some time, Muhammad received a revelation that convinced him that any suspicions were groundless. The following verse was revealed, which occurs in a lengthy legal passage on adultery, its establishment, and the rules for punishment.

> And those who cast it up on women in wedlock, and then bring not four witnesses, scourge them with eighty stripes, and do not accept any testimony of theirs ever. (24:4)

These two historical events to which the Qur'an refers, the first specifically, the second implicitly, are not occasions of revelation. Rather, an occasion of revelation is something external to the Qur'an text itself.

### *Meccan and Medinan Sūras*

Modern Western scholarship has attempted to date the Qur'an's contents in a number of ways. The most widely accepted chronology outside Islamic scholarship, which

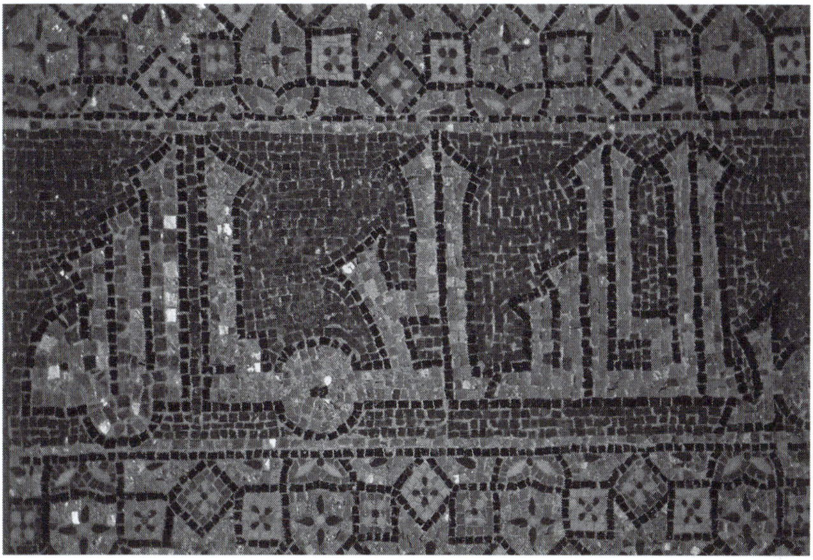

Classical Arabic Qur'anic calligraphy as mosaic architectural ornamentation.
(*Source:* Geoff Brightling/Dorling Kindersley)

tends to be based on traditional accounts, is that of the German orientalist Theodor Nöldeke (1836–1930), which is based on stylistic changes over the years of the Qur'an's revelation.[1] The sūras are divided up into the two usual groups of Meccan and Medinan periods. But Nöldeke goes farther by subdividing the Meccan sūras into three periods: early, middle, and late. The earliest sūras are generally brief, highly rhythmic, and laden with imagery. They are often introduced by oaths, as in sūra 95: "By the fig and the olive and the Mount Sinai and this land secure!"

The middle Meccan period is characterized by a quieter, more serene style. There are numerous illustrations of the truth of the divine message taken from nature and history, as well as a fuller airing of doctrinal issues. These sūras are longer and more formal. God is referred to frequently as "the Merciful" (*al-Raḥmān*), and passages are introduced with God's commanding Muhammad, "Say!" Earlier prophets are often mentioned and used as proofs of God's purposes in history.

The final Meccan period includes much of what the middle contains, but the use of "the Merciful" as a divine name ceases, and the prophet stories have an altered emphasis.

The Medinan sūras are quite different from the Meccan ones because of the changed circumstances of that period when Muhammad had become head of an independent theocratic community. The passages feature legal and social matters and are thus much more prosaic and intended for specific application to the regulation of the umma's life. The old themes of warning, judgment, punishment, reward, and God's signs in nature and history are still encountered, but their relative prominence is less frequent.

The passage just quoted about four witnesses being required before a charge of adultery may be raised is typical of Medinan passages of the regulatory and legal type.

At many points the chronologies of Nöldeke and the traditional Muslim scholars are in agreement, but their criteria for dating passages are, of course, radically different. Nöldeke's approach is a literary-critical one and depends to a great extent on internal evidence, regarding the Qur'an itself as its best source of clues. This type of scholarly-critical operation is not accepted by most Muslims, because it means treating the holy text just like any other text: generated by historical circumstances and understandable by means of historical-critical methodology. But from the scholar's perspective, there is no essential difference between dating the works of Cicero and the contents of the Qur'an, except that the former is easier because of our knowledge of the man and more precise internal evidence as well as the nature of the materials, which include letters and public orations.

### *Naming and Numbering the Sūras*

The names of the sūras are not part of the revealed message but have usually been assigned from some word by which the whole has been identified. For example, sūra 24 is called "The Poets" and sūra 16 "The Bee" because those words occur in only those two sūras. Normally, the word that names a sūra occurs early, but not always. The Muslims do not usually refer to the sūras by number, although this has become standard practice in Western scholarship (and is followed in this book.) The numbers of the sūras and verses were added later for convenience. However, Muslims do not usually use verse numberings either but instead quote the beginning of the passage in question. This practice obviously requires knowing the text by memory, an achievement that has always been most highly respected in Islam and that continues even in this age of dependence on written texts and the general loss of oral memory.

## RECITATION AND RITUAL OBSERVANCES

The *ḥāfiẓ al-Qur'ān,* literally, "the guardian of the Qur'an," that is, the one who has *memorized* it and thus helps keep it alive, is a special kind of Muslim and is looked up to as a learned and wise person. Such a person is often called a *shaykh.* Once the text is memorized, the *ḥāfiẓ* must work hard to remember it. This requires frequent repetition, which most appropriately occurs in a devotional context. Often such a person becomes a reciter (*qāri'*), who provides the necessary cycles of Qur'an recitation for the community in which he lives. Recitation is required during the salat, of course, but it is also featured in many other contexts, such as funerals, weddings, national observances, the openings of school terms, the inaugurations of officials, Ramadān nights, and social occasions in pious people's homes. During times of national emergency, as, for example, in Egypt during the Ramadān–Yom Kippur War of 1973, a popular reciter's voice was often heard chanting the Qur'an over Cairo radio. According to reports, when the recitation was being broadcast, people tended to feel secure and confident, but when it stopped, there was a noticeable tenseness and anxiety. The Qur'an soothes, supports, and strengthens the Muslims, and this is proof of its divine provenience. According to a famous prophetic saying, when the Qur'an is recited, God's *sakīna,* "peace," descends.

### *Liturgical Divisions*

In addition to the divisions by sūras and verses, the Qur'an is also arranged according to liturgical divisions, for purposes of recitation. One scheme divides the text into thirty equal parts, the number of days in the holy month of Ramadān. One part is recited each day, so that by the end of the month, the entire Qur'an has been recited. Each thirtieth of the text is called a *juz'*. These are further broken down into two smaller divisions, each called a *ḥizb,* which are further subdivided into "quarters" (*rub'*). All three, *juz'* (pl., *ajzā'), ḥizb* (pl., *aḥzāb*), and *rub'* (pl., *arbā'*) are ordinarily indicated by marks in the margins of the pages. Another arrangement is by sevenths of the Qur'an, so that it can be recited in a week.

When Muslims gather for recitation, they may choose either one sūra or the entire text. When the whole Qur'an has been finished, the occasion is one of special sacred power, and so the participants, including the listeners, break for a few moments of *du'ā'* prayer and recite some pious formulas. The actual closing of the recitation, called a *khatma,* is not completed with the final sūra of the Qur'an but with the recitation of the Fātiha, the first sūra together with the first five lines of the "Cow," which is the second sūra and the longest in the Qur'an. Thus the conclusion of one *khatma* actually is the beginning of another. The etiquette of recitation is fairly detailed. It does not include interpretation of the text but concentrates on the proper ritual uses of it. Many Muslims around the world understand little or no Arabic and need a translation in order to understand what is being said. But the recitation of the Qur'an, which is always in Arabic, is nevertheless moving and meaningful. People are frequently brought to tears and to moments of religious reflection when listening to the recitation. There is a mysterious power that is released when the Qur'an is recited, and this phenomenon has been noted since the time of Muhammad. It is for Muslims a major proof of the truth of the message and its origin with God.

### *Spiritual Significance*

The place of the Qur'an in the life of the Muslims is only in limited ways like that of the Bible in the lives of Jews and Christians. Scholars have observed that in relation to Christianity, the Qur'an may be usefully compared with Christ, in that it is believed to be God's Word that has miraculously come down into the world in history and humankind. If in Christianity the "Word became flesh," in Islam it became a book. And the book is properly appropriated and applied only when it is recited live in a context of belief and obedience.

There is an almost sacramental quality to the recitation of the Qur'an, in that God's presence is made apparent and all else is hushed before it. Muslims do not have sacraments, in the Christian sense, and that term is allowable for rough comparisons

Qur'an stall, along the wall of the Husayn Mosque, Cairo.
(*Source:* Frederick Mathewson Denny)

only and should not be applied strictly to Islam. Even the traditional definition of Christian sacrament that it is an "outward and visible sign of an inward and spiritual grace" does not quite fit the Qur'anic context. This distinction is necessary because the reciting of the sacred words is itself a participation in God's speech. This is why it must be performed as perfectly as possible. Orthoprax recitation thus serves in the manner in which the Qur'an is received, enjoyed, and transmitted.

### *Ritual Phrases*

A Muslim should not handle a copy of the Qur'an unless he or she is ritually pure; this also applies to reciting it, even if one is not using a *muṣḥaf.* One should not recite the Qur'an in unclean places or in questionable contexts. Before reciting any portion of the text, one should first "take refuge" (*isti'ādha*) by uttering the formula: "I take refuge with God from the accursed Satan" (*a'ūdhu b'illāhi min al-shayān al-rajīm*), after which is recited, whether or not it happens at that place in the text: "In the Name of God, the Merciful, the Compassionate" (*bismi-llāhi al-rahmān al-raḥīm*). This is known as the *basmala,* and it appears at the beginning of every sūra of the Qur'an, except the ninth. It is one of the most frequently uttered pious phrases of Muslims and is considered essential before embarking on any significant activity, like eating, conjugal relations, writing (in which case it is the first thing to be written down), and speaking before a group. At the close of recitation, one should say: "God Almighty has spoken truly" (*ṣadaqa Allāhu al-aẓīm*). The phrase of refuge seeking before the recitation and the closing phrase testifying to the divine truthfulness constitute a sort of verbal ritual enclosure or sanctuary around the recited text, preserving it from evil promptings and insincerity. These are a kind of *niyya* of recitation, without which the performance is profane. This interpretation is not to suggest that the Qur'an text can ever be less than sacred, only that people can recite it unworthily, thus failing to realize fully its benefits. But even profane and hardened people, like 'Umar before he became a Muslim, are affected by hearing and reading the text.

### *Technical Dimensions of Recitation*

The technical dimensions of recitation require a good knowledge of Arabic and much training and practice. Properly raised Muslim children begin reciting at an early age, mastering the difficult sounds and rhythms by ear. The art of recitation is called in Arabic ***'ilm al-tajwīd,*** "the science of euphonious recitation." It is also known by the technical terms ***qirā'a*** and ***tilāwa.*** There is a range of styles of recitation, extending from very plain, slow, almost monotonous performance (*tartīl*) according to strict rhythm all the way to highly florid, emotional, and "musical" chanting, known as *mujawwad.* The recitation should never become music, however, in the sense of secular art song, for recitation is ideally not entertainment or human-centered artistic performance. But gifted Qur'an reciters do command wide and devoted followings, which have been greatly extended since the proliferation of discs, tape cassettes, and the radio.

Egypt has long been regarded as the home of many of the best, or at least the most famous, professional reciters. A number of years ago I traveled to Cairo during the month of Ramadān in order to hear and tape-record some of these leading exponents of *tajwīd,* only to be disappointed when I discovered that most of them were out of the country, having been hired by wealthy parties to recite for them in such places as Saudi Arabia and Indonesia. Happily, there were many superb reciters who had remained at home and were heard, but they were not "stars."

Indeed, in Indonesia, Malaysia, Saudi Arabia, and other Muslim countries, Qur'an recitation contests are held periodically. Indonesia's biennial *Musābaqa Tilāwatil Qur'ān* ("contest of reciting the Qur'an") is a weeklong event of the greatest national interest, with provincial teams, parades, floats, and elaborate stadium spectacles featuring music and dance. Boys, girls, men, women, and handicapped

Advanced students engaged in Qur'an recitation at a special institute in Singosari, East Java. (*Source:* Frederick Mathewson Denny)

(visually challenged persons, mostly) compete in separate chanting classes. The president of the Republic of Indonesia and his ministers, along with the diplomatic corps from many nations, attend the gala opening ceremonies, which are held in different cities over the years.

### *Emotional Significance*

It is difficult for a Westerner, who most likely lives in a secular environment, to appreciate just how powerful and pervasive the recited Qur'an is in Muslim environments. After living in a country like Egypt, Jordan, Pakistan, or Indonesia, where recitation pours forth from the radio, television, and mosques in every neighborhood, one becomes accustomed to it before realizing how deep an impression it is making. This is made apparent when one leaves the Islamic environment and fails to hear the pleasant, pious sounds of the human voice celebrating God's message. Recitation of the Qur'an and the five daily calls to prayer punctuate and regulate the Muslim's day and are missed when they are absent. Probably Westerners have not known anything like this since the days when the monastery and church bells played the Angelus at morning, noon, and night, and monks or nuns could be heard chanting the divine services at the different times of the Christian day. The difference in the case of the Qur'an's daily recitation, other than the obvious differences of content, meaning, and context, is that nearly everyone can participate in it, not just those in the clerical orders. The reading and recitation of the Muslim scripture has been from its inception a highly democratic affair.

### *Studying the Qur'an*

For people not reared in the Islamic tradition, starting to study the Qur'an is somewhat difficult. This is because, first, it is not a narrative text, as are the Hebrew Bible and many other scriptures. There is only one sustained narrative in the Qur'an, the Sūra of Joseph (12), which in its own way parallels the biblical account of Joseph and his brothers and the saga of Israel's migration to Egypt. Throughout the Qur'an are numerous snatches of traditional stories (Jewish, Christian, Arabian) or allusions to them, and it is apparent that Muhammad's listeners knew a broad range of old narratives—legends, myths, parables, proverbs, and so forth—because they otherwise could not have understood the Qur'an at many points. And it must be assumed that a major reason for Muhammad's success with his message is that it was intelligible to most Arabs. But, second, the Qur'anic style of utterance is oracular and full of self-reinforcing repetition, giving the Westerner the impression of disjointedness and a lack of development.

Appreciation of the Qur'an is clearly an acquired taste, whether through childhood—as in the gradual acquisition of one's native tongue—or by means of study and listening because of conversion or a scholarly interest in understanding Islam. One often hears Muslims say that the Qur'an cannot be translated; it must be understood in the original if its power and beauty are to be appreciated. To the impatient and skeptical outsider, this may sound like a weak excuse for deflecting criticism from what might be considered an opaque and defective text. But it is true: a translation of the Qur'an cannot begin to do justice to either the meanings or the distinctive sounds of the original Arabic. One must earn the privilege of enjoying and being moved by the Qur'an. The mystic Jalāl al-Dīn al-Rūmī expressed it thus:

> The Koran is a bride who does not disclose her face to you, for all that you draw aside the veil. That you should examine it, and yet not attain happiness and unveiling, is due to the fact that the act of drawing aside the veil has itself repulsed and tricked you, so that the bride has shown herself to you as ugly, as if to say, "I am not that beauty". The Koran is able to show itself in whatever form it pleases. But if you do not draw aside the veil and seek only its good pleasure, watering its sown field and attending on it from afar, toiling upon that which pleases it best, it will show its face to you without your drawing aside the veil.[2]

## CONTENTS AND NATURE OF THE QUR'AN

It is not difficult to summarize the message of the Qur'an. It is essentially the five main doctrines of īmān and the five pillars, as sketched in Chapter 5. Of course, those points are covered in a variety of ways and in some cases repeatedly, but they are straightforward and fairly simple to state. In addition are a number of regulations and legal guidelines for community life. But having said this, we have not really begun to characterize either the contents or the nature of the Qur'an as they affect the lives of the faithful. One may memorize the entire text, so as to be able to do without a concordance, and yet without belief and awe, one will only be tearing away the veils that scholars imagine prevent them from discovering root meanings and causes.

It is painful for Muslims to witness certain types of historical-critical, philological, and otherwise "orientalist" scholarly treatment of their sacred book. This reaction can easily be dismissed by outsiders as fundamentalist obscurantism. But much of the modern Western scholarly investigation of the Qur'an has been a kind of plundering of its contents, to show Semitic parallels, Jewish or Christian origins for the ideas, mistakes in Muhammad's "appropriation" of the senior Abrahamic traditions (thus demonstrating Islam's inferiority because of its lack of originality), and so forth. Just as every Muslim considers criticism of Muhammad as an attack on each Muslim, so also do unsympathetic or historicist analyses of the Qur'an amount to invasions of a Muslim's sense of identity and meaning. The Prophet told his followers that their descendants would best be able to understand his soul by reading the Qur'an. The Qur'an is thus not a profane text, but the primary means of encountering God.

We have included these comments, even though they do not bear directly on the Qur'an itself, because they may be of use as the reader seeks to understand Muslims' attitudes and feelings concerning their sacred text. Secular students of the Qur'an, or any other sacred book, obviously have every right to investigate it as they see fit. Belief in the divine origin of the Qur'an is certainly not required of non-Muslims, and theoretical speculation as to its relation to the evolving mental and behavioral patterns of Muhammad is well within the boundaries of objective scholarship. Having said this, however, it remains true that any suggestion that the Qur'an is not divinely revealed, perfect and true in every respect, and totally free from historical influences (except for its arrangement, the titles of the sūras, and similar matters) is an affront to Muslim belief.

In earlier periods, non-Muslim scholars tended to equate Muhammad's words with that of the Qur'an. When quoting a passage from the scripture, one might read: "Muhammad said [thus and so]." It is certainly true that Muhammad did say what the Qur'an says, but only in the sense of repeating or reciting a text that was not composed by him in the first place. What the non-Muslim means, of course, is that Muhammad was the author, that he consciously composed the Qur'an and, by means of it, manipulated people and events. This interpretation is totally unacceptable and indeed blasphemous to Muslims, who insist upon Muhammad's illiteracy as one of the proofs of the Qur'an's divine origin. He could not have written it even if he had wanted to, the traditional view seems to be saying. Muhammad claimed that the only miracle in which he participated was the revelation of the Qur'an. Increasingly, non-Muslim scholars are altering their manner of quoting from the Qur'an, by writing or saying: "The Qur'an says [thus and so]," thus finding a common ground of usage with Muslims, without necessarily agreeing that what "the Qur'an says" came from a supernatural source. It is just good manners and does not imply either deceit or acquiescence.

### *Popular Uses*

There are many ritual uses of the Qur'an, beyond recitation in prayer and devotion. On the popular level, the Qur'an is often used as a protective device against evil spirits and influences.[3] For example, a passage from it may be written on paper and enclosed in an amulet, which is hung from the neck. Or a complete *muṣḥaf* may be mounted in a prominent place in a private auto or taxi. Or a sick person may be given a potion made by mixing water with the ink that has been used to write a Qur'anic charm. Drinking this dissolved ink is thought by some to help heal through the great *baraka* (spiritual power) of the Qur'an.

The last two sūras of the Qur'an are called "the Two Charms" and are legitimately used to ward off the evil of sorcerers and witches. The formula of "refuge taking," quoted earlier, is itself a Qur'anic command (16:98). In the Qur'anic worldview, magic is real and threatening.[4] It must sometimes be countered with magical means, of which the Qur'an is the most potent. Black magic is condemned, as is any magic that invokes any power other than God's. The power in any event is God's and not, strictly speaking, the practitioner's, although in the Qur'an, God could be said to have given to his obedient servants a powerful protector that can be used when necessary. This is basically a religious viewpoint, although there are many varieties of understanding and application of magic and the occult among Muslims.

The rituals of Muslims' social relations include phrases and expressions mined from the Qur'an. The Muslim greeting is from the Qur'an (for example, 6:54; 16:32): *al-salāmu 'alaykum* ("Peace be unto you"), and it is normally reserved for use among Muslims exclusively. The ubiquitous phrase that accompanies any human intention concerning the future is *inshā'Allāh* ("if God wills"). When someone has been complimented or praised, the speaker should immediately exclaim *mā shā'Allāh!* ("What God has willed!"). When someone is asked how her or his health is, the answer is *al-ḥamdu li-llāh* ("Praise be to God"). These and others, including the *basmala,* are so commonly uttered by Muslims, and in fact by non-Muslims living in a predominantly Muslim society, that they become habit, though they still have deep meaning.

Once when I was saying good night to a Muslim friend in Cairo, I closed by saying, "Well, I'll see you tomorrow at the stables." (A dawn riding party to the pyramids was being planned.) The Muslim friend added *"inshā' Allāh,"* whereupon I repeated, "OK, see ya then." Out came another *inshā'Allāh* but with greater intensity and some impatience. It turned out that he refused to acquiesce in any joint decision about the future until I agreed that it was finally in Allah's hands. Thus, there is a kind of magic in such phrases, too. This is especially true of *mā shā' Allāh.* It is bad form to compliment profusely a parent on his or her child, as it may indicate envy and the evil eye. But if one quickly says *mā shā' Allāh,* any harm will be averted and serene relations continued.

## INTERPRETATION OF THE QUR'AN

Until now nothing has been said about the interpretation of the Qur'an, an important and technically demanding enterprise reserved for the properly trained. But interest in exegetical matters runs high among all Muslims, who are encouraged to become as knowledgeable as possible. The Qur'an contributed to extensive literacy among Muslim peoples wherever it was taught and studied; it inculcated values as it taught the Arabic language. From the earliest Muslim times, there has been an emphasis not only on reciting the message aloud in prayer and devotion but also on understanding it. It is a mistake of method to look to Muslims for the same sorts of scriptural awareness and uses that one takes for granted in the members of the other Abrahamic traditions. The same is true for Judaism and Christianity, for all three religions have their own characteristic ideas of scripture that, though related to each other, are quite different and distinctively determined by their own histories. Christians regard and interpret the Hebrew scriptures very differently from the ways in which Jews do. They see them as leading up to Jesus, of course, but they also give them much greater play within their own tradition than do Jews. This may sound ironical, even paradoxical, but it is true. Once when I was citing an Old Testament passage while arguing for a certain view concerning Jewish belief, a Jewish colleague remarked, "Fred, forgive me, but that's a peculiarly *Protestant* error you've just committed." What he meant was that my use of the text had been made from a conceptual framework and assumptions differing from Jewish beliefs and attitudes. Although the citation from scriptures perhaps made perfect sense within a Protestant Christian framework, the citation was totally irrelevant to a Jewish understanding of the matter. Many Christians, even with their New Testament lenses polished and focused, still tend to take their Old Testament "straight," in that they do not normally feel constrained to view it through layers of exegetical tradition. This flexibility probably had its origins in the antinomian attitudes that flourished during the Protestant Reformation with respect to reading the Bible for oneself and discerning in it whatever one was personally led by the Holy Spirit to see.

But Jews appropriate their Bible through a complex and cumulative tradition of rabbinical commentary, which, layer upon layer, comprises a sort of emerging scripture in itself. The Bible is still fundamental, but it is known perfectly only when the subsequent exegetical tradition is also known. Understanding is regulated, then, by the community's scholarly experience over centuries and millennia. Judaism, like Islam, is an orthoprax religion. Law has been the characteristic preoccupation of religious scholarship in Judaism, whereas theology has been central in Christianity.

Similarly, Muslims interpret their Qur'an through layers of exegetical tradition. But the book itself is primary and closer to the forefront of every activity in a way uncommon in Judaism and Christianity. Recall the earlier comparison between the Qur'an and Christ as centers of Islam and Christianity. Just as Christianity is the religion of and about Jesus, Islam is the religion of the Qur'an. The Word comes to humankind by different means in the two traditions, but it is believed nevertheless to come definitively. The Christian can have Jesus by means of devotion to him in a variety of ways.

The Muslim cannot command the Qur'an to come into his or her heart, but there is nevertheless a personal appropriation of the Qur'an's power and meaning through the Muslim's prayerful and observant study of the text. In the Christian Eucharist the Lord is symbolically eaten in bread and wine. In Qur'an recitation, there is "real presence" also, as God's words and their power penetrate the consciousness of the listeners. "Remember God often," the Qur'an commands, and so the Muslims remember him by means of his beautiful names and other Qur'anic formulas.

We shall see in regard to Sufism that the "remembering" of God through *dhikr* is the main way in which he comes into the hearts of the Muslims, and the *dhikr,* or "mentioning," is done by means of the Qur'an. God, as a subtle and sophisticated theological conundrum expressed it, is neither the Qur'an *nor other* than it. But it can be affirmed, without recourse to such puzzling language, that God's power and blessing are in his book and that these are available for his people.

## *Technical Interpretation*

So far our discussion has been general and theoretical. But actual practice of Qur'an interpretation requires mastering some principles and terms, if it is to be understood at all. ***Tafsīr*** is an Arabic term that can be translated as "exegesis," "commentary," or "interpretation," and the like. It occurs once in the Qur'an itself (25:33). A more common Qur'anic term for exegesis is ***ta'wīl*** (for example, 3:7), but later that term takes on a special meaning as allegorical interpretation, which explores symbolic and inner meanings. This type of exegesis is especially prominent in Shī'īand Sufi (mystical) contexts. *Tafsīr* has come to represent both the entire field of Qur'an interpretation, as a generic category, and the actual operation of examining the plain text: its language, grammar, expressions, peculiarities, and so forth. At this level, the findings of *tafsīr* are not open to serious debate, although there may be a variety of alternative meanings of specific words and constructs. But at the level of *ta'wīl,* sectarian issues may affect the interpretation of passages. The sixth imām of Shī'ism, Ja'far al-Ṣādiq, stated:

> The Book of God contains four things: the announced expression (*'ibārah*), the allusion (*ishārah*), the hidden meaning related to the suprasensible worlds (*laṭā'if*), and the spiritual truths (*ḥāqā'iq*). The literary expression is for the common people (*'awāmm*); the allusion is for the elite (*khawāṣṣ*); the hidden meaning is for the friends of God (or saints) (*awliyā'*); and the spiritual truths are for the prophets (*anbiyā'*).[5]

The four-tiered hierarchy of Imām Ja'far al-Ṣādiq represents a special attitude toward Qur'an interpretation, but it is not universally accepted by Muslims.

The Qur'an represents itself as already being clear, so that the previously "unscriptured" (*ummī*) pagan Arabs would have access to God's message of judgment. Muhammad himself explained many passages to his circle, and his companions added to the growing stock of interpretations. Some of the early Muslims became skilled in such matters and even learned Christian and Jewish lore so as to extend their abilities in *tafsīr*. Over the centuries there evolved a mainstream of Qur'anic exegesis that is called *tafsīr ma'thūr*, "traditional commentary," or more literally, "commentary [that is] handed down." The greatest achievement in this type of exegesis was the extensive work by Abū Ja'far Muhammad ibn Jarīr al-Ṭabarī (d. 923), "The collection of explanations for the interpretation of the Qur'an," which in one modern edition fills thirty volumes. Ṭabarī was a great historian as well as a legal and Qur'anic scholar, and he offered much information that he gleaned from his thorough study. Reading his *tafsīr* is absorbing and illuminating; he fully reviewed the evidence and possible readings but frequently gave his own preference. Writing more than two centuries after the death of the Prophet, Ṭabarī nevertheless reproduced much of the Qur'anic commentary down to his time, which in many cases was otherwise lost. *Tafsīr ma'thūr* is the fundamental type of Qur'an commentary and is learned by all scholars, for it contains the main heritage of information and perspectives. It has continued to this day as the center of the science.

### *Speculative Interpretation*

Another main type of Qur'anic commentary is called *tafsīr bi al-ra'y*, meaning "interpretation based on individual rational judgment." This is a speculative and sometimes philosophical kind of exegesis, preferred by the more intellectual and free-thinking Muslims. It emphasizes theological issues and is, because of this preoccupation, more akin to Christian exegesis of the "biblical theology" genre. This is not to imply that the positions are in any way similar to Christian doctrinal stands. Rather, it is a matter of method and style of inquiry that makes it similar to rational investigation in other traditions. Because of *tafsīr bi al-ra'y's* predilection for rational analysis and speculation, it has frequently been attacked by the orthodox as too freewheeling and subjective. This antagonism is, in part, because of the identification of this type of exegesis with the famous Mu'tazilite ("rationalist") school of theology, which will be considered in Chapter 8. Exponents of "rationalist exegesis" include the great theologian and mystic Abū Ḥmid al-Ghazālī (d. 1111) and the Mu'tazilite al-Zamakhsharī (d. 1144), whose linguistic genius alone has caused his *tafsīr* to be studied by every aspiring *mufassir* (exegete). As Ibn Khaldūn (d. 1406), the orthodox and learned cultural historian, put it:

> Competent orthodox scholars have . . . come to disregard his [Zamakhsharī's] work and to warn everyone against its pitfalls. However, they admit that he is on firm ground in everything related to language and style (*balāghah*). If the student

> of the work is acquainted with the orthodox dogmas and knows the arguments in their defense, he is no doubt safe from its fallacies. Therefore, he should seize the opportunity to study it, because it contains remarkable and varied linguistic information.[6]

Al-Bayḍāwī (d. ca. 1286) edited and condensed al-Zamakhsharī's commentary, preserving the technical linguistic content and excising the Mu'tazilite rationalism. This relatively brief *tafsīr* is perhaps the most widely read in Sunnī Islam and has attained a kind of unofficial "scriptural" status of its own, which stems from its wide use and its being universally considered by Sunnīs as thoroughly orthodox.

***An Example of Tafsīr.*** The reader may wonder why there has been no example of *tafsīr* reproduced here. Although it is possible to do so, often Qur'anic exegesis is so caught up in linguistic discussion that it would require a knowledge of Arabic to understand it even in translation, as we observed earlier. But in the interests of authenticity and experience, a brief extract from al-Zamakhsharī is in order. Commenting on "We have not taught him [Muhammad] poetry; it is not seemly for him" (36:69ff), al-Zamakhsharī writes:

> Some took the Messenger of God to be a poet, and indeed it is related that (the Meccan) 'Uqba ibn Abī Mu'ait was one who did this. Thereupon it was said (by God): We have not taught him poetry; that is, while teaching him the Qur'ān, we have not taught him poetry. This is to be understood in the sense that the Qur'ān is neither poetry nor does it have anything to do with it, but on the contrary is far removed. Poetry contains statements that convey meaning through metre and (poetical) rhyme (*muqaffā*). Where, however, are metre and (poetical) rhyme (in the Qur'ān)? And to what extent are the themes (*ma'ānī*) to which the poets devote themselves the themes of the Qur'ān? How far removed, furthermore, is the structure (*naẓm*) of the poet's assertions from the structure and style of the Qur'ān? Thus, close investigation shows that the only relationship between the Qur'ān and poetry is that both are written in the Arabic Language.[7]

The passage goes on to say that Muhammad was not given the poetic gift, even though he loved poetry above all other ways of speaking, and that he was illiterate in any case. This example of *tafsīr* translates remarkably well into English. Even so, it is based on a sophisticated appreciation of what does and what does not constitute poetry within the Arabic context. Notice the technical terms that the translator did not dare delete in their original forms.

### Legal and Social Interpretation

The modernist Muslim scholar Muhammad 'Abduh, of Egypt (d. 1905), turned Qur'anic commentary toward consideration of the current legal and social issues. His *tafsīr* is often perfectly intelligible to the non-Arabist and non-Muslim because of its universal frame of reference, that is, its concern to ventilate crucial Islamic issues in the light of modern attitudes and habits. ʿAbduh considered the Qur'anic teaching about polygamy (for example, 4:3) to be constrained in practice, because of the virtual impossibility of treating all wives equally, which is the requirement for those who choose to have several wives. ʿAbduh was well known for advising monogamy, because of his interpretation of the Qur'an text on this issue. But he also was at pains to explain earlier Muslim practice as acceptable, even beneficial, because of peculiar circumstances:

> Polygamy had advantages in the early period of Islam, among the most important of that time being that it brought about the bond of blood relationship and of relationship by marriage, so that the feeling of tribal solidarity was strengthened. . . . Today, on the other hand, the harm (*ḍarar*) of every additional wife (*ḍarar*) carries over to her child, its father, and its other relatives. The wife stirs up enmity and hatred among them; she incites her child to enmity against his brothers and sisters, and she incites her husband to suppress the rights of the children which he has from the other wives. The husband, on the other hand, follows in the folly of the wife whom he loves the most, and thus ruin creeps into the entire family. If one wishes to enumerate specifically the disadvantages and mishaps that result from polygamy, then one would present something that would cause the blood of the believers to curdle.[8]

This is strong language, and Shaykh ʿAbduh did not escape criticism for being so outspoken.

Only a taste of *tafsīr* has been provided here, but it is sufficient for an idea of it. Although *tafsīr ma'thūr* has dominated over the centuries, at least among the Sunnis, the potential scope of Qur'anic commentary is limitless, because the message itself is so profound and mysterious. The practices of reciting and correctly copying the text were perfected during the first three centuries of Islam. Their continued cultivation is an exercise in piety and preservation of a precious and living heritage. More than that, the safeguarding and sharing of the Qur'an through recitation, copying out in beautiful script, and uttering in prayer as well as in social relations are the main ways in which the Muslims themselves are preserved and strengthened. This is the ritual use of the Qur'an in Islam, and it is as fundamental as it is broad based. The interpretation of the Qur'an, on the other hand, is much more limited, because of its great difficulty and its somewhat more idiosyncratic tendencies according to schools, sects, intellectual temperaments, and above all the possibility of multiple and layered meanings in the text itself, as was pointed out in the earlier quotation from Imām Jaʿfar al-Ṣādiq.

## THE "INIMITABILITY" OF THE QUR'AN

We shall close this chapter by returning to an earlier issue: the Qur'an's repetition and its seeming lack of structure. These dimensions have puzzled outsiders but are not regarded as defects by Muslims, because the Qur'an is first of all a divine message that provides the most authentic glimpse of God's inner nature. The text is regarded as inimitable, expressed by the phrase ***i'jāz al-Qur'ān.*** No one can produce a Qur'an, this doctrine goes, no matter how skilled in language and rhetoric. This *i'jāz,* or "miraculous" nature, applies not only to the Qur'an's unsurpassable language and style but also and especially to its truth in every detail. A remarkable phenomenon is the very repetition of the message's basic themes in practically every section of the Qur'an that might be extracted for recitation.[9] Sample the text by taking ten or fifteen verses from any portion and the likelihood is that you will have gathered its essential teaching. The lack of narrative or discursive structure, which outside observers and students have sometimes regarded as its major defect, then becomes one of its central mysteries and glories. The Qur'an is entirely self-consistent and harmonious on the level of its basic teachings, but it is discontinuous and unlike other writings, especially the Bible, which it only faintly and superficially resembles at points. This is another dimension of *i'jāz al-Qur'ān.*

The Prophet said: "The best among you is he who learns the Qur'an and teaches it." Another *ḥadīth* goes: "He is not one of us who does not chant the Qur'ān."[10] The Qur'an points out, concerning itself:

> He has sent down upon thee the Book with the truth, confirming what was before it, and He sent down the Torah and the Gospel aforetime, as guidance to the people, and he sent down the Salvation [*furıan*].
>
> • • •
>
> It is He who sent down upon thee the Book, wherein are verses clear that are the Essence [literally "mother"] of the Book, and others are ambiguous. As for those in whose hearts is swerving, they follow the ambiguous part, desiring dissension, and desiring its interpretation; and none knows its interpretation, save only God. And those firmly rooted in knowledge say "We believe in it; all is from our Lord"; yet none remembers, but men possessed of minds. (3:3–4,7)

Such ambiguous passages have been a problem in the history of *tafsīr,* as are certain passages that are considered to cancel out others. But these matters are advanced and in any case do not substantially affect what has been discussed in this chapter. They become important, however, for later legal and theological discussion. To give a hint, look at the full stop between the last and the next to last sentence in the quotation that you have just read. Some interpreters contend that there is no stop there, thus extending the true understanding of the Qur'an's meaning to "those firmly rooted in knowledge." Who could these people be? then becomes a crucial question. But the overall attitude in Islam is that one should never be overly confident in claiming special insight into the mysteries of the revelation. The great jurist Ahmad ibn Hanbal once had a dream in which he was brought into the presence of God. He made the most of the opportunity by asking God: "O Lord, what is the best way to manage to be near you?" God answered: "My Word, O Ahmad." Ibn Hanbal inquired: "With understanding or without understanding?" God replied: "With or without understanding."[11] This perfectly captures the sense of the Qur'an as a divine presence and is a warning against intellectualizing.

Another important, but technically advanced subfield in Qur'anic studies, is the "abrogated" (*mansūkh*) and "abrogating" (*nāsikh*) verses, where the former have been superceded and cancelled by the latter, which are chronologically later.

### *The Language's Beauty*

The language of the Qur'an is pure Arabic. This chapter has primarily developed a concern for its sounds, as in recitation, and its meanings, as in *tafsīr.* But it would be wrong to limit the message's significance to these two modes. The Arabic script also has great visual value. Qur'anic calligraphy developed as the single most important form of Islamic visual art and has been the only theme universally permitted in the decoration of mosques, Qur'an copies, and other religious things. Representations of humans and animals are forbidden, for fear of idolatry. The arabesque developed from writing out the Arabic language in a beautiful hand and later, as pure decoration, entered world art far beyond the boundaries of Islam. But it is only in Islamic contexts that the Arabic-Qur'anic script has its full power and meaning. The Muslim use of arabesque contains divine significance, even when it is so abstract as to be scarcely decipherable without expert guidance. The undulations and interweavings are like the mysterious and puzzling aspects of the created universe, whose divine origin and goal are discernible only to the eyes of the faithful. The sounds, meanings, and visible forms of Arabic all work together to bring the believers to the state of wondrous gratitude that is at the center of *īmān.*[12]

## NOTES

1. Theodore Nöldeke, *Geschichte des Qorans,* 3 vols, 1909–1936 (Leipzig: Dieterich'sche Verlagsbuchhandlung; repr. Hildesheim: Georg Olms Verlag, 1970). Nöldeke's collaborations over many years included Friedrich Schwally, Gotthelf Bergsträsser, and Otto Pretzl. The original edition of 1860 contained Nöldeke's essential chronology. The 1909 edition elaborated it, and the two later volumes treated the collection of the Qur'an and the history of the text. The most authoritative and accessible scholarly introduction to the Qur'an in English is by W. Montgomery Watt, *Bell's Introduction to the Qur'ān* (Edinburgh: Edinburgh University Press, 1970), a major reworking of the earlier work by Richard Bell, Watt's teacher. A major new reference work on the Qur'an is *Encyclopaedia of the Qur'ān,* ed. Jane Dammen McAuliffe (Leiden-Boston-Köln: Brill, 2001–2006). Five alphabetical volumes of topics plus a sixth, index volume.
2. A. J. Arberry, trans., *Discourses of Rumi* (London: John Murray, 1961), pp. 236–237.
3. See James Robson, "The Magical Use of the Koran," Glasgow University Oriental Society, *Transactions* 6 (1929–1933): 51–60.
4. See the article "Sir," in *Shorter Encyclopedia of Islam,* ed. H. A. R. Gibb and J. H. Kramers (Ithaca, N.Y.: Cornell University Press, 1953), pp. 545–547. Cf. "Magic," in Thomas P. Hughes, *A Dictionary of Islam* (London: W. H. Allen, 1935), pp. 303–305;

and Samuel M. Zwemer, *The Influence of Animism on Islam* (New York: Macmillan, 1920), chap. 9, "Magic and Sorcery."

5. Quoted in Seyyed Hossein Nasr, *Ideals and Realities of Islam* (Boston: Beacon Press, 1972), p. 59.
6. Franz Rosenthal, trans., *The Muqaddimah: An Introduction to History,* vol. 2 (Princeton, N.J.: Princeton University Press, 1967), p. 447.
7. From *al-Kashshāf,* as translated in Helmut Gätje, *The Qur'an and Its Exegesis,* trans. and ed. Alford T. Welch (London: Routledge & Kegan Paul, 1976), p. 60.
8. *Ibid.,* p. 250. The original is from Muhammad 'Abduh and Rashīd Riḍā', *tafsīr al-qur'ān al-ḥakīm,* 2 vols (Cairo: A.H. 1325–1353, 1907–1934 C.E.).
9. An absorbing analysis is Mustansir Mir, *Coherence in the Qur'ān* (Indianapolis: American Trust Publications, 1986).
10. Al-Baghawī, *Mishkāt al-Masābīh,* vol. 2, trans. James Robson (Lahore, Pakistan: Sh. Muhammad Ashraf, 1965–1966), pp. 446, 462ff.
11. As retold by Anwar Chejne, *The Arabic Language: Its Role in History* (Minneapolis: University of Minnesota Press, 1969), p. 12.
12. An excellent introduction is Martin Lings, *The Qur'anic Art of Calligraphy and Illumination* (London: World of Islam Festival Trust, 1976).

CHAPTER

# 7 The Prophet's Sunna as Preserved in the Ḥadīth

### KEY TERMS

***sunna* and *sunan***
***ḥadīth***
***isnād***
***matn***
***saḥīḥ***
***ḥasan***
***mawlid al-nabī***
***baraka***

## MUHAMMAD AND SCRIPTURE

The shahāda's first clause is "There is no god but God," and the Qur'an contains God's message of warning and success for those who listen and obey. But there is a second clause that must also be uttered before one is a true Muslim: "Muhammad is the Messenger of God." It does not imply worship of that human being—to do so would be idolatry—but it does imply a special character and destiny that Muslims discern in their Prophet. It is as difficult to imagine Islam without Muhammad as Christianity without Jesus, even though the two play very different roles in the religions that they founded and have different places in doctrine and practice. Both, however, were so close to the source of their inspiration and so thoroughly dominated by it that in their words and gestures people have discerned clues and demonstrations of divine activity in the historical process. For Christians, Jesus shows how God behaves among his creatures. Muhammad's life is exemplary in showing people how they should behave in the presence of God. The Muslims move heavenward through Muhammad, whereas the Christians receive their Lord in his earthward condescension, which later moves toward an ascension.

## *Sunna and Ḥadīth*

Muhammad's own voice had peculiar authority during his lifetime. While he was Prophet in Mecca and later Medina, the *qur'āns* that Muhammad received gained in prestige and power, but so did his own words and acts. Muhammad's extraordinary qualities as leader and friend seemed to be of fundamental importance in ensuring the Qur'an's acceptance, but his growing influence in turn was largely brought about by the "gracious Qur'an." The two—prophet and book—are inextricably bound up in each other in a manner perhaps unduplicated by any other scripture. Because of this, the Muslims came to recall and collect all that could be retrieved of Muhammad's life after he had died. The word **sunna** (pl. **sunan**) was used to name the Prophet's "custom," his words, deeds, and habitual practices. This word was well known in Arabic and denoted a pattern of behavior that people follow. It is then, originally, a general term. But when applied to Muhammad, it became a special term that denoted the category of exemplary words, deeds, and gestures that were destined to be authoritative in the life of the umma. The Sunna is an idea as well as a memory, and even more it is an ideal for Muslim behavior. As such it is engrained in the lives of pious Muslims and handed down by example and personal teaching.

The Sunna is also remembered and transmitted by means of a literary form called ***ḥadīth.*** The word *ḥadīth* has root meanings of "being new" and "occurring, taking place, coming to pass," and extends to talking about or reporting what has happened. Thus a *ḥadīth* came to be a "report" of something that had taken place. When such a narrative referred to Muhammad and his companions, it became a "tradition" in that it was passed down from generation to generation. The Sunna (in the collective sense of all that Muhammad left by way of teaching and example) of the Prophet, then, is preserved and communicated in a major way by means of *ḥadīths*. They were remembered and transmitted by many different people in a wide variety of contexts and regions. Eventually, scholars developed methods of sifting through and evaluating them, weeding out questionable or spurious ones and preserving authentic ones in systematically arranged collections. This process took over two centuries. But when it was completed, the Muslims had a solid second source of authoritative teaching to assist them in all aspects of their individual and corporate religious, social, civil, and legal life.

The Qur'an continued to be the most authoritative source for Islamic doctrine and practice, but in many cases the *ḥadīths* confirmed, extended, elaborated, explained, and supplemented the revelation as a scriptural complement to the Qur'an. Muhammad was obviously considered the best interpreter of the message, and beyond his explanations of Qur'anic passages, all of his words and acts gradually came to be regarded as exemplary and worthy of imitation.

This attitude led to the development of an ideal and perfect view of the Prophet. In Christianity one can distinguish between the Jesus of history and the Christ of faith, in that the former is the human being who walked the streets and byways of Galilee and ended up on a cross in Jerusalem as a criminal, and the latter is the perfect, eternal, risen savior who continues to intercede for and inspire those who love him and believe in him as the Lord of all life. Although Islam's doctrine of prophethood, and especially its understanding of Muhammad's nature, is far different from the incarnationalism of Christianity, there nevertheless is a sense that Muhammad continues to inspire and lead through his Sunna. There is, thus, a Muhammad of history and a Prophet of faith. In some sectarian views, Muhammad even takes on some of the attributes of other holy personages, such as preexistence before the creation of Adam, preeminence above all created things, and perfect wisdom. All Muslims regard Muhammad, along with all the preceding prophets, as having been sinless. There is a great range of views concerning Muhammad, from a regard for him as a hero and founder, whose example lives on in the memory of his umma, all the way to elaborate ideas of his perfection and continuing influence.

## THE FORM OF THE ḤADĪTH

Before considering specific details of the Sunna of Muhammad and related matters such as hagiography, it will be helpful to examine the form of the *ḥadīth* and how it came to be preserved and employed by the Muslims. (When the word is capitalized, it refers to the whole corpus of traditions.) The diffusion of Muhammad's teaching began with his own initiatives in advising and counseling his companions, commanding them always to remember his words and acts. From those times onward, Muslims took pains to remember everything they could about Muhammad and to disseminate this information to others. But this does not seem to have been done systematically, and so the science of *ḥadīth* did not achieve maturity until long after the Prophet's time.

The teaching of Muhammad, as distinguished from the recitation of the Qur'anic revelations, although the one took place alongside the other, was often prompted by questions and practical issues that arose in the normal course of daily life. Like Moses before him, Muhammad "judged" the people and, in the absence of a higher authority, took upon himself the responsibility of breaking new ground in many of his pronouncements and decisions. But as we pointed out earlier, Muhammad also was able to draw on custom and tribal precedent in many situations in which they did not contradict or subvert the Islamic way.

The companions passed on their memories of Muhammad's teaching and behavior in the form of *ḥadīths,* which sometimes were preserved within family lines of transmission or spread by other channels. The companions memorized, wrote down (though 'Umar opposed this), and followed the *ḥadīth,* all three being means of transmission and conservation. The last seems to have been an especially powerful means by which Muhammad's memory was grafted onto the umma and ingrained into the Muslims' attitudes and behavior patterns.

### *Parts and Arrangements of Ḥadīths*

The following is a typical *ḥadīth,* whose parts and arrangements will be explained:

> Yaḥyāibn Yaḥyā related to us: "Abu Haythama reported to us, from Abī Isḥāq, from al-Barā' [who] said: 'A man was reciting Sura al-Kahf and nearby him was

> a horse tied with two ropes, and a cloud came over him, and as it came nearer his horse began to shy from it. He went and mentioned that to the Prophet—upon whom be blessing and peace—and he replied: "That was the Sakīna which descended because of the Qur'an recitation."""[1]

***Isnād.*** This *ḥadīth* has two main parts. The first is the opening citation of the persons who transmitted it, called the ***isnād,*** a documentation process meaning "prop, support, backing." It is the chain of ascriptions by which a report is authenticated. Each link is a person who has been involved in its transmission. The second and main part of the *ḥadīth* is called the **matn,** the "main text." In this case it is the story of the horse that was startled by the sacred energy that descended in the Sakīna when the Qur'an was recited. (This is a parallel to the Jewish *shechina,* which is the "presence of God in the world.") The Muslims developed an intricate science of *ḥadīth* evaluation based on, among other things, close scrutiny of the *isnād.* It is possible to fabricate a plausible-sounding *ḥadīth,* and so the *isnād* came to be regarded as a crucial index of authenticity.

This is powerful testimony, again, to the importance of the believers in carrying on true Islamic doctrine and observance from generation to generation. A special subdiscipline known as "the science of men" (*'ilm al-rijāl*) developed, which collected all available information pertaining to every person mentioned in the *isnāds* of the growing *ḥadīth.* Such characteristics as quality of memory, reputation for telling the truth, piety, and general intelligence were considered to be important factors in evaluating the chains of authorities. Other relevant items of biographical and historical information were the contacts, travels, habits, and periods of people listed in the *isnāds.* For example, a thoroughly reliable individual may be proved to have been unable to have received from or transmitted to someone else a *ḥadīth* because he was never in the same place or lived at the same time as the other. This quickly becomes a complex matter. One collector of *ḥadīths,* al-Bukhārī, traveled very widely in pursuit of them. He is reported to have collected in all some 600,000. But many of them were duplicates, and many more were found by him to be weak or questionable, and so he finally selected 9,082 *ḥadīths* with differing *isnāds.* And when repetitions of the *matn* are counted, the number comes to only 2,602.[2]

***Collectors of Ḥadīths.*** It was the Prophet's companions who began collecting and transmitting *ḥadīths.* These came soon to exist in written as well as oral form, although like the Qur'an, the latter was preferred and regarded as more authentic. Some of the companions who collected large numbers of *ḥadīths* were Abu Hurayra, Ibn 'Umar, Anas Ibn Mālik, Ibn Mas'ūd, 'Amr ibn al-'As, the caliphs 'Umar and 'Alī, and, especially, 'A'isha. Some of these persons transmitted over 2,000 separate *ḥadīths,* but it must be remembered that these sometimes were duplicates that only had different *isnāds.* For example, Abū Hurayra is thought to have transmitted 5,374 *ḥadīths,* but many merely have different channels or *isnāds.* The actual number of separate *matns* is only 1,236, a respectable number nonetheless.[3]

### *Authenticity of Ḥadīths*

As we mentioned, the "science of men" developed so that the *ḥadīths* could be tested for their authenticity. This became an intricate as well as a historically useful and interesting field, whose sophisticated complexity can only be hinted at here.[4] There are many extant discussions of individual persons. It was essential for an individual to possess both moral character (*'adl*) and literary accuracy of the rarest quality before he could be called trustworthy (*thiqa*). Such a person's transmissions are universally accepted by *ḥadīth* scholars. The next level included transmitters whose morals were unexceptionable but whose literary skills were less than perfect. They are called *ṣadūq,* meaning "truthful." His *ḥadīths* are generally acceptable, unless contradicted by a transmitter at the *thiqa* level. Then there are other categories on a descending scale, including "weak" (*ḍa'īf*), "liar," "forger," "unknown," and others. A weak tradition is acceptable only if it is bolstered by another transmitter in a closely parallel *ḥadīth,* but such a report does not have high status. As one expert has recently put it, such a *ḥadīth* is a bit like a grade of *D* on an exam: passing but far from admirable.[5]

***Categories of Ḥadīths.*** The acceptable *ḥadīths* are graded according to the categories of ***ṣaḥīḥ.*** and ***ḥasan,*** which mean, respectively, "sound" and "acceptable" (literally, "beautiful"). These two classes are further subdivided according to their relationships with others, but we need not go into the details. Unacceptable *ḥadīths* are also divided into two groups, those that are provisionally rejected until some support can be found and those that are unconditionally rejected and will never be accepted. To give some sense of what a *ḥadīth* must be in order to be considered "sound" (*ṣaḥīḥ*), it must first have a perfectly linked and unblemished *isnād* all the way back to the first transmitter, who would be the one who received it from the Prophet himself. It should not contradict other narrations that occur in greater numbers or versions. Finally, there should be no "hidden defect," as it is called. A majority of scholars may have transmitted a *ḥadīth* from a companion as his or her statement in fact, whereas the one in question represented it as being directly from the Prophet. Such a *ḥadīth* may be regarded as sound if the *isnād* is impeccable. It was simply a mistake and is labeled as such. This does not stand as a black mark against the narrator.

We have gone into this question of authentication in some detail because it is so important to Islamic scholarship and piety. Experts in the science of *ḥadīth* are concerned about purity of transmission, and their books and discussions brim with relevant data. The average newcomer to Islamic studies typically wants to "get to the bottom" of the *ḥadīth* business, which usually means the *matn,* containing the actual narrative. This is natural and obviously important to the Muslim, too. But before the Muslim can rest easy, he or she always first examines the quality of the transmission. Books on Islamic subjects frequently have extensive appendices containing the names of the transmitters. Sometimes these books do not contain any index to the *ḥadīth matns* themselves, at least in minute detail. Rather, they will list general categories of topics.

### *Muslim Historiography*

Muslim historiography also developed using the *isnād* approach for basic documentation. In the section of al-Ṭabarī's great history that discusses the death of the third caliph, 'Uthmān, several different versions of the event are included, each with its chain of transmitters. Although this does not offer convenient sequential reading, at least for one not initiated into this type of historiography, it does lay out the entire range of extant source material together with the persons who preserved and transmitted it. In the case of 'Uthmān 's controversial end, one can read between the lines as one sees how the details and points of view differ among the various narrators. Al-Ṭabarī prudently remains silent most of the time, but his arrangement of the individual sources is significant. Similarly, both the *matns* and the *isnāds* of *ḥadīths* from, or purportedly from, the Prophet and his companions are usually worth examining. Even if a report is proved or at least suspected to be a forgery, it may nevertheless tell the scholar something interesting and useful about the party or parties that invented it.

### *Fraudulent Ḥadīths*

Modern, non-Muslim, Western scholars have tended to be highly skeptical of most *ḥadīths,* often rejecting prophetic authenticity on modern historiographical and literary-critical grounds. But even the most critical must admit that the *ḥadīths* do in fact convey extremely valuable and pertinent data about the social and intellectual world of early Islam. *Somebody* had to write them, because there is no question of their antiquity! This, of course, is a matter on which Muslim scholars cannot agree with many of their non-Muslim colleagues.[6] If an esteemed ancient authority has declared a *ḥadīth* to be sound, and that judgment has stood the test of centuries of subsequent scrutiny, then the matter is closed. And besides, such *ḥadīths* will already have been fully incorporated into the Islamic legal system as fundamental sources of doctrine and practice, second in authority only to the Qur'an.

The *ḥadīth* experts of Islam have been well aware since earliest times that many *ḥadīths* were fraudulent. Why would anyone ever fabricate a report purportedly narrating something that the Prophet said or did?[7] Sometimes this was done from sincere if misguided motives and sometimes from malice or to avoid punishment. Examples of the former are the serving of sectarian or regional interests by attributing a special saying to Muhammad. One such case involved the fabrication of *ḥadīths* about the excellence of each sūra of the Qur'an. When the perpetrator was discovered, he defended himself by saying that he was trying to protect the Muslims from a certain school of law. He had produced a pious fraud. The latter type of intentional fabrication stemmed from anti-Islamic sentiments or personal interest. All *ḥadīth* forgery is regarded as criminal behavior, but the latter types are especially detested. One forger was crucified after it was discovered that he had fabricated a *ḥadīth* suggesting that Allah might will that another prophet come after Muhammad. Thus the science of *ḥadīth* was developed in part to combat the growing misuse of the institution.

## MAJOR COLLECTIONS OF ḤADĪTH

### *Mālik*

The first substantial and carefully sifted collection of *ḥadīth* was made by Mālik Ibn Anas, who lived in Umayyad times and worked mostly in Medina. His name is given to the school of jurisprudence that he founded, the Mālikī school. Mālik was a descendant of a companion of the Prophet and was in a good position to preserve authentic materials from Muhammad's time. His greatest work is the *Muwaṭṭa'* ("beaten path"), which contains traditions of the Prophet, legal decisions of the early Muslim jurists, and reports of the companions. This work is one of the most highly respected of all *ḥadīth* collections and is still essential to scholarship and law. Imām Mālik was a brilliant scholar whose intellectual gifts were exceeded only by his legendary piety. He was also independent, even of the authorities. It is reported that when the mighty caliph Hārūn al-Rashīd visited Medina to pay his respects at the tomb of the Prophet, he greeted Mālik and asked him to come to his residence every day to teach his two sons. Mālik replied: "O Caliph, science is of a dignified nature, and instead of going to any person, requires that all should come to it."[8] Hārūn al-Rashīd was taken aback by this haughty reply, and although other rulers might have thrown Mālik in prison for insubordination and disrespect, this caliph apologized and sent his sons to Mālik 's class, where they sat among commoners to receive instruction. Toward the end of his life, Mālik withdrew into a life of spiritual reflection and died in 795 C.E. at the advanced age of eighty-five.

### *Aḥmad Ibn Ḥanbal*

Another leading collector of *ḥadīth* was the Baghdad jurisconsult Aḥmad Ibn Ḥanbal, who was active in the generation after Mālik. He was a stubbornly orthoprax Muslim who spent long periods in prison and was beaten for his rejection of the "rationalist" theological views of the Mu'tazilites, who were favored at court as the empire's official school. Aḥmad is said to have memorized a million *ḥadīths,* which he used to develop yet another law school, which bears his name. Ibn Ḥanbal compiled a collection of *ḥadīth* called the *Musnad,* so-called because it is arranged according to the *isnāds* of specific companions. This makes it very hard to use, even for experts, because there is no subject arrangement. It is estimated that the *Musnad* contains upwards of 40,000 *ḥadīths.* (They have not yet been counted.)[9] Ibn anbal died in 855 at the age of seventy-five, and reportedly nearly a million people attended his funeral. Before he died, his views were exonerated, and he even was granted a generous gift of money by the caliph, which he refused.

### *Bukhārī and Muslim*

Two of Aḥmad Ibn anbal's younger contemporaries became famous for their even greater contributions to the science of *ḥadīth,* Muhammad Ismā'īl al-Bukhārī (d. 870), from Bukharā' in Central Asia, and Muslim Ibn al-Ḥajjāj (d. 875), from the

Persian city of Nishapur. Each traveled widely in search of authentic traditions and in order to take them down orally and thus cross-checking them according to a variety of informants in a single geographical area. Each man tried to collect as many sound traditions as possible, and each finally published a collection called *ṣaḥīh,* meaning "sound" or "authentic." The two together are known as *al-ṣaḥīhān,* "The two sound [collections of *Ḥadīth*]" and are considered to be the best of all such collections. With al-Bukhārī and Muslim, the science of *ḥadīth* reached its maturity, and the student of their works will learn how perceptive, thorough, and critical historical and textual studies had become by the third century after the Prophet. Of significance is the part played by personal piety and integrity in pursuing the study and application of sacred texts like the *ḥadīth* and the Qur'an but also the supporting sources such as the biographies that examine the lives and habits of those who are mentioned in the *isnāds.* In other words, Muslim scholarship is not a disinterested affair, as modern scholarship claims to be; it was and continues to be closely related to the central concerns of faith and practice within the umma.

There is something heroic in the lives of many of the pioneering Muslim scholars. Looking back through layers of tradition and legend, it may appear that individuals like Bukhārī, Muslim, and Aḥmad ibn Ḥanbal simply rose easily to the top as great leaders and scholars. Not so. Bukhārī was quite poor and sometimes had to beg for food as he traveled alone across the central Islamic lands in search of *ḥadīths.*[10] Nor was he a sedentary scholar, aloof from the practical and worldly issues of his day. He was a fine marksman with the bow and spent time regularly in that martial art so as to be ready for *jihād* at a moment's notice. He possessed that quality known as *ḥilm* with respect to others and especially his inferiors in scholarship. Gentle and moderate in his technical criticisms of former as well as contemporary lesser lights in the science of *ḥadīth,* Bukhārī's meaning was nevertheless clear. But his manner of demonstrating the correct way in the science was by example much more than by *ad hominem* reproof and rebuttal. Once while visiting Baghdad, a group of local *ḥadīth* experts gathered to examine Bukhārī's knowledge of their subject. Ten of them each recited ten *ḥadīths,* but each (without Bukhārī's knowledge) mixed up the *isnāds* and the *matns.* As the purposely bogus *ḥadīths* were recited, Bukhārī in every instance said: "Not known to me." Most of those in attendance thought Bukhārī to be a very poor scholar, for the *matns* were familiar to everyone. But the few who were in on the test recognized the visitor's sharpness. After the last phony *ḥadīth* had been recited, Bukhārī then proceeded to correct the whole list, matching *isnād* with *matn* and explaining their fine points. You see, without the proper *isnād,* the *matn* is worthless.

### *The Sunnī Collections*

In addition to the collections of Bukhārī and Muslim, there are four collections of *ḥadīth* that are universally accepted by the Sunnīs. These collections were made by al-Tirmidhī, Abu Dā'ūd al-Sijistānī, al-Nasā'i, and Ibn Mājah, all of whom were contemporaries. These collections are called "The six books," or even "The six *ṣaḥīḥs*" and have almost a canonical prestige, although no universally "official" collection of *ḥadīth* has ever been recognized by the Muslims. After all, the Qur'an is unquestionably fundamental, perfect, and beyond question for all believers. Each of the six books of traditions is arranged according to subject, a great improvement over the earlier collections, like Ibn anbal's *Musnad,* which were arranged by *isnād.* The four other collections just listed (in addition to Bukhārī's and Muslim's) also contain *ḥasan* and even *ḍa 'īf,* "beautiful" and "weak" traditions, because of their use in legal contexts. Thus on certain topics, valuable information can be gained that is lacking in "the two *ṣaḥīḥs,*" although admittedly it does not have the authority of the sound material.

The inclusion of less surely authentic *ḥadīths* in the other four collections should not be considered unfortunate. The collectors were fully aware of the quality of materials that they included, were usually scrupulous about labeling them correctly, and even sometimes warned their readers to reject them. (Ibn Mājah did not always identify false *ḥadīths,* but his scholarship was exemplary otherwise.) These scholars included materials that before and until their time had been actually used in law as authoritative precept and precedent.

### *Other Collections*

There are many collections of *ḥadīth* beyond the ones already mentioned. The Shī'īs have their own tradition of scholarship and collecting *ḥadīths* and generally reject the Sunnīs's, although some *ḥadīths* appear in both branches. The Shī'īs recognize five collections as being authoritative and in general accept only those *ḥadīths* that were transmitted by 'Alī and his partisans. In addition to the collections of *ḥadīth* that contain reports of sayings and acts of the Prophet and his companions, there is a collection, entitled *Nahj al-Balāgha* ("The way of eloquence"), that contains sayings attributed to 'Alī, son-in-law of Muhammad and the first imām of the Shī'īs.

There is one popular and widely used collection of *ḥadīth* that draws largely on Bukhārī and Muslim but also includes many other sources. This is known as *Mishkāt al-Masābīḥ* ("Niche for lights") and was collected by Husayn al-Baghawī, who lived in the fifth and sixth Islamic centuries. This work exists in an excellent four-volume English translation by James Robson, thus extending the English-speaking student's access to authentic Islamic tradition. (This work has already been cited frequently in the notes.) Although Bukhārī's and Muslim's books are also now available in English translations, the *Mishkāt* contains a greater range of material owing to its diversity of sources. It is arranged into twenty-six books on the following list of topics: faith, knowledge, purification, prayer, funerals, zakāt, fasting, the excellent qualities of the Qur'an, supplications, God's names, the rites of pilgrimage, business transactions, marriage, emancipation of slaves, retaliation, prescribed punishments, the office of commander and *qāḍī* (judge), jihād, game and animals that may be slaughtered, foods, clothing, medicine and spells, visions, general behavior, words that soften the heart, and *fitan* ("trials and afflictions" that will come to pass before the resurrection). The subdivisions of each section are quite detailed. For example, the book about general behavior includes such topics as salutations, shaking hands and embracing, sneezing and yawning, making promises, boasting, anger and pride, and laughing. All of the traditions direct the reader toward reputable conduct as befits a Muslim. In every case Muhammad's example or explicit teaching is cited as the final authority. Because of the practical, as opposed to the scholarly, nature of the work, the *isnāds* are omitted, and all that is usually given is the final (that is, the first) transmitter, plus the collection (Muslim, Tirmidhī, or whatever) in which it was included.

## THE PROPHET'S AND HIS COMPANIONS' SUNNAS

The Prophet's Sunna is believed to be contained in the *ḥadīth,* as was stated in the beginning of this chapter. If the Qur'an unites the Muslims doctrinally and devotionally through its contents and recited cadences, then the Sunna unites them in the myriad details of daily behavior and attitudes, including correct ritual practices. Muslims who have internalized the Sunna feel at home among their brothers and sisters in the faith wherever they may be throughout the world. Although languages, foods, dress, local customs, and national identities may vary, those dimensions of belief, behavior, and attitude that are enshrined in the *ḥadīth* of the Prophet at the same time provide a unified field of meaning and action. This idea had been memorably expressed by an influential contemporary Muslim scholar:

> For nearly fourteen hundred years Muslims have tried to awaken in the morning as the Prophet awakened, to eat as he ate, to wash as he washed himself, even to cut their nails as he did. There has been no greater force for the unification of the Muslim peoples than the presence of this common model for the minutest acts of daily life. A Chinese Muslim, although racially a Chinese, has a countenance, behavior, manner of walking and acting that resembles in certain ways those of a Muslim on the coast of the Atlantic. That is because both have for centuries copied the same model. Something of the soul of the Prophet is to be seen in both places. It is this essential unifying factor, a common *Sunnah* or way of living as a model, that makes a bazaar in Morocco have a "feeling" or *ambiance* of a bazaar in Persia, although the people in the two places speak a different language and dress differently. There is something in the air which an intelligent foreign observer will immediately detect as belonging to the same religious and spiritual climate. And this sameness is brought about firstly through the presence of the Qur'an and secondly, and in a more immediate and tangible way, through the "presence" of the Prophet in his community by virtue of his *Ḥadīth* and *Sunnah.*[11]

So far only *ḥadīths* that convey something of Muhammad's Sunna, and to some extent the Sunna of his companions, have been discussed. But this latter category deserves some mention, because it has also had considerable influence. That is, Muhammad's contemporaries, specifically those who helped him develop the early umma, remain highly authoritative personages for the subsequent Muslim ages.

Although Muhammad's example is by far the most authoritative, the words and deeds of his circle also carry weight and have been incorporated into the correct pattern of life ever since.

### *The Ḥadīth Qudsī*

There is another type of *ḥadīth,* earlier mentioned briefly, that is different from the usual ones. This is the "divine saying," or *ḥadīth qudsī*, a revelation from God but couched in Muhammad's own words, according to most experts, although some regard the wording to be God's but distinct from the Qur'anic revelation and ontologically inferior because of its generation within time. By contrast, the Qur'an is viewed as eternal. The *ḥadīth qudsī* has never had an important place in the Islamic legal systems, but it has been prominent in Muslim piety, especially the more mystical varieties. Mostly these sayings are spiritual, dealing with topics closely connected with prayer, and goodness, and devotional piety. A universally known example is

> God says: "I fulfill My servant's expectation of Me, and I am with him when he remembers Me. If he remembers Me in his heart, I remember him in my heart; and if he remembers Me in public, I remember him before a public [far] better than that. And if he draws nearer to Me by a handsbreadth, I draw nearer to him by an armslength; and if he draws nearer to Me by an armslength, I draw nearer to him by a fathom; and if he comes to Me walking, I come to him running."[12]

This is a striking saying and tells us much about the special quality of the *ḥadīth qudsī* as a source of great comfort and inspiration for the Muslim in his or her private devotion. In inspiration it is regarded as originating with God, but in wording it is inferior in that it lacks the *i'jāz,* that "inimitability" that all Muslims recognize in the Qur'an.

## MUHAMMAD AS AN IDEAL HUMAN

The Muhammad of history can still be discerned in the *ḥadīths* that preserve and communicate his Sunna. But over the centuries this Muhammad became far bigger than life as popular piety came to exalt him far above ordinary mortals. This development is known by the scholarly term of hagiography, which literally means "writing about saintliness." It is known in virtually every religious tradition, and there are often similar details shared by different traditions. Typically, hagiography idealizes the heroes and saints of religion by attributing to them such things as miraculous births, wondrous deeds, and exemplary characteristics. The story, recounted earlier, of Muhammad being discovered by Bahira the Christian monk when he was accompanying the caravan to Syria, is a good example of hagiography. The mark of prophecy was discerned between the boy's shoulders, whereupon the monk warned about possible troubles from the Jews if Muhammad did not go home immediately. Likewise, the shade that was seen hovering over the boy Muhammad, even when the sun was shining all around him, is a hagiographical detail.

Muhammad is regarded as the universal human and thus the exemplary model of what full human life should be. As the Qur'an expresses it, "You have had a good example in God's Messenger for whosoever hopes for God and the Last Day, and remembers God oft" (33:21). One school of thought even regards Muhammad as the Logos that existed before the earth and its inhabitants and is in perfect union with God inwardly and active in the world outwardly. In this view, which has been championed by Sufi mystics, Muhammad is at once the original model for prophecy and its final seal. He both begins and completes what is considered to be a historical cycle of prophetic awareness and activity. Therefore, Muhammad sums up all true prophecy that has been made available to humans in the world in the whole range of religious traditions that has come into being. As one famous *ḥadīth* described Muhammad's eternal and divine nature:

> I am Aḥmad without the *mīm* [the letter *m,* without which the word becomes Ahad, "One," a name of God]: I am an Arab without the *'ayn* [the first letter, which leaves *rab(b),* meaning "Lord"]. Who has seen me has therefore seen the Truth [that is, God].[13]

A Persian mystical poem provides an interesting variant on the Aḥmad theme: "A single *mīm* divides Aḥad from Aḥmad; the world is immersed in that one *mīm.*"[14] Aḥmad is itself a variant of Muhammad and stands as the title that Muslims see as the New Testament prophecy of the Paraclete that is to come after Jesus. The Qur'anic acknowledgment of this is as follows:

> And when Jesus son of Mary said, "Children of Israel, I am indeed the Messenger of God to you, confirming the Torah that is before me, and giving good tidings of a Messenger who shall come after me, whose name shall be Aḥmad." (61:6)

(This is a debated issue between Christians and Muslims, but the former consider the Paraclete to have come on Pentecost in the Holy Spirit. The Gospel of John represents Jesus as having promised a "counselor" or "advocate" that would come after him. The Qur'anic Aḥmad, meaning "praised," is a translation of the Greek *periklytos,* meaning the same thing. But in John [14:16, 26; 15:26; 16:7] the Greek word is *parakletos,* meaning "counselor," "comforter," or "advocate." Thus the near homonyms actually have radically different meanings in Islam and Christianity.)[15]

## *The Symbology of Muhammad*

The developed Muslim view of Muhammad provides an extensive symbology by which the faithful are able to view space, time, and the human condition in satisfying ways. We shall see this richness especially in Sufism, which traces all true spiritual wisdom back to Muhammad and through him to God. Perhaps the special love and respect that Muslims have for their prophet can be better understood and appreciated by non-Muslims when they consider how much more there is to this than the historical biography of the great man who fourteen centuries ago in Hejaz called the Arabs to obedience and faith. The believers' identification with their Prophet by cultivating his Sunna is thus a way of salvation or, better, "success" (*falāh.*), both in this life and the life to come with God. It is impossible to overemphasize how much joy and inspiration Muslims experience in learning about Muhammad and striving to be worthy to emulate his Sunna, for by doing this a portion of paradise is brought into life on earth in the present age. And anyone whose name is Muhammad possesses an extra portion of the Prophet's **baraka,** "blessing."

On the occasion of the Prophet's birthday (***mawlid al-nabī***), Muslims sing songs and recite poems of praise and celebration in his honor. One such poem that has become nearly universally known and recited among Muslims is the "Mantle Ode" of the thirteenth-century Berber al-Busīrī. The name of the poem derives from the author's having been miraculously cured of paralysis by Muhammad's *burda* ("mantle"), when the Prophet came to him in a dream and spread it over the suffering man. The following brief section vividly conveys the special quality that Muslims see in their beloved hero:

> He is the one whose interior and exterior form were made perfect,
> Then the Creator of men chose him as a beloved friend.
> Far removed [is he] from having any partner in his good qualities,
> For in him the essence of goodness is undivided.
>
> • • •
>
> Ascribe to his person whatever nobility you desire,
> And ascribe to his dignity whatever grandeur you please.
> For verily, the excellence of the Apostle of Allah has no bounds,
> So that a speaker might tell of it with his mouth.
>
> • • •
>
> Every sign which the [other] noble Messengers have produced,
> Was obtained only because of his light which was with them.
> He is the sun of excellence, they are but its stars,
> Which show their light to folk [only] in the darkness.
> So that when it rises in the cosmos its guidance embraces
> The worlds, and revives all peoples.
> How excellent is the person of the Prophet! Good nature adorns him.
> Cloaked [is he] in beauty, marked by a joyful countenance.
> Like a flower in delicate freshness; like the full moon in splendor,
> Like the sea in bountifulness, and like time in aspiration.
> Even when he is alone in his majesty, it is as though
> He were in the midst of soldiers, with attendants thrown around him.
> It is as though a pearl hidden in an oyster were
> In the two mines of his speech and his smile [that is, Muhammad's teeth].
> No perfume can equal the dust that has gathered on his limbs,
> Happy is he who can sniff the odour thereof or can kiss [them].[16]

Although Muslim doctrine certainly insists that Muhammad was never more than a human like others, although without sin, the student of comparative religion is well within the responsible bounds of scholarship in characterizing the subject of such an ode as al-Busīrī's as functionally divine. Popular piety's conviction of Muhammad's virtues and graces is reinforced by the Qur'an's own high regard for him. "God and His angels bless the Prophet, O believers, do you also bless him, and pray him peace" (33:56). Therefore, when they mention their Prophet's name, devout Muslims immediately follow it with the phrase *Ṣallā Allāhu 'alayhi wa sallam,* which means "May God bless him and grant him peace." Frequently this is shortened in English to "Peace be upon him" and, in writing, to PBUH, often in parentheses following the name Muhammad or the title Prophet or Messenger.[17]

## NOTES

1. *Saḥīḥ Muslim,* vol. 6, with commentary by al-Nawawī (Cairo: al-Maṭba' al-Miṣrīya wa Maktabatuhā, 1964), p. 81-2 (Book 6, Kitāb Ṣalāt al-Musāfirīn).
2. Muhammad Mustafa Azami, *Studies in Ḥadīth Methodology and Literature* (Indianapolis: American Trust Publications, 1977), p. 89.
3. *Ibid.,* p. 26.
4. For a fuller discussion, see *ibid.,* Chapter 7.
5. *Ibid.,* p. 59.
6. Two important modern critical works are by Ignaz Goldziher, "On the Development of the *Ḥadīth,*" in his *Muslim Studies,* vol. 2 (Chicago: Aldine, 1966), pp. 17–251; and Joseph Schacht, *The Origins of Muhammadan Jurisprudence* (Oxford, England: Clarendon Press, 1950), pt. I, chaps. 1–6. Two significant Muslim critiques of the works of Goldziher and Schacht on the *Ḥadīth* are by Fazlur Rahman, *Islam* (New York: Anchor Books, 1968), chap. 3; and Muhammad Mustafa Azami, *Studies in Early Ḥadīth Literature,* 2nd ed. (Indianapolis: American Trust Publications, 1978), especially chaps. 1, 6, and 7.
7. This paragraph is based on Azami, *Methodology and Literature,* pt. I, chap. 8, "Fabrication of *Ḥadīth:* Causes and Means of Elimination," pp. 68–72.
8. Thomas P. Hughes, *A Dictionary of Islam* (London: W. H. Allen, 1935), p. 312.
9. Azami, *Methodology and Literature,* p. 86.
10. Paragraph based on *ibid.,* pp. 87–88.
11. Seyyed Hossein Nasr, *Ideals and Realities of Islam* (Boston: Beacon Press, 1972), pp. 82–83.
12. William A. Graham, *Divine Word and Prophetic Word in Early Islam* (The Hague and Paris: Mouton, 1977), p. 127.
13. Adapted from Nasr, *Ideals and Realities of Islam,* p. 89.
14. *Ibid.*
15. For a clear discussion, see Geoffrey Parrinder, *Jesus in the Qur'ān* (New York: Oxford University Press, 1977), pp. 96–100.
16. As translated by Arthur Jeffery in his anthology, *A Reader on Islam* (The Hague: Mouton, 1962), pp. 610–611. The entire "Mantle ode" appears on pp. 606–621.
17. An abundantly exampled and sophisticated appreciation of Muhammad's place in the hearts of Muslims is Annemarie Schimmel's *And Muhammad Is His Messenger: The Veneration of the Prophet in Islamic Piety* (Chapel Hill and London: The University of North Carolina Press, 1985).

CHAPTER

# 8 Muslim Creeds and Theologies: Their Purposes and Varieties

**KEY TERMS**

| | | |
|---|---|---|
| ***'ilm*** | ***'ilm al-tawḥīd*** | **Qadarites** |
| ***'ālim*** | ***mutakallim*** | **Jabarites** |
| ***'ulamā'*** | **Khārijites** | **Mu'tazilites** |
| ***'ilm al-kalām*** | **Murji'ites** | ***'aqīda*** |

## THEOLOGY

Westerners, especially those who have been influenced in their religious thinking mainly by Christianity, tend to consider theology the core concern for understanding and communicating a particular set of beliefs. This assumption carries over in the general society to educational contexts. It is common for an American college student who enrolls in an academic course in a secular religious studies department, as, for example, in a state university, to be regarded by the uninitiated as a "theology" student. Without regard for whether the course in question concerns "cargo cults," puberty rites, burial ceremonies, or religious autobiography, the uninformed will call it, before examining it, "theology." Of course we are seeing here the ignorance of both what theology is and is not and the misunderstanding of the academic study of religion. There seems to be an assumption that any intellectual inquiry concerning religion is theology. This view probably comes from theology's long dominance among the religious sciences of Christianity.

But theology is properly a religiously committed intellectual discipline, in that it seeks to provide an intellectual structure for the elements of faith and practice of persons united in a common tradition. Theologians begin with a foundation of scriptures, creeds, assertions, and doctrines and then elaborate on and systematize them by means of a disciplined discourse in order to explicate the faith for the believers and defend it against the attacks of outsiders. Theology is both a normative and constructive discipline, starting from faith and returning to it. It is not disinterested or purely intellectual, although it usually strives to be reasonable, balanced, and verifiable beyond its own borders of belief and life. In the last sense, it may be associated with evangelistic and missionary enterprises, by demonstrating the truth of religious worldview to those whom it would convert.

### *Religious Studies*

The secular academic study of religion, known as "religious studies" across much of the English-speaking world, is composed largely of descriptive disciplines, like the phenomenology, sociology, psychology, anthropology, and history of religion. Normative disciplines, such as theology or philosophy of religion, also belong, but they are regarded as quite different from the fields previously mentioned because of their interest in establishing and testing the truth of religious statements and claims. Theology usually does this within a religious tradition, but philosophy does it in the name of free intellectual inquiry and thus stakes out a more universal arena of activity in which its arguments claim to be publicly verifiable and not merely limited to the already convinced within a religious community.

To study theology or philosophy of religion is not necessarily to be engaged in a normative venture. It may be a historical and comparative inquiry that seeks simply to learn and understand what theologians or philosophers have said and written. In a religious studies department unconnected with any specific religious tradition and in no way committed to a particular religious perspective, one finds courses *about* Islamic or Christian or Buddhist convictions that are descriptive, analytical, and historical. The students and professors are not engaged in becoming better-informed Muslims, Christians, or Buddhists—although those are legitimate goals—but in learning about and understanding what people believe and why and how this affects their lives and influences those outside their communities.

By now the reader may wonder where this chapter is headed and why it has started out with a discussion of religious studies and its divisions. It has proceeded in this manner in the interests of clarity and right order, and it is hoped that the distinctions made will be of benefit not only to the study of formal Islamic thought but also to other traditions that the student may wish to examine. If theology is of central importance in the Christian tradition, so much so that in the Middle Ages in Europe it was considered to be the "queen of the sciences" (with philosophy merely its "handmaiden"), it should not be assumed that it enjoys a similar position in the other two Abrahamic traditions, Judaism and Islam. In those religions, theology is rather recessive, because the emphasis has always been much more on legal and ritual concerns. Recall, in Chapter 5, our distinction between orthodoxy and orthopraxy. Christianity, with its concern for creeds and doctrines and their clarification and defense, was characterized as being more orthodoxy centered than was either Judaism or Islam, which emphasize "right practice," orthopraxy.

### *Jewish Theology*

Years ago, when I was just starting out teaching religious studies in college, I had to prepare a number of lectures on Jewish thought for an introductory world religions course. Wanting to maintain a balance in the coverage of the Abrahamic religions, I went to a distinguished colleague who was an acknowledged expert on Judaism. When asked to suggest some possible reading materials on Jewish theology, the senior colleague laughed out loud and said something like: "Save your time. There aren't any!" After a puzzled silence on my part, he then clarified his surprising remark by explaining that Judaism has always stressed deeds rather than creeds. After that, he did give me some suggestions on reading assignments in theology, emphasizing that such activity has been regarded by Jews as neither characteristic of their tradition nor particularly important, however interesting. When Jews theologize, they do it mostly for themselves and by themselves. Not only has there never been anything like an official Jewish theology, there has never been a universal creed in Judaism. Opinions and theories by the thousand have been generated, but instead of being crystallized into a universally accepted doctrinal explication, mostly all of them have simply been included in the enormous corpus of Jewish thought. There they have had to fend for themselves in a highly contentious and skeptical intellectual environment, in which debate and disputation are a way of life—indeed, a main way of being religious.

## ISLAMIC THEOLOGY

The situation in Islam is similar to that in Judaism, although theology has been more prominent among Muslims than among Jews. Even so, in Islam, it does not approach the relative importance that it has in Christianity. The reasons for this difference will be seen as we discuss the rise of theological thinking in Islam and the development of its different forms. The nearest thing to a creed in Islam is the shahāda. But that very brief, two-part confession of belief in the oneness of God and the apostlehood of Muhammad is neither detailed nor developed enough to serve as a creed that covers the basic beliefs that unite Muslims. The shahāda does not list the five elements of *īmān,* discussed in Chapter 5, nor does it say anything about what Muslims must do, even in broad terms. What it does is simply proclaim the essential nature of God and the relation to him of his Prophet, and thus implicitly all humans. All Muslims frequently and formally (in worship) utter the shahāda, and to do so devoutly makes the outsider immediately an insider, a Muslim, upon whom all of the specific beliefs and duties are then incumbent, without further ado. But the shahāda, if it is a creed, is an extremely laconic one.

### *Kalām*

The word *theology* does not exist in Islam as an idiomatic or natural term. It can be expressed in Arabic, of course, in which it is known as *'ilm-al-lāhūt,* "the science of divinity," or *al-lāhūtīya,* which is close in meaning to "divinity" in the sense of a field of study. But those two terms are not commonly used by Muslims as names for their religious sciences. The word ***'ilm,*** "knowledge, science," is a Muslim term that is often connected with a specific branch of the religious sciences. The one who possesses expert knowledge of Islam's sources and principles and practices is called an ***'ālim,*** "one who knows" (pl., ***'ulamā',*** which has come to mean the class of specialists in Islamic Law).

The technical term that is the closest parallel in Islam to theology is *kalām,* meaning "words, discussion, discourse." ***'Ilm al-kalām*** is "the science of discourse" on divine themes. It is the Muslim equal of dogmatic or systematic theology in Christianity, although it never came to have as much importance in Islam as its analog did in Christianity. Sometimes instead of *'ilm al-kalām,* Muslims prefer the phrase ***'ilm al-tawḥīd,*** "the science of [the divine] unity." This expression reflects pious regard for the subject matter and lifts the enterprise above verbal hairsplitting and wrangling, which the word *kalām,* "talk," sometimes implies. In fact, the word *kalām* is sometimes a pejorative expression to strict Muslims, usually of a legalistic cast of mind, who distrust human reasons' attempts to understand God and his ways with humans. Similarly, the theologian, known as ***mutakallim,*** has sometimes been regarded as more clever than wise and more sharp than sincere. This is due to the sophistry that has at times come out of theological reflection and debate.

Theology has been considered to be legitimate by Muslims only when it has been subservient to the religious law, known as the *sharī'a.* The science of Muslim jurisprudence, known as *fiqh* (literally, "understanding"), is the chief Islamic science, in light of which all others are judged. *Kalām,* when it has been pursued at all in official circles, has always been subordinate to *fiqh* and in fact is a subdivision of it. Only in the activities and writings of relatively few philosophically inclined Muslim thinkers has *kalām* ever attempted to be autonomous and dominant. But such ventures have never gained the support of the majority of Muslims, who have instead given their allegiance in the analysis and interpretation of doctrinal matters to the *'ulamā',* "the scholar-jurists."

## THEOLOGICAL ISSUES

Islamic theological reflection grew out of political, social, and religious issues in the early umma. One of the most fateful was the question whether a grave sinner could still be considered a believer. The faction that seceded from 'Alī's Shī'a, known as the **Khārijites** (*khawārij,* from an Arabic word meaning "to go out" in the sense of "split off"), had a very high ideal of what the Muslim community should be. Calling themselves "the people of paradise," they pursued a perfectionist ethic as members of a charismatic community destined for salvation. But in order to preserve their pristine and righteous status under God, they sought out sin and corruption among their members and uprooted it. For those found guilty of committing grave sins, they even went to the extreme of executing them, in the belief that if they were allowed to survive, they would contaminate the rest. After 'Alī had agreed to an arbitration proceeding with his clever Umayyad challenger, Mu'āwiya, the incipient Khārijite movement split off in disgust, having concluded that their leader was not infallible and was thus unfit to govern the community. Later they rejected the Umayyads, too, and became, in effect, outlaw Muslims who zealously persisted in trying to force their vision of Islam on their brothers, especially in Iraq and North Africa but also in Arabia.

### *The Problem of the "Grave Sinner"*

The question of the "grave sinner" became a central topic of debate, for it threatened to split the umma even further than the Khārijites had. Notice that this issue is connected with social-political order and correct behavior, not abstract reflection on spiritual questions. This concern is characteristic of Islamic thought, which at its most authentic has always had a practical agenda. But not all Khārijites went to the extreme of killing grave sinners (and their families). One submovement came to control such vast portions of Arabia that it had, as a matter of practicality, to be more moderate and diplomatic. The strictest Khārijite faction, known as the Azraqites, considered theft and adultery, especially, to make the perpetrator a member of "the people of hell." Such people who were not executed were simply banished, which in the fierce tribal code obtaining in Khārijite regions amounted to the same thing. The more moderate Najdite Khārijites disciplined offenders only when they habitually sinned in a major way.

Basra, in Iraq, became a center of Khārijite theological discussion, treating in addition to the grave sin issue such topics as life under non-Khārijite rule and whether it was legitimate to lie about one's true convictions in such a circumstance and whether intermarriage should be condoned between true believers—that is, Khārijites—and ordinary Muslims surrounding and outnumbering them. A much more moderate viewpoint began to appear when some thinkers suggested that in the case of grave sinners, judgment should be suspended and left to God, who alone knows the secret things. This way of thinking led to the centrally important Murji'ite position, which held that no human could discern whether sinners were still members of "the people of paradise" or citizens of the fiery realm. The Arabic word *murji'a* is usually associated with the idea of "hope," as in Sūra 9:106, because of a delay or respite before judgment.

> And others are deferred (*murjawna*) to God's commandment, whether He chastises them or turns towards them.

This passage was used by the adherents of this school to prove that God "postpones" or "defers" judgment on certain sinners and that only he knows which ones. The **murji'ites,** then, are the "postponers," who are also sometimes called "procrastinators." They became extremely influential and provided a welcome degree of stability and security in the umma because of their moderate and tolerant views. The dominant Sunnī majority of Islam evolved from the Murji'ites.

### *Free Will and Predestination*

After the controversy over the status of the grave sinner died down and gave way to a more tolerant view, acknowledging the mystery of human virtues and vices within the complexities of human life as it actually is, a longer-lived and even more exasperating problem arose that split apart the Muslims in other ways. This was the controversy over free will and predestination. It also had its beginnings with the Khārijites, who considered humans to be free agents, responsible for their acts and thus deserving of their fates, whether to be rewarded with heaven or damned to hell. The free will position was generally anti-Umayyad on the political level and resulted in an attitude that viewed opposition to that regime as not only warranted but also desirable. The upholders of free will came to be known as **Qadarites,** from the Arabic word *qadar,* meaning "determination" or "measuring out" and including the sense of the *capacity* to determine events. It is odd that this term for predestination came to be applied to those who opposed the notion. Actually, both sides called each other Qadarites, but it stuck to the free willers. The closely related term *qudra,* meaning "power, capability" is what the free willers claimed for themselves and for all humans. It is probable that the free will position, which like predestination can be justified on the basis of Qur'anic passages, was developed and held for moral and religious reasons. That is, what is religion without responsibility, and how is responsibility to be conceived without a real capacity to act?

The opposite position, that of predestination, tended to be pro-Umayyad and stated that God had decreed that the Damascus-based caliphs should rule as protectors of Islam. Later Islamic heresiography gave the absolute predestinarians the name of **Jabarites,** from the Arabic word *jabr,* meaning "compulsion," that is, God's total power and initiative in the management of all things and events. There seems never to have been an identifiable school of this name, but it was an important tendency that cropped up in a number of different forms. The majority of Muslims came to hold a position on the issue that was more predestinarian than free will, and the Murji'ites themselves were far from asserting human capability when measured against God's might.

### *The Umma*

The most important result of the disputes and debates of the early generations of Islam, roughly down to the Abbasid revolution in 750 C.E., was the definition of what the umma was and the nature of its adherents' relationship to it. Overall, there came to be a tolerant sense of community that included diverse and even sometimes dissident groups. As long as a person proclaimed the shahāda, performed the salat, paid the zakāt, and recognized the Ka'ba in Mecca as the only *qibla,* he or she was considered to be a Muslim and entitled to dwell in the *Dār al-Islām,* the "Abode of Submission," which was over against the *Dār al-Ḥarb,* the "Household of War," the rest of humankind who were yet to embrace Islam. The consensus was that there was a difference between faith and works, which meant, among other things, that a believer who sinned was nevertheless still a believer, unless apostasy could be proved beyond the shadow of a doubt. Actually, it was not considered necessary to perform the *'ibādāt,* although naturally they were enjoined on all Muslims. Just belonging to the umma and claiming the status of Muslim was considered, especially by the extreme Murji'ites, to guarantee one a portion of paradise. There is in this division of the world a kind of cosmos-versus-chaos quality, and as the Muslims perfected their legal system and continued to extend their dominion, they became ever more convinced that their mission on this planet was to "enjoin the right and prohibit the wrong" (3:110).

## THE PLACE OF REASON

Tertullian, the North African Christian theologian of the second century, asked: "What has Athens to do with Jerusalem?" This question has as much relevance to Islam as it did to Christianity. It raises the issue of the relevance for revealed truth, whether from the Bible or the Qur'an, of Greek models of rational reflection, collectively known as *philosophy.* The Christian movement, as we observed in Chapter 1, grew up in a Mediterranean environment in which the Greek intellectual style and the Greek language both had great prestige and wide currency. This influence was true especially of the eastern Roman Empire and at least the partially Hellenized regions of Egypt and the Fertile Crescent. The Greek thinkers had virtually invented the vocabulary and techniques for speaking universally about values and transcendent realities. This is not to say that the Hebrews, Babylonians, Egyptians, Canaanites, and Arabians did not have either solid values or notions of sacred authority that demanded their reverence and obedience. But the topocosmic structures of the old Near Eastern peoples—and this applied to some extent also to the Hebrews—tended toward parochialism and particularism when set against other ways. The international and intercultural sharing of the *koiné* Greek language for several centuries following Alexander the Great's unprecedented successes in the region, the widespread Christian employment of Greek philosophical concepts and categories in the forging of an adequate Christology and theology, as well as the seminal work in Alexandria by such Jewish scholars as Philo (d. ca. 50 C.E.) created an atmosphere in which Semitic revelatory modes and symbols could not escape being translated into Greek analytical and logical forms. Conversely, Greek ideas and values also became acculturated to Eastern ways of thought and life. By the second Islamic century, there were many Christians and others whose worldview had been definitively influenced by Hellenistic modes of inquiry and discourse, in which careful empirical observation and logical testing were the hallmarks of serious investigation and analysis. The increasing sense that Islam was a universal faith and its spread among diverse peoples necessitated the development of general, transcending modes of definition and communication—or so many Muslims of wide interests apparently thought. We shall see that philosophical ideas and methods did gain some currency in Islamic thought, but both Qur'an and *Ḥadīth,* rock-solidly Arabian and Abrahamic, triumphed decisively whenever there was a controversy between reason and revelation. To alter Tertullian's classic query a bit, "What has Athens to do with Mecca? Philosophy proposes, but Allah disposes."

### *Greek Philosophy and Science*

The vogue of learning about Greek philosophy and science began in earnest with the Abbasids, who came to power in 750 C.E. Great translation projects were begun, working from both Greek and Syriac manuscripts. The latter was the scholarly language of much of eastern Christendom outside Egypt and contained large amounts of Greek philosophical, scientific, and cultural material. (It should be added that Syriac, a Semitic language closely related to Arabic, provided ready-made models for translation, which by the time of Islam had been tested in the cognate religious tradition of Christianity.) The cosmopolitan Abbasids realized the advantage of securing the best of the older cultures and intellectual traditions for themselves, in the process making them acceptable to Muslims. It should not be imagined that Greek philosophical and theological texts were alone at the center of attention. Equally important, if not more so, were medical treatises, geographies, and other scientific sources.

A distinguished series of Islamic philosophers appeared under Abbasid rule, but they never were to have wide or popular influence on the religious level, and indeed they never intended to. One of these was al-Kindī (d. ca. 870 C.E.), the only Arab who ever became a first-rate philosopher. He was heavily influenced by neo-Platonic thought, which he used in his interpretation of Islam. A devout Muslim, he nevertheless recognized the value of using Greek categories and logical procedures to develop a valid and universal Islamic theology. He apparently saw no fundamental conflict between reason and revelation and, like Jewish and Christian thinkers before him, equated prophetic revelation and the a priori, rationally derived knowledge of neo-Platonic metaphysics. Al-Kindī's influence on other advanced thinkers was notable. He had two even more influential successors: the political and philosophical thinker al-Fārābī (d. 950 C.E.) and the philosophical theologian Ibn Sīnā (d. 1037), the Avicenna of medieval Christian Latin theology in the West, both of whom are among the leading intellects of human history.

## THE MU'TAZILITE RATIONALISTS

The year 800 C.E. was a fateful one for both Christendom and Islamdom. In Rome on Christmas Day of that year Charlemagne was crowned Holy Roman Emperor by the pope, inaugurating a new age as the West began to pull out of the centuries of disintegration and chaos that had followed the barbarian invasions and the fall of Rome. In the Islamic world, Hārūn al-Rashīd was caliph of an umma as well as an empire that would never be known again in Islamic history. Hārūn was the caliph of the *Thousand and One Nights* and has captured the imaginations of countless people, non-Muslim as well as Muslim, because of the stories about him and his court in Baghdad. The Abbasid caliphate was at the height of its power and prestige in 800, whereas the Frank-led Holy Roman Empire was just beginning to pull together a diverse and fractious Europe. From the Atlantic to the borders of India, Muslim dominance was absolute, and southwestern Europe itself was solidly in the grasp of the Muslims, whose confrontations with Charlemagne were immortalized in the "Song of Roland" (although the historical Roland was killed by Basques and not Muslims). In this period a new and eventually far-reaching style of Islamic intellectual reflection and religious definition appeared in Basra and Baghdad. Its origins are obscure, but legend has it that when the Khārijites and Murji'ites were debating the fate of the grave sinner, a new position emerged halfway between them, and the holders of it "withdrew" from the conflict, thus earning their popular name of *mu'tazila,* "standing aloof."[1] There are different versions of the story, but it is certain that if such a position developed relatively early, it was not anything like the philosophical-theological school that came into being during early Abbasid times in Iraq.

### *The Mu'tazilite Movement*

The **Mu'tazilites** have been the subject of extensive study both in the history of Islamic thought and in modern Western scholarship. In the latter, they have sometimes been considered "free thinkers" who, if they had not been finally defeated and declared heretical by the eventually triumphant Sunnī "fundamentalists," might have steered Islamic theology and thus life in a direction congenial, in fact amenable, to Christian convictions and interpretations. There are superficial similarities between some types of Christian philosophical theology and Mu'tazilite ideas, especially as both value Greek logical techniques in constructive reflection. But the Mu'tazilites, far from being liberal intellectuals who wanted to accommodate the world to a vision of rationality and cooperation, were proponents of a strict and militant Islam, which they sought to impose uniformly on their wayward coreligionists and to spread to the non-Muslims by means of propaganda. They even participated in an inquisition in Iraq, imprisoning, torturing, and executing fellow Muslim religious experts and jurists who did not conform to their creed and sign a statement to that effect. We have already seen how the jurisconsult Ahmad ibn Hanbal suffered under their *miḥna,* or "ordeal," as the inquisition was called. The Mu'tazilite movement was for a number of years the official school of the Abbasid court, especially during the caliphate of al-Ma'mūn (813–833), who authorized the inquisition. But its abuses were so great and its ideas so unacceptable to grassroots Muslim religious consciousness that it was finally toppled and driven into hiding as a continuing but minority school of thought with a wide variety of styles and emphases.

***The Movement's Fall.*** What were the main points of Mu'tazilite theology by which it was able for a time to dominate in official circles but which then caused the movement to fall from power in a relatively short period? The rise and fall of the school was largely a political matter, but its intellectual dimensions continued and have been a significant if subordinate part of Islamic theology ever since. Had the Mu'tazilite proponents not sought to enforce allegiance to their theological views, those views might have become more prominent in the development of a broad consensus of Muslim thought. As it turned out, the Mu'tazilite positions acquired an *odium theologicum* that the passage of time has not been able to eradicate. Recall the words of warning that Ibn Khaldūn addressed to students who wished to read the Mu'tazilite al-Zamakhsharī's commentary on the Qur'an (Chapter 6).

## MU'TAZILITE THOUGHT

The Mu'tazilites did not choose their popular name, nor did they care to be called by it. Instead, they called themselves *ahl al-'adl wa'l-tawḥīd*, "The people of [the divine] justice and unity." They were concerned about preserving among the Muslims a ritual and doctrinal regularity and uniformity that reflected God's unity and unswerving justice at both the cosmic and historical levels of being. Theirs was essentially a religious position and not merely an intellectual or "rationalist" one, although the Mu'tazilites insisted that reason and revelation were complementary, each providing knowledge that is both reliable and essential for the proper governance of affairs in this life and the inheritance of felicity in the next.

### *The Anthropomorphism of God*

One issue that especially exercised these thinkers was many Muslims' growing tendency toward anthropomorphic conceptions of God and his ways. The Qur'an contains an abundance of imagery and description of God's way and nature that reflects attributes of his creatures. For example, the "throne" of God is mentioned, which suggests that he sits on it as a cosmic ruler (2:255). In other places the Qur'an speaks of God's hands (3:73; 36:71), his eyes (11:37), his face (2:115), and his speaking and hearing and seeing, these last three frequently. The Mu'tazilites came to regard such passages as metaphorical, intended for limited human imaginations in a scripture sent to guide and correct. They feared that if people were to become literal about such Qur'anic anthropomorphisms, then God's unity would be compromised. Indeed, these thinkers sought at all costs to avoid the Christian error of division in the godhead, even on a purely conceptual level. The Christian Trinity they regarded as a blasphemous and perverse descent into anthropomorphism and polytheism. The purposely negative way in which the Mu'tazilites discussed the whole issue of divine attributes is seen in the following brief excerpt from al-Ash'arī's (d. 935) famous discussion of their views in his book on Muslim heresies:

> The Mu'tazila agree that God is one; there is no thing like him; hearing, seeing; he is not a body, not a form, not flesh and blood, not an individual, not substance nor attribute; he has no color, taste, smell, feel, no heat, cold, moisture, nor dryness, no length, breadth nor depth, no joining together nor separation, no movement, rest nor division . . . no place comprehends him, no time passes over

> him . . . not begetting nor begotten . . . he is not comparable with men and does not resemble creatures in any respect . . . he is unlike whatever occurs to the mind or is pictured in the imagination . . . he is ceaselessly knowing, powerful, living, and will not cease to be so; eyes do not see him, sight does not attain him, imagination does not comprehend him; he is not heard by hearing; (he is) a thing not as the things, knowing, powerful, living, not as (men are) knowing, powerful, living; he is eternal alone, and there is no eternal except him, no deity apart from him; he has no partner in his rule, no vizier (sharing) in his authority, no assistant in producing what he produced and creating what he created . . . he may not experience benefit or harm, joy or gladness, hurt or pain . . . he may not cease to exist nor become weak or lacking; he is too holy to be touched by women or to have consort or children.[2]

Even with the deletions (in the interest of brevity), this is a rather thorough listing of what God is not and is one of the classic expressions of the *via negativa* ("negative way") of characterizing God in the philosophy of religion. It is akin to the Hindu concept of *neti, neti*: "not this, not that." It is even closer to the Jewish theologian Maimonides' opposition to positive attributes of God, lest he be conceived in any way as resembling his creation. The ideas of this long Mu'tazilite passage should not be supposed to be limited to that school, for they fairly express mainstream Islamic convictions concerning the ineffable and transcendent nature of God.

### *The Creation of the Qur'an*

One of the most heated issues to arise from Mu'tazilite thought was whether the Qur'an was created in time or is eternal. If the former, the question of God's knowledge as separate from his eternal nature arises. That is, how could the eternal God—in whom all Muslims believe—express himself in time, thus limiting himself by the creation of his word? The Mu'tazilites vigorously defended the doctrine of the Qur'an's having been created in time, lest the Muslims begin holding up two separate divine realities: God and his Word (that is, the Qur'an). The Mu'tazilites held the Qur'an to be the word of God, but the *created* word and not in any definitive sense part of the godhead, which is totally without attributes.

The emerging Sunnī orthodoxy, championed by such legal scholars as Aḥmad Ibn Ḥanbal, insisted that the Qur'an was indeed eternal and perfect in every respect as God's speech. This view won out, but only after a bitter political as well as theological struggle. When the Mu'tazilites for a time came to dominate the Abbasid court in Baghdad as the official theologians of the empire under Caliph Ma'mūn, among the points that they insisted on having all religious scholars agree to through a signed statement was the temporal creation of the Qur'an. Ibn Ḥanbal, among others, absolutely refused, and so the upholding of the eternal Qur'an was eventually viewed as a heroically defended view. Ironically, the doctrine of the eternal Qur'an doctrine somewhat resembles the Christian doctrine of the preexistent and divine *Logos,* "Word," of God, which in the opening of the Gospel of John is characterized as eternal and finally equivalent to God. But the Word became incarnate in the life and work of Jesus. The Mu'tazilites were concerned about just this sort of "incarnationism" slipping into Islamic doctrine and considered the position that held the Qur'an to be eternal as a main avenue for such a development. In Christianity the Word became flesh; in Islam it became a book, as we observed earlier (Chapter 6).

It should be clear by now that the Mu'tazilites, whatever they were, were not chiefly intellectuals bent on clear thinking for its own sake. They were guardians of what they considered to be true Islam, both in doctrine and in practice, including the regulation of community life. *Tawḥīd,* often translated as "unity," is actually more than that, if unity means primarily a conceptualization about the divine oneness. Indeed, *tawḥīd* properly means "making one" and so includes the servants of God who strive to reflect God's oneness through their devotion and rejection of any ideas or behavior patterns that detract from God as the sole Lord of all. Thus, upholding God's unity through *tawḥīd* is not just a mental attitude, for it is easy to mouth formulas about God's oneness without being convinced of it. Rather, *tawḥīd* requires correct acts as well as correct thinking, and this is what the Mu'tazilites were most concerned about instilling in their fellow Muslims. After God's unity-unification, they emphasized his justice (*'adl*). And here is where they attracted the most criticism, for reasons that must be understood if one is to have any grasp of Islamic theology, both in its formative period and after.

### *Free Will and Responsibility*

Following their Qadarite predecessors, the Mu'tazilites also held to a doctrine of human free will and responsibility. They did so not to assert human prerogatives and interests but to acknowledge and uphold the divine justice. God, they held, always wills what is good for his creatures. It is only humans who instigate evil in the world and, thus depending on their own acts freely chosen, determine their destinies as inhabitants of heaven or hell. In this idea the Mu'tazilites resembled the Khārijites, who were so concerned with establishing a godly society in a world in which human choices and actions had such consequences. This preoccupation with justice as the major way for "making God one," as *tawḥīd* requires, helps us understand the policies of inquisition (*miḥna*) instituted by the Mu'tazilites when they enjoyed a preferred position at the Abbasid court in Baghdad. Mu'tazilite theology did not exist in a vacuum; it was an applied process.

The Mu'tazilites argued that God was bound by his nature *always* to reward obedience and goodness and to punish disobedience and sinfulness. He could and would not do otherwise. This is necessity, a Greek rather than a Semitic notion. That is, God's acts are not just and good because he wills them; rather, God wills only things that are just and good. An abstract ideal of justice and goodness replaced the inscrutable, unpredictable, and essentially merciful but just divine decree. For the Mu'tazilites, who disregarded it as inhering in God's essential nature, reason supplanted revelation as the means of descrying God's will. The Word of God in the Qur'an, remember, was considered to be a temporally conditioned and created message, including crude anthropomorphisms fit only for crude creatures but susceptible to metaphysical interpretations by the learned scholars whose rational inclinations and techniques actually were superior to the revealed Word.

By arguing that the Qur'an must have been created in time but that reason is of the essence of God and is then shared with his creatures, the Mu'tazilites were inferring that reason would be paramount in all important matters. These thinkers certainly knew the Qur'an well and always used it as their primary source when arguing. But their method of interpreting the Qur'an made them masters rather than servants of it. The Mu'tazilites were at least consistent on this point, for they were fearful lest the Muslims hold up the Qur'an as some sort of second god.

### *Reward and Punishment*

If children who died went straight to heaven because they were children and not completely accountable, was this fair or just to older humans who presumably went to hell as a consequence of their disobedience? Is God merciful in some cases and not in others? Or is he constrained to reward nonperformance in the case of children and to punish it in the case of adults? This last sort of question, according to legend, brought about the defection of one of the most prominent Mu'tazilites, whose name was Abū al-Hasan 'Alī al-Ash'arī (d. 935). The future great *mutakallim* was with his teacher, al-Jubbā'ī, so the story goes, when they began discussing a hypothetical case of three brothers, two adults and one boy. One adult was good, and so when he died he went to heaven, having been obedient and thus meriting his reward, according to Mu'tazilite principles. The second adult brother was bad and so was consigned to hell for eternity. He got what was coming to him. The boy died but was sent to heaven, although he had never reached the age of accountability. When asked why this happened, Ash'arī's teacher is reported to have replied that God knew that the boy would have grown up to be bad and so took him at an early age and through his mercy sent him to heaven. The older brother in hell then cried to God asking why he had not done the same for him before he had grown up and too late become enmeshed in a life of sinfulness and disobedience. But al-Jubbā'ī could not give an answer to this, and there could of course be none according to strict Mu'tazilite principles. In the story, God had been unjust, which is a priori impossible.

This story obviously does not provide any reliable information about God; rather it exposes a fatal weakness in Mu'tazilite thought about the divine justice, which simply cannot be gauged by human reason. Convinced of this mysterious fact, Ash'arī is said to have left his teacher for good and the Mu'tazilite movement as well. Now, the boy in the story could have been sent to hell in the first place, but this would have been unjust, too. This story seems unlikely to be a true account of al-Ash'arī's conversion from Mu'tazilism, but it is a powerful parable and has been retold in theological circles since at least the time of al-Ghazālī (d. 1111).[3] He considered it to be a valid refutation of Mu'tazilite views (although he never connected it with al-Ash'arī, whose school he himself followed).

### *The Five Points*

Divine unity and justice are the first two of the famous "five points" that are traditionally associated with the Mu'tazilites.[4] The third concerns God's "promise and threat" (*al-wa'd wa'l-wa'īd*), which respectively refer to heaven and hell. This point includes extensive discussion of the nature and classes of sin and the relation between belief and unbelief. According to this doctrine, which is closely related to that concerning the divine justice, God always fulfills his promises and carries out his threats. If he did not, he would be a liar! Knowing this, the Mu'tazilites concluded that it was possible for human rationality to predict the final destinies of people, based on their actions in this world. God could not intervene or change his mind by relenting or forgiving, because his "promise and threat" constrained him. At the heart of this part of Mu'tazilite thought was the Qur'an's superiority as a guide for humankind over any other source, including the *Ḥadīth*. The Qur'an clearly tells what is good and what is bad, thought the Mu'tazilites.

The fourth point concerns the Muslim who is also a sinner. Called *al-manzila bayna al-manzilatayn,* "the intermediate position," it holds that the Muslim who sins is to be regarded as neither an infidel nor a believer. The Khārijites went so far as to execute the grave sinner, as has been observed, whereas the Murji'ites continued to include such a person in the full community. The "intermediate position," which seems to have been part of the Mu'tazilite identity since the beginnings of the movement, was an attempt to avoid the two extremes of the Khārijites and the Murji'ites. However, it is difficult to see how the Mu'tazilite position differed in practice in any significant degree from that of the Murji'ites, for both allowed the miscreant to live but punished him in the bargain.

The real issue seems to have been political, for the emerging schools of thought all were originally connected with partisan interests. The question of 'Uthmān and his assassination was at the core, and it continued to fester in the umma like a sore that would not heal. The Khārijites regarded 'Uthmān as a sinner in the final years of his caliphate, because of the way in which he favored his own kin over other Muslims, and other things. His assassination was, in effect, an execution. 'Alī, consequently, did not have to arbitrate, but when he did agree to arbitrate, he surrendered his authority, according to the Khārijite view.

Some of the Mu'tazilites adopted a neutral attitude toward this issue. Some scholars thus argue that their name of "those who stand aloof" arose from that. As we shall see, the political and personal question of sin and punishment are intertwined. Anyone who advocated punishment and removal from the umma was considered to be anti-Umayyad. Those who advised postponement in judging the sinner were aligned with the Murji'ites, who were generally pro-Umayyad. The Mu'tazilites preferred an intermediate position for purposes of conciliation and a unified umma. The position of 'Alī and his supporters, of course, continued to be problematic, for the Umayyads did want to bring them to justice over the killing of 'Uthmān. But the triumph of Mu'āwiya and the rise of the Umayyad dynasty effectively ended that call for revenge. The Mu'tazilites were themselves divided over the ranking of the first four caliphs. Some regarded Abū Bakr as superior to ʻAlī, and others believed the reverse. All considered Abū Bakr's caliphate to have been valid, though not as a product of divine revelation. In general, ʻUthmān's position was thought to be inferior, if only by implication, as the Muʻtazilites took the "intermediate" position on it, regarding him as neither a believer nor an unbeliever during his last years.

The fifth classical point of Muʻtazilite doctrine is that of "enjoining the right and prohibiting the wrong" (*al-amr bi al-maʻrūf wa al-nahy ʻan al-munkar*), which is a basic Qur'anic ordinance. To what extent should the Muslims make sure that their fellows follow the right way? This question is always a central concern. The Muʻtazilites held that the Muslims are obligated to "enjoin the right and prohibit the wrong" to the extent that opportunity and ability allow and with the "tongue, hand, and sword," as al-Ashʻarī put it in his authoritative discussion, introduced earlier. This policy becomes a highly charged issue when subjects start questioning whether their ruler is just or unjust, for a strict construction of the Qur'anic command could be (and occasionally was) taken as a justification for rebellion.

### *The Decline of the Muʻtazilites*

The Muʻtazilites did not last long as the official court theologians of the early Abbasids. They simply could not continue to exert such influence, partly because of their relatively small numbers but even more because they did not represent the grassroots convictions of the emerging Sunnī movement, which was much more concerned about orthopraxy and legal issues than abstract doctrine and uniformity of intellectual structure. Added to these were the Muʻtazilites' views on such things as divine justice and the Qur'an's provenance. The former repelled the majority of Muslim thinkers, who considered any rational limitation of God and his ways with his creatures as impertinent at the least and blasphemous at the worst. The illusion that one could predict God's justice tended to make tyrants out of rulers and overlooked the heart of God's nature: his mercy and forgiveness, which do not compromise his justice but fulfill it as guidance for humankind. The increasing rejection of free will, far from reducing humans to the level of puppets, instead allowed God to *be* God, infinitely above and beyond humans' capacity either to predict or to gauge his will or command. This view must be apprehended on the psychological rather than the strictly logical level, for there is a paradox at the heart of God's almightiness and decree: in total submission to them, the believer is freed from the threats and constraints of this ungodly world so as to strive for the hereafter while working to transform the current human social and political order by means of the Sharīʻa, God's law. The "freedom" of the Muʻtazilite could lead to the resignation and defeat of the sinner who too late realizes his or her wrongdoing. Although the Qur'an teaches that deathbed repentances will not be accepted, nevertheless it assures forgiveness and renewal to the person who repents while there is still time to lead an upright life.

Minarets rising above the Cairo complex of Sultan Hasan, a major *madrasa,* or theological institute, dating from the fourteenth century. (*Source:* Frederick Mathewson Denny)

By putting the burden of heaven and hell on the individual human agent, the Mu'tazilites ironically overlooked both the living God and the weakness and confusion to which humans are prone. There are excellent religious and technical doctrinal grounds, then, for the reaction against Mu'tazilism that set in even while the school was enjoying protection and support at the highest levels in Baghdad.

The Mu'tazilite venture did not die out completely, for we read of representatives of the school long after it had fallen from official status, and the Shi'ites continued to cultivate Mu'tazilite forms of discourse, with positive results. Indeed, the movement had real virtues, the greatest being the introduction of Greek-style logical argumentation into Islamic theology. So long as rationalism did not take over, the innovation was salutary, and the systematic, comprehensive structuring of Islamic belief continued afterward to be a central strength of the most viable theologies that succeeded Mu'tazilism.

## THREE MUSLIM CREEDS

The shahāda is the Muslim personal confession of faith and, as we observed in the beginning of this chapter, not quite detailed or comprehensive enough to serve as a real creed for the community as a whole. Creeds have been composed, however, but they have never developed into universally uttered summaries of doctrine in the way that the Apostles' and Nicene Creed did in Christianity. The Muslim term for creed is ***'aqīda,*** from a verb meaning "to bind" and "to contract."

### *The Greater Understanding*

One Muslim creed, known as "The Greater Understanding" (*Fiqh Akbar*), was composed for the community, according to tradition, by the great jurist Abū Ḥanīfa (d. 767), who was a leading theologian in Iraq before the period of the Mu'tazilite ascendancy.[5] This and one other, later creedal summary have been attributed to Abū Ḥanīfa, because of the scholar's great prestige and authority. It is likely that the *Fiqh Akbar I,* by which name the creed under discussion is technically known, does actually go back to the circle of Abū Ḥanīfa, if not to his own hand. Internal evidence indicates that it is pre-Mu'tazilite, because it does not touch on any of their distinctive points, a mark of later creeds. This creed is in the first person plural ("we"), which indicates that it was public at least to the extent that a school of theology embraced it. Its ten articles[6] are as follows:

1. We do not consider anyone to be an infidel on account of sin; nor do we deny his faith.
2. We enjoin what is just and prohibit what is evil.
3. What reaches you could not possibly have missed you; and what misses you could not possibly have reached you.
4. We disavow none of the Companions of the Apostle of Allah; nor do we adhere to any of them exclusively.
5. We leave the question of 'Uthmān and 'Alī to Allah, who knoweth the secret and hidden things.
6. Insight in matters of religion is better than insight in matters of knowledge and law.
7. Difference of opinion in the community is a token of divine mercy.
8. Whoso believeth all that he is bound to believe, except that he says, I do not know whether Moses and Jesus (peace be upon them) do or do not belong to the Apostles, is an infidel.
9. Whoso sayeth, I do not know whether Allah is in Heaven or on the earth, is an infidel.
10. Whoso sayeth, I do not know the punishment in the tomb, belongeth to the sect of the Jahmites, which goeth to perdition.

There has been extensive commentary on this creed, which soon becomes technical and complex. But a few issues can be discerned by the beginning student. The first article is obviously aimed against the Khārijites, who considered the grave sinner to be an infidel. The second article is taken from the Qur'an and was, long before the Mu'tazilites made it their fifth main point, the essential charge to those who ruled the Muslims, here extended to all sincere believers. The third article is directed against the Qadarites, or "free willers," who believed that humans have the capacity (*qudra*) to act on their own, without God's decree and predestination. The fourth article is aimed against the Shī'īs, who focused on 'Alī and his progeny. 'Alī was regarded by them to be superior to the other three rightly guided caliphs, who were even thought by some Shī'īs to be usurpers. The fifth article is an obvious attempt to preserve the community from further division and strife and thus expresses a centrist position between the Shī'īs and the Khārijites.

The sixth article is a curious one, which scholars trace to a very early origin before legal terminology had become technical and specific. Its essence is expressed in another version: "Understanding (*fiqh*) in religion is more excellent than understanding (*fiqh*) in law; serving Allah is better than gathering knowledge."[7] The seventh article refers to differences among the legal experts, not the theologians. "Difference" (*ikhtilāf*) here does not seem to mean contrary doctrines or disputed matters but varieties of legal opinion that can coexist. The eighth article was possibly intended as an attack on the Jews and Christians, who rejected each others' apostles (Jesus and Moses) as well as Muhammad. But it is more likely that this article was intended to lead people to view all of God's apostles as worthy of acknowledgment. Later, however, Muhammad, Jesus, and Moses were elevated to a special status, with Muhammad the chief over all. The ninth article has been thought by some commentators to oppose the view that Allah can be in one place and thus limited. Rather, this view implies that God is spiritual and beyond the confines of space and time. This would be a reasonable interpretation if the creed were post-Mu'tazilite, for that school as well as its orthodox successor, the Ash'arites, strenuously defended the view that God is transcendent and beyond place. But the early origin of this article has caused scholars to conclude that it probably refers to the Qur'nic passage (7:54) that depicts God as seated upon his throne, which Abū Ḥanīfa insisted is in heaven. The last article refers to the increasingly popular eschatological conviction that God causes some of his creatures to suffer in the tomb, before the general resurrection and judgment. The Jahmites mentioned in this article were named after Jahm Ibn Safwān, an independent theologian of late Umayyad times (d. 745–746), who denied the eternal existence of heaven and hell, instead believing that God, alone at the beginning, will be alone again at the end. This position is extreme *tawḥīd.*

### *The Testimony of Abū Ḥanīfa*

Other creeds have been composed, like the *Waṣīyat Abī Ḥanīfa,* "the Testimony of Abū Ḥanīfa," which actually represents the views of Ahmad Ibn Ḥanbal, who lived later. It consists of twenty-seven articles, some of them quite complex.[8] The nature of and relation between faith and works occupy considerable space in this creed, as do key affirmations concerning the unity and transcendence of God, the uncreated, eternal nature of the Qur'an, and the qualities of certain of the Prophet's companions and family members. The predestinarian view is upheld, as are punishment in the grave and the eternity of both heaven and hell. Interestingly, the *Fiqh Akbar I* makes very little mention of God or Muhammad so as to characterize them correctly and comprehensively, as one might expect a creed to do. The testimony of Abū Ḥanīfa, however, is much more detailed and elaborate on the nature and role of God and his apostle, even telling of the latter's intercession for his fellow humans on Judgment Day. The sense of the umma's integrity and saving nature is very pronounced, as in the fourth article: "Transgressors of the law who belong to the community of Muhammad are all of them faithful; they are not infidels."

### *Fiqh Akbar II*

The most highly developed and systematic creed is the so-called *Fiqh Akbar II,* which was possibly composed by the great opponent of Mu'tazilism, al-Ash'arī,[9] who was introduced earlier in this chapter in connection with the story of the three brothers. This sophisticated and advanced creed reflects al-Ash'arī's controversy with the Mu'tazilites and exhibits the extent to which acceptable Sunnī *kalām* had matured by the time of its composition. The doctrine of God is expressed in carefully chosen language, a few lines of which will give an idea of the delicacy and precision in talking about God.

> Allah the exalted is one, not in the sense of number, but in the sense that He has no partner; He begetteth not and He is not begotten and their is none like unto Him. He resembles none of the created things, nor do any created things resemble Him. He has been from eternity and will be to eternity with His names and qualities, those which belong to His essence as well as those which belong to His action. Those which belong to His essence are: life, power, knowledge, speech, hearing, sight and will. Those which belong to His action are: creating, sustaining, producing, renewing, making, and so on.[10]

After speaking about the eternal quality of God's qualities and names, the creed launches into a discussion of the Qur'an, which is

> the speech of Allah, written in the copies, preserved in the memories, recited by the tongues, revealed to the Prophet. Our pronouncing, writing and reciting the Kuran is created, whereas the Kuran itself is uncreated.[11]

The speech of God is a unique phenomenon, not like the speech of humans. Although God spoke to Moses, and Moses himself spoke, too, their speeches were different. God spoke before he created things, for speech is one of his eternal qualities, but it is not to be compared with human speech, even if it is uttered in history.

***Anthropomorphism.*** Recall how concerned the Mu'tazilites were about preserving God from anthropomorphism. The *Fiqh Akbar II* has clearly been influenced by this issue, but not enough to denude God of all attributes, as the "rationalists" did. Ahmad Ibn Hanbal developed a means of avoiding speculation about just how God could have hands, face, and soul. He insisted that because the Qur'an speaks of these, they must be accepted *bilā kayfa,* "without [asking] how." Al-Ash'arī also held this position. In order to avoid reducing the more concrete divine attributes to mere metaphor, the fourth article states:

> It must not be said that His hand is His power or His bounty, for this would lead to the annihilation of the quality [that is, "handness"]. This is the view of the Qadarites and the Mu'tazilites. No, His hand is His Quality, without how [bilā kayfa]. Likewise His wrath and His good pleasure are two of His qualities, without how.[12]

The Ash'arites neither anthropomorphized (*tashbīh*) God nor stripped him bare (*ta'ṭīl*) but took a middle course, known as *tanzīh,* "keeping pure," in the sense of refraining from speaking of God in human terms.

***Human Free Will and Responsibility.*** The question of human free will continued to be debated, but the parties generally tended to accept the divine ordination of all things, including human acts. Al-Ash'arī developed a puzzling view on the issue, that God intended to preserve human responsibility while asserting his divine omnipotence. It is known as the doctrine of *kasb* or *iktisāb,* a common Qur'anic root meaning "to seek, attain, earn" and so forth and came to mean "acquisition," namely, of one's acts as one's own. The sixth article of the *Fiqh Akbar II* contains the following statement about this:

> Allah did not compel any of His creatures to be infidels or unfaithful. And He did not create them either as faithful or infidels, but He created them as individuals, and faith and unbelief are the acts of men. Allah knoweth the man who turneth to belief as an infidel in the state of his unbelief; and if he turneth to belief afterwards, Allah knoweth him as faithful, in the state of his belief; and He loveth him, without change in His knowledge or His quality. All the acts of man—his moving as well as his resting—are truly his own acquisition [kasb], but Allah creates them and they are caused by His will, His knowledge, His decision, and His decree.[13]

*Kasb/ikitsāb* became the most difficult question for *kalām,* even down to the present day. The Ash'arites wanted to preserve genuine human responsibility, for else how could there be true religion? But they continued to view God as the overwhelming originator and disposer of all acts. From the viewpoint of human reason, the individual "acquires" her or his acts simply because God has willed it, not because there is any real freedom involved. Later *mutakallimūn,* as the Muslim theologians are called, sought to reserve for humans some degree of genuine responsibility. Al-Ash'arī's less well known but influential contemporary in Central Asia, al-Māturidī (d. 944), went further than his more famous fellow orthodox theologian toward upholding human free will. Later, the greatest of all Islamic religious, theological, and philosophical thinkers, Abū Ḥāmid al-Ghazālī (d. 1111), continued to assert free will and responsibility. His views on the religious life will be discussed later in this chapter and in Chapter 10, which considers Islamic mysticism.

The *Fiqh Akbar II* contains far more than can be summarized and discussed here. In addition to the points already mentioned, it asserts also the sinlessness (*'iṣma*) of the prophets, especially Muhammad, and the reality of their evidentiary signs and the miracles of saints. Certain ritual issues are included, such as the validity of prayer when one stands behind a believer, whether he or she be good or bad in behavior. More than the Qur'an's eternal nature is asserted: all of its verses have equal "excellence and greatness," although some are preeminent with regard to recitation or content: "Likewise, all of Allah's names and qualities are equal in greatness and excellence, without difference."[14]

## ORTHODOX KALĀM AND THE CHALLENGE OF PHILOSOPHY

Al-Ash'arī is generally considered to be the chief representative of what came to be orthodox Sunnī *kalām,* and his school has remained standard down to the present day. He is not to be credited with everything that his followers have held, but his name has endured as a label covering a great variety of positions. Although he was himself a friend of the Hanbalite school of jurisprudence, while remaining a Shāfi'ī (the law schools are described in the next chapter), the Hanbalīs refused to become engaged even in his revelation-championing brand of *kalām,* which they considered to be essentially un-Islamic because it relied on human reason. Their founder had, after all, devised the *bilā kayfa* position as a defense against scholastic hairsplitting.

### *Greek Philosophy*

About the time that al-Ash'arī was active, Greek philosophy was becoming more and more well known and influential among Islamic thinkers. This was true not only of the Mu'tazilites, who continued to be active and assertive even after Ash'arī, but of other thinkers as well. In fact, Platonic and Aristotelian thought entered Islamic speculation during the tenth and eleventh centuries C.E.

***Ibn Sīnā.*** Two of the greatest thinkers in Islamic history effectively used Plato and Aristotle in their systems. The first was Ibn Sīnā (d. 1037), who is known in the Latin West of Christian scholastic theology as Avicenna and who combined Islamic mysticism and Platonic idealism. Ibn Sīnā was also a celebrated physician, and his work on medicine was used in both the Islamic world and the West for many centuries.

***Ibn Rushd.*** The other great thinker was Ibn Rushd (d. 1198), a Spanish Muslim whose Latin name was Averroës. He became the most respected commentator on Aristotle and was able to combine religion and philosophy, or revelation and reason, better than anyone else of his time had. His influence on the development of Christian scholasticism was immense, especially his commentaries on Aristotle, which were translated into Hebrew and Latin.

Ibn Rushd wrote a famous rebuttal of an earlier work by al-Ghazālī, and the two works have coexisted as models of sustained argument for and against the use of philosophical techniques and assumptions in Islamic theology. Ghazālī's treatise was entitled *Tahāfut al-Falāsifa,* "The inconsistency of the philosophers," and in it he argued against several points that certain Muslim thinkers, especially Avicenna, had advanced. There were three points that were considered not only heretical but infidel,[15] a much worse offense: (1) that only spirits and not bodies are resurrected (whereas the Qur'an expressly teaches that both body and spirit are raised up on the Last Day); (2) that God knows only universals and not particulars, because of his eternal, perfect nature (but the Qur'an, which must hold the final position of authority, says that "he knows what penetrates into the earth, and what comes forth from it. . . . Not so much as the weight of an ant in heaven and earth escapes from Him . . ." [34:2–3]); and (3) that the universe is eternal, which (insisted Ghazālī) no Muslim had ever held. Ghazālī only *argued* against the philosophers; he did not suggest any replacement system. In fact, his style was heavily influenced by philosophy, especially logic, but held in a position inferior to revelation.

Ibn Rushd replied with his famous treatise entitled *Tahāfut al-Tahāfut,* or "The inconsistency of the 'inconsistency'," meaning Ghazālī's book. This long and magisterial work had enormous influence on subsequent philosophical thinking in the West, but in the Islamic world it was all but ignored and had virtually no influence. It continued to be known as an intellectual exercise, but with its appearance Greek philosophical modes of thinking had reached their limits in an Islamic intellectual community that had become more and more disinclined to engage in such speculation, preferring more existential theosophical reflection on the divine nature.

Ibn Rushd was no ivory-tower philosopher, but the chief judge of Cordova. He argued, on *legal* grounds, that philosophy was a necessity for the Muslim community, but that it should be pursued by an elite, "demonstrative" class thoroughly versed in Aristotelian logic.

***Ghazālī.*** Ghazālī, who wrote profound works about *kalām,* philosophy, logic, and other subjects, nevertheless basically distrusted the theological enterprise and considered it as essentially an apologetic tool for defense of the faith. It should not be cultivated by the masses, who would never be capable of defending their weak and untrained intellects against it. Indeed, *kalām* was likened by Ghazālī to a strong medicine that had to be prescribed and administered skillfully and precisely, lest the patient die from the treatment. Al-Ghazālī came to be convinced that God enlightened his creatures by means of his divine light and that no amount of human intellectual demonstration and search could attain to the highest knowledge. The conviction of this came not from the Qur'an but from personal experience. For some time Ghazālī had become a skeptic, "in fact though not in theory nor in outward expression":

> At length God cured me of the malady; my being was restored to health and an even balance; the necessary truths of the intellect became once more accepted, as I regained confidence in their certain and trustworthy character [this refers to mathematics and the like]. This did not come about by systematic demonstration or marshalled argument, but by a light which God most high cast into my breast. That light is the key to the greater part of knowledge. Whoever thinks that the understanding of things Divine rests upon strict proofs has in his thought narrowed down the wideness of God's mercy.[16]

This is a good point at which to end this discussion of creed and theology in Islam.

## NOTES

1. For a detailed review of the evidence, see W. Montgomery Watt, *The Formative Period of Islamic Thought* (Edinburgh: Edinburgh University Press, 1973), pp. 209–250.
2. Translated by Watt in *The Formative Period,* pp. 246–247. The original is in Abū'i-Hasan 'Alī ibn Ismā'īl al-Ash'arī, *Maqālāt al-Islāmiyyīn,* at the beginning of the section on the Mu'tazilites. Watt used H. Ritter's edition, 3 vols. (Istanbul: Society of German Orientalists, 1929–1933), p. 155ff.
3. Watt reviews in *The Formative Period,* pp. 304–307, this story and others connected with al-Ash'arī's conversion.
4. This summary of the five points is based mostly on Watt, *The Formative Period,* pp. 228–249; and H. S. Nyberg, "Al-Mu'tazila," in *Shorter Encyclopedia of Islam,* ed. H. A. R. Gibb and J. H. Kramers (Ithaca, N.Y.: Cornell University Press, 1953), pp. 425–426.
5. This discussion of Muslim creeds is based on A. J. Wensinck, *The Muslim Creed: Its Genesis and Historical Development* (London: Frank Cass, 1965), especially chaps. 6, 7, and 8.
6. *Ibid.,* pp. 103–104.
7. *Ibid.,* p. 112.
8. *Ibid.,* pp. 125–131.
9. *Ibid.,* pp. 188–197.
10. *Ibid.,* p. 188.
11. *Ibid.,* p. 189.
12. *Ibid.,* p. 190.
13. *Ibid.,* p. 191.
14. *Ibid.,* p. 196.
15. Al-Ghazālī summarizes his critique of philosophy in his famous spiritual autobiography, "Deliverance from Error" (*al-Munqidh min al-Ḍallāl*), *The Faith and Practice of al-Ghazālī,* trans. W. Montgomery Watt (London: Allen & Unwin, 1953), pp. 37–38.
16. *Ibid.,* p. 25.

CHAPTER

# 9 Law and the State in Classical Islamic Formulations

**KEY TERMS**

| | | |
|---|---|---|
| ***sharīʻa*** | ***qāḍī*** | ***faqīh*** |
| ***fiqh*** | ***ijtihād*** | ***muftī*** |
| ***ra'y*** | ***mujtahid*** | ***fatwā*** |
| ***qiyās*** | ***ijmāʻ*** | ***madhhab*** |

## ISLAM AS A WAY OF LIFE

Like Judaism, Islam is a religion and a way of life, extending into all areas of the community's existence and activity. Because of this concern for all of life, law became central from the earliest period when Muhammad was bringing the new community into being in Medina. Like Moses, Muhammad was a political leader and judge as well as a spiritual guide and teacher. He was not, of course a technical legal expert, nor was there during either his lifetime or for some time after anything resembling a legal code or system of jurisprudence. These were only gradually developed over a period of two to three centuries. But the impulse toward law was fundamental from the time of Islam's origins and eventually replaced the Arabs' customary, unwritten practices, uniting them and many other peoples into a new system of belief and order, an international umma.

## THE SHARĪʻA AND FIQH

The technical Islamic word that best conveys the sense of Islamic law, in both its character and constitution, is ***Sharīʻa.*** Literally, it means "the way to the water hole" but also includes the meaning of "the right path" to follow, and thus came to mean "law." Although it is correct to translate the word as simply "law," it is better to regard law in the strict, codified sense, as only one dimension of Sharī'a. Like the Jewish notion of Torah, Sharī'a is more than law; it is also the right teaching, the right way to go in life, and the power that stands behind what is right. The contemporary Muslim scholar Fazlur Rahman has translated Sharī'a as "the ordaining of the way,"[1] indicating the law's divine source and purposeful direction. For Muslims, God is the sole legislator, and jurisprudence—the science of the law—is but a system designed to facilitate human obedience to and service of God. As has often been said with respect to the Sharī'a, "Humankind has no rights, only duties." The Sharī'a, then, comprises all that might be positively called law and occupies the central place in the Islamic system of final authority and ordering principle. It is an ideal as well as a reality and unites and guides the Muslims in both time and space, down through the generations and across the diverse and widespread regions of Islam. The Sharī'a gives Muslims a profound sense of security and stability. Far from being an unwelcome or burdensome imposition, it is considered to be the greatest of blessings and guidance for successful individual and communal life in this world, in preparation for the hereafter.

The Sharī'a, as divine legislation, is not the same as ***fiqh,*** although it includes it. *Fiqh* means "understanding" and fairly early came to be the main term for the "science of jurisprudence." As a science with classifications, methods of argumentation, and techniques of application, it is a product of human intelligence and experience. But its sources, the essence of the Sharī'a, are revealed and immutable. Human reason cannot fully penetrate the Sharī'a, and it certainly may not question or criticize it, for it is holy. But human intellect may and indeed should be used at the levels of judgment and application, *under* the Sharī'a. This is the level of *fiqh,* of the science of law.

## THE QUR'AN AND THE LAW

When Muhammad was alive, he led the Muslims by means of the accumulating revelation of the Qur'an and by his own example and precept, as has been described in earlier chapters on the Message and the Sunna of the messenger. After the Prophet's death, the Muslims naturally turned to these sources as the most authoritative guides for the community.

### *Ra'y*

In addition to the Qur'an and the Sunna—and it must be remembered that each had its own complex and gradual developments as texts and collections of texts—early Muslim jurists also exercised personal opinion, known as ***ra'y.*** There was no systematized legal procedure until relatively late in the development of Islam's classical institutions, and so during the early generations—approximately until Abbasid times—legal thinking and decision making were carried out in an atmosphere both diverse and flexible. The Qur'an was the main authority, but gradually the *Ḥadīth* also gained wide currency and influence, as we saw earlier. To a certain extent, local custom in the countries that were converted to Islam was appropriated as part of Islamic law. This had the effect of rendering the law understandable and familiar in some respects and was a pragmatic and flexible means of extending Islamic principles in places where traditional practices posed no threat to Islam. In short, the developing Islamic legal system was quite tolerant and accommodating on practical levels. But this is not to suggest that the main source, the Qur'an, was compromised. Rather, it is to acknowledge that the community's needs far exceeded the limited and often quite general commands and prescriptions of the Qur'an.

Although all Muslims are united in the conviction that the divine legislation is first and foremost contained in the Qur'an, the sacred scripture nevertheless is impossible to use as a law by itself. It provides no clear, consistent method for its own use and in any case simply does not touch upon many areas of human life that a detailed code must consider. Even though the Qur'an may contain the essence of Islamic law and the basis for adjudicating any imaginable situation that might arise, it still does not show how to proceed on a practical level. The conviction is unexceptionable, but its application is impossible without some sort of system and method, which the Qur'an does not provide.

But the Qur'an did unite the Muslims ritually, linguistically, and spiritually and in these ways prevented any irretrievable deviations from developing even in a varied legal environment. And the Sunna of the Prophet, although it did not become fully developed and did not include the notion of Muhammad's infallibility until later, was nevertheless paired with the Qur'an from the time of the rightly guided caliphs in Medina and exploited for guidance and legislation. But in the earliest periods of the umma's development, in Medina, Kufah, and Damascus, there was not nearly the amount of *ḥadīth* material circulating that was to be available by the time of the Abbasids. To the extent that it did exist, it was simply not available in literary form, but dispersed among the companions and their descendants. The exemplary collecting and sifting of reports of such scholars as Muslim and al-Bukhārī was still far in the future, as we have seen. There is much more legislative matter in the *Ḥadīth* than in the Qur'an, and the question arose as to which was the more authoritative. Theoretically, of course, the Qur'an had to be regarded as primary, because it was held to be the word of God and not of humanity. But Muhammad, as the messenger of God, was obviously the sole authentic interpreter of the Qur'an. Thus, his words on this or that Qur'anic passage were accepted as authoritative. Gradually everything Muhammad did was to be considered infallible and thus worthy of emulation as Sunna.

## *Qiyās*

Even the Sunna did not provide all that the Muslims needed for specific legislation and legal guidance. Thus there was created a practice of analogical reasoning known as ***qiyās,*** which was nearly universally recognized as a third source of law. *Qiyās* developed from *ra'y,* "personal judgment," but was generally logically stricter and productive of a far narrower range of possible conclusions. When a problem arose that neither the Qur'an nor the *Ḥadīth* could resolve, an attempt was made to find an analogous situation in which a clear determination had already been made. There was a difference of opinion over analogical deduction, but it was finally accepted in some form by most law schools, which sometimes cited the following *ḥadīth,* relating what Muhammad asked Mu'ādh b. Jabal when he sent him to the Yemen to be a **judge** (***qāḍī***):

> "How will you decide when a question arises?" He replied: "According to the Book of Allāh."—"And if you do not find the answer in the Book of Allāh?"—"Then according to the *sunna* of the Messenger of Allāh."—"And if you do not find the answer either in the Sunna or in the Book?"—"Then I shall come to a decision according to my own opinion without hesitation." Then the Messenger of Allāh slapped Mu'ādh on the chest with his hand saying: "Praise be to Allāh who has led the messenger of the Messenger of Allāh to an answer that pleased him."[2]

### *Ijtihād*

*Ra'y* is the term used in this *ḥadīth* for "opinion," but it is immediately preceded by a verb meaning "to exercise" one's intellect, from which we get the technical term ***ijtihād,*** independent legal reasoning in search of an opinion. *Ijtihād* contains within it a sense of exertion, even struggle, and is from the same root as *jihād,* "exertion" in the way of God, including holy war if necessary. *Ijtihād* and *qiyās* are often used interchangeably, but the former is actually more general, including within its purview other forms of legal reasoning. One who exercises *ijtihād* is known as a **mujtahid.** Although this kind of intellectual exertion served as a main method in the elaboration of Islamic law in the early centuries, as positions gradually solidified and opinions were widely adopted, the Muslims tended more and more to imitate and accept on authority what their predecessors had to struggle to achieve. This development led to *taqlīd,* "imitation" and acceptance on authority, without engaging in original *ijtihād.*

### *Ijmā'*

The reason that *ijtihād* became rare and in many circles condemned was a fourth and final source of *fiqh,* "consensus of the community," known as ***ijmā'.*** It developed alongside *ra'y* and *qiyās* and, indeed, interacted with them, as they all focused on both the Qur'an and the Sunna as the ultimate source. According to a fateful *ḥadīth,* Muhammad declared: "My People will never agree together on an error."[3] Although this particular *ḥadīth* seemed not to have circulated very early in Islamic history, the idea contained in it is early. *Ijmā'* is in fact the strongest and most pervasive of the four sources of law, because it determines how or whether the other three will be used. The consensus that is regarded as authoritative is not the consensus of the

Muslims as a whole, but of those who are learned and whose opinions are respected and accepted. Of course, the acceptance of the *ijmā'* of scholars and of worthy predecessors on the part of the Muslims as a whole is an expression of general consensus. But no legal reasoning or decision reaching goes on at the popular level. *Ijmā'* became a powerful force for conformity and gradually dominated Islamic jurisprudence among the Sunnīs, for whom it provided stability and a constant source of authentication. But it would be a mistake to consider all *ijmā'* as infallible in the sense of formal truth-value. As Fazlur Rahman has observed:

> One must distinguish between authority and infallibility in this context. . . . What is regarded as infallible by the early Muslim scholars, an infallibility more assumed than expressed, is the Ijmā' *as method and principle* rather than its contents which are regarded as authoritative, not infallible. The Muslim doctrine of Ijma' has a strong practical bent and there is no talk of absolute truth-value of its content, but only of a practical rectitude-value. But rectitude values change. . . . [Ijma'] is an organic process. Like an organism it both functions and grows: at any given moment it has supreme functional validity and power and in that sense is "final" but at the same moment it creates, assimilates, modifies and rejects.[4]

The doctrine of *ijmā'* is characteristically Islamic and reflects the tradition's preoccupation with the community, the umma, as a social, political, cultural, and, above all, spiritual reality. We should add that the Arabic root from which *ijmā' derives—j-m-'*—also produces related words, such as *jamā'a,* "community" (synonym of *umma), jāmi'*, "congregational-Friday mosque," and *jāmi'a,* "university." In a real sense, then, when *ijmā'* is uttered, the Arabic speaker hears "the way of the umma," that which is "right," both resonating together.

## THE LEGAL SCHOLARS

The class of legal scholars that developed is known as the *'ulamā'* (sing., *'ālim*), which literally means "those who are learned," who possess *'ilm,* "learning" (which includes but transcends mere knowledge in the sense of information). The *'ulamā'* are not a clergy. Muslims recognize no such class. But the *'ulamā'* are leaders who offer guidance and reliable teaching on the faith. Their authority is based on their learning and their supporting traits of good character and authentic piety, not on any sort of priestly ordination or investiture. Even here a sort of popular *ijmā'* works to select those religious scholars whom the Muslims feel they can trust. There is no centralized Islamic hierarchy or religious bureaucracy, but a loose and in some ways provisional system of customs and procedures by means of which the Sharī'a is preserved and applied. This observation is not to suggest that Islamic jurisprudence is a capricious, hit-or-miss affair; rather, it is to affirm how powerful the consensus is about how things should be done that no organization is needed beyond a minimum for purposes of efficiency, record keeping, and continuity. Each Muslim locale has some sort of established procedures, and a bureaucracy to administer them.

The *'ulamā'* contain a number of different subclasses of legal experts and officials. One such is the ***faqīh*** (pl., *fuqahā'*), literally meaning "one expert in *fiqh*," a jurisconsult. This is not an official position, although one who was appointed to an official law post would have to be a *faqīh*. Sometimes the *'ulamā'* and *fuqahā* are equated, but in general the former are men of broad learning in the religious sciences (including law), whereas the latter are specialized canon lawyers, or even just casuists, and relatively minor figures.

Another title is ***muftī***, given to a legal expert who, whether or not occupying an appointed position, is recognized for his learning and skill in the law. This person, when consulted by an official or a private party, delivers a ***fatwā*** (pl., *fatāwā*), a "formal legal opinion." This opinion is not *ra'y*, in the old sense but is, rather, a carefully arrived-at position that has taken precedent thoroughly into account. In traditional Islamic countries ruled by the Sharī'a, the *muftī* has considerable authority. But in modern countries that have a modern civil code, often based on Western models, the *muftī* is able to exercise influence and authority only with the faithful and only in personal legal matters such as marriage, divorce, and inheritance. Even then, his *fatwā* is not binding in that it will be enforced by the state. A private party that is not satisfied with a *fatwā* can often go to another *muftī*, perhaps of another law school, and seek a second opinion.

## The Qāḍī

Finally, there is the *qāḍī*, the Islamic judge, appointed by the political leader and entrusted with the execution of justice in all matters of religious law, such as marriage, divorce, inheritance, and religious endowments (*awqāf*). Originally the *qāḍī* was meant to handle civil and criminal cases, too, but the tendency down through the centuries has generally been to leave those to the civil authorities, who were not of the '*ulamā*'. The ideal requirements for being a *qāḍī* are stringent and include having a blameless character and life, being a male adult Muslim, possessing a thorough grounding in the legal sciences, and even having the ability to act as a *mujtahid*. This last requirement was rendered void when the "gate of *ijtihād*" was considered closed during the third Islamic century, in the consensual belief (*ijmā'*) that all substantive legal issues had been aired and resolved. From that time forth, legal decisions were made by means of close adherence to precedent, with no independent decision making allowed. It has often been difficult to appoint a *qāḍī*, partly because of the strict requirements, but even more because of the risks involved for the incumbent. It is the *qāḍī*'s sworn and sacred duty to be fair and balanced in his deliberations, regardless of the status and power of the parties to a litigation. The *qāḍī* has often encountered attempts at bribery, retaliation, or cooptation. Indeed, some upright Muslim legal experts have refused the post of *qāḍī*, regarding it as degrading because of corrupt incumbents who have given the position a bad name. *Ḥadīths* attributed to the Prophet have even been discovered that warn against accepting the post.[5]

## SCHOOLS OF LAW

The division of Islamic jurisprudence into several distinct schools in various regions of the empire is a complex story, which can only be hinted at here. The emerging Sunnī majority finally came to recognize four main schools, whereas the Shi'ites developed three. Both branches of the Islamic community have characteristic emphases and similarities that they share in their own communities. The differences between the Sunnī and the Shīʻī law schools are much greater and rest principally in the conception of religious and political authority held by the two branches of Islam. In Sunnism the law is fixed, and so even the highest religious and political authorities are bound by it. But at the same time there is a place for consensus, although as has been pointed out, its use ended up bringing Sunnī law to a position of imitating the past (*taqlīd*) rather than creating new solutions. The result was the closing of the "gate of *ijtihād*." The Shīʻīs, or the majority of them, do not recognize *ijmā'* in law but hold up an ideal of a perfect leader, known as the imām, who continues to exert divine influence and make decisions as God's appointed agent in the world. Thus the Sunnī form of government and jurisprudence is somewhat contractualist, whereas the Shīʻī is more authoritarian. At this level of the discussion, we are forced to venture into the area of political theory and the concept of the state. A fuller consideration of political authority and governance among Muslims will come later in this chapter. Law and political matters are not sharply distinguished from each other, whether among Sunnīs or Shīʻīs, as both are bound up with the Islamic worldview and way of life.

### *Regional Centers*

Islamic legal theory and practice had several different regional centers in the early empire of the rightly guided caliphs and the Umayyads and Abbasids. Medina was the most important early center, for obvious reasons, but Syria and Iraq also actively fostered the development of schools. A "school" of Islamic law is called a ***madhhab*** (pl., *madhāhib*), literally meaning a "way." All of the law schools came to agree that there are many human issues and activities that do not come under the law at all but are indifferent, having neither a positive nor negative status in the Qur'an or Sunna. Although Islam is a religion of law, it cannot fairly be characterized as a religion of litigiousness, or frequent going to court. Most "legal" issues that touch Muslims' daily lives pertain to matters that do not require a *faqīh* or *muftī* or *qāḍī*. That is because they can be mastered and followed by the ordinary Muslim who has discretion and a healthy conscience. Muslims learn early what the Sharīʻa requires in the way of devotional life—worship, almsgiving, and the rest of the pillars—and by adulthood they generally are aware also of social and familial responsibilities. In short, Islam's "orthoprax" dimensions are widely understood and observed on the individual and group levels. Law therefore is internalized in the community and is not the preserve of specialists. This is not to say that the canon lawyers are not necessary, far from it; but to conceive of Islamic law, or rather the Sharīʻa, strictly in terms of professionalism would be to miss the peculiar quality of the popular Islamic passion for obedience to God's commands. The legal specialists did not create the Sharī'a idea or the umma as the context for its application; *they* were created by *them.*

## THE FIVE PRINCIPLES

There are five categories of acts that Islamic law recognizes and that appear in all books of *fiqh.* These five *aḥkām,* or "principles," are known by various names, but their meanings are clear to Muslims:

1. *farḍ* or *wājib*—duties and acts that are required of all Muslims and whose performance is rewarded and whose omission is punished (e.g., prayer, almsgiving, and fasting).
2. *sunna, masnūn, mandūb,* or *mustaḥabb*—duties and acts that are recommended but not required. Performance of them is rewarded, but omission is not punished (for example, certain supererogatory prayers during the salat or visiting Medina after the pilgrimage).
3. *jā'iz* or *mubāh*—indifferent actions, whose performance or omission is neither rewarded nor punished.
4. *makrūh*—actions that are disapproved but not punished or forbidden (there is a wide divergence of opinion about this category).
5. *ḥarām*—actions that are both forbidden and punished (e.g., fornication, drinking wine, and stealing).

This is an outline that does not take into account the subtle distinctions within and between categories. One example will suffice: at the *farḍ* level can be distinguished actions that are obligatory for every individual Muslim, like salat and zakāt; this is called *farḍ 'ayn.* But there is also a class of actions that is obligatory for only some Muslims, known as *farḍ kifāya.* An example is attending funeral prayers; it is sufficient that only a representative group of Muslims attend in a particular community, but some Muslims *must* attend. As long as this condition is met, others who stay at home need not fear that they have sinned.

The *aḥkām al-khamsa,* as the five qualifications or principles are known in Arabic, are both legal and ethical. They show a broad range of shadings in human activities and leave some room for flexibility. For example, what some legists might consider to be indifferent (*mubāh*), others might regard as *makrūh.* And what some would condemn as forbidden (*ḥarām*), others might hold to be merely "almost illegal," and thus *makrīh.*

There is also the simpler division of acts and things into the two categories of *ḥarām,* "forbidden," and *halāl,* "permitted." This distinction will be taken up in Chapter 12 with reference to food regulations.

## SUNNĪ LAW SCHOOLS

### *The Ḥanafī School*

In Sunnī Islam a number of different law schools developed, but only four survived and have continued to be important down to the present. The oldest was founded in Iraq in early Abbasid times by Abū Ḥanīfa (d. 767), who was one of the most gifted and liberal of the Islamic legists. *Ra'y* was prominent in the school's method, reflecting earlier Iraqi prototypes, but over the years the *madhhab* became more restrictive in its use. The Ḥanīfī school, as it is known, is the most liberal and flexible of the four Sunnī *madhāhib*. *Qiyās* as a sophisticated method of reaching legal judgments was pioneered and perfected by Abū Ḥanīfa, who refused to accept an appointment as a *qāḍī*. Today the Ḥanafī *madhhab* is dominant in Central and Western Asia (Afghanistan to Turkey), Lower Egypt (Cairo and the Delta), and the Indian subcontinent.

### *The Mālikī School*

The second surviving school is that founded in Medina and the Hejaz by Mālik ibn Anas (d. 795). He was a great collector of *ḥadīths* but even more a supporter of the "living tradition" of Medina. Medina, in turn, was the earliest center of Islamic law and government, which was thereby steeped in prestige and authoritative precedent. Mālik's great book, *Al-Muwaṭṭā'* ("The beaten path"), is an influential compilation of his opinions and judgments and the sources he used to reach them. The Mālikī *madhhab* is prominent today in North Africa and Upper Egypt.

### *The Shāfi'ī School*

The third great *madhhab* is that of the Shāfi'īs, founded by Muhammad ibn Idrīs al-Shāfi'ī (d. 819), who was without doubt the single greatest legal scholar in Islamic history. Al-Shāfi'ī came originally from southwest Palestine, but he traveled extensively during his life, studying under Mālik in Medina, teaching and practicing law in Baghdad, and finally taking up residence in Egypt, where he produced his major works before his death there. Al-Shāfi'ī developed the main principles of Islamic jurisprudence (*uṣūl al-fiqh*) and systematized them into a coherent unity. The subsequent standardization on major issues among the four surviving Sunnī schools is due to his pioneering and definitive work.

Al-Shāfi'ī's greatest contribution was in the distinguishing and preferring of prophetic Hadīth from the "living tradition" of Medina that his teacher Mālik had cultivated. This resulted in the Prophet's prestige and authority rising ever higher and being second only to the Qur'an in theory and in some cases higher in practice. How al-Shāfi'ī accomplished this is laid out in his *Risāla* ("Treatise"), which is available in an English translation. The close relationship in Islamic law between the Qur'an and the Sunna of the Prophet was definitively and finally established by al-Shāfi'ī. In addition, al-Shāfi'ī refined even further the use of *qiyās,* which he rather severly curtailed, in comparison with the freer employment of it by the Ḥanafis. But in addition to establishing the Prophet's Sunna as the second of the four "roots" (*uṣūl*) of law, al-Shāfi'ī defined *ijmā'* in its classical form and invested it with the power that enabled it to oust *ijtihād* from jurisprudence, except in the most limited sense. That is, *ijmā'* came to be the principle as well as the procedure that the legists of all the Sunnī schools increasingly used in order to determine what was authentically Islamic. Thus *ijmā'* extended even to the authentication of *ḥadīth.* It is in this context that the fateful *ḥadīth* attributed to the Prophet ("My people will never agree together on an error") takes on meaning. If the earlier decisions of the legal experts and judges were gradually accepted through *ijmā'* as definitive, then what more was there to do in new cases but examine them for guidance as correct precedents? The Shāfi'ī *madhhab* is today predominant in the Malaysian-Indonesian archipelago, southern Arabia, East Africa, Lower Egypt, and most of the Indian Ocean littoral.

### The Ḥanbalī School

The fourth and last of the classical Sunnī schools was founded by a younger contemporary of al-Shāfi'ī, Amad anbal (d. 855), who carried al-Shāfi'ī's enthusiasm for and trust in *Ḥadīth* farther than any other legist had. We met Ibn Hanbal earlier in this book in connection with the persecutions that he and his fellow traditionalist legists suffered under the Mu'tazilites during the reign of al-Ma'mūn in Baghdad. He was an extremely conservative and combative religious thinker and leader of deeply Qur'anic and *ḥadīthī* convictions who spawned a rather fundamentalist school that has had a dramatic history down to the present. Ibn Taimīya, the thirteenth-century self-proclaimed *mujtahid,* and the seventeenth-century Wahhābī reformation in Arabia that was influenced by his thought were Ḥanbalī in orientation, and this school has continued for two centuries to be the official and dominant one in northern and central Arabia (modern Saudi Arabia).

The four Sunnī schools all are regarded by one another as fully orthodox, and in practice there is no fundamental difference among them. Their histories have varied, and the regions of the Dār al-Islām in which they have prospered retain characteristic cultural aspects and differences, but in essence they all uphold an ideal of the Sharī'a that unites them and their adherents in a common Sunnī "orthopraxy." The same cannot be said when one compares the Sunnī with the Shī'ī law schools, although even between those two great heritages and communities, the *dīn,* or religious observances, are essentially the same.

***The Fiqh Books.*** In the voluminous books of *fiqh* generated down through the centuries in both Sunnī and Shī'ī contexts, there is a twofold separation into what might be called "ritual matters," known as *'ibādāt* (literally, "worships") and *mu'āmalāt,* "social matters." The books always open with ritual matters, because they are of the greatest importance to those who would be God's "adoring worshipers" (*'ābidīn,* from the same root as *'abd,* "slave"). Thus, beginning with purification, the *fiqh* books treat in minute detail the pillars and related matters before dealing in the *mu'āmalāt* sections with social relations, such as marriage, inheritance, and property. This twofold division in no way suggests that one is "religious" and the other "secular" or profane. All of Islamic life is of religious significance in some sense, but not everything is connected with the specific acts of worship.

## SHĪ'Ī LAW SCHOOLS

The Shī'ī law schools are distinguished from one another by the branches of Shī'ism that they represent, but on selected issues and sources, they all differ markedly as a group from their Sunnī counterparts. Both Shī'ī and Sunnī law schools recognize the Qur'an and the Sunna as the basic sources of jurisprudence, but the versions of the sunna received and cultivated in the two traditions sometimes differ. The Shī'īs place great trust in their imāms, or divinely guided leaders, and there are traditions unique to them and passed down by them. Complicating the situation are the imāms that were recognized at different times and in different places in the early centuries of Islamic history. Of course, all imāms descend from the Prophet through 'Alī and Fātima.

But the three most prominent branches of Shī'ism are the small community known as the Zaydīs (who are closest to Sunnīs in that they do not regard their imāms as having been more than human); the Ismā'īlīs, who recognize an unbroken chain of imāms down to the present, though they focus their adoration on the seventh in the original line, Ismā'īl, the elder son of Ja'far al-Ṣādiq, who was not recognized by the Shī'ī majority (this has given the Ismā'īlīs their alternative name of "Seveners"); and the Ithnā-'asharīs, meaning "Twelvers," or the Imāmīs, who contend that there were twelve imāms, the last of whom left the world in 874 and is alive, but in a mysterious hiding or "occultation," whose technical term is *ghayba.* Both the Seveners and the Twelvers reserve room in their legal systems for the doctrine of the imām, who is infallible and divinely guided and not at all subject to consensus in the way that Sunnī law is.

Shī'ism is highly authoritarian, with its adherents' strong conviction that God teaches and guides his people through his imāms. Authority flows from above to below, whereas in Sunnism the relationship is the other way around, at least in theory. In Shī'ism, moreover, *ijtihād* has continued to be prominent and effective, especially among the Imāmīs, whose hidden imām necessitates a succession of scholars (*mujtahids*) to manage juristic affairs until he returns again in a future messianic age. In Ismā'īlī Shī'ism, the uninterrupted succession of living imāms provides constant legislative and legal guidance. In practice, Shī'ī law bears some resemblance to Sunnī *fiqh,* in that although *ijtihād* continues to operate, the tendency is to revere and maintain what has long been regarded as authoritative in the teachings and opinions of the early legists of their communities. One great difference between Shī'ī—more particularly, Twelver—law and Sunnī law is a form of temporary marriage, known as *mut'a,* that the Shī'ī community recognizes but that most Muslims (and all Sunnī schools) regard as little different from legalized

Islamic studies seminar at Cairo's Al-Azhar University Mosque.
(*Source:* Frederick Mathewson Denny)

prostitution. Other major divergences from Sunnī legal practice are a much stricter form of repudiation in divorce law than countenanced by the Sunnīs and a different inheritance procedure, which among the Twelvers provides a better treatment of certain female relatives and does not favor certain male ones in the way that Sunnī law does. The most prominent Shī'ī law school is the Ja'farī, named after its founder, Ja'far al-Ṣādiq, the sixth imām.

## ISLAMIC POLITICAL INSTITUTIONS: FORMS, FUNCTIONS, AND THEORIES

### *The Split between the Shī'īs and the Sunnīs*

As we saw in the beginning of Chapter 4, the caliphate (*khilāfa*) was founded in an atmosphere of urgency right after the death of the Prophet, who seems not to have prescribed any specific procedures or institutions for when he would no longer be the leader of the Muslims. The Shī'īs, of course, contend that he had designated 'Alī as his successor, a view that carries with it the corollary assumption that all other Islamic heads outside the Prophet's line through 'Alī and Fātima have been usurpers. The split between the Shī'īs and Sunnīs since the earliest period has been mainly political, and the Shī'īs presented an identifiable alternative quite early, with their characteristic ʻAlid loyalism (which was not restricted to Shīʻīs). But the Sunnī movement itself, whose name is short for *ahl al-sunna w'al-jamāʻa,* "the people of the [prophetic] sunna and the community," did not take on its definitive characteristics until well after Shīʻism had established itself in various forms. The Sunnī movement was solidified about the time of Ahmad ibn anbal (800s), when the grassroots *ʻulamā'* and pious Muslims had agreed that rational speculation, such as that of the Muʻtazilites, was wrong and that only by means of obedience to and conformity with the prophetic sunna, a rather literalistic interpretation of the Qur'an, and imitating and transmitting the opinions and decisions of the learned and respected scholars of the past (especially the first generations) could the umma truly carry out the commands of the Sharīʻa and live in security. But Sunnīsm had potent antecedents and forebears, which the finally dominant majority traced back to the rightly guided caliphs: Abū Bakr, ʻUmar, ʻUthmān, and ʻAlī. So, if Sunnism only very gradually developed into the more or less unified form that it enjoyed by the third Islamic century, it nevertheless regarded itself as the original and continuing orthodoxy from the beginning.

*Ijmāʻ* was a powerful engine of this attitude formation, for it appropriated to itself the past and applied it in an authoritarian manner to the present and each succeeding generation. The very word *Sunnī* is a powerful clue to the way in which the Prophet's prestige and person had become the perfect standard for orthodoxy, and the word *jamāʻa,* "community," whose roots also produce *ijmāʻ,* indicates social and political conviction. If you are a member of the true community, the Jamāʻa, which implies the "majority," then you are in the right all the way. The Shīʻīs, however, can in no way be characterized as having been any less devoted to the Prophet's Sunna. If anything, they were more so than the Sunnīs, because they gave centrality to the Prophet's family in determining who should be the true imāms down through the descending generations. But Shīʻī political and religious authority did not reside in the community, whose decisions by its qualified leaders in jurisprudence were believed to be correct. It lay in the actual imāms, who then exercised their right to rule as superior, essentially superhuman representatives of God.

### *The Sunnī Caliphate*

The Sunnī Caliphate lasted for more than six centuries before it was extinguished by the Mongols when they invaded Baghdad in 1258. Later it continued in greatly reduced form as part of Ottoman legitimacy. Its long career was very erratic, and only in the early periods, approximately down to the time of Hārūn al-Rashīd and his immediate successors (ca. 800), can it be said to have been a truly powerful political institution. By the fifth Islamic century its actual territorial dominance barely extended to the outskirts of Baghdad, where in fact it was a sort of honored prisoner in its own house, because most of its regions had been taken over by local princes and military leaders, who were, in one conspicuous case, Shīʻī. These Buwayhid amīrs, as they were known, could easily afford to prop up the caliph for symbolic and expedient reasons. Nevertheless the *idea* of the caliphate continued to be compelling to the Sunnīs, and there was even a separate caliphate in Spain for more than half a century under the remarkable Abd al-Rahmān III (reigned 912–961), who made the audacious claim in the name of the Umayyads who had ruled there since the Abbasid takeover in 750. The theory as well as the practice of Sunnism had been to recognize only one caliph: as God's religion is only one, reflecting the divine unity, so should God's "best umma" (Sūra 3:110) be one. Later political theorists acquiesced in multiple caliphs provided that their domains were separated by a sea. This approach to the problem of a declining institution is only one example of the sort of after-the-fact rationalization that increasingly characterized Islamic political theory.

***The Definition of a Caliph.*** What is a caliph and what is he supposed to do?[6] As we shall see, the answer to these questions could be supplied only after the institution was weakened beyond recuperation. In the first place the caliph was the Prophet's "deputy," *khalīfa,* and it has often been agreed that he was responsible for what Muhammad had been responsible for, except for the prophetic function, which ceased at his death. The majority of Muslims have held that the caliph should be (like Muhammad) of Qurayshī descent, but only the Shī'īs insisted that he be in the Prophet's line. The extremist Khārijites, on the other hand, held that any Muslim was eligible to be caliph, even a non-Arab or slave. The Sunnīs also held that the believers should obey the caliph, because to do so was tantamount to obeying God. To buttress this authoritarian position, the term *khalīfat Allāh,* as was noted earlier, "Vicegerent of God," came into use in Umayyad times, as did "Shadow of God on Earth" by Abbasid times. As early as 'Umar, the title "Commander of the Faithful" (*amīr al-mu'minīn*) was also in use. It is said that a messenger arrived at 'Umar's headquarters one day and asked: "Where is the Commander of the Faithful?"[7] 'Umar was pleased with this new form of address and adopted it. In succeeding periods many applied that title to themselves, although regional princes who remained loyal to the Abbasid caliph in Baghdad changed the title, so far as it applied to themselves, to "Commander of the Muslims" (*amīr al-muslimīn*).

Although the first four caliphs had been in some sense elected to the office, this election later became merely a formality, known as the *bay'a,* an oath of allegiance taken by the leading figures of the court and the assembled body that heard the proclamation of a new caliph. The *bay'a* can be traced back to a pre-Islamic Arabian custom of shaking hands on an agreement. But most Muslim leaders have historically been military strong men whose *bay'as,* when exacted, were a far cry from the old Arabian practice, which must have looked increasingly idealistic in retrospect.

***The Idea of the Caliphate.*** The idea of the caliphate is not only political but religious as well, because the institution was believed to be essential to maintenance of the Sharī'a. The caliphate was not a necessary or even an inevitable institution, as has been amply demonstrated in Islamic history. But as an ideal it has exerted great influence as an attempt to fulfill God's legislation for humankind. Adam was the first *khalīfa,* and the Qur'an mentions others, like David, the king of Israel. All humans are called to be "deputies" of God on earth, and this is the highest calling possible for humans. Obeying the Muslim caliph, then, came to symbolize obedience to God and his Sharī'a. The Sharī'a precedes the caliphate or any other form of Islamic government that could be developed. That is, there is no prescribed form of Muslim government, either in the Qur'an or the Sunna; there are only guidelines and principles that can be followed as Muslim peoples do their best to order society wherever they may be. The umma is not a governmental idea in the administrative sense; rather it is the totality of Muslims in the world upholding the Sharī'a however they can.

There is neither church nor state in Islam in any fundamental and enduring sense. The umma is at most a provisional and adaptive reality, directly dependent on God for its being and its meaning. Its great strength as both an ideal and a reality is seen best in the devotional discipline and unity of Muslims around the world. No government or religious establishment regulates or enforces their prayers and other formal observances, although official agencies may sometimes maintain stability and facilitate the activities of mosques and pious foundations. But the institutions, such as ministries of *waqfs* (charitable religious trusts), that are found in every Muslim country are there to serve the religion and not to be served by it. The conviction that God is transcendent and sovereign makes Muslims chary of any sorts of human structures, especially hierarchical ones like the Roman Catholic Church. The Sharī'a is served by the state, and there are many ways that this may be accomplished. The caliph is as subject to the Sharī'a as is the humblest peasant Muslim.

***The Function of the Caliphate.*** The caliphate, even when it became weakened and increasingly ineffective politically and militarily, nevertheless symbolized for the Muslims a link with the past all the way to the time of the Prophet and the rightly guided caliphs. This nostalgia for that golden age was so strong by the time of the Shī'ī Buwayhid amirs in Baghdad that a scholar was commissioned to prepare a special study of the institution, describing its nature and function and relating the caliph to the whole governmental and social structure, particularly to the type of military princes that had wrested the true power from the caliphs. The author of this remarkable treatise was a Shāfi'ī jurist, who served as *qāḍī* in Baghdad under the Abbasid caliphs al-Qādir (d. 1031) and his son al-Qā'im (d. 1075). His name was al-Māwardī (d. 1031), and he was educated in the Islamic sciences and especially good at analyses of governmental and legal issues. His views on the caliphate, as set forth in his *Al-Aḥkām al-Sulḥāniya* ("The governmental statutes"), have been respected as definitive and thorough, even if idealistic and practically impossible to fulfill. For our purposes, the essential points of his treatment can be briefly summarized.[8] Before proceeding, it should be said that his use of the terms *imām* and *imāma* ("imāmate") is synonymous with *khalīfa* and *khilāfa* ("caliph" and "caliphate") and in no sense carries a Shī'ī meaning.

The imāmate is made necessary by revelation, not reason, a position originally taken by al-Ash'arī in his debates with the Mu'tazilites. The office was filled by election rather than by designation (the Shī'ī way), and even only one valid vote could elect a caliph. The candidate must be of the Quraysh tribe. Even if there is only one candidate, there still must be an election, a view that is in keeping with the treatise's anti-Shī'a bias. There is much detail on potential disputes concerning claimants to the office. A caliph may nominate his successor (almost all the Umayyads and Abbasids did, but al-Māwardī does not reveal his opinion on the validity of a caliph's nominating his son). The caliph may not carry the title *khalīfat Allāh* (he is properly *khalīfa rasūl Allāh*—"The Deputy of the Messenger of God"). There is a long final discussion of circumstances under which the caliph might have to give up his office: evil conduct, heresy, mental illness, bodily incapacity, loss of liberty to function as caliph (the nub of the issue and the probable reason for composing the treatise). The caliph who would have lived up to all of al-Māwardī's conditions would have been a superior leader, indeed. In a manner characteristic of his biases, Māwardī says that the caliph would have had to know *fiqh,* so as better to protect the legal system and uphold the Sharī'a.

Other scholars wrote similar works, but al-Māwardī's treatise is one of the more thorough, and it came out of an active public career and familiarity with actual issues. Two centuries later the caliphate was a memory, although attempts to continue and revive it have been made down to the twentieth century, when the last vestige of it in the Ottoman Empire was abolished in 1924 by Mustafa Kemal Atatürk after the Turkish revolution. The caliph, even and perhaps most when he did *not* have direct political control of territories, has been a symbol of the unity of the umma under the Sharī'a.

***If the Caliph Is a Bad Ruler.*** One of the Muslims' most difficult problems has been how to behave under a bad ruler. The *'ulamā'* decided that it was legal to depose a caliph, but there was no procedure. A Sunnī population that initiated the procedure would be admitting error, because there had to be a *bay'a* in the first place. But the pledge of loyalty was considered to be void if the incumbent violated the terms of his office, terms that were never written down in a job description, to be sure, but that were nevertheless agreed on by consensus. Most caliphs actually held their positions by force, and the *bay'a* was more a fiction than a contract. Possibly if a constitutional model for the caliphate along the lines of al-Māwardī's treatise had been ratified (by *ijmā'*) early in the umma's history, many tragic developments could have been avoided. But to speculate in this manner is to stray from the historical, social, and political realities of Islam in its classical phases of development.

The Muslims tended to suffer bad rulers, partly because they concluded that as long as such a leader at least enforced the Sharī'a, things would work out. Their greatest fear seemed to be of a general disorder and confusion as well as the very real threat of damnation, should the Sharī'a be suspended even for a day. One of the ruler's main responsibilities was to maintain the *'ulamā'* and provide an orderly legal environment. It perhaps does not need to be pointed out that a basically wicked ruler could be punctilious in this for purely political purposes, for it would cost him nothing and increase his support, however grudging that might be. There was a degree of fatalism in the way that later Muslim theorists looked at such matters.

In addition to his thorough treatment of the caliphate, Al-Māwardī included a section in his book on "amirate by seizure." The amīr was the commander of the armies and thus the real power in the later Abbasid state. In his time the Buwayhids held this post, as we pointed out. Ideally, al-Māwardī argued, the caliph should select the amīr. But if the amirate should be seized, and the new incumbent cannot be removed, then put up with him. But this went against the Sunnī commitment to the "election" of rulers (it was certainly acknowledged that the amīr was the real power). Al-Māwardī got himself into difficulty here, but it was a real and not merely a theoretical problem, not of his invention. He attempted to mitigate the harshest implications of his position by stating that obedience should be rendered to an "amirate by seizure" only if the strong man delegates enough power to the *'ulamā'* to enforce the Sharī'a.

### *The Sultanate*

The title *sulṭān* originally pertained to temporal power only, especially military power. The sultāns were more ambitious than the amīrs in that they later attempted to assume religious titles, like caliph, and to present themselves as guardians of the true faith. Some political treatises of late Abbasid times and after never mention the caliph but instead speak of "monarchs" and "sultans" and "kings." The view matured among them that kingship and religion were true brothers, each needing the other to survive and maintain order. Kingly rule guards against anarchy, whereas religious authority leads the struggle against evil. This position is a functionalist view of religion, not regarding it as an end in itself but as a useful, indeed indispensable, ally of government. But Islam is understood by Muslims to be both *dīn* and *dawla,* "religion" and "government."

After the fall of the caliphate the sultan was the supreme Islamic ruler. All idealism was swept away with the old system, and the Muslims realized that in the sultan they were dealing with naked force. A certain Egyptian Sunnī jurist by the name of Ibn Jamā'a put forth the extreme view that when an unqualified person imposes himself on the nation by military might alone, his *bay'a* (it was thought that a pledge was still needed for rulers after the caliphate had perished) was automatic and therefore legal. This view is similar to the old imperial Chinese notion of the Mandate of Heaven's being transferred from one incumbent to another, for example, after a revolution. The winner is thought to have heaven's favor. In the Muslim case it was thought that such a ruler would at least be able to restore unity among the Muslims. This was an unfortunate development, though, for it resulted in legitimating coups d'état. Ibn Jamā'a failed to refer to the Sharī'a as the centrally important authority, and this was the fatal flaw in his rationalizations about power politics. He was not taken seriously, therefore, except by the Mamluke rulers of Egypt who had taken power in that country by force.

***Ibn Taimīya.*** A Ḥanbali jurist from Syria, Ibn Taimīya (d. 1328 C.E.), took Ibn Jamā'a sternly to task for his views and over his long career carried on such a vitriolic attack against the accommodators and vacillators, both in this field and in others (like saint cults), that he was constantly thrown into prison and regarded as unbearable by the rulers. A pamphleteer and popular preacher, Ibn Taimīya wanted to rid Islam of the abuses that had crept into the religious and the political spheres. Ibn Taimīya was both a first-rate theologian and legal and political theorist, in some ways the prototype of the balanced Muslim thinker. His devotion to both the letter and the spirit of the Sharī'a as the ideal for the umma was developed in his own important work, *Al-Siyāsa al-Shar'īya,* "Administration [according to the] Sharī'a."[9] In it Ibn Taimīya exhibits no interest in the caliphate, holding that neither was it a necessary institution nor did its historical existence have any peculiar virtues.

The caliphate, Ibn Taimīya argued, was not required by the Qur'an, the Sunna, or the consensus of the companions. The only valid caliphs were the first four, but after them Islamic leaders could only be called imāms, whether in the religious or the political sense (though not in the Shi'ite sense.) There is no election or selection of a leader by some fiction of providing legitimacy. Governance is a political matter, and it should be carried out so far as possible for the welfare of the people, but always in light of the Sharī'a. The ruler should enable the *'ulamā'* to function properly. God is the real sovereign, and he demands obedience on all levels of the population. Two contracts are at work here, and this insight is original with Ibn Taimīya: the Muslim community associates with its fellow members under the Sharī'a, thus enjoying a spiritual and symbolic unity; specific Muslim communities or nations make a pact of government, entering into a contract with the ruler and rendering obedience to him on condition that he cooperates with and facilitates the work of the *'ulamā',* upholding and enforcing the Sharī'a. If the ruler does not live up to this second contract, the pact with him will be dissolved. It is up to the Muslims to establish governments in the best way they can and to get rid of bad rulers if the people's consensus is that the Sharī'a has not been served. This idealistic doctrine is also a realistic one in that it anchors itself in the actual world and does not get tangled up in inconsequential stipulations about caliphs and their qualifications, which were never practically effective, anyway.

"Sharī'a politics" is another way to translate *siyāsa shar'īya.* Ibn Taimiyya's uncompromising approach to the governance of the Muslims was sustained by a religious energy that welled up in the midst of life as an ecstasy of obedience. Ibn Taimīya's theories were also supported by commitment to their application. His views were not influential during his lifetime, but four centuries later they provided a theological and theoretical underpinning for the Wahhābi reforms in Arabia, whose reverberations are still being felt today. It is hard to categorize Ibn Taimīya, because he fell into no particular school. Although he was a Ḥanbalī jurist, he engaged in theological disputation and writing. And although he was a practical, this-worldly Muslim activist, he was also a Sufi mystic whose funeral in Damascus was attended by over 200,000 people. And even though he attacked the veneration of saints and visits to their tombs for blessing and intercession, after his death the simple pious adopted the practice of making pilgrimages to his tomb to pay their respects and seek the benefits of his spiritual power (*baraka*). His long periods in prison enabled him to compose many formal treatises as well as pamphlets. (The despondency brought on by the removal of his writing materials is said to have caused his death.) Finally, although he was loyal to his Ḥanbalī *madhhab,* he nevertheless considered himself to be a *mujtahid* and insisted that without *ijtihād,* the umma would make an idol out of its own past tradition, which was the prisoner of *taqlīd,* "blind imitation." The only indisputably authoritative voices of the past were the Qur'an, the Sunna, and the pious *salaf,* or the companions and other leaders of the first generation of Islamic history.

### *The Shī'ī Imamate*

The word *imām* has been used in connection with Sunnism as well as Shī'ism. It is a Qur'anic expression, meaning "pattern," "model," "leader," but never in any sense that reflects the later definitions of the term. All Muslims use the term to refer to the one who stands before the congregation to lead the prayer. Eminent religious scholars are also called *imām.* In Cairo, for example, everyone knows that the bus that follows the "imam" route ends up at the square near the magnificent tomb of Imām al-Shāfi'ī, the greatest of the Sunnī legal scholars. And as we saw in the previous section, the Sunnī caliph was also known as the imām, because he was the supreme leader of the community.

Shī'ism preserves its own developed and variegated doctrines and lore concerning its leaders, the greatest of whom are given the title of imām. The Shī'ī approach to governance is not reducible merely to a political difference of opinion about rule. Rather, Shī'ī convictions about their imāms are essential to their linking of human affairs to divine purposes. Both Sunnī and Shī'ī ideas about religion and the state are politics of God, but they differ in character, although they each are recognizably and essentially Islamic.

Both Shī'ism and Sunnīsm are original and early dimensions of the Islamic tradition, each with overlapping characteristics. As Seyyed Hossein Nasr succinctly put it:

> Sunnism and Shi'ism, belonging both to the total orthodoxy of Islam, do not in any way destroy its unity. The unity of a tradition is not destroyed by different applications to it but by the destruction of its principles and forms as well as its continuity. Being the "religion of unity" Islam, in fact, displays more homogeneity and less religious diversity than other worldwide religions. Sunnism and Shi'ism are dimensions within Islam placed there not to destroy its unity but to enable a larger humanity and differing spiritual types to participate in it. Both Sunnism and Shi'ism are the assertion of the *Shahādah, Lā ilāha ill'Allāh,* expressed in different climates and with a somewhat different spiritual fragrance.[10]

As we saw in our brief discussion of Shī'ī law, that collection of Islamic subcommunities by no means agrees on who their authentic leaders were. The one thing that Shī'is do agree on, however, is that the only true imām is one that descended from the Prophet through the line of 'Alī and Fātima. Imam and caliph were not the same thing for Shī'īs, although they were for Sunnīs: imām is a far more exalted idea for Shī'īs.

The numerical proportion of Shī'īs to Sunnīs does not indicate the importance of the minority group, which amounts to perhaps as much as 20 percent of the umma. The small subgroup of Shī'īs known as the Zaydīs, who are today dominant only in North Yemen, constitute the most moderate of the Shī'ī sects. They are not insistent on a specific lineage of imāms but have recognized various descendants of Hasan or Husayn, sometimes more than one at the same time. One strict stipulation is that imāms may not succeed one another by inheritance so as to create a dynasty. In theology, they are Mu'tazilite, and they tend to be anti-Sufi. In *fiqh,* Zaydīs have pursued a variety of methods, in practice not being much different from the four Sunnī schools.

***Legal Concept of the Imamate.*** Both the Ismā'īlīs and Imāmīs, introduced earlier in this chapter, have a very strong doctrine of the imām as a divinely appointed and sustained leader with perfect wisdom and judgment to guide the Muslims. The imāms, according to these two main Shī'ī branches, are a sort of continuation of the work of Muhammad. In contrast with the Zaydīs, the Ismā'īlīs (Seveners) and Imāmīs (Twelvers) insist on a hereditary descent and recognize their respective lines of imāms as possessing the esoteric knowledge of religion that was first passed on by 'Alī.[11] This secret or, rather, inner gnosis distinguishes the true imāms from other worthy individuals who may also be descended from 'Alī and who deserve the respect and prayers of the faithful as being among the *ahl al-bayt,* the "people of the [Prophet's] house."

Our outline has been overly sketchy, for the development of imām doctrines in these two communities was complex and, especially in the case of the Ismā'īlīs, difficult to trace because of the secrecy shrouding the sect's most sacred doctrines. In general, Imāmī Shī 'ism maintains a balance between its inner and outer doctrines, whereas the Ismā'īlīs tend to emphasize the esoteric, or *bāṭinī,* dimension.

Both schools consider the world of appearance to be underlaid by a more real and enduring world of realities. The imāms are uniquely qualified by means of a divine light, known as the *nūr muḥammadī,* "the Muhammadan light," to serve as authoritative teachers for the Muslims during this historical phase of the cosmos's existence. The historical epoch of the universe's being has been divided into two cycles: the cycle of prophecy (*nubuwwa*) and the cycle of interpretation, known as *wilāya,* meaning "sainthood," specifically of one who is a close associate or "friend" of God. Muhammad was the last in the cycle of prophecy, whereas 'Alī began the cycle of *wilāya,* which will continue until the Judgment Day.

The cycle of *wilāya,* then, is the period during which the imāms dominate and guide.[12] The imāms, in a sense, are representatives and continuators of prophecy. God always maintains an imām for the Muslims, even though that imām may be hidden and apparently powerless. They serve as intercessors between humans and God and in all ways preserve the Shī'īs from error. The light that they all have shared transcends each individual imām, who remains a human being, but an elevated human being, because of the graciousness of his office and the powers associated with it. The Shī'īs make a very large place in their religious life for visiting the tombs of the past imāms. The Sunnī parallel would be visits to the shrines of famous saints whose remains are believed to possess great spiritual power for blessing and intercession. Not all Sunnīs, however, consider saint veneration and visits to tombs to be acceptable, and the practice is, in fact, forbidden in Saudi Arabia because of the puritannical Wahhābi dominance there since the eighteenth century.

## ISLAMIC LAW AND THE STATE IN THE PRESENT ERA

This chapter has introduced Islamic Law and the State in their classical meanings, ideals, and functions during the rise of Muslim governments, such as the Sunni Caliphate and the Shi'i Imamate in premodern times. Much of what has been covered in this chapter still functions in ways that reflect enduring respect for Islam's legal traditions generally, but often with adaptations to modern ways of life and the development of national legal systems that draw on principles and practices based both on Islamic values and common law as developed in European models. The landscape of modern Muslim legal thought and governance according to Islamic principles is both exceedingly complex and diverse.

Specific examples of how Muslim legal thinkers have dealt with the challenges as well as opportunities of modernity and imperialist colonialism are addressed in Chapter 14: "Major Movements and Trends in Renewal and Reform." Generally speaking, in the modern era the greatest continuing influence of classical Shari'a standards and regulations has been in the area of personal status law, covering marriage, divorce, and inheritance. And personal status debate and deliberation is by no means restricted to Muslim majority states and regions. With so many Muslims now living in Western countries, both in Europe and the Americas, secularist national governments are increasingly being asked to enact legislation that recognizes Islamic legal practices in personal status matters as acceptable for their Muslim citizens.

A 2005–2007 Gallup poll of unprecedented scope, based on tens of thousands of interviews with residents of thirty-five nations with Muslim majority or at least substantial Muslim populations, learned that "majorities in most countries, with the exception of a handful of nations want *Sharia* as at least 'a' source of legislation."[13] The poll also found that substantial majorities also favor some form of democratic rule, but not necessarily Western models. Both the concepts of *Sharī'a* and democracy have wide ranges of meaning, as the poll discovered. And the study cited above also provides an important way of distinguishing the *Sharī'a* from Islamic law as follows:

> To clarify the distinction between *Sharia* and "Islamic law," think of *Sharia* as a compass (God's revelation, timeless principles that cannot change) and Islamic law (*fiqh*) as a map. This map must conform to the compass, but it reflects different times, places, and geography. The compass is fixed; the map is subject to change.[14]

## NOTES

1. Fazlur Rahman, *Islam* (New York: Anchor Books, 1968), p. 117.
2. "Ḳiyās," in *Shorter Encyclopedia of Islam,* ed. H. A. R. Gibb and J. H. Kramers (Ithaca, N.Y.: Cornell University Press, 1953), p. 267.
3. Ibn Mājah, from his collection of *Ḥadīth, "Fitan"* section.
4. Rahman, *Islam,* pp. 83–84. Rahman's emphasis.
5. "Ḳāḍī," in *Shorter Encyclopedia of Islam,* pp. 201–202.
6. This section relies heavily on E. I. J. Rosenthal, *Political Thought in Medieval Islam: An Introductory Outline* (Cambridge, England: Cambridge University Press, 1958), Part I, chap. 2, "The Caliphate: Theory and Function."
7. As reported in Ibn Khaldūn, *The Muqaddimah,* vol. 1, trans. F. Rosenthal (Princeton, N.J.: Princeton University Press, 1967), p. 466.
8. An excellent English translation is Al-Mawardī, *The Ordinances of Government,* trans. Wafaa H. Wahba (Reading, U.K.: Garnet Publishing, Ltd., 1996). A reliable summary is by H. A. R. Gibb, "Al-Mawardi's Theory of the Caliphate," in the collection of his articles edited by S. J. Shaw and W. R. Polk as *Studies on the Civilization of Islam* (Boston: Beacon Press, 1962), pp. 151–165. See also H. A. R. Gibb's "Some Considerations on the Sunni Theory of the Caliphate," in the same volume, pp. 141–150. Both essays have informed the present discussion.
9. Available in English as *Ibn Taimiyya on Public and Private Law in Islam,* trans. Omar A. Farrukh (Beirut: Khayats, 1966).
10. Seyyed Hossein Nasr, *Ideals and Realities of Islam* (Boston: Beacon Press, 1972), p. 148.
11. See Abdulaziz Abdulhussein Sachedina, *The Just Ruler in Shi'ite Islam* (New York: Oxford University Press, 1988). A study of the authority of the jurist in imāmī *fiqh.*
12. See Nasr, *Ideals and Realities of Islam,* pp. 174–176 for a clear and fairly detailed explication of this and related Shī'ī doctrines.
13. John L. Esposito and Dalia Mogahed, *Who Speaks for Islam? What a Billion Muslims Really Think* (New York: Gallup Press, 2007), p. 48.
14. *Ibid.,* p. 53.

PART FOUR

# The Sufi Way of Mysticism and Fellowship

CHAPTER

# 10 Islamic Mysticism and the Disciplines of Esoteric Piety

### KEY TERMS

| | | |
|---|---|---|
| ***ṣūfī*** | ***āyāt*** | ***fanā'*** |
| ***taṣawwuf*** | ***walī*** | ***baqā'*** |
| ***bāṭin*** | ***faqr* and *faqīr*** | ***malāma* and *malāmatīya*** |
| ***ẓāhir*** | ***ma`, rifa*** | ***maqām* (pl. *maqamāt*)** |
| ***dhikr*** | ***ṭarīqa*** | ***ḥāl* (pl. *aḥwāl*)** |

## SUFISM

There are many Muslims who would put this chapter much earlier in an account of Islamic religion. That it is included toward the end of this book in no sense implies that it is less significant or influential than, say, law or political forms or systematic theology. In some ways the mystic path of Islam undergirds and inspires all else, because it is more closely linked to the fundamental sources of Islamic religious life: the Qur'an and the Prophet. Logically, given the *quality* of what will be considered in the following pages, it should have come before our treatment of history, law, and theology. But chronologically and institutionally, it comes later. That is, although it can be convincingly argued that a deeply mystical sensibility was operative in the life and work of Muhammad and certain of his companions, especially 'Alī, it took generations, even centuries, for it to develop and find expression in such institutionalized and regularized forms as societies, literary genres, meditation patterns, artistic traditions, and systematically articulated doctrines.

To some extent, Sufism was the inner power of Islam from the beginning, but in another sense it has been a renewing and reforming response to developments and trends that have from time to time sapped Islam of its vitality and spontaneity. For example, as mosque-centered worship and devotional life became more formalized and dominated by the *'ulamā',* many Muslims yearned for a warmer, more spontaneous daily spiritual life, in the English poet William Cowper's words, "a closer walk with God." Similarly, when the Islamic empire had reached a position of enormous power and wealth, there were thoughtful people who asked: Is this all there is? Were we created on this earth to get rich and then die? The people who would come to be known as Sufis decided to strike out on a spiritual quest for permanent meaning, beyond the structures and rhythms of *ḥayāt al-dunyā,* "the life of this world." Sufism is not a sect, but a widespread and many-sided dimension of Islamic piety.

### The Term Sufism

The English word *Sufism* derives from the Arabic word ***ṣūfī,*** an "adept of the mystical path" of Islam. But *ṣūfī* is in turn most likely derived from the Arabic root *ṣūf,* "wool," of which the coarse-woven garments of early Muslim ascetics were made. An alternative theory is that the original root is *ṣafā,* meaning "purity." There is much written on the origin of the term *ṣūfī,* but convention came to prefer the "wool" theory, though admitting that other hypotheses also had much to recommend them. The word *ṣūfī* strictly applies only to quite advanced mystics, ones who could be masters to beginners. The related term *mutaṣawwif* means "novice," one who is just learning. A third rank is the *mustaṣwif,* one who wants to be admired as a seeker after spiritual truth but who is essentially a "phony." When the Sufis came to be admired by the Muslims, they were accompanied by charlatans and fakes who wore patched woolen frocks and wanted to be respected and given charity as saintly persons. An old saying goes: "The *Mustaṣwif* in the opinion of the Sūfīs is as despicable as flies, and his actions are mere cupidity; others regard him as being like a wolf, and his speech unbridled, for he only desires a morsel of carrion."[1] The technical term by which the Muslims identify Sufism is ***taṣawwuf.*** The two will be used interchangeably here.

### The Sources of Sufi Spirituality: Qur'an and Prophet

Sufism has been of great interest to Western scholars and to a larger intellectual population interested in "Eastern" spirituality. This interest stems from the literary excellence of Sufi-inspired poetry and prose, as well as the appealing qualities of much of Sufi theosophy: its breadth of spirit, its tolerant attitudes toward other paths, and its subtle appreciation of the human condition, couched often in paradoxical, even punning language. Until relatively recently, there was a tendency among Western scholars to attribute much, if not most, of Sufism to pre-Islamic and extra-Islamic sources, such as Gnosticism, Buddhism, Hinduism, Zoroastrianism, and Christian and Jewish forms of mysticism. Although extra-Islamic influences cannot be denied, the major roots of Sufism are indigenous to Islam. These are the Qur'an and the Prophet Muhammad. Sufis themselves have always traced their spiritual lineages back to Muhammad and God. The suggestion that essential elements of the tradition originated outside is unintelligible as well as impertinent. Also, Western self-congratulation on discovering the authentic Islamic roots of Sufism is fatuous. But the purpose of this chapter is to provide an overview of Sufi ideas and practices, not a history of scholarship.[2]

***Sufi Interpretation of the Qur'an.*** The Qur'an is the primary source of Sufi sensibility and the model and continuing guide for its sustenance. Although all Muslims look to the same Qur'an, there are many ways in which it is appropriated and interpreted. As we observed in Chapter 6, there are two basic types of exegesis of the text: *tafsīr,* which is a plain investigation of literal meaning, and *ta'wīl,* which tends toward allegorical and symbolic interpretation. The Sufis became deeply involved in *ta'wīl* and in fact incorporated it into their overall approach to God. That is, allegorical and spiritual interpretation is part of their true religious quest, and not something preliminary to it. To Sufis there is always a hidden and higher, as well as an evident and plain, meaning of Qur'anic passages, just as there is a hidden (***bāṭin***) and obvious (***ẓāhir***) meaning to other dimensions of life.

The word **dhikr,** "remembrance," "mentioning," and its verbal forms occur frequently in the Qur'an and have special meaning for Sufis. "Mention God often" (3:41) is interpreted by the Sufis both literally and symbolically, so that the constant remembering of God through recitation of the Qur'an, praise, and prayer came to constitute a distinctive pattern of spiritual discipline known as *dhikr.* It took on a variety of forms, some musical and ecstatic, others quiet and inward, and in the case

Shrine and burial place of Shaykh Rukn al-Dīn Multānī. Fourteenth century C.E. Multan, Southern Punjab, Pakistan. (*Source:* Frederick Mathewson Denny)

of the Mawlāwīs of Jalāl al-Dīn Rūmī, centered in a sacred dance performed by "whirling dervishes," as they are romantically called by tourists. Some of the details of *dhikr* will be outlined in Chapter 11.

The Qur'an speaks often of the "signs" ***(āyāt)*** of God in nature and in history, which, for those who can "see" and understand them, provide spiritual lessons and a special sense of closeness to God. The Sufis have meditated on these signs with the conviction that having been sent by God, they lead back to him as well. More than that, God knows what man's "soul whispers within him, and We are nearer to him than the jugular vein" (50:16). The wonderful as well as awful nearness of God is often remembered by the Sufis.

> And when My servants question thee concerning Me—I am near to answer the call of the caller, when he calls to Me. (2:186)

> To God belong the East and the West; whithersoever you turn, there is the Face of God; God is All-embracing, All-knowing. (2:115)

This latter verse is one of the most mysterious ones in the Qur'an that the Sufis ponder, especially when paired with the following verse:

> All that dwells upon the earth is perishing, yet still abides the Face of thy Lord, majestic, splendid. (55:27)

The attaining of a right relationship with God is not accomplished simply by means of meditation, as we see in the following Qur'an verse:

> And give the kinsman his right, and the needy, and the traveller; that is better for those who desire God's Face; those—they are the prosperers. And what you give in usury, that it may increase upon the people's wealth, increases not with God; but what you give in alms, desiring God's Face, those—they receive recompense manifold. (30:38–39)

The expression "Face of God" should not be taken literally, for it pertains to his inner essence and attributes, which are invisible and eternal. "Face" is a vivid metaphor for God's personal nature, and it is through a deep personal relationship that the mystic draws near to his or her Lord. And God is the one who turns first toward his creatures so that they might turn toward him (for example, 9:118): The initiative is God's.

The Sufis emphasize God's love more than his justice, without, of course, denying the latter in any sense. The mutuality between God and his creatures is expressed in a passage that the Sufis have never tired of quoting:

> O believers, whosoever of you turns from his religion, God will assuredly bring a people He loves, and who love Him, humble towards the believers, disdainful towards the unbelievers, men who struggle in the path of God, not fearing the reproach of any reproacher. . . . Whoso makes God his friend, and His Messenger, and the believers—the party of God, they are the victors. (5:54,56)

The word for *friend* in Arabic is ***walī,*** which also carries the meanings of "kinsman," "patron," "neighbor," and "protector." Applied to humans, it has come to mean "saint" and as such is a potent title throughout the Islamic religious system, particularly on the popular level, of which more will be said in Chapter 13. The intimacy suggested by the term is notable, and love more than justice befits such a personal relationship. There is something about life itself that causes the Sufi—or perhaps any sensitive person—to catch his or her breath and occasionally stare wide eyed in gratitude. The modern question of whether God exists is rather beside the point when humans come to realize their own existence. To "seek the Face of God" is to seek what offers enduring satisfaction. In a sense, the search is itself the goal, and the Sufis realize that future joy and contentment are not different in kind from the ecstasy of their present relationship with God, with each *walī* to the other. The relation of friend and patron is not a propositional matter, but an experienced state. It is "tasted," as al-Ghazālī said, rather than cogitated.

***The Qur'an and the Prophet.*** It is not possible to distinguish completely the Qur'an as the main source of Sufi inspiration and doctrine from the Prophet Muhammad, who is so intimately related to the message. "You have a good example in God's Messenger for whosoever hopes for God and the Last Day, and remembers God oft" (33:21). The Sufis see their beloved Prophet as thoroughly saturated by the Qur'anic message, and they believe that in reading it Muhammad's soul is made manifest. They especially delight in recalling Muhammad's mysterious "night journey" up through the seven heavens to the presence of God (see 17:11). In this initiatory experience Muhammad was given the special power and wisdom that the Sufis consider to be the charter of their own continued existence, because they trace their lineage back to Muhammad and through the "night journey" to God himself. Likewise, Muhammad's first encounter with his Lord is a potent testimony for the Sufis.

> By the Star when it plunges, your comrade is not astray, neither errs, nor speaks he out of caprice. This is naught but a revelation revealed, taught him by one terrible in power, very strong; he stood poised, being on the higher horizon, then drew near and suspended hung, two bows-length away, or nearer, then revealed to his servant that he revealed. His heart lies not of what he saw . . . indeed, he saw one of the greatest signs of his Lord. (53:1–11,18)

The Qur'an is itself the most powerful spiritual source of Sufism, but Muhammad's own intimate acquaintance with God and his having been the human means by which the message was transmitted to the world make him inextricably related to it. We have seen how the Qur'an and the prophetic Sunna are fundamental to Islamic law; they are similarly essential as the bases of Sufism, although they are appropriated and applied in very different ways and for different ends.

***The Sufi Ḥadīth.*** The Sufi collections of Ḥadīth include many of the same ones that are accepted by orthodox jurisprudence as sound. But much else is also included, and so legal scholarship came sometimes to suspect the Sufis as deficient in their standards relating to traditions of the Prophet. The modern British expert on Sufism, A. J. Arberry, has observed that of the two general classifications of Sufi Ḥadīth[3]—those that deal with the Prophet's ascetic views and practices and those that are more theosophical—orthodox Muslims have tended to suspect the latter far more than the former. Whatever the case may be with respect to their historicity, the traditions that the Sufis have actually pondered and transmitted have been significant to the development of Islamic mystical thought and practice. One type of *ḥadīth* (discussed in Chapter 7) that Sufism has especially stressed is the "divine saying" (*ḥadīth qudsī*), a third category of utterance among the Qur'an, God's own speech, and Muhammadan traditions, which the Muslims consider to be reports of Muhammad, a human being. The divine saying purports to be God's speech, but not part of the Qur'an. The following examples should convey some idea of their appeal for mysticism.

> When Allah decreed the Creation He pledged Himself by writing in His book which is laid down with Him: My mercy prevails over My wrath.[4]

> I am with My servant whenever he remembers Me and his lips move (in mention of Me).[5]

> My Earth and My Heaven contain Me not, but the heart of my faithful servant containeth Me.[6]

> I was a hidden treasure, and I desired to be known; therefore I created the creation in order that I might be known.[7]

These and many other divine sayings provide an array of ideas and insights for Sufi meditation and devotion. This type of source appeared very early in Islamic piety, and according to William A. Graham, a contemporary specialist in the subject, gives us a valuable insight into earliest Sufism, before it developed into schools with specific and distinctive methods of spiritual cultivation. But such sources have had no significant impact on Islamic jurisprudence and very little on Sunnī dogmatic theology. In Shī'ī Islam they have had much greater influence and are deeply ingrained in the religious sensibilities of Shi'ite Muslims in general. This preponderance is not surprising considering the great devotion to the Prophet's family within that branch of Islam.

The Prophet soon became much more than a man in the ordinary sense. As we noted earlier, the Muhammad of history became, after his death, the Prophet of faith. One prophetic *ḥadīth* even goes so far as to identify God and his messenger: "He that hath seen me hath seen God."[8] This is not as radical a notion as it first appears, when another *ḥadīth* is recalled: "Consult thy heart, and thou wilt hear the secret ordinance of God proclaimed by the heart's inward knowledge, which is real faith and divinity."[9] That is, God has implanted something of himself in the basic constitution of his human creatures, so that when they are thinking and living truly, they cannot help but reflect God's glory. All of this goes to show how intimate the relationship between God and humans is, according to the types of sources Sufism has cultivated and made central. This has led to the characterization of Sufism as the "heartbeat of Islam."

Some claim that far from being heterodox, enthusiastic, somewhat radical, and personalistic, Sufism is in fact *normative* Islam, by which other forms must be gauged. This is implied in a famous saying of Abū'l-Hasan Fushanjī, who lived in the third century after the Hijra: "Today Sufism is a name without a reality, but formerly it was a reality without a name."[10] That is, in the time of the Prophet and his companions and for the early generations, Islam was spontaneous, alive, and authentic. Sufi reality was its heart but did not need to be identified as such. Then there were no *mustaṣwifs,* "phony Sufis" who wanted to be admired and emulated. As al-Hujwīrī concluded his gloss on this saying: "Formerly the practice [that is, of *taṣawwuf*] was known and the pretense unknown, but nowadays the pretense is known and the practice unknown."[11]

All Muslims venerate the Prophet to a greater or lesser degree, and the cultivation of his Sunna has united them through the ages. Muhammad as a guide to the right way to God is seen in the conviction that whenever a Muslim raises up the salat, he or she is making a personal *mi'rāj* or ascension to God, just as the Prophet did in his miraculous journey. The special character of Muhammad's guidance is discerned in the doctrine of the "Muhammadan light" (*al-nūr al-muḥammadī*), which Shī'īs consider to be present in the imāms, generation after generation, giving them authority to interpret the Qur'an and preserving them from error. Beyond Shī'ism, Sunnis also sing hymns to the Prophet, in which he is regarded as preexistent and perfect; human yes, but in the sense that a gem is also a stone, but polished and translucent.[12] The characteristics that Muslims discern in their Prophet were discussed in Chapter 7. Sufis have been influential in extending the role and symbolism of Muhammad to that of universal human, the model for authentic existence in union with God.

## ASCETICISM IN EARLY ISLAMIC CONTEXTS

When the Islamic empire reached its peak of power and wealth under the Umayyads and early Abbasids, thoughtful Muslims began to cultivate simpler lives and eschew material possessions. People looked back on the Prophet and the rightly guided caliphs and others of the first generation and period of conquests as having generally lived sober and simple lives. There is no reason to doubt that Muhammad and his companions were not corrupted by worldly luxuries, but later legend holds them up as paragons in this regard, mostly because their successors often indulged themselves excessively in hedonistic pursuits. Something of Muhammad's simplicity and relative poverty has already been described. Among his immediate successors as caliphs, Abū Bakr and 'Umar stand out as especially self-denying. But extreme asceticism was not condoned by Muhammad, nor does it seem to be suggested in the Qur'an. This is especially true if it includes celibacy, which Islamic practice rejects in all but the most unusual circumstances.

The Sufis have regarded Abū Bakr as a model of renunciation, the technical Arabic term for which is *zuhd.* Abū Bakr embraced poverty voluntarily, as al-Hujwīrī illustrates in his interesting discussion of the first caliph, who is said to have prayed: "O God, give me plenty of the world and make me desirous of renouncing it!" This odd utterance is glossed by al-Hujwīrī as follows:

> This saying has a hidden sense, viz.: "First bestow on me worldly goods that I may give thanks for them, and then help me to abstain from them for Thy sake, so that I may have the treble merit of thanksgiving and liberality and abstinence, and that my poverty may be voluntary, not compulsory."[13]

'Umar, whose shabby garments became legendary, provides the inspiration for the Sufis' patched cloak, the emblem of the life of renunciation and spiritual poverty, known as **faqr.** So central is this idea of poverty that ***faqīr*** ("poor one") early became a synonym for *mutaṣawwif.* There is, of course, a gentle irony in the title *faqīr,* for the truly poor are the truly wealthy in the attributes and virtues that matter with God. The Prophet himself is reported to have exclaimed, "In poverty is my pride."

### *Hasan of Basra*

Probably best known among early Sufis for ascetism and a general distrust of the sensual world was al-Ḥasan al-Baṣrī (d. 728), who was also a theologian and a famous preacher whose sermons affected many in Basra. Hasan lived in perpetual fear of God's judgment and was said never to laugh or talk in a lighthearted way. He admonished his fellow believers to avoid dealing with rulers, to keep a safe distance from women—however virtuous—by never being alone with them, and not to listen to what others say in conducting one's life. Hasan was not so much a technical mystic, in the sense that he provided a distinct system of meditation and attainment of union with God, as he was a powerful witness to the saintly life of reverent fear and world renunciation. His weeping for the sins of himself and the world was legendary in his own time, and this aspect of him approaches the "pathological," as William James defined the type in his discussion of mysticism in *The Varieties of Religious Experience.* But Hasan was not at all disabled by his melancholy nature and tragic view of life. He made major contributions to the development of *kalām* and always maintained a balance between speculative issues and questions of personal piety. All Sufis afterward looked back to him as one of their heroes, a trailblazer of the religious life and inspiration for all Muslims.

Hasan of Basra is somewhat of an exception among early Sufis in his having been also a *mutakallim* whose *kalām* activities were in the center of Islamic thought and as near to what might be called *orthodox* as could be hoped. He was, in other words, what has been called a *sober* Sufi in that nothing he did or taught was suspect in the eyes of other observant, pious Muslims of Qur'anic grounding. This statement raises the issue of Sufism as a heterodox or even heretical form of Islam, and there did develop a great variety of doctrines, views, and practices among mystically inclined believers, which ran the gamut from Hasan of Basra's conservative and centrist teaching to rather extreme positions in which esoteric doctrines and devotional excesses predominated. In some cases, even the Sharī 'a was rejected as being a veil between humankind and God and a form of idolatry. This "antinomian" form of

Sufism, which actually took on different forms and was by no means always shockingly anti-Sharī'a, was never a major type of piety, although by its nature it drew attention to itself. A third form was characterized by a sort of intoxication, brought about by a feeling of ecstatic union with God.[14]

## *Rābi'a*

Asceticism did not necessarily mean that a person had to spend his or her adult life sorrowing and weeping in fearful reverence of God and dread of the Last Day. Asceticism was also a form of liberation from the things of this life and a preparation for the afterlife in dependence on God alone and in hope of his satisfaction (*riḍā'*). If Hasan of Basra exemplifies the fear of God, a later Basran, the woman Sufi Rābi'a al-'Adawīya (d. 801), introduced an emphasis on love, and this became ever after a characteristic of Sufism in all its forms. Rābi'a was austere in her lifestyle but joyful in her communion with God. Many men desired to marry her and proposed, but she always refused, asserting that she belonged entirely to God and could not give herself to anyone else. Her ecstatic love for God, expressed in language and symbols of passionate intensity and longing, was nevertheless a disinterested love. That is, she loved God for himself alone and neither from fear of hell nor hope of heaven. God alone could satisfy her, just as God's satisfaction alone was sufficient for his slaves. She was bold in her approach to God when compared with Hasan, who was so very fearful. She prayed to God at night:

> O Lord, the stars are shining and the eyes of men are closed and kings have shut their doors, and every lover is alone with his beloved, and here am I alone with Thee.[15]

Her doctrine of the kind of love that one must have for God is epitomized in the following famous poem:

> I have loved Thee with two loves, a selfish love and a love that is worthy (of Thee).
> As for the love which is selfish, I occupy myself therein with remembrance of Thee to the exclusion of all others,
> As for that which is worthy of Thee, therein Thou raisest the veil that I may see Thee.
> Yet there is no praise to me in this or that,
> But the praise is to Thee, whether in that or this.[16]

Although they almost surely never met face to face, Rābi'a having been only a young slave girl when Hasan of Basra was very old, there are many legends linking the two. One of them has Hasan refuse to remain at any gathering that did not include Rābi'a. Another displays Rābi'a's wit in turning down Hasan's proposal of marriage. She posed to him a riddle in four parts, each of which dealt with her situation with respect to God on Judgment Day. He confessed that the answer was a hidden affair in each case, known only to God, to which she replied:

> Since this is so, and I have these four questions with which to concern myself, how should I need a husband, with whom to be occupied?[17]

Hasan wept profusely and often. Once when Rābi'a was passing beneath his window, she felt some drops of moisture fall on her. Looking up and finally ascertaining that it was Hasan's tears and not rain or something else, Rābi'a reportedly exclaimed:

> O teacher, this weeping is from pride of self; rather weep tears (as a result) of looking into your heart, that within thee they may become a river such that within that river you will not by searching find your heart again unless you find it in the Lord of Might.[18]

This remark is said to have silenced the self-occupied old saint.

***Ibrāhīm ibn Adham.*** Rābi'a had many disciples, and she also was on equal terms with other prominent Sufis, who did not condescend to her because of her sex. Indeed, in many cases she was regarded as clearly the superior because of her penetration and authority. She was apparently able to reprehend important or phony people without making them hate her, as she did with regard to Hasan's dripping tears. One legend has the famous Ibrāhīm ibn Adham, another contemporary, making his way excruciatingly slowly across the desert to Mecca. It took him fourteen years to reach it, because at every prayer place he stopped to perform two prostrations. Finally arriving at the great sanctuary he looked up only to find the Ka'ba missing. Thinking he must be blind, he was told by a mysterious voice, "No harm has befallen your eyes, but the Ka'ba has gone to meet a woman, who is approaching this place."[19] It was, of course, Rābi'a. He was furious with jealousy and exasperation, but she upbraided him for his having taken fourteen years to reach Mecca because of his neurotic obsession with ritual.

Ibrāhīm ibn Adham, it must be added in all fairness, was no small person but a profound and powerful spiritual guide to many. He had been a prince in his native Balkh, but when he was out hunting one day an animal—some say an antelope—addressed him in moving words. "Wast thou created for this, or wast thou commanded to do this?"[20] Like the young Buddha Guatama, with whom he is often compared, Ibrāhīm renounced his royal title and lifestyle and took to the road as a wandering dervish, living for a long period in the desert, where it is reported that he was taught mystical truth by al-Khiḍr, the wonderful, legendary "Green One" of Near Eastern religious folklore, who is believed to be the mysterious companion of Moses in the Qur'an story (18:66–83). Often when a person has reached mystical maturity and "enlightenment" (known in technical Sufi terminology as **ma'rifa**) without the aid of a human master, it is said that al-Khiḍr has conferred the *khirqa,* the cloak that symbolizes initiation into the select company of Sufi adepts. The great Spanish Sufi of a later age, Ibn 'Arabī (d. 1240), was also said to have been invested with the *khirqa* by al-Khiḍr, and throughout his long and intellectually as well as physically adventurous life, he continued to insist on being taught by an inner light. His independence and radical recasting of basic Islamic doctrines concerning the divine unity (he was accused of pantheism) and other matters nearly led to his being assassinated in Egypt. Such individualism has frequently been a mark of Sufism.

## SUFI SYMBOLISM

If Sufism developed early a characteristic ascetic style with respect to material possessions and comforts, it also cultivated a variegated system of symbols and signs based on interior reflection and meditation and expressed often in arresting, sometimes sublime poetry. Some of Islam's greatest literary productions were inspired directly by Sufism. Arabic became a major medium for Sufi poetry, but ultimately much of the greatest verse was composed in Persian, for example, couplets written by Jalāl al-Dīn Rūmī.

### *Ibn al-Fāriḍ*

The greatest Arabic-speaking poetic exponent of Sufism was Ibn al-Fāriḍ (d. 1235), who appeared when the movement had established most of its characteristic positions and practices. He is said to have composed his verse while in a state of ecstatic trance, during which "he would now stand, now sit, now repose on his side, now lie on his back, wrapped like a dead man; and thus he would pass ten consecutive days, more or less, neither eating nor drinking nor speaking nor stirring."[21] Although not precisely a theologian or philosopher, Ibn al-Fāriḍ nevertheless thought and composed at the very highest theosophical level, but through the aesthetic means of poetic art rather than the formal medium of academic discourse. It is possible to say things, or to allude to them in verse, when to articulate them in prose would be risky as well as inadequate. Ibn al-Fāriḍ, like his great contemporary Ibn 'Arabī, was pantheistic in leaning, and throughout their work can be seen the vision of the unity of being centered in the absolute oneness of God.

> All thou beholdest is the Act of One.
> In solitude, but closely veiled is He.
> Let him but lift the screen, no doubt remains:
> The forms are vanished, He alone is all;
> And thou, illumined, knowest by His light
> Thou find'st His actions in the senses' night.[22]

These lines are from Ibn al-Fāri's long poem, the *Tā'īya,* so-called because of its 760 verses, all of which end in *t* (*tā'* = *t* in Arabic). This masterpiece is available in a translation by R. A. Nicholson, the greatest scholar of Ibn al-Fāriḍ in English. Another poem is the "Ode to wine," or *Khamrīya,* which takes as its subject the intoxication of divine love.

> . . . a vintage that made us drunk before the creation of the vine.
>
> • • •
>
> But for its perfume, I should not have found the way to its taverns; and but for its resplendence, the imagination would not have pictured it.
>
> • • •
>
> Seek it in the tavern, and there to the accompaniment of tuneful notes bid it display itself, for by means of music it is made a prize.
> Wine never dealt with Care in any place, even as Sorrow never dealt with Song;
> And though the intoxication with it have but the life of a moment, thou wilt regard Time as a slave obedient to thy command.
> Joyless in this world is he that lives sober, and he that dies not drunk will miss the path of wisdom.
> Let him weep for himself—he whose life is wasted without part or lot in wine![23]

Wine is a metaphor for God's love, of course, and the tavern is the source, where music is also found that lifts the soul to God. These themes occupied much of Sufi poetry, especially in that in Persian, in which wine and its effects are much more graphically described and celebrated than in the relatively chaste but bold verses for the paradoxically sober "drunk," Ibn al-Fāriḍ. The lusty drinking song of the Jāhilīya desert Arab was transformed into the ode to Sufi ecstasy. Ibn al-Fāriḍ's poetry strongly evokes desert settings. He was a native of Egypt, but spent a long time in the Hejaz, which he loved and whose influences on his art can be seen in many places. The *Tā'iyya* has been likened by the French specialist on Sufism, Louis Massignon, to the *kiswa,* the richly embroidered black velvet covering of the Holy Ka'ba in Mecca, because it is for spiritual pilgrims who through mystical discipline and meditation make their way to God at his center.[24]

### *Wealth and Poverty*

By Ibn al-Fāriḍ's time (he died in 1235), we are no longer in the early Islamic period. Sufi doctrines had advanced to their highest points by then, and there were numerous variations on central themes. An ascetic discipline continued to be basic, even though it was by no means always extreme in its practices. Sufis had come to realize that material poverty and spiritual poverty are not necessarily coterminous. The Sufis often argued about whether poverty or wealth was better, both being conditions or attributes of human existence. The learned Persian Sufi al-Hujwīrī declared that God alone was wealthy and that his wealth was of a different kind from worldly possessions:

> Wealth is a term that may fitly be applied to God, but one to which Man has no right; while poverty is a term that may properly be applied to Man, but not to God. Metaphorically a man is called "rich," but he is not really so. Again, to give a clearer proof, human wealth is an effect due to various causes, whereas the wealth of God, who Himself is the Author of all causes, is not due to any cause. Therefore there is no community [that is, an attribute common to both God and humans] in regard to this attribute. It is not allowable to associate anything with

> God either in essence, attribute, or name. The wealth of God consists in His independence of anyone and in His power to do whatsoever He wills: such He has always been and such He shall be for ever. Man's wealth, on the other hand, is, for example, a means of livelihood, or the presence of joy, or the being saved from sin, or the solace of contemplation; which things are all of phenomenal nature and subject to change.[25]

Another element in this discussion is purity (*ṣafwa*), which some regarded as not only the supreme virtue of mysticism but also the word whose root is the true source of the term *taṣawwuf,* "sufism."[26] Purity is the perfection of annihilation, some argued, whereas poverty (*faqr*) relates to things, if only by their absence, and therefore pertains to the phenomenal world. Purity, *ṣafwa,* is beyond the conditions of created existence and subsistence and thus in another realm, so to speak (although to be "in" any thing or condition is to be bound by spatial–temporal categories, and *ṣafwa,* according to the debates, may not legitimately be considered to be subject to categories).

In everyday human life, it is possible to distinguish two kinds of poverty: *faqr,* the poverty of renunciation of worldly goods, and *maskana,* the poverty of lowliness, with an absolute minimum of livelihood. The latter is not a state that persons seek or desire, but one that most people simply find themselves in: a bare means of getting along in regard to food and shelter and clothing. Some Sufis argue that the *faqīr* (spiritually poor) is superior to the *miskīn,* (materially poor) because the former relies on God alone and not on worldly means, however meager, whereas the *miskīn* would gladly change places with the rich person. Other Sufis argue that *maskana* is superior to *faqr,* because the former condition is given, the acceptance of which makes one paradoxically independent of material goods, whereas the latter is a deliberate means to approach God and therefore is, paradoxically, unbelief. The debate has never been concluded to everyone's satisfaction.

## SUFISM AS AN ESOTERIC DISCIPLINE: THE ṬARĪQA OR WAY

The Sharī'a, as we learned in the preceding chapter, is the Way of the Muslims in the sense of the divine law and the proper ordering of society on earth. There is another term, ***ṭarīqa,*** that means "way," and more than way, in the sense of a highway or road, it means "method," "system," "procedure," and even "creed." It also means a specific type of Sufi brotherhood or order, and this meaning will be the central topic of the next chapter. But here we shall investigate what *ṭarīqa* means as a discipline of the Islamic spiritual life. The Sharī'a often stands for the external way of all Muslims, embodied in acts of worship, regulations for community life, "enjoining the right and forbidding the wrong," as the Qur'anic phrase puts it. The Tarīqa, on the other hand, often means the inner way, beyond adherence to the Sharī'a. The Sharī'a, then, provides the structure of *exoteric* Islam, know as the *ẓāhir,* and the Tarīqa embodies the *esoteric,* known as the *bāin.* Remember the discussion of Qur'anic exegesis in

Chapter 6 in which we distinguished between *tafsīr,* "plain interpretation," "correct literal meaning," and *ta'wīl,* "allegorical interpretation," which explores inner, hidden meanings. Sharī'a and Tarīqa are to each other what *tafsīr* and *ta'wīl* are. The two should be balanced and mutually complementary, neither one arrogating to itself exclusive rights or truths. Generally, the Sharī'a is regarded as the greater of the two, because it applies to all Muslims and is sufficient unto salvation if obeyed and preserved. By the time one reaches the more mysterious and difficult and select level of the Tarīqa, one should have cultivated an exemplary Muslim life under the Sharī'a. That is, ascending to the somewhat elite level of Sufi spiritually does not excuse one from Sharī'a responsibilities. In fact, some Sufis fulfilled them to excess. Sufis have disagreed on this issue, some insisting that at the higher levels the mere performance of *'ibādāt* and other aspects of Sharī'a-centered life is a veil separating the seeker from ultimately realizing gnosis and union with God. Sharī'a, for this point of view, is more or less a pedagogical and ordering system that is finally only a provisional discipline for the majority who have not yet attained the higher elevations of the mystic path.

Many Muslims, especially of the more Sharī'a-minded sort, have, because of such a view, doubted the Islamic authenticity of Sufism. If certain people believe that they are beyond the Sharī'a, then what does this imply for the maintenance of the umma, which requires a motivated and disciplined communal commitment to the externals of Islam, as laid down in the Qur'an and the Sunna? Some Sufi extremists have also tended to focus on themselves and their own special mystical abilities, thus taking the focus from God, the transcendent one. The Sufi novice has traditionally been commanded to present himself to his master as submissively as the corpse is presented to the one who washes it before burial. This view has also led many Muslims to doubt the Sufi way. Because of these problems, the great early systematizer of Sufi theory, Sarī al-Saqaṭī (d. ca. 867) defined the true *taṣawwuf* as

> a name including three ideas. The sufi is he whose light of divine knowledge does not extinguish the light of his piety; he does not utter esoteric doctrine which is contradicted by the exterior sense of the Koran and Sunna; and the miracles vouchsafed to him do not cause him to violate the holy ordinances of God.[27]

Sarī's definition is a brief memorandum of what he and other Sharī'a-minded Sufis of his day and later regarded as abuses and excesses.

Most of the great earlier and Abbasid-period Sufis, down to the time of and including Abū Ḥāmid al-Ghazālī (d. 1111), belong to this sober, Sharī'a-obedient group, among whom should be mentioned such individuals as Hasan of Basra, Rābi'a al-'Adawiya, ārith al-Muḥ āsibī, Ibrāhīm ibn Adham, and Sarī's own nephew, the celebrated Baghdad master al-Junayd (d. 910), who was arguably the greatest single Sufi theoretician during the first half-millennium of the movement, not excluding al-Ghazālī, whose greatness lies in a different sphere, as we shall explain shortly.

## AL-JUNAYD AND SOBER SUFISM

Al-Junayd's development of the central Sufi doctrine of ***fanā'***, "annihilation," within a unified and self-consistent system has remained standard down to the present. He was a profound scholar as well as a meditative genius who could penetrate the secrets of his disciples and provide exactly the right guidance. This psychological skill is found in Sufi masters—it is one of the prime requisites for the position, you might say—but not all masters have had an intellectual understanding and control of it; most have operated at a more intuitive, even charismatic level. As might be said today, al-Junayd understood Sufism and maintained a "professional" level of ethics and competence among his disciples and colleagues. In short, al-Junayd was a mature human being, with all that that adjective implies, *ẓāhir* and *bāṭin,* externally and internally.[28]

Al-Junayd is said to have refused to discuss Sufi doctrine while his revered uncle Sarī was still living. Sarī, a humble and truthful man, had once declared that his nephew was superior in spiritual rank to himself, even though the older man was master to the younger. Later, in a dream, al-Junayd was commanded by the Prophet to teach the people for the sake of their salvation. Awaking, Junayd mused that his state was indeed higher than that of his uncle, because no less than the Prophet had spoken to him. Then a disciple of Sarī arrived telling Junayd that he would have to teach now that Muhammad had commanded him. He could refuse his uncle and the many others in Baghdad who had begged the young man to teach, but he could not refuse the Prophet. Stunned by this news from his uncle and master, Junayd exclaimed:

> I perceived that Sarī was acquainted with my outward and inward thoughts in all circumstances, and that his rank was higher than mine, since he was acquainted with my secret thoughts, whereas I was ignorant of his state. I went to him and begged his pardon, and asked him how he knew that I had dreamed of the Apostle. He answered:"I dreamed of God, who told me that He had sent the Apostle to bid you preach."[29]

Junayd was master of the religious sciences of the day and merely specialized in mystical lore. This breadth is characteristic of the orthodox, or "sober," Sufis, who took seriously their positions of influence and leadership and strove to conduct themselves within the Sharīʻa boundaries, while plumbing the depths and appreciating their limits. Here lies a mystery, for if God really does reveal his will and provide guidance in the externals of the Qur'an and Sunna and legislation, then the Muslim already has all that earth and heaven can embrace, and there is no need to leave the common ground of Muslim faith and practice. One simply journeys inward, never leaving the Sharīʻa behind. Put another way, the Sharīʻa can never be exhausted, for it is God's legislation and, more, the way to him. Recall that the term *sharīʻa* originally had as one of its meanings "the way to the water hole."

### *Union with God*

Al-Junayd was no mere intellectual or theorizer, a sort of distinguished professor who had a thorough scholar's knowledge of his subject and related fields. He longed to be in union with God and to give up the things of this passing world. Yet no mortal, Junayd knew, could ever be united with the One; there must always be a distinction between God and his creatures. But if a person can die to this present self and life, then all that remains is God. Everything that exists among created things is "perishing (*fānin*) yet still abides the Face of thy Lord" (Sūra 55:27) came to have a potent meaning for Junayd and gave to him the technical term *fanā*, "annihilation," "cessation of being," "extinction." If this extinction is achieved, then there will be only life in God, which is called ***baqā',*** literally, eternal "continuance" or "abiding." This sort of thing cannot be thought to make it happen; it must be experienced. It requires complete denial of the self in order to have that self perfected in God. *Fanā'* is reached by means of mystical states, including trancelike meditation. When one is united with God, one is absent from this world and the self. But then the Sufi returns to his or her normal self and the mundane world and in returning experiences great sadness and suffering. But, as Junayd insisted, it is like the suffering of being separated from a loved one, the sweet pain of lovers longing to be united over vast distances. The suffering is itself a sort of mark or proof of the relationship's reality. It is also a form of sobriety after the intoxication of union, and Junayd believed that this was a higher state than mystic intoxication in which the subject lost all sense of the self.

> Now I have known, O Lord,
> What lies within my heart;
> In secret, from the world apart,
> My tongue hath talked with my Adored.
>
> So in a manner we
> United are, and One;
> Yet otherwise disunion
> Is our estate eternally.
>
> Though from my gaze profound
> Deep awe hath hid Thy Face,
> In wondrous and ecstatic Grace,
> I feel Thee touch my inmost ground.[30]

***Criticism of Junayd's Doctrine.*** Al-Junayd was fully aware that some of his contemporaries were not satisfied with his doctrine, wanting instead to be lost in the bliss of union with God in a sort of intoxication that thrills and transforms without ill effects. Al-Junayd did not trust the sort of mystical ecstasy that people always want if they can have it, believing that it was not the highest station of spiritual maturity. Paradoxically, one must be separate from God to appreciate and stand in awe of his majesty and unity. But in this separateness one can also be perfected by God and brought into communion with him, and this is what *baqā* was to Junayd. It is not an egoistic desire to rise to God; rather, it is a longing to be purified and sustained by and within God, with all base things annihilated and left behind. This is finally a mystery to be pondered and believed rather than an intellectual problem to be solved by logical methods. Junayd habitually spoke and wrote in a sort of oblique and elliptical language, fearing both the trap of intellectual pride and the misunderstanding of most orthodox religious leaders and teachers, who were becoming increasingly critical and suspicious of Sufi teachings and practices.

The age of al-Junayd was the period following the overthrow of the Mu'tazilite supremacy in Baghdad. Sunnism had established itself with an increasingly narrow and law-centered focus. Independent reasoning (*ijtihād*) was on the wane, and the official mosque-oriented religion of the *'ulamā'* and normal ritual duties were alone to be regarded as authoritative and acceptable. The Sufis and their disciples were considered to be serious rivals to the orthodoxy that had emerged after major struggles in the legal and theological spheres. Just as in the field of *kalām,* with its tradition of relatively independent and rational inquiry, so also in regard to Sufism, with its emphasis on the interior and hidden dimensions of piety and speculation, there was a suspicion of deviation on the part of the legists, whose definition of heresy centered in the Arabic word *bid'a,* literally meaning "innovation." Some Muslims felt that the orthodoxy achieved by the Sunnī dominance constricted and inhibited authentic religious life, and so there developed a separate but by no means regulated variety of ways of cultivating inwardness and spontaneity. The Sharī'a-oriented Islamic life, in other words, was becoming too regimented and formal for people who were convinced that devotion to God was best achieved in warm, interpersonal contexts and in contact with guides who had themselves experienced higher states of consciousness. Al-Junayd and others like him provided an option to the official round of devotional life centered in the mosque. These "orthodox" Sufis did not in any sense consider their teachings or their example to draw Muslims away from the basic duties of Islam. But Islamic experience could not be and was not to be constrained by the *'ulamā's* vision of Islam.

## ANTINOMIAN SUFISM

A second major form of Sufi independence was *antinomian,* a rejection of the Sharī'a, at least the letter of it, in favor of pure dependence on God alone. One branch of this movement took its name, **Malāmatīya**, from the word ***malāma,*** "blame," whose root occurs in the Qur'an in the following passage:

> O believers, whosoever of you turns from his religion, God will assuredly bring a people He loves, and who love Him, humble towards the believers, disdainful towards the unbelievers, men who struggle in the path of God, not fearing the reproach (*lawma* = *malāma*) of any reproacher. (5:54)

### *Malāmatīya Sufism*

In its original form in the ninth century, Malāmatīya Sufism was concerned with following God in a sincere manner, without ostentation or self-righteousness. The true Muslim life was simple and unaffected and did not indulge in excessive or obvious piety. The admiration and approval of the world were thought to be snares for such people. Religion, it was learned, could become a barrier rather than a highway to God. Some of the Malāmatīs openly disobeyed the divine law, in one celebrated case by an obscene act (urinating publicly in an unacceptable manner) so as to earn the Muslims' reproach (*malāma*).[31] Such people internally thought themselves to be sincere in their devotion to God, especially as they cut off themselves from the approval of their fellow Muslims. It is not difficult to grasp the ironic dimension of this movement and even to admire it to some extent. But al-Hujwīrī, in a severe critique, considered the Malāmatīs to be no better than anyone else, because they were still unduly influenced by the responses of people and not singularly devoted to God.[32] By rejecting the approved religious duties, they exerted their own egos and thus succeeded in doing what they most wanted to avoid: appearing to be pious, however perversely.

Al-Hujwīrī's chapter on the Malāmatīya movement is subtle and wise; it recognizes that some kinds of blame come naturally to people who are misunderstood or resented for their uprightness. Such are not reproved by the great shaykh. But anyone who intentionally "abandons the law and commits an irreligious act, and says that he is following the rule of 'blame,' is guilty of manifest wrong and wickedness and self-indulgence."[33]

The best path to follow for one who seeks freedom from praise is not to reap blame but to become "nonexistent," as al-Hujwīrī put it. One must hide both pious works and shameful deeds from others, so as to be considered an object of indifference. Such a withdrawal requires pure devotion, for some desire admiration, and others have what appears to be a masochistic craving for mortification. Both are attachments to this world and thus impediments to the mystic life.

This problem is common to all religions and not unique to Islam. There is an old Japanese Buddhist story of a disciple whose spiritual master one day turned him out into the world, saying that his training was now finished and that he could go and teach others. While spending a night in a country inn on his travels, the mystic overheard a group of fellow travelers in the next room talking about him in low, awed tones, with one of them saying that he had observed something rare and wonderful about the solitary traveler in the next room. The disciple immediately packed his duffle and returned straight to his master, insisting that he was not ready to be sent out from him yet, because "there was still some light shining through."[34] Al-Hujwīrī seemed to agree that the obvious Sufi is not the real Sufi.

## INTOXICATED SUFISM: AL-ḤALLĀJ

The Malāmatīs provide an absorbing study and reveal most of the pitfalls as well as the potentialities of the mystic life. But there is another type of Sufi that has much in common with the blame seekers but goes on to surrender to intoxicating union with God at all costs. This is the third major category of Sufis. One of the early Sufis, the Persian Abū Yazīd al-Bistāmī (d. 875), upon discovering God in his own soul, exclaimed: "Glory to Me! How great is My Majesty!"[35] He was not praising himself as a mortal but acknowledging the presence of the living God. Nevertheless, his utterances shocked the pious and brought extreme censure. He was the first major exponent of the intoxicated Sufism that proved to be such a troubling yet powerful tendency, both in live witnessing to union with God and in literary products of the highest merit. Abū Yazīd was highly regarded in his time even by "sober" Sufis like al-Junayd, who wrote a commentary on his sayings that interpreted them in an orthodox manner. Abū Yazīd adopted the ascension of Muhammad as a central theme in his spiritual quest and thus started a trend continued by others.[36]

### Al-Ḥallāj

Al-Junayd had a would-be disciple who carried Abū Yazīd's type of intoxication to its logical limits by identifying himself with God in a manner that even the great Baghdad master could not condone. This was usayn ibn Man ūr al-allāj (d. 922), one of the most appealing and disturbing figures in Islamic history, over whom Muslims are seriously divided, even to this day.[37] As a young *mutaṣawwif,* Hallāj drifted from master to master without asking permission, thus violating a major propriety and inviting the scorn of the masters in Baghdad and other regions. He wanted to become al-Junayd's disciple, but the latter refused him, considering him to be mad as well as impetuous and self-centered. Hallāj was a brilliant young man who wrote many mystical texts, whose quality was considered to be mixed in both accuracy and propriety: he was independent. As a contemporary admirer observed, Hallāj was never considered authoritative either in his writings or his teaching, because he was never "confirmed," that is, formally approved by a recognized master. He was not, as we might say today, a member of the "union." He led an extremely ascetic life and traveled widely to Mecca, India, Persia (his native country), Central Asia, and other places. He seemed to have a deep knowledge of Hinduism, Buddhism, and especially Christianity, while remaining always a conscientious Muslim in faith and practice. He attracted a substantial following of disciples, although he was not part of the Sufi establishment, which at that time was dominated by al-Junayd and other orthodox types.

***Al-Hallāj's Blasphemy.*** Al-Hallāj ended up as a martyr for his convictions. His most famous utterance and the one that, because he refused to recant it, cost him his life, was *anā al-Ḥaqq,* "I am God" (literally, "I am truth" or "reality"). Another thing that caused him great trouble was his claim to have miraculous powers. Others accused him of magic. This strange mystic became the most extreme of the intoxicated Sufis, identifying absolutely with God, his beloved. One of his most fondly remembered allegories is about the moth that, circling ever closer to the candle's flame through fascination with the light, finally unites with it and is consumed. The human soul is like the moth, and God is like the flame. In 922, Hallāj was crucified in Baghdad for his blasphemy. Years earlier, someone had overheard a conversation between al-Junayd and al-Hallāj, in which the old master predicted death on the gallows for the young seeker. The "passion" of Hallāj bears some resemblance to that of Christ, and there seems to have been a conscious identification of the former with the latter. Hallāj is said to have approached his cross laughing and, after performing a final salat, to have raised up thanks to God for revealing to him "the raging fires of Thy Face" and hidden, mysterious things that no other was permitted to see. Before his slow execution was begun, Hallāj prayed:

> And these Thy servants who are gathered to slay me, in zeal for Thy Religion, longing to win Thy favor, forgive them, Lord. Have mercy on them. Surely, if Thou hadst shown them what Thou has shown me, they would never have done what they have done; and hadst Thou kept from me what Thou has kept from them, I should not have suffered this tribulation. Whatsoever Thou wilt do, I praise Thee! Whatsoever Thou dost will, I praise Thee![38]

Then Hallāj was executed in a hideous manner over a period of many hours without crying out, "nor did he plead for pardon," the source says.

More than three centuries later, Jalāl al-Dīn Rūmī composed a brief discourse on the subject of identification with God. Taking as his text Hallāj's immortal phrase *Anā 'l-ḥaqq,* he continues:

> People imagine that it is a presumptuous claim, whereas it is really a presumptuous claim to say *Ana 'l-'abd* "I am the slave of God"; and *Ana 'l-Ḥaqq* "I am God" is an expression of great humility. The man who says *Ana 'l-'abd* "I am the slave of God" affirms two existences, his own and God's, but he that says *Ana 'l-Ḥaqq* "I am God" has made himself nonexistent and has given himself up and says "I am God," i.e., "I am naught, He is all; there is no being but God's." This is the extreme of humility and self-abasement.[39]

There were those in Baghdad who understood what Hallāj was saying and, as in the case of Abū Yazīd al-Bistāmī, were willing to view it in a favorable, if qualified, manner. But what seems to have most aroused the religious leaders was Hallāj's *public* proclamation of what were really advanced doctrines that the masses were unable to appreciate and that consequently would be harmful to them. Had Hallāj kept his views to himself or to a small circle, he might not have been martyred. But he was surrounded by powerful political forces that threatened anyone who might spiritually arouse the populace. Hallāj's free approach to God and the religious life did not sit well with the religious establishment, which wanted conformity and control within traditional patterns. But as it turned out, and as is typically the case, the martyr's power after death is far greater than the preacher's power in life. Since Hallāj's time, mystics and others across the Islamic world have continued to be inspired by his free decision to die so as to be one with God. One hymn, universally known among the Sufis, begins: "Kill me, o my trustworthy friends, for in my being killed is my life . . ."[40] Hallāj is one of two great examples in Islamic history of the power of redemptive suffering. The other is, of course, al-Husayn, the martyr of Karbala.

## STATES AND STATIONS

By the time of Hallāj's death, Sufism was a fairly well-established movement, with a great variety of styles and emphases. Key doctrines that were to become classic elements of the system had been worked out. Among them was the hierarchy of "stations" (***maqām;*** pl., ***maqāmāt***) and "states" (***ḥāl;* pl., *aḥwāl***), a more or less systematic, although varying, sequence of "spiritual attainments" and "moods" (as Arberry characterizes the terms) that the novice was expected to pass through on his path to *gnosis,* the "saving knowledge" that the Sufis call *ma'rifa,* after which comes the unitive life in God. The "station" or *maqām* is a level on the ascending path to God that is achieved by the novice, and most authorities consider it permanent. There is a more or less set sequence of stations, and it is not considered proper—or even possible—to violate the order in which they may be attained. As al-Hujwīrī put it.

> Thus, the first "station" is repentance (*tawbat*), then comes conversion (*inābat*), then renunciation (*zuhd*), then trust in God (*tawakkul*), and so on: it is not permissible that anyone should pretend to conversion without repentance, or to renunciation without conversion, or to trust in God without renunciation.[41]

The ascending order includes a total of some twenty stations, according to one authority. After reaching *riḍā',* "satisfaction," "pleasure" [as in Sūra 5:119—"God was well-pleased with them (his truthful servants), and they were well-pleased with Him"], the traveler has reached the transition point between the stations and the states. The *ḥā l,* or "state," is considered to be a gift that God bestows on a person. It is a sort of "irresistible grace," to borrow St. Augustine's famous phrase. The novice cannot repel a *ḥāl* or attract or earn one. Al-Hujwīrī considered states to be transitory, "like flashes of lightning," as al-Junayd expressed it.[42] This is because the states are from God and cannot properly be made part of the attributes of a human being. But al-Muḥāsibī, another subtle and respected master (d. 781), whose name derives from the word for "self-examination," held that the state may be permanent. He centered his conviction in love, *maḥabba,* which all Sufis consider to be a state and thus a free gift from God. If love does not become a part of the Sufi, then he or she cannot be a lover, which is absurd. The love of the servant for the Lord is not a fleeting thing, but it is a permanent state that once bestowed, transcends logical or even psychological analysis. It is, according toal-Qushayrī, the next-to-the-last *ḥāl* on the ascending path, followed by *shawq,* the "yearning to be constantly with God."

Another characteristic dimension of the Sufi path is *dhikr,* the "remembrance" and "mentioning" of God, which the Qur'an commands should be done often (33:41) and which is calming to the heart (13:28). *Dhikr* is of two general types, one that is uttered aloud through the mouth and the other coming silently from the heart. There are further distinctions that different Sufi orders made and that became special features of their spiritual disciplines and methods, which we shall describe in the following chapter.

Solitary worshiper in a mosque in Isfahan, Iran. (*Source:* Ellen Fairbanks-Bodman)

## AL-GHAZĀLĪ AND THE RECONCILIATION OF SHARĪ'A AND ṬARĪQA

As the umma approached its five hundredth anniversary, a milestone that many regarded as auspicious, an unusual combination of motives, views, and experiences found their focus in a single life. The person who lived that life has been called the second greatest Muslim after Muhammad. He was Abū Ḥāmid Muḥammad al-Ghazālī, a Persian born in Tūs in 1058 who, after a long and eventful life of learning, teaching, traveling, and seeking wisdom, died in his native town in 1111, or 505 of the Hijra, having lived long enough to traverse that very special five hundredth anniversary and be hailed as a *mujaddid,* "renewer" of Islam. (It is traditionally believed that God will raise up such a renewer each century.) Orphaned as a youngster, Ghazālī and his brother, who himself became an influential and much-respected Sufi master, were brought up with the best available education. Abū Hāmid was finally trained by the greatest systematic theologian of the period, al-Juwaynī (d. 1083), known as the Imām of the Two Sanctuaries (that is, Mecca and Medina). (Juwaynī was a great logician and did much to strengthen *kalām* by means of logic.) Ghazālī, still at a relatively young age, was brought to the capital, Baghdad, and installed in what now would be called a university chair in the new theological institute, the Nizāmīya, named after its founder and patron, the *wazīr* Nizām al-Mulk, the most powerful political figure in the Islamic world of that time.

### *Ghazālī's Teachings*

Ghazālī was thirty-three when Nizām al-Mulk appointed him to his Islamic college. Over the next four years he earned an exalted reputation there as a teacher, with lecture audiences numbering in the hundreds. Ghazālī also produced many fundamental scholarly writings, especially on philosophy, *fiqh,* logic, and theology. A follower of the Ash'arite school, which was the closest thing Sunnīsm had to an orthodox brand of *kalām,* Ghazālī advanced it in some ways before deciding that rational theology of any kind was dangerous and not conducive to the authentic religious life. Ghazālī dealt philosophy a mortal blow in his celebrated *Tahāfut al-Falāsifa* ("The incoherence of the philosophers"), as we observed in Chapter 8, on creeds and theologies. But in the process he became a master of both *kalām* and *falsafa,* and his works in both fields are first-rate and have remained textbook models for generations of theological students.

***Spiritual and Physical Crisis.*** At the height of his success as a professor, al-Ghazālī contracted a serious physical ailment that rendered him literally speechless. His physical and emotional state also deteriorated until some began to fear for his life. At the core was a profound spiritual crisis. Ghazālī felt torn between his comfortable and rewarding life at the Nizāmīya and the growing sense that he was condemned to damnation. As he wrote in his spiritual autobiography, *Deliverance from Error:*

> It had already become clear to me that I had no hope of the bliss of the world to come save through a God-fearing life and the withdrawal of myself from vain desire. . . . I considered the circumstances of my life, and realized that I was caught in a veritable thicket of attachments. I also considered my activities, of which the best was my teaching and lecturing, and realized that in them I was dealing with sciences that were unimportant and contributed nothing to the attainment of eternal life. After that I examined my motive in my work of teaching, and realized that it was not a pure desire for the things of God, but that the impulse moving me was the desire for an influential position and public recognition. I saw for certain that I was on the brink of a crumbling bank of sand and in imminent danger of hell-fire unless

> I set about to mend my ways. . . . One day I would form the resolution to quit Baghdad and get rid of these adverse circumstances; the next day I would abandon my resolution. I put one foot forward and drew the other back. If in the morning I had a genuine longing to seek eternal life, by the evening the attack of a whole host of desires had reduced it to impotence. Worldly desires were striving to keep me by their chains just where I was, while the voice of faith was calling, "To the road! To the road! What is left of life is but little and the journey before you is long. All that keeps you busy, both intellectually and practically, is but hypocrisy and delusion. If you do not prepare now for eternal life, when will you prepare? If you do not now sever these attachments, when will you sever them?" (Translator's emphasis)[43]

After months of indecision and tension, Ghazālī's physical impediment appeared. He could barely eat food and could not talk. He turned toward God and was not disappointed. "He made it easy for my heart to turn away from position and wealth, from children and friends."[44] He declared publicly that he was going to Mecca on a pilgrimage, a thing that no one would ever question. But he privately planned to travel to Syria where he would spend time in retreat. He secretly decided never to return to Baghdad, but he could hardly announce that in light of his fame and his position as the personally appointed professor of Nizām al-Mulk, who had meanwhile been murdered by the Ismā'īlī Shī'ī group that gave its name to a new word, "assassins" (*al-Ḥashshāshūn,* "eaters of hashish"). There was possibly some real danger to Ghazālī from the Seljuk sultan in Baghdad, who had executed Ghazālī's uncle shortly before Ghazālī left Baghdad and his position as professor.

***Ghazālī and Sufism.*** Ghazālī became a Sufi and spent the next eleven years traveling and writing in Syria, Palestine, and Hejaz. He lived as a very poor man and wrote his masterpiece *Iḥyā' 'ulūm al-dīn,* "The revivification of the sciences of religion," a long work that in its modern edition fills four large volumes. Ghazālī finally returned to his native Persia, living for a while in his hometown of Tūs before accepting an invitation to teach once again. He did not continue long in this but returned to Tūs and founded a Sufi retreat center where he taught his disciples about the *ṭarīqa* and counseled and shaped them. This was one of the first, if not the first, Sufi hermitage or cloister, known in Persian as *khānqāh* and in Arabic as *zāwiya.*

Ghazālī came to the Sufi way after his other studies and accomplishments. He was especially influenced, as he admitted, by some of the great masters of the past, some of whom have been considered in this chapter: al-Muhāsibī, Abū Yazīd al-Bistāmī, al-Junayd, and al-Shiblī. He came to be convinced that

> what is most distinctive of mysticism is something which cannot be apprehended by study, but only by immediate experience (*dhawq*—literally "tasting"), by ecstasy and by a moral change. . . . I apprehended clearly that the mystics were men who had real experiences, not men of words, and that I had already progressed as far as was possible by way of intellectual apprehension. What remained for me was not to be attained by oral instruction and study but only by immediate experience and by walking in the mystic way.[45]

And that is what he did.

Al-Ghazālī achieved something that perhaps no one else could have done. His theoretical work on theology and Sufism was never as original or innovative as that of others, but the way he combined the fundamental themes of Islamic religion in his thought, teaching, writings, and especially example was unique. He was highly regarded by disparate parties that did not get along well with one another: Sunnī jurists, Ash'arite *mutakallims,* and Sufis. By means of a judicious blending of the key elements of all three, Ghazālī forged a new synthesis of what the Muslim life should be. His views of the Sharī'a were informed by spiritual sensitivity, and his Sufi devotion never went beyond the bounds of the holy law found in the Qur'an and the Sunna. Sarī al-Saqatī's definition of "true *taṣawwuf,*" quoted earlier in this chapter, applies perfectly to al-Ghazālī, who was the soberest of Sufis and did much to present the Tarīqa as normative Islam.

## NOTES

1. 'Alī ibn 'Uthmān al-Jullabī al-Hujwīrī, *The Kashf al-Maḥjūb: The Oldest Persian Treatise on Sufism,* ed. Reynold A. Nicholson (London: Luzac, 1936), p. 35. The title may be loosely translated as "The Uncovering of the Veiled." This magisterial work explores most of the dimensions of Sufism present by the eleventh century.
2. For a detailed history of scholarship of Sufism, see A. J. Arberry, *An Introduction to the History of Sufism* (London: Longman, 1943). A briefer survey is by Annemarie Schimmel, *Mystical Dimensions of Islam* (Chapel Hill: University of North Carolina Press, 1975), pp. 3–22.
3. Arberry, *Sufism* (New York: Harper Torchbooks, 1970), p. 25.
4. *Forty Ḥadīth Qudsi,* selected and translated by Ezzeddin Ibrahim and Denys Johnson-Davies (Beirut and Damascus: Dar al-Koran al-Kareem, A.H. 1400–A.D. 1980), p. 40.
5. William A. Graham, *Divine Word and Prophetic Word in Early Islam* (The Hague and Paris: Mouton, 1977), p. 130.
6. Arberry, *Sufism,* p. 28.
7. *Ibid.*
8. *Ibid.*
9. *Ibid.*
10. Al-Hujwīrī, *Kashf,* p. 44.
11. *Ibid.*
12. Seyyed Hossein Nasr, *Ideals and Realities of Islam* (Boston: Beacon Press, 1972), p. 88.
13. Al-Hujwīrī, *Kashf,* pp. 70–71.
14. I am indebted for this threefold categorization into "sober," "antinomian," and "intoxicated" to H. A. R. Gibb, "The Structure of Religious Thought in Islam," in *Studies on the Civilization of Islam* (Boston: Beacon Press, 1962), pp. 209–211.
15. "Rābi'a al-'Adawīya," in *Shorter Encyclopedia of Islam,* ed. H. A. R. Gibb and J. H. Kramers (Ithaca, N.Y.: Cornell University Press, 1953), p. 462.

16. Margaret Smith, *Rābi'a the Mystic and Her Fellow Saints in Islam* (Cambridge, England: Cambridge University Press, 1928), pp. 102–103.
17. *Ibid.,* p. 12.
18. *Ibid.*
19. *Ibid.* For additional anecdotes about Rābi'a, with many of her sayings, see Michael Sells, ed. and trans., *Early Islamic Mysticism: Sufi, Qur'an, Mi'raj, Poetic and Theological Writings* (New York: Paulist Press, 1996), pp. 151–170. Sells explains how the later Persian Sufi poet Farīdu d-Dīn 'Aṭṭār (d. ca. 1229) greatly influenced history's high opinion of Rābi'a as an extraordinarily wise and saintly person. 'Aṭṭār collected most of what we have concerning Rābi'a's life and sayings in his Persian book *Memorial of the Friends of God,* a strongly hagiographical treatment of seventy-five Sufi masters. The Rābi'a that is characterized in this chapter has been definitively shaped by 'Aṭṭār's much later, idealized accounts and not by much in the way of records that can be confirmed from Rābi'a's actual historical era.
20. Al-Hujwīrī, *Kashf,* p. 103.
21. Arberry, *Sufism,* p. 94.
22. Reynold A. Nicholson, *Studies in Islamic Mysticism* (Cambridge, England: Cambridge University Press, 1921), "The Odes of Ibnu 'l-Fārid," p. 191.
23. *Ibid.,* pp. 184, 188.
24. Louis Massignon, "La Cité des morts au Caire," *Bull. de l'Inst. Français d'Archéologie Orientale,* Le Caire, LVII, 1958, 79 pp.; repr. in Louis Massignon, *Opera Minora,* 3 vols, vol. 3. (Paris: Presses Universitaires de France, 1969), pp. 233–285. Cited in Schimmel, *Mystical Dimensions of Islam,* pp. 276–277.
25. Al-Hujwīrī, *Kashf,* pp. 21–22.
26. See Al-Hujwīrī, *Kashf,* pp. 58–61.
27. As quoted in Gibb, "Structure of Religious Thought in Islam," in *Studies,* pp. 209–210.
28. A well-rounded study is by A. H. Abdel Kader, *The Life, Personality and Writings of al-Junayd* (London: Luzac, 1962).
29. Al-Hujwīrī, *Kashf,* p. 129.
30. Arberry, *Sufism,* p. 59.
31. Schimmel, *Mystical Dimensions of Islam,* p. 86.
32. Al-Hujwīrī, *Kashf,* pp. 62–69.
33. *Ibid.,* p. 65.
34. I am indebted to Gary Snyder for this version, heard at a religious poetry seminar, University of Colorado, Boulder, August 9, 1983.
35. Arberry, *Sufism,* p. 54.
36. *Ibid.*
37. This sketch of al-Hallāj's life and work is based mostly on the section, "A Saint and His Fate," in Eric Schroeder's collection of sources, *Muhammad's People: A Tale by Anthology* (Portland, Me.: Bond Wheelwright, 1955), pp. 520–554. A profound yet accessible scholarly study of al-Hallāj is Louis Massignon, *Hallāj: Mystic and Martyr,* Abridged Edition, Herbert Mason, trans. and ed. Bollingen Series XCVIII (Princeton, N.J.: Princeton University Press, 1994), based on Mason's four-volume 1982 English

translation (also published by Princeton University Press) of Massignon's monumental *La Passion de Husayn Ibn Mansūr Hallāj; martyr mystique de l'Islam exécuté à Baghdad le mars 26 922; étude d'histoire religieuse* (Paris: Gallimard, 1922; nouvelle édition 1973). Massignon (1883–1962), a leading Roman Catholic intellectual and longtime professor at the Collège de France, spent his whole career studying al-Hallāj and fostering Muslim-Christian dialogue.

38. *Ibid.,* p. 553.
39. *Rūmi: Poet and Mystic (1207–1273): Selections from His Writings,* trans. and ed. Reynold A. Nicholson (London: Allen & Unwin, 1950), p. 184.
40. Schimmel, *Mystical Dimensions of Islam,* p. 69.
41. Al-Hujwīrī, *Kashf,* p. 181.
42. *Ibid.,* p. 182.
43. In W. Montgomery Watt, *The Faith and Practice of al-Ghazālī* (London: Allen & Unwin, 1953), pp. 56–57.
44. *Ibid.,* p. 58.
45. *Ibid.,* p. 55.

CHAPTER 11

# Masters and Disciples: The Forms and Functions of Sufi Orders

### KEY TERMS

| | | |
|---|---|---|
| ***silsila*** | ***al-insān al-kāmil*** | ***mathnawī*** |
| ***murīd*** | ***quṭb*** | ***ṭā'ifa*** |
| ***khirqa*** | ***mawlid*** | ***samā'*** |
| ***ribāṭ*** | ***ziyāra* (pl. *ziyārāt*)** | ***waḥdat al-wujūd*** |

## THE RISE OF SUFI ORDERS

Sufism cannot operate in a vacuum or without concrete forms of human association and structuring. During its centuries of doctrinal and meditational development it coexisted with the other forms of institutional Islam, not striking out in radically independent forms. Those more rebellious and freewheeling Sufis, like the Malamātīya, tended toward radicalism without settling into enduring institutional modes. Great spiritual guides like Hasan of Basra, Rābi'a al-'Adawīya, Hārith al-Muhāsibī, and al-Junayd operated close to the accepted structures of mosque and academic-legal discourse. Small groups of Sufis also clustered together in homes and meeting houses for training in meditation. But in its early periods, Sufism was much more of an elite spiritual preoccupation than a large-scale, popular movement. It was not until the time of al-Hujwīrī and al-Ghazālī, in the eleventh century, that more permanent, organized associations came into being, with representation from all levels of society and with an increasingly international scope in membership and influence. Ghazālī seems to have been one of the first to establish a definite brotherhood or order, with a governing discipline or rule and a residential, conventlike establishment, called a *khānqāh* in Persian (and *ribāṭ* or *zāwiya* in Arabic). In the century after

Ghazālī there were founded the great Sufi orders that endure to this day, about which more will be said later.

## SHAYKHS AND FAQĪRS: THE MASTER–DISCIPLE RELATIONSHIP

Before the Sufi orders were created, institutionalized expression was developed in the relationship between the master (*shaykh* in Arabic, *pīr* in Persian) and the disciple (*faqīr* or *murīd* in Arabic, *shāgird* in Persian). Unusually potent spiritual personalities emerged who attracted disciples, often in large numbers. These people traced their authoritative teaching back to acknowledged earlier masters, like al-Junayd, who in turn traced theirs back earlier, and so forth all the way to such figures as 'Alī and then to Muhammad himself, whose special relationship to God, as in the miraculous night journey, was universally attested. Thus there came into being the notion of a chain, called a **silsila,** extending backward in time all the way to Muhammad and God. In such contexts these spiritual lineages came to serve in a precisely parallel functional manner to the *isnāds* that scholars attached to *ḥadīths,* attesting to their authenticity. The *silsila* as "spiritual *isnād*" linked Sufis—both masters and their disciples—in a living bond with the past and in a real sense with the future also, for the teachings were handed down from master to disciple generation after generation. Tomorrow's shaykh was yesterday's *faqīr* or ***murīd.*** A kind of spiritual "grafting" took place that ensured the continuity of doctrine and correct discipline in each *ṭarīqa.* With the development of specialized orders, the term *ṭarīqa,* "path" or "method," came also to mean an actual communal organization of Sufis, centered in whatever method was pursued. (Hereafter tarīqa will mean the "Sufi Way"; *ṭarīqa* will be used for specific orders or methods.)

### *Defining the Master–Disciple Relationship*

Joachim Wach, a leading twentieth-century historian of religions, explained that the master–disciple relationship differs significantly from the teacher–student relationship, which it nevertheless resembles in certain respects.[1] The latter relationship is based on a common interest in a subject matter and a willingness to transmit knowledge of it. It is not necessary that the teacher and student have a personal relationship beyond mutual respect and courtesy and a willingness to cooperate according to the respective roles of the relationship. After the training is completed, the student and teacher may part ways, for the transaction—if it may be called that—is complete. If they continue to be in contact, whether socially or professionally or both, their relationship will nonetheless be not as it was when one was teacher and the other was student. The master–disciple relationship may also entail imparting knowledge and techniques, but it goes beyond that into a personal dimension of intense mutual engagement. The master and disciple are not brought together primarily for a transaction involving objective knowledge or techniques but, rather, for a spiritual reason and a desire to transform awareness in the inferior party under the superior wisdom and spiritual power of the master. As the Sufis say in this connection, the *faqīr* must present himself to his *shaykh* as a corpse to the one who washes it before its final commitment to the grave.

The disciple will always be the disciple in relation to his master, even though he may himself become master to other disciples in turn. A disciple may go on to another master, but in Sufism this is not permitted unless the previous master allows it. Recall that this was one of the main reasons why al-Hallāj had such a difficult time with the masters of his day. He never received the "confirmation" that has always been regarded as essential before a person may himself aspire to mastership. But there must come a day, as Wach observed, when the disciple and his master part ways. A certain sadness is associated with this, because of the intensity of the relationship. Something of the master's soul goes with the disciple, and something of the disciple's spirit remains with the master, and so there is a bond of love that endures after the physical separation. In the case of the *shaykh–faqīr* relationship in Sufism, the *shaykh* passes on the central doctrines of the *ṭarīqa* to his disciples, and they in turn maintain the tradition of brotherhood, because of their common master.

This *shaykh–faqīr* structure enabled Sufism to develop strong permanent institutions and to reach into all sectors of the societies and cultures in which it took root. The immediate disciples taught the principal ideas and techniques as well as the biographies of former masters, and there were also learners and listeners who were farther from the center yet devoted to the aims and ideals of brotherhoods. Organizations of craftsmen, like medieval guilds in Christian Europe, and young men's associations dedicated to Islamic ideals of courage and honor were created, often in close association with a Sufi *ṭarīqa,* which provided a sacred center and a means of communication with other idealistic Islamic organizations in far-off places. It is significant that when the umma's political order reached its lowest point in regard to unity and common purposes, the Sufi brotherhoods arose and provided a type of spiritual unity that proved in many ways to be much more powerful even than the caliphate in its glory.

## THE QĀDIRĪ ORDER: ISLAM'S MAJOR INTERNATIONAL SUFI BROTHERHOOD

The first great Sufi brotherhood was founded by the Persian 'Abd al-Qādir al-Jīlānī (1078–1166).[2] As a student of Ḥanbalite *fiqh* in Baghdad, he came under the influence of Sufi masters and after a long novitiate was finally invested with the **khirqa,** the tattered woolen robe certifying authentic Sufi status. It is said that some of his fellow *mutaṣawwifs* had resented having a legal scholar in their midst, especially a Ḥanbalite. When 'Abd al-Qādir was about fifty, he began preaching publicly, and soon his audiences grew so large that a special place had to be set aside. Followers established a ***ribāṭ*** (retreat) for him, which included several buildings that were used as a religious school with 'Abd al-Qādir as its head. People came to live at the retreat and spent long periods in association with the Ḥanbalite jurist who had become a Sufi shaykh. A number of 'Abd al-Qādir's disciples went on to become great figures themselves. His teaching was well within the tradition of "sober" Sufism and included much orthodox matter, whether on law or the Qur'an. He exerted his principal influence as a preacher to all levels of society, from the rich, influential, and well educated all the way down to the very humblest people. Even rulers and high government officials came under his sway. From 'Abd al-Qādir's time onward, this power was a special feature of *ṭarīqa* Sufism in many places. So powerful did the spiritual masters become and so widespread their followings that rulers were sometimes made or unmade by them. They served as advisers and spiritual guides and represented a sort of Islamic ideal of God's rule in the midst of the believers, especially after the caliphate's demise. The Sufi masters became part of a grand hierarchy of saints extending all the way up to a spiritual master called the **perfect man,** or ***al-insān al-kāmil,*** who served as a "pole" (***quṭb***) around which the world revolved and from which it received guidance and strength and meaning. This ***quṭb*** was placed in the cosmos by God, through whom he worked his will in the world and sustained it.

### *'Abd al-Qādir's Teachings*

'Abd al-Qādir did not himself subscribe to such a bold theosophy: his message was relatively simple and straightforward. But after a generation or two, his followers began to ascribe miracles and wonderful things to 'Abd al-Qādir, so that eventually he became the center of a real cult with a full-blown liturgy and hagiography linking him with the saints of the past and all the way back in a *silsila* to the origins. It is doubtful that 'Abd al-Qādir ever intended to establish a permanent order, but that was the effect of his teaching and influence. His disciples maintained his authority and passed on his teaching and spiritual power, or *baraka,* to others in a continuous chain.

'Abd al-Qādir's sermons did not contain advanced Sufi terminology or concepts; they were popular. Yet the great master did teach the necessity of asceticism before anyone could embark on a path of serious devotion to God. All created things separate humans from their creator, acting as *veils,* a term frequently encountered in Sufism. 'Abd al-Qādir had a clear sense of his own authority, but after his death people came to regard him as on a level near to that of the Prophet Muhammad, a result of the adulation of his school.

'Abd al-Qādir had forty-nine children, and after him one of his sons carried on the order's activities, and after him, his son, and so on. Some of 'Abd al-Qādir's followers started spreading his teaching during his lifetime, promising heaven to those who joined. The Qādirī order thus became prominent in many parts of the Islamic world, but especially in the Indian subcontinent and North Africa, where it also spawned suborders like the Rifā'ī order, founded by 'Abd al-Qādir's nephew Ahmad al-Rifā'ī (d. 1182). This order was from the beginning more exuberant than its parent and featured such practices as extreme mortification of the flesh, walking on fire, glass eating, and other things.

Unlike other major orders, the Qādirīya did not have a distinctive form of *dhikr,* nor did its founder ever develop one. The order is quite orthodox and tolerant, not requiring its members to break with the piety of normal observant Muslims. Although the *dhikr* and other practices required no great divergence from the normal religion of the masses, the cult of the founder was nevertheless extreme, in that 'Abd al-Qādir's rank was at the very top of all saints, and rivaled, as we observed, the Prophet himself. Some of the titles given to 'Abd al-Qādir are "Light of Allah," "Sword of Allah," "Proof of Allah," "Pole of Allah," and "Command of Allah."

## OTHER CLASSIC SUFI ORDERS

### *The Suhrawardīya Order*

Before considering two other major orders, we shall list the more prominent ones, together with the regions in which they prospered. The second of the greater orders to be founded was that named after Shihāb al-Dīn 'Umar ibn 'Abd Allāh al-Suhrawardī (1144–1234) [not to be confused with his famous townsman Abūal-Futūh, who was executed for his heretical (pantheistic) ideas in 1168; that native of Suhraward is known as al-Suhrawardī *al-maqtūl,* which means "Suhrawardi martyr"]. Shihāb al-Dīn gained wide fame, and his moderate doctrines, close to orthodoxy, drew many Muslims of all classes to his movement. The Suhrawardīya has been very influential in India, especially in Bengal and what is now Bangladesh.

### *The Shādhilīya Order*

Another major order was founded in North Africa by Nūr al-Dīn Ahmad ibn 'Abdallāh al-Shādhilī (1196–1258) and is known as the Shādhilīya. It became prominent in North Africa, Egypt, the Arabian Peninsula, and Syria. Although wide in its appeal, the Shādhilīya order is more extreme in its practices than are the other large orders, like the Qādirīya, with which it often coexists and with which it has also spawned other orders.

### *The Bektāshīya Order*

Among the Turks a very prominent order was that of the Bektāshīs, which for centuries was closely associated with the Ottoman military elite: the Janissary corps. The Bektāshī order was quite independent from the orthodox Islam of the *'ulamā'* and mosque and included Christian and traditional folk elements in its doctrines and rituals. Regarding the external duties of Islam, such as the salat, as nonessential, the Bektāshīs held to an esoteric doctrine centering in 'Alī, Muhammad, and Allah and recognizing the twelve imāms of Shī'ism. When new members were received, a sort of communion service featuring wine, bread, and cheese was held. The adherents confessed their sins to their leaders, and women also participated as equals in the rituals. The Bektāshīs gathered in their distinctive meeting places, known in Turkish as *tekkes* (cf. *zāwiya, khānkāh, ribāṭ*). There is much of the Turkish soul in the history of Bektāshī mysticism, for the order gained a secure foothold in many Turkish villages and neighborhoods. Some of the finest Sufi lyric poetry was composed by Bektāshīs. The order was officially disestablished in 1925 by the new secular government of Mustapha Kemal Atatürk, although it had been gradually waning since 1826 when the Ottoman Janissaries were abolished and exterminated.

### *The Badawīya Order*

A very old order with a wide peasant following and a blending of heterogenous elements is the Badawīya in Egypt, founded by Sayyid Ahmad al-Badawī in the thirteenth century.

***Sīdī Ahmad.*** Sīdī Ahmad, as he was known, was born in Morocco of parents who descended from an old Hejazi family that had been traced back even to 'Alī. Sīdī Ahmad grew up as a superb horseman and invincible fighter, admired by the extremely *macho* types with whom he associated, especially in Mecca, where as a young man he lived for a number of years. One scholar has translated his picturesque Arab nickname *Abū 'l-Fityān* as "Champion Bruiser,"[3] but it could also be rendered "Master Chevalier," for it certainly pertained to his horsemanship and martial skills.

The mosque–tomb–school complex of Sayyid Ahmad al-Badawī in Tanta, Egypt. The huge crowds are attending his autumn birthday celebration *(mawlid)*. (*Source:* Frederick Mathewson Denny)

The *Khalīfa* or head of the Badawīya order, who rides at the end of the festival procession through the streets of Tanta on the final day of the *mawlid*. (*Source:* Frederick Mathewson Denny)

***Sīdī Ahmad and Sufism.*** When Sīdī Ahmad reached about age thirty, he underwent a profound transformation and became a Sufi. He studied some *fiqh* and a great deal of Qur'anic science. His personality change included withdrawal from the world and long periods of silence, practices that contrasted sharply with his earlier life of brawling. He had visions that led him and his older brother to travel to Iraq, where they paid their respects at the shrines of 'Abd al-Qādir al-Jīlānī and Ahmad al-Rifā'i, whose then relatively young *ṭarīqas* had already come to dominate spiritual life in the Middle East. Sīdī Ahmad then traveled from Iraq to Egypt, where he took up residence in the delta city of Tanta, a place where there was already a considerable amount of Sufi activity and several prominent masters. In Tanta, Sīdī Ahmad became the center of a new order that eventually took his name. His activities there included unusual feats of spiritual athleticism, like standing on a roof and staring at the sun for long periods and engaging in lengthy periods of total silence or prolonged screaming, as well as going without food or drink for extended periods. The stories about him include many miracles.

Other Sufi masters in Tanta greatly resented him as a foreign intruder, but he gradually eclipsed them and came to be associated with Tanta and spirituality all over Egypt. This is a rare achievement for a non-Egyptian, because although the Egyptians are a very hospitable people, they have a clear sense of who is and who is not one of them. Sīdī Ahmad came to be the greatest saint of Egypt, a position that he holds to the present day.

***Sīdī Ahmad's Birthday Celebrations.*** There are several ***mawlids,* birthday celebrations**, held each year in Sīdī Ahmad's honor, but the autumn one—significantly dated according to the old solar calendar—is the largest and most lavish. It is a huge country fair, with crowds of peasants clogging the streets of Tanta for a week or more. The Sufi brotherhoods gather in gaily colored tents and perform their *dhikrs* far into the night. Sword swallowers and musicians and dancers can be seen in the streets, and hundreds of people hawk all kinds of wares, especially festival foods. Some of the practices associated with Sīdī Ahmad's *mawlid* and with his cult in general center in fertility, both of soil and humans, and earlier scholars hesitated to describe all of the activities that were observed. The saint is able to impregnate or make barren women fertile, it is said, and there are rituals associated with visitations to his tomb, housed in a cluster of buildings in the center of Tanta. But besides the folk aspects, some of which extend back well before the coming of Islam or even Christianity, there is a sense of Sīdī Ahmad's representing an authentically Islamic form of popular religion. The theological institute associated with the great mosque in Tanta is in all of Egypt second only to Cairo's great Azhar University.

People all over Egypt and beyond venerate the saint's burial place and make visits (***ziyārāt***) there in order to receive his *baraka.* Egyptians cry out for aid and intercession, saying: "Ya Ahmad! Ya Badawi!" I have myself participated in conversations with Egyptian peasants (*fellāḥīn*) who were convinced that Sīdī Ahmad could hear us talking about him and that we therefore had to be very circumspect in our language—and this was in Cairo, some sixty miles from Tanta. The Badawīya order is very different from the more restrained and orthodox Qādirī order, although both have wide appeal. Red is the color associated with Sīdī Ahmad, and in each generation, the *khalīfa,* his successor, wears a bright red robe. Each year on the final day of the great autumn *mawlid,* a grand and colorful processional of Sufi orders, craft guilds, soldiers, and schoolchildren marches for several hours through the streets of Tanta. The current *khalīfa* rides at the rear on an elaborately adorned horse and is accompanied by men riding camels on which they beat big copper kettledrums. The *zaffa,* or parade, ends when the procession reaches the great mosque and performs the Friday salat, with the red-robed *khalīfa* being in the place of honor, as he represents for each age the power and guidance of Sīdī Ahmad himself and carries his doctrine down in a continuing *silsila.* The year that I attended the autumn *mawlid,* officials estimated the number of visitors to be more than one and a half million. Thus, it rivals the hajj in its ability to attract crowds and in the past has even exceeded it.

Master of a chapter of one of the Badawīya orders in the *zaffa*, or procession, during the autumn *mawlid* for Sayyid Ahmad al-Badawī in Tanta. Notice the men at bottom right in attitude of *du'ā*, personal petitionary prayer to God. The presence of such a holy man radiates *baraka*, "blessing," to those nearby, according to popular belief. (*Source:* Frederick Mathewson Denny)

## JALĀL AL-DĪN AL-RŪMĪ AND THE MAWLAWĪS

In the popular Western mind, the whole world of Islamic, indeed, "Oriental" mysticism is romantically associated with the order popularly known as the "whirling dervishes" because of the characteristic dance that the members perform as their unique form of *dhikr*. This order, whose actual name is the Mawlawīya, in honor of its founder Mawlānā ("our master") Jalāl al-Dīn al-Rūmī, was founded in Konya, Asia Minor, in the thirteenth century. (In its native Turkey the order is called the Mevlevi order.) Rūmī, the name, means "Roman" and refers to Asia Minor and points west, which were known in medieval Islam as Rūm, because they housed part of the eastern Roman Empire and its capital, Constantinople. Rūmī, the man, was born in Balkh in northern Afghanistan. His father was a distinguished theologian who also had an interest in Sufism, toward which he turned his son. Escaping the approaching Mongol invaders, the family traveled for a long time through Iran and other Near Eastern countries, going all the way to Mecca before returning through

Syria to take up permanent residence in Anatolia, or Rūm, as it was then known. They finally settled in Konya, ancient Iconium, which is situated in the peninsula's southwest central region.

Jalāl al-Dīn married and had a son, Sultān Walad, who continued his father's work and spread the name of the Mawlawīs. Jalāl al-Dīn's father became the spiritual counselor to one of the Turkish sultans, and so the family's position was secure and comfortable. At age twenty-five Jalāl al-Dīn became a serious student of Sufism and ten years later was elevated to the rank of *shaykh.* In addition to mastering all of the levels of Sufi training, Jalāl al-Dīn also was well schooled in traditional Islamic sciences, as his father had been before him. Sultān Walad has left us a most valuable narrative of his father's life,[4] and so we have, in many cases, more accurate information about Rūmī (Jalāl al-Dīn) than we do about many other Sufi masters, whose stories are so full of hagiography as to be almost worthless from a historical standpoint.

### *Shams*

After Jalāl al-Dīn became a *shaykh,* he began a series of encounters with unusual spiritual guides who came to reside in Konya. The most important of these was Shams al-Dīn al-Tabrīzī, who arrived in 1244 and quickly attracted Jalāl al-Dīn as an embodiment of the "divine beloved," whom he had been hoping for years to encounter. There is a dimension of wild longing after God in Rūmī's (Jalāl al-Dīn's) poetry that probably began before his meeting with Shams but took on definitive form as a result of their friendship, which had a tragic outcome. Rūmī became so devoted to Shams's company that he cut himself off from all others for a long period of time, thus earning his disciples' anger and jealousy. The disciples in turn reprimanded Shams for taking their master from them. Shams had to run for his life to Damascus. However, Sultan Walad was dispatched to fetch him back to his father's side, as he was inconsolable without his beloved friend. A second outburst among the disciples caused Shams to repair once again to Damascus, from where he was again retrieved. Shortly, the situation in Konya became bitter once again because of Rūmī's total preoccupation with Shams. He neglected family and disciples, everything except his beloved. Finally, a number of the disciples, including another son of Rūmī, murdered Shams by stabbing him and then hid him in a well. Sultan Walad lied to his father, telling him that Shams was merely missing and that all were searching for him, but secretly he pulled the body from the well and buried it, concealing the grave with plaster. Incredibly, the tomb was discovered only a few years ago by the director of the museum in Konya that houses objects associated with the Mawlawīs.

Because of Rūmī's losing his beloved companion, in whom he thought that God came to Rūmī and communed with him, he began to compose poetry. Over the remaining years of his life (ca. 1247–1273), he produced what is considered to be some of the finest Persian poetry. It is conjectured that out of the tragedy of Shams also evolved the characteristic whirling dance of the Mawlawīs, together with the plaintive music that accompanies and inspires it. There had been mystical dance before the time of Rūmī, but he and his order developed it into the highest ritual art.[5]

### *The Whirling Dervishes*

The dancers, with flowing robes that spread out as they spin, circle around their shaykh, who, like the sun or the *axis mundi,* stands still in the center of the cosmos and provides a focal point, a beginning and an end for the planetary and galactic revolutions of the ecstatic dervishes. The symbolism of the music and dance work together to form an affecting and transforming *dhikr.* There are numerous descriptions of the dance and its variations. In recent years a group of Mawlawīs from the home *tekke* in Konya have made successful Western tours, performing their dances before large audiences in many cities in Europe and America. This sort of performance is, of course, very different from the original setting in the order. But since its revolution after World War I, Turkey has restricted its Sufi organizations, fearing their mass appeal and emotionalism, which are considered to be inconsistent with a modern, secular society. The *ṭarīqas* also could pose a real political threat.

## RŪMĪ'S POETRY

Rūmī composed thousands of rhymed couplets in Persian, known as ***mathnawīs.*** These were collected together into an epic work of 25,000 couplets known as the *Mathnawī,* although Rūmī himself called it the "Book of Husām," after a disciple who late in the poet's life became another intimate associate and after Rūmī's death succeeded him as head of the order. Rūmī considered himself to be like a flute through which Husām al-Dīn played the sad music of the soul. The *Mathnawī* opens on this note:

> Hearken to this Reed forlorn, breathing even since 'twas torn
> From its rushy bed, a strain of impassioned love and pain.
>
> The secret of my song, though near, none can see and none can hear.
> Oh, for a friend to know the sign and mingle all his soul with mine!
>
> 'Tis the flame of Love fired me, 'Tis the wine of love inspired me.
> Wouldst thou know how lovers bleed, hearken, hearken to the Reed![6]

The devotee of God is like a reed flute, which becomes a living instrument only when its natural life is torn from its roots in the earth. The pain of separation from one form of existence ushers in the ecstasy of the new mode as a vehicle of heavenly breath. Even as God caused the reed to be created in its watery nursery, so also did God raise it up to a higher level as his own means of communicating the love and union that he desires with all of his creation.

God's purposes are worked out on the level of temporal, earthly existence in real lives that must respond freely to what has happened to them. This is a paradoxical state of affairs. But Rūmī could see some sort of necessity at work in the troubled life he himself lived, with his beloved coming intermittently to him in the forms of Shams al-Dīn al-Tabrīzī and others after him. Rūmī's glimpses of the divine beloved were sufficient to sustain a celebration of God's works at all levels of his creation in the purest poetry possible. The poetry itself is a primary vehicle for God's expression, although Rūmī himself did not claim to produce verses of revelation, in the sense of the Qur'an. Yet his great output, especially the *Mathnawī,* has been characterized as a "religious picture book,"[7] a sort of companion or complement to the Qur'an. There are seemingly countless passages in the *Mathnawī* that stun the reader with their freshness and originality, even after centuries and despite the limitations of time, language, and place. Rūmī had that rare genius that enabled him to transcend such conditions because of the penetration of his thought and the poetic expression that he developed from study and meditation. Like his contemporary, the Egyptian poet-mystic Ibn al-Fāriḍ, who was introduced in the previous chapter, Rūmī was able to inhabit simultaneously the time of the enraptured mystic in union with God and the time of the disciplined and aware creative artist who works toward his goal of perfect expression. Consider the somewhat unexpected turn of thought that occurs in one of his poems from the *Mathnawī,* one that deals with women:

> If you rule your wife outwardly, yet inwardly you are ruled by her whom you desire,
> This is characteristic of Man: in other animals love is lacking, and that shows their inferiority.
> The Prophet said that woman prevails over the wise, while ignorant men prevail over her; for in them the fierceness of the animal is immanent.
> Love and tenderness are human qualities, anger and lust are animal qualities.
> Woman is a ray of God; she is not the earthly beloved.
> She is creative: you might say she is not created.[8]

Rūmī is not always complimentary to women, nor are most traditional Islamic writers, who often regard women as seductresses and symbols of the sensual world. But in this poem Rūmī sets forth a vision of woman as a transcendent being or principle, a symbol of God the Creator. Rūmī's great contemporaries, Ibn al-Fāriḍ and Ibn al-'Arabī, also held the feminine principle in high esteem as symbolic of God's love and beauty. Ibn 'Arabī even suggested that women are among the hierarchy of saints that ascends up to the pole himself or herself.[9]

Rūmī was not fond of the *'ulamā'*, or dogmatic theologians, because of their hairsplitting, calculating ways. They would choke truth rather than follow it:

> Learn from thy Father! He, not falsely proud,
> With tears of sorrow all his sin avowed.
> Wilt thou, then, still pretend to be unfree
> And clamber up Predestination's tree?—
> Like Iblīs and his progeny abhorred,
> In argument and battle with their Lord.
> The blest initiates *know:* what need to *prove?* From Satan logic, but from Adam love.[10] (Translator's emphasis)

The "Father" is Adam who, according to Sūra 7:22, repented his sin and wept bitterly over it. Adam had sinned freely, the poem contends; therefore, theologians should not blame God. It is suggested that predestinarian theology is the work of Iblīs (Satan). The "blessed initiates" are the Sufis who have attained *ma'rifa,* gnosis. Logical demonstration and argumentation are signs of alienation from God, emphasizing distinction and difference, whereas love is the quality of union and concord with God. Adam contained within himself the *fiṭra,* that God-given constitution that is at the core of every human being, whose mystery is love.

### *Rūmī's Legacy*

Rūmī died in 1273 after producing some of the greatest Sufi poetry. He was not, however, a retiring writer who observed the world from a slight distance. He was fully engaged in the life of his order and produced his mature thought out of the activities associated with being a spiritual master in charge of many disciples. His stressful life contributed to his ongoing growth.

At the core of Rūmī's thought was his conviction that God was both hidden and revealed; that is, he was beyond his creation and, at the same time—paradoxically—immanent in the world of appearances. It is mainly through the Qur'an that God has revealed himself. The *Mathnawī* can be read as an extended and illustrated commentary on the Qur'an, but at the level of *ta'wīl* and not *tafsīr.* It goes beyond the scriptural text and weaves folklore and traditional tales, as well as neo-Platonic, biblical, and Christian ideas, into a tapestry of mature Sufi thought. Rūmī was not a systematic or academic thinker or poet; his work poured forth from him more often in ecstatic exuberance than in reflective composition. He is reported to have been a joyful person who wanted always to share his sense of God's love with all around him. His message is a message for all seasons of human life. Even the modern religious skeptic or agnostic must be moved to reflection by his poem about the person who cries constantly to his Lord, saying "Allah! till his lips grew sweet with praising Him." But the devil spoke up and asked the person where Allah's response was. This broke the worshiper's heart, and so he ceased calling for God. In a dream, al-Khiḍr asked the downcast person why he had stopped praying:

> He answered. "No 'Here am I' is coming to me in response:
> I fear that I am turned away from the Door."
> Said Khadir, "Nay, God saith: That 'Allah' of thine is
> My 'Here am I,' and that supplication and grief
> And ardour of thine is My messenger to thee. Thy fear and
> love are the noose to catch My Favour:
> Beneath every 'O Lord' of thine is many a 'Here am I' from Me."[11]

The longing for God in the worshiper's heart is a testimony to the presence and power of God, who speaks through his servant.

## THE SILSILA OR SPIRITUAL LINEAGE

As we observed earlier in this chapter, the *silsila* is the "chain" by means of which Sufi orders trace their heritage directly through authoritative masters all the way to the Prophet. Sufism preserves a sense of authenticity and stability as a pure form of Islam and strongly suggests that from the very beginning Sufism was the interior dimension of the movement. The Tarīqa and the Sharī'a, then, coexisted in a mutually complementary manner from Muhammad's time, and both are solidly based on the Qur'an and the Sunna. This is a regulating principle among Sufis and testifies to their concern to be regarded as orthodox. But it is not an acceptable version for all Muslims, especially not for those moderns who have seen in Sufism the seeds of weakness and passiveness that have robbed Islam of its power and confidence as a triumphalist religion. More will be said on this topic in the last two chapters.

The *silsila* as a formal written lineage appeared relatively late in the development of Sufism and did not become critical until the rise of major orders in the twelfth and thirteenth centuries. According to J. Spencer Trimingham, the earliest extant *silsila* dates from the tenth century.[12] It belonged to Ja'far al-Khuldī (d. 959), who took the *ṭarīqa,* or "method," from al-Junayd, who received it from Sarī al-Saqatī, who in turn took it from Ma'rūf al-Karkhī, who got it from Farqad al-Sabakhī, who received it from Hasan al-Basrī, who took it from Anas ibn Mālik, who received it from the Prophet Muhammad. Al-Junayd, Sarī al-Saqatī, and Hasan al-Basrī are frequently encountered in *silsilas.* The Shī'īs also include the imāms, and, later, most Sufi *silsilas,* whether Sunnī or Shī'ī, traced their lines back to Muhammad through 'Alī. But 'Alī does not appear in the Sufis' earliest *silsilas,* although he was, of course, of central concern to Shī'īs who were not necessarily Sufis. Al-Junayd is frequently the main link between the earlier Sufis with the Prophet and the more prominent orders that arose after him. All of the major orders that have been described in this chapter trace their lineages back through al-Junayd and thus belong to the Junaydīya family (not to be confused with a later Indian order of that name), as Marshall Hodgson dubbed it.[13] This does not mean, of course, that all of these orders, some very different from one another in doctrine and style, trace the same lines back to al-Junayd himself. Rather, it was at Junayd that the various individual links diverged.

The *silsila* became important when the master–disciple relationship achieved a central position in Sufism, to the point that individual masters' teachings and bodily remains became the basic elements in the continuing cults of the founders. Thus, although 'Abd al-Qādir al-Jīlānī was in some sense the founder of the *ṭarīqa* that bears his name, the *silsila* attached to his order, although it goes back to him, must also continue back behind him to the Prophet. The Qādirīya as a specific *ṭarīqa* does not go all the way back to the Prophet, but the interior aspects of the doctrine do. Muhammad, it is believed, taught an esoteric doctrine to select persons, and this teaching has been passed down through the many *silsilas* linking him with the *ṭarīqas.* This theory allows for the rise of individual organizations within the historical process while at the same time it connects them with a constant grounding in the original and perennial doctrine.

### *Ṭarīqa and Ṭā'ifa*

The *ṭarīqa* thus is passed down by means of the *silsila.* So far in our discussion of Sufism the term *ṭarīqa* has had to serve a variety of purposes because of its different meanings. Although the term is used to refer to the actual "orders" of Sufism in the organizational and social senses, a more precise technical term for this is ***ṭā'ifa,*** an Arabic word that literally means "association" or "organization." It is at this level that historical novelty can occur, because *ṭā'ifas* are only concrete contexts for *ṭarīqas,* which conceptually go all the way back to the Prophet, even though they were introduced by actual Sufi masters. The *silsila* should not be regarded merely as a kind of family tree that proves a historical linkage back to the Prophet. It does that, to be sure, but it is more a spiritual chain, a kind of rope or "lifeline"[14] that connects one with God, both horizontally, that is, back through time on the terrestrial level, and vertically, for God is the present "friend" of his adoring servants. The correct way to God is known through the *ṭarīqa,* which is handed down by the *silsila.* But the *living* relationship with God by means of this *ṭarīqa* is a current matter.

## DHIKR AND SAMĀ': REMEMBRANCE AND THE SPIRITUAL CONCERT

*Dhikr* is a frequently used Qur'anic word meaning "remembering," "mentioning," and, by extension, "prayer." Some examples from the text: "So remember Me, and I will remember you; and be thankful to Me; and be you not ungrateful towards Me." (2:151). "Recite what has been revealed to thee of the Book, and perform the prayer; prayer forbids indecency and dishonor. Remembrance of God [*dhikr*] is greater; and God knows the things you work." (29:45 Arberry translated the Arabic as "God's remembrance," which is misleading.) "And remember the Name of thy Lord, and devote thyself unto Him very devoutly." (73:4)

Among Sufis *dhikr* became the central means of worshiping God and invoking his presence in both the individual and the group. *Dhikr* may either be silent or spoken, but it does follow a pattern, or a variety of patterns, depending on the Sufi *ṭarīqa* in which it is practiced. On the ritual level, it is the type of *dhikr* that distinguishes one *ṭarīqa* from another more than anything else. On the simplest level, *dhikr* can be practiced by anyone at any time and in any place, because it is voluntary and spontaneous. But Sufis developed *dhikr* into elaborate forms of meditation and worship.

### *The Principle of Dhikr*

The principle of *dhikr* is that it brings together God and the believer and works to purify the worshiper of all that is bad. If one concentrates on remembering God through the repetition of his names and attributes, taking them from his message, then one gradually will draw closer and closer to God. Or he comes closer and closer to his servant. If anyone could perform *dhikr* in the time before Sufism had developed into established forms, by the time the master–disciple relationship became regulative, one had to receive instruction in it from a shaykh who knew the correct practice. Thus there really are two levels of *dhikr:* a sort of "generic" *dhikr* that can be performed at will and a specific *dhikr* that is transmitted as an esoteric technique within a *ṭarīqa.* The two coexist in Islam. The generic type may be performed, for example, with the aid of the *subḥa* (a string of beads like a rosary), which helps the worshiper maintain an orderly repetition of pious formulas. Advanced Sufis do not normally use the *subḥa,* regarding it as a veil between them and the object of their meditation. But the *dhikr* itself can also be an obstacle to union with God.

### *Three Forms of Dhikr*

As a technique on the path to full awareness and union, *dhikr* takes three main forms.[15] The first is *dhikr al-awqāt,* the set *dhikrs* of each day, following at least two of the obligatory salats. This *dhikr* is regulated by one's master, who gives permission for it and prescribes its specifics. The Qādarīs, for example, often recite the following three phrases thirty-three times each: *subḥan Allāh* ("Glory be to God!"), *al-ḥamdu l'illāh* ("Praise be to God!"), and *Allāhu akbar* ("God is greatest!"). Next comes the *dhikr al-khafī,* which is a personal recollection under the guidance of one's shaykh. This type of *dhikr* emphasizes breath control and becomes quite elaborate in some *ṭarīqas,* requiring long periods of solitary practice to master. Trimingham (a contemporary expert on the orders) has translated the following description of a simplified *dhikr khafī,* based on the *tahlīl* formula of the first part of the shahāda (*Lā ilāha illā 'llāh,* "There is no god but God"), which contains both a negation and an affirmation. The *Lā ilāha* is uttered while exhaling, and the *illā 'llāh* is said while inhaling. This is a basic element of many *dhikrs,* but soon the process becomes more complex, as the following Naqshabandī (a major *ṭarīqa*) passage suggests:

> He [the worshiper] must keep the tongue pressed against the roof of his mouth, his lips and teeth firmly shut, and hold his breath. Then starting with the word *lā,* he makes it ascend from the navel to the brain. When it has arrived at the brain he says *ilāha* to the right shoulder and *illā 'llāh* to the left side, driving it forcefully into the pineal heart through which it circulates to all the rest of the body. The phrase *Muḥammad rasūl Allāh* is made to incline from the left to the right side, and then one says, "My God, Thou art my goal and satisfying Thee is my aim."[16]

The third type of recollection is *dhikr al-ḥaḍra,* "the *dhikr* of presence," a communal, shared type. The "presence" is that of the Prophet, who in later developments of *ṭarīqa* Sufism was increasingly featured as a supreme guide and active participant. Earlier, this group-recitation *dhikr* was known as *samāʿ*, literally meaning "listening" but connoting a "spiritual concert" with music and sacred dance. This group *dhikr* often becomes elaborate and thrilling to hear and participate in. I have joined in lengthy evening *dhikrs* and can attest to the warm feelings of love and brotherhood that are generated when a large congregation chants beautiful odes to the Prophet or remembers liturgically the "most beautiful names of Allah" (*al-asmā' al-ḥusnā*). When incense is burned and candles are lighted, the fragrance and light help transport one into another time and another place. This is the special time of the *dhikr,* and the subjective experience is that of feeling very close to God. Sometimes a spontaneity is released that carries along the assembly.

The master of a chapter of a Sufi order is not necessarily the one who leads the group *dhikr* in the actual performance sense. A special singer, called a *munshid,* does this. The *munshid* is sometimes a virtuoso, both musically and spiritually. Some *munshids* have popular followings, as in Egypt. Earle H. Waugh, a Canadian scholar, has conducted extensive field research on the *munshid* in the Cairo region and collected examples of *dhikr* texts and rendered their melodies on the Western musical staff. The techniques of drumming have also been described by Waugh.[17]

The group *dhikr* is not always musical, for some orders disapprove of emotionalism. Formal Islamic worship, as in the salat, contains no musical expression. The rhythmical recitation of the Qur'an is not regarded as music, and when it wanders into a kind of musical form resembling art song or entertainment, it is censured as such. But Sufism has provided the opportunity for Muslims to lift their voices in song to God, and most orders encourage it. Sufi singing does not occur in the mosque, normally, but in the convent type of settings of the individual orders or in someone's home. The typical *ḥaḍra* includes a lengthy recital of the order's central doctrines and traditions and then much praise of God and blessing of the Prophet.

### *The Samā'*

The ***samā'*** is an elaborate form of *ḥaḍra* centered in music and dance as a means of ecstasy. Sober Muslims of a legal cast of mind have generally regarded it as an illicit form of devotion because of its sensuousness, which could and sometimes did degenerate into sensuality. Abū Ḥāmid al-Ghazālī (the theologian) composed a famous treatise[18] on this subject and advised caution when coming into contact with *samā'*. His brother, Ahmad, on the other hand, favored the *samā'* as an indispensable aid to authentic *dhikr.* A portion of his own treatise on the subject is instructive in the way it defines movements of dance, whirl and leap:

> The dancing is a reference to the circling of the spirit round the cycle of existing things on account of receiving the effects of the unveilings and revelations; and this is the state of the gnostic. The whirling is a reference to the spirit's standing with Allāh in its inner nature (*sirr*) and being (*wujūd*), the circling of its look and thought, and its penetrating the ranks of existing things; and this is the state of the assured one. And his leaping up is a reference to his being drawn from the human station to the unitive station.[19]

The most highly developed form of dance in Sufism was that of the Mawlawīs of Jalāl al-Dīn Rūmī, as we observed earlier. Music and dance were, for Rūmī, the very substance of heaven. Each of us is born with a remembrance of this, but it has to be reawakened for us to realize its eternal origin and goal:

> We, who are parts of Adam, heard with him
> The song of angels and of seraphim.
> Our memory, though dull and sad, retains
> Some echo still of those unearthly strains.
>
> Oh, music is the meat of all who love,
> Music uplifts the soul to realms above.
> The ashes glow, the latent fires increase:
> We listen and are fed with joy and peace.[20]

Our discussion of the *dhikr* and the *samā'* has been both general and selective. They have many aspects and a literature that describes and regulates the techniques and theories connected with them. The *dhikr* is, after all, the center of Sufi doctrines and practices and, like the Hindu *yoga*—which it resembles in some ways—has many separate but related varieties, from the simple and elementary to the sophisticated. Although not a secret practice, the *dhikr* is nevertheless an esoteric discipline that requires intense application under the guidance of a master. It can be dangerous, especially the breathing exercises and the sometimes extended periods of ecstasy in which the adept may go without food and water. More subtle are the dangers to the soul when a freelancer dabbles in an unregulated fashion in such powerful psychological and spiritual processes. One can easily fool oneself and think that one really knows and controls what is happening, when in reality one is adrift on a sea of emotionalism and subjective responses.

The great twentieth-century Algerian shaykh, Ahmad al-'Alawī, was once conversing with his French physician, a Dr. Carret, when the voice of a solitary Sufi novice was heard calling upon God, from a remote location in the *zāwiya* that was ruled by the old shaykh.

> "A . . . l . . . lā. . . h!"
> It was like a cry of despair, a distraught supplication, and it came from some solitary cell-bound disciple, bent on meditation. The cry was usually repeated several times, and then all was silence once more.
>
> "Out of the depths have I cried unto Thee, O Lord."
>
> "From the end of the earth will I cry unto Thee, when my heart is overwhelmed: lead me to the rock that is higher than I."
>
> These verses from the Psalms came to my mind [130:1, 61:2]. The supplication was really just the same, the supreme cry to God of a soul in distress. I was not wrong, for later, when I asked the Shaikh what was the meaning of the cry which we had just heard, he answered:
>
> "It is a disciple asking God to help him in his meditation."
> "May I ask what is the purpose of his meditation?"
> "To achieve self-realization in God."
> "Do all the disciples succeed in doing this?"
> "No, it is seldom that anyone does. It is only possible for a very few."
> "Then what happens to those who do not? Are they not desperate?"
> "No: they always rise high enough to have at least inward Peace."[21]

Dr. Carret had thought that "inward Peace" was sufficient, but the Shaykh al-'Alawī later told him that beyond that was the true union with God, which requires mastery of the order's doctrine.

## SUFI THEOSOPHY: THE THOUGHT OF IBN 'ARABĪ

No treatment of Sufism would be complete without considering certain significant intellectual contributions to Islamic self-definition and reflective expression, however atypical. Recall that Abū Hāmid al-Ghazālī was a major philosophical theologian who turned to mysticism as the highest and truest form of the Muslim life. His lasting contribution was the monumental "Revivification of the sciences of religion" (*Iḥyā' 'ulūm al-dīn*). This is not primarily a work of theology or philosophy, although it is informed at places by those disciplines, and it could not have been composed without a thorough grounding in them, which included an awareness of their limitations. Al-Ghazālī always maintained a distance from and a distinction between the Sufi and his Lord so that perfect union was impossible, if such union meant what someone like al-Hallāj did. The intoxicated Sufis might contemplate their final absorption in God, but al-Ghazālī and other sober types of mystics sustained an orthodox respect for God's transcendence.

A contemporary of Rūmī, the Spanish-born and -reared Sufi Ibn 'Arabī (1165–1240), brought Sufi thought to its highest point of subtlety and sophistication in his philosophy of ***waḥdat al-wujūd,*** "the oneness of being," a seemingly monistic doctrine that has had a controversial career in Islamic intellectual history.

Ibn 'Arabī was a well-trained scholar in all of the religious sciences, which he turned toward his distinctive interests. Although he was orthodox in his religious observance, he was convinced that he was led in his thinking by an inner light that came from God. He considered all created things to be manifestations of God, which is not to say that he equated creation with God. Some critics down through the ages have called his thought pantheistic, that is, holding that God is immanent in his creation and can be identified with it and it with him. Others have simply called Ibn 'Arabī a monist, a label that itself does not do justice to the subtlety as well as the contradictions or confusions of his system. He viewed the universe as both relative being and external to God, yet linked to God by archetypes in the divine mind, from which they originally emanated in the process of creation. The divine names in the Qur'an are continuing images that draw together God and his creation in a mutual relationship that is perhaps best characterized as a sort of spiritual alchemy. Put another way, things exist because they have been perceived by God. But these things were willed into being in the first place, because God did not want to be alone in the universe. He wanted to be appreciated as a "hidden treasure," according to a *ḥadith qudsī* that Ibn 'Arabī featured in his system.

### *The Concept of Waḥdat al-Wujūd*

*Waḥdat al-wujūd,* as recent scholarship has demonstrated, is a richer concept than the English translation "oneness of being" can suggest. Annemarie Schimmel (a leading expert on Sufism), following Marijan Molé (another contemporary specialist), has pointed out that in Arabic there is no verb *to be.*[22] *Wujūd* means, rather, "finding" and "discovery," but it has traditionally been translated as "being" or "existence" and then accommodated to Western philosophical ideas of existence. Instead of the Western emphasis on the substance ideas connected with a static concept of being, there is in the Arabic *wujūd* a characteristically Semitic quality of dynamism, centered not in the substance or identity of "stuff" but in the unity of perception and being found, a sort of consummation of a relationship. Ibn 'Arabī was a *muwaḥḥid,* a "unitarian," which reflects what Islam always espoused in the doctrine of *tawḥīd,* "divine unification."

### *Ibn 'Arabī's Works*

Ibn 'Arabī wrote many works; one estimate numbers them as high as 500. Among his best-known and most influential works are *Al-Futūḥāt al-Makkīya,* "Meccan openings," an encyclopedic treatment of Sufism; *Fuṣūṣ al-Ḥikam,* "Bezels of wisdom," a discussion of prophets as vehicles of divine wisdom; and *Tarjumān al-Ashwāq,* "The interpreter of longing," a collection of verses expressing the author's admiration and love for a certain Persian lady whom he had met in Mecca, whose learning and graciousness captivated him. Her image can be glimpsed in other of Ibn 'Arabī's works, which more than any other Islamic speculative theology assigns an exalted position to the feminine principle.

***Love and Muhammad's Nature.*** At the heart of Ibn 'Arabī's thought was love, not as a mere principle for theosophical reflection, but as the central truth and dynamic of the universe. This love allowed him to be tolerant of other religions, which he tended to regard as amounting to much the same thing. This tolerance, as Schimmel has pointed out, was reserved for only those others who had attained a lofty station so as to be able to realize the truth of the "oneness of *wujūd.*"

Ibn 'Arabī was not alone in regarding Muhammad as the highest of humans, but he carried the theory of Muhammad's nature further than most did. For him, Muhammad was and is the "complete human," *al-insān al-kāmil.* This phrase is most often translated as "perfect man," but that does not fully convey the meaning. *Insān,* though it can be rendered as "man," does not carry a strong sense of male gender, because it can also be translated as "human being." *Kāmil* contains the meanings "integral," "whole," "perfect," "complete," and "finished." *Al-insān al-kāmil* really means one who is the model of what authentic human existence should be. It is a normative concept. Muhammad is this paradigm through whom God expresses his nature by means of the Qur'an and the Sunna. More than that, God sustains and regulates the created cosmos by means of the "complete human," who exists at the peak of a great hierarchy of saints and acts as a mediator between God and creation.[23]

## NOTES

1. Joachim Wach, "Master and Disciple: Two Religio-Sociological Studies," *Journal of Religion* 42 (January 1962): 1–21.
2. For a more detailed sketch and bibliographies, see the articles "'Abd al-Ḳādir," and "Ḳādiriyya" in *Encyclopedia of Islam,* new ed., ed. H. A. R. Gibb et al. (Leiden: E. J. Brill, 1960). The most informative ready reference to the major Sufi orders is by J. Spencer Trimingham, *The Sufi Orders in Islam* (New York: Oxford University Press, 1973).
3. Joseph Williams McPherson, *The Moulids of Egypt* (Cairo: N.M. Press, 1941), p. 288. This eccentric, delightful book contains much lore about both Muslim and Christian saint festivals in Egypt.
4. The biographical matter of this as yet untranslated (into English) Persian work is briefly summarized by R. A. Nicholson in *Rūmī: Poet and Mystic* (London: Allen & Unwin, 1950), pp. 17–22. A much more substantial summary of Rūmī's life and work is found in Annemarie Schimmel, *Mystical Dimensions of Islam* (Chapel Hill: University of North Carolina Press, 1975), pp. 308–328, and more extensively in her *The Triumphal Sun: A Study of the Works of Jalāloddin Rumi* (London and The Hague: East-West Publications, 1980), pp. 3–58. See also a culminating work of Schimmel's career-long devotion to Rumi studies: *I Am Wind, You Are Fire: The Life and Work of Rūmī* (Boston and London: Shambala Publications, Inc., 1992).
5. Al-Hujwīrī condemned dance as a means of spiritual exercise, *The Kashf al-Maḥjūb: The Oldest Persian Treatise on Sufism,* new ed. by Reynold A. Nicholson (London: Luzac, 1936), p. 416. Abū Ḥāmid al-Ghazālī wrote a lengthy treatise on the place of music in devotion but included only a few observations on dance. This work has been translated by Duncan Black MacDonald, "Emotional Religion in Islam As Affected by Music and Singing, Being a Translation of a Book of the Iḥyā' 'Ulūm ad-Dīn of al-Ghazzālī," *Journal of the Royal Asiatic Society* (April 1901): 195–252; (October 1901): 705–748; (January 1902): 1–28. The author's moderate views on dance are found in the final installment, pp. 11–13.
6. Nicholson, *Rūmī: Poet and Mystic,* p. 31.
7. H. A. R. Gibb, "Structure of Religious Thought in Islam," in *Studies on the Civilization of Islam* (Boston: Beacon Press, 1962), p. 211.
8. Nicholson, *Rūmī: Poet and Mystic,* p. 44.
9. Schimmel, *Mystical Dimensions,* p. 431.
10. Nicholson, *Rūmī: Poet and Mystic,* p. 165.
11. *Ibid.,* p. 91.
12. Trimingham, *Sufi Orders in Islam,* p. 261.
13. Marshall G. S. Hodgson, *The Venture of Islam,* vol. 2 (Chicago: University of Chicago Press, 1974), p. 214.
14. Martin Lings, *What Is Sufism?* (Berkeley and Los Angeles: University of California Press, 1975), p. 38.
15. This description is based mostly on Trimingham, *The Sufi Orders in Islam,* pp. 194–217.

16. As quoted in *ibid.,* p. 202, from Tāj al-Dīn ibn Zakarīya Mahdī Zamān al-Rūmī, *Risālat fī sunan al-Ṭā'ifat al-Naqshabandiyya,* (Cambridge, Add. MS., 1073), pp. 4–5.
17. Earle H. Waugh, *The Munshidīn of Egypt: Their World And Their Song* (Columbia, S.C.: The University of South Carolina Press, 1989).
18. Al-Ghazālī, in MacDonald, "Emotional Religion in Islam," cited above, n. 5.
19. As quoted in Trimingham, *The Sufi Orders in Islam,* p. 195, from *Tracts on Listening to Music,* ed. and trans. J. Robson (London, 1983), pp. 99–100.
20. Nicholson, *Rūmī: Poet and Mystic,* p. 32.
21. Martin Lings, *A Sufi Saint of the Twentieth Century* (Berkeley and Los Angeles: University of California Press, 1973), p. 22.
22. Schimmel, *Mystical Dimensions,* p. 267. Marijan Molé, *Les mystiques musulmanes* (Paris: Presses Univeritaires de France, 1965), pp. 59–62.
23. A detailed and sophisticated interpretation of Ibn 'Arabī's mystical theology, with a translation of portions of his "Meccan Openings" (*al-futūḥāt al-makkīya*), has been done by William C. Chittick in *The Sufi Path of Knowledge: Ibn 'Arabī's Metaphysics of Imagination* (Albany: State University of New York Press, 1989). Chittick has observed that nowhere does Ibn 'Arabī himself appear to use the phrase *waḥdat al-wujūd,* although "the idea permeates his works," p. 79.

PART FIVE

# Patterns of Islamic Personal and Communal Life

CHAPTER

# 12 The Islamic Life Cycle and the Family

## KEY TERMS

| | | |
|---|---|---|
| *aqīqa* | *khitān* | *mahr* |
| *kunya* | *khafḍ* | *ṭalāq* |
| *nasab* | *nikāḥ* | *ribā* |
| *laqab* | *'awra* | *maḥram* |
| *nisba* | *ẓinā* | *ḥarām* |
| *basmala* | *'urs* | *ḥalāl* |

## ISLAMIC DOMESTIC RITES, CEREMONIES, AND CUSTOMS

As we have seen throughout this book, Islam is a complete way of life and not merely a system of belief and ritual practices. This chapter will treat some of the more down-to-earth customs of Islamic life, beyond either the obligatory ritual duties of worship and the other pillars or the somewhat rarefied world of Sufism and its related activities. Instead, our interest will be on such things as birth, naming, education, and childhood; entry into adult status and marriage; marital responsibilities and privileges and the raising of children; divorce and remarriage; the structure and function of the Muslim family at both the nuclear and extended levels; the inheritance of property; death and the rites connected with it; and everyday domestic activities such as sleeping, eating, and entertaining visitors. The following chapter will take us out into the street and the wider community of Muslims to be found in the mosque, occupational contexts, markets, cafés, schools, entertainment and sports, and other public settings. It will also deal with the relations between Islamic beliefs and observances and popular, regional attitudes and practices.

## RITES OF INFANCY AND CHILDHOOD

### *Birthing*

There is no Qur'anically prescribed rite connected with birth or the first period of life, but there are certain *ḥadīths* and customs concerning what Muslims should do. As soon as a child is born and after it has been washed and swaddled, some male, either a religious guide or a relative, pronounces the call to prayer (*adhān*) in the baby's right ear and the call to perform the prayer (*iqāma*) in the left, in imitation of Muhammad, who is reported to have done this on the occasion of the birth of Hasan, his grandson. Then, again following the Prophet's example, the same person chews a small amount of date flesh and then puts the softened morsel into the baby's mouth. This marks the first feeding outside the womb and with the mouth. Then the Fatiha is recited for the protection and health of the infant, and people come bearing gifts.

The seventh day after birth is important, for this is when the child is usually named and a sacrifice is often performed, although it is not absolutely required. The ***'aqīqa*** sacrifice, as it is known, dates back to pre-Islamic Arabia. The word *'aqīqa* refers to the infant's hair, which is shaved off and weighed, after which an equivalent amount of silver is given as alms. The sacrifice consists of two male sheep or goats for a boy and one for a girl. This reflects a notion of the comparative superiority of males over females, and although the birth of either a girl or boy is an occasion for rejoicing, the birth of a boy is especially auspicious and satisfying.

### *Naming*

Although the naming may be done at birth, it is very often done on the same day as the *'aqīqa.* People name their children after relatives, or saints, or sometimes auspicious events. But it is most common to follow the Prophet's suggestions, which include 'Abdallāh, "Slave of God," 'Abd al-Rahmān, "Slave of the Merciful," the names most loved by God, and Muhammad's own name as well as those of his family and companions. Muhammad did not allow the use of both his given name and his surname (Abū'l-Qāsim, "Father of Qāsim"), but either one or the other. The infant is given his or her own name, but there are other names that the individual will acquire over time. For example, when one has become a parent, one is entitled to use the **kunya,** an honorific name, prefaced by *Abū,* "father," or *Umm,* "mother." The child bears a **nasab,** either *Ibn,* "son of," or *Bint,* "daughter of." Thus, Abū Zayd is "Father of Zayd," Umm Zaynab is "Mother of Zaynab," Ibn 'Umar is "Son of 'Umar," Bint Ahmad is "Daughter of Ahmad," and so forth. Another type of name is the **laqab,** an honorific or nickname that is acquired through special circumstances such as superior accomplishment, a trade, or something unusual. An example of the first would be Abū'l-Fityān, "Champion Bruiser," given to Sīdī Ahmad al-Badawī for his skill in the martial arts. An example of the second could be al-Hallāj, the "Carder," namely, of wool (although this became a *laqab* with a double meaning as "carder" of hearts). The third type could be something like al-Jāhiz, the "Goggle-eyed," a nickname actually given to one of the greatest prose writers of Abbasid times. There are also names that indicate the place of origin or some other special association. Abū Hāmid al-Ghazālī, for example, means Abū Hāmid from Ghazāla, the town in which he was born and reared and to which he later returned. Such a name is called **nisba**.

Because so many Muslims bear the old Arabic names of early Islam, it is sometimes difficult to identify individuals precisely. Because of this practice, other names in addition to the given names are especially useful. In addition to Muhammad and the names of the companions, the names of the prophets contained in both the Bible and the Qur'an are held in esteem. A well-known *ḥadīth* says, concerning the use of the Prophet's name: "There is no people holding a consultation at which there is present one whose name is Muhammad or Ahmad, but God blesseth all that assembly."[1]

The naming of the child is not actually part of the *'aqīqa* ceremony and does not even have to be done on the seventh day but may be done shortly after birth or on the eighth day, if the birth occurred in the afternoon.

On the fortieth day after the birth the mother is purified and thus able to resume the ritual duties from which she was excused during her pregnancy, parturition, and confinement. This is an important day in the lives of both mother and child, and there is often festivity connected with it.

### *Learning the Qur'an*

As soon as the young one begins to talk, he or she is taught the frequently uttered consecration phrase known as the **basmala** ("In the Name of Allah, the Beneficent, the Merciful") and other simple phrases and devotional formulas. Traditional schooling was centered in the Qur'an, which became the textbook for countless millions of people over the centuries. Traditionally, the child started learning how to read the Qur'an at about age seven. It is impossible to overestimate the significance of this in ingraining Islamic values and attitudes, which have always also been inseparable from the linguistic and literary forms in which they were originally revealed. Nowadays, most Muslim children go to modern schools, but if the dominant ethos of the region is Islamic, they will be taught something about the Qur'an and its proper recitation, sometimes in optional afterschool sessions.

### *Circumcision of Boys*

Often, Muslim boys pass through their major status change—**circumcision (*khitān*)**—when they have recited the entire Qur'an once through. In Malaysia and other regions where this procedure is followed, the boy undergoes the operation at ten to twelve years of age. It is thus a real puberty rite, separating the boy from childhood and introducing him into a new, higher status. There is much anxious anticipation of circumcision at the age of puberty, because the initiand is increasingly aware of his own sexuality and needs also to demonstrate his bravery and honor. The adults talk a lot about the fearsomeness of the circumciser and make frightening remarks right up to the time of the event, which in some cases is semipublic, although it is more and more often performed in a clinic or hospital.[2] In any event, there is much festivity, with music, special foods, and many guests. While the actual event is taking place, one may hear praise of God, partly, as some observers have suggested, to drown out the boy's cries. But the procedure is relatively safe, and those who perform it are usually trained and experienced.

I have witnessed very peremptory circumcision operations in small booths close to the wall of the great Tanta mosque in Egypt during the autumn *mawlid* or birthday celebration of the saint Sīdī Ahmad al-Badawī. There, peasant parents simply bring their little boys, from infancy up to ages seven or eight, and the circumciser and usually an assistant hold the boy down while his foreskin is removed. Sometimes a man plays on a flute or beats a drum. Afterward the child will be given sweets, like ice cream, and paraded off in honor and triumph as if he were a little prince. Whether the celebration is makeshift and humble or ceremonious and lavish, it is a significant moment in the life of a boy and his parents and siblings. Afterward, if the circumcision takes place around puberty, the boy will enter into full participation in Islamic ritual life, although he may have performed prayers and fasting before, either regularly or occasionally.

Circumcision is not mentioned in the Qur'an, but Muslims everywhere regard it as essential, and the *Ḥadīth* record it as a practice enjoyed by all past prophets.[3] Significantly, it is also known by a euphemism: *ṭahāra,* meaning "purification." The age at which it is performed varies from region to region and even from family to

Qur'an school near Jakarta, Indonesia. This *kuttāb* is located in a neighborhood mosque and meets after regular public school has ended for the day. Sandals are deposited outside, because the session is held in a ritually pure place. (*Source:* Frederick Mathewson Denny)

family, but most often age seven is preferred, although it is known from as early as the seventh day following birth all the way up to puberty. Adult converts to Islam have traditionally been required to undergo the operation, but this practice is not universally considered to be essential, especially if there is a health risk. Of course, in the Bible there are reports of circumcisions of adult males and mention of the period of healing that was required afterwards (for example, Gen. 17:9–14, 23–27; Josh. 5:2–9). The ancient Israelites considered circumcision to be a sign of the covenant between them and Yahweh, a mark on each male indicating his membership in the special community. The Jews have continued the practice to this day.

### *Circumcision of Girls*

Muslim girls are also sometimes "circumcized," a practice that can be traced back in Islam to a *ḥadīth* in which Muhammad is reported to have said: "Do not cut severely, as that is better for a woman and more desirable to a husband."[4] This operation, called in classical Arabic ***khafḍ*** (literally, "decreasing"), involves cutting away a part or all of the clitoris or simply making a slight scar on it. This operation, unlike the circumcision of boys, is done in private and without any celebration whatsoever. Although it is not practiced universally, it is known in such diverse regions as Egypt and the Sudan, Arabia, Africa south of the Sahara, and Southeast Asia. It is known among non-Muslims, too, for example, the Coptic Christians of Egypt, who possibly have continued the practice from pre-Islamic, even pharaonic times.[5] The farther one travels up the Nile valley into central Africa, the more severe a version of the operation one will find. Modern governments are concerned about stemming the practice, and it is now illegal in Egypt.

Emotions sometimes run high over female "circumcision," pro and con. Orthodox Muslim opinion is mixed on the subject and appears to differ on the precise meaning of the preceding quoted *ḥadīth.* Some take it to mean that Muhammad disapproved of the practice, which seems to have been well ingrained in Jāhilīya Arabia. Others take it to mean that it is recommended though not absolutely required, and still others regard it as required. In some regions—for example, in Indonesia—it is, interestingly, known by the euphemism *sunnat* (from *sunna*), "recommended."

The reasons for clitoridectomy are varied. Some insist it is to reduce the female sexual drive, which, it is thought, would otherwise be uncontrollable. Others argue that the clitoris is an incipient penis that, if not excised or reduced would make a woman hermaphroditic and therefore unmarriageable. This folk rationale is prevalent, and it has profound implications when compared with ethnographies of widely dispersed peoples that practice some form of genital mutilation.[6] All agree that it is part of the larger category of purification, *ṭahāra* (and is sometimes referred to by this term), and that is reason enough for the practice of both male and female circumcision, as far as many Muslims are concerned. Although there is much male domination and regulation of the female sexual drive and its expression implied in clitoridectomy, it should be emphasized that it is frequently women who enforce the old practice, and it is often a specialty of midwives (e.g., in Egypt). Indeed, female "circumcision" is not an essentially Islamic practice; it is more a pattern of culture in those regions where it is practiced.

## MARRIAGE (*NIKĀḤ*)

Muslims are urged to marry and have children as early in life as is feasible. Celibacy and renunciation of the sexual urge are forbidden, except in rare cases and during certain periods of an individual's life. The Prophet disapproved of monasticism as such, although he seems to have respected the spirituality of monks. He did not allow anyone to prefer God so exclusively as to give up marriage, for this would be to reject God's gift of good things in this life. As we have seen, even the ascetic Sufis generally were married and raised children. (Rābi'a was an exception, who independently preferred God to all else, and without apology.) There was a tendency in early Islam toward renunciation and a semimonastic style of religious life that Muhammad had to discourage. Yet he did not force people to marry, as the following well-attested *ḥadīth* indicates:

> Young man, those of you who can support a wife should marry, for it keeps you from looking at strange women and preserves you from immorality, but those who cannot should devote themselves to fasting, for it is a means of suppressing sexual desire. (Al-Bukhārī and Muslim)[7]

Muslims have generally believed that one should not wait too long before marrying, and that relying too heavily on the cautionary and conditional side of a phrase like "those who can support a wife" is misguided. As the Qur'an states: "Marry the spouseless among you, and your slaves and handmaidens that are righteous; if they are poor, God will enrich them of His bounty. . . . And let those who find not the means to marry be abstinent till God enriches them of His bounty" (24:32,33). Here there is a strong sense that God will provide for those who serve him. The urge to obey God by marrying gives young adults a sense of seriousness and industry and serves to deflect them from drifting to and fro in late-adolescent sexual confusion.

### *Selection of Marriage Partners*

In Islamic marriage (known as ***nikāḥ***), a legal contract is the basis of the union, with the rights and duties plainly laid out and mutually agreed upon by both parties. Marriage is not a sacrament, as are most Christian marriages, but Muslims do consider marriage a solemn affair blessed by God. Even in modern times, an Islamic marriage is usually arranged by the parents of the bride and often of the groom, too. Islamic marriage is a uniting of *families* as much as individuals. A first-time bride must be represented by a guardian (*walī*), who may be her father, grandfather, or other male relative, or if such is not available, someone else, like a male adult appointed by an official. The bride's guardian, whether parent or another, is essential in that only he can "give her away," by signing the marriage contract. It is possible for potential marriage partners to see each other before deciding to marry and before marrying, but their meeting must be done only with a proper chaperon. It is considered dishonorable for a marriageable man and woman to socialize together otherwise. Thus, among properly observant Muslims, dating in the Western sense is not condoned, nor is courtship.

***Basis for Selection.*** Muslims may not be married without their consent, but in the case of a virgin, silence is interpreted by her *walī* as consent. (There are many details concerning marriage law, especially when different *madhhabs* are considered; here we shall describe only the more common and basic elements.) Although family interests are often paramount in selecting a spouse—because of wealth, status, need to marry off daughters, and other things—it is permissible for men and women to indicate preferences and desired qualities in a partner. The Prophet reportedly said: "A woman may be married for four reasons, for her property, her rank, her beauty and her religion; so get the one who is religious and prosper" (Al-Bukhārī and Muslim).[8]

Generally it is the male (or his mother) who is most active in seeking a mate, as this *ḥadīth* implies. And he may proceed on his own, unlike the woman. In the West, romantic love has for a long time been the major factor in selecting a spouse, whether from the man's or the woman's viewpoint. But this is not the case among most Muslims, as is clear from the foregoing. Moreover, romantic love is regarded as a feeble basis for something as important as marriage. The Muslim view is that love should grow out of the marriage but that at the outset, commitment, honor, mutual respect, and friendliness are most important.

## *The Wife's Duties*

In the marriage bond, both partners are legal individuals. The woman retains her own property and can do with it what she pleases. The man is responsible for providing for his wife, and she in turn is obligated to manage the domestic side, and so there is ideally a complementary balance. The two are required to preserve their sexual life exclusively for each other, and the wife especially must properly comport herself and cover her body in the presence of other men. These days it is common in urban, industrial societies for Muslim women to work outside the home and have careers and professions of their own. But the requirements of dignity and proper dress and behavior still apply. Strictly following the most conservative Islamic dress code means that only a woman's face and hands should be visible. Her hair, arms, and other parts may be seen only by her husband and close blood relations. (Only the husband may see his wife's intimate areas, which include the back.) This pattern is not universally observed, whether in the West or in parts of the Muslim world like Indonesia, but it is making a strong comeback these days. Even in North America, one has only to visit a large university campus to see Muslim women in "proper" dress, covering their ***'awra,*** the technical term that means everything but the face and hands and, among some interpreters, feet.

### Adultery

Most readers of this chapter will likely be unacquainted with Islamic life patterns. What we have just described will possibly be absorbed with a mixture of disapproval and fascination by liberal Westerners. It should not be concluded that Muslims are either Victorian or prudish in matters pertaining to sexuality. To the contrary, they are both realistic and frank, but they are also fully aware of the temptations of human sexuality and the ways in which yielding to them can be injurious both on the personal-individual and the social levels. Sexuality is viewed by Muslims as one of God's greatest gifts, but they believe it must be enjoyed and applied only within the honorable and responsible institution of marriage. No deviant forms of sexual expression are permitted by Islam. Homosexuality (male or female), prostitution, premarital and extramarital sex, and the varieties of sexual practices that are typically referred to under such headings as sodomy and bestiality all are *ḥarām,* that is, absolutely forbidden and punishable by God. What is more, the lustful consideration of another person is tantamount to fornication, precisely in the sense that Jesus meant when he declared, "You have heard that it was said, 'You shall not commit adultery.' But I say to you that every one who looks at a woman lustfully has already committed adultery with her in his heart" (Matt. 5:27–28). ***Zinā,*** "adultery" or "fornication" of the eyes, is a well-attested danger in Muslim lore.[9]

### Polygyny

The Qur'an permits a man to marry up to four wives at the same time. "Marry such women as seem good to you, two, three, four; but if you fear you will not be equitable, then only one" (4:3). This passage has been interpreted in different ways and sometimes as implying that monogamy is the preferred practice. Later in the same sūra, we read: "You will not be able to be equitable between your wives, be you ever so eager" (4:129). Polygyny is thought by Muslims to be very rare in practice, and it is. Nevertheless, Muslims have most often considered polygyny to be permissible and in certain cases desirable, particularly when there has been a surplus of women, such as after a period of warfare. Again, every Muslim man and woman is strongly encouraged to marry and have offspring, but what will happen if there are not enough men to go around? Women will be denied the opportunity to fulfill their potential as human beings. If women have been widowed or abandoned, marriage confers on them a protected and honorable status.

No one denies, however, that multiple marriages often impose problems of rivalry, jealousy, hurt feelings, frustration, and inequity. Only rarely would it appear possible for a polygynous household to run smoothly. It is difficult to imagine it in a modern setting, and such marriages are thus exceedingly rare among Muslims who have left behind the traditional patterns of tribal peasant life.

Polygyny is often quite distasteful to such Muslims, even though they grant its validity in limited cases, such as those just mentioned. The rather strict Qur'anic conditions for the practice, furthermore, appear to be improvements over the loose and unregulated practices of the Jāhilīya period in Arabia. Muhammad's marriage to Khadīja was monogamous and lasted twenty-five years. For various reasons, after her death he contracted marriages with a number of wives. But his was a special case, and the political, social, and humane advantages and considerations connected with those unions were recognized and approved by all. Muhammad's treatment of his wives, although things did not always go smoothly, was honorable, and it has become an important part of his Sunna.

### *The Marriage Ceremony*

Marriage is legal and complete without any sort of festivity, but it would be hard to imagine Muslim marriage that did not feature merrymaking, with many guests, music making, dancing, wonderful foods, Qur'an recitations, and brightly colored decorations. This traditional celebratory phase that comes after the signing of the marriage contract by the groom and the bride's *walī* is universal but takes many different specific forms in the umma's various regions and cultures. In Arabic, it is called ***'urs,*** a root that gives us *'arūs,* meaning "bride" or "bridegroom."

Sometimes the festivities go on for days, as in the older tribal societies. But in modern settings, the *'urs* may be a large party in a rented ballroom or club or in the home. I attended a wedding party in Yemen that featured singing and eating and dancing far into the night, with the men and boys gathered together in an upper chamber and the women collected in a separate large apartment just across the alleyway. The two separated parties could hear each other's joyful celebrating but, because of strict social tradition, were prohibited from mingling (nor did they wish to). After a while the men descended to the street and escorted the groom back and forth in front of the house where the bride and her entourage were gathered. The women looked down on the parade in the street through curtained windows and cried out loudly in that shrill ululation characteristic of the joyful exultation of Arab women. Meanwhile the men continued to sing, thereby protecting their hero, the groom, from danger and filling him with courage for the critical moments to come when he and his bride would be closeted together for the consummation.

On the wedding night everyone anxiously awaits the outcome of the first coupling, and in many traditional villages, particularly in the Arab world, a bloodstained sheet may be exhibited as positive proof of the bride's virginity. But the woman is not the only focus of this archaic ritual (which appears to go back to biblical times).[10] A study based on field research in Oman reveals that the bloody-sheet routine is actually as much a test of the groom's potency as it is of the bride's virginity. Indeed, this absorbing study concludes that the real pressure on the *laylat al-dukhla,* the "wedding night," is on the groom.[11]

The foregoing excursion into what for Westerners must appear to be exotic lore has not been recounted for reasons of entertainment, although a Yemeni wedding is certainly a fascinating social phenomenon, even for Yemenis. Nor will the seeker of quaint folk practices always find a bloody-sheet display after a village wedding. But old practices are still observed in more traditional settings, and for many Muslim peoples, they provide a sense of enduring values and satisfy inherited needs for

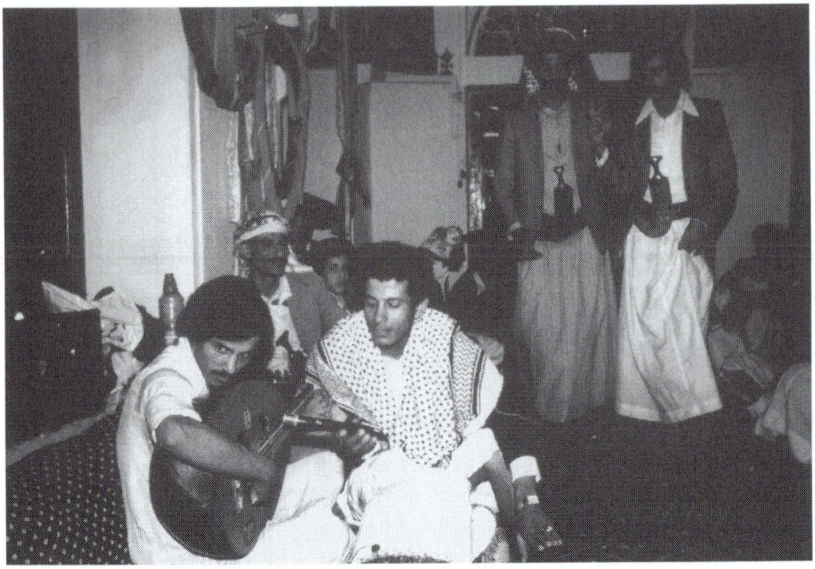

Men's wedding party in San'a, North Yemen. The women enjoy a party of their own across the street. Their joyful cries can be heard as a counterpoint to the music the men make singing and playing the *'oud.* Men take turns dancing up and down the narrow guest hall. (*Source:* Frederick Mathewson Denny)

certainty. There are many old customs connected with marriage and weddings in Islamic regions, as can be seen in the anthropological literature. The interested reader should consult such classic studies as Edward Alexander Westermarck's *Ritual and Belief in Morocco* and Edward William Lane's *Manners and Customs of the Modern Egyptians,* as well as more recent analyses such as Abdulla M. Lutfiyya's *Baytīn: A Jordanian Village,* which shows the continuity of old social forms and practices, especially those concerning marriage festivities.[12]

***The Bridal Gift.*** One of the fundamentals of the marriage contract is an appropriate bridal gift from the groom. This **mahr,** as it is known, has its root in the pre-Islamic "bride price," but with the coming of Islam the idea of purchasing the wife was replaced by the idea of a gift. Even so, certain legal discussions reflect the *mahr*'s earlier transactional quality. The marriage contract is null and void without payment of the *mahr,* and when it is signed, the amount or type of *mahr* is announced. It is often a matter of great interest to others, but it need not be lavish or conspicuous. During the time of the Prophet, even a pair of shoes was given as a *mahr.* Whatever it is, this gift becomes the property of the bride (technically, but it often winds up in the hands of her family). It is given at the time of the marriage or sometime after or even in installments. If the husband divorces his wife after the marriage has been consummated, then she keeps the whole amount; if before consummation, she is entitled to one half. The law books contain much detail about this bridal gift.

## DIVORCE (*ṬALĀQ*)

The Prophet declared that God considered divorce (*ṭalāq*) to be the most detestable of permitted things, and the Qur'an counsels immediate arbitration between spouses when there is the danger of a split (4:35). Islamic divorce traditionally was a fairly straightforward affair, in which the man had the advantage in initiating the proceeding and carrying it out. Today the woman has almost as much power, however, if there has been written into the marriage contract a conditional divorce formula covering any number of eventualities. For example, the contract may stipulate that the husband must fulfill certain obligations; if he does not, then the marriage will immediately be null and void. In some modern Muslim countries, divorce by repudiation (*ṭalāq*) has been outlawed or legally restricted, as has been polygyny.

### *Repudiation*

But tradition still has the greater influence, and in most places divorce is achieved in the old ways. The best-known and most controversial form is *ṭalāq,* "repudiation" of a wife by her husband in a most peremptory manner. The husband does not have to state grounds, although it is recommended that he do so. The formula "I divorce you" is uttered three times, the first and second being followed by a prescribed waiting period during which reconciliation is permitted without formalities. During this period, the couple may cohabit and then remarry. But once the third *ṭalāq* has been uttered, the divorce is final and no reconciliation is possible. If for some reason the couple wishes to remarry, then the divorced wife must first contract a marriage to another man. The marriage is not consummated, and so the second husband can divorce the woman immediately. This is a complex legal issue with much written about it, both for and against the practice. In general, such a marriage of convenience is disapproved, even condemned. If, however, the second marriage is consummated, there is less disapproval. Obviously, such a consummation is unlikely to occur in such cases, because the intervening husband is just a legal pawn who is paid for his troubles.

A more severe form of *ṭalāq* has also been practiced through the years. It involves uttering the three repudiations all at one time. This procedure is regarded as valid, although it is not recommended. Under the three *ṭalāq* procedures just described, there was a waiting period after the first two repudiations, lasting the length of three menstrual periods. During these periods the couple could be reconciled and remarry. But when the *ṭalāq* is uttered all at once, there is no chance for reconciliation. There is, however, still a waiting period of three menstrual periods, because the wife may be pregnant. If so, she is entitled to support until her confinement is over.

### *Legal Aspects*

Divorce is a highly complex legal field in Islam, and only a hint of its possible forms and ramifications can be given here. Some forms of divorce include the wife's purchasing her freedom, with part of her *mahr,* for example. This type of divorce carries the risk of a man's making extortionate demands on a wife who desires and needs to be free from an oppressive or undesirable husband, who nevertheless continues to abide by the marriage agreement and the Muslim law.

Another form of divorce takes place when the husband accuses his wife of being pregnant by another man. This *li'ān* ("mutual cursing"), as it is known, is based on an oath by the husband that his wife has committed adultery. No proof is required, and the husband is not subject to the usual Qur'anic punishment for false witness in such an affair. He simply swears four times that his wife is an adultress and then a fifth time that if he is lying, God's wrath may fall on him. The wife, for her part, swears four times that she is innocent and a fifth that if her husband is telling the truth, God's wrath may fall on her. This procedure is based on Sūra 24:6–9. When the oaths have been taken, the marriage is over.

Still another form of divorce is actually annulment and known as *faskh* or *ṭafrīq*. It is initiated by the wife or her *walī* because of the nonfulfillment of some requirement or because of such things as the husband's insanity or nonpayment of the rest of the *mahr.*

Divorce in Islamic countries is fairly common, partly because it is, at least for the man, so easy. With the advent of "no-fault" divorce and other easy and speedy procedures in the West and the drastic decrease in Christian conservatism regarding divorce, there is, consequently, more divorce there than in traditional Muslim populations. But strongly Roman Catholic countries have fewer divorces, because of the very strict canon law that since earliest times has declared divorce to be forbidden except under the most extreme circumstances; even then, it is actually considered annulment.

## INHERITANCE

The Muslim law of inheritance, which is based on the Qur'an (4:11–12), is very complex, or can be if the heirs are numerous and qualified to inherit according to a "fixed share" system that is detailed in the Qur'an and elaborated in later sources and discussions. The basic Qur'anic regulations are that male children receive twice what female children do; and in any case, the children of the deceased receive all or most of the estate, after expenses and debts have been paid and certain other possible heirs have been covered, according to a formula. If there is no son, one daughter gets one half of the total or shares two-thirds if there is more than one daughter. The parents and spouse of the deceased also have certain rights. The details can be found in books on Islamic law, but in general, the Muslim law of inheritance strives to be equitable and just. A person may make a will, bequeathing up to one-third of his or her estate as he or she chooses, but the remainder is regulated by law. The Islamic inheritance law and its numerous details worked out over the centuries were a great improvement over pre-Islamic Arabian inheritance practices, which favored the principal fighting males of the paternal line and gave absolutely nothing to women or even to male minors who could not as yet bear arms. The wife of the deceased received nothing; in fact, she was considered as part of the former husband's property and so was herself passed on to the husband's heirs.

## PROPERTY

Islamic inheritance law does tend to divide up property so that it is impossible for any individual in a large family to retain an unequally big portion. This becomes a problem for families that have established businesses that they wish to maintain through the generations. But Muslim jurists have been able to devise procedures for minimizing the losses to families in this regard. One way is to establish a charitable trust, known as a *waqf.* It is not subject to the inheritance law, but neither is it considered by most legal experts an ethical way to defeat the procedures and aims of the Qur'anic regulations concerning the proper division of an inheritance. *Waqfs* were designed for religious philanthropy, and so their proper object is the establishment of such institutions as mosques, schools, libraries, waterworks, hospitals, market buildings, and the like. A proper family *waqf* would continue to provide an income to several legitimate beneficiaries, but in a regulated and continuing manner. If it were a large rental property, for example, it could continue to be exploited in a businesslike way without its becoming so hopelessly divided up as to be impossible to administer profitably and rationally. On the other hand, until modern times, so much property in Muslim lands ended up in some sort of trust that it became very difficult for governments to regulate property matters so as to promote economic progress and stability. Recently, attempts have been made to put property back into circulation and thus increase its value. This approaches the realm of property law and management and not inheritance, but it is an important field that the serious student of Islamic economics cannot overlook.

## INTEREST

Another aspect of Islamic economic doctrine is the prohibition of interest, known in Arabic as ***ribā***. This term means "usury," but Qur'anic and later Islamic opinion has it that any increase in wealth by means of a loan is usurious. Some Qur'anic passages dealing with interest are "Those who devour usury shall not rise again except as he rises, whom Satan of the touch prostrates; that is because they say, 'Trafficking is like usury.' God has permitted trafficking, and forbidden usury" (2:275); "O believers, devour not usury, doubled and redoubled . . . " (3:130); and "And what you give in usury, that it may increase upon the people's wealth, increases not with God; but what you give in alms, desiring God's Face, those—they receive recompense manifold" (30:38).

The prohibition of interest naturally complicates dealings in the modern, international worlds of banking and commerce. Observant Muslims do not accept interest on bank accounts or loans, although some consider it permissible to donate any accrued interest to charity, recognizing that it is impossible in today's world for money not to earn interest if it is invested or deposited in institutions that are in business to make a profit. Across the Islamic world banking institutions are being established that seek to follow the Qur'anic law concerning *ribā* while exploring ways to enhance Islamic society and institutions through imaginative new procedures and programs. And in Western nations, Muslims are developing Islamic banking and finance companies to help the community with mortgages, auto loans, and investments. The key point in Islamic economics is goodwill for others, especially the less fortunate and the public or general welfare. It is significant that alms, or *zakāt,* are considered by the Qur'an to be like a loan to God on which God increases the value. But this is not "interest," because the wealth that a person gives came from God in the first place. A profit made on an investment that has entailed some risk is not considered *ribā.*

## FAMILY LIFE

Something has already been said about family life in connection with birth, childhood, marriage, and inheritance. But beyond that is a world of attitudes and activities centered in the nuclear and extended families, because it is there that life is lived at all its levels: economic, social, sexual, recreational, ritual, and protective. The Islamic family has been a bulwark against general instability and chaos, providing mutual protection and support and a setting for the proper care of children, women, and old people. The extended family structure works to protect against the isolation and abandonment of bereaved or handicapped individuals. This idea is not unique to Islam, of course, for other religions and cultures also put much store by the family, for example, Jews, Italians, and Greeks, not to mention the Chinese, whose filial devotion and solid family loyalty are legendary.

A common Islamic view of marriage is that a husband and wife need each other in order to be complete and fulfilled. The division of labor needed to maintain a household normally means that the husband works outside the home in the public sector, earning a livelihood for himself, his wife, and their children, and the wife concentrates her energies and talents in managing the family's domestic affairs. This type of marriage is of course under attack in the modern West, where it is branded as unfair to women. Without turning our discussion into a debate, it should be said that thoughtful and observant Muslims and others are both aware of and sensitive to the issues of injustice and subjugation, whether of women, children, or men; but they are also bent on preserving a traditional family structure because they believe that it is the most stable and honorable form for intimate social relations and the inculcation of ethical values, religious principles, and the formation of mature character. Muslim families, whether in traditional urban settings, like Cairo, Lahore, or Istanbul, or in

European or American locales, are experiencing most of the pressures and limitations of contemporary economic life. There are one-parent families, working mothers, and "latchkey" children who are Muslims, too.

### *The Extended Family*

The extended Islamic family brings all members into a close mutual relationship. This includes money matters, for if someone needs assistance, a loan or gift may be made, and always without interest. If a brother or sister or niece or nephew is abandoned or destitute, then it is the responsibility of the others to provide for that person. This is expected within a nuclear family even in the West, but it is not so common to see it applying beyond it. Extended families are close because they provide for their members a continuing form of entertainment and recreation by means of visits, shared meals, and constant consultations.

I have lived for long periods in Egypt and Indonesia, two culturally very different Islamic environments. In both places, families carry out unending and close social activities within the family circle and do not normally go beyond it, except in the immediate community. That is because of the sanctity of the ***maḥram*** relationship, as we know it from the Qur'an. *Maḥram* means "taboo" or "unlawful" in the sense of being one whom it is impossible to marry because of close blood ties. *Maḥrams* are relatives like father, mother, son, daughter, grandparents, uncles, aunts, nephews, nieces, as well as in-laws, adoptive parents or children, and anyone who has been nursed by the same breast. Thus, there is sharper distinction between private and public in Islamic contexts than there is in the modern West.

It is possible for persons to socialize outside the *maḥram* status, provided they are properly chaperoned by a *maḥram* or a spouse. For example, a Muslim woman may not entertain a non-*maḥram* male or be alone with him in a setting that could raise questions of propriety or be even potentially compromising. But it is perfectly permissible for a wife to receive non-*maḥram* guests, either with her husband or with members of her family or even with other adults of the same sex present. (Not all would agree with the last example.) One day while visiting Egypt, I had the inauspicious experience of arriving for lunch at the home of a Muslim couple, knowing that the husband was out of town but that there would be other adult females present. Although this was an unusual arrangement, it was apparently acceptable because I was a special guest. But because of unforeseen circumstances, the other women at the last minute could not come after all, and the hostess was put in the predicament of having to be hospitable to me while realizing that our being alone in the house, with only her son and her servant girl present, would raise eyebrows. As it turned out, the couple were known to have many Western acquaintances, and their neighbors apparently realized that in this case, hospitality was more sacred than violation of the *maḥram* code.

On another occasion, I was hiking in the hills of Jordan enjoying the scenery and hoping to find some old artifacts in the sand, when I inadvertently trespassed into the territory of a Bedouin family. Only the wife and a child were at home, and the young woman beckoned earnestly and insisted that I stay for tea. She was extending to me the hospitality of her poor home, although according to strict Muslim observance, we could not properly socialize together beyond exchanging greetings. At the same time, if she had *not* offered hospitality, it would have reflected poorly on her husband, because I was a stranger and to be treated somewhat differently from others who lived there and knew better.

Similar things have happened to me in other parts of the Muslim world, including Indonesia, which is far from the old central lands of Islam. It would be easy to offer more anecdotes, but my point is to illustrate both the propriety of Muslim social customs and at the same time the spontaneous and generous flexibility that Muslims exercise when appropriate. Islamic social life is not based on the fear of making mistakes or avoiding simple human contact. The rules and customs do, however, provide a sense of seemliness and predictability that enhances rather than hinders social intercourse.

## FOOD AND EATING HABITS

### *What Can Be Eaten?*

Meals are at the center of much Muslim family and social life, as they are of most peoples in the world. As in other aspects of life, most things pertaining to food and eating are indifferent in the eyes of the law; that is, they are permitted, though by no means necessarily recommended. But certain types of substances are forbidden, and are thus ***ḥarām.*** Permitted things are ***ḥalāl.*** These two technical terms divide up the world for Muslims and relate to practically everything imaginable. In the case of food, there is a further distinction within the *ḥalāl* category, between what is *ṭayyib,* that is, "good" and "pure," and what is not, although it falls within the general classification of permitted things. For example, beef, which is *ḥalāl,* may not be eaten if it has not been slaughtered properly and the blood drained off. Nor should one eat spoiled food. The Qur'an expressly forbids four kinds of food: carrion, blood, pork, and anything sacrificed and dedicated to other than God (2:173). By carrion is meant any creature that dies spontaneously, whether from illness, old age, being killed improperly, or whatever. However, the skin may be used for nonfood purposes. All four of these prohibited foods parallel the Jewish prohibitions. The forbidding of blood refers to flowing blood, as when someone punctures a living animal to draw off its blood for food. It is permissible to consume the blood that remains in the flesh of a properly slaughtered animal, as long as there has been an attempt to drain it off. Interestingly, sea creatures and locusts that have died spontaneously are considered to be *ḥalāl.* All marine animals (i.e., those that cannot live out of the water) are *ḥalāl,* whether they have been caught, slaughtered, or died spontaneously, for the sea is considered to be essentially pure.[13] Even shellfish may be consumed, and this is contrary to Jewish dietary regulations. Certain other land creatures are prohibited, even though they are not mentioned in the Qur'an: for example, predators (both animals and birds), dogs, and, for some jurists, donkeys. The *'ulamā'* have also condemned crocodiles, weasels, pelicans, otters, foxes, elephants, ravens, and insects. Often, the predators and some of the animals just mentioned are regarded as *makrūh,* "detestable," but not *ḥarām.*

Not only is what is eaten of importance, but Muslims also must consider with whom it is eaten. Here there is a general rule that, first, any *ḥalāl* food that has been slaughtered properly, including invoking the name of God, is permitted. If there is doubt but no evidence that the food was dedicated to other than God, then the Muslim may simply pronounce the *bismillāh al-Rahmān al-Rahīm* over it ("In the Name of God, the Merciful, the Compassionate"). The food of the People of the Book (the Jews and Christians) is generally acceptable, because those folks are fellow monotheists. Of course, this applies only to *ḥalāl* foods. Christians eat pork and sometimes blood in special dishes like black pudding. Jews and Muslims have similarities as to specific foods, as has been noted, except that the Jewish list of *ḥarām* items is longer because of the prohibited marine species. (Some Muslims avoid shellfish, but the majority find no authority for the practice.)

### *How It Is Eaten*

Observant Muslims invoke God by means of the *basmala* when they prepare to eat. In traditional settings, many Muslim peoples eat with their hands, although utensils like spoons may be used, too. The Prophet is reported to have sometimes used a knife when there was meat. As was pointed out in Chapter 5, only the right hand may be used, because the left is reserved for unclean duties associated with the toilet. Recall that the preference for the right extends to all social relations: One offers a gift or object and receives something only with the right hand. One should also not touch another person with the left hand. The use of the right hand in eating is especially important when a common dish is provided, as in the Arab world. (In South Asia a common dish is rather uncommon.) In such a case, one should not pick and poke about in the dish but simply grasp what is near at hand. Nor should one eat in a reclining posture or eat while standing. One should never complain of food that one dislikes or the manner of preparing a dish, but one may simply—and silently—not eat it.

Generally, in more traditional households, especially in the Arab world but also in South Asia, the men will eat first, and then the women and children. When guests are present, the man of the house will eat with them apart from the rest of the family, although this is not absolutely required. Different patterns are found in different places. In Indonesia, for example, it is much more common for people to eat in solitude, even though at something like a festival they will begin together before turning aside to consume their meals.

In many parts of the world, mealtime is for eating above all. The Western custom of making table conversation is rare at best, and sometimes it is absent altogether. There are always exceptions, though, especially when a non-Muslim guest is present. At such times, the host and perhaps other members of his family will engage the visitor in pleasant conversation and keep offering food. Occasionally an honored guest will be fed first to indicate his or her social status. In general, Muslim practice favors eating in company with others and using mealtime as an opportunity to praise and thank God.

A very important Islamic prohibition relates to wine and any other intoxicating beverage or substance. The Qur'an explicitly forbids the consumption of wine: "O believers, wine and arrow-shuffling, idols and divining-arrows are an abomination, some of Satan's work; so avoid it; haply so you will prosper (5:90)." The Prophet uttered a number of sentences regarding intoxicants, and the overall purport is that all are *ḥarām* in any quantity and in any context.[14] Nor can alcohol be bought or sold by Muslims or given or received as a gift, even to or from non-Muslims, or used in cooking or even in medical prescriptions, except when absolutely necessary and under the supervision of a Muslim professional of sound morals and religion.

## CLOTHING, ORNAMENTATION, AND TOILET

Muslims emphasize personal bodily cleanliness, and this naturally pertains to purity while engaged in ritual practices such as prayer, as well as at other times. Clothing is not precisely regulated, and so Muslims enjoy a great variety of styles and fabrics. As we noted earlier in connection with the hajj, the men don the *iḥrām,* the white, seamless cotton garment of ritual dedication, whereas the women are permitted to wear their normal native garb. The two sexes thus together bear witness to both the unity of the community and its diversity. The *'awra* (private areas) must be covered in both sexes, of course. Men should not wear clothes made of pure silk, but women are permitted to do so. Silk is not a *ḥarām* fabric, but it does suggest luxury and ease as well as conspicuous consumption, all of which ill befit a sincere Muslim male, who should work hard and spend the excess of his earnings for the improvement of the general welfare, specifically in charitable works. (It is necessary to distinguish between observant and nonobservant Muslims, of course.) Neither should men wear gold, but it is allowable for women. Both sexes are permitted to wear silver. Silk, gold, and silver are allowable for women, as befits their status as the weaker sex. (Their acquisition may also be considered as a premodern form of banking.) Neither women nor men are allowed to wear seductive clothing, nor may they wear clothing inappropriate to their sexes. Children are to follow their parents' example, but the distinction in dress between boys and girls is not necessarily maintained strictly at all times, because their sexuality does not become important until puberty or just before.

As for styles of coiffure, men are encouraged to grow mustaches and to let their beards grow if they do not become annoying or interfering. It is recommended that they be trimmed regularly. It is also permissible, indeed in some traditional opinions desirable, to dye the hair so as to be distinct from other peoples, especially the Christians and the Jews.[15] But Muslims should not tattoo or indulge in surgery to alter the appearance of the skin or shape the teeth in an unnatural manner. (But these

Indonesian Qur'an reciters at an advanced institute in Java. Their head covering and dress are proper for Muslim ladies. Some Muslims cover the hair entirely, but this is not universally regarded as essential. (*Source:* Frederick Mathewson Denny)

practices are known, for example, among Bedouin women.) The wearing of wigs and hairpieces is forbidden, because it is a "forgery."

Perfume is recommended, especially before visiting the mosque on Friday. Women should also use scent after menstruation. One of the main elements in the Muslim aesthetic of everyday life is the desirability of pleasant odors, for they are a reminder of paradise. The Prophet is reported to have declared that three things were especially beautiful to him: the company of women, prayer, and perfume. The olfactory sense is in the present day still very prominent. Floral bouquets and vials of pleasant scent are often exchanged as gifts among Muslims, and it is not at all out of the ordinary for men to share whiffs of perfume with one another rather than to offer cigarettes, especially in this age of awareness of the dangers of tobacco. But Muslims have always enjoyed beautiful smelling substances, because of their intrinsic excellence as well as the Prophet's clear predilection for them.

## DEATH RITUALS

When a person approaches death, if possible his or her family or a fellow Muslim should turn the dying person's face toward Mecca and the *qibla,* and utter the first shahāda, "There is no god but God." It is believed that the deceased will need to remember this most profound of confessions so as to be ready for his or her judgment before God. It is recommended that someone recite Sūra *Yā Sīn* (36), which is particularly appropriate for anyone on the verge of death. As a prophetic *ḥadith* testifies: "If anyone recites *Yā Sīn* out of a desire for God's favour, his past sins will be forgiven him; so recite it over those of you who are dying."[16] This sūra deals with death and resurrection and is one of the best known and most often memorized of all sections of the Qur'an. Key verses touching on death are

> Surely it is We who bring the dead to life and write down what they have forwarded and what they have left behind; everything We have numbered in a clear register. (verse 12)
>
> • • •
>
> And the Trumpet shall be blown, then behold, they are sliding down from their tombs unto their Lord.
> They say, "Alas for us! Who roused us out of our sleeping place? This is what the All-merciful promised and the Envoys spoke truly."
> "It was only one Cry; then behold, they are all arraigned before Us. So today no soul shall be wronged anything, and you shall not be recompensed, except according to what you have been doing. See, the inhabitants of Paradise today are busy in their rejoicing, they and their spouses, reclining upon couches in the shade; therein they have fruits, and they have all that they call for. "Peace!"—such is the greeting, from a Lord All-Compassionate." (verses 50–57)

### *Burial Rites*

As soon as a person has died, the body must be washed and prepared for burial.[17] If the person dies in the morning, then the burial should be that day, but if in the afternoon, then the next morning. There is particular merit in performing the final full ablution (*ghusl*) for the deceased. Females perform this rite for females and males for males, except in the case of children or spouses. During the washing, the private parts should be covered. The parts that are washed first are those that are normally washed during the *wuḍū,* or minor ablution; then the rest of the body is washed in proper order, with appropriate prayers uttered at each step. Scent is recommended to be added to the washing water, but it must not contain alcohol. No embalming is permitted, but the remains should be as clean as possible, including the major orifices. Soap and water are used for the washings, which generally number three, but the last washing should contain scent instead of soap. If more washings are needed, then the number must be odd, usually five or seven. Each time, the right side is cleansed first. The hair must be unbraided, washed, and combed. Women's hair may then be rebraided in three braids. The body is dried with a clean cloth, with perfume added to the head, forehead, nose, hands, knees, eyes, armpits, and perfumed cotton placed over the lower orifices. A simple white cotton shroud, sometimes in two pieces like the *iḥrām,* is wrapped around the corpse, but more often three pieces of cloth completely wrap a male and five a female. The final wrapped body should contain indications of where the head and the feet are, for the laying in the grave requires proper orientation toward Mecca, with the body lying on its right side.

It is not necessary to place the deceased in a coffin, although it is permissible. No costly materials should be used either in the grave clothes or in the construction of the coffin or grave. Sometimes the body is carried to a mosque, where the special prayer service, known as *ṣalāt al-janāza* ("salat over the dead"), is performed. But this location is not necessary; the home of the deceased or any clean place will suffice. The service may even be performed in the graveyard itself, if there is enough space, though this is not recommended. The salat is led either by a close male relative or by a professional *imām.* The deceased, whether in a coffin or on a bier, is placed in front of where the worshipers will stand; the *imām* stands between them and the midsection of a deceased male or the shoulders of a female.

### *Funeral Prayers*

The entire service is performed standing and consists of four *takbīrs* (saying "*Allāhu akbar*"—"God is most great"), each followed by *du'ā'*. The first *takbīr* alone is performed while raising the hands, as at the beginning of any of the daily salats, and is followed either by a *du'ā'* or a recitation of the Fātiha (*Sūra 1*), depending on the *madhhab.* The details vary among the schools, but generally the funeral salat consists mainly in prayer for the deceased. If a child is being buried, then there is no asking forgiveness for sins, for a child is not accountable until puberty. Taking part in the *ṣalāt al-janāza,* as in the procession to the burial place afterward, is a *farḍkifāya;* that is, it must be done, but it is "sufficient" (*kifāya*) that a representative number of Muslims perform the rite. The *du'ā'* prayer following the *takbīrs* is usually taken from those uttered by the Prophet, but other prayers may be used. A typical sequence after each of the four *takbīrs* is al-Fātiha, a prayer for the Prophet Muhammad, a prayer for the deceased, and, finally, a prayer for all the Muslims, with the whole concluded by *al-Salāmu 'alaykum* ("Peace be upon you"). The following is an example of a funeral prayer first offered by Muhammad. It is the one after the third *takbīr,* which is for the deceased:

> Allah, do forgive him and have mercy on him and make him secure and overlook his shortcomings, and bestow upon him an honoured place in Paradise, and make his place of entry spacious, and wash him clean with water and snow and ice, and cleanse him of all wrong as Thou dost clean a piece of white cloth of dirt, and bestow upon him a home better than his home and a family better than his family and a spouse better than his spouse, and admit him into Paradise, and shield him from the torment of the grave and the torment of the Fire. (Muslim)[18]

The relater of this *ḥadīth* declared that after hearing the Prophet's prayer, he wished he himself could have been the corpse.

### *Time of Burial*

The burial should be done quickly, for as the Prophet is reported to have advised: "Should the deceased be righteous you would speed him towards good and should he be otherwise you would be laying aside evil from your necks" (Bukhārī and Muslim).[19] The bier is carried on the shoulders of men, usually four, who generally take turns with four new bearers, and then an additional four, and so on, until the burial ground is reached. The grave is normally four- to six-feet deep, with a niche carved out on the side (called a *lahd*), into which the body is placed on its side, with its head facing Mecca. The body should preferably rest directly on the ground, but a coffin is sometimes used instead. A green brick may be used to rest the head on, but never a pillow. The *lahd* is covered, usually with unfired bricks, and then the main pit is filled in with earth. Each mourner drops in three handfuls of soil. At the moment of placing the body in the *lahd,* the one doing this should say, "In the Name of God and according to the Way of the Prophet." It is also a common (although not universal) practice to recite from the twentieth sūra of the Qur'an: "Out of the earth We created you, and We shall restore you into it, and bring you forth from it a second time" (verse 55).

After the grave has been filled in, at least symbolically by the handfuls of earth, someone delivers a brief address to the deceased, reminding him or her of the central truths of God's oneness, Muhammad's messengership, the reality of heaven

Funeral procession in Cairo. It is a duty for Muslims to follow a procession such as this to the grave-site, but it is sufficient that only a few do so. Men may take turns carrying the coffin. (*Source:* Amy Newhall)

and hell, the religion of the Qur'an, and the solidarity of the Muslim brotherhood that takes the Ka'ba as its prayer point. Or, if such an address is not delivered, the group together recites a Fātiha, and then after walking about forty paces from the grave, they offer another, because it is believed that the buried one is already beginning to undergo interrogation by the angels Munkar and Nakīr. If the deceased was not reminded of the first shahāda ("There is no god but God") on the deathbed, then this is uttered in his or her ear when the body is placed in the grave niche, before it is walled in. This last is done so that the deceased will be able to answer correctly the questioning angels.

## MOURNING CUSTOMS

The foregoing has been an abbreviated description of a typical, orthoprax Muslim funeral and burial. There are many regional and cultural variations in detail, but the basic form nevertheless persists and regulates all else. After the burial, it is customary to remember the deceased periodically by means of special meals, prayers, Qur'an recitation sessions, and other things. Observances go on for the first forty days after the funeral and at set times thereafter, but the actual period of mourning is only the first three days after the burial, during which the bereaved avoid wearing jewelry or perfume and go about in unwashed clothing. Widows must mourn like this for four months and ten days. It is a widespread practice to wail for the dead, and often special woman wailers are employed for the purpose, but strict observance (based on prophetic *ḥadīths*) severely condemns this practice and warns that it increases the deceased's suffering in the grave.

Usually the grave site is raised in a mound several inches above the level ground, though this is disapproved by the strictest *'ulamā',* who also condemn embellishing the grave by means of any structures or elaborate headstones. It is acceptable to place a small marker, however, naming the deceased and containing a pious formula, such as the Fātiha. Despite prohibitions and even violent razings, as by the Wahhābī reformers in eighteenth-century Arabia, Muslim cemeteries have nevertheless often contained elaborate and costly mausoleums, some of which are masterpieces of Islamic architecture. An assortment of these can be seen in the great necropolises of Islamic Cairo, for example.

The fetus who dies because of miscarriage or abortion is buried without ceremony in a cloth wrapping, after first having received a name.[20] The martyr is buried without washing or prayer, in the clothes he or she was wearing when struck down. Purification is not needed, because such a person is already ritually pure and destined for paradise. One of the Muslims' central beliefs concerning the body in the grave is that it undergoes punishments in the intermediate period between the burial and the general resurrection. This period is known as *barzakh* and is a kind of purgatory. There is some difference of opinion among the legal scholars as to whether all dead people undergo punishment or only the sinners and infidels, but the majority contend that the true believers experience only a kind of dreamless sleep

Muslim cemetery in Surabaya, East Java. Sufis, especially, have always emphasized the benefits of meditating in burial places. Notice the lone figure reading, left of center. (*Source:* Frederick Mathewson Denny)

until the general Judgment. Muslims everywhere view the visiting of cemeteries as a meritorious act and conducive to proper reflection about one's own demise. Sufis, especially, have cultivated this practice as part of the *ars moriendi,* the "art of holy dying." Abū Hāmid Al-Ghazālī, in a great treatise on the religious life, tells his fellow Muslims how one should go to bed at night:

> When you want to go to sleep, lay out your bed pointing to Mecca, and sleep on your right side, the side on which the corpse reclines in the tomb. Sleep is the similitude of death and waking of the resurrection. Perhaps God most high will take your spirit this night; so be prepared to meet Him by being in a condition of purity when you sleep. Have your will written and beneath your head. Repent of your faults, seek pardon, resolve not to return to your sin, and so sleep. Resolve to do good to all Muslims if God most high raises you up again. Remember that in like manner you will lie in the tomb, completely alone; only your works will be with you, only the effort you have made will be rewarded.[21]

The topics and examples considered in this chapter on Islamic life-cycle rites, ceremonies, and customs have been selected and described so as to give a general idea of typical behavior. It must be understood that this is a huge field of inquiry and that actual practices as well as attitudes vary considerably from one place to another, while remaining properly Islamic in the minds of the believers. The Islamic law provides for a wide range of opinion as to what is acceptable or not, and there can be circumstantial considerations touching upon most dimensions of human behavior. It is hoped that the materials considered here have given the reader a better sense of the actual life of Muslims, beyond the more formal aspects of doctrines and jurisprudence.

## NOTES

1. Edward William Lane, *Arabian Society in the Middle Ages: Studies from the Thousand and One Nights,* ed. Stanley Lane-Poole (New York: Barnes & Noble, 1971), p. 190. Muslim naming practices also include many regional variations, using names from other than the Arabic–Islamic tradition in addition to such classic names as Muhammad, Fatima, ‘Umar, and ‘Ali. See the excellent study by Annemarie Schimmel, *Islamic Names,* "Islamic Surveys" (Edinburgh: Edinburgh University Press, 1989).
2. There is a nicely detailed and illustrated description of circumcision and related rituals in Hajji Mohtar bin H. Md. Dom, *Traditions and Taboos* (Kuala Lumpur: Federal Publications, 1979), pp. 35–43.
3. Both al-Bukhāri and Muslim. See al-Baghawī, *Mishkāt al-Masābīh,* vol. 3, trans. James Robson (Lahore, Pakistan: Sh. Muhammad Ashraf, 1965–1966), p. 929.
4. *Ibid.,* p. 934.
5. Otto Meinardus, *Christian Egypt: Faith and Life* (Cairo: American University in Cairo Press, 1970), pp. 318–341, contains a detailed examination, with an extensive bibliography. See also the article "Khitān," by A. J. Wensinck, in *The Encyclopaedia of Islam,* new ed., vol. V, Fasc. 79–80 (Leiden: E. J. Brill, 1979), pp. 20–22.
6. See, for example, Bruno Bettelheim, *Symbolic Wounds: Puberty Rites and the Envious Male* (Glencoe, IL: Free Press, 1954).
7. al-Baghawī, *Mishkāt,* vol. 2, p. 658.
8. *Ibid.*
9. Yusuf al-Qaradawi, *The Lawful and the Prohibited in Islam (Al-Halal Wal Haram Fil Islam)* (Indianapolis: American Trust Publications, n.d.; first published in Arabic in 1960), p. 153.
10. Raphael Patai, *Sex and Family in the Bible and the Middle East* (New York: Double-day, 1959), "The Bloodstained Garment," pp. 66–70.
11. Unni Wikan, *Behind the Veil in Arabia: Women in Oman* (Baltimore and London: Johns Hopkins University Press, 1982), p. 225ff.
12. Edward Alexander Westermarck, *Ritual and Belief in Morocco,* 2 vols. (London: Macmillan, 1926); Edward William Lane, *Manners and Customs of the Modern Egyptians,* first published in 1836, with numerous subsequent editions and printings; Abdulla M. Lutfiyya, *Baytīn: A Jordanian Village* (The Hague: Mouton, 1966).
13. Al-Qaradawi, *The Lawful and the Prohibited in Islam,* p. 52. For a thorough discussion of Islamic regulations pertaining to food, drink, slaughtering, and related topics, see pp. 39–79.
14. A representative sampling is in al-Baghawī, *Mishkāt,* vol. 2, pp. 776–779 and vol. 3, pp. 908–909. The Prophet Muhammad used to drink *nabīdh,* a beverage made from dates, raisins, honey, wheat, barley, and other things, but only before it fermented. I was once treated to a coconut drink in East Java, which bubbled and had a piquant taste.

Some of the company declined to sample it. When I asked what the Islamic legal status of the beverage was, I was told, with a smile, "between *ḥalāl and ḥarām!*"

15. Al-Qaradawi, *The Lawful and the Prohibited in Islam,* pp. 92–93.
16. al-Baghawī, *Mishkāt,* vol. 2, p. 460.
17. This description of burial practices and rites is based on Abdul Rauf, *Islam: Creed and Worship* (Washington, DC: The Islamic Center, 1974), pp. 40–42, 96–100; and Mohammad Abdul Aleem Siddiqui, *Elementary Teachings of Islam* (Dacca, Bangladesh: n.d.), pp. 62–64, and the appendix, "Preparation of the Deceased and Janaza Prayers." For *ḥadīths* on death, burial, and funerals, see al-Baghawī, *Mishkāt,* vol. 1, pp. 320–370.
18. *Gardens of the Righteous: Riyadh as-Salihin of Imam Nawawi,* trans. Muhammad Zafrullah Khan (London: Curzon Press, 1975), p. 176, number 939.
19. *Ibid.,* p. 177, number 945.
20. The Sharī'a position on abortion is that it is absolutely prohibited, except when the life of the mother is threatened beyond a reasonable doubt. See Al-Qaradawi, *The Lawful and Prohibited in Islam,* pp. 201–202.
21. W. Montgomery Watt, *The Faith and Practice of al-Ghazālī* (London: Allen & Unwin, 1953), "The Beginning of Guidance," p. 115. For details on Islamic ideas concerning death and afterlife, see Jane Idleman Smith and Yvonne Yazbeck Haddad, *The Islamic Understanding of Death and Resurrection* (Albany: State University of New York Press, 1981).

# CHAPTER 13 Ideals and Realities of Islamic Community Life

**KEY TERMS**

***qubba*** ***ziyāra* (pl. *ziyārāt*)** ***ta'ziya***

## THE CLOSENESS OF THE COMMUNITY

Just as the Islamic family has its own patterns and style and provides the primary setting for the life-cycle rites of birth, naming, circumcision, marriage, and death, so also has the larger community typical structures and functions that both express and accommodate to an Islamic vision of life. That is, at both the family and the wider community levels Muslims regulate their lives by means of both transcending Islamic norms and values and regional customs and practices. Islam's inherent adaptability to a variety of local contexts is a testimony to its enormous success as a world religion. Muslims on Sumatra feel a close brotherhood with Muslims in Pakistan, Central Asia, and Europe, and at the same time they feel proud and special for being Minangkabau or Batak or Acehnese, three of the distinct cultures on Sumatra. This chapter seeks to discern typical forms of Islamic community life through a description of the town, the city, and the ways people gather together for trade, work, business, education, recreation, and worship. When appropriate, we shall point out differences among peoples, as well as when strict Islamic teaching and local customs diverge and even conflict. It is not possible in the brief confines of a single chapter to do justice to the variety of data that would be required for a thorough treatment of Muslim community life. Rather, we shall present the typical as well as examples of the exceptional, so that the reader will be aware of the texture and quality of Muslim societies and begin to understand how they function.

## THE MOSQUE

From its origins, Islam has been closely identified with settled forms of social and economic life, in both the town and the city. The romantic and Western associations of Bedouin of the desert and a monotheism born from meditation in vast expanses under a brilliant sky are far from the facts. As we observed in Chapter 4, Muslims have always preferred to live where people gather together for worship. Making a *hijra* to a settled community has traditionally been a meritorious act, for it both symbolizes and embodies the intention to live responsibly with others for the common good.

### *The Mosque's Uses*

The center of the Islamic town or city is the Friday mosque, and this has been so since the earliest times.[1] Adjacent to the mosque, which must be architecturally and structurally complete and enclosed, is the market or bazaar (Arabic, *sūq*). In large towns and governmental centers, there traditionally is a palace, or the house of the ruler or his representatives, which is fortified. Sometimes the governor's house is at the edge of town, for security reasons. Often, also, in the center is the public bath (*ḥammām*), which provides a place for ritual purification, especially after major impurity. The Friday mosque is a multipurpose building where important public

Worshipers gathered for Friday noon Salat in a busy section of Cairo. The great crowd has forced an overflow congregation to use the sidewalk and street outside. A mosque is not primarily a building, but a place set aside for worship. The street here has been converted into mosque-space for the duration of the worship service. (*Source:* Frederick Mathewson Denny)

announcements and proclamations are made, crowds are gathered in times of crisis—for example, to rally support for defense or holy warfare—and where at the Friday worship service, the ruler's name is mentioned in the sermon, thus demonstrating his continued authority. (When the sovereign's name has not been mentioned, this has often indicated a change in government. During times of conflict, citizens listen closely to the Friday sermon.) The major mosque also often has an educational function, with learned shaykhs holding forth either in the mosque itself or in special attached buildings or arcades. The mosque provides a place for men to rest, to socialize, to take time out from a busy day in order to meditate for a while, even to eat, as well as, of course, to perform the obligatory daily salats. After school, boys may go to the mosque for instruction in Qur'an recitation or, nowadays in crowded, noisy cities like Cairo, to do homework. If the mosque is famous for being also the burial site of a famous saint, then many people, women included, will visit the place for blessing and intercession. But in large cities, there will be a variety of saints' tombs connected with mosques that are not necessarily Friday mosques but that nevertheless provide a focus for the life of individual quarters.

Friday mosque, Cairo, Egypt. This imposing structure, patterned on traditional architectural lines, is an example of recent strides in government-sponsored building in Egypt. (*Source:* Frederick Mathewson Denny)

The shops and workshops closest to the mosque typically deal in candles, incense and perfumes, religious objects such as rosaries and amulets and books, together with the leather-working establishments that bind the books as well as manufacture slippers and other products. When I was living and studying in Cairo, my shaykh at a large mosque occasionally sent a boy out into an alley close by to find a certain book or pamphlet. There were always little eating establishments nearby, too, where a quick lunch of falafel, goat cheese, Syrian flatbread, and greens and onions could be purchased for a few pennies, the boy usually going to a separate little vending stand for each item. When such a simple but satisfying repast is spread out on a mat in a quiet corner of the mosque, it is not long before a small group gathers to have a bite or two. Although most people do not use the mosque for a brown-bag lunch, it is normally permissible to consume food on the premises. On occasions when large numbers of travelers descend upon a town or city, it has traditionally been normal for people without accommodations to sleep in the mosque. And during the last ten days of Ramadān, pious Muslims like to keep nightly prayer and recitation vigils (known as *i'tikāf*) in the mosque. Men also use the sanitary facilities that most large mosques have, such as toilets and ablution taps.

Minangkabau women in their finest business attire dominate the marketplace in Bukittinggi, west central Sumatra. The Minangkabau have traditionally been a matrilineal society, but they are also strict Sunnī Muslims. Islamic law allows for wide variations in local custom. Minangkabau women own most of the land, whereas the men engage in business activities far and wide, returning at harvesttime to help with the farmwork. (*Source:* Frederick Mathewson Denny)

***The Mosque's Hospitality.*** Several years ago I received a telephone call from a representative of the district attorney's office of an American city in which there had arisen a controversy over a local mosque, which happened to be in a residential neighborhood. The premises were being used as a sleeping place for visiting and transient Muslims. The legal representative wanted me to appear as an expert witness for the prosecution by saying that such behavior was not typical of or approved by Islam. I immediately replied, "But, oh, yes, it is!" The caller's ardor for my cooperation instantly cooled. I agreed that this particular pattern of social life would understandably arouse the anxieties of the neighbors about the value of their property, because they viewed the mosque as what in the most charitable terms could only be called some sort of "crash pad." Of course, in an Islamic context one who finds it necessary to put up in a mosque for the night is hardly considered to be a hippy or a bum. On the other hand, such a person would not be turned out of a mosque if he came seeking shelter and had no place else to go. Hospitality and protection of the stranger and wayfarer are sacred in Islam.

## THE MARKETPLACE

Not far from the central mosque in a large town there traditionally is a closed shopping area with warehouses for textiles and other valuable products. Either in these enclosed structures or nearby are shops with metal products for cooking or ornament; however, the actual smithies or forges will be some greater distance away, but possibly no farther than a back alley. Rather than a grid plan, as in the ancient Greek and Roman cities of the Mediterranean basin—influential in the West with their sense of municipality with its own authority and structures of civic involvement and expression—the classic Muslim city of the central regions, at least, has grown out from the center according to separate and partially separate quarters. Ethnic and tribal groups sharing a religious identification nevertheless lived in separate enclaves from earliest times. Non-Muslims settled in their own city sectors and the Jews often as close as feasible to the governor and his guard, for protection in times of persecution and unrest.

### *The Protection of the Marketplace*

The inhabitants of the Muslim town or city have always had some anxiety, even fear, about being attacked, either in the individual quarter—which may have a bitter feud with another quarter—or from the outside. Of course, walled fortifications are not unique to the Muslim world, for they were the means by which people protected themselves in medieval Europe, too.

The positioning of the quarters and associated trades and occupations has often been hierarchical, with the elite and powerful being near the center.[2] Often the individual quarters have also their own gates and security systems. The maze of small streets and alleys that double back on themselves and generally end in the quarter contrasts with the grid pattern or the modern rationalized system of streets and boulevards and public squares and gardens. These last have not been part of traditional Muslim settlements, because of the extreme privacy at the family level that Islamic life requires. The typical single dwelling usually has a central courtyard of some sort, secure from the eyes of outsiders, and the main entrance is constructed so as to conceal what is immediately inside the house. Windows on the street are fashioned so as to make it impossible for strangers to see in and to enable the women of the house to spend as much time as they want peering out. In the Arab world, these *mashrabiyya*-screened windows, often beautifully crafted, are now dying out as new, high-rise Western-style apartment complexes take over. There are many aspects of Muslims' houses that have deep religious significance, such as their social separations, their use as prayer space, and their inviolability from the outside and the necessity of preserving and protecting family honor.[3]

## PUBLIC BEHAVIOR

In the street of a traditional Muslim town or city, and this is as true today as in the past, the male sex dominates. The few females that are seen are usually veiled and go about their business in the market or wherever without making any social contact with anyone else. As one writer has put it, the women are socially "invisible," although they physically must make their way from place to place in the town.[4] The sense of personal space and privacy in public places is quite different in Islamic cities than in the West. In traditional settlements, for example, there was a place, usually an open field, where people could relieve themselves in a ditch or on the ground. Both women and men simply squat, the former perhaps being completely concealed as to their identity.

### *Affection in Public*

All Muslims consider it to be extremely bad form for a couple to demonstrate affection for each other in public, and in some societies husband and wife walk together—if they ever do—at some distance apart from each other. On the other hand, members of the same sex may be quite affectionate in public. Years before, when I visited Egypt for the first time, I heard from a returning international businessman that all the men of Cairo were gay, evidently because they strolled up and down the city's streets arm in arm and hand in hand. I was skeptical but wondered what such behavior meant. When I finally settled in Cairo for an extended period of study, I learned that several men could be seen at any particular time in the always-crowded streets walking close together and often arm in arm. I was fortunate to have Egyptian friends and to live in a somewhat traditional quarter of Cairo, and so I soon learned that friends like to be physically close to each other, that it is a sign of trust and mutual regard, and that in such a teeming metropolis it is practically impossible to walk the streets with someone and carry on a conversation without being physically attached: the passers-by would drive you farther and farther apart unless you kept pushing people aside. Two people walking arm in arm are considered one person, and others make way!

American men, particularly of northern European extraction, are typically uneasy about close physical contact or even proximity with other males. It is a cultural difference and may or may not have to do with uneasiness or uncertainty about sexual orientation. As every social scientist knows who has had the job of acclimatizing people to life in the Middle East, for business or government occupations, it is necessary to break through stereotypes and fears of different cultural and social patterns. A typical illustration is of an Arab and an American who meet to discuss a possible business deal. The Arab moves closer to his colleague, and the colleague pulls away, perhaps with exquisite delicacy. The Arab thinks, "He doesn't like me, what have I done wrong?" and the American imagines that the Arab is becoming overly friendly and maybe a little strange. Both are usually mistaken. Or an American, in his office, tilts back in his chair and puts his feet up on the desk, a seemingly innocent and idiomatic posture that is, however, deeply insulting and repulsive to a Middle Easterner and to many peoples from all over the Islamic world, because it points the bottoms of the feet (which have been in contact with dirt) at the guest. It is common for men to embrace each other in Islamic countries, especially the Middle East, and to kiss each other on the cheek, first one and then the other. This is not a pattern, however, in Southeast or most of South Asia, though perhaps the reason that it is common among Pakistanis is the strong Arab influence there.

Parade float in Indonesia's 1985 national Contest of Reciting the Qur'an (*Musabaqa Tilawatil Qur'an* in Pontiak, West Kalimantan, on the island of Borneo). (*Source:* Frederick Mathewson Denny)

### *The Cafés*

In many parts of the Islamic world, but especially in the Middle East and North Africa, men spend a good deal of time outside the house and in the café. Each neighborhood has cafés for socializing, playing games like backgammon, checkers, chess, and cards. This is a pattern of Mediterranean life, and the café is common too in the Christian countries on the northern shores. In a large city like Cairo, one has only to walk a short distance away from the modern, main thoroughfares to enter an area where people, often from the same country district, have settled over a period of generations or even centuries. Late into the evening the little openfront cafés will do a steady business, serving Turkish coffee in small cups, strong but very sweet tea in glass tumblers, and water pipes (*nārjīla, sheesha*). When prayer time arrives, some of the men will go to a mosque, and there is always one nearby. Afterward, the worshipers will probably return to the café to see what is going on and who is around. This routine is repeated day after day, year in and year out. People keep in close touch, and everyone knows just about everything there is to be known about everyone else.

### *Public Violence*

The neighborhood street and the café actually provide a considerable amount of stability in a given neighborhood: rarely is there violence in an area where the people have lived for a long time, know one another and are concerned about personal, family, and, indeed, community honor and propriety. In Cairo there is an old joke that two men will never get into a punching match unless there is close at hand a crowd large enough to pull them apart, and soon. This behavior does not, by the way, indicate cowardice; rather, Egyptians, at least those from Lower Egypt, are extremely reluctant to engage in physical violence unless it is for a very good reason, like a national emergency or a threat to family honor. Upper Egypt is another matter, but even there when tempers flare, the men are as often hovering at the brink of hilarity as on the verge of killing.

The expression of hostility and violence varies greatly across the Muslim world, mostly according to the cultural and social values in the regions. Egyptians are quite nonviolent as a rule, whereas Yemenis continue to express some of the old Arabian fighting spirit. The fearsome curved daggers that Yemeni men wear in their belts are not just for fashion's sake, and the rivalries and territorial protectiveness of the hinterland tribes generate many little feuds and even minor wars. Often the violence in a still somewhat medieval region like Yemen is caused by the mountain tribes' traditional distrust of centralized government. Similar patterns are found from the mountains of Morocco in the west, through Afghanistan in Central Asia, all the way down to Sumatra, especially Aceh and the Batak regions, but also on Madura.

Public behavior among Muslims continues to be strongly influenced by the Sunna of Muhammad, especially with regard to the details of etiquette and proper demeanor. When Muslims come together, and barring any particular hostilities related to current strife or international disputes, they know what is expected of them with respect to proper behavior, and they try to live up to it. That is why it was such a shock to the world some years ago when the Grand Mosque in Mecca was seized by terrorist dissidents: it went against all that the Muslims hold sacred, both with regard to space—it is the central sanctuary—and to proper behavior.

## RECREATION

Although in traditional Islamic towns and cities the pattern of daily life is closely connected with the quarter and the neighborhood within the quarter, Muslims do not limit their interests exclusively to the café and the home front. The festivals of the Muslim year provide entertainment and diversion, as do such domestic events as weddings, circumcisions, and the entertaining of guests. In addition, there have always been other forms of recreation, like organized sporting events, hunting, and the martial arts. Falconry is one of the oldest and noblest of hunting sports among the Arabs, and it is still practiced. Hunting gazelles and dangerous predators were favorite medieval outdoor pursuits, and there are many miniature paintings and poems and stories describing them.[5]

### *Sports and Games*

The Prophet is reported to have enjoyed footraces, and his companions competed in them. Another approved sport is wrestling, which Muhammad also is said to have enjoyed. Archery was approved by the Prophet, but not using living targets, like chickens, as the pre-Islamic Arabs were known to do. But Muhammad forbade fighting contests between animals—like cockfights and bullfights—because of the unnecessary suffering caused. Muhammad even allowed his Abyssinian soldiers to play with their deadly spears right in the mosque in Medina. The famous story about 'A'isha's watching the men at their games of spear throwing is testimony to the Prophet's relaxed and approving attitude toward nondestructive sports and amusements. Horseback riding is approved as entertainment as well as necessity, and racing is also acceptable, including the awarding of prizes and even betting under certain conditions (that the bettor is not a competitor and that there be no "winner-take-all" provision).[6]

Gambling in any form is forbidden and is considered to be at the level of drinking alcohol, worshiping idols, and divining with arrows, the other three great sins forbidden in a single Qur'an passage (5:90). Even backgammon is regarded by many legists as *ḥarām,* because it uses dice, although others consider it to be *makrūh,* "detested," if no betting is done. Chess also has had its supporters and detractors, but it is nowadays considered permissible as long as no betting accompanies it, it does not interfere with prayers, and the players do not use foul language when playing it.[7] The skill required by the game is highly approved, and this is what sets it apart from games of chance, like backgammon. Modern athletic contests, like soccer, tennis, basketball, and such sports as one sees in Olympic competition are acceptable, and Muslim nations regularly field teams in them. Swimming is approved, but the exposure of the body must be according to the rules for *'awra,* at least among strictly observant Muslims.

### *Movies*

Movies are acceptable, provided they do not depict immoral themes or acts or deflect people from religious duties and responsible living. Many Western films and television programs, especially American, are deeply offensive to pious Muslims, because they show people engaged in immoral behavior, whether in social situations with mixing and touching between the sexes or actual sexual activity (as in X-rated movies) or in glorifying criminal or immoral behavior, violence, materialism, and cruel humor. But movies are enormously popular throughout the Islamic world and in many villages and remote places offer one of the few chances to expand the people's horizons and relieve the dulling routine and inescapable poverty. One type of movie, usually made in India, has a romantic plot, but usually no kissing or even touching. Films depicting the martial arts are popular, especially with men, and so many films seem to concentrate on violence, sometimes extreme. Posters advertising such films can be seen on theater marquees and billboards from North Africa to Java: The masses are strongly attracted to them, though usually the pious deplore them.

It is true that an enormous amount of visual trash is produced in the West and in Japan. But the worldwide market for it requires a balanced view as to who is moral and who is not. Islamic nations attempt to produce television shows and movies that are in keeping with their religious values. In such places as Egypt, Pakistan, and Indonesia, one can view dramas, educational presentations, news programs, children's features, and the like during broadcasting hours, which are usually restricted to a few per day because of the enormous expense of programming and the limited resources available in most countries, including some European nations. This is one of the reasons that American programs are so ubiquitous around the world; the producers have something to market, and national media organizations find themselves compelled to purchase packages of shows as well as certain productions that at least make it possible to plan television schedules. Slick situation comedies and melodramas are undeniably appealing to many people. But in Islamic nations they are often countered by generous amounts of Qur'an recitation and the coverage of religious news. In Saudi Arabia, where there are no movie theaters, people buy video cassettes and show them at home in the family circle. And in North America, where the Muslim population is growing rapidly, Islamic television and radio fare is reaching out to Muslim markets, especially in urban locales. Global satellite TV is very influential, as is the Internet.

### *Nightlife*

Nightclubs and social dances and balls are condemned by the pious if they involve the serving of alcoholic beverages, the improper mixing of the sexes (beyond *maḥram* relationships), and indecent types of entertainment. During Egypt's food riots in January 1977, bands of strictly observant and indignant Muslims swept into many casinos and nightspots in Cairo and vandalized them in the name of religion. This reaction was not only against sinful luxuries, it was also a blow at the materialistic, wealthy minority who were prospering in Egypt while the masses were descending ever deeper into poverty. Egypt has been sharply criticized by more conservative Muslim countries because it allows such decadent Western institutions as nightclubs and casinos to operate, complete with the selling of alcoholic beverages. The Egyptian authorities are also increasingly aware of and responsive to severe disapproval among the country's Muslim citizens of activities and institutions which they consider to be Western, immoral, and unislamic. In Pakistan, for example, there are restaurants and social clubs and even discotheques, but they are very sedate, family-oriented establishments, with absolutely no liquor, beer, or wine sold. This strictness is because of the efforts at "islamization" that have been taking place in Pakistan in recent years. In Indonesia there is much more flexibility. Although liberal Jakarta has many Western-style entertainment opportunities, Java as a whole is a peasant, or at least a village-based, island society, in which the loss of poise and the excessive show of emotion—as might be produced by overindulgence in drinking—are considered to be extremely bad form and to be avoided at all costs.

### *Smoking*

One type of recreation, if it can be called that, is smoking tobacco, usually in cigarette form. Smoking is very common in Muslim nations, particularly in the Arab world and Southeast Asia. As in the West, there are warnings to people of the dangers of smoking, but also, as in the West, many people seem to be oblivious to them. There is not much in the way of enforced prohibitions of smoking in public places and conveyances, possibly because of the extreme reluctance of people to interfere with others who are indulging in a practice that is not condemned by religion. There is a special atmosphere associated with smoking in the Indonesian environment because of the clove-scented cigarettes that most of the inhabitants prefer. The visitor is very conscious of this aroma from one end of the archipelago to the other, and it seems to fit very well the exotic, mysterious, and sensual ambience of that beautiful equatorial nation, where in addition to Western movies and television programs, traditional artistic forms, like shadow plays and gamelan music, are still popular. The shadow plays, performed by masters of puppetry behind illuminated sheets, depict the Hindu characters of the great epics, like the *Mahabharata.* The Indonesians love these plays for their convincing dramatization of the mysterious interweaving of the forces of good and evil in human life.

## OFFICIAL ISLAM

Throughout Islamic history there have been attempts to define and enforce true Islam. As we saw in our earlier discussions of the Ḥadīth, jurisprudence, *kalām* theology, and Sufism, Muslim thinkers and leaders have often been at pains to clarify sources and issues in the interest of authentic religion, which came generally to mean those based on the Qur'anic revelation and the Sunna of the Prophet Muhammad. But the mastery of the interpretation and even the correct transcription of the Qur'an as well as the discernment of sound as opposed to weak or unacceptable *ḥadīths* were themselves protracted projects that required crucial decisions at every step along the way. Orthodox Islam, then, was an achievement and not a given. It demanded the best intellectual, moral, and leadership efforts of the Muslims who came to realize that, like the Church, the umma must continuously reform and purify itself. This sense of urgency is very much alive today in Islamic circles, just as it was in other great periods of Muslim history, such as during the Abbasid revolution, the Mu'tazilite "inquisition" *(miḥna)* that descended upon staunch conservatives like Ahmad ibn anbal, the vehement denunciations of saint veneration and idolatry of Ibn Taimīya, and the Wahhābi reforms in Arabia of the eighteenth century, which were influenced by the writings of that great Damascus jurist who lived four centuries earlier.

Robert Redfield, an American anthropologist who wrote influential theoretical works around the middle of the last century, distinguished between "great" and "little" traditions in his study of peasant life. The world's major religions represent great traditions, with their transcending doctrinal, symbolic, ethical, and value systems and institutions; and local or regional attitudes, values, and practices—whether religious or secular—comprise the little tradition in a given place. Part of the appeal and success of the world religions is their ability to transcend cultural and geographical and ethnic boundaries, to respect and to preserve regional beliefs and practices—at least those that are not contrary to the principles of the major religion—and in the process to adapt them to their own vision. Sometimes this happens quickly and decisively, as in the early Muslim conquests in Palestine and Iraq, whereas at other times it is a gradual process, involving compromise and adjustment, as in parts of sub-Saharan Africa and in Southeast Asia, where ancient traditions still exert enormous influence. In Arabia, the little tradition of pilgrimage, veneration of local sacred centers, and the Abrahamic legends of Arabian origins were successfully integrated into the new synthesis brought about by the Qur'an and Muhammad. In a sense, Islam coopted what it valued as the best in the old system and then gave it the sanction of revelation. The result was a new tradition that gradually became a "great tradition" as Islam developed into a world religion.

Generally, for the majority, "true" Islam has been considered to be Sunnism, based on the Qur'an and *Ḥadīth,* the interpretations and teachings of the early jurists, and the four great law schools. Together these comprise the Sharī'a and its institutionalized expressions. There has been a certain flexibility in this model, notwithstanding the "closing" of the gate of *ijtihād* in the fourth Islamic century. That is, there never developed a set creed uniting Muslims, nor has there ever been any kind of ecclesiastical hierarchy, as in Christianity, whose task was to ensure that the community remain "One, Holy, Catholic, and Apostolic." There has been a high degree of uniformity across the umma in matters of worship. At the ritual level, the Shī'ī minority have also been included as full and equal participants, as it makes much more sense to view the two dimensions as an essentially unified tradition but offering a variety of emphasis and style. The variety is important, and it would be untrue to both the spirit and forms of authentic Islamic devotion to regard the majority's habits and beliefs as "orthodox" and the minority's convictions and practices as "heterodox," for at the center both are one. Beyond the Sunnī–Shī'ī distinction are additional specific and local customs and observances that contribute to the richness and, at points, the confusion of what can be called Islam only at the anthropological level. Here we are talking not about definitions and ideals but about actual behavior and symbolic processes.[8]

## POPULAR ISLAM

In Chapter 11 there is a brief description of the popular cult of the Sufi *ṭarīqa* of Sīdī Ahmad al-Badawī in Tanta, Egypt. Although the order's teachings are well within the boundaries of Islam, at least as it was accepted widely after the time of al-Ghazālī and sober Sufism, some of the practices connected with the Badawīya are of the folk variety and belong to a very old little tradition that goes back well before Islam's arrival in Egypt. The fertility cult elements especially seem to indicate roots of an older cult or pattern of beliefs and practices. But the order combines both the great tradition of classical Islam and the local, little tradition that, in fact, spread its influence throughout Egypt and even beyond. A similar pattern can be seen across the Islamic world: the great tradition, often represented by classical Sufism, with its *silsilas* extending back all the way to the Prophet, and local traditions that reveal the different ways of being religious. Sufism, because of its tolerance, is generally the vehicle by which the little and great traditions come together in a harmonious balance, expressing regional ideas and practices while imposing on them some roughly orthodox Islamic standard.

## THE VENERATION OF SAINTS

The major structure of ritual behavior that is at the same time nearly universal in the Islamic world and frequently questioned if not condemned is the veneration of saints. It is often, although not always, connected with popular Sufism. The Qur'anic term *walī (awliyā')* is most often translated as "saint," but it does not mean quite that in Arabic. Rather, it means "friend," "benefactor," "patron," "helper," "one who is near," and so forth, depending on the context. The classic passage is found in Sūra 10:62: "Surely God's friends *(awliyā')*—no fear shall be on them, neither shall they sorrow." God is also a *walī,* in the sense of a protector: "God suffices as a protector, God suffices as a helper" (Sūra 4:45). Thus according to the Qur'an, God and humans are in a relation of *walī* to one another. The Qur'an also forbids the taking of a *walī* other than God (for example, 42:31), a practice that is a form of *shirk.* The community of *walīs* is clearly set forth in Sūra 5:55: "Whoso makes God his friend, and His Messenger, and the believers—the party of God, they are the victors." According to the Qur'an, anyone who is a believing servant of God is his *walī,* and

God is *walī* to that person, too. All sincere Muslims, then, comprise the *awliyā'*, the community of "saints."

But as time passed, the term came to be more and more often applied to special humans who, often after their death, were considered to possess *baraka* and the ability to intercede with God on behalf of the living. Special tomb structures were erected over their burial places, which in some cases were highly elaborate and sumptuously appointed. The mosque–tomb complex of Sīdī Ahmad al-Badawī is an example. But most saint shrines are relatively humble affairs. In Egypt, for example, they are square buildings with a dome over the burial place. These **qubbas,** as they are known (from "dome"), can be seen in virtually every corner of inhabited Egypt, and they are still being erected because saints are still being produced. Villagers love to visit the tombs of their favorite saints, seeking blessings, boons, and just soaking up the power of such places. Indeed, any place without a *qubba* dedicated to a *walī* is thought to be poor. Sometimes a person has a dream that a departed spirit comes to him demanding that a proper tomb be built to house his earthly remains. This is always a disturbing experience, especially when the dream visitation is accompanied with threats that if a tomb is not erected, then dire consequences will follow.

### *Regional Differences in Veneration*

The veneration of saints in Islam takes on different forms wherever it occurs, but the basic pattern is the same. In Morocco, it is a highly developed phenomenon that has great political importance, because of the lineages of important persons in the Prophet's line (known as *sharīfs*), who continue to exert influence generation after generation. In Pakistan it is powerful everywhere, as in India. In Indonesia it is also widespread and sometimes possesses a peculiar quality because of the mixture of religious and cultural elements in which both the indigenous Javanese past, for example, and the Hindu–Buddhist past persist in symbolic and ritual forms.

***The Saint of Giri.*** In northeast Java, there is a famous shrine at the burial place of Raden Paku, a semilegendary figure who is credited with establishing Islam near the seaport of Gresik in the fifteenth century. "Prince Paku" is recognized as one of the *wali songo* ("honored saints"), the nine apostles of Islam who brought the true religion to Java.[9] Raden Paku attracted thousands of persons to Islam and also became famous as a great warrior who fought and prevailed against a punitive expedition of the great Hindu Majapahit kingdom, which was soon to pass from the scene because of vigorous Muslim advances. The fateful battle occurred at the hill in Giri where Raden Paku had built a mosque and where he taught Islam to the many who were attracted by his charisma. It is said that the attacking Majapahit forces were miraculously defeated by Raden Paku's pen, which had turned into a *keris,* the curved blade that is an accessory and symbol of male honor and courage in Java. Although Raden Paku is the given name of the warrior saint, he is nevertheless remembered and venerated as Sunan Giri, which roughly translated is "the saint of Giri."

A typical *qubba,* erected over the grave of a *walī* in Egypt. This one is in the Delta, a few miles from Tanta. Egyptians consider a settlement or quarter without a saint's shrine to be poor indeed, because of the absence of spiritual benefits that are so essential in everyday life. Both Muslims and Christians venerate saints and even visit each other's shrines and festivals in Egypt.
(*Source:* Frederick Mathewson Denny)

To this day, multitudes of pilgrims visit Sunan Giri's tomb and mosque complex in Gresik, and there is an elaborate, crowded annual *mawlid* celebration. It is situated atop a conical hill, oddly enough some distance from the original Giri hill, which seems to have become forgotten over the centuries but whose archaeological deposits have recently been unearthed and include the ablution cisterns as well as the *miḥrāb* ("prayer niche") of the original mosque. The traditional site is dominated by an imposing mosque with a three-tiered roof, reminiscent of Buddhist architecture in the archipelago. There are also several peripheral buildings, plus a large cemetery with numerous smaller mausoleums and many gravestones. Many notable Muslims are buried on the premises, all of the graves being on the west side of the mosque so as to be situated between Mecca and the worshiping congregation. This by no means implies worship of the departed saints; it simply symbolizes their priority of position as they repose in proper Islamic fashion facing the *qibla.* Sunan Giri's tomb is the most resplendent of all and occupies a lovely, low, tile-roofed building. Some of the symbols used to decorate the site are Hindu, significantly, and testify to the continuing power of that great tradition which over the centuries of islamization since Sunan Giri's time became part of East Java's little tradition.

The entrance to the actual inner tomb chamber is guarded by *nāgas,* sculptured images of the Hindu serpent deity that traditionally guards temples and tombs. The main entrance to the hilltop cemetery is likewise guarded by two enormous stone *nāgas,* one on each side of the stairway. The actual cubical burial chamber of Sunan Giri is made of precious wood, carved in a graceful and ornate lotus motif, another Hindu religious symbol.

The syncretism of symbolic elements in no way indicates continuing Hindu convictions, except that in Java everything conspires to provide meaning in a mysterious and mystical manner. The actual mosque, in which no one is buried, reflects a Buddhist architectural tradition, although it is nevertheless every centimeter a Muslim house of worship, but in a Javanese style. The ceiling is decorated with exquisite Arabic calligraphy. The *qibla* wall has two *miḥrābs,* one marking the direction of prayer and the other containing the *minbār,* which, if it is functionally identical with the raised pulpits of the Middle East, at the same time resembles a chariot or a sedan chair such as might have symbolized the throne of a Hindu divinity in the pre-Islamic Javanese past.

***Sīdī Abū al-Haggāg.*** In Upper Egypt, there is another active saint complex in the famous tourist town of Luxor, which can be traced back to the thirteenth century. It is located on the remains of the great Muslim saint Yusuf Abū al-Haggāg (Ḥajjāj), whose elaborate mosque–tomb complex rises from the ruins of the great Temple of Amon in Luxor, which itself dates back to the Empire period of pharaonic times, about the fourteenth century B.C.E. Just as in the case of the Badawī *mawlid* in Tanta, there is an elaborate *zaffa,* or parade, through the town, ending at the mosque–tomb. An interesting feature is the boats carried along in the processional, one of which is a large replica of a nineteenth-century Nile steamboat. The presence of boats is traced to a miracle of the saint, who reportedly saved the ship on which he and his companions were sailing home from the hajj in Mecca.[10] Because of the legend, there have always been boats connected with the cult. During the *mawlid,* the boats are carried by representatives of the various Sufi orders (*ṭuruq*) and are filled with children whose parents claim descent from Sīdī Abū al-Haggāg himself. This identification is a variation on the *silsila,* which traces spiritual descent from a line of shaykhs. Of course, the *silsila* is also present at the *mawlid* in connection with each of the orders.

There may be a very ancient source of the boat motif, because in pharaonic times the pharaoh was transported on a royal barge, along with the gods Mut and Khons, each in his own vessel.[11] Ancient royal funerals featured the sailing of the deceased's boat across the Nile from the east bank to the west, for burial in the necropolis of Thebes and eternal life in the Land of the Westerners, which was what the abode of the dead was called, in connection with the setting sun. The Abū al-Haggāg festival boats do not actually sail on the Nile, however.

Some years ago I was in Luxor serving as lecture-guide for a group of American tourists. As soon as I had some free time, toward the end of a long day sight-seeing among the pharaonic tombs, I paid a visit to the pale yellow stucco buildings belonging to the saint complex within the walls of the Temple of Amon.

Drums for calling the faithful to prayers. Mosque of Sunan Ampel, Surabaya, East Java. These great drums are beaten when the call to worship is intoned, but their loud summons does not replace the traditional *adhān*. Drums have traditionally been used to call assemblies together in Southeast Asia and were easily adapted to Islamic practice in the region. (*Source:* Frederick Mathewson Denny)

The substantial *qubba*-dome and minarets rise just above the crumbling pillars and pylons. At night, the word *Allah* can be seen in green neon lights high up on the structure. When I reached the top of the stairway from the village side and was about to enter the door of the tomb, I was greeted by a caretaker who smilingly suggested that I had lost my way and must be looking for the pharaonic temple, as are the majority of visitors to Luxor from the West. I said "No, I have come to visit Sīdī Abū al-Haggāg," whereupon the kind old gentleman threw open the door and guided me by the arm to the various points of interest inside, introducing me at the same time to several other people connected with the establishment. We stopped at several burial places (a number of saints repose there) and said some prayers and then sat on the carpeted floor for a while, enjoying tea and quiet conversation.

Although it is highly unusual for a non-Muslim foreigner to visit this tomb, in fact Sīdī Abū al-Haggāg is known in his native land as one of the most powerful and wonderful of all saints, especially in Upper Egypt. Anyone who visits Luxor and does not pay respect to Sīdī Abū al-Haggāg at his tomb has missed the chance of being in touch with a vibrant spiritual tradition that, unlike pharaonic religion, continues to provide guidance and blessing for countless Egyptian peasants, who look to Luxor as a sort of regional *axis mundi* and make their little *"hajjes"* there on the saint's birthday party *mawlid* each year.

The folk Islam of Abū al-Haggāg's cult is linked to numberless other saint complexes across Egypt, the Near East, and the entire Islamic world by the great tradition of the Qur'an, the Sunna, and the pillars of worship, alms, fasting, and pilgrimage; for whatever else goes on of a strictly local or regional nature—whether it be boats in the Luxor *zaffa* or fertility charms in Tanta—the devotees of the saints are also devout Muslims. The local cults enable people, particularly those with little education and livelihood and little or no chance of travel or change in their condition, to have a meaningful and active religious life. Islam is not a religion of books and rules, but a total way of life. Its ability to adapt and be adapted is at the core of Islam's success as a world religion, as we observed earlier. The great tradition—Islam—"stoops to conquer" in the world of saint veneration, elevating what otherwise might remain merely local superstitions and cults to a general level of religious life that shares its ideals with Muslims everywhere.

***The Absence of Saint Veneration in Saudi Arabia.*** Significantly, only Saudi Arabia prohibits saint veneration and considers it to be idolatry (*shirk*) and heretical innovation *(bid'a),* sanctioned by neither the Qur'an nor the Prophet. The greatest Islamic "saint" is, of course, Muhammad, but no one is allowed to behave in an emotionally demonstrative or obviously adoring manner within the precincts of his tomb in Medina or at the many sites there and in Mecca, as well as other places where the heroes and heroines of early Islam are buried. In the eighteenth century, during the violent Wahhābi campaign against saint cults, many mausoleums, mosque–tomb complexes, and burial markers were pulled down and obliterated in the name of a reforming, puritan Islam that traced its roots through the Hanbali jurist Ibn Taimīya (d. 1328) to the primitive period of Islam's formation on the foundations of the Qur'an, the Sunna, and the opinions and consensus of the salaf, the pious "ancestors" of the first generations. Today, because of the continuing influence of Wahhābism as the official theology and religious ethic of Saudi Arabia, even kings receive nothing more than a simple inscription marking their burial places, which otherwise have no conspicuous features. The austere fundamentalist movement founded by Muhammad Ibn 'Abd al-Wahhāb (1703–1792) is only one of a number of strict reform movements that have occurred in Islamic history. There are many Muslims today who agree with the principles of that movement and regard it as pure Islam. Many others, though perhaps preferring not to respect a school of fundamentalism that serves to bolster a royal dynasty—as Wahhābism does and always has in Saudi Arabia—nevertheless agree with its austere standard of limiting the human activities that can be considered as true Islam. This means that folk dimensions, like saint cults and many other things, must be scrutinized and most probably excised as idolatry and superstition.

Shrine of Shaykh Yusuf Abū al-Haggāg in the midst of the ruins of the Temple of Luxor, Upper Egypt. This *walī* is perhaps second only to Sayyid Ahmad al-Badawī in all Egypt. (*Source:* Frederick Mathewson Denny)

## DISTINCTIVE SHĪʿĪ RITUAL PRACTICES

Despite the differing opinions regarding the acceptability of saint veneration and visits to saints' tombs among Sunnī Muslims, the reverence paid to the imāms and other heroes and heroines of the faith is very much a central part of Shīʿī Islam. In Chapter 4 we introduced the Shīʿī movement as an early political faction based on the claim that the Prophet had designated his cousin and son-in-law ʿAlī to be his successor as leader of the umma. ʿAlid loyalism has taken various forms, but it has always been conscious of tragedy and has cultivated the hopeful expectation that at the close of history God will vindicate his faithful followers who have remained true to Islam as it was defined by the succession of imāms. As we saw in Chapter 9, even the Shīʿīs split up into further divisions over the precise number and identity of the imāms.

### *Shīʿī Commemorations*

***Visits (ziyāra; pl., ziyārāt)*** to the tombs of Shīʿī saints are integral to that form of Islam and should not be regarded as mere "folk Islam," local superstition, or "little tradition." Although the Shīʿīs certainly share to the fullest extent in the observances known as the "pillars of Islam," along with their fellow Muslims of the Sunnī tradition, they also observe additional rites. The tenth day of the Muslim month of Muḥarram, known as ʿAshūra, is sacred to all Muslims because of its association with a voluntary fast that Muhammad adopted from Judaism after he settled in Medina. After the break with the Jews, Ramadān became the obligatory fast for the Muslims, but 'Ashūra has remained to this day a voluntary observance, especially among the Sunnīs. But the Tenth of Muḥarram was also the day on which Husayn was killed in the great battle at Karbala. Thus, on the ninth of the month Shi'ites fast, and on the next day they commemorate the death of their redemptive hero Husayn. It is thought that God works through Husayn for the salvation of all the truly faithful. So holy became the city of Karbala that people wanted to die there in proximity to their savior or to have their remains transported there. Over time, Karbala became a vast Shī'ī necropolis. On the Tenth of Muḥarram Shī'īs make their *ziyārāts* to the city and the grave of Husayn. But the city is also a major goal of Shi'ite pilgrimage at other times, such as on the birthday of the twelfth imām. Other major pilgrimage sites are at Kufa, where 'Alī was struck down by an assassin; Najaf, in Iraq, where 'Alī's tomb is (and which is often visited by Shī'īs just before their hajj to Mecca); Qum, Iran, the burial place of Fātima al-Ma'sūma, who was the wife of Imām 'Alī Ridā', the eighth in the line of successors to 'Alī; and Mashhad, Iran, where the remains of the eighth imām repose (alongside those of the Abbasid caliph Hārūn al-Rashīd, who also died there). Another site, equally revered by the Shī'īs and the Sunnīs, is the mosque of Sayyidnā ("Our Master") Husayn in Cairo. It is believed that in the twelfth century the head of Husayn was transported to Egypt by the Shī'ī Fātimid rulers and buried in a special mosque, which has since disappeared. A very imposing Turkish-style building now shelters the relic and also serves as a major Friday worship place for that part of Cairo.

### *Ta'ziya*

A distinctive form of religious drama grew up around the Karbala tragedy. It is known as **ta'ziya,** which in Arabic means "consolation." This "passion play," as it is often characterized in English, is performed in a variety of forms and with different scripts in many towns and cities of Iran, Iraq, and the Indian subcontinent where Shī'īs are prominent. The first third of the month of Musarram is the *ta'ziya* "season," with the tenth being the most favored, for obvious reasons. *Ta'ziya* is the only form of theater that ever developed as an indigenous Islamic art or ritual form.[12] But it is not like Western theater, except perhaps for the antecedents of it in medieval mystery and morality plays, which also were more than entertainment because of their didactic and religious dimensions. The *ta'ziya* tells not only the central story of Husayn's martyrdom but also of the other principal characters and their roles in the larger struggle of the Shī'īs against the Umayyads. There is no sharp distinction between the performers and the audience, because of the emotions shared by all and the identity with those heroes of long ago, whose virtues and saving influence are reborn and passed on at each reenactment of the sacred events. That is, this is a participatory dramatic ritual that pulls everyone in at one or another level. The audiences weep when it is appropriate, and then they laugh or exult when things are going well, even though they know the tragic ending. Processionals accompany the performance, with young men, the prototypes of Shīʿī martyrdom in all ages, flagellating themselves with chains and smearing their faces and bodies with blood. This aspect of Muḥarram became widely publicized during the Iranian revolution in 1979 and during the long American hostage crisis.

In the beginning, *ta'ziyas* were performed on street corners or in mosques until in recent centuries special buildings were designed and built for them. They often resemble "theaters in the round," thus enhancing the sense of audience participation and identification. Husayn and his supporters typically wear green, the color associated with Muhammad, and the hated Umayyad forces wear red. The two colors distinguish the values of the two opposing forces in the minds of the viewers.

During the referendum for the new Islamic constitution in Iran after the Islamic revolution of 1979, the ballots were colored green and red, the green being "in favor" and the red "opposed." The symbolism continues as strong as ever in the present day. It should not be imagined, however, that green and red are invariably opposed as implacable symbols of truth against falsehood, for red is also the color associated with Husayn's tomb at Karbala, and his brother Hasan is associated with green because of his treaty with Muʿāwiya. Green stands for peace in this case, and red stands for struggle.[13]

In addition to actual dramatic performances of *ta'ziya,* there are also storytellers who travel around the countryside with cartoonlike pictorial representations that they unfold while telling the story to people in the streets.[14] The telling is done in a singing style, as indeed poetry has been recited traditionally in the Islamic world,

*Ta'ziya* in cartoon form, painted on canvas. Traveling storytellers go from village to village in Iran singing the tragic story of Husayn's martyrdom, unrolling the canvas scroll as they proceed. (*Source:* Peter Chelkowski)

both in Persian and Arabic. There are also public paintings, sometimes in tilework, representing the martyrdom of Husayn. The general Islamic prohibition of images in religious contexts does not apply to Shi'ism, which delights in remembering its heroes by means of figural representational art. Besides dramatic and pictorial representations of Karbala, during the months of ritual mourning—Muḥarram and afar—in Shī'ī locales can be seen black-draped bazaars and buildings. On the ninth and tenth of Muḥarram, in addition to *ta'ziya* performances and processionals of flagellants, young men's societies march carrying portable shrines, called *ṭabaqs*, containing pictures of 'Alī or other imāms. They may also contain photos of recently deceased persons, who are then incorporated into the general mourning rites. A *ṭabaq* may be constructed and carried in the name of any fellow Shī'ī who has died during the preceding year, but young men are most often memorialized in this manner. Also, Shī'ī graves often commemorate a young man who is buried there, with a headstone on which is carved the figure of a horse and rider, symbolizing chivalry and manly strength. There also are memories of Husayn in this case, because of the association in people's minds of his battle horse (named Duldul) with its holy owner.

By visiting these holy places, the Shī'īs retain their sense of being a special community of Muslims. As this chapter has demonstrated, Muslims of all types seem to need religious practices that are more emotional and spontaneous than the pillars, although they still consider them to be basic. The practices we discussed here include a strong sense of regularity and propriety, and each has its separate lore, thus enhancing the Shī'ī's sense of spiritual heritage. There is no problem with the emotional Shī'ī pilgrimage and *ta'ziya* in their being heretical, innovative, or superstitious. Sunnīs sometimes labor under the criticisms and reproaches of the stricter "*ulamā*" when they venerate their saints and seek intercession. But not so the Shī'īs, who remain confident that their special practices are not only beautiful and spiritually fulfilling but also correct and proper, being rooted as they are in the great epic of their forebears.

## NOTES

1. See Gustave E. Von Grunebaum, *Islam: Essays in the Nature and Growth of a Cultural Tradition* (London: Routledge & Kegan Paul, 1961), chap. 7, "The Structure of the Muslim Town," p. 142ff. Cf. Xavier de Planhol, *The World of Islam* (Ithaca, N.Y.: Cornell University Press, 1959), p. 2ff.; and Ira Lapidus, ed., *Middle Eastern Cities* (Berkeley and Los Angeles: University of California Press, 1969), especially Oleg Grabar, "The Architecture of the Middle Eastern City from Past to Present: The Case of the Mosque," pp. 26–46.
2. See Lapidus's article, "Muslim Cities and Islamic Societies," in *Middle Eastern Cities,* pp. 47–74, for details on classes and their spatial positioning in cities and towns. Another excellent study of the market and its Islamic dimensions is *Meaning and Order in Moroccan Society,* ed. Clifford Geertz, Hildred Geertz, and Lawrence Rosen, (Cambridge, England: Cambridge University Press, 1979), especially C. Geertz's long section, "Suq: The Bazaar Economy in Sefrou."

3. See the pioneering study, based on extensive field research in Egypt, of Juan Eduardo Campo, *The Other Sides of Paradise: Explorations into the Religious Meanings of Domestic Space in Islam* (Columbia, S.C.: University of South Carolina Press, 1991).
4. Michael Gilsenan, *Recognizing Islam: An Anthropologist's Introduction* (London and Canberra: Croom and Helm, n.d. [ca. 1983]), pp. 171–173. This collection of essays and articles contains astute observations about everyday life in Muslim contexts.
5. Sharī'a regulations governing hunting are summarized in al-Qaradawi, *The Lawful and the Prohibited in Islam* (Indianapolis: American Trust Publications, n.d.; first published in Arabic in 1960), pp. 63–70.
6. *Ibid.,* p. 297.
7. *Ibid.,* pp. 298–299.
8. See Clifford Geertz, *Islam Observed: Religious Development in Morocco and Indonesia* (New Haven, Conn.: Yale University Press, 1968), for a sophisticated discussion of what "Islam" means in differing cultural contexts.
9. It is not easy to find materials on the Wali Songo in English. For brief summaries of the islamization of northeast Java, see H. J. De Graaf, "South-East Asian Islam to the Eighteenth Century," in *The Cambridge History of Islam,* vol. 2, ed. P. M. Holt, Ann K. S. Lambton, and Bernard Lewis (Cambridge, England: Cambridge University Press, 1970), pp. 130–135; and Thomas W. Arnold, *The Preaching of Islam: A History of the Propagation of the Muslim Faith* (Lahore, Pakistan: Sh. Muhammad Ashraf, 1961), pp. 380–391.
10. Joseph Williams McPherson, *The Moulids of Egypt* (Cairo: N.M. Press, 1941), p. 306.
11. *Ibid.,* p. 307.
12. See the excellent collection of articles on the *ta'ziya* in Peter Chelkowski, ed., *Ta'ziya: Ritual and Drama in Iran* (New York: New York University Press, 1979). See also the same author's article "Ta'ziya," in *The Encyclopaedia of Islam,* new ed., vol. X (Leiden: Brill, 1999), pp. 406–408.
13. I am grateful to Dr. Abdulaziz A. Sachedina, of the University of Virginia, for this information on the symbolism of red and green in Shī'ī contexts.
14. This paragraph is based on information generously provided by Dr. Ann Betteridge, of Tucson, Arizona, who has conducted anthropological field work on the subject in Iran.

PART SIX

# Islam in the Modern World

CHAPTER 14

# Major Movements and Trends in Renewal and Reform

**KEY TERMS**

| | | |
|---|---|---|
| ***Dār al-Islām*** | ***taqlīd*** | ***Santris*** |
| ***Dār al-Ḥarb*** | ***bid'a*** | ***Abangan*** |
| **Wahhābīs** | ***mahdī*** | ***Priyayi*** |
| **shirk** | ***falāḥ*** | ***pancasila*** |

## THREE PHASES OF ISLAMIC HISTORY

### *The First Phase*

It was long conventional in Western characterizations of Islamic history to divide it into three major phases. The first was from its origins to the Mongol conquests of the thirteenth century C.E. This was the "classic" period of a distinctive and brilliant Islamic civilization, extending from Spain and Morocco in the west to Southeast Asia and Sumatra in the east. During this period there was a clear superiority of sciences, armaments, literature, arts, crafts, and philosophy in the Islamic world that other civilizations were to benefit from as well as contribute to. The diverse Muslim peoples reached such a level of international and intercultural cooperation and community that being a Muslim in that civilization was like being a Roman citizen during the Roman Empire period. Trade routes, sea-lanes, and governmental institutions (like the post office) were remarkably secure and stable for Muslim travelers and merchants, and individuals could traverse the vast distances between Morocco and Egypt and Baghdad and Iran and Central Asia always to find waiting a predictable environment in which the stranger, as long as he was also a Muslim brother, had an honored and recognized niche. Even the law-abiding non-Muslim was guaranteed security and enjoyed hospitality. The uniformity of religious ritual and social etiquette, based on the Qur'an and prophetic Sunna and codified in the law schools, was as reassuring on the practical, everyday level as it must have seemed providential.

Muslims were well aware of the privilege of living in the ***Dār al-Islām,*** the Abode of Submission that was starkly contrasted with the ***Dār al-Ḥarb,*** the Abode of Warfare, outside the secure and religiously regulated Islamic umma where, regardless of what local government was in power, there was a conviction that human life should be based on "enjoining the right and forbidding the wrong," as the Qur'an commands (e.g., 22:41). These two entities, Dār al-Islām and Dār al-Ḥarb, are also ideas that can be analyzed according to the mythic model of cosmos versus chaos. The Islamic world is based on fundamentals, regardless of the struggles necessary to sustain a balanced order. The non-Islamic world, although it obviously enjoyed its own territories and seasons of prosperity and power, finally lacked the cosmic foundation that could give it lasting and definitive legitimacy and security. There was, then, a missionary urgency to spread the benefits of Islam through *da'wa,* "call," and *jihād,* "exertion," and the remarkable extent of islamization down to Mongol times is testimony to the fervor and industry of many generations to extend the Dār al-Islām.

### *The Second Phase*

Then came the Mongols, and a second era was ushered in, marked at the outset by widespread devastation and death in Central Asia, Iran, Mesopotamia, and points west. Although great Islamic nations continued to arise in the future, like the Sāfavids in Persia, the Mughals in India, and the Ottomans in the eastern Mediterranean and beyond, the characteristic genius of Islamic civilization no longer produced as much brilliant and original expression as had been known in classical times, especially in theology, literature, the arts, and science. Rather, there was thought to be a general degeneration in Islamic institutions and a corresponding diminution in the self-confidence and associated military and political power that the umma could muster and apply.

All the while, from the time of the Crusades to the period of European exploration and discovery, the West was steadily gaining in self-confidence, cohesion, and purpose. Spain expelled the last of the Moors in 1492, the fateful year that also witnessed the arrival of the Italian Christopher Columbus in the New World. The Protestant Reformation was about to begin, which in its successive developments in various nations, plus the vigorous countermeasures and innovations launched by the Roman Catholic church, spread Western ways and purposes into regions of previously unknown and unexploited resources. The development of southern trade routes by means of which the Europeans were able to reach distant Asian ports without traveling through Muslim lands and transport goods and people more cheaply and safely than before did much to accelerate the atrophying of Muslim trade dominance and control of routes that the umma had enjoyed in the eastern and southern Mediterranean and Spain, and farther east in Asia and Africa.

It was not so much that the Muslims declined rapidly during the Protestant Reformation and later as that the Islamic world remained relatively static while the West advanced dramatically in all areas of human endeavor.[1] The West also had expanded its sphere of influence to the Western Hemisphere, which was the preserve of the Christian nations, and to old civilizations and societies of Asia and the South Seas.

The Portuguese and Dutch came to dominate the Malaysian-Indonesian archipelago, and the British later ruled India, Burma, and other South Asian regions. This ushered in the long period of Western colonialism, which was a difficult challenge to Muslim honor as well as the Islamic way of life in a world ruled by infidels, who were so perversely successful in their enterprises. The domination by outsiders afflicted Hindus and Buddhists, too, and it also altered when it did not obliterate Native American as well as African societies and cultures.

It is hazardous to distinguish historical periods of Islam's career across such a great range of geographic and cultural frontiers, if by such periods is intended a consistent characterization of the umma's fortunes vis à vis other traditions. For example, toward the end of the fifteenth century, as we mentioned, the last of the Muslims were driven from the Iberian Peninsula under King Ferdinand and Queen Isabella, thus marking the end of a long era of Muslim presence in Spain, which in earlier centuries dominated there. But in the Middle East and India, Islamic empires were thriving, with power and prestige that were never reached in earlier times, even when the Abbasid Empire was at its peak. This period saw the steady increase of Islamic influence in the Malaysian-Indonesian archipelago, with Muslim communities appearing along the coasts of populous islands such as Sumatra and Java.

### *The Third Phase*

The third, or modern, era in the umma's history can be said to begin around 1800, but this date requires many qualifications. It marks the time when Napoleon and his forces were in Egypt (they actually entered in 1798) and opened it up to Western influences, development, and exploitation in a manner that was reflected and imitated in other southern and eastern Mediterranean as well as Asian Muslim lands throughout the nineteenth and up to the mid-twentieth century. There were modern Western influences in Egypt and other countries before 1800, but by that time such influences had gained sufficient momentum to change fundamentally the ways Muslim peoples viewed themselves and the world. And their world shrank more with each decade until in the present day there are continuous communications between even the most backward places and the rest of the globe. Even such traditional, medieval outposts as Yemen are rapidly being incorporated into modern life by means of the mass media, transportation, and economic development.

### *Influences on Islam*

It would be a mistake to attribute the changes in Islam during the past two or so centuries solely to Western influences and modernity. Before the time of Napoleon and without any external influences, significant reform movements were begun in the umma itself. In India there was a fundamental reform in the eighteenth century instigated by Shāh Walī Allāh of Delhi (1702–1762). In Arabia during the same period a powerful puritan movement arose under the leadership of Muhammad ibn ‘Abd al-Wahhāb (1703–1792). It is instructive to consider these two quite different developments, which Fazlur Rahman has called “premodernist reform movements”[2] because of their indigenous character and the fact that they arose as a result of forces and issues that were wholly within the Islamic scheme of history and self-interpretation. The Wahhābī reforms especially offer valuable insights into Islam’s tendency to purge and reform itself from time to time in obedience to the radical demands of *tawḥīd* and its earthly task of “enjoining the right and forbidding the wrong.”

***Sufism.*** Sufism had a fateful influence on the reforms of Shāh Walī Allāh, who incorporated it into his vision of a purified Islam that balanced the various elements of theology, law, society, economics, and politics into a just system in which abuses of the poor, on the one hand, and the deterioration of Muslim power, on the other, would be checked. By the eighteenth century, the old Mughal dominance in India had waned considerably, and Hindu rebellions and revival movements were exerting great influence in the subcontinent, where the Hindus were in the majority. Some Muslim leaders thought that a return to strict orthodoxy was desirable so as to stem Hindu assertiveness. But both Shāh Walī Allāh, and Shaykh Ahmad Sirhindī before him, wanted to maintain the spiritually invigorating and humane virtues of Sufism while excising its sometimes antinomian and relativistic tendencies, which were being increasingly blamed for weakening the Islamic community. This developed into a major modern critique of Sufism that is far from abating even today. Shāh Walī Allāh’s high-minded reform did have some effect on Muslim rulers of his time, who shared his desire to restore Islamic power in India. But it was too late to turn back to the great Mughal times of the preceding centuries. Thus the Sufi part of Shāh Walī Allāh’s vision of a coherent Islamic synthesis was gradually replaced by a zealous brand of puritanism that resembled, even as it reflected, Wahhābīsm, to which we now turn.

## THE WAHHĀBĪS

In order to understand the peculiar force and point of the **Wahhābī** movement in Arabia, it is necessary to go back several centuries earlier to that Hanbali maverick, Ibn Taimīya (d. 1328), whom we met earlier in Chapter 9. Remember that Ibn Taimīya, although he was conservatively antirationalist and suspicious of Sufism—at least the freewheeling sorts—nevertheless considered himself to be a *mujtahid* and, indeed, insisted that the revelation and prophetic traditions be interpreted and applied anew in each generation. The Qur’an and *Ḥadīth* are perfect and immutable, but in a world of change and chance, the alert Muslim must be able to analyze the times and in the process bring them under the scrutiny and authority of the Sharī‘a.

Added to this flexible fundamentalism based on an "ecstasy of obedience," as we observed in Chapter 9, was a fanatical opposition to the cult of saints, which by his time had become a prominent feature of popular Islam in the Near East and beyond. At the heart of Ibn Taimīya's repudiation of saint veneration was a conviction about the divine unity (*tawḥīd*) that considered any suggestion of religious respect for a creature tantamount to **shirk,** "idolatry," the single unforgivable sin, according to the Qur'an (4:48). Ibn Taimīya, remember, did not insist on any particular form of government for Muslims; it was sufficient that whatever form of rule and order was instituted, it be a "Sharī'a politics" (*siyāsa shar'īya*).

If Ibn Taimīya thought his reliance on the Qur'an and especially the Sunna was fundamental, preserving him and all who followed those sources from innovation and error, it was also true that to rely on the Sunna was to base oneself on the early generations of Muslim scholars and jurists, who had made the Sunna a corpus of literature and source of law. The prophetic Sunna did not appear as an accomplished fact to the Muslims upon the death of the Prophet, as we observed in Chapter 7, on the *Ḥadīth* literature. It was a long time in the making in the form that came to be regarded as acceptable and authoritative. Ibn Taimīya led the struggle in his day against ***taqlīd,*** "blind imitation" of the consensus of earlier scholar-jurists, and he was himself also committed to a kind of *taqlīd,* for his acceptance of the Sunna was not as radical as he seemed to think, nor could his position accurately be characterized as a "back to the Qur'an" movement.[3] But his contribution to a fresh consideration of basic problems did have a positive effect on people who came after him, especially the Wahhābīs of Arabia.

### *Ibn 'Abd al-Wahhāb and Ibn Sa'ūd*

As a young man, Muhammad ibn 'Abd al-Wahhāb traveled widely in the central Islamic lands, studying theology, philosophy, and jurisprudence as well as Sufism.[4] In Iran he became a Ḥanbalī, after which he took to preaching a strict doctrine of *tawḥīd,* which brought him difficulties as well as supporters. At Dar'īya in Najd he came to be associated with the local leader Muhammad ibn Sa'ūd, with whom he later worked out a scheme whereby Ibn 'Abd al-Wahhāb would provide religious leadership and teaching for the people and Ibn Sa'ūd would serve as political head and highest worldly authority. This partnership evolved into the strong partnership of Sa'ūdī royalty and Wahhābī religious sectarianism that still dominates today in the Kingdom of Saudi Arabia. As the house of Sa'ūd's power and prestige increased and spread throughout the peninsula, so also did the Wahhābī brand of reformed Islam.

### *Heresy and Annihilation of Saint Veneration*

Ibn 'Abd al-Wahhāb followed the lead of Ibn Taimīya and returned to the Qur'an, the Sunna, and the Sunnī legal positions that were worked out in the first three centuries, especially as represented in the Ḥanbalī *madhhab.* He and his followers denounced all else as **heresy** (***bid'a***) and worked to rid Arabia of it. Saint veneration was singled out for annihilation, and the early Wahhābīs did succeed in razing any mosques, shrines, and tombs that were in any way dedicated to the memory or centered in the ongoing cult of *walīs*. Sufism was also fiercely attacked, largely because it was so actively engaged in saint cults and pilgrimages to local shrines. Cemeteries were purged of anything more elaborate than a simple tomb marker. In those days in Arabia, as in other old Muslim centers, there was much imposing funerary architecture. In Arabia it was obliterated. Simplicity in architecture as in the religious life became the watchword for Arabia. Wahhābī mosques even did without minarets and ornaments beyond the most basic furnishings. Anything resembling *shirk* was stamped out, such as seeking intercession with God through anyone other than Muhammad (and he only on the Last Day, as the Qur'an allows), making a vow to any but God, denying the divine decree and predestination in all things, and including the name of any creature (angel, prophet, saint) in prayer.

The Wahhābīs constituted (and still do) a sort of religious police force that severely reprimanded any and all offenders and went beyond even the strict Hanbalī majority in certain matters. For example, believers were *required* to participate in congregational worship. Merely reciting the shahāda was not considered sufficient for full membership in the umma; in addition, one's character had to be examined. Smoking, shaving the beard, and using abusive language were to be punished, for example, by whipping. Even the use of the *subḥa* (rosary) in prayer and meditation was disallowed, because it was not known to have been practiced or countenanced by the Prophet and was thus to be considered "innovation" (*bid'a*), that peculiarly Islamic term for *heresy.* (But it was permitted to count God's most beautiful names on the knuckles, as Muhammad had done.)

### *The Success of the Wahhābīs*

The Wahhābīs had great successes as well as serious setbacks over many years, but on the whole they became permanently established in Arabia, and at their height (ca. 1811) their influence was felt very strongly as far away as Aleppo in the north, to the Red Sea in the west, all the way to the Indian Ocean in the east. Later, Wahhābism put down roots in India as well as in parts of Central Asia. Its indirect influence and inspiration were felt throughout the umma, even in places where its doctrines were received unsympathetically and its violent methods, based on *jihād* against fellow Muslims, deplored. The Wahhābīs sacked the holy Shī'ī city of Karbala in 1802 and massacred the inhabitants. Of course, Shi'ism was regarded by the Wahhābīs as especially idolatrous, with its cult of imāms and pilgrimage practices.

Although the Wahhābīs were opposed to Sufism, much more so than even Ibn Taimīya had been, they nevertheless resembled a Sufi order to some extent, as Fazlur Rahman has pointed out.[5] They called themselves and their system the *ṭarīqa Muḥammadīya* and even organized into agricultural communes and villages called *ikhwāns,* "brotherhoods," which were to be always ready for *jihād,* according to various categories and under different chains of command.

Opposition to the Wahhābīs was partly based on their rejection of all rational theology and, even more, their prohibition and censoring of many beliefs, attitudes, and practices that were widely accepted and liked, including all veneration of *walīs*. The most serious reason for opposition, however, was the Wahhābīs' violent means of attempting to enforce their system and spread it to Muslims everywhere. As Rahman has observed, they resembled the violent and fanatical Khārijites of early Islam.[6] And even though they did preach a return to *ijtihād,* as indeed they had to, considering their program, their rejection of rational speculation, whether in jurisprudence or theology (which they did not approve in any case), made them ineffectual. One cannot have responsible independent decision making without systematic, independent thinking. It is largely on the practical levels of worship, social organization, and the fostering of an egalitarian common Islamic lifestyle that the Wahhābīs succeeded in any positive manner. But their call for *ijtihād* has continued to this day to be heard by highly diverse Muslim individuals and groups. Unfortunately, unlike their hero and inspirer Ibn Taimīya—who was very able in theological dialectic and imaginative legal and political discourse—they were not able to follow him by putting into practice his example and his suggestions for applying the revelation and Muhammad's principles in a real *siyāsa shar'īya* that would be universally acceptable and reformative.

Wahhābism continues to dominate Saudi Arabian religious, legal, and moral life in the early twenty-first century. Its influence is strong in worldwide programs of spreading its ultraconservative views and practices, aided by vast oil wealth. The Taliban movement that ruled Afghanistan for a number of years until the post–9/11, 2001, American invasion and occupation of that country was profoundly influenced by Wahhābism's extremely puritanical vision of Islam.

## OTHER REFORM MOVEMENTS

### *North Africa*

The nineteenth century witnessed a variety of reforming tendencies in different parts of the Islamic world. In North Africa (Libya), the Sanūsī movement used social action to combat European colonialism. The Sanūsīya, named after its founder, a Berber from Algeria, was a combination of Sufi organization and a free-ranging though basically orthodox Sunnism. The founder established several *zāwiyas* in Cyrenaica and finally died there. But his sons continued the movement after him, and it has persisted to this day.

In the Sudan there arose a Mahdist movement, led by Muhammad Ahmad ibn 'Abd Allāh (1834–1885),[7] a self-proclaimed **messiah (*mahdī,* guided one)** who organized his followers for military action and considered *jihād* against all evils to be second only to the congregational salat among his substitute list of pillars, which also included a shahāda, including belief in Muhammad Ahmad's Mahdihood, recitation of the Qur'an, obedience of God's commandments, and observance of certain *dhikrs* that the Mahdi had developed and published. The hajj was dropped. The movement became powerful in the Sudan and saw its task to be overthrowing the

Egyptians and their Turkish masters who ruled the Sudan, followed by the actual conquest of Egypt, Arabia, Syria, and the Ottoman capital itself. Many thoughtful Muslims in the Sudan were offended by Muhammad Ahmad's extreme claims concerning himself as well as his opposition to scholarship. He did exert a powerful influence, however, by means of his egalitarian policies that enabled slaves and masters to cooperate and fight side by side. There was an enthusiasm among the masses, who were carried along in a seemingly spontaneous flow of eschatologically meaningful action and adventure. The movement's asceticism, possibly derived from Wahhābism, provided a sense of spiritual superiority and strength.

The Sudanese Mahdist uprising attracted the attention of the whole world in 1885 when the British defender of Khartoum, General Charles George "Chinese" Gordon, was killed after a long siege of his garrison ended in a decisive victory for the Mahdists, who stormed it. Muhammad Ahmad himself died in the summer of 1885 at Omdurman, where a *qubba* was erected over his grave. Even before his death, Muhammad Ahmad was considered to be a saint, even though he forbad saint veneration and visits to shrines.[8] The Mahdist domination of the Sudan continued until 1898, when it was brought to an end by a punitive expedition led by British General Kitchener.

### *West Africa*

A vital and far-ranging Sunni reform movement arose early in the nineteenth century in the Sokoto region of northwestern Nigeria. Usuman dan Fodio (1754–1817 C.E.), a very devout and respected Sunni scholar and Sufi shaykh and a member of a Fulbe clan in the Hausa kingdom of Gobir, led the movement. Dan Fodio and his line of orthodox Sunni scholars had been spreading strict Sunni doctrines and practices throughout Gobir and neighboring areas for many years. Dan Fodio, whose honorific name was the Shehu (the Hausa language name for *shaykh*), urged the Gobir leaders to cease tolerating traditional, rather flexible, spiritual practices and conform strictly to the Shari`a as defined by Sunni Islam. His puritanical writings condemned such local, to him, un-Islamic Hausa cultural practices as music, singing, elaborate dress, building designs, and regional social customs and mores. This eventually led to a military type of *jihād* against the Gobir leadership, with military units organized and led by devoted followers of dan Fodio. The campaigns lasted from 1804 to 1808, with the Sunni forces facing much larger forces than they could deploy, and ended with the establishment of a sizable Sunni Islamic state that dan Fodio's followers called a "caliphate," remembering the golden age of Muslim power under the Abbasids in Baghdad.

Usuman dan Fodio was by this period growing old, although he provided much in the way of inspiration and policy advice. The final years of the Shehu's life were spent advising on administrative matters in the caliphate, teaching spiritual wisdom from his Qadiriyya Sufi order's tradition, and writing influential religious books and poetry that had a very large following. Near the end of his life the Shehu was increasingly regarded by his devoted followers—who by then were very numerous—as a *walī*, a true saint who is near to God and can bestow blessings on people who would come to be near him, touching him and wanting to experience his spiritual power and presence. He strongly denied being a *walī,* but did admit to authentic spiritual inspirations and insights. He died in 1817 and was buried in his home on the outskirts of the new capital Sokoto. The home became a shrine, attracting visitors seeking blessings and help as occurs at such saint shrines throughout most of the Muslim world.

Dan Fodio's son Muhammadu Bello succeeded his father as leader of the new state and was very successful in that role. The long-term results of dan Fodio's work was the spreading of a much more orthodox type of Islam and Muslim living in the region than what had preceded him.

The Sufi aspects of his teaching did not continue notably, in part because of an increasing Wahhābī influence in West Africa. But dan Fodio's great corpus of spiritual writings and beautiful poetry continue to inspire and delight readers. Following is an example of his poetry from a major work of 106 stanzas praising the Prophet Muhammad and dan Fodio's deep love for him:

> My friends, I begin my praise in order to comfort my loneliness,
> Into my heart he keeps coming in,
> I am longing to see him, the Most Excellent of Prophets,
> Muhammad, Ahmad, for he excels them all.
> In my heart I sing his praises.
>
> • • •
>
> When I drink the waters of his praise, truly,
> I feel nothing except love for him.
> Whenever I go out, the direction I am following
> Is that of the motion of my eyes, they are desiring the east,
> That they may succeed in seeing my Lord, the Prophet,
> When I go out, in whatever direction I turn my eyes,
> It is as if I see him and hear him speak.
>
> • • •
>
> When I am silent my heart is not tardy,
> In all my thoughts I desire to see him,
> When I hear the words, "Peace be upon you," then I will remember him,
> Whenever I exchange greetings, it is as if he and I exchange them,
> It is as if I take his hand in mine.[9]

### *India*

In India during the nineteenth century there were several reform movements, one led by Sayyid Ahmad Barelwī of Raē Barēlī, who is thought by some to have been inspired by Wahhābism.[10] Whatever the truth of that, Sayyid Ahmad's puritanical reforms resembled Wahhābism but went further by denying allegiance to any or all Sunnī schools of law. *Jihād* became the core of the movement, both against the Sikhs and later the British. Sayyid Ahmad died in battle in 1831. The nineteenth century was a very difficult one for Indian Muslims, who were deprived of any semblance of power and had to console themselves with religious reforms and dreams of driving out the British. An influential reforming theological seminary was established at Deoband in 1876, in which moderation predominated, without, however, suggesting an abandonment of traditional Islamic principles, including the duty of Muslims to rule themselves.

### *Sufism and Reform*

Fazlur Rahman has observed that although Sufism was influential in a number of premodern reform movements, it was a transformed Sufism, largely divested of its medieval doctrines and practices, especially those that were so heavily informed by the theosophical cosmology of Ibn ʿArabī, with its hierarchy of saints and "perfect human" (*al-insān al-kāmil*).[11] Sufi organization and discipline were turned instead toward activism, with the figure of the Prophet dominating through an emphasis on his interior moral and spiritual nature. The old medieval Sufism continued, however, and it can still be seen today, although it has long since ceased to be very influential for the masses. The old Sufism came increasingly to be regarded as a weakening and corrupting factor in an Islamic community that needed to overcome serious disabilities, whether spiritual, moral, legal, or political.

***Need to Reform.*** A sense that things had gone wrong in the umma seems clearly to antedate the kinds of Western challenges that later convinced Muslims everywhere that reform was not only necessary but inevitable. The Wahhābīs were horrified by the degenerate behavior that could be witnessed in Mecca, the central Muslim sanctuary. Morals were lax and superstitious practices rife there and throughout the Hejaz. The Sanūsī movement in Libya was aimed at fighting the tribal violence, moral decay, and economic deterioration of Muslim peoples who were not at the time very much concerned with the West.

## SOME MODERNIST THINKERS

Movements such as those led by Shāh Walī Allāh of Delhi, Ibn ʿAbd al-Wahhāb, and the Sudanese Mahdi were powerful in their own day and continued to exert influence long after, especially Wahhābism. But in the nineteenth century, Islamic thinkers attempted to come to grips with science, technology, and Western political and economic domination over most of the globe. If the older movements were essentially indigenous products of the umma, the latter were responses to outside ideas and forces. Sometimes they were apologetic, seeking above all to defend Islam against the secularizing and relativizing tendencies of modern thought. At other times they were militantly anti-Western, dedicated to the overthrow of imperialism, especially of the British Empire. Sometimes the responses were accommodating and adaptive, viewing the West and science as a mixed blessing, with elements to be admired and imitated, while resisting beliefs and behavior thought to be incompatible with Islamic principles.

All Islamic reformers, whether hot, lukewarm, or cold toward Western science and institutions, were nevertheless aware of the umma's weakness and desirous of doing whatever was possible for renewal and reform. A common theme was, and remains, the reopening of the gate of Ijtihād. Not only Sufism, with its quietist and often superstitious beliefs and practices, but also the great majority of the *'ulamā'* were locked into old patterns and unable to wake the Muslims to the challenges of the modern era. The perception of the umma's deteriorated state came about internally, as was evidenced in the premodernist movement. The strength to deal with it also came from native Islamic resources of conviction and responsibility. The story of Islamic reform and the purification of institutions and thought down to the present is not imaginable without the Muslims' faith in the proper destiny of the umma under the Sharī'a. Muslim peoples did not adopt Western religious or ideological systems wholesale, nor did they seek to shed their Islamic traditions and life patterns. The assertive dimensions of Islam, as most dramatically expressed in *jihād,* never died out, even though the Muslim nations' institutional structures were tottering and sometimes ineffective.

## Al-Afghānī

One of the most energetic and original of all Islamic reformers in the last century was Jamāl al-Dīn al-Afghānī (1839–1897), a tireless activist who traveled from country to country calling his fellow Muslims to wake up and drive out Western influences from their midsts. This could be accomplished only by internal renewal, purification, and reorganization. That is, it was not enough to get rid of outside forces; the umma also needed to be reformed, both according to enduring Islamic principles and procedures and with the admitted benefits of modern science and thought. Afghānī was not a narrow fundamentalist but a humanistic champion of basic rights and sympathetic to the masses of poor, powerless people across the Near Eastern and Asian world of his day.[12] In a sense, he was a harbinger of Third World causes that have become such a prominent aspect of the poor nations' struggle for survival today.

Al-Afghānī was more a social and political activist than a thinker, but he did appreciate the power of the press and published his ideas in articles and pamphlets that were read from Europe to India, although wherever they were in control, the British tried to suppress them. With his younger admirer and colleague, the Egyptian Muhammad 'Abduh (1849–1905), Afghānī published in Paris a little paper that took its name from a society they had founded: *Al-'Urwa al-Wuthqā,* "The most firm handle," taken from a phrase in the Qur'an: "Whosoever disbelieves in idols and believes in God, has laid hold of the most firm handle, unbreaking . . . " (2:256). The articles had a wide range of subject matter, but they all were composed for purposes of action and not simply intellectual reflection. They treated political, social, cultural, and economic as well as religious and theological issues. Although they appear to reflect Afghānī's thinking, the pieces also reveal the developing thought of the greater thinker 'Abduh, although he was not recognized until after he returned to Egypt from exile in Paris. Afghānī stirred up strong anti-imperialist feelings among Muslims and convinced many that a pan-Islamic movement would help renew and reunite the umma. Afghānī finally died in Istanbul, where he had spent the last five years of his life under a kind of house arrest, luxuriously looked after and allowed to receive visitors but unable to leave the city.

### *'Abduh*

Muhammad ʻAbduh was born in 1849 to a poor peasant family in Upper Egypt. He early showed great intellectual ability and was sent to study religious sciences at the famous mosque-school in Tanta, which was associated with the tradition of Sayyid Ahmad al-Badawī, the great Sufi saint. Later he entered the Azhar University in Cairo, where he much later became its modernizing and thus controversial rector. From his teens, ʻAbduh was interested in mysticism and sometimes meditated and observed an ascetic withdrawal. Because of his contact and, for a time, close association with Jamāl al-Dīn al-Afghānī, ʻAbduh's world broadened to take in Western thought and science and areas of Islamic tradition that he had not known well before.

ʻAbduh's thought and activities were marked by restraint and reflective tolerance, even though he shared with his mentor Afghānī the hope of seeing Islam strengthened and Western influences and power withdrawn from the Islamic nations. ʻAbduh was a rational theologian, a sort of neo-Muʻtazilite, who saw no essential conflict between reason and revelation and religion and science. ʻAbduh looked back to the scientific and philosophical thought of classical Islam and argued that Islam at its most authentic had always been on the side of science and progress in a universe in which a kind of natural law of discernible cause and effect operates under a benevolent and righteous God.

Ethics were at the core of ʻAbduh's thought, and because of that, he was an active person who could not retire from the world and view it abstractly or in a detached, intellectualist manner. The reform of Islam was his life's work, and it had to be grounded in real-life situations. One of the central points of his thinking and activism was patriotism, and he did much to foster Egyptian nationalism, believing that a people that is proud of its native land would be much better able to protect it from enemies, whether from without, like the imperialist West, or from within, where strong men's despotic rule had been the norm for centuries.

Toward the close of his life, ʻAbduh was often at the center of controversy. He claimed the right of *ijtihād* for himself and others and, in a respectful manner, worked outside the old fashioned *fiqh* or *taqlīd* to urge people to return to the Qur'an and the Sunna. He was also critical of saint veneration, although higher forms of Sufism informed his conscience and shaded his style toward tolerance, without giving up firmness. He was not a champion of the old medieval Sufi worldview, with its theosophy of saintly hierarchy. For ʻAbduh, that sort of thinking was no longer viable in a world in which science and realism mattered most. This realism led him to emphasize ethics over reflection and the rational exploitation of what he regarded as primitive and, therefore, pure Islam.

For all his spirituality and crusading for enlightened beliefs and practices in the modern world, ʻAbduh was also very resilient. In his autobiography, the young, blind Taha Husayn tells of the respect the Azhar students had for 'Abduh and the excitement he aroused with his efforts to bring the venerable institution into the modern world in curriculum and teaching methods. Husayn tells of the young men in his dormitory preparing for the evening lecture, when they "would talk about the Imam himself, discussing his extraordinary qualities, recalling his judgment on the sheikhs, or theirs on him, and repeating the crushing replies with which he used to silence questioners or objectors and make them a laughingstock to their fellows."[13]

'Abduh always relied on the Qur'an and began a great modernist commentary on it that was finished by others after his death. Although he recognized universal laws of nature, he also constantly called upon his fellow believers to look beyond those laws to their creator. The regular and beneficent workings of nature provide signs (*āyāt*) by which we may contemplate and love God.

Jamāl al-Dīn al-Afghānī was not closely identified with any single country, because he tirelessly traveled throughout the Dār al-Islām and beyond—even for a time to America—spreading his doctrine of pan-Islam and renewal, free from the great powers. Muhammad 'Abduh also traveled and for a time was banished from his native land, but he always worked to improve his Egyptian environment and remained there in his later years to serve his country as well as his religion through hard, practical work. His example was not to be forgotten, for as far away as Indonesia his ethic of social action and improvement of people's daily lives through education and proper health care had results. The liberal-minded Indonesian Islamic service organization, *Muhammadiyah,* with its female counterpart, *Aishiyah,* were founded because of 'Abduh's inspiration and thinking.

### *Sayyid Ahmad Khān*

A third modernist Muslim thinker was Sayyid Ahmad Khān (1817–1898), who is almost entirely identified with India, where in 1875 he founded the famous Anglo-Muhammadan College at Aligarh (now the Muslim University of Aligarh). Sayyid Ahmad Khān was a liberal Muslim thinker of marked philosophical leanings. He admired the modern West and sought in his experimental college to bring to India the best of Western educational content and methods. Generations of young men were graduated from Aligarh and took their places as leaders in modern fields. But Aligarh did not provide much Islamic education, and this increasingly became a liability for the college as more assertively conservative Islamic movements emerged.

Al-Afghānī was highly critical of Ahmad Khān and accused him of being a materialist (*dahrī*) and even the Antichrist (*al-Dajjāl*) in a vitriolic repudiation of Indian materialists that appeared in *Al-'Urwa al-Wuthqā,* the paper he edited with 'Abduh. Another term applied to Ahmad Khān was *nechari,* after "nature," because of his peculiar views of natural cause and effect that operate, in his view, autonomously and without God's managing. Here Ahmad Khān was more radical than Muhammad 'Abduh, who continued to see divine providence behind the observable and somewhat predictable flow of natural causes and effects.

## A Global Map of Muslim Populations

*Estimated population percentage by country, approximately 1.57 billion globally*

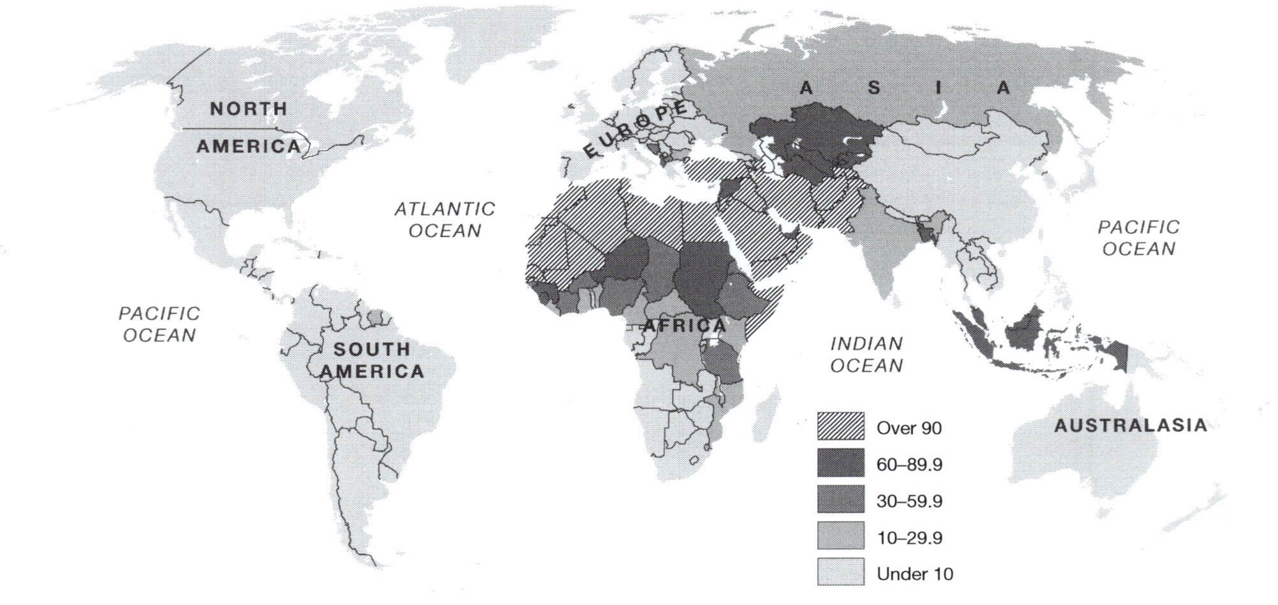

Ahmad Khān lived a long, useful life and did much to encourage improvement in education and other social arenas. In his own day he came to be regarded as too sympathetic with the West and lacking in the Islamic militancy that his *jihād*-prone coreligionists increasingly preached. It is interesting to speculate whether his materialism would have been forgiven by Afghānī if he had not so admired the hated British, upon whom the gentle Ahmad Khān believed that God had bestowed "all good things spiritual and worldly" in greater abundance than anywhere else.[14]

### Influence of the Three Thinkers

Afghānī, 'Abduh, and Ahmad Khān present us with three quite different types of positions and temperaments. Each was born into a traditional Islamic environment that was beginning to experience change. Afghānī blew like a fresh wind over the territories and oceans of the Dār al-Islam, although those places were not then ruled by believers. But the umma and the Abode of Surrender need not have at any given time a specific form of government or nation status in order to be Islamic in some sense. Even while foreign powers were ruling in India and Egypt and corrupt Muslim leaders held power in places like Persia and Istanbul, Afghānī called for renewal and reform at the level of the common people. His work was not in vain, and to the present he has continued to be a beacon of Islam. 'Abduh was actually a greater thinker than Afghānī was, and his social activism also continues to be found in the Muslims' ethical deliberations and policy formulations across the world. But he was more restrained, somehow more "Egyptian," if by that is understood a tolerance of others and a patience combined with determination in getting tasks accomplished. It was characteristic of Afghānī to have provided the ideas for *Al-'Urwa al-Wuthqā* while the hardworking, careful 'Abduh served as actual editor and got out the journal. Afghānī was assertive and combative, but 'Abduh was somewhat of a theological apologist, who took pains to demonstrate that Islam also contained scientific and philosophical thinkers who did not suffer by comparison with those of the modern West. 'Abduh seems to have been convinced of this, and it is not difficult to see in his thought something of the attractiveness of the Mu'tazilite positions when observed in a *taqlīdī* environment.

Sayyid Ahmād Khān was far more liberal and accommodating to Western scientific and philosophical thought than either of the other two was. He went outside Islamic sources and procedures in his break with tradition and fundamentalism. Perhaps this was because he lived in an environment that was witnessing the increasing isolation of Muslims in an overwhelmingly Hindu population. If, from the perspectives of reformers like Afghānī and even 'Abduh, he seemed out of place in his own time, he looks even odder today when leaders like the late Ayatollah Khomeini in Iran, Osama bin Laden and al-Qaeda, and fundamentalists in many parts of the Islamic world uniformly reject Western values, social customs, and cultural modernity. Afghānī and 'Abduh appear to have fostered ways of being Islamic in the modern world by emphasizing abiding Islamic beliefs and values and retaining a recognizably Islamic social and political ordering of life.

Sayyid Ahmad Khān's educational reforms, however, are not to be regarded as a human failure, for most Muslim children now are schooled in modern subjects and want to be included in the good things of this life that are made possible through technology and rational ordering of the means of production and consumption. Of course, material success and prosperity are not Islam's final goals of human life. But they are legitimate aims, and it would be reading Islamic history wrongly to see it as predominantly interested in the afterlife. The conviction that God has prepared for his obedient servants an abode of bliss and reward has not made the Muslims dreamy and passive; on the contrary, it has enabled them to be active in the life of this world, whether politically, economically, socially, or culturally, centering all in God and his religion. This brings ***falāḥ***, success, the characteristic Islamic word for "salvation," both in this world and the next.

## ISLAM AND NATIONALISM

One of the most notable trends of modern times has been the establishment of independent national states. In the eighteenth and nineteenth centuries, this occurred mostly in Europe and the Americas, although in Asia and the Middle East there were movements in this direction that were concluded in the twentieth century, especially after World War II and the end of most colonial establishments across the globe, such as the Dutch East Indies (which became the Republic of Indonesia), British India (which later split into India, Pakistan, and Bangladesh), French North Africa (which after liberation became the independent nations of Morocco, Tunisia, and Algeria), and others. Turkey, almost alone among the Middle Eastern nations was created without having experienced the degradation and humiliation of colonization and foreign rule. Turkey emerged after World War I under the leadership of the remarkable Mustafa Kemal, whose adopted name Atatürk ("Father of the Turks") suggests something of his importance. The Ottomans themselves had been powerful colonialists for centuries, having come close to extending their rule as far as Vienna (in 1683) and absolutely dominating the Arab world and North Africa well into the nineteenth century, when Egypt was lost (and then ruled by Britain) and other places were taken over by France, Italy, Russia, and Greece (which gained its independence in 1829).

### *Turkey*

Turkey emerged in Anatolia when the decrepit Ottoman Empire collapsed under the victorious French and British campaigns in World War I. It could easily have become a European colony had it not been for the powerful support of Atatürk in central Anatolia in the name of the Turkish people and army, without any permission from what remained of the continuing, but feeble Ottoman government in Istanbul. By means of decisive military moves, including the expulsion of the Greeks in 1921 and 1922 and the establishment of a new capital in Ankara (in the heartland), Atatürk led the new nation to international recognition by 1923. He then abolished the sultanate, that final vestige of the caliphate on which many Muslims had continued to place their hopes for an international Muslim revival. Atatürk then proceeded to disestablish Islam by canceling the Sharī'a, outlawing Sufi brotherhoods and activities, requiring the salat to be performed in Turkish, adopting the Roman alphabet (and thus rendering future generations incapable of reading Arabic, whose script the old Ottoman Turkish had been written in), and even forbidding the wearing of the fez. Atatürk insisted that progress lay in Westernization, and so he proceeded to try to make Turkey into a "European" country.

The idea of emphasizing things Turkish was itself fairly new, for the old Ottoman regime had been internationalist and committed to pan-Islamic symbols and customs, which were useful for the imperial administration across the Muslim lands that it had so long dominated. In the early twentieth century, as if in anticipation of Atatürk, intellectuals like Ziya Gök-Alp (1875–1924), under the influence of the French sociologist Émile Durkheim, developed a modernization program based on the three coordinated ideas of "Turkification, Islamization and Modernization."[15] Gök-Alp's ideas were certainly radical, for "Islamization" meant a return to a primitive Islam when he imagined there was the freedom to innovate and think freely, before the characteristic classical legal and religious institutions had developed and come to dominate Muslims. The Turkish language, culture, and customs were revived and enhanced so as to render the most meaningful symbols and structures for national life. Religion and state were separated in a secularizing revolution that nevertheless recognized Islam as the proper religion for Turks, but without adopting pan-Islamic or theocratic programs.

Atatürk went much farther even than the intellectual Gök-Alp, by sponsoring a Turkism that went, in Kenneth Cragg's word, into "irreligion."[16] Since Atatürk's time, the Turks have continued to carry on in a more or less secularist fashion. But after World War II there was rebirth of theological education, and the Sufis became slightly visible, even though their activities technically are still prohibited. But mysticism is a part of the Turkish soul and the great renewal that is occurring among Muslims everywhere is attractive to Turkish sympathy and participation.

The worldwide Islamic revival of the late twentieth century and the present is challenging Turkey's secular government very assertively by means of various forms of Turkish Muslim activism in politics, education, publishing, and cultural behavior (particularly the adoption of strict Islamic dress codes such as veiling of girls in public schools and women in universities and the workplace).

### *Saudi Arabia*

Since Turkey emerged as a new and independent national entity, many other predominantly Muslim peoples have also achieved nationhood. Although most have sought to modernize their governments and economies, as well as their education, health, and planning, some have made it their explicit goal to do so through Islam. The modern kingdom of Saudi Arabia, although not a democratic nation by any means, is nevertheless dedicated to using its oil wealth to improve its citizens' conditions of life, while at the same time maintaining a strictly fundamental Wahhābi-based religious posture, at least officially. The handsome green and white flag of Saudi Arabia has a sword over which is written the shahāda, with no mention of either Arabia or the royal dynasty.

The few remaining Muslim monarchs are feeling great pressure these days from revolutionary forces, whether religious or secularist, and it is unlikely that they can last indefinitely. The Saudis see it as their task to protect and maintain the holy cities of Mecca and Medina as well as to foster Wahhābī-slanted Islamic religious, social, and educational programs throughout the world. These activities have led to the building of mosques, schools, Islamic centers, and publishing operations in such diverse places as Britain, Indonesia, Pakistan, the United States, Egypt, and Australia. The Saudis also see it as their duty to use their wealth in the service of fellow Muslims who are the victims of natural calamities, such as earthquakes, floods, and famines, although in the last category there is far more need than even the Saudis and other wealthy Arab oil states can provide. When several years ago, there was a violent attempt to take over the Grand Mosque in Mecca, people around the world, especially Muslims, were shocked by such an event's taking place in the sacred precincts of the Ka'ba itself. That siege was just one indication of how militant Muslims sometimes can be when they dedicate themselves wholly to what they conceive to be the restoration of "true Islam."

### *Pakistan*

The state of Pakistan was established after World War II as an attempt to build an Islamic nation populated by a variety of Muslim peoples already living in the northwest and northeast of the main Indian subcontinent, as well as many who emigrated from the new republic of India in order to live in the new Islamic nation. As we noted earlier in this chapter, the nineteenth century saw Muslim power and prestige on the decline in India, so that by the start of the twentieth century, anxiety over the political rights of Muslims there led to the formation of the Muslim League (1906), which provided a voice for Muslims and a forum for considering alternatives in anticipation of the eventual British withdrawal from the region. There periodically were conflicts between the Hindu and Muslim communities, despite efforts at conciliation and cooperation by such leaders as Mohandas ("Mahatma") K. Gandhi (d. 1948) on the Hindu side and the poet-philosopher Muhammad Iqbal (d. 1938) on the Muslim side. After all, it was in the interests of both Muslims and Hindus to free the subcontinent from British rule. But there turned out to be too much separating the two religious communities for there ever to be a joint national arrangement.

Iqbal proposed in 1930 the establishment of an administratively separate Muslim region in four northwestern provinces and because of this later gained the title "Father of Pakistan." Some Indian Muslim students in Britain adopted the name of the new nation from the Urdu words *pak* ("pure") and *stan* ("country"), with the added meaning of *pak* plus the letter *s* as an acronym of *P*unjab, *A*fghanistan, *K*ashmir, and *S*ind, the four provinces in question. But Iqbal did not live to see the birth of Pakistan. In 1940, the politician Muhammad Ali Jinnah led the Muslim League in its call for the establishment of Muslim statehood in the regions where Muslims comprised a majority. After the war, Britain agreed to a separate Islamic nation in connection with Indian independence, which was granted in 1947. That fall, there were massacres of Hindus and Muslims, especially in Punjab, during the frantic exchange of large sectors of populations struggling to reach the safety of their majority groups. More than a million people were killed before relative stability could be established. In East Bengal, which became East Pakistan and then Bangladesh, there was much less violence.

After the partition of India and Pakistan it was obvious that India had the advantage of bureaucratic machinery, diversified population and economy, and a central geographic position. Pakistan started off with crippling deficiencies in nearly all of these areas, but with the conviction that a pure Islamic order could be established and serve as an example to other Muslim peoples. During the years since its founding, Pakistan has had periodic conflicts with India, particularly over the status of Kashmir.

The burial place of Muhammad Ali Jinnah, the Qā'id-e-A'zam ("Great Leader") who led Pakistan as founder and first president (d. 1948). Karachi. (*Source:* Frederick Mathewson Denny)

In 1971 East Pakistan declared its independence and took the name Bangladesh, which led to a civil war, with West Pakistan troops entering the former eastern province and committing horrible atrocities against the weaker population, millions of whom fled to India as refugees. India supported the new nation of Bangladesh and fought a brief war with Pakistan, which led eventually to a cease-fire and the restoration of order, with the new state established. Since that time Pakistan was ruled for a long time by a military government that backed a program of strict islamization of the society and its institutions. For two brief periods, Pakistan had a woman—Benazir Bhutto—as prime minister (1988–1990, 1993–1996), but her administrations were swept from power through judicial proceedings fueled by allegations of corruption and incompetence.

Although Pakistan today is a relatively poor nation, Bangladesh is destitute. Yet in Pakistan, at least, there is an Islamic spirit that, through educational programs, large-scale publishing efforts, and foreign missions, provides some of the most vigorous Islamic religious leadership worldwide. Although the islamizing spirit is strong in Pakistan, the country also has a large, sophisticated intellectual class thoroughly at home in the worlds of modern science, philosophy, and religious reflection. Sir Muhammad Iqbal, the Father of Pakistan, was a world-class thinker whose legacy continues among his people, regardless of the practical problems of developing a truly Islamic national venture in the complex modern world.

Pakistan has exerted enormous influence beyond its borders through the activist organization Jamaat-i-Islami, founded by the scholarly journalist Mawlana Abu-l-A'la al-Mawdudi (1904–1979). The Jamaat-i-Islami seeks to bring about islamization of all levels of life, at the same time benefiting from and contributing to modern scientific and technological advances that are consistent with Islamic principles, such as education, health care, and social services. Pakistan is a nuclear power, as is neighboring India. Some view the former country's weapon as an "Islamic bomb," although interpretations of just what that means vary widely.

### *Indonesia*

The inhabitants of the former Dutch East Indies began to call for independence early in the twentieth century, but it was not until the Japanese occupation during World War II when it appeared that definite progress could be achieved after the Allied victory. In 1945 the great nationalist leader Sukarno and his close associates proclaimed Indonesian independence. Over the next four years there was a constant struggle with the Dutch colonialists, who had reestablished themselves after the war. But in 1949 independence was finally won and a parliamentary type of government established.

The formation of Indonesia from the many different peoples, languages, customs, and regions was a miracle. Today the nation ranks fourth in the world in population (now approaching 240 million) and first in the number of Muslims, approaching 90 percent. Although basically an agricultural nation, Indonesia nevertheless contains some of the major world supplies of natural resources, like petroleum, tin, bauxite, and timber. Islam arrived in the islands late but was well established by the close of the sixteenth century, especially along the coasts of Java and Sumatra. The religion was carried largely by Muslim traders from India, although Arabs regularly reached its shores, too. Sufi piety and organization were dominant in the Islam that was planted, and they proved to be a perfect fit for the mystically inclined and reflective peoples of the archipelago, where Hinduism and Buddhism had long provided a refined and sophisticated symbolism, coupled with indigenous beliefs and practices, especially on Java.

Indonesian Islam is different from the Islam of the Near East or South Asia, in that it exists harmoniously with other religions, whether major ones like Christianity and Hinduism or regional belief and behavior patterns. On Java, the most populous island and the center of the government, culture, and economy, there are three generally recognized classes of Muslims. First are the ***Santris,*** who are quite orthodox and to some extent arabicized and conscious of their relationship with Muslims everywhere. Then there is the ***Abangan*** category, the majority, who are Muslim but syncretized with traditional regional beliefs and customs. Finally there is the ***Priyayi*** class, Muslims, but deeply influenced by their aristocratic past as Javanese, with older Indian-influenced attitudes and behavior patterns. This threefold classification should be used cautiously, because the social reality is complex and subtle, with overlapping and blending of components.

The strict Muslim groups were disappointed at independence with their leaders' decision not to make the Sharī'a the law of the land. This was done, it was said, in the interests of national unity. Instead, a compromise of **five principles,** in Indonesian ***pancasila,*** was promulgated as the basis of Indonesian nationhood: monotheism, humanism, national unity, democracy, and social justice. This program has continued to the present to provide Indonesia with guidance and relative harmony, although there continue to be forces in favor of the islamization of the government and the society, led by the Santris. Neither Sukarno, whose rule came to an end in 1965 amidst a bloodbath of Muslim-led anti-Communist hatred—in which possibly as many as one million people were slaughtered—nor his successor, Suharto, had been content to allow the Muslim domination of their regimes.

Nevertheless, under President Suharto, Indonesian Islam thrived, judging from the projects that have been sustained, like mosque building, the development of Islamic schools everywhere, the establishment of a national system of Islamic universities that train religious teachers and leaders for small towns and villages, and government policy that favors Islam on the old bitter issue of whether religious bodies should have the right to proselytize.[17]

This last problem emerged anew after the Abangan Muslims were persecuted politically by Santris following the 1965 massacre of Communists. Hundreds of thousands of these Abangans converted to other religions—Buddhism, Hinduism, and especially Christianity.[18] Anyone who might have been suspected of lacking in religious zeal was in danger of being regarded as a Communist and, therefore, an atheist. Thus a religion was a port in a storm, but the large-scale conversion to Christianity was a surprise. All the same, Islam is securely established as the majority religion in Indonesia. It remains to be seen whether a Santri-led Muslim wave will succeed in capturing the government and establishing the Sharī'a as the law of the land, as happened in revolutionary Iran and as is still being attempted in Pakistan. Probably the tolerant live-and-let-live attitudes of the Indonesians, especially the Javanese, will prevail, and the practical approach of Pancasila will continue to enable the leaders to preserve a balance among the factions and populations. But the question remains: Is Islam true to its origins and its destiny if it does not strive to make God's religion one and God's people one? The Santris, although they are a minority among Indonesian Muslims, nevertheless are linked to the global renaissance of Islam and thus tend to want Sharī'a rule in Indonesia.

An economic downturn caused great instability in Indonesia in 1998, which in turn led to President Suharto's resignation in the face of widespread protests and violence. In 1999, Abdurrahman Wahid, a prominent Muslim leader, was elected president. Although he was a moderate, not favoring the formation of a Muslim state in Indonesia, he nevertheless was driven from office in 2001 and replaced by Megawati Sukarnoputri, the republic's founding father Sukarno's daughter.

### *Iran*

The final example of Islam and modern national entities is also the most dramatic in form and fateful in results, which have not yet ended. The Shī'īrevolution in Iran in 1978–1979 brought to a brutal end the long period of Shah Reza Pahlavi's program of modernization of that ancient nation's economy, society, educational system, and military. The shah was an autocrat who dealt very harshly with his opponents, to the point of maintaining a large secret police that arrested people on the slightest suspicions or pretexts and often imprisoned them without trial, tortured them, and, in many cases, executed them. On the surface and in the public, the shah tried to present an image of a benevolent monarch bringing his people into prosperous and progressive modern times. And many people in the middle and upper classes did indeed prosper, especially from the country's oil wealth. Western-style recreations, fashions, social life, music, entertainment, and consumer goods were abundantly available in all the cities and large towns, accompanied by garish posters, billboards, and shop fronts. Women in the cities went about in short dresses and without the traditional Islamic covering of the hair and arms, something shocking and unacceptable to more conservative Muslim sensibilities, which were all the time still very strong, although beneath the surface and waiting to reemerge. The shah's repressive internal security measures, combined with his Westernizing ways and the increasingly hostile relationship between popular modern culture and Islamic values and customs, led to a situation that was exploited by the *'ulamā'* and other religiously or ideologically oriented factions, whether conservative, middle of the road, or radical.[19]

There had long been rivalry and competition and, at times, bitter conflicts between the rulers of Iran and its religious scholars, who regarded themselves as rulers of that Shī'ī nation by divine right, which they have also imagined coincides with the real wishes of the masses. This is not a fantasy in Shī'ī countries, because of the people's continuing identification with the special legacy that has descended to them from Muhammad through ʻAlī and Fātima and their martyred son Husayn. The Iranians were not always dominantly Shīʻī, although there has been since early Islamic history a goodly representation of them. It was not until the Sāfavid dynasty (1501–1732) that Shīʻism was established as the state religion. Since then, Shīʻī convictions have had a firm grip on Iran's popular beliefs, attitudes, and customs as well as religious, educational, and social institutions.

Shīʻism was appropriate for Iran, because of its tendencies toward a metaphysical dualism of good versus evil, light against darkness, and a view of history that sees in the future a final showdown between God's true worshipers and the wicked. These and other notions reflect something of Iran's Zoroastrian past, even as they go beyond it in new, Islamic ways with symbols and observances appropriate to the triumphal religion. (During the American hostage crisis and later, when Iranian leaders and their ayatollah have cried out against the "Great Satan," whether with reference to Washington, Moscow, or some other adversary, they have used a title that has its roots not only in the Qur'an but also in the old Iranian symbol system. Satan, as a potent religious concept of adversary to God, was possibly born in Iran, from whence it influenced post-Exilic Judaism and later Christianity and Islam.)[20]

The close association between religion and rule is also an old Iranian emphasis, which contributed to the rise of sacral kingship during pre-Islamic times and continued to live on in the Abbasid caliphate in Baghdad, albeit in Islamic garb. In postrevolutionary Iran there is, however, no kingship. The Ayatollah Khomeini, the architect and guiding spirit of Islamic Iran, declared years ago that Islam does not have kings.

Worshipers in a classic mosque in Isfahan, Iran. The men and women are separated by a sheet. The *mihrāb* (prayer niche) is to the left. Note the strict Islamic covering of the two women. (*Source:* Yvonne Haddad)

Faisal Mosque, Islamabad, Pakistan. This largest of south Asian Mosques also houses the International Islamic University. (*Source:* Frederick Mathewson Denny)

Instead, the "priests" have taken power in the name of God. Of course, the Iranian *'ulamā'*, the "mullahs," are strictly not a priesthood. But they are a bona fide "clergy," because of the peculiarly Shī'ī doctrines of authority and leadership that insist on so much divine inspiration and empowering of the imāms and their representatives who rule in their place until the Last Day. (Ayatollah means "sign of Allah/God" and is a title bestowed on the most highly respected mullahs in Iran.)

One of the most appealing aspects of the late Ayatollah Khomeini's rule was his activism, which viewed Islam as a revolutionary movement aimed at changing the world and not as a system of mere worship and pattern maintenance that withdraws from the challenges of the modern age. This theme has been a lasting dimension of Islamic reform since the Wahhābi rising. Only members of the *'ulamā'* are considered fully fit for leadership, according to Khomeini, because only they have the requisite knowledge of the sacred law. And in these times only the Ayatollah Khomeini seemed to have the authority to exercise what the Iranian Shī'ī's call *valayat-i faqih,* "rule exercised by an eminent *mujtahid* in the absence of the imam."[21] Many Iranian Muslims did not hesitate to call their hero "Imām," thus using the sacred title of the one who went into occultation and is expected to return and usher in a final, golden age of the Shī'ī's vindication.

The traditional Shī'ī tendency to follow their religious leaders—*mujtahids, 'ālims, ayatollahs,* and so forth—in the conviction that they possess God's guidance and enlightenment was illustrated during the revolution when an Iranian gentleman was being interviewed on American television about the upcoming referendum in which the citizens of revolutionary Iran would vote on whether to accept or reject the draft Islamic constitution. The person being interviewed admitted that there were some parts of the document about which he had some questions and doubts but that he was going to vote in favor of it anyway, "Because I trust Imām."

Iran today is one of the most vigorous and radical contexts of Islamic revival and reform, with many efforts to influence and change other Islamic nations, whether Shī'ī or Sunnī. There is a conviction that the old sectarian (Shī'ī–Sunnī) split no longer makes any sense but serves only to divide and confuse Muslims in a manner that delights their enemies in the West and other places. The post-Khomeini era in Iran has seen some signs of pragmatism as more moderate leaders seek to reestablish economic and commercial ties with Europe and the Americas. However, at this writing there is considerable resentment on the part of a large proportion of the Iranian population that a continuing clergy-prone government deprives citizens of basic human and civil rights.

## NOTES

1. See Marshall G. S. Hodgson's analysis of the origins of modernity and the "transmutation" of the "Technical Age" in the West in *The Venture of Islam*, vol. 3 (Chicago: University of Chicago Press, 1974), especially pp. 176–200.
2. Fazlur Rahman, *Islam* (New York: Anchor Books, 1968), chap. 12.
3. *Ibid.*, p. 243.
4. There is still no full-scale study in English of the Wahhābi movement and its founder. This review is based largely on the article, "Wahhābīya," in *Shorter Encyclopedia of Islam*, ed. H. A. R. Gibb and J. H. Kramers (Ithaca, N. Y.: Cornell University Press, 1953), pp. 618–621. See also H. St. John B. Philby, *Saudi Arabia* (New York: Arno Press, 1972); and the same author's *Arabia of the Wahhabis* (New York: Arno Press, 1973). For a sharply critical summary of contemporary Wahhābism, with extensive citation of Arabic sources, see Khaled Abou El Fadl, "The Ugly Modern and the Modern Ugly: Reclaiming the Beautiful in Islam," in *Progressive Muslims: Justice, Gender, and Pluralism*, ed. Omid Safi (Oxford, U.K.: Oneworld, 2003), pp. 49–62, 69–76.
5. Rahman, *Islam*, pp. 245–246.
6. *Ibid.*, p. 246.
7. See "Muhammad Ahmad B. 'Abd Allāh," in the *Shorter Encyclopedia of Islam*, pp. 407–408. A solid historical study is by Peter M. Holt, *The Mahdist State in the Sudan, 1881–1898: A Study in Its Origins, Development and Overthrow*, 2nd ed. (Oxford, England: Clarendon Press, 1970).
8. "Muhammad Ahmad B. 'Abd Allāh," in the *Shorter Encyclopedia of Islam*, p. 408.
9. Mervyn Hiskett, *The Sword of Truth: The Life and Times of the Shehu Usuman dan Fodio* (New York: Oxford University Press, 1973) p. 55f. Translated from Hausa by the author. For a more detailed overview of this subject, see the article "'UTHMĀN B. FŪDĪ," by D. M. Last, in *The Encyclopaedia of Islam*, Vol. X, new ed. (Leiden: Brill, 2000), pp. 949–951.

10. This is doubted by Fazlur Rahman, *Islam,* p. 253.
11. *Ibid.,* pp. 253–254.
12. *Ibid.,* p. 266.
13. Taha Hussein, *The Stream of Days: A Student at the Azhar,* trans. Hilary Wayment, 2nd ed. (London: Longman, 1948), p. 24.
14. Quoted in Kenneth Cragg, *Counsels in Contemporary Islam* (Edinburgh: Edinburgh University Press, 1965), p. 49.
15. See *ibid.,* pp. 144ff., for a compact summary of Gök-Alp's main ideas.
16. *Ibid.,* p. 147.
17. See Nurcholish Madjid, "Islam in Indonesia: Challenges and Opportunities," in *Islam in the Contemporary World,* ed. Cyriac K. Pullapilly (Notre Dame, Ind.: Cross Roads Books, 1980), p. 349, for details on Islamic resurgence, especially on university campuses.
18. *Ibid.,* p. 346.
19. John Obert Voll, *Islam: Continuity and Change in the Modern World* (Boulder, Colo.: Westview Press, 1982), p. 295ff.
20. The name "Satan" is not Iranian, but Semitic. For a review of the origins of the concept, see the article "Satan," in *The Interpreter's Dictionary of the Bible,* vol. 4 (New York and Nashville: Abingdon Press, 1962), pp. 224–228, especially p. 226, 3e, "Iranian Influence."
21. Shahrough Akhavi, "Shi'i Social Thought and Praxis in Recent Iranian History," in *Islam in the Contemporary World,* ed. Pullapilly, p. 183.

CHAPTER 15

# Three Forms of Islamic Revival: "Fundamentalism," Feminism, and Establishing the Umma in North America

**KEY TERM**

***da'wa***

Modern Islam is a vigorous, complex amalgam of peoples, movements, and goals, and not the monolithic, centrally coordinated, hostile enterprise that outsiders sometimes assume it to be. Anyone who has looked closely at the history of Islam and has come to appreciate the strength of its community mindedness will realize that Islamic solidarity on certain issues—proper social relations, resistance to domination by secularist and otherwise non-Islamic political and cultural forms, obedience to the Qur'an and the Sunna, and the vision of a unified umma under the Sharī'a to solve the world's ills—is a hallmark of the tradition, with roots in the early period. There is no doubt that many, if not most, Muslims would like to see their religion spread to all places. This is at the heart of ***da'wa,*** the "call" to Islam that is the basis of the missionary endeavors which have been effective in recent decades in Africa, Asia, Europe, and the Americas.

## FUNDAMENTALISM

The term *fundamentalism* has been widely used since the 1970s to characterize various forms of Islamic revivalism. The term originated in America early in the twentieth century, when it was applied to ultraconservative Protestant Christian biblical literalists and inerrantists who propounded a list of "fundamentals" that all true Christians should follow. Because of the American Protestant origins of the term, many observers, Muslim and non-Muslim alike, believe that it should not be applied to Islam. But language descriptive of human belief and behavior, especially in religion and politics, is often adapted from striking and original historical phenomena. Terms like *church, sect, prophet, sage, guru, tabu, mana, discipleship, liberal, conservative, charisma,* and *shaman* have classical contexts of meaning as well as wider applications in typifying characteristics and behavior beyond the original cases.[1]

The editors of the University of Chicago's monumental, five-volume "Fundamentalism Project" did not hesitate to deploy the term cross-culturally. They saw it as "here to stay" because no other term (e.g., *conservatism or traditionalism*) quite expresses its "fighting" character. Fundamentalists, according to the editors, (1) "fight back," (2) "fight for" (their "worldview"), (3) "fight with" (their "resources, weapons"), (4) "fight against" ("others"), and (5) "fight under" (God, or "some transcendent reference").[2]

Probably the wide media use of the terms *fundamentalism* and *fundamentalist* with reference to Islam makes it impossible to avoid applying the term to Islam. And Muslims themselves often use it, both positively and negatively. In the former case they completely divorce it from any Christian connotations and simply use it to refer to the fundamental teachings and practices of Islam. In this case, the term has some utility. But most Muslims have a strong dedication to the fundamentals of the religion, although they may have different styles of expressing it. Other terms that demarcate singularly committed Muslims from others, often with radical reformist programs in mind, include the following: activist, Islamist, Islamicist, extremist, fanatic, and militant. Bruce Lawrence, a specialist on Islam and comparative religion, argues that *fundamentalist* is a global term that defines a common reality applicable to a variety of religions. He defines fundamentalism as

> the universal affirmation of religious authority as holistic and absolute, admitting of neither criticism nor reduction; it is expressed through the collective demand that specific creedal and ethical dictates derived from scripture be publicly recognized and legally enforced.[3]

Lawrence's definition is global, but when used with respect to specific traditions it has to be considered in terms of the specific circumstances of each tradition. His definition generally applies to a wide range of Muslim movements, which themselves have varied styles, temperaments, and methods for realizing their goals.

John O. Voll, a specialist on Islam in the Arab world, also accepts the term *fundamentalism* as useful and defines it in a manner similar to Lawrence's definition.

Both consider fundamentalism to be something quite different from ordinary sincere piety, because fundamentalists have a great sense of urgency. As Voll sees it,

> those commonly referred to today as "fundamentalists" adopt an identifiable approach to this common obligation [that Muslims of all kinds have of affirming the truth of the Qur'an and implementing it in personal and collective life], an approach marked by an exclusivist and literalist interpretation of the fundamentals of Islam and by a rigorist pursuit of sociomoral reconstruction. Islamic fundamentalism is, in other words, a distinctive mode of response to major social and cultural change introduced either by exogenous or indigenous forces and perceived as threatening to dilute or dissolve clear lines of Islamic identity, or to overwhelm that identity in a synthesis of many different elements.[4]

Our preference is to avoid characterizing Muslims as fundamentalists whenever possible and, instead, to treat movements and schools case by case. Fundamentalism as a term too often serves as a negative label obscuring what we are trying to understand and appreciate. For example, the Wahhābīs (introduced in Chapter 14) are often viewed as a reform movement that gave rise to fundamentalism. Wahhābism continues to thrive today in Saudi Arabia. To call it "fundamentalist" alongside other quite dissimilar but equally activist movements in other parts of the Muslim world does not much advance our understanding. And the frequent association of the term (especially in the media) with terrorism, backwardness, "medieval" mentality, and general closed-mindedness may reveal more about the people using the term than its referent(s).

### *The Muslim Brotherhood*

Between the time when modernizing Muslim reformers such as Muhammad 'Abduh, Jamāl al-Dīn al-Afghānī, and Sayyid Ahmad Khān were active and the recent worldwide Islamic revival were other Islamic movements that provided much of the ideology and methods of current activism, especially in the Sunni world. In a symbolic sense, and for Westerners, particularly, the global Islamic revival may be dated from the 1973 OPEC oil price increases, which had such a dramatic impact on the oil-dependent Western industrial nations and provided oil-rich Islamic countries with a new sense of power and promise. One of the most influential activist movements was the Muslim Brotherhood (*al-Ikhwān al-Muslimūn*), founded in Egypt in 1928 by Ḥasan al-Bannā' (1906–1949). Al-Bannā' was well educated in Islamic subjects although not an aspirant to the ranks of the *'ulamā'*. As a young man, he rejected Western influences in the Islamic world as subversive of Islamic values and society. Secularism, materialism, free mixing of the sexes, alcohol, and ethical relativism, among other things, were seducing and destroying Muslims in his view. Al-Bannā' gathered members to his Brotherhood for devotions, study, and general Islamic revitalization. The founder's militant approach and charismatic preaching caused the movement to spread rapidly, first in the cities and villages of Egypt, and then to Syria, the Sudan, Palestine, and other Arab countries.

Although al-Bannā' had admired Sufism as a young man, he later considered its contemporary forms to be too quietist and passive. Yet he incorporated Sufilike measures in the discipline and organization of the Muslim Brotherhood (e.g., required devotions featuring prayer and *dhikr*) but dedicated them to outward-directed service for social and religious welfare, as well as political activism. The Brotherhood appealed especially to urban Muslims of the working classes and has been likened to an "activist labor union" in its organization.[5] Al-Bannā' defined the movement as a

> Salafiyya (i.e., pertaining to the founders of Islam) message, a Sunni way, a Sufi truth, a political organization, an athletic group, a cultural–educational union, an economic company, and a social idea.[6]

But al-Bannā' did not want the Brotherhood to be a mere organization. It was, rather, to be a human community

> not a benevolent organization, nor a political party, nor a local association with strictly limited aims. Rather, you are a new spirit making its way into the heart of this nation and revivifying it through the Qur'an.[7]

The Muslim Brotherhood fell upon hard times as it came into increasing conflict with the Egyptian government, first during World War II and then under the regime of King Farouk. A Brotherhood member murdered the Egyptian prime minister in 1948, and al-Bannā' was murdered the following year. From that time on, the Brotherhood was suppressed by the government, and its members were kept under close watch as well as limited in their operations. Under the revolutionary government of Gamal Abdel Nasser, which began in 1952, the Brotherhood came under increased governmental pressure. Many of its members were imprisoned, and the movement was essentially brought to an end. But it remained underground and continued to have a circumscribed existence until the period of rapprochement with moderate Islamic opposition groups initiated by Egyptian president Hosni Mubarak in the 1980s.

This period came after the assassination of President Anwar Sadat during a military review in 1981 by a team organized by Khālid al-Islāmbūlī, members of an extremist and militant Muslim group called Al-Jihād. When the Egyptian president fell dead, his killer shouted, "I am Khālid al-Islāmbūī, I have killed Pharaoh, and I do not fear death!"[8] Sadat had been considered by most Egyptians to be a modernist, too pro-Western and elitist, a traitor who had made peace with Israel, and one who had expressed contempt for true (i.e., "fundamentalist") Muslims by incarcerating them in great numbers. Thus he was an archenemy, like the evil Egyptian ruler of ancient times as portrayed in both the Bible and the Qur'an. The most extreme Muslim groups take it upon themselves to denounce even fellow Muslims as infidels. One such group is known as *Takfir wa'l-Hijra,* "Excommunication (i.e., by declaring someone a *kāfir,* "infidel") and Emigration (withdrawing from infidel society)."

The Muslim Brotherhood continues to exist and during the last two decades has become increasingly involved in Egyptian politics with representation as elected members of the National Assembly. Although the organization continues to be strongly activist, it is prone neither to violence nor to programs and policies that would alienate the broad middle consensus of sincere Muslim sentiment, which has become increasingly influential in the Islamic revival in Egypt. The Brotherhood, like similar nonviolent Muslim activist movements elsewhere, wants to bring national life under the authority of the Sharī'a and establish as far as possible a truly Islamic society, with due respect for and protection of religious minorities.

### *Sayyid Quvb and "Jāhiliyyah"*

There is not enough space here to survey the many and varied contemporary Islamic movements of activist character. But the example of one extremely influential person can provide some idea of the kind of Islamic aspiration and energy that informs many Muslim individuals and groups in their quest for authentic Islamic life today. That person is the Egyptian contemporary of Ḥasan al-Bannā', and a leading member of the Muslim Brotherhood, Sayyid Quvb (1906–1966).

Quṭb was raised in a religious manner and received a thorough education in Cairo, finishing with a degree in Arabic literature. He was not trained to be a professional religious leader, but like Ḥasan al-Bannā', reflected deeply on Islam and its problems as a thoughtful and concerned layperson. Quṭb came to believe that the only authentic source for survival, let alone revival, of Islam was the Qur'an, which he had memorized by age ten. He later wrote a clear and accessible commentary on the Qur'an, which has profoundly influenced educated Muslims around the world. The commentary does not emphasize the traditional issues of grammar and philology but expounds the message as a guide and awakener for Muslims of all conditions.

Quṭb became a prolific writer, establishing himself as a literary specialist before he turned increasingly to religious writing. Although while growing up he discovered an admiration for Western ways, especially in literature, he later developed a deep antipathy for the West and what it had done to the world of Islam through colonialist imperialism and export of secularism, sexual immorality, and materialism. His 1948 book *Social Justice in Islam* is a strong call for Muslims to return to their true mission on earth as a just and balanced system of social life, governance, economy, and worship. His thesis is that Islam has been revealed by God as a complete and perfect way of life under the Sharī'a and that to inject foreign elements into Muslim faith and order is to weaken and corrupt the umma, which had in fact happened.

After publishing *Social Justice in Islam,* Quṭb traveled to the United States to study educational administration in Washington, D.C., and California. The sojourn in the United States was not a happy one, partly because of the ubiquitous, uncritical media support for the new state of Israel and its accompanying rejection of Palestinian rights and, implicitly, of all Arabs. Also, as Yvonne Y. Haddad, an Arab

American specialist on Islam and the Middle East, has suggested, Quṭb's dark complexion possibly made him aware of, as well as vulnerable to, the prevalent racism of America.[9] During a period of study at the Colorado State College of Education (now known as the University of Northern Colorado) in Greeley, Colorado, Quṭb was appalled at the free and open social contact between male and female students and what he considered to be their immodest dress standards. Greeley could hardly be considered a liberal environment in that period, at least by American standards in general.

Returning to Egypt in 1950, Sayyid Quṭb joined the Muslim Brotherhood and turned his attention to writing on Islam. During the ensuing years he developed a comprehensive Islamic ideology, extremely critical of the West and of what he considered to be corrupt Islamic regimes—particularly Egypt's. Quṭb argued that whereas the Sharī'a is God's enduring and immutable legislation, the science of jurisprudence (*fiqh*) enables Muslims to adapt and apply it to changing conditions and needs.

After the Egyptian revolution and during the Nasser years, Quṭb developed a systematic critique of the regime and spent long periods in prison for his trouble. It was after his release from prison in 1964 that Quṭb wrote his final and most influential book, *Milestones,* which, in historian John O. Voll's words, "presented unambiguously the radical fundamentalist indictment of Muslim society of the 1960s and proposed immediate and direct steps toward the establishment of an authentically Islamic society."[10] Quṭb considered all Islamic societies to be inauthentic, no better than that of non-Muslim peoples. He argued that the root cause of humankind's straying from the right way is *jāhiliyyah,* "ignorance." Islam regards the pre-Islamic era in Arabia as the "Age of Jāhiliyyah," as was noted in Chapter 2. Quṭb extended this idea to the present.

> If we look at the sources and foundations of modern modes of living, it becomes clear that the whole world is steeped in *jāhiliyyah,* and all the marvelous material comforts and advanced inventions do not diminish its ignorance. This *jāhiliyyah* is based on rebellion against the sovereignty of Allah on earth. It attempts to transfer to man one of the greatest attributes of Allah, namely sovereignty, by making some men lords over others. It does so not in the simple and primitive ways of the ancient *jāhiliyyah,* but in the more subtle form of claiming that the right to create values, to legislate rules of collective behavior, and to choose a way of life rests with men, without regard to what Allah has prescribed. The result of this rebellion against the authority of Allah is the oppression of His creatures. Thus the humiliation of the common man under the communist systems and the exploitation of individual[s] and nations due to the greed for wealth and imperialism under capitalist systems are but a corollary of the rebellion against the authority of Allah and the denial of the dignity of man bestowed upon him by Allah. . . . How to initiate the revival of Islam? A vanguard must set out with this determination (i.e., of bringing total submission to Allah into a "concrete form") and then keep going, marching through the vast ocean of *jāhiliyyah* which encompasses the entire world. During its course, this vanguard, while distancing itself somewhat aloof from this all-encompassing

> *jāhiliyyah* should also retain contacts with it. . . . The milestones (i.e., along the path) will necessarily be determined in the light of the first source of this faith—the Noble Qur'an—and from its basic teachings.[11]

President Nasser regarded the Muslim Brotherhood, and the ideological work of Quṭb, especially, as hostile and subversive. Many members were imprisoned. But followers made hand copies of Quṭb's work and secretly shared them, so that *Milestones* became a sort of manual of Islamic revival. Because of the book, Quṭb was arrested in 1965, condemned to death and executed in 1966. He was buried in an unmarked grave. Nevertheless, he became an authentic martyr of Islamic revival, and his reputation has continued to grow to the present day. Quṭb's *Milestones* was a major text for the extremist groups that arose in Egypt in the 1970s, and the assassins of Sadat took it to heart as a program for dealing with the *jāhiliyyah* that they considered modern "Pharaonic" Egypt to be. Quṭb is thought by many to have become rigid and intolerant in his final years and some of his most extremist followers certainly embody those traits.

Whenever I attend Islamic conferences in North America I find copies of *Milestones* available for sale in abundant supply. Muslim college and university students, especially, herald its virtues as a blueprint for making what Quṭb called *hijra* ("emigration") from the world of *jāhiliyyah* to the society of authentic Muslim faith and order, just as Muhammad and his companions emigrated from Mecca to Medina in the great Hijra to establish the umma in 622. Quṭb's idea of *hijra* is that true Muslims must create a provisional society separate from the structures of *jāhiliyyah* and develop a disciplined core that will carry on the struggle, indeed the *jihād,* required to transform the world according to Islamic principles. Many Muslims have been inspired by Sayyid Quṭb's example and his idea of working toward that end by founding a wide variety of movements that usually qualify in the world media as "fundamentalist," whatever their specific programs and methods, whether gradualist or militant.

Sayyid Quṭb's legacy in the Islamic revival is matched by few others. However, mention should be made of Ali Shari'ati (1933–1977), the Western-educated Iranian intellectual whose writings did much to inspire the Iranian Islamic revolution under the leadership of Ayatollah Khomeini. As the American specialist on Shi'ism Abdulaziz A. Sachedina has argued persuasively, Shari'ati succeeded in turning Shi'ite concerns from quietist to activist forms, reflecting and indeed replicating the force and focus of early Shi'ism.[12]

A final figure, introduced briefly earlier, is Abū Alā Mawdūdī (1904–1979) of Pakistan, founder of the powerful and influential Jamaat-i-Islami, a strongly ideological and political Islamist movement whose activities have a global scope. Mawdūdī wrote many influential books and a commentary on the Qur'an. Some of his ideas influenced Quṭb, who read the Pakistani reformer's works. Mawdūdī also experienced persecution and imprisonment for his principles, but the outcome was far different in that he and his movement succeeded in gaining the backing of many key Pakistanis, who have been and still are dedicated to islamizing that country, which had its origins as an Islamic state after World War II.[13]

## ISLAM AND THE STATUS OF WOMEN

Perhaps no subject attracts the attention of Western observers of Islam and Muslims as much as the status of women within what is perceived to be a strongly male-dominated system of beliefs, practices, and social institutions. Western media often focus, for example, on the practice of seclusion of females and requiring them to cover their bodies completely and conceal their faces with a veil. This practice is known as *purdah* in South Asia and *ḥijāb* in Arabic, and it has various degrees of observance, from a total concealing of the person from view—which may extend to being sequestered in private quarters at all times—to simply covering the hair with a scarf while pursuing an independent social and business life in public. The Qur'an prescribes veiling in Sūra 33:53, but some commentators believe that the passage applied only to the Prophet's wives, who were subject to much public annoyance in the center of things in Medina. "When you ask any of the wives of the Prophet for something, ask from behind a curtain (*ḥijāb*). That is purer for your hearts and for their hearts."[14] In any event, veiling of the face and head was practiced in the ancient Near East long before Islam, and it seems also to have been practiced by the upper classes in Arabia, too.

Another topic that arouses emotions is Islam's permitting males to have up to four concurrent wives, while females may marry only one spouse. Moreover, Muslim males may marry Jewish and Christian women, whereas Muslim females may wed only Muslims. Divorce, which is permitted for both men and women, is in practice generally much easier for males to obtain. And although most marriages in Muslim societies are arranged by the parents or other guardians, males usually have more freedom than females in choosing a spouse.

In very conservative and traditional Muslim societies, such as Saudi Arabia, females and males are rigidly separated in schools, mosques, and the workplace. Women are not permitted to drive or to go about uncovered in public, a circumstance that led to a bold demonstration by Saudi women during the Persian Gulf crisis of 1990–1991, when a number of them drove vehicles in direct violation of the law.

Westerners are often very critical of Islam for its treatment of women. This is often deeply resented by Muslims as meddlesome, hypocritical, inaccurate, and even sinful. Males and females, according to Muslim teaching, are of equal status before God and enjoy equal religious duties and privileges. The Qur'an explicitly addresses both males and females in important passages, as in the following verse concerning the virtues of true Muslims:

> For Muslim men and women—
> For believing men and women,
> For devout men and women,
> For truthful men and women,
> For men and women who are
> Patient and constant, for men
> And women who humble themselves,
> For men and women who give
> In charity, for men and women

> Who fast (and deny themselves),
> For men and women who
> Engage much in Allah's praise—
> For them has Allah prepared
> Forgiveness and great reward. (Sūra 33:35, A. Y. Ali tr.)

This and other Qur'anic passages indicate a balanced relationship of the sexes before God. Contemporary Muslim thinkers, and especially feminists, have devoted considerable attention to the Qur'an's teachings regarding sex and gender matters and have found it often to be at odds with the frankly male chauvinist and patriarchal institutions and customs of Islamic societies since early times.

There is no question that females around the world, and in different societies and cultures, have most often occupied positions of inferior status and been made objects of abuse at the hands of males and male-dominated institutions. Judaism, Christianity, and Islam, each in their own ways, have sorry records on treatment of and attitudes toward females. The emancipation of women in Western countries is a relatively recent development and is still unfolding. So when Westerners heap criticism on Islam and Muslims for their sex and gender customs and practices, they often forget that their own histories have contained similarly unjust and abusive assumptions and practices that do not reflect the highest aspirations of their faiths' teachings. This observation is not assuming that because one group's experience is questionable another's is thereby absolved of responsibility for its own sins. Rather it is to provide a context for judgment and for viewing change over time.

Feminism in the Islamic world is often dated to the nineteenth century, when Egypt, especially, came into contact with the West and sent many of its citizens to Europe for modern education, especially in science and technology. The discussions about women's rights were usually carried on in the context of Islamic family law as Western legal systems began to be known and adapted to Middle Eastern countries, largely as a result of imperialism. Muhammad 'Abduh, who was introduced in Chapter 14, called for a reform in Islam's treatment of females in line with Qur'anic teachings, which he saw as differing considerably in favor of women's rights compared to the unhappy status of women in actual Muslim societies of the nineteenth century. He observed that

> the Muslims have erred in the education and training of women, and not teaching them about their rights; and we have failed to follow the guidance of our religion, becoming an argument against it.[15]

As was shown in Chapter 6, with the quoted passage from 'Abduh's Qur'an commentary condemning the practice of polygamy, the great scholar did not shrink from controversy. His views on polygamy and other aspects of Muslim law influenced his contemporary Qāsim Amīn (ca. 1863–1908), who took up the feminist cause in Arab society as a whole, beyond the theological and legal context on which 'Abduh focused. Amīn's 1899 book, *The Emancipation of Women* (*Tasrīr al-mar'a*), created a great controversy and instigated passionate debate in Egypt and beyond both for and against his views. The book called for removing the veil (*ḥijāb*), educating females, outlawing polygamy and divorce by repudiation (*ṭālaq*), and granting equal rights with men. All of these things had been suggested and discussed well before Amīn's time, but his book brought them to a focus during a period of great change, when modern Western ideas were circulating in Egypt and other Islamic countries and traditionalists were feeling increasingly set upon by the new wave of social reformist discourse. As Leila Ahmed, an Egyptian specialist on Women's Studies now teaching in America, has written in her book *Women and Gender in Islam: Historical Roots of a Modern Debate,*

> The anger and passion Amīn's work provoked become intelligible only when one considers not the substantive reforms for women that he advocated but rather, first, the symbolic reform—the abolition of the veil—that he passionately urged and, second, the reforms, indeed the fundamental changes in culture and society, that he urged upon society as a whole and that he contended it was essential for the Egyptian nation, and Muslim countries generally, to make. The need for a general cultural and social transformation is the central thesis of the book, and it is within this thesis that the arguments regarding women are embedded: changing customs regarding women and changing their costume, abolishing the veil in particular, were key in the author's thesis, to bringing about the desired general social transformation.[16]

It was not until long after Qāsim Amīn's death when upper-class women in Egypt were freed from wearing the veil. The leading and probably most widely known Muslim feminist of the time was the Egyptian Madame Hūdā Sha'rāwī (1879–1947). At no point in her long and influential career as a feminist reformer did her activism appear more dramatically than on the day in May of 1923 when she and a friend returned from the International Women's Alliance meeting in Rome. Upon alighting from the train at Cairo station, the two took off their veils. Applause broke out among the waiting women, some of whom also removed their veils.[17] This highly symbolic act marked an opening of the way for women in Egypt and other Muslim countries.

In 1926 secondary education for girls was introduced with a curriculum equivalent to that for boys. In the intervening years, Egyptian women—at least of the urban higher classes—gained considerable ground with respect to rights and lifestyle options. This has been true also of other urbanized regions of the Islamic world, such as in Iraq, Syria, Algeria, prerevolutionary Iran, Pakistan, Bangladesh, Malaysia, and Indonesia. But the vast majority of Muslim women experience more traditional and patriarchal forms of social life, which the Islamic revival has reinforced in its zeal to institute Sharī'a-minded ways, if not at the legislative level, then at least in disciplined subcommunities of strict observance.

If "feminism" in a Muslim region may be said to have appeared first in late nineteenth century Egypt, "*Islamic* feminism" is a term that started to circulate widely only recently. There is a rich and varied women's movement across the Muslim world that seeks liberation and improvement of conditions according to Islamic principles. That is, Muslim feminists, whether male or female, generally reject Western forms of women's liberation as incompatible with Islam. Modernization is one thing and it generally is acceptable to these people, whereas Westernization is not. Whether the one can be enjoyed without the acceptance of the other is, of course, a vexed issue with numerous levels of discourse not limited to sex and gender roles and rights. As Yvonne Haddad writes, in her survey article on the subject "The Global Islamic Feminist Movement,"

> Islamic feminism is the latest phase in the struggle for women's liberation in the Muslim world. While some have dismissed the term as an oxymoron, it has become the identity of choice for some Muslim scholars and activists both in the United States and overseas.
>
> It was coined in the 1990s, in the milieu of the UN's Fourth World Conference on Women in Beijing, whose slogan was "Women's Rights are Human Rights."[18]

Today there is much interest in and dedication to Islamic feminism as the best chance for women's rights and for improvement of life across the globe for all Muslims, regardless of gender. The amount of new books, articles, Web site forums, and conferences on the subject is growing exponentially. There is no unified definition of the subject, because some Muslim feminists seek development of their discourse and practices fully within the Islamic heritage, whereas others, as Haddad observes, "seek change through recourse to secular ideas as well as those who attack the faith as misogynist at its core." The Muslim feminists developing their agenda fully within the faith community continue to respect and follow the Qur'an as the highest standard of truth and ethics, although they do have strong motivations to overcome patriarchal interpretations and legal applications of it.

It must be remembered that Islam is, at base, a profound religious belief and action system with great spiritual appeal to both women and men. As was suggested above, the original teachings of Islam, as contained in the Qur'anic revelation, may be seen to be quite liberating to women, whereas the subsequent history of the umma saw the triumph of absolute male domination, not only of the institutions of Islamic civilization but also of the sources, principles, and procedures of its discourse. Muslim feminists—that is, sincere Muslim monotheists who believe in the truth of the Qur'an's message and Muhammad's teaching—are calling for a return to the Qur'an as the ultimate and sufficient source for a renewed and egalitarian Islamic social order where males and females enjoy equal dignity and rights. Such Muslim reformers tend to accept basic traditional aspects of Islamic social and family life, so long as they are not left solely in the hands of males or observed without flexibility and informed consent. Thus it may be that a Muslim woman will feel called to wear the veil, or enter into a marriage where she will be in charge of domestic matters as a fulltime occupation. But some reformers insist that Muslim women should have a choice within a sufficiently broad range of options for living life Islamically.

It is worth repeating, however, that vast numbers of Muslims, including women, continue to embrace the traditional ways with respect to sex and gender roles. The 1970s saw the return of the veil in many Islamic regions where it had been abandoned for years. The reasons for this visible affirmation of Islamic identity are complex and varied, but they are closely related to the global Islamic revival, which we surveyed earlier in this chapter. In Iran, the *chador* (a black cloth that completely covers the female head and body) is required for all women in public; some women accept this as appropriate, while many others submit lest they suffer severe punishment at the hands of zealous male enforcers. In other places, where the veil is not required, many Muslim women nevertheless wear it—at least so far as covering their hair in public—as a way of conforming to strict piety and thus escaping criticism and being considered un-Islamic. And many women find very modest dress and covering of the hair, if not the face, to be liberating and preferable to the Western sexist preoccupation with physical appearance and attracting men.

The increasing numbers of Muslims in the West is providing a variety of challenges for traditional Muslims. It is also producing new possibilities for those who want the spiritual rewards of Islam along with lifestyles in keeping with free acceptance of modernity and pluralism in secular societies where religious people sustain their own systems of community and faith with tolerance for each other. With this observation, we move to a consideration of the unprecedented growth of Muslim populations in the West, especially North America.

## ISLAM AND MUSLIMS IN NORTH AMERICA

The European exploration, settling, and development of the Americas occurred during a period when Islamic political power and intellectual creativity experienced a steady decline in most regions of the Dār al-Islām. Although Europeans and Muslims of North Africa, the Nile-to-Oxus regions, and South and Southeast Asia would often be obliged to deal with each other (at times amicably and at others antagonistically), the Americas were the West's own preserve for exploitation of natural (and human) resources and the spreading of Christianity and European civilization. And although Muslims were occasionally present in the Western hemisphere, substantial numbers arrived only under the conditions of slavery, which, in the lands that became the United States, lasted from the early 1600s until abolition in 1863. Slavery had an even earlier beginning in Spanish America and was finally abolished during the nineteenth century.

Scholars estimate that between 14 percent and 20 percent of African slaves brought to the Americas were Muslim. Surviving accounts from the American South reveal that Muslim slaves, including some with Arabic literacy, struggled to sustain their religious beliefs and practices in a very adverse environment. We read of slaves who refused to eat pork or drink alcohol.[19] In the twentieth century, African Americans have steadily increased their sense of African cultural and spiritual traditions, including, for many, a desire to recover a lost Islamic heritage. These and other factors have caused the population of African American Muslims now to number as much as a third of the total Muslim population in the United States.

### *Muslim Immigration to North America: Some Sociological Generalizations*

Middle Eastern Muslims, mostly unskilled and uneducated laborers from the Syrian regions of the Arab world, began arriving in America in the late nineteenth century.[20] After World War I many more immigrants arrived. Following a cessation during World War II, Muslim immigration, mostly from Arab countries but also from Eastern Europe and the Soviet regions, picked up again from the mid-1940s to the mid-1960s. This third "wave" (as the specialist on Muslims in America Yvonne Yazbeck Haddad characterizes the phases)[21] of immigrants was generally better educated and more skilled than the earlier waves. Although economic motivations have always been central in immigration patterns to America, the third wave of Muslim immigration was often motivated, also, by the desire to escape political oppression and persecution. Since 1967, when new U.S. immigration laws took effect, immigrants of all kinds have included a high proportion of well-educated professionals who speak English and have a sophisticated, global perspective.

Sharon McIrvin Abu-Laban, a Canadian sociologist, has divided Muslim immigrants to North America into three cohort types: "Pioneer" families (nineteenth century to World War II), "Transitional" families (post–World War II to 1967), and "Differentiated" families (1968 to the present).[22] The pioneer cohort represents the first two waves of immigrants, introduced above. The early generations were disproportionately male, usually without knowledge of English, and unskilled. Although these people had a strong Muslim identity, there was not much opportunity for Islamic instruction and guidance. When mosque communities were eventually established, they were as much community centers as places of prayer. They resembled other American religious congregations in this regard more than traditional mosques. For these early males especially, Muslim spouses were in short supply. Therefore, many married outside the faith if they did not succeed in acquiring a spouse from back home. Succeeding generations of the pioneer cohort experienced erosion of their linguistic heritages, greater intermarriage with non-Muslims, and general assimilation to the American way of life. Abu-Laban tells the story of a third-generation pioneer Muslim student, who remarked after learning that Muslims were forbidden to drink alcohol: "Beer? What's wrong with beer? What do you mean we aren't supposed to drink beer?"[23] The pioneer cohort, which continues to reproduce itself, is not receptive to the more traditionalist, nonassimilated ways of Muslim immigrants who have arrived more recently.

Abu-Laban's "transitional" cohort, whose first numbers arrived between World War II and 1967, included many students from Arab countries and South Asia. Most were males from elite backgrounds who, to the extent that they remained in North America, constituted the first significant "brain drain" from their native countries. There has been a tendency to characterize the transitional Muslim immigrants as "'Īd Muslims," that is, those who attend the mosque and participate in religious observances only at the two festivals of the Islamic year. As with the first cohort, this one also experienced large-scale marriage with non-Muslims, thus increasing assimilation. The transitional cohort, especially in the second generation, has had to face increasing anti-Muslim sentiment, as expressed in media stereotyping and biased curricular materials and unpleasant encounters in school and the workplace. Abu-Laban observes that such difficulties afflict the transitional generation severely, due to their relative lack of strong Islamic institutional affiliations, whether in the traditional family or the mosque.

The third and largest cohort is the differentiated Muslim families that started to arrive in the United States, particularly, in 1968 (when U.S. immigration laws were liberalized) and continue to arrive, from many different countries. A general characteristic shared by this cohort is a general lack of interest in assimilating into American life, with a distinct preference for maintaining their own ethnic and religious ways. This cohort has come into existence during the period of the worldwide Islamic revival and frequently shares many of its objectives. Among these is Islamic dress, especially women's, which often includes a complete covering of the hair and sometimes (although rarely) even a veil over the face. Strong emphasis on *ḥalāl,* that is, permitted foods, is another signifier of the differentiated cohort. The increased organizing of Islamic centers and the construction of mosques—often with adjoining school facilities—although not limited to the differentiated cohort by any means, is nevertheless evidence of Muslims feeling the need for their own space, where community formation and sustenance can occur.

Immigrant Muslims in North America outnumber all others, with African American Muslims in second place regarding numbers, and indigenous others—mostly white, middle-class people—in third. The umma ideal of Islam has always emphasized egalitarianism and mutual loyalty and support. But for the first time, the bewildering variety and diversity of Muslims from around the world are represented in a common social and political environment, as in North America (where the differences between Canada and the United States are not significant and free association across borders is obtained). It is ironic that a microcosm of the global umma should find its first realization in an environment that is non-Islamic, pluralistic, free, and highly secularized. Indeed it could not have happened otherwise: It is one thing for the world's Muslims to love each other and cooperate during the pilgrimage, but it is quite another for them to come together into a multicultural and multinational federation under their own auspices. The obstacles are too great. But Muslims migrating to these shores as members of both religious and ethnic minorities are automatically thrust into the free market of religious affiliation and preaching that has characterized religious life in North America since European contact.

The religious free market in America is unsettling and even threatening to Muslim sensibilities, who usually prefer a situation where their community is in a superior position of power and protected from attempts at proselytization from Christian missionaries, especially. But Muslims also realize that the free market can be a distinct advantage to their interests, because it protects them from persecution and restrictions and allows them latitude to spread their own message through preaching and example.

The majority of immigrant Muslims have come from the Arab world, South Asia (Afghanistan, Bangladesh, India, and Pakistan), Iran, and Turkey. But some large

The Islamic Center of Greater Toledo, located near the intersection of two major highways in Perrysburg, Ohio. The center's large membership includes people from more than thirty different national and ethnic backgrounds. (*Source:* Frederick Mathewson Denny)

Islamic centers, such as the Islamic Center of Greater Toledo, in Ohio, and the Islamic Center of Southern California, in Los Angeles, have more than thirty different nationalities and ethnicities represented in their memberships. It is not uncommon to find mosques where Sunnīs and Shī'ites worship together and conduct their community affairs in harmony and with common purpose. But it is also not uncommon to find ethnic mosques and Islamic centers—Turkish, Iranian, Pakistani, and others—where other Muslims are welcome, but where they also might feel somewhat uncomfortable because of a strange language, different customs, clannishness, and poor prospects of ever becoming intimately connected with the group. African American Muslims and immigrants recognize their common Islamic bond and amicably worship together, but they do not often intermarry or have much social contact.

### *African Americans and Islam*

The relatively large numbers of African American Muslims is due to at least three main causes. The first is the increasing consciousness of an Islamic heritage from Africa before slavery, as was mentioned earlier. The second is the proliferation of new African American religious movements with some identification with Islam in this century. The third is the trend of African American conversion to Islam in prisons.

A strong reaction against white, Christian culture has often marked the rise of new African American religious movements. An early example is the Moorish Science movement founded in Newark, New Jersey, in 1913 by Timothy Drew (1886–1929), a North Carolinian of humble beginnings. Noble Drew Ali, as his followers came to call him, taught that black Americans must discover their true identity and destiny by means of an educative process centered in learning *The Holy Koran,* an idiosyncratic text unrelated to the Qur'an of Islam. Noble Drew Ali considered his people to be "Asiatics," or "Moors" (from Morocco), and not "negroes." The movement spread among northern cities in the United States, but soon split up and now exists only marginally.

In 1930 a peddler—whether from Arabia, Turkey, Iran, or elsewhere is uncertain—named variously Wallace D. Fard, Walli Farad, Farad Mohammad, and other names, began preaching in Detroit a message aimed at black people. According to this message, black people had originally been Muslims, but due to white treachery and oppression had lost their identity and purpose. Fard called the blacks the "Lost–Found Nation of Islam in the Wilderness of North America" and sought to include them in a new movement based on education, a common ritual, and strong community defense. After Fard's mysterious disappearance in 1934, one of his leading associates, Elijah Poole (1897–1975), assumed leadership under the name Elijah Muhammad. He held sway over the growing movement in an absolute manner until his death.

Although the name *Islam* is used to identify the movement, in fact the Nation of Islam from its beginning bore little, if any, resemblance to true Islam. For one thing, members came to regard W. D. Fard as Allah incarnate and Elijah Muhammad as his prophet. Moreover, the supremacy of the blacks was assumed, with the whites regarded as devils. But at the center of the movement, whatever its ties to authentic Islamic convictions, was hard work and commitment to bettering the lot of black people in America and beyond. Although mostly poor people joined and found new lives of dedication and accomplishment, upper-class blacks also joined and provided the movement with a modicum of respectability among the African American community. The larger American society, however, regarded the "black Muslims," as they came to be called, as a threat to whites and the body politic. Members were investigated and observed by law enforcement agencies throughout the country. Even so, the movement made headway, especially in the development of schools, strong family life, and black business enterprises. Elijah Muhammad was a stern leader who taught his followers the virtues of thrift, abstinence, hard work, and separation from the corrupt society surrounding them, which he prophesied would be punished at the end of time.

The Nation of Islam had organizations—represented by mosques and temples—throughout urban America by the 1960s, when it reached its peak. One of Elijah Muhammad's most outstanding ministers was a former convict, Malcolm Little (1925–1965), who learned about Islam in prison and set about transforming his life, through study and activism, as a member of Elijah Muhammad's movement. He received the name "Malcolm X," thus, as with so many other converts to the movement, ridding himself of his white, "slave" name. Malcolm X's stern visage, in newspapers and television reports, came to represent the radical black power movement across the United States by the early 1960s. African Americans came to regard Malcolm X as a noble and courageous spokesman who militantly confronted the white establishment. He provided a stark contrast to the Reverend Martin Luther King, Jr., who advocated nonviolence in the struggle for racial justice.

After being suspended from his role as one of Elijah Muhammad's top ministers in 1963 (because of a scandal caused by Malcolm X's declaring, upon President John F. Kennedy's assassination, that "the chickens have come home to roost"), Malcolm X traveled to the Middle East and completed the *ḥajj* at Mecca. The *ḥajj* experience, vividly described in his autobiography, of mixing amicably and joyfully with Muslims of all colors and nationalities transformed Malcolm X's awareness and led him to embrace authentic Islam. He broke from the Nation of Islam and founded the Muslim Mosque, Inc., in New York City. But his leadership was short lived, because he was assassinated in 1965 by two members of the Nation of Islam. Since that time, Malcolm X's reputation as a courageous and visionary proponent of racial justice and civil rights has steadily grown. He is now regarded throughout the umma as one of the twentieth century's most significant Muslim reformers. His example has led multitudes of African Americans to accept Islam.

There are other African American Islamic movements, but the Nation of Islam had the greatest influence. In 1975 Elijah Muhammad died whereupon his son Wallace (Warith) Deen Muhammad assumed leadership, having been previously designated by his father. Warith Deen, who had studied Arabic and Islamic subjects in a thorough manner, quickly and decisively led the movement in the direction of normative Islam, replacing his father's teachings with the Qur'an and divesting the movement of its racist exclusivism. The name of the movement was dropped and replaced by successive others, including "The World Community of Islam in the West" and "The American Muslim Mission." Warith Deen Muhammad and his followers finally decided that the members should simply call themselves "Muslims" and blend into the umma. Warith Deen Muhammad resigned as leader of the approximately ca. 2.5-million-member organization, currently known as the American Society of Muslims, in 2003. The weekly newspaper the *Muslim Journal* continues to be published in Chicago and covers news of interest to all Muslims in the United States and abroad. Warith Deen Muhammad does not have the commanding presence of Malcolm X or the spellbinding rhetorical skills of Minister Louis Farrakhan. But he does possess genuine charisma in his evident spirituality, combined with a plainspoken, nonflamboyant personal style.

African American Muslims, the vast majority of whom are now mainline Sunni Muslims, do not quite blend into the umma, although great progress has been made in that direction. There is still a Nation of Islam, with Minister Louis Farrakhan at its head. The old doctrines have been modified and softened somewhat, but the emphasis is still on economic and social justice for blacks worldwide, who are perceived to be oppressed by white people. Minister Farrakhan is a charismatic speaker who sometimes commands wide media attention because of his support of political candidates and controversial statements, which have been characterized as both racist and anti-Semitic. Such wide coverage has helped sustain an image of "black Muslims" as a dangerous and subversive element of society by the larger American public. Membership in the continuing Nation of Islam is largely from the poor, unemployed sector, whereas the ongoing component that embraced normative Islam tends to be middle class. However, there are indicators that the Nation of Islam may be on the brink of embracing mainstream Islam.

### *Muslims in Corrections*

The third major cause of African American participation in Islamic movements is the high rate of conversion in U.S. prisons. A disproportionately large number of minorities and poor people are involved in the U.S. criminal justice system. One authoritative source has reported that "almost one in four (23 percent) black men in the age group 20–29 is either in prison, jail, on probation, or parole on any given day."[24] Many people of the so-called American "underclass" have come to view time in prison as an unavoidable part of life. The question for corrections policy makers is whether prisons should rehabilitate or punish, not to mention removing dangerous and offensive people from society.

One leading Muslim prison chaplain, Imam Warithu-Deen Umar, formerly a high official with the State of New York Department of Correctional Services and president of the National Association of Muslim Chaplains, has counselled that rehabilitation of many offenders is not possible because they have not yet been *habilitated.* But Islam has proven to be an appealing path for many inmates, especially African Americans, who find fellowship, protection, a new identity, and hope for a productive and disciplined life in submission to Allah and following his ways. Although a certain percentage of converts to Islam (or other religions) in prison is an expression of "jail-house religion" (defined as a temporary phenomenon with various manifestations), estimates of up to a third of African American inmates converting to Islam make an enduring commitment that continues to deepen after their release from prison.

The strict observance of Islamic practices can consume an individual and totally reorient life. Prison time is often harsh and boring. But a strong commitment to a demanding religious regimen—including the study of Arabic and the reading of the Qur'an and *ḥadīth*—in fellowship with a powerful support group can transform the prison experience into a positive, even triumphant struggle against adversity and aimlessness. A sort of habilitation to a fulfilling way of life is brought about that permits the individual to make a new start. Prison administrations, although once fearful of the many Nation of Islam members in their facilities in the 1950s and 1960s, have come to respect Muslims in prison for the positive dimensions of their lives, which complement and even augment the objectives of the corrections programs.

A major concern of Muslims in prison is rights to such things as: regular prayer times, to be served *ḥalāl* food, to wear Islamic garb, and to grow facial hair. The record of granting such rights is mixed around the nation, but steady progress has occurred with an impressive record of successful litigation to show for it.[25] The prospects for Muslim inmates vary according to how long the sentence is and where it is being served. In the state of New York, for example, there are more than three dozen professional Muslim chaplains and a record of humane regard for prisoners' religious rights. New York City has a similar record, and its head chaplain, a Muslim, is also supervisor of the chaplains representing the other religions. But other states have not advanced as far as New York in providing adequate services and facilities for prisoners. Eliminating pork, for example, from prison diets would entail an expensive and controversial shift of food suppliers. But Muslims are increasingly demanding *ḥalāl* food—not just a porkless diet, but foods that have been properly prepared for Muslim consumption. Moreover, the observance of the Ramadan fast requires a special arrangement for Muslims to take their meals at times that conflict with prison schedules.

The length of the prison sentence has a significant impact on the quality of inmate life. Short termers need to prepare themselves for productive, disciplined lives after release—a concern that Muslim chaplains take seriously in their counseling and preaching. Long termers, however, need to find a way of dealing with despair and hopelessness. Islam's doctrine of forgiveness and divine recompense helps many lifers to live as full and hopeful a life in prison as possible, with the expectation of a blessed afterlife.

A great challenge to the Muslim community as a whole in the United States is the disappointingly high rate of recidivism of released Muslim inmates. The main reason for this is the lack of special programs and facilities, such as Muslim halfway houses, to help former inmates make a successful transition to life outside the corrections facility. The strong bonds of the prison-based Muslim community, once left behind, are not replaced by a similarly disciplined structure of living and learning on the outside. The mosque congregations, Islamic centers, and other Muslim organizations in the United States are beginning to recognize the urgent need for action and resources to help fellow Muslims in distress, and progress is being made.

### *Establishing an Islamic Environment in North America*

Muslims in North America, as across the global Muslim Umma, observe the five Pillars of Islam as Muslims everywhere do: (1) reciting frequently the shahada, a witnessing to the oneness of God and the messengerhood of the Prophet Muhammad; (2) observing the five daily *salat* worship services, whether in a formal mosque—particularly for Friday noon worship—or at home or work; (3) the annual giving of zakāt (alms); (4) the annual fasting (sawm) during the holy month of Ramadan; and (5) the Hajj, or "Pilgrimage," to Mecca once during one's lifetime, if resources, health, and other circumstances permit.

Increasingly, Muslim cemeteries are being established in both Canada and the United States, indicating a new dimension of integration into the wide range of funeral and memorializing practices of the general population, a kind of being "planted" as an enduring faith community that will be generally recognized and respected, as have earlier religious populations since the early settlements began. Islamic schools are also growing in number and curricular options, often associated with mosque congregations. Sufi mystical societies also exist, as in most Muslim lands, and although that dimension of Muslim spirituality is not required by the Shari'a Law, or the Qur'an, it does provide deep devotional opportunities and sustains a joyful faith while also fulfilling the standard beliefs and practices of all Muslims. As the North American Muslim population continues to grow and prosper, it will increasingly be accepted as a valuable part of spiritual and civic life as a whole. Jews, Christians, and Muslims increasingly engage in interreligious dialogue, and there are fine examples of mutual help and support when difficult situations may develop for whatever reason.

The great challenge to Muslims in North America is to establish an Islamic environment so as to be able to live securely with Islamic norms of belief and behavior. This is an exceedingly difficult task, for obvious reasons. But major Islamic organizations, such as the Islamic Society of North America (ISNA), are struggling to mobilize support and resources for Islamic education, community building, interest-free loans, responsible interpretations and applications of Islamic law within the constraints of North American life, and other things.

ISNA is the largest Muslim umbrella organization in North America, with individual and institutional members all over Canada and the United States. Its annual convention attracts several thousand people who spend two-and-a-half days attending panels, joining in the daily *ṣalāt* services, and engaging in endless conversations and debates about the progress of building the umma here. Booths containing vast displays of books, cassettes, Islamic clothing, *halāl* food suppliers, jewelry, perfume, sanitary facilities (for ablutions and toilet use in the home), Islamic banking and financial services, schools, and special-interest organizations like Muslim Scouting and relief efforts for Somalis, Kurds, Kashmiris, and other oppressed Muslim peoples are set up at the convention.

It is too early to predict how North America's Muslims will organize themselves in the long run. Other religious traditions—Protestants, Catholics, and Jews—have sorted out according to denominational and sect-like entities. But Islam, although it has sects, does not have denominational groupings that would compare with Baptists, Methodists, Episcopalians, Lutherans, and Congregationalists. Protestant denominations have emerged from doctrinal differences. Muslims do not have the kinds of theological and doctrinal differences that are found in Christianity. Nor does Islamic liturgy admit of significant variations across sectarian groupings. As Shī'ites and Sunnīs often say, there are historic and continuing political differences between them, but the *dīn,* the religious belief and action system, is essentially one.

Jews in North America, however, have subdivided into denominations: Orthodox, Conservative, Reconstructionist, and Reformed. Jews do not have major differences over theological issues that Christians have; but then, theology in Judaism, as in Islam, has traditionally been a much less important matter than in Christianity. There are significant differences between Jewish communities on details of worship and the permissibility of innovations, on sex–gender roles, on the extent to which kosher regulations are observed, and other things. Islam, like Judaism, is strongly concerned with orthopraxy. Unlike Judaism, in Islam there is near consensus on worship and the

Imam Siraj Wahhaj, of Masjid Taqwa, Brooklyn, New York, addressing the audience at the annual meeting of the Islamic Society of North America in Dayton, Ohio, in 1991. (*Source:* Frederick Mathewson Denny)

regulation of social life, including sex–gender roles and responsibilities. If major and enduring Islamic associations are successful in North America, they may resemble denominations in their organizational and outreach concerns, but they will not exhibit diversity of doctrine or worship, even though they will spread across a spectrum from liberal to traditionalist in matters of social life and regulation of the sexes. The more assimilated and "Americanized" Muslim communities, such as the large and independent-minded ones in Toledo and Los Angeles, will provide models for the liberal approach, whereas the traditionalist types, such as are often found in university communities where large Muslim foreign student populations exist, will uphold old-fashioned, unassimilated values and practices.

No one is certain about how many Muslims live in North America, but a recent reasonable estimate is 2,54,000 in the United States and 657,000 in Canada.[26] The number is steadily growing, due to conversion, immigration, and birth. Soon the Muslim populations of both the United States and Canada will likely be larger than their Jewish populations. Conversion to Islam should increase steadily, as more North Americans come to learn of its strong ethic of social justice, its ideals of global community and egalitarianism, and its powerful commitment to solid family structures and morality.

Islam and Muslims are still somewhat exotic presences in North America, but their domestication is gradually taking place. We have become used to visiting mosques and other Islamic congregational settings over the years in traditional locales in the Middle East and South and Southeast Asia. Visiting most mosques in North America is, at this time, like visiting mosques in a Muslim country. But when one visits Friday worship at the strongly African American congregation in Oakland, California, for example, and hears the American *imām* deliver the sermon in English, with appropriate references to American life and issues, one begins to sense that one is in an environment that is both Islamic and American. This is even more evident after the service, when one enjoys greeting and mingling with congregants—male and female—outside in the beautiful courtyard where food, books, and other items are sold after Friday *alāt.* The Oakland community has a mosque and adjoining fulltime Sister Clara Muhammad Islamic School (a name that came from the old Nation of Islam's successful educational venture) in buildings that once belonged to a Christian congregation. Looking up at the Gothic, arched windows while hearing the chanting of the Arabic Qur'an does not seem at all unusual when seated amidst the congregation, which includes a number of immigrant Muslims as well as African Americans.

## NOTES

1. See Joachim Wach's suggestive article, "The Concept of the 'Classical' in the Study of Religions," in his collection of essays *Types of Religious Experience: Christian and Non-Christian* (Chicago: University of Chicago Press, 1951), pp. 48–57.
2. Martin S. Marty, and R. Scott Appleby, eds. *Fundamentalisms Observed,* "The Fundamentalism Project," vol. 1 (Chicago: University of Chicago Press, 1991), pp. viii–ix.

3. Bruce B. Lawrence, *Defenders of God: The Fundamentalist Revolt Against the Modern Age* (San Francisco: HarperSanFrancisco, 1989), p. 27. A reprint, with a new author's preface, was published in 1995 by the University of South Carolina Press. Lawrence places fundamentalism in opposition to modernism and interprets its progress in Christianity, Judaism, and Islam.
4. John O. Voll, "Fundamentalism in the Sunni Arab World: Egypt and the Sudan," in Martin E. Marty and R. Scott Appleby, eds., *Fundamentalisms Observed, op. cit.*, p. 347.
5. *Ibid.*, p. 362.
6. *Ibid.*, quoted from Richard P. Mitchell, *The Society of the Muslim Brothers* (London: Oxford University Press, 1969), p. 14.
7. *Ibid.*, quoted from Hasan al-Bannā', *Five Tracts of Hasan Al-Bannā' 1906–1949,* trans. Charles Wendell (Berkeley: University of California Press, 1978), p. 36.
8. A reliable and absorbing account of Sadat's assassination and the movement that was responsible for it is Gilles Kepel's *Muslim Extremism in Egypt: The Prophet and Pharaoh,* trans. Jon Rothschild (Berkeley: University of California Press, 1985).
9. Yvonne Y. Haddad, "Sayyid Quṭb: Ideologue of Islamic Revival," in *Voices of Resurgent Islam,* ed. John L. Esposito (New York: Oxford University Press, 1983), p. 69. I am generally indebted to and closely follow Haddad's interpretation of Quṭb in this section. I have also followed the treatment of Quṭb by John O. Voll in his "Fundamentalism in the Sunni Arab World," *op. cit.*, pp. 369–372.
10. "Fundamentalism in the Sunni Islamic World," *op. cit.*, p. 370.
11. Sayyid Quṭb, *Milestones,* translated from Arabic (Indianapolis, Ind.: American Trust Publications, 1990), pp. 8–9.
12. Abdulaziz A. Sachedina, "Activist Shi'īsm in Iran, Iraq, and Lebanon," in *Fundamentalisms Observed, op. cit.*, pp. 403–456, especially pp. 434–436. See the same author's "Ali Shariati: Ideologue of the Iranian Revolution," in John L. Esposito, ed., *Voices of Resurgent Islam, op. cit.*, pp. 191–214.
13. See Charles J. Adams, "Mawdūdī and the Islamic State," in John L. Esposito, ed., *Voices of Resurgent Islam, op. cit.*, pp. 99–133 and Mumtaz Ahmad, "Islamic Fundamentalism in South Asia: The Jamaat-i-Islami and the Tablighi Jamaat of South Asia," in *Fundamentalisms Observed, op. cit.*, pp. 457–530.
14. As translated by Leila Ahmed in her *Women and Gender in Islam: Historical Roots of a Modern Debate* (New Haven, Conn.: Yale University Press, 1992), p. 54. Ahmed provides a detailed, illuminating discussion of this and related passages.
15. As quoted in translation in John L. Esposito, *Women in Muslim Family Law* (Syracuse: Syracuse University Press, 1982), p. 50. Originally published in 'Abduh's journal, *Al-Manar,* which was published in 1912 in Cairo in a collected edition by Manar Press (although the quoted passage was written around the turn of the century).
16. Leila Ahmed, *Women and Gender in Islam, op. cit.*, pp. 145–146.
17. See *ibid.*, p. 176. Also, Hūdā Sha'rāwī, *Harem Years: The Memoirs of an Egyptian Feminist* (1879–1924), trans. and ed. Margot Badran (New York: The Feminist Press at the City University of New York, 1987), pp. 4, 1129–1130.
18. Posted June 8, 2009 on the website: http://www.themosqueinmorgantown.com/forum/feminism-and-islam

19. See Allan D. Austin's *African Muslims in Antebellum America: A Sourcebook* (New York: Garland Publishers, 1984). Statistical information on numbers of Muslim slaves, their characteristics and places of origin is on pp. 29–36.
20. I am indebted to the following sources for this review of Muslim immigration to America: Abdo A. Elkholy, *The Arab Moslems in the United States* (New Haven, Conn.: College and University Press, 1966), pp. 15–30; Sharon McIrvin Abu-Laban, "Family and Religion among Muslim Immigrants and their Descendants," in *Muslim Families in North America,* ed. Earle H. Waugh, Sharon McIrvin Abu-Laban, and Regula Burckhardt Qureshi (Edmonton: University of Alberta Press, 1991), pp. 12–31; and Yvonne Yazbeck Haddad and Adair T. Lummis, *Islamic Values in the United States: A Comparative Study* (New York: Oxford University Press, 1987), pp. 3–16 and *passim.*
21. *A Century of Islam in America,* "The Muslim World Today," Occasional Paper No. 4 (Washington, D.C.: The Middle East Institute, 1986), p. 2.
22. "Family and Religion among Muslim Immigrants and their Descendants," in *Muslim Families in North America, op. cit.,* pp. 12–26.
23. "Family and Religion," *op. cit.,* p. 17.
24. Marc Mauer, "Young Black Men and the Criminal Justice System," *Corrections Compendium,* XV, no. 2 (March 1990): 4.
25. See Kathleen Moore, "Muslims in Prison: Claims to Constitutional Protection of Religious Liberty," in *The Muslims of America,* ed. Yvonne Yazbeck Haddad (New York: Oxford University Press, 1991), pp. 136–156.
26. As estimated in a comprehensive study of more than 200 countries by The Pew Forum on Religion and Public Life study "Mapping the Global Muslim Population: A Report on the Size and Distribution of the World's Muslim Population," Copyright Pew Research Center 2009, p. 25. www.pewforum.org

CHAPTER

# 16 Whither Islam and the Muslims? Progressive Muslims with a Vision of an "Islam without Borders"

**KEY TERM**

***gharb zadegi***

In 1932 Sir Hamilton Gibb, one of the twentieth century's leading Western historians of Islam, published an edited volume with the title *Whither Islam? A Survey of Modern Movements in the Moslem World.* In his introduction, Gibb sketched what he called the crisis of Islam in the modern era. He predicated his understanding upon a conceptual framework that he called a medieval constitution of Islamic society that was struggling to cope with

> the intrusion of new ideas and new tendencies . . . [that would] inevitably . . . bring about, sometimes with startling suddenness, a whole chain of movements, social, political, economic, and religious, by which its intellectual and material outlook was profoundly stirred. The rapidity with which these movements have manifested themselves of late years, and the violence with which they have at times reacted against old traditions and old customs, have produced throughout the Moslem world a condition of unsettlement and pyschological strain which involuntarily recalls the crisis through which Europe passed during the Renaissance and the Reformation, though, of course, with many special features of its own. It is this unsettlement which constitutes the present-day problem of Islam.[1]

Whereas today most Muslims are strongly in favor of modernization of Muslim societies in the scientific and technological spheres, they are generally opposed to Westernization if that means adopting such perspectives as secularity, universal human rights based on the Enlightenment rather than religion, and equality of the sexes. Gibb wrote that "the impingement of the culture of Western Europe upon the Moslem world has been responsible for the present crisis of Islam."[2] However, in stark contrast to the contemporary situation, Gibb went on to say that "the most remarkable feature of the Moslem world in these early decades of the twentieth century is not that it is becoming westernized, but that it desires to be westernized."[3]

## WESTOXICATION

With respect to the intrusion and importation of Western cultural norms and attitudes into the Muslim world, there has for some time now been a running discourse in Iran about **Westoxication (*gharb zadegi* in Farsi)**, a term coined by the Iranian Heideggerian philosopher Ahmad Fardid in his university lectures. It was Jalal Al-i Ahmad (1921–1969) who made the term popular through his book *Gharbzadagi* (sic) ("Westoxication"), which was banned in prerevolutionary Iran under the Shah.[4] Ahmad's book "alerted us to the onset of a case of terminal cultural cancer," as contemporary Iranian philosopher and progressive Muslim activist Abdolkarim Soroush sees it.

> What Al-i Ahmad meant by Westoxication was the coming of Western customs, manners, and technology, causing eviction from our native home, the sacrifice of our noble and gracious traditions at the feet of the Western practices and industry. It meant the nauseating imitation of everything Western even at the expense of immolating the most eminent cultural assets and legacies of our own: speaking with their tongue, thinking with their brain, looking through their eyes, and wailing their pain.[5]

Soroush discerns two main types of Westoxication. One is acquiesence to Western domination as a "historically determined fate" that cannot be avoided. Islam and Islamic civilization are legacies of the past, now being replaced by a new epoch. The other type is a flexible, critical assessment of Western culture, science, and technology. "It says that a calamity, or to put it more accurately, an accident has occurred but one must keep one's head: The West must be carefully examined but vigorously resisted. The useful elements must be absorbed and the harmful rejected. Traditions must be evoked as a bulwark of resistance, and the slumbering culture must be awakened."[6]

## MODERNITY AND WESTERNIZATION IN THE POST 9/11 WORLD

In some ways the current revitalization of Islam around the world—whether in extremist and fundamentalist ways as addressed in the preceding chapter, or in more moderate and liberal ways—is a rejection of Westernization, while at the same time it is an embracing of modernity in such areas as science, technology, and medicine. Islamic civilization was, during its golden age (ca. 700–1200 C.E.), the world leader in science, mathematics, astronomy, medicine, and other advanced fields. Muslims today have no problem adopting and developing science and technology, even though their modern forms have largely developed in the industrial West. And, as we saw in the preceding chapter, large numbers of Muslims today are migrating to the West and taking their religious and cultural beliefs and values with them. Once Muslims settle in the West, they inevitably adopt and conform to Western patterns of culture and custom in varying degrees.

Also, as we observed in the preceding chapter, the free marketplace of American religion is unsettling and even threatening to some people, particularly immigrants from the Muslim world. Muslims enjoy religious freedom in America as well as in other Western countries, but that does not mean that their life is necessarily easy. For example, Muslims routinely experience Christian proselytization initiatives at greater or lesser levels of energy in varying locales. This is extremely unsettling and stressful, because in countries governed by Islamic law no non-Muslim religions may proselytize among Muslims. Only Muslims may preach their religion publicly and seek converts in countries such as Iran, Saudi Arabia, and Pakistan. There are legal safeguards for religious minorities under the Shari'a, but there are also restrictions that may be traced back to early Islamic history. Of course, the freedom of the Christian evangelist in secular countries is also the freedom of the Muslim missionary who can negotiate the free religious marketplace, too. Muslims actually welcome a great many converts to their community in North America, as in many other parts of the world.

A few years ago, at a Muslim social scientists conference in the Detroit area, a panel on the "domestication" of Islam in North America drew a large audience. During the discussion period, a Muslim of South Asian origin started complaining about the strange messages being propagated by some African American inner-city religious movements claiming to be Muslim. The commentator sharply reminded the assembly that such freelancing with questionable doctrinal content would never be tolerated in a truly Islamic society and should not be in America, either. He declared, with great passion, "Something must be done about this!" The moderator, a longtime resident of the United States but a native of Gambia, gently but firmly responded that if there were an official religious form of enforcement that could do something about this or that, it most assuredly would not be of Islamic persuasion. "We would not even be here having this discussion," he added, were there a religious authority that oversaw and regulated the religious beliefs and activities of American citizens.

Indeed, the moderator concluded that Muslims in North America are enjoying a good life and freedom alongside other Muslims, as well as people of other peaceful religious faiths, because of the First and Fourteenth Amendments, among other things. Then the moderator suggested, "Brother, go out yourself into the streets of Philadelphia, New York, and Washington, D.C., and make your case about true Islam to your brothers and sisters who, in your eyes, are astray. You have every right to do so!" A large number of attendees at the session responded enthusiastically by saying, "Allahu akbar!" ("God is Most Great") three times, meaning strong approval of the moderator's remarks.

Roger Williams (1603?–1683), founder of the Rhode Island colony and its capital, provides in a "Letter to the Town of Providence" (ca. January 1654/55) a model for a religiously pluralistic and tolerant "ship of state" in quite literal terms.

> There goes many a Ship to Sea, with many a Hundred Souls in one Ship, whose Weal and Woe is common; and is a true Picture of a Common-Wealth, or an human Combination, or Society. It hath fallen out sometimes, that both *Papists* and *Protestants, Jews,* and *Turks,* may be embarqued into one Ship. Upon which Supposal, I do affirm, that all the Liberty of Conscience that ever I pleaded for, turns upon these two Hinges, that none of the *Papists, Protestants, Jews,* or *Turks,* be forced to come to the Ship's Prayers or Worship; nor, secondly, compelled from their own particular Prayers or Worship, if they practice any. I further add, that I never denied, that notwithstanding this Liberty, the Commander of this Ship ought to command the Ship's Course; yea, and also to command that Justice, Peace, and Sobriety, be kept and practiced, both among the Seamen and all the Passengers.[7]

The "Turks" in Williams's letter are, of course, the Muslims, who in his era were often characterized according to the real and perceived military threats that they posed for Christendom. There was an Ottoman Turkish siege of Vienna in 1529 and a second in 1683, the year of Williams's death. Both sieges were unsuccessful, but they did greatly alarm Europeans because of the depth of their penetration into the heart of Europe. Europeans have long regarded Islam and Muslims as real and enduring threats to their existence, whereas Muslims have reciprocated by viewing Europeans as "Crusaders" bent on conquering their lands and subjecting them to extreme oppression. The record of relations between Islam and the West is in many ways tragic, with chronic recurrences over centuries. In 1998, Osama bin Laden, the leader of the al-Qaeda terrorist organization, formed the "World Islamic Front for the Jihad ["struggle, holy war"] Against the Jews and the Crusaders." Other Islamist activists also consider Westerners, and particularly Americans, to be modern Crusaders as they have occupied two Muslim countries, Afghanistan and Iraq, beginning in 2001 and 2003, respectively. And the stationing of American military personnel and weapons in Saudi Arabia during the Gulf War of 1991 caused great consternation, resentment, and humiliation among Muslims, who view such an infidel presence in the land of the two holy sanctuaries of Mecca and Medina as a sacrilege. The American military presence in Saudi Arabia was one of the most compelling factors in Osama bin Laden's launching of a terrorist *jihād* against America.

The events of September 11, 2001, changed many things in the world and in Americans' perceptions of the world. However, the causes and dynamics of the destructive attacks were not new, nor did their catastrophic carnage strike some peoples of the developing world as out of the ordinary when placed alongside their own ongoing experiences of deprivation, death, and destruction. Somalia, Sudan, Afghanistan, Rwanda, Kashmir, Palestine, and the Balkans come to mind. Political Islam, including its most extremist, violent forms, has precedents extending back to early Islamic history and such uncompromising puritanical movements as the Kharijites, who attacked and killed fellow Muslims for not being righteous and pious enough. Modern forms may be traced to the Wahhābī reformers of eighteenth century Arabia and their continuing descendants in Saudi Arabia and the al-Qaeda network. The latter's commitment to terrorism against people, Muslims and non-Muslims alike, deemed deserving of destruction is influenced by extremist ideologues such as Sayyid Quṭb (treated in the preceding chapter), the Egyptian Muslim reformist who was executed by President Nasser's government in 1966. Quṭb's legacy continues with great force in the ranks of al-Qaeda and similar movements bent on punishing, in particular, what their followers perceive to be a secular, materialistic, ungodly West and its multitudes of corrupt and misguided Muslim imitators. Although Quṭb did not himself advocate a doctrine calling for the mass killing of unbelievers that al-Qaeda fosters, his extremist teachings about the need for a *jihād* against corrupt Muslim Middle Eastern leaders, as well as non-Muslims, have influenced Muslim terrorists who would go much further than Quṭb prescribed to achieve their goals. The vast majority of Muslims do not consider *jihād* ("effort," "holy war") to be in any way related to terrorism, regardless of how extremists seek to justify such measures as mass killings as an authentic expression of *jihād*. *Jihād* is a sanctified obligation—sometimes characterized as the "sixth Pillar" of Islam—that Muslims must fulfill in a variety of ways, ranging from personal self-discipline in the struggle to be righteous to armed combat, as stipulated in the Shari'a.[8]

Many negative and hurtful things are being said, or thought, about Islam and Muslims in America and around the world. There are abusive and violent assaults on Muslims occurring in North America and Europe, where some elements of the societies are calling for the expulsion of Arabs, Muslims, and people who are thought to resemble them. But positive attitudes and actions are also being directed toward protecting, respecting, and reassuring Arabs and Muslims in America of their worth, their dignity, and their rights as citizens.

Considerable numbers of Muslims now live and prosper in many Western countries, in Europe and the Americas, as well as in Australia. For example, as of 2004 the Muslim population of France was approaching 10 percent. The United States, with as many as six to seven million Muslims, is the closest thing in history to a microcosm of the richly diverse umma, the global Muslim community. Muslims in America include both converts and immigrants in large numbers and from many racial and ethnic groups: African American, South Asian, white, Middle Eastern, and more. Most of the world's Muslims are horrified and disgusted by the events of September 11; additionally, many feel defiled and humiliated by the actions of their extremist coreligionists. Islam was, according to many Muslims' view, to some degree hijacked on September 11 by Osama bin Laden and his supporters, and Islamist terrorism, whether sponsored by al-Qaeda or other organizations, continues to be a major threat in many parts of the world. It will take time and soul-searching to heal great hurts and to remove the additional stigma that Muslims now bear on top of their long, discouraging struggle to be respected, appreciated, and trusted by the rest of the human family.

Islam possesses high spiritual and moral ideals and principles, as has been documented throughout this book, and Muslims have a rich and honorable heritage as one of the greatest and most humane civilizations in human history. Muslims today are seeking strength to face the awesome and complex burden of putting their house(s) in order so that they may live with the rest of the world—indeed with each other, as well—in peace, dignity, and mutual respect. One of the greatest challenges for many Islamist as well as all violently extremist Muslims is accepting cultural modernity and secularity, or at least tolerating them, in open, pragmatic ways. They may be able to learn gradually and peacefully from an emerging population of fellow Muslims, who are increasingly characterizing themselves as "progressive Muslims," and who are courageously and creatively venturing in the direction of a peaceful, global discourse in an "Islam without borders" without losing their deep Islamic faith, proud Muslim identity, and enduring moral values. Traditionalist Muslims, who often feel the need to circle the wagons in defense against "the Other"—whether that is the West or fellow Muslims considered to be astray—may need to conduct extremely thorough, and perhaps unpleasant and painful, examinations of their political, social, economic, religious, and ethical habits, convictions, and institutions. This applies particularly in areas such as human rights, the status of women, social justice, democratic principles and institutions, and freedom of religion, opinion, and expression.

We have addressed some issues and developments that Muslims are challenged to think about in light of the events of September 11, 2001, and ways in which those events' percussive force has marked a fateful transition in both American national and global awareness, as well. It is equally urgent that Americans and others strive to understand problems and predicaments that Muslim peoples face in the postcolonial world, where they have so often been victims of injustice, marginalization, and abuse of varied kinds and from various sources. There needs to be encouragement and support of effective educational programs that will inform citizens about the beliefs, hopes, ideals, achievements, and aspirations of Muslims and other minorities, who deserve respect and understanding as fellow citizens and bearers as well as sharers of their valuable spiritual and cultural resources. The struggle to remove the motives for terrorism, as well as to reprioritize and develop more just policies and practices in international relations as well as in economic globalization, will be long and arduous.

The freedoms that Muslims enjoy today in Western countries in some cases provide cover for the development of radical expressions of religious activism, including terrorist activities. Since al-Qaeda's attacks on America on September 11, 2001, an increasing amount of intelligence information has been collected on such activities, whether based in mosques or in sleeper cells in numerous parts of the world, including Western countries. But in far more cases, Muslims in the West are positively adopting and adapting to Western ways of life and in the process contributing significantly to them. By no means is Islamist extremism the only threat to freedom, whether in the West or in Muslim countries. The price of freedom is considerable, and threats to it can emanate from an indefinite number of sources other than religious zealotry of whatever origin. The USA Patriot Act, hastily passed by the U.S. Congress after 9/11, contains elements that many see as threats to the civil liberties of all Americans.[9]

## PROGRESSIVE MUSLIMS

If *fundamentalism* and *fundamentalist* can be charged terms in the Muslim context, an even more problematic and frequently avoided or evaded term is *liberal.* Almost as bad to many Muslim ears is *modernist,* if applied to Islamic beliefs and standards. Today, a trend among thoughtful Muslims who feel challenged, threatened by, and even alienated from conservative and often authoritarian Muslim interests and institutions is to refer to themselves as "progressive Muslims." I first came across this term when living in Indonesia in the 1980s. Once, in a discussion with Islamic scholars in the Muslim university where I was a visiting professor, I referred to an imaginative and flexible Muslim thinker's views as "rather liberal." One of my ever gentle and diplomatic Indonesian academic hosts encouraged me to consider using the term *progressive* instead of *liberal.* I thought to myself that a euphemism is a euphemism, but the term stuck with me and took life as a positive, constructive notion that survives in the target range of conservative criticism and dismissal.

The term "progressive Islam" was first "popularized," according to Farid Esack, by Suroosh Irfani in his 1983 book *Revolutionary Islam in Iran—Popular Liberation or Religious Dictatorship?*[10] According to Esack, before that time the term was used by some as an alternative to "modernist" or "liberal" Islam, or as representing "simply an antiauthoritarian or anticonservative Muslim discourse."[11] Irfani developed an idea of progressive Islam for leftist activists in postrevolutionary Iran. He wrote that the

> progressive Islamic movement is anti-imperialist, and in the economic domain, its opposition to capitalism and the exploitative system on which capitalism rests is unequivocal. It believes that Islam as an ideology can mobilize the Muslim masses by its appeal to social justice and the challenge it poses to the status quo.[12]

The first systematic attempt to define progressive Islam was undertaken in 1998 by an Internet community of Muslim activists and scholars known as the Progressive Muslim Network (PMN). That group drafted a document titled

"Progressive Islam—A Definition and Declaration." The following definition is contained in the document:

> Progressive Islam is that understanding of Islam and its sources which comes from and is shaped within a commitment to transform society from an unjust one where people are mere objects of exploitation by governments, socioeconomic institutions and unequal relationships. The new society will be a just one where people are the subjects of history, the shapers of their own destiny in the full awareness that all humankind is in a state of returning to God and that the universe was created as a sign of God's presence.[13]

In 2003 a book of essays titled *Progressive Muslims: On Justice, Gender, and Pluralism* was published.[14] The editor, Omid Safi, of The University of North Carolina at Chapel Hill and fourteen Muslim colleagues, six female and nine male, who teach at various institutions of higher education in the United States and beyond, developed the collection of essays through long, detailed deliberations. Topics addressed include "The Ugly Modern and the Modern Ugly: Reclaiming the Beautiful in Islam"; "In Search of Progressive Islam Beyond 9/11"; "Islam: a Civilizational Project in Progress"; "The Debts and Burdens of Critical Islam"; "On Being a Scholar of Islam: Risks and Responsibilities"; "Transforming Feminism: Islam, Women, and Gender Justice"; "Progressive Muslims and Islamic Jurisprudence: The Necessity for Critical Engagement with Marriage and Divorce Law"; "Sexuality, Diversity and Ethics in the Agenda of Progressive Muslims"; "American Muslim Identity: Race and Ethnicity in Progressive Islam"; "Islamic Democracy and Pluralism"; "How to Put the Genie Back in the Bottle? 'Identity' Islam and Muslim Youth Cultures in America"; and others.

The essays address theological matters here and there but they are not a major focus. Only one deals with Islamic law in a sustained manner (the one on marriage and divorce). None treats the Qur'an specifically, although there are citations from the scripture as well as references to it. There is little direct criticism of strictly conservative, puritanical, or fundamentalist Muslim interests or movements except for UCLA law professor Khaled Abou El Fadl's challenging critique, "The Ugly Modern and the Modern Ugly," which opens the collection.

The emphasis of the book is the emphasis of the progressive movement generally and it is heralded in the book's subtitle: *On Justice, Gender, and Pluralism,* all of which are integral to social justice. The group that conferred on the design and purpose of the book entertained a number of other possible terms to characterize their principles and goals (e.g., "Islamic reformation," "liberal Muslims," and "critical Muslims") but settled on "progressive Muslims." The term *progressive* has its problems, according to editor Omid Safi, but it has enough virtues to win out over the alternatives, he maintains. As Safi summarizes the discussions,

> There is something about this term 'progressive.' It is more than anything else an umbrella term that signifies an invitation to those who want an open and safe space to undertake a rigorous, honest, potentially difficult engagement with tradition, and yet remain hopeful that conversation will lead to further action.[15]

In addition to "progressive Muslims," "progressive Islam" was also considered. However, that option was adamantly set aside, for reasons that help us understand more clearly the goals of the discourse. Safi relates that one of the contributors stated, "Islam has always been progressive. It is Muslims that have not always been so." Safi adds that

> we are also wary of falling into the easy dichotomy of I love Islam, it is those darn Muslims that I have a problem with. For better or worse, in truth and ignorance, in beauty and hideousness, we call for an engagement with real live human beings who mark themselves as Muslims, not an idealized notion of Islam that can be talked about apart from engagement with those real live human beings. . . . To keep the focus on the responsibilities of human beings, we have titled this volume "Progressive Muslims," rather than "Progressive Islam."[16]

Although progressive Muslims do not see themselves, in this context, as embracing an ideology or belonging to a denomination, sect, or other sharply defined Muslim organizational entity or subgroup, they do generally share the vision that has thus far been described. The final chapter of *Progressive Muslims,* "What Is the Victory of Islam? Towards a Different Understanding of the *Ummah* and Political Success in the Contemporary World," is by Malaysian political scientist, human rights activist, and columnist Farish A. Noor. His chapter puts forth an "Islam without borders" (Arabic: *Islām bi lāḥ udūd*), by which Noor means a truly universal Islam with Muslims living and engaged in the whole world in all its diversity and need. Noor contrasts this with the traditional Muslim religiopolitical notion of a separate *Dār al-Islām,* the "Household of Submission," sharply demarcated from the rest of the human family, which is still signified in traditionalist Muslim circles as the *Dār al-Ḥarb,* the "Household of Warfare," to be ultimately subdued and converted to Islam. Noor writes,

> We need to forge a new chain of equivalences that equates universal concerns with Muslim concerns and universal problems with Muslim problems. The Muslim heart cannot bleed only when it sees Muslim tears. If we are not moved by the plight and suffering of others, if we cannot feel the pain and anxieties of others, if we cannot share the joy and aspirations of others, then we cannot claim the same rights and entitlements for ourselves. . . . Our concerns for justice, equity, rights, and freedom need to be articulated in a borderless world where our audience is not only ourselves but the world as a whole, both now and in the future.[17]

## PROGRESSIVE ASSERTIVENESS

Khaled Abou El Fadl, one of the most assertive progressive Muslims in the world, receives numerous threats for his views and is often under police protection. His opening chapter in *Progressive Muslims,* "The Ugly Modern and the Modern Ugly: Reclaiming the Beautiful in Islam," views what he calls supremacist (Muslim) puritanism as a politically oriented "siege mentality" that has marginalized free rational discourse on religion and ethics among Muslims. Abou El Fadl describes the current

> doctrinal dynamic as the predominance of the theology of power in modern Islam, and it is this theology that is a direct contributor to the emergence of highly radicalized Islamic groups, such as the Taliban or al-Qaeda, and the desensitization and transference with which Muslims confront extreme acts of ugliness. Far from being authentic expressions of inherited Islamic paradigms, or a natural outgrowth of classical tradition, these groups, and their impulsive and reactive modes of thinking, are a by-product of colonialism and modernity.[18]

Abou El Fadl does not stop there. He sees supremacist puritanism as a state of mind that views Islam not as a

> moral vision given to humanity . . . [but as] the antithesis of the West. . . . This type of Islam . . . is akin to a perpetual state of emergency when expedience trumps principle, and illegitimate means are consistently justified by invoking higher ends. . . . In this siege mentality, there is no room for analytical or critical thought, and there is no room for seriously engaging the Islamic intellectual heritage. There is only room for bombastic dogma, and for a stark functionalism that ultimately impoverishes the Islamic heritage.[19]

One of the darkest dimensions of Abou El Fadl's siege mentality diagnosis is supremacist puritanism's

> rabidly aggressive form of patriarchy that responds to feelings of political and social defeatism by engaging in symbolic displays of power that are systematically degrading of women. . . . [T]here is a certain undeniable vehemence and angst in the treatment of women, as if the more women are made to suffer, the more the political future of Islam is made secure. Puritan orientations do not hesitate to treat all theological arguments aimed at honoring women, by augmenting their autonomy and social mobility, as if a part of the Western conspiracy was designed to destroy Islam.[20]

## AN IRANIAN SHI'ITE MUSLIM'S VOICE IN HUMAN RIGHTS AND RATIONAL DISCOURSE

One of the most widely known advocates of a progressive discourse is the Iranian philosopher Abdolkarim Soroush, introduced earlier in this chapter with his remarks on "Westoxication" (*gharab zadegi*). Although Soroush was a strong supporter of the Iranian Islamic revolution of 1979 under Ayatollah Khomeini, since that time he has developed a rigorous critique of the revolutionary regime and its domination by fundamentalist Shi'ite clerics, most of whom have been extremely narrow minded, repressive, and authoritarian. Although he had a theological education in Iran, as well as a university background in science and philosophy, Soroush later pursued postgraduate studies in England in chemistry and the philosophy of science. He then moved on to studies in philosophy of history and philosophy of religion, with a particular emphasis on ethics. He has been writing and lecturing, principally in his native country, in characteristically independent and open-minded ways, on such topics as ethics, human rights, religion and democracy, secularism and modern worldviews, freedom, faith and reason, tolerance, and theological approaches to revival and reform. Soroush has a growing following of Iranians and Muslims from other countries, as well, who think that the time has come for moderate and liberal voices to challenge the kinds of hidebound traditionalism that Iran's mullahs and Muslim leaders in so much of the world represent.

Because of his daring criticisms of Islamism in its many forms, the Western writer Robin Wright has dubbed Soroush the "Luther of Islam."[21] Challenging Iran's clerical establishment, as Soroush is openly doing, is to some people reminiscent of Martin Luther's nailing his "95 Theses" to the door of the Castle Church in Wittenberg, Germany, in 1517, disputing some of the Roman Catholic Church's teachings and practices. To be sure, comparing any Muslim reformer to Luther is meaningful primarily to Westerners, but the occasional necessity for reform is as much a dimension of Islamic as of Christian institutional awareness, because ethical monotheism in its varied expressions has traditionally upheld exacting standards pertaining to proper faith and order. But reform does not have to go necessarily in the direction of puritanism and punishment; it can also move in the direction of flexibility and pragmatism. For example, the Sudanese Sunni legal scholar and human rights activist Abullahi Ahmed an-Na'im, now a law professor at Emory University in Georgia, has not hesitated to use reforming language in his progressive scholarship, as may be seen in the title of his controversial 1990 book *Toward an Islamic Reformation: Civil Liberties, Human Rights, and International Law.*[22] An-Na'im explicitly moves in the direction of reforming Islamic law so that it can work in harmony with modern constitutionalism, democracy, and the three important areas named in the subtitle of his book.

One of the greatest areas of contemporary concern around the world is human rights. Some Islamic declarations of human rights have been published in recent years, thus adding to the trend that started with the United Nations sponsored Universal Declaration of Human Rights (UDHR) of 1948. The UDHR did not base its principles in any way on religion, but explicitly refrained from such an approach. The UDHR does include "freedom of thought, conscience and religion . . . [including] freedom to change [one's] . . . religion or belief" as one of its articles, but the basis of rights is not religion in any sense, but "recognition of the inherent dignity and of the equal and inalienable rights of all members of the human family [as] the foundation of freedom, justice and peace in the world" (preamble to the UDHR).

Islamic law does not permit converting from Islam to any other religion but considers it to be a capital offense, similar to treason. So, in Islamic human rights declarations, such as the Cairo Declaration of Human Rights in Islam of 1990, although many rights are included, since the declaration is intended for Muslims, Islam is the only approved religion and thus "it is prohibited to exercise any form of compulsion on man or to exploit his poverty or ignorance in order to convert him to another religion or to atheism" (Cairo Declaration, Article 10). The freedom to be a Muslim is, of course, covered by the UDHR, so the Cairo Declaration may be viewed as a supplement to the UDHR specifically covering Muslim contexts. Further, the Cairo Declaration explicitly states, in its concluding Article 25, "The Islamic Shari'ah is the only source of reference for the explanation or clarification of any of the articles of this Declaration." The Cairo Declaration was sponsored by the fifty-seven member states of the Organization of the Islamic Conference (OIC), the world's largest international Muslim organization with headquarters in Jedda, Saudi Arabia.[23]

Abdolkarim Soroush has a characteristically independent view of human rights when viewed from a traditional Islamic perspective. Soroush is not afraid to use, in a positive manner, the word *liberal* either, with respect to an Islamic understanding of rights. In his article "The Idea of a Democratic Religious Government," Soroush writes,

> [a main] issue concerning human rights is the false assumption that sensitivity to human rights is a surrender to relativistic liberalism. Such an assumption is at once ignorant of the nature of liberalism and an insult to religion; it gives liberalism more credit than it deserves and religion less: liberalism is not the fount of all human rights, nor is religion their antithesis.[24]

Soroush's views on human rights are completely different from the type of discourse that the 1990 Cairo Declaration puts forward, where everything must finally be subject to the Shari'a. The following is from the same article just quoted:

> The first issue concerning human rights is that it is not a solely legal [*fiqhī*] intrareligious argument. Discussion of human rights belongs to the domain of philosophical theology [*kalām*] and philosophy in general. Furthermore, it is an extrareligious area of discourse. Like other debates on matters that are prior to yet influential in religious understanding and acceptance, such as the objectivity of ethical values, the problem of free choice, the existence of God, and the election of prophets, human rights lies outside the domain of religion. A religion that is oblivious to human rights (including the need of humanity for freedom and justice) is not tenable in the modern world. In other words, religion needs to be right not only logically, but also ethically.[25]

Soroush, like most Shi'ite thinkers, is quite open to a rationalistic style of theological thinking pioneered in early Islamic theology by the Mu'tazilites (described in Chapter 8). The Sunnis eventually outlawed Mu'tazilite theology as an acceptable general discourse for Islamic doctrine and law, although individual thinkers continued to produce significant theological thought along the rational lines of that broadly defined trend of theology. Soroush is quite critical of the lack of sufficient rational processes in the contemporary conduct of Islamic theological, legal, and ethical discourses.

> The role of rationality in the arena of religion has, thus far, been that of a timid and discreet servant of understanding and defense of religion. However, defense and affirmation cannot be complete without critique and analysis. The enterprise of rationality is an all-or-nothing project. One may not employ reason to attest to the truth of one's opinions, without leaving the door open to its faultfinding critique. The attempt to enjoy the sweet affirmation of reason without tasting its bitter reproach is pure self-delusion.[26]

The passage just quoted appears in the previously cited essay on democratic religious government, which can function, as he argues, only in a climate of "examined religiosity." Religious democracy, for Soroush, entails a "thoroughgoing project of religious rationality, a rationality that contains gains along with losses. It is an invitation to a determined methodology with undetermined results, an invitation to examined versus emulated religiosity."[27]

Abdolkarim Soroush, Khaled Abou El Fadl, Abdullahi Ahmed an-Na'im, and an increasing number of fellow progressive Muslims are being heard far and wide, debated, discussed, and received as part of an important new trend in Islamic thought that has an activist rather than an ivory-tower, academic agenda. The progressive Muslims that are contributors to Omid Safi's *Progressive Muslims: On Justice, Gender, and Pluralism* are mostly academic professionals, to be sure. But they are also deeply engaged participants in their local Muslim communities and beyond. They are committed, Islamically and indeed within the entire range of human discourse and cooperation on values and peace, to "thinking globally and acting locally."

## MUSLIM WOMEN SCHOLAR-ACTIVISTS

Thus far, we have introduced only male progressive Muslims. There are also many Muslim women who support the broad aims of progressive Muslim thought and action. The book *Progressive Muslims* contains six contributions by Muslim women scholars out of a total of fifteen chapters. An earlier book, *Windows of Faith: Muslim Women Scholar-Activists in North America,* edited by Gisela Webb, contains eleven chapters, all written by women.[28] Although that book does not employ the adjective "progressive" in connection with the contributions, the content and spirit of the chapters is well within the framework of what we have been describing in broad terms. To borrow from the twentieth-century philosopher Ludwig Wittgenstein's useful concept, there is a "family resemblance" between what is presented in *Progressive Muslims* and *Windows of Faith.*

Muslim women have long endured having others—males and Western feminists, for example—speak for them. Gisela Webb's editor's introduction to

*Windows of Faith,* titled "May Muslim Women Speak for Themselves, Please?" argues that Muslim women have too often been represented in Western media and popular opinion as a class suffering continual abuse in their patriarchal societies, as "oppressed or mute victim[s]." Webb sees the reality as much more complex, with American Muslim women fostering varieties of empowering "scholarship-activism" that "must include attention to the practical, immediate issues involved in actualizing the Qur'anic mandate of social justice and concomitantly, that any consideration of 'practical' solutions to problems and injustices faced by women must have sound theological grounding in the Qur'anic worldview."[29]

The volume opens with a vigorous essay by Amina Wadud, "Alternative Qur'anic Interpretation and the Status of Muslim Women." Wadud, a respected Qur'anic exegete at home in traditional Islamic as well as contemporary global hermeneutical theory and method, argues that the Qur'an is the fundamental authority for all of Islamic life and being and that it promises a much better range of options for the nurture of human identity and dignity than any of the secondary discourses, mostly jurisprudential, that were developed over the centuries in the name of Islam. There is a fundamental, though certainly not "fundamentalist," scripturalism at work in Wadud's discourse that is increasingly found across the landscape of Muslim activist feminism. Wadud focuses on "being" rather than "doing," as she seeks human, including female, "actualization" as an agent of Allah/God on earth.[30]

Although Muslim women activist scholars are generally strongly focused on the Qur'anic revelation as the highest authority for Islamic life, some are also engaging Islamic jurisprudence in ways that may provide new interpretations and applications of the sources of law within traditionally accepted juristic methodologies. Maysam al-Faruqi's chapter "Women's Self-Identity in the Qur'an and Islamic Law" provides a strong argument against the ways in which traditional jurists have interpreted two fateful Qur'anic passages: Sūra 2:228 and Sūra 4:34, where commentators "started implying a biological difference in intelligence, capacity, and piety between men and women."[31] Following are translations of the two passages:

> Divorced women shall wait by themselves
> for three periods; and it is not lawful
> for them to hide what God has created
> in their wombs; if they believe in God
> and the Last Day. In such time their mates
> have better right to restore them, if they
> desire to set things right. Women have
> such honorable rights as obligations, but
> their men have a degree above them; God is
> All-mighty, All-wise. (Sūra 2:228)
>
> • • •
>
> Men are the managers of the affairs of women
> for that God has preferred in bounty
> one of them over another, and for that

> they have expended of their property.
> Righteous women are therefore obedient,
> guarding the secret for God's guarding.
> And those you fear may be rebellious
> admonish; banish them to their couches,
> and beat them. If they then obey you,
> look not for any way against them;
> God is All-high, All-great. (Sūra 4:34)

The divine authorization for husbands to beat rebellious wives (*w'aḍribuhunna*) in 4:34, although a correct literal translation above by Arberry (who was not a Muslim), is interpreted as follows by a respected modern Muslim translator, 'Abdullah Yūsuf 'Alī, who inserts a widely accepted compassionate interpretation, as seen in his parentheses: "As to those women on whose part ye fear disloyalty and ill conduct, admonish them (first), (next), refuse to share their beds, (and last) beat them (lightly); but if they return to obedience, seek not against them means (of annoyance): for Allah is Most High, Great (above you all)." Regardless, beating is permitted in the passage and opinions have varied as to how intensive it may be.

Al-Faruqi's refutation of traditional, male-biased readings of the passages is technically sophisticated, complex, and lucid. Especially significant is that she is tackling the issue *within* accepted modes of Islamic legal discourse and not from an alien perspective. Al-Faruqi is, in other words, claiming legal ground within an acceptable Islamic jurisprudential framework that fellow Muslims will be required to respond to and not ignore. The increasing interest and skillful activity of Muslim women in the arena of Islamic law is a significant development in modern Islamic legal discourse. This is not to say that such women legal activists are universally welcomed or tolerated by the mostly very conservative and male legal guild at this time.

A final example of the kind of scholarship that *Windows of Faith* presents is Asifa Quraishi's chapter, "Her Honor: An Islamic Critique of the Rape Laws of Pakistan from a Woman-Sensitive Perspective," which seeks to demonstrate that, although the laws in question are indeed bad for women, the impression that many women have of Islam is not true. Some deeply disturbing cases are described, including one in which a nearly blind, teenaged domestic servant charged that her employer and his son had repeatedly raped her. She was the only witness against them, whereas the Qur'an requires four eyewitnesses, strictly speaking. The case against the men was dismissed. However, the servant became pregnant, and being unmarried was charged with "fornication," and convicted, based on her condition. Quraishi argues that "cultural patriarchy has . . . coloured the application of certain Islamic laws in places such as Pakistan, resulting in the very injustice that the Qur'an so forcefully condemns."[32] Providing important technical details about rape as viewed by Islamic law and custom, she concludes that Pakistan's current law is not truly Islamic, and concludes with a call for a "modern Islamic gender egalitarian law of rape."[33]

## CONCLUSION

The book *Progressive Muslims* makes little mention of fundamentalism and fundamentalists—Muslim or other—and where it does, principally in one chapter,[34] it does not focus exclusively on Islam but addresses what the author calls a "clash of twin fundamentalisms," one being Muslim extremism and the other the Western-dominated global market. Progressive Muslims seek not to be confrontational, but proactive. They prefer to invite participation rather than give orders. They strive to have open minds and hearts backed up by strong commitments, based on their Islamic principles and practices, but extending in peaceful and nonjudgmental ways to all people.

Islamists, fundamentalists, supremacist puritans, and other conservative traditionalists disapprove and even condemn some of the causes and positions that progressive Muslims support. The progressives hope that as they try to engage their fellows in civil, respectful dialogue in a global Umma without borders, a vast Muslim community that is as varied and diverse as can be imagined will define and celebrate itself in all its creative diversity. Progressive discourses continue to develop and spread, in such areas as human rights; feminist thinking and activism; peacebuilding; social, economic, political, and environmental justice; interreligious relations; and, recently, a constructive addressing of diversity in sexual orientation (e.g., there is a lively Web site for gay, lesbian, bisexual, and transgendered Muslims; the organization's name is "Al-Fatiha," "the Opening," which is also the title of the first Sūra of the Qur'an).

There is a considerable amount of interest across the Muslim world in the open and frank sharing of ideas, sustaining lively discussions, inviting people to Islam, and general networking in this age of the Internet. It may well be that that momentous technological phenomenon will propel progressivism, as well as other Muslim initiatives, in a manner that would have been impossible before its appearance on a global scale.[35]

## NOTES

1. H. A. R. Gibb, *Whither Islam? A Survey of Modern Movements in the Moslem World* (London: Victor Gollancz Ltd., 1932), pp. 22–23.
2. *Ibid.,* p. 318.
3. *Ibid.,* p. 319.
4. Jalal Al-I Ahmad, *Occidentosis: A Plague from the West,* trans. Robert Campbell, ed. Hamid Algar (Berkeley, CA: Mizan Press, 1984).
5. Abdolkarim Soroush, "The Three Cultures," in *Reason, Freedom, and Democracy in Islam: Essential Writings of Abdolkarim Soroush,* translated, edited, and with a critical introduction by Mahmoud Sadri and Ahmad Sadri (New York: Oxford University Press, 2000), p. 160. Soroush observes that "the three cultures that form our common heritage

are of national, religious, and Western origins. While steeped in an ancient national culture, we are also immersed in our religious culture, and we are at the same time awash in successive waves coming from the Western shores" (p. 156).

6. *Ibid.,* p. 161.
7. *The Correspondence of Roger Williams: Volume II, 1654–1682,* ed. Glenn W. LaFantasie (Hanover and London: Brown University Press/University Press of New England, 1988), p. 424.
8. For information about al-Qaeda and other extremist "Jihadi" movements and their ideologies, see Jessica Stern, *Terror in the Name of God: Why Religious Militants Kill* (New York: HarperCollins, 2003), pp. 115, 117, 269–271 and *passim.*
9. Georgetown University law professor David Cole has addressed this matter in a well-documented book, *Enemy Aliens: Double Standards and Constitutional Freedoms in the War on Terrorism* (New York and London: The New Press, 2003).
10. (London: Zed, 1983).
11. Farid Esack, "In Search of a Progressive Islam Beyond 9/11," in *Progressive Muslims: On Justice, Gender, and Pluralism,* ed. Omid Safi (Oxford: Oneworld, 2003), p. 79.
12. Irfani, *Revolutionary Islam in Iran,* p. 33, as quoted in Esack, *op. cit.*, p. 80.
13. Progressive Muslim Network Web site: http://www.progressivemuslims.com/index2.html
14. Publication details are in note 13.
15. *Progressive Muslims,* p. 18.
16. *Ibid.*
17. *Ibid.,* p. 332.
18. *Ibid.,* p. 43.
19. *Ibid.,* p. 44.
20. *Ibid.*
21. Writing in *The Los Angeles Times,* January 27, 1995, p. 2.
22. (Syracuse: Syracuse University Press, 1990).
23. The text of the Cairo Declaration may be found in Ann Elizabeth Mayer, *Islam and Human Rights: Tradition and Politics,* 3rd ed. (Boulder, CO: Westview Press, 1997), Appendix B, pp. 203–208.
24. Abdolkarim Soroush, *Reason, Freedom, and Democracy in Islam, op. cit.*, p. 129.
25. *Ibid.,* p. 128.
26. *Ibid.,* p. 154.
27. *Ibid.,* p. 155.
28. Gisela Webb, ed., *Windows of Faith: Muslim Women Scholar-Activists in North America* (Syracuse: Syracuse University Press, 2000). The material contained in this section was originally published in my review of the book in *Journal of Law and Religion,* XV, no. 1 & 2 (2000–2001): 535–539. Used here by permission.
29. *Ibid.,* pp. xi–xii.
30. *Ibid.,* p. 21.
31. *Ibid.,* p. 82.
32. *Ibid.,* pp. 102–103.
33. *Ibid.,* pp. 134.

34. Chap. 2: "In Search of Progressive Islam Beyond 9/11," by Farid Esack, particularly pp. 87–93.
35. The Internet is used energetically across the considerable spectrum of Muslim interests and causes, from fundamentalist and militant to peacebuilding and progressive. In between is an enormous amount of accessible information and resources such as Qur'an texts and exegesis, Ḥadīth collections, and legal guides. Two book-length studies by Gary Bunt provide extensive information and absorbing analysis as well as extensive guidance to online resources: *Virtually Islamic: Computer-Mediated Communication and Cyber Islamic Environments* (Cardiff: University of Wales Press, 2000), and *Islam in the Digital Age: E-Jihad, Online Fatwas and Cyber Islamic Environments* (London and Sterling, Virginia: Pluto Press, 2003). A very useful and varied collection of chapters is *Muslim Networks from Hajj to Hip Hop*, ed. miriam cooke and Bruce B. Lawrence (Chapel Hill and London: The University of North Carolina Press, 2005).

# Suggestions for Further Reading

## PART ONE

## RELIGION AND COMMON LIFE IN THE PRE-ISLAMIC NEAR EAST

### *General*

**Corrigan, John, Frederick M. Denny, Carlos M. N. Eire,** and **Martin S. Jaffee.** *Jews, Christians, Muslims: A Comparative Introduction to Monotheistic Religions.* Upper Saddle River, N.J.: Prentice Hall, 1998.

**Frankfort, Henri.** *Kingship and the Gods: A Study of Ancient Near Eastern Religion As the Integration of Society and Nature.* Chicago: University of Chicago Press, 1948.

**Frankfort, Henri, H. A. Frankfort, John A. Wilson, Thorkild Jacobsen,** and **William A. Irwin.** *The Intellectual Adventure of Ancient Man.* Chicago: University of Chicago Press, 1946. (Absorbing and accessible surveys of the Ancient Near Eastern Civilizations.)

**Gaster, Theodor H.** *Thespis: Ritual, Myth and Drama in the Ancient Near East.* New York: Harper Torchbooks, 1966.

**Hallo, William W.** and **W. Kelly Simpson.** *The Ancient Near East: A History,* 2nd ed. New York: Harcourt Brace Jovanovich, 1997.

**Kramer, Samuel Noah,** ed. *Mythologies of the Ancient World.* Garden City, N.Y.: Anchor Books, 1961.

**Leeming, David.** *Jealous Gods and Chosen People: The Mythology of the Middle East.* New York: Oxford University Press, 2004.

**Pritchard, James B.,** ed. *Ancient Near Eastern Texts Relating to the Old Testament,* 3rd ed. Princeton, N.J.: Princeton University Press, 1969.

### *Mesopotamia*

**Heidel, Alexander.** *The Babylonian Genesis,* 2nd ed. Chicago: University of Chicago Press, 1951.

**Jacobsen, Thorkild.** *The Treasures of Darkness: A History of Mesopotamian Religion.* New Haven, Conn.: Yale University Press, 1976.

**Kramer, Samuel Noah.** *Sumerian Mythology.* New York: Harper & Row, 1961.

**Oppenheim, A. Leo.** *Mesopotamia: Portrait of a Dead Civilization.* Chicago: University of Chicago Press, 1964.

### *Egypt*

**Černý, Jaroslav.** *Ancient Egyptian Religion.* London: Hutchinson's University Library, 1952.

**Frankfort, Henri.** *Ancient Egyptian Religion.* New York: Columbia University Press, 1948; Harper Torchbooks, 1961.

**Morenz, Siegfried.** *Egyptian Religion.* London: Methuen, 1973.

**Shafer, Byron E.,** ed. *Religion in Ancient Egypt: Gods, Myths, and Personal Practice.* Ithaca, N.Y.: Cornell University Press, 1991.

**Wilson, John A.** *The Culture of Ancient Egypt.* Chicago: University of Chicago Press, 1951. (Originally entitled *The Burden of Egypt.*)

## The Ancient Israelites and Judaism

**Baron, Salo W.** *Social and Religious History of the Jews,* 16 vols. New York: Columbia University Press, 1952 *et seq.*

**Bright, John.** *A History of Israel,* 4th ed. Louisville, KY: Westminster John Knox Press, 2000.

**Brueggemann, Walter.** *An Introduction to the Old Testament: The Canon and Christian Imagination.* Louisville, KY: Westminster John Knox Press, 2003.

**Goitein, S. D. B.** *Jews and Arabs: Their Contacts Through the Ages.* New York: Schocken, 1955.

———. *A Mediterranean Society: The Jewish Communities of the Arab World As Portrayed in the Documents of the Cairo Geniza,* 5 vols. Berkeley and Los Angeles: University of California Press, 1967 *et seq.*

**Neusner, Jacob.** *The Way of Torah: An Introduction to Judaism,* 7th ed. Belmont, Calif.: Wadsworth, 2003.

**Newby, Gordon Darnell.** *A History of the Jews of Arabia: From Ancient Times to their Eclipse Under Islam.* Columbia, S.C.: University of South Carolina Press, 1988.

## Christianity

**Atiyah, Aziz Suryal.** *Eastern Christianity.* London: Methuen, 1968.

**Attwater, Donald.** *The Christian Churches of the East,* 2 vols. Milwaukee: Bruce Publishing, 1947–1948.

**Barrett, C. K.,** ed. *The New Testament Background: Selected Documents.* New York: Harper Torchbooks, 1961.

**Bettenson, Henry,** ed. *Documents of the Christian Church,* 3rd ed. Oxford, England: Oxford University Press, 1999.

**Browne, Laurence E.** *The Eclipse of Christianity in Asia: From the Time of Muhammad till the Fourteenth Century.* Cambridge, England: Cambridge University Press, 1933.

**Crossan, John Dominic.** *The Historical Jesus: The Life of a Mediterranean Jewish Peasant.* San Francisco: HarperSanFrancisco, 1991.

**Meeks, Wayne A.** *The First Urban Christians: The Social World of the Apostle Paul.* New Haven, Conn.: Yale University Press, 1983.

**Pelikan, Jaroslav.** *The Christian Tradition: A History of the Development of Doctrine,* vol. 1, *The Emergence of the Catholic Tradition* (*to A.D. 600*). Chicago: University of Chicago Press, 1971.

**Walker, Williston.** *History of the Christian Church,* 4th ed. New York: Scribner's, 1985.

## Pre-Islamic Arabia

**Allouche, Adel.** "Arabian Religions," in *The Encyclopedia of Religion,* vol. 1, ed. Mircea Eliade et al. New York: Macmillan, 1987, pp. 363–367.

**Arberry, A. J.** *The Seven Odes: The First Chapter in Arabic Literature.* London: Allen & Unwin, 1957.

**Bravmann, M. M.** *The Spiritual Background of Early Islam.* Leiden: E. J. Brill, 1972.

**Gabrielli, Francesco,** ed. *L'antica società beduina.* Rome: Centro di Studi Semitici, Istituto di Studi Orientali, Università di Roma, 1959, especially the chapters by Walter Dostal, "The Evolution of Bedouin Life," and Joseph Henninger, "La Religion Bedouine Préislamique," The latter article is now available in English translation in Merlin L. Swartz, ed. *Studies on Islam.* New York and Oxford, England: Oxford University Press, 1981, pp. 3–22.

**Gibb, H. A. R.** "Pre-Islamic Monotheism in Arabia," *Harvard Theological Review* 55 (1962): 269–280.

**Goldziher, Ignaz.** *Muslim Studies [Muhammedanische Studien],* trans. S. M. Stern and C. R. Barber. Chicago: Aldine, 1966. "Muruwwa and Dīn," vol. 1, pp. 11–44; "The Arabic Tribes and Islam," vol. 1, pp. 45–97; "What Is Meant by 'al-Jāhiliyya'," vol. 1, pp. 201–208.

**Hitti, Phillip K.** *History of the Arabs,* 9th ed. New York: St. Martin's Press, 1967.

**Ibn al-Kalbī.** *The Book of Idols,* trans. Nabīh Amīn Fāris. Princeton, N.J.: Princeton University Press, 1952.

**Levi della Vida, Giorgio.** "Pre-Islamic Arabia," in *The Arab Heritage,* ed. Nabih A. Faris. Princeton, N.J.: Princeton University Press, 1944, pp. 25–57.

**Lyall, Sir Charles.** *Translations of Ancient Arabian Poetry.* London: Williams and Norgate, 1930.

**O'Leary, DeLacy.** *Arabia Before Muhammad.* London: Kegan Paul, Trench, and Trübner, 1927.

**Ringgren, Helmer.** *Studies in Arabian Fatalism.* Uppsala: Lundequistska Bokhandeln, 1955.

**Shahid, Irfan.** "Pre-Islamic Arabia," in *The Cambridge History of Islam,* vol. 1, ed. P. M. Holt, Ann K. S. Lambton, and Bernard Lewis. Cambridge, England: Cambridge University Press, 1970, pp. 3–29.

**Smith, W. Robertson.** *Kinship and Marriage in Early Arabia.* London: A. and C. Black, 1903.

———. *The Religion of the Semites.* New York: Meridian Books, 1956.

**Stetkevych, Jaroslav.** *Muhammad and the Golden Bough: Reconstructing Arabian Myth.* Bloomington and Indianapolis: Indiana University Press, 1996.

**Wolf, Eric R.** "The Social Organization of Mecca and the Origins of Islam," *Southwestern Journal of Anthropology* 7 (1951): 329–356.

# PART TWO

# THE COMING OF ISLAM: THE PROPHET, HIS PEOPLE, AND GOD'S RELIGION

## *Reference Works and General Introduction to Islamic Religion*

### *Bibliographic Aids*

**Adams, Charles J.,** ed. "Islām," in *A Reader's Guide to the Great Religions,* 2nd ed., ed. Charles J. Adams. New York: Free Press, 1977, pp. 407–475. (Thorough and with valuable annotations and discussions.)

*Index of Islamic Literature.* Supplement to the *Muslim World Book Review.* Leicester, U.K.: The Islamic Foundation, 1980– . (Covers materials in English only.)

*Oxford Islamic Studies Online* (*www.oxfordislamicstudies.com*). (Highly useful for people beginning the study of Islam. Basic definitions and information. Published and maintained by Oxford University Press).

*The Muslim World Book Review.* Leicester, U.K.: The Islamic Foundation, 1980– . (Scholarly reviews.)

**Pearson, J. D.,** comp. *Index Islamicus, 1906–1955: A Catalogue of Articles on Islamic Subjects in Periodicals and Other Collective Publications.* Cambridge, England: W. Heffer, 1958. (This indispensable resource for the serious student of Islam has several supplemental volumes and will, one hopes, be continued indefinitely. Multilingual coverage.)

**Sauvaget, Jean.** *Introduction to the History of the Muslim East: A Bibliographical Guide.* Berkeley and Los Angeles: University of California Press, 1965. (Based on the second edition as recast by Claude Cahen.) (Of special value for the advanced student, because it covers original sources and their editions.)

## *Reference Works*

*Encyclopaedia of Islam,* new ed. Leiden: E. J. Brill, 1954– . (A basic reference that covers all aspects of Islamic religion, history, culture, and literature. The articles are arranged according to their *vernacular* terms [for example, *masdjid* for "mosque," *fiḳh* for "jurisprudence"], so that the reader must expend some effort in order to use the work efficiently).

*Encyclopaedia of the Qur'ān.* Jane Dammen McAuliffe, general. ed. 6 vols. Leiden-Boston-Köln: Brill, 2001–2006 . (Authoritative entries on a vast variety of topics by leading scholars.)

**Esposito, John L.,** Editor in Chief. *The Oxford Encyclopedia of the Modern Islamic World,* 4 vols. New York and Oxford: Oxford University Press, 1995. (Comprehensive and accessible).

**Fārūqī, Ismā'īl al-** and **Lois Lamyā al-Fārūqī.** *The Cultural Atlas of Islam.* New York: Macmillan, 1986.

**Glassé, Cyril.** *The New Encyclopedia of Islam* 3rd ed. Lanham, Md.: Rowman and Littlefield Publishing Group, 2008. (An unusually comprehensive, authoritative and sympathetic guide. Much easier to use by the nonspecialist than the *Encyclopaedia of Islam.*)

**Hughes, Thomas Patrick.** *A Dictionary of Islam.* London: W. H. Allen, 1935. (Old, but contains many items lacking in the *Encyclopaedia of Islam.*)

**Kennedy, Hugh,** ed. *An Historical Atlas of Islam,* 2nd, rev. ed. Leiden Boston-Köln: Brill, 2002.

**Nanji, Azim A.**, ed. *The Muslim Almanac: A Reference Work on the History, Faith, Culture, and Peoples of Islam.* Detroit: Gale Research Inc., 1996.

**Rippin, Andrew,** ed. *The Islamic World.* London and New York: Routledge, 2008. (A comprehensive, deeply absorbing and up-to-date guide to the whole range of Islamic faith and culture, treating the geo-political Muslim world, religious life, intellectual life, Muslim biographies, cultural dimensions, and social issues).

**Weekes, Richard V.,** ed. *Muslim Peoples: A World Ethnographic Survey,* 2nd ed., 2 vols. Westport, Conn.: Greenwood Press, 1984. (Authoritative and absorbing, with excellent bibliographies.)

## *Journals*

*Arabica: Journal of Arabic and Islamic Studies/Revue d'etudes arabes et islamiques.* (Addresses contemporary problems in Arab societies through multidisciplinary approaches).

*British Journal of Middle Eastern Studies.* (Covers a wide range of topics from the rise of Islam to the present).

*Bulletin of the School of Oriental and African Studies.* Published by the University of London. Covers Asia, Africa and the Middle East. (Many articles and reviews on Islam-related subjects, although the journal covers all aspects of religions, politics, history, literatures and cultures of the regions).

*Die Welt des Islams.* (A highly respected German journal on modern Muslim history and culture from 1800 to the present. In French, English, and German).

*Islamic Studies.* (An excellent English language journal published by the Islamic Research Institute in Pakistan. Wide range of coverage).

*International Journal of Middle East Studies.* Published by the Middle East Studies Association of North America. (Wide range of topics and fields, including political, anthropological, sociological and cultural topics that often relate to Islam and Muslims).

*Journal of Islamic Studies.* Published by the Oxford Centre for Islamic Studies. (Multidisciplinary and wide-ranging).

*Journal of Near Eastern Studies.* Published by the University of Chicago since 1941. (Focuses on the Near East from ancient times before Islam down to modern times. Articles on Islam are regularly published).

*Studia Islamica.* (Established in 1953, continues to provide articles on topics in all historical periods, but focusing mostly on southwest Asia and the Mediterranean Basin. In French and English).

*The Muslim World: A Journal Devoted to the Study of Islam and Christian-Muslim Relations in Past and Present.* (Established in 1911, this journal continues to be an import forum relating to the mission in its title).

## *Anthologies of Sources on Islamic Religion*

**Cragg, Kenneth** and **R. Marston Speight,** eds. *Islam from Within: Anthology of a Religion.* Belmont, Calif.: Wadsworth, 1980.

**Jeffery, Arthur,** ed. *Islam: Muhammad and His Religion.* New York: Liberal Arts Press, 1958. (Good for beginners.)

———. *A Reader on Islam: Passages from Standard Arabic Writings Illustrative of the Beliefs and Practices of Muslims.* The Hague: Mouton, 1962. (A monumental resource for the more advanced.)

**McNeil, William H.,** and **Marilyn R. Waldman,** eds. *The Islamic World.* New York: Oxford University Press, 1973.

**Peters, F. E.** *A Reader on Classical Islam.* Princeton, N.J.: Princeton University Press, 1994. (Richly varied original sources in translation with clear and interesting running commentary.)

**Rippin, Andrew** and **Jan Knappert,** eds. *Textual Sources for the Study of Islam.* Chicago: University of Chicago Press, 1990.

**Williams, John Alden,** ed. *The Word of Islam.* Austin, Tex.: University of Texas Press, 1994. (Classical sources accessible to beginners.)

## *General Introductions to Islam*

**Ahmad, Khurshid,** ed. *Islam: Its Meaning and Message.* Leicester, U.K.: The Islamic Foundation, 1976. (Authoritative essays on various aspects of Islam by leading Muslim scholars.)

**Berkey, Jonathan P.** *The Formation of Islam. Religion and Society in the Near East, 600–1800.* Cambridge: Cambridge University Press, 2003.

**Cragg, Kenneth.** *The House of Islam.* Belmont, Calif.: Wadsworth, 1975.

**Denny, Frederick M.** *Islam and the Muslim Community,* 2nd ed. San Francisco: HarperSanFrancisco, 1992. (Focuses on the concept of *umma.*)

**Endress, Gerhard.** *Islam: An Historical Introduction,* 2nd ed., trans. Carole Hillenbrand. Edinburgh: Edinburgh University Press, 2002. (A highly sophisticated survey with helpful appendices–names and titles, language and script, the Islamic calendar–a detailed chronological table and a very extensive bibliography).

**Esposito, John L.** *Islam: The Straight Path,* expanded ed. New York: Oxford University Press, 1991. (Strong on contemporary issues.)

**Gibb, H. A. R.** *Mohammedanism: An Historical Survey,* 2nd ed. New York: Oxford University Press, 1962. (Succinct and brilliant.)

**Goldziher, Ignaz.** *Introduction to Islamic Theology and Law,* trans. Andras and Ruth Hamori. Princeton, N.J.: Princeton University Press, 1981. (First published in 1910 in German as *Vorlesungen über den Islam.* An interpretative work of fundamental scholarship, based on original sources throughout. More advanced than Cragg or Gibb.)

**Hodgson, Marshall G. S.** *The Venture of Islam: Conscience and History in a World Civilization,* 3 vols. Chicago: University of Chicago Press, 1974. (A global treatment of great authority and empathy. Difficult but well worth the effort.)

**Martin, Richard C.** *Islamic Studies: A History of Religions Approach.* Upper Saddle River, N.J.: Prentice Hall, 1996. (Currently the best brief survey for the beginner.)

**Nasr, Seyyed Hossein.** *Ideals and Realities of Islam.* Boston: Beacon Press, 1972. (An eloquent appreciation by a leading Muslim thinker.)

**Peters, F. E.** *Allah's Commonwealth: A History of the Near East 600–1100 A.D.* New York: Simon & Schuster, 1973. (Particularly good on intellectual currents, magisterially explained.)

**Rahman, Fazlur.** *Islam,* 2nd ed. Chicago: University of Chicago Press, 1979. (Challenging discussions by a leading Muslim intellectual make this work as much primary source as textbook.)

**Rippin, Andrew.** *Muslims: Their Religious Beliefs and Practices,* 2nd ed. London and New York: Routledge, 2001. (A highly sophisticated yet accessible survey.)

**Schimmel, Annemarie.** *Islam: An Introduction.* Albany: State University of New York Press, 1992.

**Speight, Marston.** *God Is One: The Way of Islam.* New York: Friends Press, 1989. (A deeply sympathetic portrayal, especially recommended for use by Christians interested in interreligious dialogue with Muslims.)

**Von Grunebaum, Gustave E.** *Mediaeval Islam.* Chicago: University of Chicago Press, 1953. (A stimulating study for the more advanced reader.)

## Muhammad

**Asani, Ali S.** and **Kamal Abdel-Malek,** in collaboration with Annemarie Schimmel. *Celebrating Muhammad: Images of the Prophet in Popular Muslim Poetry.* Columbia, S.C.: University of South Carolina Press, 1995.

**Buhl, Frants.** "Muhammad," in *Shorter Encyclopaedia of Islam,* pp. 390–405. (Based on the Danish author's great biography of the Prophet, *Das Leben Muhammeds,* 2nd ed, trans. H. H. Schaeder. Heidelberg: Quelle & Meyer, 1955.)

**Haykal, Muhammad Husayn.** *The Life of Muhammad (Ḥayāt Muḥammad),* trans. Ismā ʿīl R. al-Fārūqī. Indianapolis: American Trust Publications, 1976. (Very popular modern Egyptian treatment, first - published in Arabic in 1935.)

**Ibn Isḥāq.** *The Life of Muhammad: A Translation of Isḥāq's Sīrat Rasūl Allāh,* trans. Alfred Guillaume. London: Oxford University Press, 1967. (The standard early Islamic biography.)

**Lings, Martin.** *Muhammad: His Life Based on the Earliest Sources.* New York: Inner Traditions International, 1983.

**Peters, F. E.** *Muhammad and the Origins of Islam.* Albany: State University of New York Press, 1994. (High-level scholarship in a very accessible form.)

**Rahnema, Zeinolabedin.** *Payambar the Messenger,* translated from Persian by L. P. Elwell-Sutton. Lahore, Pakistan: Sh. Muhammad Ashraf, 1964. (This three-volume work, although based on original sources, is written like a historical novel and provides a good sense of Muslims' love for Muhammad.)

**Rodinson, Maxime.** "A Critical Survey of Modern Studies on Muhammad," translated by Merlin L. Swartz, in the translator-editor's *Studies on Islam.* New York and Oxford, England: Oxford University Press, 1981.

———. *Mohammed,* trans. Anne Carter. New York: Vintage Books, 1974.

**Siddiqui, Abdul Hamid.** *The Life of Muhammad.* Lahore, Pakistan: Islamic Publications, 1969.

**Watt, W. Montgomery.** *Muhammad at Mecca.* Oxford, England: Clarendon Press, 1953; and *Muhammad at Medina.* Oxford, England: Clarendon Press, 1956. (The standard works in English, written with close attention to traditional sources and displaying great sympathy with the subject. The two volumes are abridged as one in *Muhammad: Prophet and Statesman.* London: Oxford University Press, 1961. This is best for the beginner.)

## Basic Beliefs and Duties of Islam

**Abdalati, Ḥammudah.** *Islam in Focus.* Indianapolis: Islamic Trust Publications, 1977.

**al-Baghawī, Husayn,** and expanded by **Walī al-Dīn al-Khatīb al-Tibrīzī.** *Mishkāt al-Maṣābih* ("The niche for lamps"), 4 vols, trans. James Robson. Lahore, Pakistan: Sh. Muhammad Ashraf, 1964–1966. (This vast collection of *ḥadīth* includes much matter pertaining to worship and ritual practices.)

**Calverly, E. E.** *Worship in Islam,* rev. ed. London: Luzac, 1957. (A detailed description of the salāt, with a translation of Abū Hāmid al-Ghazālī's "Book of Worship" from his *Iḥyā' 'Ulūm al-Dīn* ["Revivification of the sciences of religion"].)

**Denny, Frederick M.,** and **Abdulaziz A. Sachedina.** *Islamic Ritual Practices: A Slide Set and Teacher's Guide,* vol. 7. Asian Religions Media Resources. New Haven, Conn.: Paul Vieth Christian Education Service of the Yale Divinity School, 1983. (180 photo slides and commentary.)

**Farāhāni, Mirza Moḥammed Ḥosayn.** *A Shi'ite Pilgrimage to Mecca 1885–1886* [the *Safarnāmeh*], ed., trans., and annotated by Hafez Farmayan and Elton L. Daniel. Austin: University of Texas Press, 1990. (A close-up, absorbing account.)

**Haneef, Suzanne.** *What Everyone Should Know About Islam and Muslims.* Chicago: Kazi Publications, 1982. (Gives a good sense of the daily religious life of Muslims. Written especially for prospective Muslims.)

**Kamal, Ahmad.** *The Sacred Journey, Being a Pilgrimage to Mecca.* New York: Duell, Sloan and Pearce, 1961.

**Nasr, Seyyed Hossein, Hamid Dabashi,** and **Seyyed Vali Reza Nasr,** eds. *Shi'ism: Doctrines, Thought, and Spirituality.* Albany: State University of New York Press, 1988. (Wide-ranging selection of sources and commentaries.)

**Padwick, Constance E.** *Muslim Devotions: A Study of Prayer Manuals in Common Use.* London: S.P.C.K., 1961. (A sensitively arranged and moving discussion, with very generous translated examples of prayers.)

**Rauf, Muhammad Abdul.** *Islam: Creed and Worship.* Washington, D.C.: The Islamic Center, 1974. (Detailed description of major religious observances, with useful photos and drawings.)

## *The Arab-Muslim Conquests and the Development of Islamic Civilization*

**Afsaruddin, Asma.** Excellence and Precedence: *Medieval Islamic Discourse on Legitimate Leadership.* Leiden: Brill, 2002.

**Arnold, Thomas W.** *The Preaching of Islam: A History of the Propagation of the Muslim Faith,* 2nd ed. Lahore, Pakistan: Sh. Muhammad Ashraf, 1961.

**Bosworth, Clifford Edmund.** *The Islamic Dynasties: A Chronological and Genealogical Handbook.* Edinburgh: Edinburgh University Press, 1967.

**Brend, Barbara.** *Islamic Art.* Cambridge, Mass.: Harvard University Press, 1991.

**The Cambridge History of Islam.** (Mentioned earlier.) (Historical articles.)

**Crone, Patricia.** *God's Rule: Government and Islam.* New York: Columbia University Press, 2004. (Comprehensive, advanced survey of major issues down to the end of the Abbasid Caliphate in 1258 CE).

**Crone, Patrica and Martin Hinds.** *God's Caliph: Religious Authority in the First Centuries of Islam.* Cambridge: Cambridge University Press, 1986.

**Daniel, Norman.** *Islam and the West: The Making of an Image.* Edinburgh: Edinburgh University Press, 1960; reprinted Oxford: Oneworld, 1997. (Classic study.)

**Donner, Fred McGraw.** *The Early Islamic Conquests.* Princeton, N.J.: Princeton University Press, 1981.

**Esposito, John L.,** ed. *The Oxford History of Islam.* New York: Oxford University Press, 1999. (A superb general history with magnificent black and white and color illustrations.)

**Hodgson, Marshall G. S.** *The Venture of Islam.* (Mentioned earlier.)

**Hooker, M. B.** *Islam in Southeast Asia.* Leiden: E. J. Brill, 1983.

**Hourani, Albert Habib.** *A History of the Arab Peoples.* Cambridge, Mass.: Belknap Press of Harvard University Press, 1991.

**Jafri, S. H. M.** *The Origins and Early Development of Shī'a Islam.* London and New York: Longman, 1979.

**Kennedy, Hugh.** *When Baghdad Ruled the Muslim World: The Rise and Fall of Islam's Greatest Dynasty.* USA: Da Capo Press, 2005. (First published in the United Kingdom by Weidenfeld and Nicholson, 2004, under the title *The Court of the Caliphs.* A very good read by a leading expert).

**Khalidi, Tarif.** *Classical Arab Islam: The Culture and Heritage of the Golden Age.* Princeton, N.J.: Darwin Press, 1985.

**Khan, Ruqayya Yasmine.** *Self and Secrecy in Early Islam.* Columbia, S.C.: University of South Carolina Press, 2008. (A groundbreaking study of early texts–the Qur'an, ethical discourses, and love poetry–that reveal a nuanced understanding of fundamental dimensions of early Arabo-Muslim civilization's interrelated religio-ethical, social, cultural, political, and psychosexual realities).

**Lapidus, Ira M.** *A History of Islamic Societies.* Cambridge and New York: Cambridge University Press, 1988.

**Lassner, Jacob.** *The Shaping of 'Abbāsid Rule.* Princeton, N.J.: Princeton University Press, 1980.

**Levtzion, Nehemiah,** ed. *Conversion to Islam.* New York: Holmes and Meier, 1979.

**Madelung, Wilferd.** *The Succession to Muhammad: A Study of the Early Caliphate.* Cambridge: Cambridge University Press, 1997.

**[al]-Mawardi, 'Ali ibn Muhammad.** *The Ordinances of Government: A Translation of Al-Ahkam al-Sultaniyya w'al- Wilayat al-Diniyya,* by Wafaa H. Wahba. London: Garnet Publishing Limited, 1996.

**Momen, Moojan.** *An Introduction to Shi'i Islam: The History and Doctrines of Twelver Shi'ism.* New Haven, Conn. and London: Yale University Press, 1985.

**Schacht, Joseph** with **C. E. Bosworth,** eds. *The Legacy of Islam,* 2nd ed. Oxford, England: Clarendon Press, 1974.

**Schimmel, Annemarie.** *Calligraphy and Islamic Culture.* London: Tauris, 1990 [1984].

**Shaban, M. A.** *The 'Abbāsid Revolution.* Cambridge, England: Cambridge University Press, 1970.

———. *Islamic History A.D. 600–750 (A.H. 132): A New Interpretation.* Cambridge, England: Cambridge University Press, 1971.

**Tabari.** *The History of al-Ṭabari.* Albany: State University of New York Press, 1989– . (A multivolume English translation of the most important classical history of Islam.)

**Watt, W. Montgomery.** *A History of Islamic Spain.* Edinburgh: Edinburgh University Press, 1965. (With additional sections on literature by Pierre Cachia.)

**Wellhausen, Julius.** *The Arab Kingdom and Its Fall.* London: Curzon Press, 1973. (Long the standard critical history.)

———. *The Religio-Political Factions in Early Islam,* trans. R. C. Ostle and S. M. Walzer. Amsterdam: North-Holland, 1975.

**Yücesoy, Hayrettin.** *Messianic Beliefs and Imperial Politics in Medieval Islam: The 'Abbasid Caliphate in the Early Ninth Century.* Columbia, S.C.: University of South Carolina Press, 2009. (A deeply absorbing study of early Islamic messianic beliefs and motivations at a critical period of political history).

# PART THREE

# THE ISLAMIC RELIGIOUS SYSTEM

## *The Qur'an*

### *Translations*

**Ali, A. Yusuf.** *The Koran: Text, Translation and Commentary.* 1934, various reprintings. Especially recommended is the New Revised Edition, *The Holy Qur'ān: Text, Translation and Commentary.* Brentwood, Md.: Amana Corporation, 1409 A.H./1989 C.E. (With Arabic text and extensive explanatory notes.) (Useful to the beginning student of Arabic, because the Arabic text is on facing pages.)

**Arberry, A. J.** *The Koran Interpreted.* London: Allen & Unwin, 1955; New York: Macmillan, 1964. (This author's preference, but every translation is at best an interpretation of the original.)

**Dawood, N. J.** *The Koran: With a Parallel Arabic Text.* London and New York: Viking Penguin, 1990. (A highly reliable modern rendering.)

**Kassis, Hanna.** *A Concordance of the Qur'ān.* Berkeley: University of California Press, 1983. (Invaluable reference.)

**Pickthall, Mohammad Marmaduke.** *The Meaning of the Glorious Koran.* New York: New American Library and Mentor Books, n.d. (Widely available and with useful notes. The project was approved by Muslim authorities in Egypt.)

**Sells, Michael,** translation and commentary. *Approaching the Qur'ān: The Early Revelations.* Ashland, Oreg.: White Cloud Press. (Includes audio CD.)

### Studies

**Baljon, John.** *Modern Muslim Koran Interpretation.* Leiden: E. J. Brill, 1961.

**Bell, Richard.** *Bell's Introduction to the Qur'ān.* Completely revised and edited by W. Montgomery Watt. Edinburgh: Edinburgh University Press, 1970. (The best handbook in English and from a Western scholarly viewpoint.)

**Cragg, Kenneth.** *The Event of the Qur'an: Islam in Its Scripture.* London: Allen & Unwin, 1971. (The background and setting of the Qur'an.)

———. *The Mind of the Qur'an: Chapters in Reflection.* London: Allen & Unwin, 1973. (The most penetrating study of the sacred text yet by a non-Muslim. Intellectually demanding.)

**Esack, Farid.** *The Qur'an: A User's Guide-a Guide to its Key Themes, History and Interpretation.* Oxford: Oneworld, 2005.

**Gade, Anna M.** *Perfection Makes Practice: Learning, Emotion, and the Recited Qur'ān in Indonesia.* Honolulu: University of Hawaii Press, 2004.

**Izutsu, Toshihiko.** *Ethico-Religious Concepts in the Qur'ān.* Montreal: McGill University Press, 1966.

———. *God and Man in the Koran: Semantics of the Koranic Weltanschauung.* Tokyo: Keio Institute of Cultural and Linguistic Studies, 1964. (Both books by Izutsu reward close examination.)

**Jansen, J. J. G.** *The Interpretation of the Koran in Modern Egypt.* Leiden: E. J. Brill, 1974.

**Jeffery, Arthur.** *The Qur'ān As Scripture.* New York: Russell F. Moore, 1957.

**Jomier, Jacques.** *The Bible and the Koran.* Chicago: Henry Regnery, 1967.

**Mir, Mustansir.** *Coherence in the Qur'ān.* Indianapolis: American Trust Publications, 1986.

**Nelson, Kristina.** *The Art of Reciting the Qur'ān.* Austin: University of Texas Press, 1985.

**Parrinder, Geoffrey.** *Jesus in the Qur'an.* New York: Oxford University Press, 1977.

**Quasem, Muhammad Abul.** *The Recitation and Interpretation of the Qur'ān: Al-Ghazali's Theory.* Kuala Lumpur: University of Malaya Press, 1979.

**Rahman, Fazlur.** *Major Themes of the Qur'ān.* Minneapolis and Chicago: Bibliotheca Islamica, 1980. (A penetrating and authoritative review.)

**Welch, Alford T.** Ḳ"ur'ān," in *Encyclopedia of Islām,* new ed., vol. v. Leiden: E. J. Brill, 1981, pp. 400–429.

### Qur'anic Commentary (tafsīr)

**Ayoub, Mahmoud.** *The Qur'ān and its Interpreters.* Albany: State University of New York Press, 1984.

**Gätje, Helmut.** *The Qur'an and Its Exegesis,* trans. Alford T. Welch. London: Routledge & Kegan Paul, 1976. (First published in German in 1971, this anthology of traditional and modern commentary is unique in English. Highly recommended.)

**Maudūdī (Mawdoodi), Abū 'Ala.** *The Meaning of the Qur'an.* Lahore, Pakistan: Sh. Muhammad Ashraf, 1967. (A translation and commentary that has been appearing gradually in small fascicules. Widely studied by English-speaking Muslims.)

**Rippin, Andrew,** ed. *Approaches to the History of the Interpretation of the Qur'ān.* Oxford: Clarendon Press, 1988.

**Smith, Jane I.** *An Historical and Semantic Study of the Term "Islam" As Seen in a Sequence of Qur'ān Commentaries.* Missoula, Mont.: Scholars Press, 1975. (Contains much information on the nature and varieties of *tafsīr,* with generous examples in translation.)

### The Ḥadīth

**al-Baghawī,** and **Walī al-Dīn al-Tibrīzī.** *Mishkāt al-Maṣābīh.* (Mentioned above in "Basic Beliefs. . . . ") (A vast collection of *ḥadīth* -reports on a wide range of topics taken from Sunni collections).

**al-Nawawī.** *Gardens of the Righteous: Riyadh as-Salihin of Imam Nawawi,* trans. Muhammad Zafrullah Khan. London: Curzon Press, 1975. (A famous collection of *ḥadīth* by a famed Shāfi'ī jurist. Topically arranged.)

**'Alī, Muhammad.** *A Manual of Ḥadīth,* 2nd ed. Lahore, Pakistan: Ahmadiyyah Anjuman Ishā'at Islām, n.d. (Conveniently arranged according to major topics of belief and practices. With Arabic text. Based heavily on al-Bukhārī's canonical collection.)

**Azami, Muhammad Mustafa.** *Studies in EarlyḤadīth Literature,* 2nd ed. Indianapolis: American Trust Publications, 1978. (Technical.)

———. *Studies in Ḥadīth Methodology and Literature.* Indianapolis: American Trust Publications, 1977. (Good for beginners.)

**Brown, Jonathan.** *The Canonization of al-Bukhārī and Muslim: The Formation and Function of the Sunnī Hadīth Canon.* Leiden and Boston: Brill, 2007.

**Goldziher, Ignaz.** "On the Development of the adīth," in his *Muslim Studies,* vol. 2, pp. 17–251. (Mentioned earlier.) (The most important technical analysis by a modern Western scholar.)

**Graham, William A.** *Divine Word and Prophetic Word in Early Islam.* The Hague and Paris: Mouton, 1977. (Contains a generous sampling of the *ḥadīth qudsī,* with Arabic text, translation and notes.)

**Juynboll, G. H. A.** *The Authenticity of the Tradition Literature.* Leiden: E. J. Brill, 1969.

**Muslim ibn al-Ḥajjāj al-Qushayrī.** *SaḥīḥMuslim: Being Sayings and Doings of the Prophet Muhammad as Narrated by His Companions and Compiled Under the Title al-Jami'-us-Sahih by Imam Muslim,* trans. Abdul Hamid Siddiqi. Lahore, Pakistan: Sh. Muhammad Ashraf, 1971–1973. (One of the two most authoritative collections, the other being the one by al-Bukhārī.)

**Rahman, Fazlur.** *Islamic Methodology in History.* Karachi, Pakistan: Central Institute of Islamic Research, 1965. (Technical analysis of *ḥadīth* development.)

**Robson, James.** *An Introduction to the Science of Tradition.* London: Royal Asiatic Society of Great Britain and Ireland, 1953. (Text and translation of a classic work by Al-Ḥakīm al-Nīsābūrī, *Al-Madkhal ilāMa'rifat al-Iklīl.*)

**Wensinck, Arendt Jan.** *A Handbook of Early Muhammadan Tradition: Alphabetically Arranged.* Leiden: E. J. Brill, 1960. (A useful guide to *ḥadīths,* topically arranged in alphabetical order. It is almost essential to know Arabic to gain full use of this fine reference work, because the entries are keyed to standard Arabic texts of the *ḥadīths.*)

## *Creeds, Theologies, and Philosophies*

**'Abduh, Muhammad.** *The Theology of Unity (Risālat al-Tawḥīd),* trans. Kenneth Cragg and Ishaq Musa'ad. New York: Humanities Press, 1966.

———. *Ethical Theories in Islam,* 2nd ed. Leiden: E. J. Brill, 1994.

**Al-Ghazālī.** *Deliverance from Error,* trans. and ed. R. J. McCarthy. Louisville, Ky.: Fons Vitae, n.d. (Reprint of original edition entitled *Freedom and Fulfillment.*) New York: Twayne, 1980. (Five important texts of one of Islam's greatest thinkers and spiritual guides.)

**Al-Hillī, Al-Hasan Ibn Yūsuf.** *Al-Bābu 'l-Ḥādī 'Ashar: A Treatise on the Principles of Shi'ite Theology,* trans. William McElwee Miller. London: Royal Asiatic Society, 1928. (Standard Imāmi-Twelver explication.)

**Goodman, Lenn.** *Jewish and Islamic Philosophy: Crosspollinations in the Classic Age.* New Brunswick, NJ: Rutgers University Press, 1999.

_____. *Islamic Humanism.* New York: Oxford University Press, 2003. A richly detailed and elegantly written survey of human-centered, even secular dimensions of classical Islamic civilization—its poetry, music, wine, war, love, play, hunting, dress/display, ethics, theology, epistemology, metaphysics and grand tradition of Arabic universal history.

**Fakhry, Majid.** *A History of Islamic Philosophy,* 2nd ed. New York: Columbia University Press, 1983.

**Ibn Bābawayh, Muhammad ibn 'Alī.** *A Shiite Creed,* A translation of Fyzee, Asaf A. A. *Risālat 'l-I'tiqādat.* London: Oxford University Press, 1942. (Comprehensive and useful for Shī'ī-Sunnī doctrinal comparisons.)

**Jackson, Roy.** *Fifty Key Figures in Islam.* London and New York: Routledge, 2006. Includes solid and informative brief biographies of leading spiritual, legal, theological, philosophical, ethical and historical thinkers from early Islamic history to the present. Lists major works and further reading for each entry.

**Leaman, Oliver.** *An Introduction to Medieval Islamic Philosophy.* Cambridge: Cambridge University Press, 1985.

———. *Averroes and his Philosophy.* Oxford: Clarendon Press, 1988.

**MacDonald, Duncan Black.** *Development of Muslim Theology, Jurisprudence and Constitutional Theory.* New York: Russell & Russell, 1965.

———. *The Religious Attitude and Life in Islam.* New York: AMS Press, 1970. (Excellent chapters on al-Ghazālī.)

**Marmura, Michael E.** *Islamic Theology and Philosophy: Studies in Honor of George F. Hourani.* Albany: State University of New York Press, 1984. A richly diverse collection of articles by leading scholars in the two fields.

**McCarthy, Richard J.** *The Theology of al-Ash'arī: The Arabic Texts of al-Ash'arī's Kitāb al-Luma' and Risālat Istiḥsān al-Khawḍfi 'Ilm al-Kalām.* Beirut: Imprimerie Catholique, 1953. (With translations.)

"Mu'tazila," by H. S. Nyberg, in *Shorter Encyclopaedia of Islam,* pp. 421–427.

**Netton, Ian Richard.** *Allah Transcendent: Studies in the Structure and Semiotics of Islamic Philosophy, Theology and Cosmology.* London and New York: Routledge, 1989.

**Peters, F. E.** *Allah's Commonwealth.* (Mentioned earlier.) (Clear and comprehensive chapters on the development of theology and philosophy.)

**Peters, J. R. T. M.** *God's Created Speech: A Study in the Speculative Theology of the Mu'tazilī Qadi . . . ibn Ahmad al-Hamadani.* Leiden: E. J. Brill, 1976.

**Rahman, Fazlur.** *Prophecy in Islam: Philosophy and Orthodoxy.* London: Allen & Unwin, 1958. (Treats several major thinkers.)

**Reinhart, A. Kevin.** *Before Revelation: The Boundaries of Muslim Moral Thought.* Albany: State University of New York Press, 1995. (Addresses difficult issues pertaining to ethical judgment of acts before the Qur'an).

**Watt, W. Montgomery.** *The Formative Period of Islamic Thought.* Edinburgh: Edinburgh University Press, 1973. (Traces the Mu'tazilite schools.)

———. *Free Will and Predestination in Early Islam.* London: Luzac, 1948.

———. *Islamic Philosophy and Theology.* Edinburgh: Edinburgh University Press, 1962. (Not as much on philosophy as on theology, but a good book for beginners.)

**Wensinck, Arendt Jan.** *The Muslim Creed: Its Genesis and Historical Development.* Cambridge, England: Cambridge University Press, 1932. (Examples of creeds, with full explication and notes.)

**Winter, Tim, ed.** *The Cambridge Companion to Classical Islamic Theology.* Cambridge: Cambridge University Press, 2008. (Comprehensive, substantial articles on a wide range of interrelated subjects e.g. ethics, philosophy, theology, mysticism, worship, cosmology, jurisprudence.)

**Wolfson, Harry Austryn.** *The Philosophy of the Kalam.* Cambridge, Mass.: Harvard University Press, 1976.

## *Islamic Legal and Political Thought*

**Arjomand, Said Amir.** *The Shadow of God and the Hidden Imam: Religion, Political Order, and Social Change in Shi'ite Iran from the Beginning to 1890.* Chicago: University of Chicago Press, 1984.

**Arnold, Thomas W.** *The Caliphate.* New York: Barnes & Noble, 1966.

**Cook, Michael.** *Commanding Right and Forbidding Wrong in Islamic Thought.* Cambridge: Cambridge University Press, 2000.

**Coulson, Noel J.** *A History of Islamic Law.* Edinburgh: Edinburgh University Press, 1964.

**Fyzee, Asaf Ali Asghar.** *Outlines of Muhammadan Law,* 3rd ed. London: Oxford University Press, 1964. (Especially good on the modern period.)

**Gibb, H. A. R.** *Studies on the Civilization of Islam,* ed. S. J. Shaw and W. R. Polk. Boston: Beacon Press, 1962. Chap. 8, "Some Considerations on the Sunni Theory of the Caliphate," Chap. 9, "Al-Mawardi's Theory of the Caliphate," and Chap. 10, "The Islamic Background of Ibn Khaldun's Political Theory."

**Hallaq, Wael.** *A History of Islamic Legal Theories: An Introduction to Sunni Usūl al-Fiqh.* Cambridge: Cambridge University Press, 1999.

———. *Authority, Continuity and Change in Islamic Law.* Cambridge: Cambridge University Press, 2001.

**Hamīdullāh, Muhammad.** *Muslim Conduct of State,* 7th rev. ed. Lahore, Pakistan: Sh. Muhammad Ashraf, 1977. (Islamic law and international relations.)

**Ibn Taimīya.** *Ibn Taimiyya on Public and Private Law in Islam (Al-Siyāsa al-Shar'īya).* Translated by Omar A. Farrukh. Beirut: Khayyats, 1966.

**Kamali, Mohammad Hashim.** *Principles of Islamic Jurisprudence.* Selangor Darul Ehsan, Malaysia: Pelanduk Publications, 1989. (The most useful technical survey in English.)

**Khadduri, Majid.** *The Islamic Conception of Justice.* Baltimore: Johns Hopkins University Press, 1984.

**Khadduri, Majid.** *War and Peace in the Law of Islam.* Baltimore: Johns Hopkins University Press, 1955. (On *jihād* and related matters.)

**Liebesny, Herbert J.** *The Law of the Near and Middle East: Readings, Cases, and Materials.* Albany: State University of New York Press, 1975.

**Peters, Rudolph.** *Jihad in Classical and Modern Islam.* Princeton, N.J.: Markus Wiener Publishers, 1996.

**Roberts, Robert.** *The Social Laws of the Quran: Considered and Compared with Those of the Hebrew and Other Ancient Codes.* London: Curzon Press, 1971.

**Rosenthal, E. I. J.** *Political Thought in Medieval Islam: An Introductory Outline.* Cambridge, England: Cambridge University Press, 1958. (The most useful and informative single survey.)

**Sachedina, Abdulaziz Abdulhussein.** *The Just Ruler in Shi'ite Islam: The Comprehensive Authority of the Jurist in Imamite Jurisprudence.* New York: Oxford University Press, 1988.

**Schacht, Joseph.** *An Introduction to Islamic Law.* Oxford, England: Clarendon Press, 1964. (Critical Western analysis of great intellectual power, but in certain respects offensive to Muslims because of the author's skepticism concerning traditionally accepted Muslim sources and procedures.)

**Shāfi'ī, Muhammad ibn Idris, al-.** *Islamic Jurisprudence: Shāfi'ī's Risāla,* trans. Majid Khadduri. Baltimore: Johns Hopkins University Press, 1961. (The "treatise" on how the greatest Muslim jurist derived the *fiqh* from the Qur'an, the prophetic Ḥadīth (sunna), consensus (*ijmā'*), and analogical reasoning (*qiyās*). An important work.)

## PART FOUR

## THE SUFI WAY OF MYSTICISM AND FELLOWSHIP

**Arberry, A. J.** *An Introduction to the History of Sūfism.* London: Longman, 1942. (A history of scholarship on Sufism.)

———. *Sufism: An Account of the Mystics of Islam.* New York: Harper Torchbooks, 1970. (A good first book on the subject.)

**Archer, John Clark.** *Mystical Elements in Mohammed.* New Haven, Conn.: Yale University Press, 1924.

**As-Sulamī, Abū 'Abd ar-Raḥmān.** *Early Sufi Women,* trans. Rkia E. Cornell. Louisville, Ky.: Fons Vitae, 1999. (Invaluable collection of sources by and about Sufi women, with Arabic texts as well as translation.)

**Bashir, Shahzad.** *Messianic Hopes and Mystical Visions: The Nurbakhshiya Between Medieval and Modern Islam.* Columbia, S.C.: University of South Carolina Press, 2003.

**Burckhardt, Titus.** *An Introduction to Sufi Doctrine,* trans. D. M. Matheson. Lahore, Pakistan: Sh. Muhammad Ashraf, 1959. (A penetrating discussion by a leading Western Sufi. Intended to enlighten seekers rather than simply to inform scholars.)

**Chittick, William C.** *The Sufi Path of Knowledge: Ibn al-'Arabi's Metaphysics of Imagination.* Albany: State University of New York Press, 1989. (The fullest study of the great Andalusian mystic's thought in a Western language, with copious translated passages.)

———. *Faith and Practice of Islam: Three Thirteenth Century Sufi Texts.* Albany: State University of New York Press, 1992. (An excellent introduction to Islam from a normative Sufi perspective.)

**Corbin, Henry.** *Avicenna and the Visionary Recital.* New York: Pantheon, 1960.

———. *Creative Imagination in the Sufism of Ibn 'Arabī.* Princeton, N.J.: Princeton University Press, 1969. (Advanced.)

**Ernst, Carl W.** *Words of Ecstasy in Sufism.* Albany: State University of New York Press, 1985.

**Hodgson, Marshall G. S.** *The Venture of Islam,* vol. 2, "The Ṣūfism of the Ṭarīqa Orders, c. 945–1273," pp. 201–254. (Shows how Sufism offered a sense of order and stability to international Islam.)

**Hoffman, Valerie J.** *Sufism, Mystics, and Saints in Modern Egypt.* Columbia, S.C.: University of South Carolina Press, 1995.

**Hujwīrī, 'Alī ibn 'Uthmān al-Jullabī.** *The Kashf al-Maḥjūb: The Oldest Persian Treatise on Sufiism,* new ed., trans. Reynold A. Nicholson. London: Luzac, 1967. (One of the most informative and balanced surveys ever written.)

**Ibn al-'Arabi, Muḥyī al-Dīn.** *The Tarjumán al-Ashwáq, a Collection of Mystical Odes,* tran. R. A. Nicholson. London: Royal Asiatic Society, 1911.

**Kader, A. H. Abdel.** *The Life, Personality and Writings of al-Junayd.* London: Luzac, 1962.

**Keshavarz, Fatemeh.** *Reading Mystical Lyric: The Case of Jalal al-Din Rumi.* Columbia, S.C.: University of South Carolina Press, 1998. (Emphasizes the great mystical poet's thoroughly realized identity as a creative artist in relation to his life and times).

**Lings, Martin.** *A Sufi Saint of the Twentieth Century.* Berkeley and Los Angeles: University of California Press, 1973. (Absorbing study of the Algerian master Ahmad al-'Alawī and his order in North Africa. Possibly the most engaging book on Sufism in a Western language.)

**Massignon, Louis.** *The Passion of al-Ḥallāj: Mystical Martyr of Islam,* trans. H. Mason, 4 vols. Princeton, N.J.: Princeton University Press, 1983. (A monumental work. Places al-Hallāj in the whole tradition.)

**Nasr, Seyyed Hossein.** *Sufi Essays.* London: Allen & Unwin, 1972. (Penetrating insights that will be enlightening for the modern reader.)

———. *Three Muslim Sages: Avicenna, Suhrawardi, Ibn 'Arabī.* Cambridge, Mass.: Harvard University Press, 1964. (Very accessible to the beginner but based on profound knowledge of the sources.)

**Nicholson, Reynold A.** *The Mystics of Islam.* London: Routledge & Kegan Paul, 1966. (Concentrates on more elite forms.)

———. *Rūmī: Poet and Mystic (1207–1273: Selections from His Writings).* London: Allen & Unwin, 1950. (Good introduction.)

———. *Studies in Islamic Mysticism.* Cambridge, England: Cambridge University Press, 1978. (Translations and commentaries of such leading figures as Ibn al-Fārid.)

**Schimmel, Annemarie.** *Mystical Dimensions of Islam.* Chapel Hill: University of North Carolina Press, 1975. (The best survey of Sufism, drawing from a vast range of sources in many languages.)

———. *The Triumphal Sun: A Study of the Works of Jalāloddin Rumi,* rev. ed. London and The Hague: East-West Publications, 1980.

**Sells, Michael A.** *Early Islamic Mysticism.* New York: Paulist Press, 1996. (Important original sources in English translation.)

**Smith, Margaret.** *Al-Ghazālī, the Mystic.* London: Luzac, 1944. (Very good on the man as well as his context.)

———. *Rābi'a the Mystic and Her Fellow Saints in Islam.* Cambridge, England: Cambridge University Press, 1928. (Additional materials on women and Islamic spirituality make this a timely as well as inherently interesting study.)

**Trimingham, J. Spencer.** *The Sufī Orders in Islam.* Oxford, England: Oxford University Press, 1971. (Very detailed and solid survey.)

**Watt, W. Montgomery.** *The Faith and Practice of al-Ghazālī.* London: Allen & Unwin, 1953. (Translations of two works of the great theologian and Sufi.)

**Waugh, Earle H.** *The Munshidīn of Egypt: Their World and Their Song.* Columbia: University of South Carolina Press, 1989. (Sufi singers in contemporary Egypt.)

_____. *Memory, Music, and Religion: Morocco's Mystical Chanters.* Columbia, S.C.: University of South Carolina Press, 2005. (A field-based study of Sufi singers at the other end of North Africa, with their differences from their Egyptian Sufi brothers and sisters.)

# PART FIVE

## PATTERNS OF ISLAMIC PERSONAL AND COMMUNAL LIFE

**'Abd al 'Aṭī, Hammūdah.** *The Family Structure in Islam.* Indianapolis: American Trust Publications, 1977. (Thorough, technical, and authoritative.)

**Ahmad, Imtiaz,** ed. *Ritual and Religion Among Muslims in India.* New Delhi: Manohar Publications, 1981. (Well-informed social-scientific articles.)

**'Ali, Muhammad.** *The Religion of Islam.* Lahore, Pakistan: Ahmadiyyah Anjuman Isha'at Islam, 1950, and various reprints. (Comprehensive on such legal matters as marriage, divorce, debts, banking, foods, and punishments.)

**Ammar, Hamed.** *Growing Up in an Egyptian Village: Silwa, a Province of Aswan.* New York: Octagon Press, 1966.

**Banu, U. A. B. Razia Akter.** *Islam in Bangladesh.* Leiden: E. J. Brill, 1992. (Sociological study of religious life and customs.)

**Blackman, Winifred Susan.** *The Fellāhīn of Upper Egypt.* London: Frank Cass, 1968. (Good on folk religion and daily life. Illustrated.)

**Bowen, Donna Lee** and **Evelyn A. Early,** eds. *Everyday Life in the Muslim Middle East,* 2nd ed. Bloomington and Indianapolis: Indiana University Press, 2002. (Absorbing portraits and snapshots of daily life through stories, poems, and essays.)

**Bowen, John R.** *Muslims through Discourse: Religion and Ritual in Gayo Society.* Princeton, N.J.: Princeton University Press, 1993. (Excellent ethnographic study of a regional Muslim culture in the Gayo Highlands of Sumatra.)

**Campo, Juan Eduardo.** *The Other Sides of Paradise: Explorations into the Religious Meanings of Domestic Space in Islam.* Columbia: University of South Carolina Press, 1991.

**Canaan, Taufik.** *Mohammedan Saints and Sanctuaries in Palestine.* London: Luzac, 1925.

**Chelkowski, Peter J.,** ed. *Ta'ziyeh: Ritual and Drama in Iran.* New York: New York University Press, 1979.

**cooke, miriam** and **Bruce B. Lawrence,** eds. *Muslim Networks from Hajj to Hip Hop.* Chapel Hill and London: The University of North Carolina Press, 2005. (Muslims have cultivated effective social, religious, commercial, political and military networks in their umma/community throughout Islamic history. This collection of probing essays traces effective Muslim networking practices down to the current era of the Internet).

**De Planhol, Xavier.** *The World of Islam.* Ithaca, N.Y.: Cornell University Press, 1959. (Illuminating study of the relationship between geography and religious life in Muslim countries.)

**Eickelman, Dale F.** *Moroccan Islam: Tradition and Society in a Pilgrimage Center.* Austin: University of Texas Press, 1976.

**Fernea, Elizabeth W.** *Guests of the Sheik.* New York: Anchor Books, 1968. (Absorbing study of the author's life among the women of a traditional village in Iraq.)

**Fischer, Michael M. J.** and **Mehdi Abedi.** *Debating Muslims: Cultural Dialogues in Postmodernity and Tradition.* Madison: University of Wisconsin Press, 1990.

**Gaudefroy-Demombynes, Maurice.** *Muslim Institutions,* trans. John P. MacGregor. London: Allen & Unwin, 1950.

**Geertz, Clifford.** *The Religion of Java.* Glencoe, Ill.: Free Press, 1960. (A modern classic on the relation between religion and culture, with a sensitive treatment of normative and folk Islam.)

**Geertz, Clifford, Hildred Geertz,** and **Lawrence Rosen.** *Meaning and Order in Moroccan Society.* Cambridge, England: Cambridge University Press, 1979. (For a ground-breaking analysis of the ways in which religious symbols and sensibilities inform economic and social behavior, see especially Clifford Geertz's long section, "Suq: The Bazaar Economy in Sefrou." The book also has a fine photo essay.)

**Geertz, Hildred.** *The Javanese Family: A Study of Kinship and Socialization.* Glencoe, Ill.: Free Press, 1961. (Technical but clear, containing much valuable information for understanding religious attitudes and behavior.)

**Gilsenan, Michael.** *Recognizing Islam: An Anthropologist's Introduction.* London and Canberra: Croom and Helm, 1983. (A collection of essays that offers unusual insights into actual life in Muslim contexts, with analyses of signs, gestures, cultural clues, and spatial orientations.)

**Granqvist, Hilma Natalia.** *Birth and Childhood Among the Arabs: Studies in a Muhammadan Village in Palestine.* New York: AMS Press, 1975.

———. *Marriage Conditions in a Palestinian Village,* 2 vols. New York: AMS Press, 1975.

———. *Muslim Death and Burial: Arab Customs and Traditions Studied in a Village in Jordan.* New York: International Publications Service, 1965.

**Koentjaraningrat.** *Javanese Culture.* Singapore: Oxford University Press, 1985. (Chapter 5, on "Javanese Religion," contains valuable data and reflections on Islam in the Javanese context.)

**Lane, Edward William.** *An Account of the Manners and Customs of the Modern Egyptians.* Originally published in 1836. Many editions and reprints, for example, New York: Dover, 1973. (A great work, still very reliable in many details, especially among the *fellāḥīn* [peasants]. Profusely illustrated.)

**Lapidus, Ira,** ed. *Middle Eastern Cities.* Berkeley and Los Angeles: University of California Press, 1969.

**Levy, Reuben.** *The Social Structure of Islam.* Cambridge, England: Cambridge University Press, 1957. (Not clearly organized but repays close reading.)

**Lutfiyya, Abdulla M.** *Baytīn: A Jordanian Village.* The Hague: Mouton, 1966.

**Massé, Henri.** *Persian Beliefs and Customs.* New Haven, Conn.: Human Relations Area Files, 1954. Originally published in 1938 in French. (Good on Shī'ī life.)

**McPherson, Joseph Williams.** *The Moulids of Egypt* ("Egyptian saint's days"). Cairo: N. M. Press, 1941. (Describes scores of festivals throughout Egypt. A wonderful excursion into the Egypt of the 1920s and 1930s.)

**Möller, André.** *Ramadan in Java: The Joy and Jihad of Ritual Fasting.* Lund Studies in History of Religions. Department of History and Anthropology of Religions, Lund University, Lund, Sweden. Stockholm: Almqvist and Wiksell International, 2005.

**Qaradawi, Yusuf al-.** *The Lawful and the Prohibited in Islam (Al-Halal Wal Haram Fil Islam).* Arabic ed. 1960; Indianapolis: American Trust Publications, n.d. (Otherwise difficult-to-find information on a wide range of topics, such as foods, clothing, games, sports, and sexual behavior.)

**Rauf, Muhammad Abdul.** *The Islamic View of Women and the Family.* New York: Robert Speller, 1977.

**Rugh, Andrea B.** *Reveal and Conceal: Dress in Contemporary Egypt.* Syracuse: Syracuse University Press, 1986. (Regional variations and religious meanings; illustrated.)

**Schimmel, Annemarie.** *Islamic Names.* Edinburgh: Edinburgh University Press, 1989. (Absorbing, detailed, technical survey with much discussion of religious meanings in a variety of Muslim cultures.)

**Smith, Jane Idleman** and **Yvonne Yazbeck Haddad.** *The Islamic Understanding of Death and Resurrection.* Albany: State University of New York Press, 1981. (Treats both classical and modern attitudes.)

**Sweet, Louise E.,** ed. *Peoples and Cultures of the Middle East,* 2 vols. Garden City, N.Y.: Natural History Press, 1970. (Expert articles on many aspects of life in the region.)

**Von Grunebaum, Gustave E.** *Islam: Essays in the Nature and Growth of a Cultural Tradition,* 2nd ed. London: Routledge & Kegan Paul, 1961. Especially Chap. 7, "The Structure of the Muslim Town."

**Waardenburg, J. D. J.** "Official and Popular Religion As a Problem in Islamic Studies," in *Official and Popular Religion As a Theme in the Study of Religion,* ed. Pieter Hendrik Vrijhof and Jacques Waardenburg. The Hague: Mouton, 1979.

**Westermarck, Edward Alexander.** *Ritual and Belief in Morocco,* 2 vols. London: Macmillan, 1926. (Massively detailed descriptions, based on extensive field work. A classic.)

**Woodward, Mark R.** *Islam in Java: Normative Piety and Mysticism in the Sultanate of Yogyakarta.* Tucson: University of Arizona Press, 1989.

# PART SIX

# ISLAM IN THE MODERN WORLD

## *General*

**Adams, Charles C.** *Islam and Modernism in Egypt.* London: Oxford University Press, 1933. (Especially good on Muhammad 'Abduh and his circle.)

**Ahmad, Aziz.** *Islamic Modernism in India and Pakistan, 1857–1964.* London: Oxford University Press, 1967.

**Akbarzadeh, Shahram** and **Benjamin MacQueen,** eds. *Islam and Human Rights in Practice: Perspectives Across the Ummah.* London and New York: Routledge, 2008.

**Akhtar, Shabbir.** *A Faith For All Seasons: Islam and the Challenge of the Modern World.* Chicago: Ivan R. Dee, 1990.

**An-Na'im, Abdullahi Ahmed.** *Toward an Islamic Reformation: Civil Liberties, Human Rights, and International Law.* Syracuse: Syracuse University Press, 1990.

_____. *Islam and the Secular State: Negotiating the Future of Shari'a.* Cambridge, MA and London, UK: Harvard University Press, 2008.

**Antoun, Richard T.** *Muslim Preacher in the Modern World: A Jordanian Case Study in Comparative Perspective.* Princeton, N.J.: Princeton University Press, 1989.

**Berkes, Niyazi.** *The Development of Secularism in Turkey.* Montreal: McGill University Press, 1964.

**Boland, B. J.** *The Struggle of Islam in Modern Indonesia.* The Hague: Martinus Nijhoff, 1971.

**Brockopp, Jonathan E.,** ed. *Islamic Ethics of Life: Abortion, War, and Euthanasia.* Columbia, S.C.: University of South Carolina Press, 2003.

**Bunt, Gary.** *Virtually Islamic: Computer-Mediated Communication and Cyber Islamic Environments.* Cardiff: University of Wales Press, 2000.

———. *Islam in the Digital Age: E-Jihad, Online Fatwas and Cyber Islamic Environments.* London and Sterling, Va.: Pluto Press, 2003.

**Cragg, Kenneth.** *Counsels in Contemporary Islam.* Edinburgh: Edinburgh University Press, 1965. (Masterful analyses of Islam and modernity in a variety of countries. Very extensive bibliography of works in several languages.)

**Esposito, John L.** and **John O. Voll.** *Makers of Contemporary Islam.* New York: Oxford University Press, 2001.

_____ and **Dalia Mogahed.** *Who Speaks for Islam? What a Billion Muslims Really Think.* Based on Gallup's World Poll—the largest study of its kind. New York: Gallup Press, 2007.

**Feener, R. Michael,** ed. *Islam in World Cultures: Comparative Perspectives.* Santa Barbara, Ca.: ABC-CLIO, 2004. (Regional specialists provide abundant data and analysis to show the cultural diversity of the contemporary Muslim world).

**Foltz, Richard C., Frederick M. Denny,** and **Azizan Baharuddin,** eds. *Islam and Ecology: A Bestowed Trust.* Cambridge: Harvard University Press, 2003.

**Geertz, Clifford.** *Islam Observed: Religious Development in Morocco and Indonesia.* New Haven, Conn.: Yale University Press, 1968. (Masterful comparative study.)

**Gerholm, Tomas** and **Yngre Georg Lithman,** eds. *The New Islamic Presence in Western Europe.* London and New York: Mansell, 1988.

**Gibb, H. A. R.** *Modern Trends in Islam.* Chicago: University of Chicago Press, 1947. (Lays out nearly all the issues. Dated as to details, but intellectually dateless.)

**Gladney, Dru C.** *Muslim Chinese: Ethnic Nationalism in the People's Republic.* Cambridge, MA: Harvard University Press, 1996.

**Hourani, Albert.** *Arabic Thought in the Liberal Age, 1798–1939.* London: Oxford University Press, 1962. (A classic study.)

**Iqbal, Sir Muhammad.** *The Reconstruction of Religious Thought in Islam.* Lahore, Pakistan: Sh. Muhammad Ashraf, 1951. (A profound philosophy of religion for modern times, by the "Father" of Pakistan.)

**Israeli, Raphael.** *Muslims in China: A Study in Cultural Confrontation.* London: Curzon Press, 1980.

**Keppel, Gilles.** *Muslim Extremism in Egypt: The Prophet and the Pharaoh*, trans. Jon Rothschild. Berkeley: University of California Press, 1985.

**Kerr, Malcom H.** *Islamic Reform: The Political and Legal Theories of Muhammad 'Abduh and Rashīd Riḍā.* Berkeley and Los Angeles: University of California Press, 1966.

**Krämer, Gudrun** and **Sabine Schmidtke,** eds. *Speaking for Islam: Religious Authorities in Muslim Societies.* Leiden and Boston: Brill, 2006.

**Kurzman, Charles,** ed. *Liberal Islam: A Sourcebook.* New York: Oxford University Press, 1998.

**Lewis, I. M.,** ed. *Islam in Tropical Africa.* London: Oxford University Press, 1966.

**Marty, Martin E.** and **R. Scott Appleby,** eds. *Fundamentalisms Observed,* The Fundamentalism Project, vol. 1. Chicago: University of Chicago Press, 1991. See the following chapters: "Fundamentalism in the Sunni Arab World: Egypt and the Sudan," by John O. Voll, pp. 345–402; "Activist Shi'ism in Iran, Iraq, and Lebanon," by Abdulaziz A. Sachedina, pp. 403–456; and "Islamic Fundamentalism in South Asia: The Jamaat-i-Islami and the Tablighi Jamaat of South Asia," by Mumtaz Ahmad, pp. 457–530.

**Mayer, Ann Elizabeth.** *Islam and Human Rights: Tradition and Politics,* 3rd ed. Boulder and Oxford: Westview Press, 1999.

**Mitchell, Richard P.** *The Society of the Muslim Brothers.* London: Oxford University Press, 1969. (The standard work.)

**Mottahedeh, Roy.** *The Mantle of the Prophet: Religion and Politics in Iran.* New York: Simon & Schuster, 1985.

**Norris, Harry.** *Islam in the Balkans.* Columbia, S.C.: University of South Carolina Press, 1993.

**Quṭb, Sayyid.** *Milestones.* Indianapolis: American Trust Publications, 1990 [originally published in Arabic in 1964]. (Enormously influential with Muslim fundamentalists.)

**Rahman, Fazlur.** *Islam in Modernity: The Transformation of an Intellectual Tradition.* Chicago: University of Chicago Press, 1982. (A candid critique.)

**Reid, Anthony** and **Michael Gilsenan,** eds. *Islamic Legitimacy in a Plural Asia.* London and New York: Routledge, 2007. (Addresses thorny issues of pluralism and co-existence of Muslims with non-Muslims in South and Southeast Asia in the present day).

**Safi, Omid,** ed. *Progressive Muslims: On Justice, Gender, and Pluralism.* Oxford: Oneworld, 2003. (Ground-breaking essays by Muslim scholar-activists with independent views of an "Islam without borders.")

**Said, Edward.** *Covering Islam: How the Media and the Experts Determine How We See the Rest of the World.* New York: Pantheon, 1981. See also the author's famous study of Western colonialist-minded scholarship on the Middle East and Asia. *Orientalism.* New York: Pantheon, 1978.

**Sardar, Ziauddin.** *The Future of Muslim Civilization.* Petaling Jaya, Malaysia: Pelanduk, 1988.

**Schubel, Vernon James.** *Religious Performance in Contemporary Islam: Shi'i Devotional Rituals in South Asia.* Columbia, S.C.: University of South Carolina Press, 1993.

**Smith, Wilfred Cantwell.** *Islam in Modern History.* Princeton, N.J.: Princeton University Press, 1957. (An excellent analysis by a scholar who had a rare grasp of Islamic history and religious studies as a whole.)

———. *Modern Islam in India.* London: Victor Gollancz, 1946; Lahore, Pakistan: Sh. Muhammad Ashraf, 1969. (Detailed study down to World War II.)

**Soroush, Abdolkarim.** *Reason, Freedom, and Democracy in Islam: Essential Writings of Abdolkarim Soroush,* trans., ed., Introd. by Mahmoud Sadri and Ahmad Sadri. New York: Oxford University Press, 2000.

**Van Bruinessen, Martin** and **Julia Day Howell,** eds. *Sufism and the "Modern" in Islam.* London and New York: I.B. Tauris, 2007. (Interesting and timely articles on a wide variety of Sufi-related situations, issues, challenges, and developments in diverse locations around the contemporary Muslim world).

**Vogt, Kary, Lena Larsen,** and **Christian Moe,** eds. *New Directions in Islamic Thought: Exploring Reform and Muslim Tradition.* London and New York: I.B. Tauris and Co., Ltd., 2009.

**Voll, John O.** *Islam: Continuity and Change in the Modern World,* 2nd ed. Syracuse: Syracuse University Press, 1994.

## *Islam and Muslims in North America*

**Fischer, Michael M.** and **Mehdi Abedi.** *Debating Muslims: Cultural Dialogues in Postmodernity and Tradition.* Cited earlier; treats Houston, Texas Muslims.

**Haddad, Yvonne Yazbeck,** ed. *The Muslims of America.* New York: Oxford University Press, 1991.

**Haddad, Yvonne Yazbeck** and **Adair T. Lummis.** *Islamic Values in the United States: A Comparative Study.* New York: Oxford University Press, 1987. (Note the extensive bibliography.)

**Hasan, Asma Gull.** *American Muslims: The New Generation.* New York and London: Continuum, 2001.

**Husaini, Zohra.** *Muslims in the Canadian Mosaic: Socio-cultural and Economic Links with their Countries of Origin.* Edmonton, Alberta: Muslim Research Foundation, 1990.

**Lee, Martha F.** *The Nation of Islam: An American Millenarian Movement.* Lewiston, N.Y.: Edwin Mellen Press, 1988.

**Leonard, Karen Isaksen.** *Muslims in the United States: The State of Research.* New York: Russell Sage, 2003.

**Lincoln, C. Eric.** *The Black Muslims in America,* rev. ed. Boston: Beacon Press, 1973.

**Malcolm, X.** with **Alex Haley.** *The Autobiography of Malcolm X.* New York: Ballantine, 1973.

**Marsh, Clifton E.** *From Black Muslims to Muslims: The Transition from Separatism to Islam, 1930–1980.* Metuchen, N.J.: Scarecrow Press, 1984.

**McCloud, Aminah Beverly.** *African American Islam.* New York and London: Routledge, 1995.

**Smith, Jane I.** *Islam in America.* New York: Columbia University Press, 1999.

**Waugh, Earle H., Baha Abu-Laban,** and **Regula B. Qureshi,** eds. *The Muslim Community in North America.* Edmonton: University of Alberta Press, 1983.

**Waugh, Earle H., Sharon McIrvin Abu-Laban,** and **Regula Burckhardt Qureshi,** eds. *Muslim Families in North America.* Edmonton: University of Alberta Press, 1991.

## *Women and Islam*

**Abbott, Nabia.** *Aishah, the Beloved of Muhammad.* Chicago: University of Chicago Press, 1942.

**Abou El Fadl, Khaled.** *Speaking in God's Name: Islamic Law, Authority and Women.* Oxford: Oneworld, 2001.

**Ahmed, Leila.** *Women and Gender in Islam: Historical Roots of a Modern Debate.* New Haven, Conn.: Yale University Press, 1992.

**Ali, Ayaan Hirsi.** *The Caged Virgin: An Emancipation Proclamation for Women and Islam.* New York: Free Press, 2006.

**Atiya, Nayra.** *Khul-Khaal: Five Egyptian Women Tell their Stories.* Syracuse: Syracuse University Press, 1982.

**Badran, Margot.** *Feminism Beyond East and West: New Gender Talk and Practice in Global Islam.* New Delhi: Global Media Publications, 2007. (Samples data on the subject from Middle Eastern African and Asian countries as well as the West.)

**Beck, Lois** and **Nikkie Keddie,** eds. *Women in the Muslim World.* Cambridge, Mass.: Harvard University Press, 1978.

**cooke, miriam.** *Women Claim Islam: Creating Islamic Feminism through Literature.* New York and London: Routledge, 2001.

**Esposito, John L.** *Women in Muslim Family Law.* Syracuse: Syracuse University Press, 1981.

**Fernea, Elizabeth Warnock** and **Basima Qattan Bezirgan,** eds. *Middle Eastern Muslim Women Speak.* Austin: University of Texas Press, 1977.

**Jeffery, Patricia.** *Frogs in a Well: Indian Women in Purdah.* London: Zed Press, 1979.

**Kandiyoti, Deniz,** ed. *Women, Islam and the State.* Philadelphia: Temple University Press, 1991.

**Keddie, Nikki R.** *Women in the Middle East: Past and Present.* Princeton and Oxford: Princeton University Press, 2007. (A combination of previously published and new work in three "books": An important history of women in the Middle East, followed by theoretical and methodological considerations of approaches to the study of Middle Eastern women, and ending with an autobiographical interview of the author with an updated supplement.)

**Macleod, Arlene Elowe.** *Accommodating Protest: Working Women, the New Veiling, and Change in Cairo.* New York: Columbia University Press, 1991.

**Maududi, Abul A'la.** *Purdah and the Status of Woman in Islam,* 10th ed. (first published in Urdu in 1939). trans. and ed. Al-Ash'ari. Lahore: Islamic Publications Limited, 1990. (A highly influential treatise along ultra-conservative lines.)

**Mernissi, Fatima.** *Beyond the Veil: Male–Female Dynamics in Modern Muslim Society,* rev. ed. Bloomington and Indianapolis: Indiana University Press, 1987. (Radical Muslim feminist critique of patriarchal Muslim societies.)

———. *The Veil and the Male Elite: A Feminist Interpretation of Women's Rights in Islam,* trans. Mary Jo Lakeland. Reading, Mass.: Addison-Wesley, 1991. (Continues from the above by examining the classical textual sources of Islamic history, institutions, law, and theology concerning sex and gender roles in Islam.)

**Najmabadi, Afsaneh.** *Women with Mustaches and Men without Beards: Gender and Sexual Anxieties of Iranian Modernity.* Berkeley: University of California Press, 2005.

**Nouraie-Simone, Fereshte,** ed. *On Shifting Ground: Muslim Women in the Global Era.* New York: The Feminist Press of the City University of New York, 2005.

**Saadawi, Nawal.** el-. *The Hidden Face of Eve: Women in the Arab World,* trans. and ed. Sherif Hetata. London: Zed Press, 1980. (A radical, angry book by an Egyptian Muslim feminist physician. Discusses love, sex, clitoridectomy, abortion, and women's liberation in Islamic societies.)

**Shaaban, Bouthaina.** *Both Right and Left Handed: Arab Women Talk About Their Lives.* Bloomington and Indianapolis: Indiana University Press, 1991. (Frank testimonies of Algerian, Lebanese, Palestinian, and Syrian women on a wide range of topics connected with marriage, family, work, and social life.)

**Shaarawi, Huda.** *Harem Years: The Memoirs of an Egyptian Feminist (1879–1924),* Intro., trans. and ed. Margot Badran. New York: The Feminist Press at the City University of New York, 1987.

**Siddiqi, Mohammed Mazheruddin.** *Women in Islam.* Lahore: Institute of Islamic Culture, [1952] 1990.

**Siddiqi, Muhammad Iqbal.** *Islam Forbids Free Mixing of Men and Women.* Lahore: Kazi Publications, 1983.

**Souaiaia, Ahmed E.** *Contesting Justice: Women, Islam, Law, and Society.* Albany: State University of New York Press, 2008.

**van Nieuwkerk, Karin,** ed. *Women Embracing Islam: Gender and Conversion in the West.* Austin: University of Texas Press, 2006.

**Waddy, Charis.** *Women in Muslim History.* London and New York: 1980. (Informative sketches of the lives of Muslim women from the Prophet's time to the present time.)

**Wadud, Amina.** *Qur'an and Woman: Rereading the Sacred Text from a Woman's Perspective.* 2nd ed. New York: Oxford University Press, 1999.

_____. *Inside the Gender Jihad: Women's Reform in Islam.* Oxford: Oneworld, 2006.

**Walther, Wiebke.** *Woman in Islam.* London and Montclair, N.J.: George Prior, 1981. (Historical survey with many illustrations.)

**Webb, Gisela,** ed. *Windows of Faith: Muslim Women Scholar-Activists in North America.* Syracuse, N.Y.: Syracuse University Press, 2000.

**Women and Islam.** special issue of *Women's Studies International Forum,* vol. 5, no. 2. New York: Pergamon Press, 1982.

**Zuhur, Sherifa.** *Revealing Reveiling: Islamist Gender Ideology in Contemporary Egypt.* Albany: State University of New York Press, 1992.

# Glossary

**Abangan** The broad peasant class of syncretistic Muslims in Indonesia, especially Java.
**'Abbāsids** Great dynasty of classical Islamic civilization (750–1258 C.E.).
**'Abd** "Slave," "servant," especially of God. 'Abd Allāh means "slave of God."
**Abrahamic** Pertaining to the patriarch, to whom Jews, Christians, and Muslims all trace their spiritual origins.
**Adhān** The "call" to *ṣalāt* ("worship"), uttered by the *mu'adhdhin.*
**Al-aḥkām al-khamsa** The "five principles" of Islamic law relating to acts: *farḍ* ("obligatory"), *sunna* ("recommended"), *mubāh* ("indifferent"), *makrūh* ("reprehensible"), and *ḥarām* ("forbidden").
**Ahl al-'adl wa 'l-tawḥīd** "The People of Justice and (Divine) Unity," the formal name that the Mu'tazilites gave themselves.
**Ahl al-Bayt** "People of the House," namely the family of the Prophet.
**Ahl al-Kitāb** "People of the Book," meaning especially the Jews and Christians, but also the Zoroastrians. Tolerated as *dhimmīs* by Muslim governments.
**'Alid** One who has special respect for 'Ali and his line. Extends to the political sphere but does not necessarily imply Shī'ī partisanship.
**'Ālim** One learned in *'ilm,* "religious knowledge" (pl., *'ulamā'*).
**Allāh** "God." A contraction of Arabic *al-ilāh,* "The God."
**Anṣār** "Helpers," namely, the Medinans who joined with Muhammad and his Meccan Muslim followers in establishing the umma.
**'Aqīda** A creedal statement in summary of basic religious beliefs.
**'Aqīqa** Ceremony of haircutting seven days after birth of Muslim child.
**'Aṣabiya** Strong group feeling, as of Arab tribes.
**Asbāb nuzūl al-Qur'ān** The "occasions of revelation" of the Qur'an. Historical events connected with times of specific revelations.
**'Āshūrā'** The "tenth" of the Muslim month of Muharram. A traditional day of fasting for Jews and, later, Muslims. Especially sacred to the Shī'īs, because Imām Husayn was martyred on that day at Karbalā'.
**Al-Asmā' al-Ḥusnā** "The most beautiful Names" of God, said to number ninety-nine.
**'Awra** Literally, "genitals." The portions of the body that should be properly covered; males—from navel to knees, females—all but the face, hands, and feet (according to the strictest observance).
**Āya (pl., āyāt)** "Sign" of God in the created universe. Also means "verse" of the Qur'an.
**Āyat Allāh** "Ayatollah." Literally, "sign of God," but in Iranian Shī'ism, the title of an especially revered member of the *'ulamā'*.

**Baqā'** Sufi technical term for eternal "abiding" with God.
**Baraka** "Blessing," "spiritual power" (pl., *barakāt*).
**Barzakh** "Isthmus" or "interval" between death and resurrection. A kind of Muslim "purgatory."
**Basmala** The name of the invocation: *Bismillāhi 'l-Raḥmāni 'l-Raḥīm* ("In the Name of God, the Beneficent, the Merciful.")
**Bāṭin** "Interior," "esoteric," particularly with respect to saving knowledge, or *gnosis.*
**Bay'a** Oath of allegiance to a ruler, especially a caliph.
**Bid'a** "Innovation," meaning heresy in the context of Islamic law and doctrine.
**Bilā kayfa** "Without (asking) how," Ahmad ibn Hanbal's formula concerning the Qur'an's literal sense, including anthropomorphisms, which must be accepted, *bilā kayfa,* regardless of rational objections.

**Dahr** "Time," or "fate," among the pre-Islamic Arabs.
**Dār al-Islām** "The Abode of Islam," meaning those territories of the umma that are under Muslim control. The rest of the world is known as the *Dār al-Ḥarb,* "The Abode of Warfare," because it has not "surrendered" to God and come to enjoy the benefits of Sharī'a rule.
**"Daughters of Allah"** The three Arabian goddesses: al-Lāt, al-'Uzzā, and Manāt, named in Sūra 53:19–20. The Qur'an rejects them.
**Da'wa** "Call," "bidding," to Islam. Missionary activity of Muslims.
**Dhikr** "Mentioning," "remembering" God. The central Sufi form of spiritual discipline, with many specific types.
**Dhimmī** A member of the "People of the Book" (*Ahl al-Kitāb*), who is protected in his or her minority status when living under Muslim rule, in exchange for certain obligations such as paying the "head tax" (*jizya*). From *dhimma,* a covenant of "protection."
**Dīn** "Religion," especially in practice. *Al-Dīn al-Islāmī means "the Islamic religion."*
**Du'ā'** "Calling" upon God in supplication or petition. Spontaneous and individual prayer, as distinguished from the formal prayer service of salāt.

**Falāḥ** "Success," "prosperity." The most idiomatic Islamic parallel to the English word *salvation.* Applies to this life and the hereafter.
**Falsafa** "Philosophy." A philosopher is called in Arabic a *faylasūf* (pl., *falāsifa*). Borrowed from the Greek *philosophia.*
**fanā'** "Passing away," "extinction." The Sufi technical term for the ceasing to be before attaining final union with God.
**faqīh** One expert in *fiqh;* a jurist (pl., *fuqahā'*).
**faqīr** "Poor person." In Sufism, one who is a mendicant. *Faqr* is voluntary, that is, spiritual poverty as well as normal poverty.
**farḍ** "Obligatory" duty, as the five daily salāts.
**Al-Fātiḥa** "The Opening," meaning the first sūra of the Qur'an. It is a prayer frequently uttered in many contexts.
**Fatwā** A learned legal opinion produced by a *muftī,* "jurisconsult" (pl., *fatāwa*).
**Fiqh** "Understanding" of the law, and therefore jurisprudence.
**Fitna** "Trial," "testing." In Islamic history, great trials and tribulations experienced by the umma, as in the early dissensions (pl., *fitan*).
**Fiṭra** Humankind's natural constitution or disposition, which is believed to be sound.
**Furqān** "Criterion" between right and wrong. A name for the Qur'an. Sometimes translated "salvation," as is *falāḥ,* but neither term means "redemption."

**Ghayba** "Occultation," a sort of mysterious concealment. The Imāmī Shī'īs believe that their twelfth imām is concealed by *ghayba* but still ruling the world.
**Ghazwa** "Raiding," as in pre-Islamic Arabia. The chief object was camels.
**Ghusl** The major ablution, entailing a full ritual bath, after major *ḥadath.*

**Ḥadath** Impurity, of which there are two kinds recognized by the Islamic law: "minor" (*asghar*) and "major" (*akbar*). The first refers to ritual impurity of a part of the body, the second to the whole body. Minor *ḥadath* is removed by *wuḍū';* major by *ghusl.*
**Ḥadīth** "Report," "event," "news." A literary form that communicates a *sunna* of the Prophet Muhammad (pl., *aḥādīth*).
**Ḥadīth Qudsī** "Divine saying." God's thoughts expressed in Muhammad's words. Occupies an exalted position between the Qur'an and the prophetic Ḥadith.
**Ḥāfiẓ** "Guardian," "keeper." One who knows the Qur'an by heart (pl., *ḥuffāz*).
**Ḥajj** "Pilgrimage" to Mecca during pilgrimage month (*Dhū 'l-Hijja*). A male pilgrim is a *ḥājjī,* and a female a *ḥājja,* which are terms of considerable honor.
**Ḥāl** Sufi "state," an unearned grace on the mystic path to God (pl. *aḥwāl*). Contrasted with *maqām,* an earned "station" on the path.
**Ḥalāl** "Permissible," "lawful," as regarding food and activities. The opposite of *ḥarām,* "forbidden."
**Ḥanafiya** *Madhhab* of Sunni law founded by Abū Hanīfa (adj., *Ḥanafī* or Hanafite).
**Ḥanbalīya** *Madhhab* of Sunni law founded by Ahmad ibn Hanbal (adj., *Ḥanbalī* or Hanbalite).
**Ḥanīf** In the Qur'an, means a pure or "generic" monotheist, such as Abraham, who was not Jew, Christian, or qur'anic Muslim (pl., *ḥunafā'*).

**Ḥaram** "Sanctuary," such as Mecca or Medina. The two together are called in Arabic *Al-Ḥaramayn,* "the two sanctuaries." *Ḥaram* also means "sacred," "forbidden," "taboo," "holy."

**Ḥarām** In Islamic law, means "forbidden," and punishable. Can also mean "sacred" and therefore also forbidden in the sense of taboo. Both *ḥaram and ḥarām* express the ambivalence of the sacred, its terrible as well as its sublime sides.

**Ḥarīm** "Harem," meaning the private quarters of a traditional Arab Muslim home where the women and children reside inviolate and out of sight of strangers.

**Ḥijāb** "Cover, curtain, veil." The Muslim practice of veiling women, either by covering the hair, or the entire head and face. In South Asia this is called *purdah,* and may also mean the seclusion of females.

**Hijra** "Emigration," especially of the Prophet and his companions in 622 from Mecca to Medina.

**Hilāl** The new crescent moon, which marks the beginning of months and sacred seasons in Muslim countries. A symbol of the Islamic religion.

**Ḥilm** "Forbearance," the mark of a superior man in pre-Islamic Arabia. Possessed only by the person of great spiritual as well as physical strength and courage. One of the names of God is *Al-Ḥalīm,* "The Gently Forbearing."

**Ḥizb** One sixtieth of the Qur'an, a division recognized for systematic recitation of the entire scripture. A *rub' ḥal-izb,* "one quarter of a (sixtieth) section," is recited in ten or fifteen minutes, and is a typical "turn" when several are reciting together.

**'Ibāda** "Worship," especially the five pillars. Literally, "service."

**'Īd** "Festival." There are two canonical festivals recognized by Islamic law: the great feast, known as *al-aḍḥā,* "The Feast of Sacrifice," and the minor feast, called *'Īd al-fiṭr,* "The Feast of Breaking the Ramadān Fast."

**Iḥrām** State of ritual purity and sanctity, achieved by renouncing certain activities and donning a special garb (also called *iḥrām*) when commencing the hajj, or pilgrimage to Mecca.

**I'jāz al-Qur'ān** "Miraculous nature," especially of the Qur'an. *Mu'jiza* means "miracle."

**Ijmā'** "Consensus," one of the four sources of Sunnī *fiqh.*

**Ijtihād** Independent legal reasoning, engaged in by a *mujtahid.*

**'Ilm** "Knowledge," "science" (pl. *'ulūm,* "sciences"). Those who possess knowledge of the religious sciences are called the *'ulamā'.*

**'Ilm al-rijāl** "The science of men," a branch of Ḥadīth sciences that focuses on the transmitters of *ḥadiths* and their *isnāds,* to determine their trustworthiness and soundness.

**Imām** "Leader," as in the daily salāts. The Shī'īs hold an exalted view of their imāms, who have been invested with infallible guidance by God. An imām may also be a religious teacher with no special sacrality.

**Imāmā** Referring to the "Twelver" branch of Shī'ism, which recognizes twelve holy imāms.

**Īmān** "Faith," a religious virtue that is more highly regarded by the Qur'an than *islām,* "surrender." One who has faith is a *mu'min.*

**Al-Insān al-Kāmil** "The Complete Human" or "Perfect Man." A Sufi theosophical concept of an exalted human who rules the universe as God's agent. The *Insān Kāmil* is at the top of the hierarchy of saints.

**'Irḍ** "Honor," especially of pre-Islamic Arabian males.

**Islām** "Surrender," "submission." The name of the religion of the Qur'an. One who surrenders is called a *muslim.*

**Ism** Personal given name, such as 'Umar, Zaynab.

**Ismā'īlī** A major Shī'ī branch, which takes its name from Ismā'īl, the sixth imām, Ja'far al-Sādiq's older son, who is regarded as the true successor to Ja'far. His position in the succession gives the alternative name of "seven-imām Shī'ism" to the Ismā'īlīs. The Ismā'īlīs have a complex, esoteric doctrine of the imām.

**Isnād** The process of providing authentication for *ḥadīths.* A *sanad* (pl. *asnād*) is a "prop" or "support," in the sense of a person who has transmitted the report. The *isnād* is the connection of the chain of transmitters of a given *ḥadīth.*

**Isrā'** A night journey, especially Muhammad's miraculous flight from Mecca to Jerusalem on the night of his ascension (*mi'rāj*) to heaven.

**Isti'ādha** "Seeking refuge" in God from Satan and evil, especially when beginning recitation of the Qur'an.

**I'tikāf** Spiritual retreat, especially during the last ten days of Ramadān, when Muslim men often seclude themselves in mosques for prayer.

**Ja'farīya** The major Shī'ī school of law, named after Imām Ja'far al-Sādiq.
**Jahannum** The qur'anic term for hell, paralleling the Hebrew *gehenna*.
**Al-Jāhilīya** The pre-Islamic Arabian era of "barbaric ignorance."
**Jamā'a** "Community," "group." A synonym for the umma, but it has more restricted meanings, too.
**Janāba** A form of major *ḥadath* (ritual impurity), usually related to sexual activities, such as seminal emission, orgasm, and intercourse.
**Janāza** "Funeral bier" and rites associated with burial.
**Al-Janna** "The garden," a major Qur'anic concept of the hereafter of the blessed.
**Jihād** "Striving," "exertion," especially in the religious path or holy war.
**Jinn** "Genies," a class of spirit creatures made of fire that are often, but not always, evil or mischievous. They appear in the Qur'an (Sing., *jinnī*).
**Juz'** One thirtieth part of the Qur'an, for reciting the whole in a month, by reading one section each day.

**Ka'ba** Literally "cube." The main Islamic sanctuary in Mecca.
**Kāfir** "Infidel." The root, *kufr*, includes the meaning "ingratitude."
**Kāhin** Soothsayer, diviner, especially in Jāhilīya Arabia.
**Kalām** "Speech," "discourse," especially on religious matters. *'Ilm al-Kalām* is dialectical or systematic theology.
**Khalīfa** "Successor," "deputy," especially of the Prophet. Caliph.
**Khilāfa** The caliphate.
**Khānqāh** Persian term for Sufi retreat or cloister.
**Khātam al-Anbiyā'** "Seal of the Prophets," a title of Muhammad, who was last and who validated the true prophecies of former times.
**Khatmat al-Qur'an** A recitation of the entire Qur'an, often on special occasions.
**Khawārij** Khārijites. The strict sect of early Islamic history.
**Al-Khiḍr** "The green one," a mysterious figure in Near Eastern folklore, who is thought sometimes to bestow blessings, protection, and mystical initiation. He is considered to be a special agent of God.
**Khirqa** The tattered woolen "mantle" of the Sufi, symbolizing poverty (*faqr*).
**Khitān** Circumcision.
**Khuṭba** The "sermon" preached at the Friday congregation salat, by the *khaṭīb*, "preacher."
**Kiswa** The richly brocaded cloth that covers the Ka'ba.
**Kitāb** "Writing," "book," "scripture."
**Kunya** An honorific name of relationship, such as *Abū*, "father" (of), *Umm*, "mother" (of), for example, Abū Bakr, Umm Kulthūm.

**Lahd** The hollowed-out side of a grave wall where the corpse reposes in Muslim burial. It is on the *qibla* side.
**Laqab** An honorific or nickname based on special circumstances pertaining to the bearer. For example, Abū Hurayra received his *laqab*, meaning "Father of the Kitten," because he was so fond of felines.

**Madhhab** "Way" of acting, "procedure." School of Islamic law (pl., *madhāhib*).
**Mahdī** "Guide," "leader." Messianic figure who will appear at the end of the world and usher in a new order. There are various theories.
**Mahr** The "bridal gift" or dowry that the groom is required to give to his wife at the time of marriage.
**Maḥram** "Forbidden, taboo." In Islamic law *maḥram* refers to the boundaries of legal consanguinity, within which males and females are forbidden to marry and thus are permitted to associate freely with fathers, daughters, brothers, sons, nephews, etc.
**Malāmatīya** An antinomian Sufi movement, based on the conviction that those who bring censure or blame (*malāma*) upon themselves will be specially protected by God for relying on him alone (and not on obedience of the Sharī'a).
**Mālikīya** The Mālikī *madhhab* of Sunni *fiqh*, founded by Anas Ibn Mālik.
**Manāsik** Sacred rituals, particularly of the hajj.
**Maqām** A sufi "station," considered to be an earned stage on the path to union with God.
**Ma'rifa** Mystical knowledge, understanding. Gnosis.
**Masjid** "Place of prostration," mosque.
**Masjid jāmi'** "Friday mosque."

**Matn** The text of a *ḥadīth,* containing the "story."

**Mawla** Adopted member of an Arab tribe; non-Arab Muslim convert in early Islamic history (pl., *mawālī*). Also, "master."

**Mawlid** "Birthday," especially that of a saint with its festivities. *Mawlid al-Nabī* is the "Birthday Festival of the Prophet."

**Miḥrāb** The niche in the wall of a mosque marking the *qibla,* direction of Mecca.

**Minbār** The raised pulpit in a mosque from which the *khaṭīb* delivers the *khuṭba* (sermon).

**Mi'rāj** "Ascension," particularly that of the Prophet up to heaven.

**Mu'adhdhin** "Caller to salat" by means of the *adhān.* (Sometimes spelled "muezzin.")

**Mufassir** Qur'an commentator-exegete.

**Muftī** Jurisconsult learned in the Qur'an, the Sunna, and *fiqh.* Gives learned opinions, called *fatāwā* (sing., *fatwā*).

**Muhājirūn** "Emigrants," especially those who accompanied Muhammad on the Hijra.

**Muḥrim** One who is in the ritual state of *iḥrām,* as on the hajj.

**Mujaddid** "Renewer" or "reformer" of Islam. It is traditionally held that God appoints a *mujaddid* at the turn of each century. Al-Ghazālī was believed by many to be the *mujaddid* of his time.

**Mujtahid** One who exercises *ijtihād,* "independent legal reasoning."

**Mulla** Persian form of *mawlā,* "master" of religious sciences, member of the *'ulamā'.*

**Mu'min** "Believer," one who has *imān,* "faith."

**Murīd** Sufi disciple, literally "one desiring" to be guided in a *ṭarīqa* ("spiritual path") by a master (*shaykh, murshid, pīr*).

**Murji'a** "Postponers." The broad-based early school of *kalām* that left to God the decision about the fate of the grave sinner.

**Murūwa** "Manliness." The Jāhilīya virtue enbracing courage, honor, generosity, and chivalry.

**Muṣḥaf** "Codex," "volume," especially of the Qur'an (*al-Muṣḥaf al-Sharīf,* "the noble volume") (pl. *maṣāḥif*).

**Muslim** "One who has surrendered" to God through the act of *islām.*

**Mustaṣwif** A pretender to the Sufi path who desires honor and admiration but is basically insincere.

**Mutakallim** One who practices *kalām;* systematic theologian (pl., *mutakallimūn*).

**Mutaṣawwif** Sufi novice or one who continually aspires to higher levels of mystical attainment.

**Mu'tazila** The celebrated "rationalist" school of *kalām* whose name comes from a word that means "to stand aloof."

**Muwaḥḥid** "Unitarian," that is, a believer in *tawḥīd,* divine "unity" and "making the unity" constant in thoughts and actions (pl., *muwaḥḥidūn*).

**Nabī** "Prophet."

**Najāsa** Polluting matter that touches the worshiper, his or her clothes, or the prayer place. Examples: wine, urine, blood, excrement, and the saliva and other fluids of pigs and dogs.

**Al-Nār** "The fire" of hell.

**Nawāfil** Supererogatory prostrations in worship (sing., *nāfila*). Any voluntary acts of piety.

**Nikāḥ** "Marriage" and the legal issues pertaining thereto.

**Niṣāb** The minimum amount of wealth that a person must possess before zakāt can be computed on it.

**Nisba** Part of a person's name, indicating place of origin or some other special relationship. For example, Jamāl al-Dīn al-Afghānī; the last part of the name is the *nisba,* indicating Afghan origin. *Nasab* is a lineage link, e.g., *ibn,* "son" of.

**Niyya** "Intention," especially before any ritual act, such as the salat. Without proper *niyya,* the act is invalid.

**Al-Nūr al-Muḥammadī** "The Muhammadan light," believed by Shī'is to be the inspired essence of all prophecy, which is handed down from imim to imām.

**Pancasila** The Indonesian "five principals" of monotheism, humanism, national unity, democracy, and social justice.

**"Pillars of Islam"** The five principal categories of worship (*'ibāda*): *shahāda* ("testifying" to the unity of God and the messengerhood of Muhammad), *ṣalāt* (obligatory "prayer service" five times daily), *zakāt* (legal "alms"), *ṣawm* (Ramadān "fast"), and *ḥajj* ("pilgrimage" to Mecca). The "pillars" represent a minimum level of religious observances for pious Muslims. (The term *pillars* is not universally used by Muslims.)

**Pīr** Spiritual guide in Sufism. The Persian equivalent of *shaykh* is standard in Iran and the Indian subcontinent.

**Priyayi** Indonesian, especially Javanese, Muslims of the upper class of ancient Hindu-Buddhist background, whether of royalty or the governmental bureaucracy.
**Purdah** See *ḥijāb.*

**Al-Qaḍā' wa'l-Qadar** "The divine decree and predestination."
**Qāḍā** Islamic "judge," officially appointed by the ruler. In contrast with those of the *muftī* and the *faqīh,* the Qāḍi's judgments are binding, whereas the others' are merely advisory.
**Qāri'** Qur'an "reciter." The professional *qārī'* has memorized the Qur'an and may be employed for a wide variety of contexts in which he recites. Some *qāri's* become very famous and sought after. May be of either sex.
**Qibla** The direction of Mecca, toward which Muslims orient themselves in the salat. The *qibla* is marked by a niche, called a *miḥrāb,* in the wall of a mosque.
**Qiyās** Legal decision making and argumentation by means of "analogy." One of the four sources of Sunni *fiqh.*
**Qubba** A domed structure, typically erected over the burial site of a saint.
**Qur'ān** "Recitation," especially the Islamic scripture.
**Quraysh** The leading tribe in Mecca at the time of Muhammad, who was a member of the Qurayshī clan of Banū Hāshim.
**Quṭb** "Pole," in the sense of an *axis mundi.* In Sufi cosmology, *Al-Quṭb* is at the head of the hierarchy of saints and is identified with *Al-Insān al-Kāmil,* "The Perfect Man."

**Rak'a** The basic cycle of postures in the salat, consisting of standing, bowing, prostrating, and sitting.
**Ramaḍān** The holy month of fasting, when the Qur'ān was first revealed.
**Rasūl** "Messenger." A type of prophet entrusted with a special divine message for a specific people. All *rasūls* are *nabīs,* but the reverse is not the case.
**Ra'y** Personal "opinion," especially in legal decisions.
**Ribā** Usury; any gain from the loan of goods, property or cash.
**Ribāṭ** A military outpost or fort on the boundaries of a Muslim country. Has come to mean a Sufi retreat or cloister.
**Ridda** "Apostasy," especially from Islam. Also called *irtidād.*

**Ṣadaqa** Charity, given freely and at any time. Not to be confused with zakāt, which is a formal religious tax.
**Ṣaḥīḥ** "Sound," especially of *ḥadīth.*
**Sakīna** God's "tranquility" which descends on his faithful servants, for example, when the Qur'an is recited. (Compare Hebrew *schechina,* "God's presence in the world.")
**Ṣalāt** The formal prayer-worship service observed five times daily.
**Samā'** Literally "hearing," but in Sufism, the participation in an ecstatic spiritual recital or concert involving music and dance.
**Santri** Indonesian Muslims of rather strict religious observance, avoiding syncretism as far as possible.
**Ṣawm, Ṣiyām** "Fasting" from dawn until dark during the month of Ramaḍān.
**Sa'y** The "running" ritual during the hajj, which commemorates Hagar's frantic search for water for her child, Ismā'īl.
**Shāfi'īya** The Sunnī *madhhab* founded by Muhammad ibn Idrīs al-Shāfi'ī.
**Shahāda** The "bearing witness" to God's unity and Muhammad's messengerhood (*Lā ilāha illā Allāh. Muhammadun rasūl Allāh* means "There is no god but God. Muhammad is the Messenger of God.") Saying the shahāda once in one's life, with belief, makes one a Muslim.
**Shā'ir** "Poet." Muhammad was thought by some to have been an inspired *shā'ir* instead of a prophet.
**Sharī'a** Literally, the "way to the water hole." Came to mean the Islamic law based on the Qur'an and the sunna.
**Shaykh** Among the many meanings are elder, religious scholar, Sufi master, tribal or clan chief, ruler, and pious gentleman. *Shaykha* is the female form.
**Shayṭān** "Satan," evil spirit, demon (pl., *shayāṭīn*).
**Shī'a** "Party," "faction," "sect." The adherents of 'Alī, who believed that Muhammad had chosen him and his descendants as rightful successors and rulers of the Muslims. There are various subbranches.
**Shirk** "Association," especially of anything with God; idolatry. One who commits *shirk* is a *mushrik.* This is the one unforgivable sin, according to the Qur'an (4:48).

**Silsila** "Chain," which in Sufism means a spiritual lineage traced back to the Prophet through a succession of shaykhs. The *silsila* has been called a "spiritual *isnād*" because it authenticates the doctrines of a *ṭarīqa,* just as the *isnād* documents a *ḥadīth.*

**Siyāsa** Governmental administration, politics.

**Subḥa** Muslim prayer beads, usually strung in a loop of eleven, thirty-three, or ninety-nine, with suitable marker beads to aid in progressing through ritual repetitions of "the most beautiful names" (numbering ninety-nine), and other formulas.

**Ṣūfī** Wearer of course woolen frock; adept of the Islamic mystical path. (From *ṣūf,* "wool.")

**Sunna** "Custom," "usual procedure" or "way of acting," especially of Muhammad. The Prophet's sunna is remembered and transmitted by means of the literary form known as *ḥadīth* ("report"). *Sunna* also is a legal term that means "recommended."

**Sunnat** A widely encountered synonym for circumcision, especially of females.

**Sunnī** Popular name for the Muslim majority, which is technically known as *Ahl al-Sunna wa 'l-Jamā'a,* "The People of the (established) Custom and the Community" (in the sense of a single, normative political entity). (The name does not imply that the Sunnīs follow the Prophet's sunna more than do the Shī'is.)

**Sūra** Chapter of the Qur'an.

**Tafsīr** "Explanation," "commentary," especially of the Qur'an.

**Ṭahāra** Purification, including the various ritual means to that end. Sometimes used as a synonym for circumcision.

**Tahlīl** To utter the phrase *lā ilāha illā Allāh:* "There is no god but God." Also means rejoicing, jubilation, as in Halleluja!

**Ṭā'ifa** Literally "part," "portion," "sect." In Sufism it means a religious order, as in a specific organization.

**Tajwīd** The science of euphonious recitation of the Qur'an.

**Takbīr** The uttering of *Allāhu Akbar:* "God is Most Great."

**Ṭalāq** Divorce.

**Talbiya** The uttering of the pious formula *Labbayk allahuma labbayk . . . : "I am here, O my God, I am here." Talbīya* literally means obeying or complying with a command or request. Pilgrims utter the *talbīya* frequently on hajj as a joyous expression of obedience.

**Tanzīh** Deeming God as beyond anthropomorphic conceptions.

**Taqlīd** Acceptance of a legal position or theological assertion on mere authority without independent inquiry; blind imitation.

**Ṭarīqa** The Sufi "way." A *ṭarīqa* may be a method of spiritual discipline with specific techniques of meditation, or it may be an actual order in the organizational sense, like *ṭā'ifa* (pl., *ṭuruq*).

**Tartīl** Slow, clear, rhythmic recitation of the Qur'an.

**Taṣawwuf** The Sufi way.

**Tashahhud** "Testimony" (cf. *shahāda*) to the oneness of God and the messengerhood of Muhammad while in the sitting position in the salat, with the index finger of the right hand extended as a physical symbol of the divine unity.

**Tashbīh** Having anthropomorphic conceptions of God. The opposite of *ta'ṭīl.*

**Taslīm** The benediction at the end of the salat: "The peace and mercy of god be with you." Uttered facing to either side.

**Ta'ṭīl** Divesting God of all attributes, whether or not anthropomorphic. The opposite of *tashbīh.*

**Ṭawāf** The ritual circumambulating of the K'aba.

**Tawba** "Repentance," the first station on the Sufi path to God.

**Tawḥīd** Maintaining God's unity. This is the central theological fundamental of the Islamic religion.

**Ta'wīl** Allegorical or symbolic interpretation, for example, of the Qur'an.

**Tayammum** Ritual ablution by means of clean earth (sand, dust) instead of water. Allowable only under certain circumstances.

**Ta'ziya** "Consolation," more specifically the Shī'ī passion drama that commemorates the martyrdom of Imām Husayn at Karbalā'.

**Tekke** Turkish term for Sufi retreat center (cf. *zāwiya, khānqāh, ribāṭ*).

**Tilāwa** Recitation of the Qur'an.

**'Ulamā'** The learned class of religious and legal scholars (sing., *'ālim*).

**Umayyad** Pertaining to the Qurayshī clan of Banū Umayya, which became the first Muslim dynasty, with its capital at Damascus (661–750).

**Umma** A community having a common religion. The Muslim community.
**'Umra** The "lesser hajj," entailing only the rites performed in the vicinity of the K'aba. This visitation may be performed at any time of the year, whereas the hajj proper must be observed on the set days of the hajj month.
**'Urs** Marriage festivities, as distinguished from the actual contract-signing ceremony, which is known as *nikāh.*
**Uṣūl** "Roots," meaning basic principles, as in the case of the sources of jurisprudence (*uṣūl al-fiqh*) (sing., *aṣl*).

**Waḥdat al-wujūd** "Unity of being," a controversial doctrine of Sufi theosophy because of its susceptibility of monistic and pantheistic interpretation.
**Wahhābīya** The sternly puritanical reform movement founded in Arabia in the eighteenth century by Muhammad Ibn 'Abd al-Wahhāb.
**Waḥy** Inspiration; the way in which the Qur'an was revealed to Muhammad, including both the ideas and the words.
**Wājib** Obligatory, as a duty (cf. *farḍ*).
**Walī** One who is close, like a friend, relative, protector, helper. Muslim "saint" (pl. *awliyā*).
**Waqf** A charitable trust dedicated to some pious or socially beneficial purpose (pl., *awqāf*).
**Wuḍū'** The lesser ablution before certain ritual activities, such as salat or Qur'an recitation.
**Wuqūf** The "standing" ceremony performed at 'Arafāt during the hajj.

**Yathrib** The oasis town to which Muhammad and his fellow Meccan Muslims migrated in the Hijra in 622. Also and most particularly known thereafter as *Madīnat al-Nabī,* "The city of the prophet" (Medina).

**Zaffa** Procession of people, as at a *mawlid* commemorating a saint's day.
**Ẓāhir** The external dimension of something, the plain and obvious meaning. Opposite of *bāṭin,* the interior or esoteric dimension of scripture or doctrine.
**Zakāt** Legal almsgiving, calculated on the basis of one's wealth. One of the categories of Islamic worship (*'ibāda*). (Zakāt is not the same thing as charity, *ṣadaqa;* the latter should be dispensed spontaneously and continually.)
**Zamzam** The well near the Ka'ba in Mecca. Considered sacred.
**Zāwiya** Literally, "corner," of a mosque or other building. A Sufi retreat or cloister.
**Zaydiya** One of the major Shi'i branches. As a *madhhab,* it is close to Sunnism. Prominent in North Yemen.
**Ziyāra** "Visitation," as to a holy shrine like Medina or Karbalā' (pl., *ziyārāt*).
**Zuhd** Asceticism.

# Acknowledgments


*The author gratefully acknowledges permission to reprint copyrighted material (listed approximately in order of quotation):*

*The Intellectual Adventure of Ancient Man,* by Henri and H.A. Groenewegen Frankfort, John A. Wilson, Thorkild Jacobsen and William A. Irwin. Copyright © 1946 by The University of Chicago. Published by the University of Chicago Press. Used by permission.

*Temples, Tombs and Hieroglyphs,* by Barbara Mertz. Copyright © 1964 by Barbara G. Mertz. Published by Dodd, Mead and Company, New York.

*The Oxford Annotated Bible with the Apocrypha,* Revised Standard Version of the Bible, copyrighted 1946, 1952 © 1971, 1973 by the National Council of the Churches of Christ in the U.S.A. Published by Oxford University Press.

*The Seven Odes: The First Chapter in Arabic Literature,* by A. J. Arberry. Copyright © 1957 by George Allen & Unwin, Ltd., London. Reprinted by permission of HarperCollins Publishers Ltd.

*Mishkat Al-Masabih,* 4 volumes, by Al-Baghawī and Al-Khaṭīb Al-Tibrīzī (translated by James Robson). Copyright © 1966 by Sh. Muhammad Ashraf, Publishers, Lahore, Pakistan.

*The Koran Interpreted,* by A. J. Arberry. Copyright © 1955 by George Allen & Unwin, Ltd., London, and Macmillan Publishing Co., New York. Reprinted by permission of HarperCollins Publishers Ltd. and Simon & Schuster, Inc.

*The Life of Muhammad: A Translation of [Ibn]Ishāq's Sīrat Rasūl Allāh,* by A. Guillaume. Copyright © 1955 by Oxford University Press.

*Islam: Creed and Worship,* by Muhammad Abdul Rauf. Copyright © by M. A. Rauf, 1974. Washington, D.C.: Islamic Center.

*Discourses of Rumi,* by A. J. Arberry. Copyright © 1961 by John Murray (Publishers), Ltd., London.

*Ideals and Realities of Islam,* by Seyyed Hossein Nasr. Copyright © 1966 by George Allen & Unwin Ltd., London. Published by Beacon Press, Boston as a Beacon paperback in 1972 by arrangement with George Allen&Unwin Ltd. Used by permission of Kazi Publications.

*The Qur'an and Its Exegesis: Selected Texts with Classical and Modern Interpretations,* by Helmut Gätje, trans. and ed. Alford T. Welch. Copyright © 1976 by Routledge & Kegan Paul Ltd, London. Second edition copyright © 1996, Oneworld Publications. Reproduced by permission of Oneworld Publications.

*Divine Word and Prophetic Word in Early Islam,* by William A. Graham. Copyright © 1977 by Mouton and Company, The Hague and Paris.

*A Reader on Islam,* by Arthur Jeffery. Copyright © 1980 by Ayer Company Publishers. Used by permission.

*The Formative Period of Islamic Thought,* by W. Montgomery Watt. Copyright © 1973 by Edinburgh University Press, Scotland.

*The Muslim Creed: Its Genesis and Historical Development,* by A. J. Wensinck. Copyright © 1932 by A. J. Wensinck. Reprinted with the permission of Cambridge University Press.

*The Faith and Practice of Al-Ghazālī,* by W. Montgomery Watt. Copyright © 1953, 1994 by William Montgomery Watt. Reproduced by permission of Oneworld Publications.

*Rabi'a the Mystic and Her Fellow-Saints in Islam,* by Margaret Smith. Copyright © 1928 by Cambridge University Press. Reprinted with the permission of Cambridge University Press.

*Studies in Islamic Mysticism,* by Reynold A. Nicholson. Copyright © 1921 by Cambridge University Press. Reprinted with the permission of Cambridge University Press.

*Sufism,* by A. J. Arberry. Copyright © 1950 by A. J. Arberry. Reprinted by permission of HarperCollins Publishers Ltd.

*Muhammad's People: A Tale by Anthology,* by Eric Schroeder. Copyright © 1955 by Bond Wheelwright Company, Freeport, Maine.

*The Kashf al-Mahjūb: The Oldest Persian Treatise on Sūfism,* by 'Alī ibn 'Uthmān al-Jullabī al-Hujwīrī (translated by Reynold A. Nicholson). Copyright © 1911, New Edition 1936, by Luzac & Company, Ltd., London.

*Mystical Dimensions of Islam,* by Annemarie Schimmel. Copyright © 1975 by The University of North Carolina Press, Chapel Hill, North Carolina.

*A Rūmī Anthology,* Reynold A. Nicholson. © 2000, by Oneworld Publications. (Previously published as *Rūmī: Poet and Mystic* by George Allen & Unwin, Ltd., London, 1950.)

*The Sufi Orders in Islam,* by J. Spencer Trimingham. Copyright © 1971 by Oxford University Press.

*A Sufi Saint of the Twentieth Century,* by Martin Lings. Copyright © 1961, 1971 by George Allen & Unwin, Ltd.

*Gardens of the Righteous: Riyadh As-Salihin of Imam Nawawi,* translated by Muhammad Zafrullah Khan. Copyright © 1975 by Muhammad Zafrullah Khan. Published by Curzon Press Ltd., London.

*The Sword of Truth: The Life and Times of the Shehu Usuman dan Fodio,* by Mervyn Hiskett. Copyright © 1973 by Oxford University Press. By permission of Oxford University Press, Inc.

*The Lawful and the Prohibited in Islam,* by Yusuf al-Qaradawi (Translators: Kamal El-Helbawy, M. Moinuddin Siddiqui, Syed Shukry). Copyright © n.d. by American Trust Publications, Indianapolis, Indiana.

*Milestones* by Sayyid Qutb. Copyright © 1990 by American Trust Publications, Indianapolis, Indiana.

*Whither Islam? A Survey of Modern Movements in the Moslem World,* by H. A. R. Gibb. Copyright © 1932 by Victor Gollancz Ltd., London.

*Reason, Freedom, and Democracy in Islam: Essential Writings of 'Abdolkarim Soroush,* translated, edited, and with a Critical Introduction by Mahmoud Sadri and Ahmad Sadri. Copyright © 2000 by 'Abdolkarim Soroush. Published by Oxford University Press. By permission of Oxford University Press, Inc.

*The Correspondence of Roger Williams: Volume II. 1654–1682,* ed. Glenn W. LaFantasie. Copyright © 1988 by University Press of New England, Lebanon, NH. Reprinted with permission.

*Progressive Muslims: On Justice, Gender, and Pluralism,* © 2003, Omid Safi. Published by Oneworld Publications. Reproduced by permission of Oneworld Publications.

*Journal of Law and Religion,* Vol. XV, Numbers 1 & 2 (2000–2001), pp. 535–539. Review by Frederick M. Denny of *Windows of Faith: Muslim Women Scholar-Activists in North America,* Gisela Webb, ed., published 2000 by Syracuse University Press. Excerpts from the review reprinted by permission of *JLR*.

# Index

**Note:** The locators followed by 'ill' refer to illustrations cited in the text.